The Official Precious Moments® Collector's Guide to FIGURINES

FOURTH EDITION

John & Malinda Bomm

COLLECTOR BOOKS

A Division of Schroeder Publishing Co., Inc.

Front cover: 79540B Bride (Asian); 104850 Mom, You're A Sweetheart; 824719 Our Love Will Never Be Endangered
Back cover: 521000 There Is No Greater Treasure Than To Have A Friend Like You; 588059 Our Love Will Flow Eternal; E-5213 God Is Love.

Cover design by Terri Hunter
Book design by Terri Hunter
Layout by Beth Ray

COLLECTOR BOOKS
P.O. Box 3009
Paducah, Kentucky 42002-3009

www.collectorbooks.com

The current values in this book should be used only as a guide. They are not intended to set prices, which vary from one section of the country to another. Auction prices as well as dealer prices vary greatly and are affected by condition as well as demand. Neither the authors nor the publisher assumes responsibility for any losses that might be incurred as a result of consulting this guide.

Searching for a Publisher?

We are always looking for people knowledgeable within their fields. If you feel that there is a real need for a book on your collectible subject and have a large comprehensive collection, contact Collector Books.

Proudly printed and bound in the United States of America.

A Banner Of Hope, A Symbol Of Pride, **117581**

Contents

Beautiful And Blushing, My Baby's Now A Bride, 117802

Share The Gift Of Love™

A Note From The Authors

Prices listed in this publication are secondary market value pricing. Pricing is determined by location, condition of item, coloring, presence or absence of box, and of course, demand. The authors of this book take no responsibility for variations in pricing. Pricing should be used only as a generalization, not an actual. All information in this book has come from sources such as collectors, dealers, and a wide range of research. Any errors are misinformation received.

Any changes needed should be sent to the authors of this book. This is the only way we can finally get accurate descriptions, marks, and errors.

If anyone has any information not found in this book, please contact John and Malinda Bomm at pmguides@hotmail.com. Please list the information with corrections, pictures, etc.

Happiness Is Being A Mom, 115926

Acknowledgments

Special thanks goes to Jamie Benson for all the pictures sent to me.

Thanks also to Susan Brock, Precious Moments Inc. Marketing Project Manager, and her crew for all their help finding pictures and information.

Thank you to both the Clinton Library and the George H. Bush Library for taking picutes of the Precious Moments pieces these presidents received. It has made this book extra special.

Thank you to the Precious Moments Museum for the pictures that were taken of the few rare pieces for this book.

Malinda and I would like to thank our mother for all the input, information collecting, and phone calling she had to do to make this book possible. She spent many, many hours of work helping put this book together.

An extra special thanks goes out to PMI employees: Karen Bellgrad, Rachel Perkal, and Debbie Fiorenza. Without their help we would not have all the new information found in this edition.

An extra special thanks to Ginny Gully for all her help getting us pictures and information.

About The Authors

John and Malinda Bomm are residents of Orlando, Florida. John was born in Amityville, New York, in 1962. He, his younger brother, and his parents stayed in New York until 1972, when his father was transferred to Pennsylvania. They lived in the beautiful Amish country there for three years until John's father was transferred again, this time to New Jersey. John completed his education in New Jersey and at the age of 16 started working for Pathmark Supermarkets as a cart boy and cashier. When John turned 18 he started building a race car, one of his passions through his growing years. He is now a "stay-at-home" dad taking care of his four children.

Malinda was born in 1962 on Naha Air Force Base in Okinawa, Japan. Her father was an Air Force Master Sergeant at the time. Her mother was a native of Okinawa. Malinda and her parents lived in Okinawa for nine years until they moved to Langley Air Force Base in Virginia. Malinda completed her education at Tabb High School in Virginia. She moved to New Jersey in 1987 where she met John Bomm. When John's parents moved to Florida, John and Malinda made the move with them. They were married on Valentine's Day, 1991. John and Malinda have adopted four children: Eric, 17; Gerard, 15; Ramey, 12; and Sirjesim, 11. Malinda is now a health claims examiner for a large city agency.

Through Malinda, John developed a love of Precious Moments collectibles. Malinda and John's collection has expanded from five Precious Moments figurines to approximately 1,300 pieces, including bisque figurines, dolls, plates, water globes, and much more. Several rooms in their house showcase their collection. They authored several editions of *The Official Precious Moments Guide to Figurines* and one edition of *The Official Precious Moments Collector's Guide to Company Dolls,* also published by Collector Books, in 2003.

The History Of Precious Moments

Sam Butcher

Samuel John Butcher was born on January 1, 1939. He was the third of five children who grew up in a very poor family. As a child, he spent hours underneath the dining room table writing stories and illustrating them. Even in kindergarten, his dream of becoming an artist was evident, when he illustrated *Little Black Sambo* and made a box with a movie crank that worked like a movie screen — the whole school admired it. At this young age his talent was recognized by both family and friends.

When Sam was in high school in the fall of 1957, he met Katie Cushman, whom he married on December 27, 1959. They had five children: Jon, Philip, Tammy, Debbie, and Timmy. Though life was very busy, Sam continued following his dream of becoming an artist.

Over the years Sam found the Lord and devoted his life to him. His strong spiritual commitment led him to employment at the International Child Evangelism Fellowship in Grand Rapids, Michigan. It was there that he learned how to study the Bible, and his desire to spread God's love to others grew. It was also there that he met Bill Biel, who later became his dear friend and business partner. In 1971 Sam and Bill decided to leave their jobs and go out on their own as commercial artists. With no money, a bit of poster paint, and the talents God gave them, they formed their own company, "Jonathan & David," with Sam as illustrator and Bill as designer.

In 1975 Sam and Bill were invited to attend the Christian Booksellers Convention in Anaheim, California. It was then that they began preparing greeting cards featuring teardrop-eyed children, and Bill came up with the name "Precious Moments." This idea was a huge success at the convention, and their tiny booth was overrun with customers — $10,000 worth of orders were placed. All the men needed was the money to produce the cards and fill the orders. They went to the bank with orders in hand, but were turned down. They decided to try the Christian Businessmen's Association, who told them to put their trust in the Lord. And eventually, Sam met a wealthy man who offered to loan him $25,000 to start up his business.

That first year (1975) Sam and Bill's first major projects were Christmas cards and Bicentennial cards. To offset their costs and help pay bills, they also painted Christmas scenes on store windows and garages. During the second CBA convention in Atlantic City, Sam and Bill introduced four posters: *Jesus Loves Me, Praise the Lord Anyhow, Prayer Changes Things,* and *God Is Love.* At the same time, their Precious Moments greeting cards ministry continued to grow in acceptance to those associated with the growing company of Jonathan & David. Through all the struggles, Sam and Bill kept their senses of humor, and asked the Lord to guide and direct them in sharing the Gospel through the ministry of the Precious Moments greeting cards.

Early in 1978, Sam and Bill were both in the studio when a man by the name of Eugene Freedman called. He was the president and chief executive officer of Enesco Imports Corporation, a company heavily involved in the giftware industry, headquartered in the Chicago suburb of Elk Grove Village. Freedman had seen some of the Precious Moments cards, including *I Will Make You Fishers Of Men.* Freedman wanted to know if Sam and Bill would be interested in making Precious Moments into three-dimensional art through porcelain figurines.

Sam and Bill had a special relationship. Sam was an artist, not a businessman. The two decided to part ways in March of 1984. Sam sold his interest in Jonathan & David, Inc., the greeting card company, to Bill. They remained friends for many years.

The collection is now well over 1,500 pieces with new introductions offered each year. Members of collectors' clubs continue to be found throughout the world. Even more telling, since its opening in 1989, Precious Moments Park in Carthage, Missouri, has welcomed approximately 400,000 visitors every year.

In July 2005, PMI became the distributor of Precious Moments Gift Products after taking back the license from Enesco during its bankruptcy.

Today the company is run by Sam's son, Don Butcher, and long-time business partner and friend, Jim Malcolm. Sam's daughter, Debbie Butcher, serves as the VP of Creative.

The new product development team has introduced exciting figurines like the co-branded Disney collection and the new seasonal promotions. In addition, the team of licensing experts will focus on licensing strategy and bringing new looks to the licensed products.

***Happiness Is A Song From Heaven,* 112969**

Prototypes, Production, And Manufactured Pieces

We have received important information pertaining to some problems encountered in our previous issues of this book. Individual Precious Moment figurines do not all look the same, even though they have the same number or name. The company has made these individual pieces at different times, looking just a bit different.

A prototype is a piece that was made, but because of a flaw in production, had only one piece manufactured. Prototypes were sometime used by salesmen trying to acquire sales.

A production piece is a piece made but for some reason not manufactured. For example: a piece has a small animal, finger, or other such piece that will not adhere correctly. Once the figurine is fired and ready to paint, the problem piece keeps falling off. Instead of throwing away all the figurines, only the pieces completed were put on sale. The production was a one time and mark only.

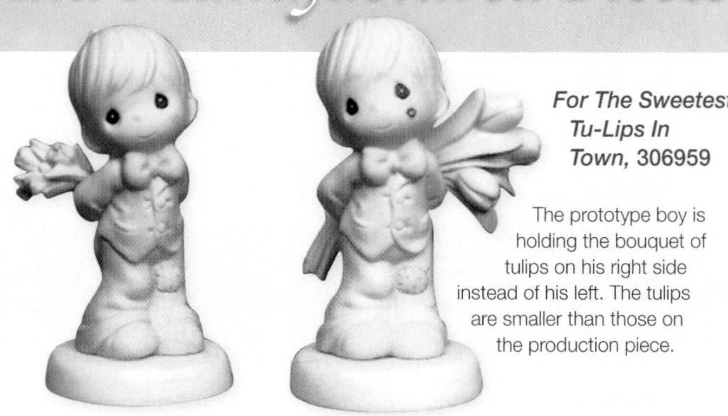

For The Sweetest Tu-Lips In Town, 306959

The prototype boy is holding the bouquet of tulips on his right side instead of his left. The tulips are smaller than those on the production piece.

A manufactured piece is a piece that has been made for several years. Each piece is the same. The marks change each year of production.

This is the first time any of this information has come to our attention. If anyone has an odd piece that is not in the book, please email me at pmguides@hotmail.com. I will be happy to research the item and get it into the next edition.

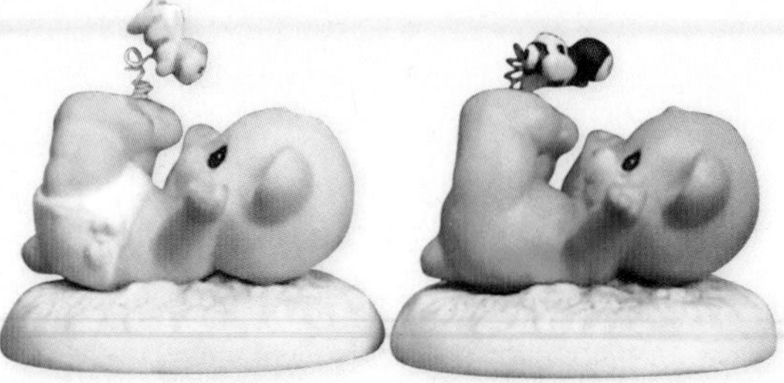

You're My Honey Bee, 487929

The first bear was the prototype with the bear having a lighter skin tone and wearing a diaper. The bee was a light gray and yellow with pink feet. Eyeglasses mark.

No prototype pieces had the title or production number on the base; they instead came with stickers of the numbers.

Wishing You A Ho Ho Ho, 527629

The color of the prototype was more red, whereas the production piece was pinker.

How To Clean Your Precious Moments

Here are some tips to help keep your collection clean and safe. The most important thing is to keep your pieces in a safe, smoke-free area and out of direct sunlight. PMI recommends hand washing your pieces using warm water and any mild soap and wiping them with a damp cloth. Place something soft underneath the area in which you are working just in case the piece gets dropped. When finished, wipe the item off with a soft towel and set it aside to dry completely. If you have intentions of reselling the pieces, try to keep all the original packaging. There is a higher resale value on the secondary market if everything is complete.

A Tub Full Of Love, 112313

What Is Sam Butcher's Signature Worth?

No one can put a value on Sam Butcher's signature on a Precious Moments figurine. Appraisers have set a higher value on a signed piece since he is the artist. The system they seem to use averages out to approximately $30.00 on easily acquired pieces and approximately $50.00 on pieces that are harder to find. With certain special pieces the price could go up to an additional $100.00. Eugene Freedman's signature does not increase the value of a piece, yet Yasuhei Fujioka-San's signature could add $25.00 and Shuhei Fujioka's (his son) could add $15.00.

SamB

Errors And Variations

B-0102 *A Smile's The Cymbal Of Joy*
The word "Cymbal" was misspelled "Symbol" on some Charter Member figurines.

E-0202 *But Love Goes On Forever*
Some of these pieces were reproduced after production was ended. Those pieces were sent to Canada and are identified with the Dove mark.

E-0535 *Love Is Patient — Boy* (Ornament)
Some pieces have been found with the "Merry Christmas" upside down.

E-1373B *Smile, God Loves You*
The boy sometimes has a black eye and sometimes a brown eye.

E-1374B *Praise The Lord Anyhow*
On some pieces the puppy has a brown nose and on some it has a black nose.

E-1377B *He Careth For You*
The inscriptions on E-1377A (*He Leadeth Me*) and this piece were sometimes swapped.

E-2013 *Unto Us A Child Is Born*
Pieces have been reported with the words placed on the pages incorrectly.

E-2362 *Baby's First Christmas* (Ornament)
In variation one, the girl's straight hair appears curly. In variation two, the girl has curly hair, but the decal on the bottom of the piece is missing.

E-2372 *Baby's First Christmas* (Ornament)
The inscription did not come with the first pieces that were produced. Right before the piece was suspended, an inscription was included.

E-2395 *Come Let Us Adore Him* (set of 11)
The original set included a boy holding a lamb. Later he was replaced by a shepherd wearing a turban.

E-2805 *Wishing You A Season Filled With Joy*
The figurine with the dove year mark shows a dog with both eyes painted black instead of one single painted eye.

E-2837 *Groom*
Two different molds were used for this piece; on one, the boy's hands are hidden by his sleeves, and on the other, the boy's hands can be seen.

E-2854 *God Blessed Our Year Together With So Much Love And Happiness*
"God Blessed Our Years" (plural) is the error on some of the decals of these first anniversary pieces.

E-3106 *Mother Sew Dear*
Some pieces have only half the "M" printed on the embroidery.

E-3110B *Loving Is Sharing — Boy*
Pieces have been found with the dog missing or with the boy's lollipop unpainted.

E-3111 *Be Not Weary In Well Doing*
Some pieces had the inscription printed as *Be Not Weary And Well Doing.*

E-4724 *Rejoicing With You*
Sometimes the "e" in Bible is covered by the girl's hand.

E-5200 *Bear Ye One Another's Burdens*
The original figurine shows the boy with a smile yet others have been found with a little circle mouth.

E-5214 *Prayer Changes Things*
In some cases, the words "Holy Bible" were put on the back of the book. Some were found with "Holy Bible" on the figurine upside down.

E-5379 *Isn't He Precious*
This piece has been seen completely without paint.

E-5624 *They Followed The Star* (set of 3)
It has been noted that the camels originally came without blankets.

E-5629 *Let The Heavens Rejoice*
The Precious Moments decal is missing on some of the pieces.

E-7156R *I Believe In Miracles*
The variation is the lack of the inscribed "Sam B" on the bottom of the pieces. The boy's head is also smaller on some.

E-9266 & *Our Love Is Heaven-Scent*
E-9266B *I'm Falling For Somebunny*
Both pieces were made with the incorrect inscription *Somebunny Cares.*

E-9268 *Nobody's Perfect!*
On this figurine, the boy has either a smile or a frown on his face.

PM-831 *Dawn's Early Light*
A Dove mark has been found on the bottom of some of these pieces.

PM-961 *Teach Us To Love One Another*
Pieces have been found with decals upside down.

PM-971 *You Will Always Be A Treasure To Me*
Has been found with a heart mark.

12238 *Clown Figurines* (A-B-C-D)
On many of these clowns the inscription was written as "CROWN."

12262 *I Get A Bang Out Of You*
This figurine has been found with a *Lord Keep Me On The Ball* understamp.

12416 *Have A Heavenly Christmas* (Ornament)
On some of the 1987 wreaths the words "Heaven Bound" are upside down.

102229 *O Worship The Lord*
Many collectors have found this piece missing the "O."

111155 *Faith Takes The Plunge*
Some of the figurines that debuted in 1988 and 1989 had smiles and some had frowns.

115231 *You Are My Main Event*
The strings on the balloons are sometimes pink instead of white.

115915 *You Are The Apple Of My Eye*
Some of the apples were yellow.

128708 *Owl Be Home For Christmas* (Ornament)
This 1996 ornament has been found with the date missing.

136204 *It's A Girl*
Pieces have been found with one shoe not painted.

136255 *Age 6*
On some pieces, the heart with the age number is missing. Most pieces that should have decals are often missing them, but this piece has the entire heart missing.

183873 *Age 10*
Some pieces are missing the bowling pins.

192368 *Give Ability A Chance*
Has been found without the Easter Seals Lily mark.

260940 *From The Time I Spotted You I Knew We'd Be Friends*
The word "Know" has been found on some pieces instead of "Knew." The monkeys on some pieces are very dark brown instead of light brown.

261130 *Have You Any Room For Jesus*
The word "Bowling" has been found misspelled on the calendar.

306843 *20 Years And The Vision's Still The Same*
On a small number of the commemorative figurines, the Sword and Eyeglasses marks both appear.

306916 *Friendship Hits The Spot*
Many pieces have been found with the table missing. Decals were incorrectly spelled "Freindship."

455830 *Warmest Wishes For The Holidays*
Some pieces came with a green star and a little cat on the base.

520748 *Friendship Hits The Spot*
Variation one has a misspelling: *Freindship Hits The Spot*. On variation two, the table between the two girls is missing.

520756 *Jesus Is The Only Way*
Dates have been omitted on some and have been placed incorrectly on others.

520772 *Many Moons In Same Canoe, Blessum You*
Over the years, the Indians' hair has been darkened.

520802 *My Days Are Blue Without You*
Some pieces have a frown or puckered mouth instead of a smile.

522279 *A Reflection Of His Love*
Pieces have been found with a white or blue water reflection in the fountain.

522317 *Merry Christmas, Deer*
All figurines with the Bow and Arrow mark had no Precious Moments logo.

523011 *There's A Christian Welcome Here*
On some of the Chapel Exclusive pieces, the angel's hair hides his right eyebrow.

523704 *May Your Christmas Be A Happy Home* (Ornament)
This ornament shows a boy wearing either a yellow or blue shirt. The yellow shirt is considered the variation.

524204 *Love Is Color Blind*
Pieces have been found with no butterfly on the girl.

524352 *What The World Needs Now*
Pieces have been found with the Bible missing from the table.

524425 *May Only Good Things Come Your Way*
Some pieces have the butterfly on top of the net while others have the butterfly on the right side of the net, upside-down.

526053 *Pretty As A Princess*
On some pieces one point on the princess's crown is not painted gold.

527106 *He Is Not Here For He Is Risen As He Said*
On the sign outside the tomb some exclusives pieces read "Math" instead of "Matt."

528609 *Sending My Love Your Way*
Variation one, the kite held by the girl is missing its stripes. Variation two, the kitten is sometimes missing completely.

529540 *Park Bench*
Pieces were found glazed over and unpainted.

531634 *Who's Gonna Fill Your Shoes?*
Some pieces have been found with no bows on the girl's shoes.

531952 *Dropping In For The Holidays*
Pieces have been found with the "Egg Nog" and the decal upside-down. The cup of this piece came in either pink or blue.

649732 *Hay Good Lookin'*
Some pieces have the cat in front of the girl.

730068 *The Future Is In Our Hands*
On some pieces, the girl is holding a cardinal instead of a bluebird.

930004 *Will You Share Your Heart With Me?*
This figurine comes with a red heart ring box or a lavender ring box. The original came with the red box. It was later decided that the ring box would change to lavender as a running change.

The Original "21"

The original 21 figurines were introduced in 1979.

Jesus Loves Me (boy), E-1372B

Jesus Loves Me (girl), E-1372G

Smile, God Loves You, E-1373B

Jesus Is The Light, E-1373G

Praise The Lord Anyhow, E-1374B

Make A Joyful Noise, E-1374G

Love Lifted Me, E-1375A

Prayer Changes Things, E-1375B

Love One Another, E-1376

He Leadeth Me, E-1377A

He Careth For You, E-1377B

God Loveth A Cheerful Giver, E-1378

Love Is Kind, E-1379A

God Understands, E-1379B

O, How I Love Jesus, E-1380B

His Burden Is Light, E-1380G

Jesus Is The Answer, E-1381

We Have Seen His Star, E-2010

Come Let Us Adore Him, E-2011

Jesus Is Born, E-2012

Unto Us A Child Is Born, E-2013

Precious Moments Figurines' Stories

Focusing In On Those Precious Moments, C-0018

Sam attended a collectibles show in Edison, New Jersey, in the spring of 1999. He presented this special version of the 1998 club figurine to Rosemarie who belongs to the Happiness Is Belonging Club and the Precious Moments Collectible Treasures website. Sam states, "She is one of the most giving, kindest people and has a huge giving heart."

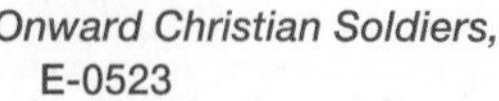

Onward Christian Soldiers, E-0523

Sam could hardly wait to paint this idea. This little soldier carried the message to Sam to keep going when things got tough.

His Eye Is On The Sparrow, E-0530

This figurine was first made as a card for a man who Sam had met. It was later made into a figurine. The man's son had committed suicide after returning home from war. The family was sent many cards at the death of their son, but Sam's card really touched them. The painting helped the family know that God had it in his hands from the very beginning.

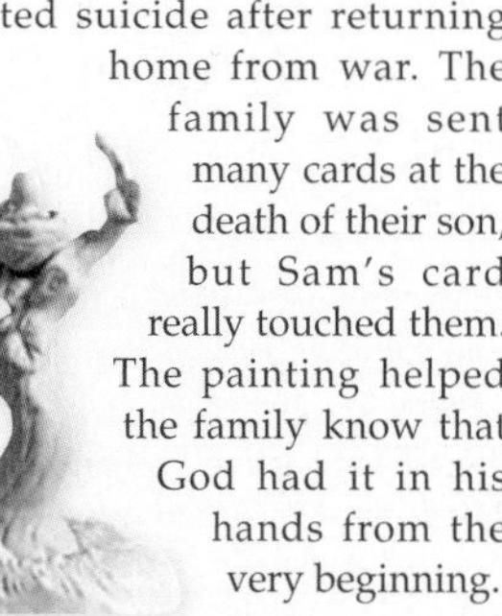

Praise The Lord Anyhow, E-1374B

Philip, Sam's second son, was the inspiration for this figurine. Sam said you couldn't spend much time with Philip before you threw up your hands lovingly and said, "Praise The Lord Anyhow!"

Make A Joyful Noise, E-1374G

This figurine is one of the original "21" introduced in 1978. Sam and Bill were driving on a country road when they came across a woman with a bumper sticker on her car that read, "Honk If You Love Jesus." Sam honked the car horn; she looked up, forgetting the instruction on her bumper sticker, thinking they were very rude young men. She gave them a dirty look and mouthed some nasty words. He pointed to the sticker, honked again, and drove away. Sam was inspired by this and created the image of a little girl nose-to-nose with a goose. It was originally called *Honk If You Love Jesus.* The title was changed before production.

Love One Another, E-1376

This was the first Precious Moments drawing. Tammy, Sam's daughter, sat by "Uncle Bill" on a stool back-to-back and the love she portrayed for Uncle Bill was the inspiration for the first Precious Moments figurine. The original art was stolen from the Jonathan & David Company.

God Loveth A Cheerful Giver, E-1378

Debbie, Sam's daughter, inspired this piece. Sam will probably never forget Debbie, with her box full of puppies, asking him if any of his friends needed a pet.

Love Is Kind, E-1379A

Sam's son Timmy was the subject for this figurine. Timmy is a boy who liked to spend a lot of his time alone with nature when he was small. He also enjoys painting and music.

O, How I Love Jesus, E-1380B

Through Sam's ministry with the Child Evangelism Fellowship, he met a very special member of the Pitt River Indians. This man had a difficult childhood. He learned to overcome his problems and became an excellent teacher. This figurine was dedicated to that man from the mountains of Northern California.

His Burden Is Light, E-1380G

This little Indian girl figurine is another result of Sam's experience with the Pitt River Indians. Though life was not easy for them, the Indians kept their traditional ways and never gave their burdens to the Lord. As time went on they left their old traditions and embraced the Lord.

To God Be The Glory, E-2823

Sam will never forget the day he saw Fujioka-San's sculpture of *To God Be The Glory*. He says it captures the story of his life. He feels that the Lord has been good to him and has blessed all his work.

***I'm Sending You A White Christmas,* E-2829**

Sam's mother was born in Michigan, but moved to Florida at an early age. After the death of her father, her mother moved the family back to Michigan. Sam's mother was only five years old and had never seen snow. The first time she saw snow, his mother was found packing snowballs in a box to mail to her relatives in Florida.

***God Sends The Gift Of His Love,* E-6613**

Sam's grandniece inspired him to create this piece. She looked precious in her frilly Christmas dress her mom made for her. Sam felt the little child was God's special gift to her parents.

***I Believe In Miracles,* E-7156**

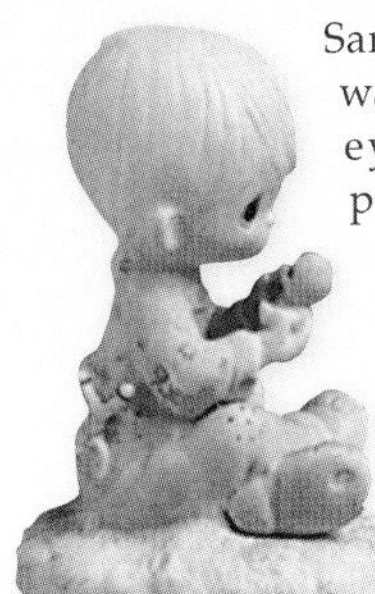

Sam's former partner, Bill, was given no hope for his eyesight, but through prayer Bill's sight was restored. This figurine also became the official gift of Child's Wish, an organization for terminally ill children.

***Part Of Me Wants To Be Good,* 12149**

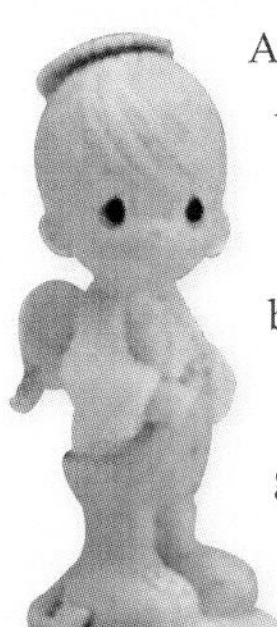

A very special young man, Albern Cuidad, who lived in the Philippines, was the inspiration for this figurine. He was always getting into trouble but he was so loveable you couldn't help but like him. He often said, "Please forgive me, I really meant to be good." The little boy in the figurine *Part Of Me Wants To Be Good* is modeled after Albern.

***Lord, I'm Coming Home,* 100110**

A collector who was a winner in one of the company's idea contests inspired this figurine. Her brother, who loved to play ball, died at the young age of 19. Sam was moved by the collector's story and her idea for a figurine, so he created this piece.

***God Bless The Day We Found You,* 100145**

Heather was the adopted daughter of the Butchers. She was five years old when she was adopted. They were struggling to make ends meet but knew they wanted her for a daughter. Because of his love for Heather, Sam created *God Bless The Day We Found You,* to celebrate the love that comes with an adopted child.

***The Lord Giveth And The Lord Taketh Away,* 100226**

After a trip to the Philippines, Sam arrived home and found total chaos. He found his wife Kate standing beside the tipped-over birdcage looking at bird feathers all over the floor. The cat had eaten the canary. Though it was a sad experience, Sam envisioned this figurine, *The Lord Giveth And The Lord Taketh Away.*

***No Tears Past The Gate,* 101826**

No Tears Past The Gate was painted to comfort Sam's assistant in the Philippines, Levi, whose sister was dying. She was 18 when she died. The painting was presented to Levi just a few weeks afterwards. Levi became one of Sam's most devoted workers. He was promoted to manager, then vice-president, and later president of the company.

***Only One Life To Offer,* 325309**

While speaking at a Bible camp, Sam met a young man named Larry who had been in and out of trouble. Sam took him under his wing and helped turn this young man around. Larry completed Bible school and went into youth ministry. When Larry was less than 40 years old, he called Sam and asked for money for an operation; he had stomach cancer. The surgery was not successful. He died, leaving a wife and two children. This figurine was dedicated to him.

***The Good Lord Will Always Uphold Us,* 325325**

A special friend of Sam's was a missionary in South Africa. Even though she had had rheumatoid arthritis since childhood, she faithfully served the Lord. This figurine was designed to honor Sam's faithful friend, Lory Burg.

***Heaven Must Have Sent You,* 521388**

Nancy Laptad, an employee in Sam's office, was always there when he needed financial advice. Nancy, though she was seen on a daily basis, did not realize how important she was. The figurine was dedicated to Nancy because she was always there when she was needed.

***Merry Christmas, Deer,* 522317**

A five-year-old girl adopted from an orphanage wanted all her Christmas gifts except one sent to her friends at the orphanage. All she wanted to keep was a stuffed reindeer. On the way home from delivering the toys, her reindeer got stuck in the door of a subway train and was lost forever. Several years ago, this lady wrote to Sam and asked him to help her find the Precious Moments ornament of a little reindeer with a teddy bear on his back. Sam sent the ornament from his private collection. The story inspired Sam to create this figurine of a little girl hanging ornaments on the antlers of a reindeer.

Count Your Many Blessings, 879274

In July 1994, a Canadian collector named Penny, and her husband, Rod, made a trip to the chapel hoping to meet Sam Butcher. When they finally met Mr. Butcher, he told Penny she "wasn't worth a cent" (a pun on her name). In 1996 Penny received a note from the chapel telling her that Sam had put the artwork for the "Jest One Penny" piece into production. Sam presented the figurine to Penny in 2000. It was called *Count Your Many Blessings*.

Collecting Friends Along The Way, PM-002

Sam has met many people that have been touched by the Precious Moments collection, and he says it brings him joy to see how much the figurines mean to them. This figurine was designed to honor all the special people in our lives, be they family, friends, or club members. There are 20 animals sculpted on the figurine in commemoration of the twentieth anniversary of the club.

Hello, Lord, It's Me Again, PM-811

Jon, Sam's oldest son, inspired this figurine after a romantic setback. Sam envisioned this little guy with a Dear Jon letter. He is on the phone and there is a tear running down his cheek. He's saying, "Hello, Lord, It's Me Again." Jon later found Patti and married her.

Smile, God Loves You, PM-821

Sam believes that outward appearances don't matter and that "you can't judge a book by its cover."

Put On A Happy Face, PM-822

This figurine was made to inspire collectors to show their happy side. Sam says it's really hard to take off your mask and show a "sunny side." This little clown figurine became an instant success and won the hearts of collectors.

Trust In The Lord To The Finish, PM-842

Sam began the painting for this figurine on his way to the Philippines. His youngest brother, Hank, always loved driving race cars.

The Lord Is My Shepherd, PM-851

Sam's daughter, Debbie, was the inspiration for this figurine. She has a warm, sensitive spirit and has contributed greatly to the Precious Moments line. She could handle all the very difficult problems in her life. This piece is a symbol of God's promise that, he, as the Good Shepherd, is always there to meet our every need.

I Love To Tell The Story, PM-852

Inspired by the old Christian song, this piece was dedicated to Pastor Royal Blue, who led Sam to the Lord Jesus. The child is speaking to a lamb, which symbolizes a pastor feeding God's flock with the bread of life, the word of God.

Grandma's Prayer, PM-861

This figurine is a loving tribute to Sam's grandmother, who reminded Sam often that she was praying for him.

I'm Following Jesus, PM-862

After encountering a jobless Filipino friend, Carlito, Sam was inspired to create this figurine. Carlito and his family trusted the Lord to take care of their needs. Eventually, Carlito got his own cab, which has a sign in the window that reads, "I'm Following Jesus."

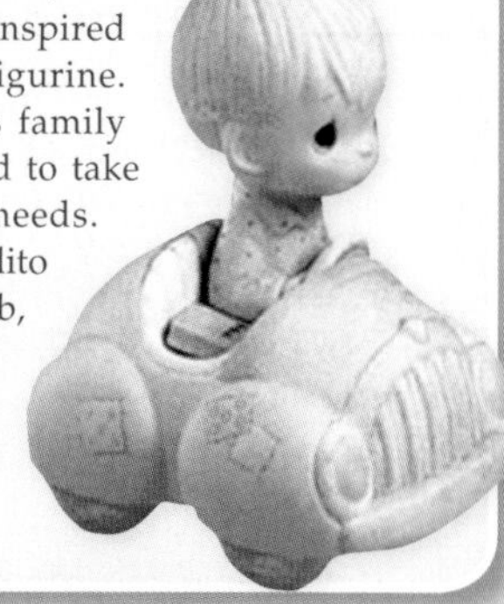

In His Time, PM-872

Sam Butcher said, "One day while Steve (Sam's son-in-law) was working in the garden, I visualized a boy patiently waiting for a tiny seed to grow. In my thoughts, the seed became a symbol of Steve's faith and patience as he waited for it to protrude from the ground."

Annual Production Marks

The annual production marks, located on the bottoms of the bases of Precious Moments figurines, reveal the year of the figurine's production and symbolize an inspirational message.

UM No Mark, before 1981

Triangle, Mid-1981
Symbol of the Holy Trinity — God the Father, God the Son, and God the Holy Ghost.

Hourglass, 1982
Represents the time we have on earth to serve the Lord.

Fish, 1983
Earliest symbol used by believers of the early apostolic church.

Cross, 1984
Symbol of Christianity recognized worldwide.

Dove, 1985
Symbol of love and peace.

Olive Branch, 1986
Symbol of peace and understanding.

Cedar Tree, 1987
Symbol of strength, beauty, and preservation.

Flower, 1988
Represents God's love for his children.

Bow & Arrow, 1989
Represents the power of the Bible.

Flame, 1990
For those who have gone through the fire of life and found comfort in believing.

Vessel, 1991
A reminder of God's love which flows through the vessel of life.

G-Clef, 1992
Symbolizes the harmony of God's love.

Butterfly, 1993
Represents the rebirth of man who comes from darkness into the light.

Trumpet, 1994
Represents loving, caring, and sharing; also signifies a battle cry and a herald of victory.

Ship, 1995
Ships, which are mentioned many times in the Scriptures, symbolically portray a message of hope.

Heart, 1996
Symbol of love.

Sword, 1997
From Hebrews 4:12, *For the Word of God is quick and powerful, and sharper than any two edged sword.*

Eyeglasses, 1998
Symbolizes Precious Moments' twentieth year and "the vision's still the same."

Star, 1999
From Matthew 2:2, *Where is He who has been born King of the Jews? For we have seen His star in the East and have come to worship Him.*

Egg, 2000
From Sam Butcher: *I have chosen the egg because it symbolizes the new millennium and a new beginning. Just as we know little of what the twenty-first century will bring, no one knows what is taking place inside an egg. Nor will they completely understand until it is hatched and God's wonderful plan is revealed. The egg speaks of birth, of new things to come — things known only to God alone.*

Sandal, 2001
The sandal represents our journey with the Lord.

Cross in Heart, 2002
Keeping faith in his heart, Sam chose a cross surrounded by a heart to symbolize faith. It is representative of the importance of faith now and in the next century.

Crown, 2003
The crown represents glory, dignity, and sovereignty. This is what Sam Butcher feels Precious Moments is all about.

Three-Petal Flower, 2004
In the world of Precious Moments, each petal in this flower symbolizes part of the message "loving, caring, and sharing."

Bread, 2005
Jesus said to them, *I am the bread of life; he who comes to me shall not hunger, and he who believes in me shall never thirst.* John 6:35

House, 2006
From Psalm 122:1-2, *I was glad when they said to me, Let us go to the house of the Lord! Our feet have been standing within your gates, O Jerusalem.*

Hammer, 2007
Hebrews 3:4, *For every house is built by someone, but God is the builder of everything.*

Stylish Heart, 2008
Celebrates "The Gift of Life" Proverbs 4:23, *Above all else, guard your heart, for it is the well spring of life.*

Sheaf of Wheat, 2009
John 6:35, *I am the Bread Of Life: he who comes to Me shall never hunger, he who believes in Me shall never thrust.*

Tree, 2010
Psalms 1:3, *He is like a tree planted by streams of water, which yields its fruit in season and whose leaf does not wither. Whatever he does prospers.*

Special Production Marks

Diamond
Appears on #103004, *We Belong To The Lord.*

Rosebud
Appears on #525049, *Good Friends Are Forever.*

Art of Disney
Appears on Walt Disney Showcase pieces.

Easter Seals Lily
Appears on annual figurines that benefit Easter Seals.

Flag
Appears on 1991 editions of *Bless Those Who Serve Their Country* figurines.

Flag
Appears on 1992 editions of *Bless Those Who Serve Their Country* figurines.

Four-Star Flag
Appears on 2002 *America Forever* series.

Know The Secondary Market

How do you find out about the production of Precious Moments pieces? Where do you start searching for these items? Precious Moments figurines have been produced since 1978. Finding outdated pieces can be difficult or easy, depending on the piece for which you are searching. The secondary market is the place to find these difficult Suspended, Retired, or Closed pieces.

The secondary market helps when a piece is no longer available at retail stores or at the retirement of the piece. When a piece is Retired, production is stopped on that piece. As the piece is sold out in the stores it becomes almost impossible to purchase. This same piece becomes more valuable on the secondary market and the collector is more willing to pay a higher price, thus increasing the value of the item. The collector today has more opportunity in the market because of the internet. Most collectors have computers and can go to different websites that deal with the secondary market. The collector can check out these sites to purchase some of those difficult to find pieces. We have listed some of these on page 293.

There are several ways to end the production of a piece. When a piece is Retired, the mold is broken and cannot be produced again. No notice is given to the collector when a piece is Retired. The collector is given only a small amount of time to purchase a piece that will be pulled out of production. Suspended pieces are temporarily taken out of production but can be brought back into production at a later date with a change of some sort to the piece. Dated figurines or pieces with a limited production time are called Closed pieces. They were produced for a limited time, possibly for one year, or in a limited quantity.

In addition to these pieces there are others produced for certain occasions or events. These are called Special Event, Limited Edition, and Club Member Exclusive figurines. Dated Annual means that the piece was issued for one year and includes a date on the figurine; Annuals were issued for one year only, but do not have dates on them. The ongoing, or Open, pieces can be purchased at retail dealers or on internet sites. Pieces produced before mid-1981 had no symbol on the understamp and are called Unmarked (UM). Precious Moments plates and ornaments were not marked until 1984.

Know the item you are purchasing on the secondary market and examine it for damage. Watch for dings, hairline cracks, paint discoloration, or other damage. Watch for fakes! There are some out there. Know your collection, read price guides, know what you are looking at. Only you can determine what you want in your collection — with or without boxes, damaged pieces bought at a good price, or pieces in mint condition. It's all up to you.

How To Use Your Precious Moments Price Guide

Many collectors confuse the copyright date with the date of issue. You must refer to the annual production symbol, not the date, to determine what year your pieces were manufactured. This price guide shows the suggested retail price for each piece. It lists when it was introduced and shows the changes in production symbols for the piece.

This guide lists items in the index at the back of the book in numerical order. The pieces manufactured from 1982 to the present are numbered on the understamp. If you do not know the number but do know the name of the piece, check the general index in the back of the book. The quickest and most accurate means of identification is the item number that appears on the understamp of most items manufactured from 1982 to the present. This number also appears in ads, brochures, and catalogs.

Remember: Errors are made all the time; unmarked pieces can sometimes be pieces that were just not marked.

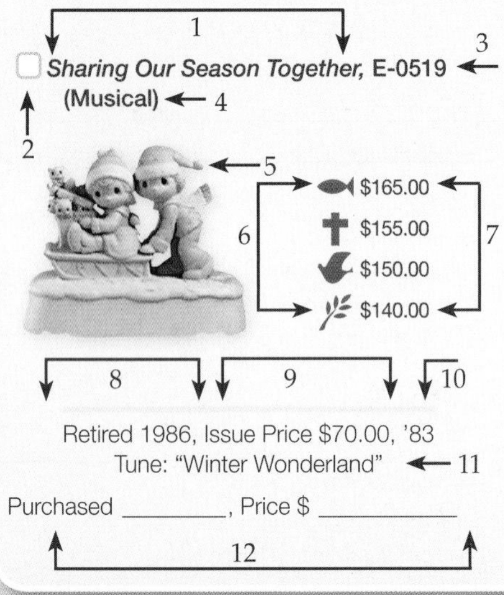

1. **Title** — Spiritual name given to the piece.
2. **Checkbox for inventory** — Box to check to keep track of a personal collection.
3. **Item Number** — The quickest and most accurate means of identification; appears on the understamp of most items.
4. **Object** — Tells whether item is something other than a figurine — ornament, musical, frame, plate, plaque, box, etc. (If nothing is listed in parentheses, it is a figurine.)
5. **Picture** — Photo of the item. We did not have photos of all items, but included any information known about the piece.
6. **Production symbols** — Annual Production Symbols; shows all symbols used for a particular figurine.
7. **Secondary market value** — The cost of the item when it is sold on the secondary market, according to production mark.
8. **Production status** — States if the piece has been Suspended or Retired, is a Limited Edition, Annual or Dated Annual, Club Member Exclusive, Special Event, or Open (still available). Date is included if known.
9. **Issue price** — The cost of the item at the time it was first introduced.
10. **Year introduced** — Lists the year the piece was first issued.
11. **Collector information** — Gives important facts about the piece: series, number in set, or name of tune played by musical pieces.
12. **Purchase information** — Gives the collector space to record information on the purchase date and price paid for each piece.

General Figurines

☐ *Sharing Our Season Together,* E-0501

$195.00
$185.00
$178.00
$172.00

Suspended 1986, Issue Price $50.00, '83

Purchased ________, Price $ ___________

☐ *Jesus Is The Light That Shines,* E-0502

UM $85.00
$80.00
$77.00
$75.00
$73.00

Suspended 1986, Issue Price $22.50, '83

Purchased ________, Price $ ___________

☐ *Blessings From My House To Yours,* E-0503

UM $100.00
$95.00
$93.00
$91.00
$89.00

Suspended 1986, Issue Price $27.00, '83

Purchased ________, Price $ ___________

☐ *Christmastime Is For Sharing,* E-0504

$135.00
$125.00
$120.00
$115.00
$110.00
$105.00
$100.00
$98.00

Retired 1990, Issue Price $37.00, '83

Purchased ________, Price $ ___________

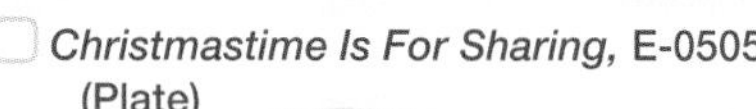

☐ *Christmastime Is For Sharing,* E-0505 (Plate)

UM $95.00
$90.00

Dated Annual 1983, Issue Price $85.00
Series: *Joy Of Christmas,* Second Issue

Purchased ________, Price $ ___________

☐ *Surrounded With Joy,* E-0506

$100.00
$95.00
$89.00
$85.00
$83.00
$79.00
$75.00

Retired 1989, Issue Price $21.00, '83

Purchased ___________

Price $ ___________

☐ *God Sent His Son,* E-0507

$110.00
$75.00
$73.00
$70.00
$69.00

Suspended 1987, Issue Price $32.50, '83

Purchased ________, Price $ ___________

☐ *Bringing God's Blessing To You,* E-0509

$110.00
$100.00
$95.00
$92.00
$90.00

Suspended 1987, Issue Price $35.00, '83

Purchased ________, Price $ ___________

☐ *Tubby's First Christmas,* E-0511

$58.00
$55.00
$53.00
$50.00
$48.00
$48.00
$48.00
$45.00
$43.00
$43.00
$40.00

Suspended 1993, Issue Price $12.00, '83
Nativity Addition

Purchased________ , Price $________

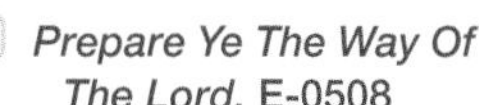

☐ *Prepare Ye The Way Of The Lord,* E-0508

$250.00
$225.00
$215.00
$200.00

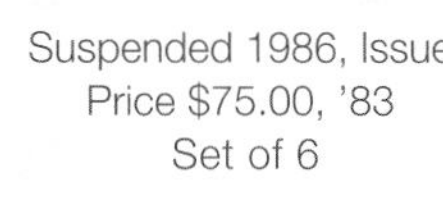

Suspended 1986, Issue Price $75.00, '83
Set of 6

Purchased ___________

Price $___________

It's A Perfect Boy, E-0512

[Fish] $80.00
[Cross] $77.00
[Dove] $71.00
[Olive Branch] $68.00
[Cedar Tree] $65.00
[Flower] $60.00
[Bow & Arrow] $58.00
[Flame] $55.00
[Vessel] $55.00

Suspended 1990, Issue Price $18.50, '83
Nativity Addition

Purchased ________, Price $ ____________

Surround Us With Joy, E-0513 (Ornament)

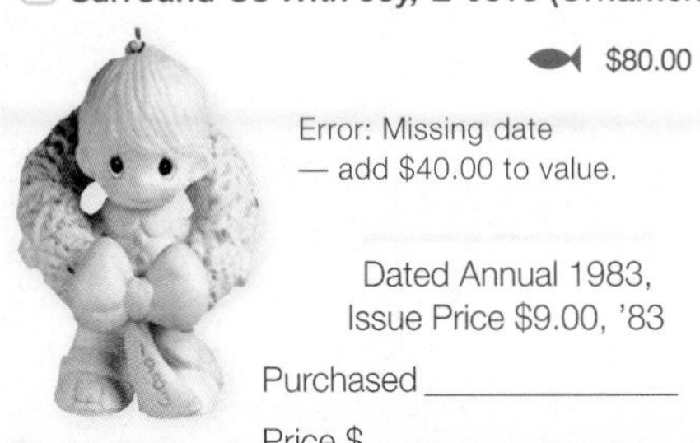

[Fish] $80.00

Error: Missing date — add $40.00 to value.

Dated Annual 1983, Issue Price $9.00, '83

Purchased ______________

Price $ ________________

Mother Sew Dear, E-0514 (Ornament)

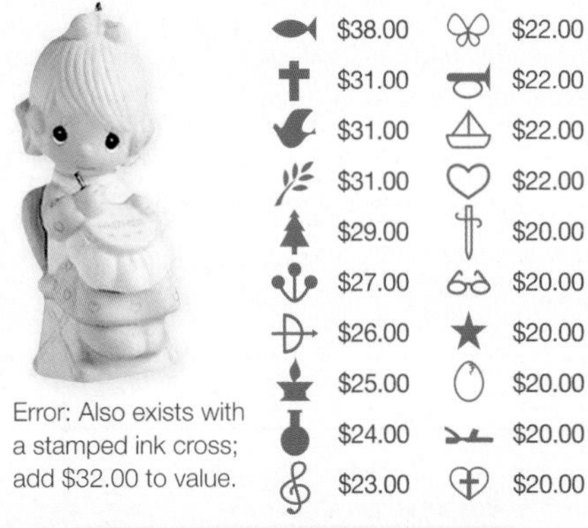

[Fish] $38.00
[Cross] $31.00
[Dove] $31.00
[Olive Branch] $31.00
[Cedar Tree] $29.00
[Flower] $27.00
[Bow & Arrow] $26.00
[Flame] $25.00
[Vessel] $24.00
[G-Clef] $23.00
[Butterfly] $22.00
[Trumpet] $22.00
[Ship] $22.00
[Heart] $22.00
[Sword] $20.00
[Eyeglasses] $20.00
[Star] $20.00
[Egg] $20.00
[Sandal] $20.00
[Cross in Heart] $20.00

Error: Also exists with a stamped ink cross; add $32.00 to value.

Retired 2002, Issue Price $9.00, '83

Purchased ________, Price $ ____________

To A Special Dad, E-0515 (Ornament)

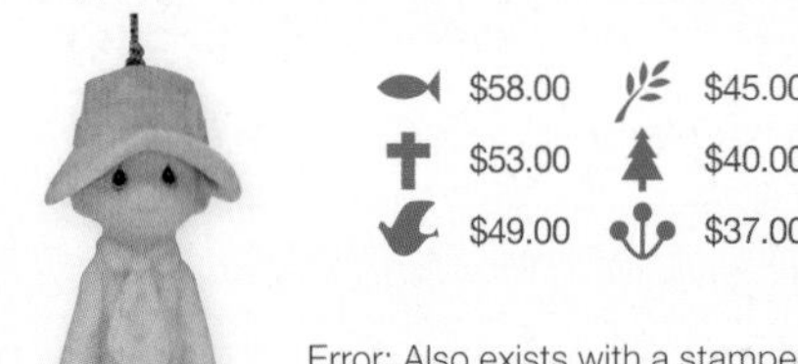

[Fish] $58.00
[Cross] $53.00
[Dove] $49.00
[Olive Branch] $45.00
[Cedar Tree] $40.00
[Flower] $37.00

Error: Also exists with a stamped ink cross; add $50.00 to value.

Suspended 1988, Issue Price $9.00, '83

Purchased ________, Price $ ____________

The Purr-fect Grandma, E-0516 (Ornament)

[Fish] $50.00
[Cross] $40.00
[Dove] $36.00
[Olive Branch] $33.00
[Cedar Tree] $31.00
[Flower] $31.00
[Bow & Arrow] $31.00
[Flame] $31.00
[Vessel] $30.00
[G-Clef] $30.00
[Butterfly] $29.00
[Trumpet] $29.00
[Ship] $27.00
[Heart] $27.00
[Sword] $26.00
[Eyeglasses] $25.00
[Star] $24.00
[Egg] $23.00
[Sandal] $22.00
[Cross in Heart] $21.00

Error: Also exists with a stamped ink cross; add $55.00 to value.

Retired 2002, Issue Price $9.00, '83

Purchased ________, Price $ ____________

The Perfect Grandpa, E-0517 (Ornament)

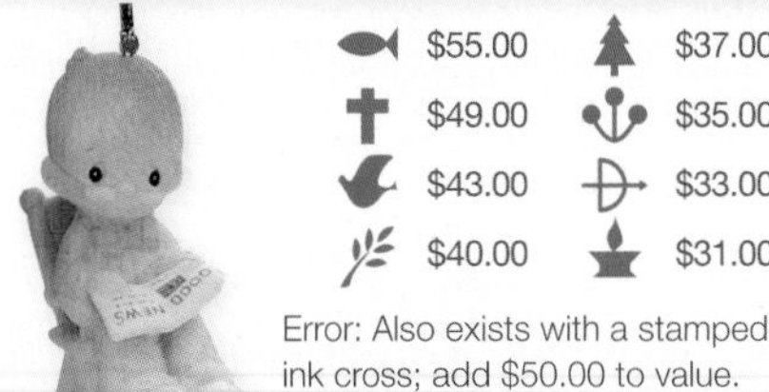

[Fish] $55.00
[Cross] $49.00
[Dove] $43.00
[Olive Branch] $40.00
[Cedar Tree] $37.00
[Flower] $35.00
[Bow & Arrow] $33.00
[Flame] $31.00

Error: Also exists with a stamped ink cross; add $50.00 to value.

Suspended 1990, Issue Price $9.00, '83

Purchased ________, Price $ ____________

Blessed Are The Pure In Heart, E-0518 (Ornament)

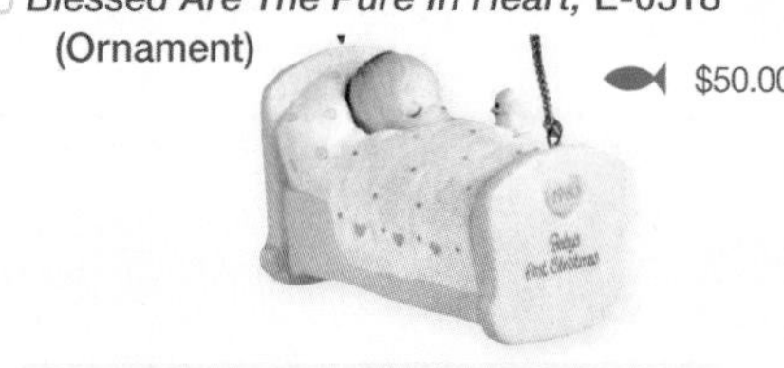

[Fish] $50.00

Dated Annual 1983, Issue Price $9.00, '83
"Baby's First Christmas"

Purchased ________, Price $ ____________

Sharing Our Season Together, E-0519 (Musical)

[Fish] $225.00
[Cross] $215.00
[Dove] $205.00
[Olive Branch] $195.00

Retired 1986, Issue Price $70.00, '83
Tune: *Winter Wonderland*

Purchased ________, Price $ ____________

Wee Three Kings, E-0520 (Musical)

[Fish] $155.00
[Cross] $145.00
[Dove] $135.00
[Olive Branch] $125.00

Suspended 1986, Issue Price $60.00, '83
Tune: *We Three Kings*

Purchased ____________

Price $ ______________

Blessed Are The Pure In Heart, E-0521 (Frame)

[Fish] $75.00
[Cross] $65.00
[Dove] $60.00
[Olive Branch] $57.00
[Cedar Tree] $54.00

Suspended 1987, Issue Price $18.00, '83
"Baby's First Christmas"

Purchased ________, Price $ ____________

Surrounded With Joy, E-0522 (Bell)

UM $70.00 [Fish] $70.00

Error: Has been reported missing date; add $45.00 to value.

Dated Annual 1983, Issue Price $18.00, '83

Purchased ______________

Price $ ________________

Onward Christian Soldiers, E-0523

UM $270.00
[Fish] $75.00
[Cross] $72.00
[Dove] $71.00
[Olive Branch] $70.00
[Cedar Tree] $69.00
[Flower] $68.00
[Bow & Arrow] $67.00
[Flame] $66.00
[Vessel] $65.00
[G-Clef] $64.00
[Butterfly] $63.00
[Trumpet] $62.00
[Ship] $61.00
[Heart] $60.00
[Sword] $59.00
[Eyeglasses] $58.00
[Star] $57.00
[Egg] $57.00
[Sandal] $55.00
[Cross in Heart] 55.00

Though very rare, Unmarked pieces could have been produced in any of the years of production. Consider Fish as the first mark. Also exists with a decal Fish; add $115.00 to value.

Retired 2002, Issue Price $24.00, '83

Purchased ________, Price $ ____________

☐ ***You Can't Run Away From God*, E-0525**

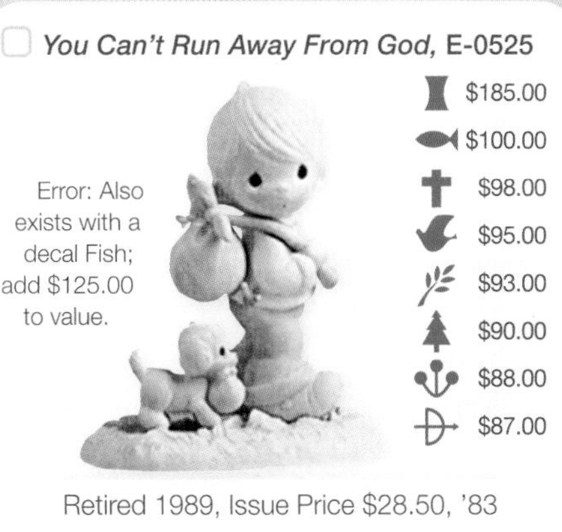

Error: Also exists with a decal Fish; add $125.00 to value.

$185.00
$100.00
$98.00
$95.00
$93.00
$90.00
$88.00
$87.00

Retired 1989, Issue Price $28.50, '83

Purchased ________, Price $ ___________

☐ ***He Upholdeth Those Who Fall*, E-0526**

UM $175.00
$125.00
$115.00
$105.00

Unmarked pieces could have been produced in any of the years of production. Consider Fish as the first mark. Also exists with a removable inked Fish; add $120.00 to value.

Suspended 1985, Issue Price $28.50, '83

Purchased ________, Price $ ___________

☐ ***His Eye Is On The Sparrow*, E-0530**

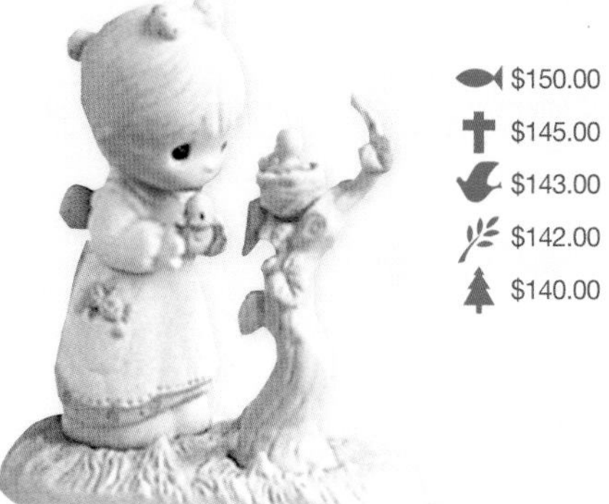

$150.00
$145.00
$143.00
$142.00
$140.00

Retired 1987, Issue Price $28.50, '83

Purchased ________, Price $ ___________

☐ ***O Come All Ye Faithful*, E-0531 (Ornament)**

$60.00
$55.00
$53.00
$50.00

Suspended 1986, Issue Price $9.00, '83

Purchased ______________

Price $______________

☐ ***Let Heaven And Nature Sing*, E-0532 (Ornament)**

$55.00
$51.00
$49.00
$45.00

Retired 1986, Issue Price $9.00, '83

Purchased ________, Price $ ___________

☐ ***Tell Me The Story Of Jesus*, E-0533 (Ornament)**

$56.00
$51.00
$48.00
$45.00
$45.00
$45.00

Suspended 1988, Issue Price $9.00, '83

Purchased ________, Price $ ___________

☐ ***To Thee With Love*, E-0534 (Ornament)**

$60.00
$55.00
$52.00
$50.00
$49.00
$45.00
$44.00

Retired 1989, Issue Price $9.00, '83

Purchased ________, Price $ ___________

☐ ***Love Is Patient*, E-0535 (Ornament)**

$63.00
$60.00
$55.00
$51.00

Suspended 1986, Issue Price $9.00, '83

Purchased______________

Price $______________

☐ ***Love Is Patient*, E-0536 (Ornament)**

$70.00
$65.00
$63.00
$63.00

Suspended 1986, Issue Price $9.00, '83

Purchased ________, Price $ ___________

☐ ***Jesus Is The Light That Shines*, E-0537 (Ornament)**

$60.00
$55.00
$53.00

Suspended 1985, Issue Price $9.00, '83

Purchased ________, Price $ ___________

☐ ***Wee Three Kings*, E-0538 (Plate)**

UM $55.00
$54.00
$53.00
$52.00

Limited Ed. 15,000, Issue Price $40.00, '83
Series: *Christmas Collection* – Third Issue; Individually Numbered

Purchased ________, Price $ ___________

☐ ***Katie Lynne*, E-0539 (Doll)**

UM $225.00
$200.00
$197.00
$190.00
$188.00
$186.00
$185.00

Suspended 1988, Issue Price $150.00, '83

Purchased ________, Price $ ___________

☐ *Jesus Loves Me,* E-1372B

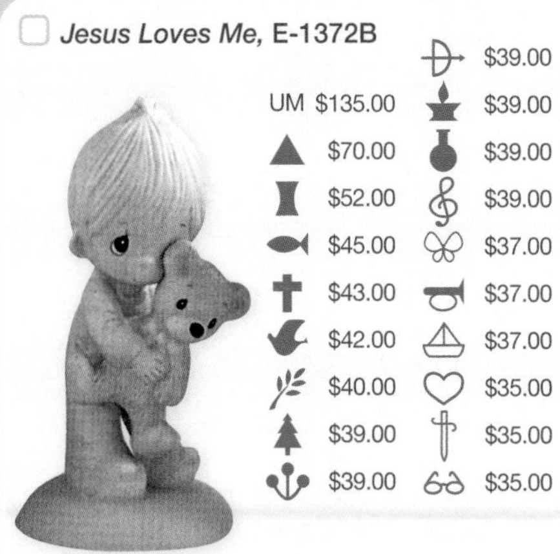

Mark	Price	Mark	Price
UM	$135.00	[bow & arrow]	$39.00
▲	$70.00	[flame]	$39.00
[hourglass]	$52.00	[vessel]	$39.00
[fish]	$45.00	[G-clef]	$39.00
[cross]	$43.00	[butterfly]	$37.00
[dove]	$42.00	[trumpet]	$37.00
[olive branch]	$40.00	[ship]	$37.00
[cedar tree]	$39.00	[heart]	$35.00
[flower]	$39.00	[sword]	$35.00
		[eyeglasses]	$35.00

Retired 1998, Issue Price $7.00, '79
One of the Original "21"

Purchased ________, Price $ ___________

☐ *Jesus Loves Me,* E-1372G

Mark	Price	Mark	Price
UM	$150.00	[G-clef]	$48.00
▲	$90.00	[butterfly]	$46.00
[hourglass]	$80.00	[trumpet]	$45.00
[fish]	$70.00	[ship]	$44.00
[cross]	$65.00	[heart]	$43.00
[dove]	$62.00	[sword]	$42.00
[olive branch]	$59.00	[eyeglasses]	$41.00
[cedar tree]	$57.00	★	$40.00
[flower]	$55.00	[egg]	$40.00
[bow & arrow]	$52.00	[bird]	$40.00
[flame]	$50.00	[cross in heart]	$40.00
[vessel]	$48.00	[crown]	$40.00

Retired 2003, Issue Price $7.00, '79
One of the Original "21"

Purchased ________, Price $ ___________

☐ *Smile, God Loves You,* E-1373B

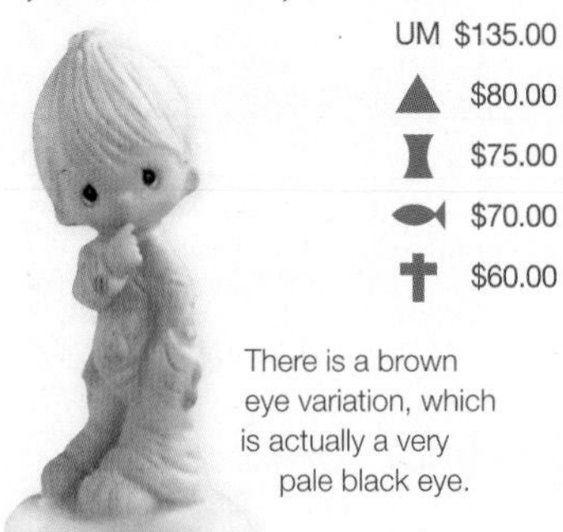

UM	$135.00
▲	$80.00
[hourglass]	$75.00
[fish]	$70.00
[cross]	$60.00

There is a brown eye variation, which is actually a very pale black eye.

Retired 1984, Issue Price $7.00, '79
One of the Original "21"

Purchased ________, Price $ ___________

☐ *Jesus Is The Light,* E-1373G

Mark	Price	Mark	Price
UM	$140.00	[cross]	$65.00
▲	$80.00	[dove]	$65.00
[hourglass]	$75.00	[olive branch]	$65.00
[fish]	$75.00	[cedar tree]	$55.00
		[flower]	$50.00

Retired 1988, Issue Price $7.00, '79
One of the Original "21"

Purchased ________, Price $ ___________

☐ *Praise The Lord Anyhow,* E-1374B

UM	$140.00
▲	$125.00
[hourglass]	$100.00

There are variations in the color of the dog's nose (brown or black) and variations in the color of the ice cream.

Retired 1982, Issue Price $8.00, '79
One of the Original "21"

Purchased ________, Price $ ___________

☐ *Make A Joyful Noise,* E-1374G

Mark	Price	Mark	Price	Mark	Price
UM	$130.00	[cross]	$68.00	[G-clef]	$45.00
▲	$80.00	[dove]	$65.00	[butterfly]	$45.00
[hourglass]	$80.00	[olive branch]	$60.00	[trumpet]	$45.00
[fish]	$70.00	[cedar tree]	$55.00	[ship]	$45.00
		[flower]	$55.00	[heart]	$45.00
		[bow & arrow]	$52.00	[sword]	$45.00
		[flame]	$50.00	[eyeglasses]	$45.00
		[vessel]	$45.00	★	$45.00
				[egg]	$45.00

Figurine has experienced mold shrinkage problems; variations in the position of the goose are common.

Retired 2000, Issue Price $8.00, '79
One of the Original "21"

Purchased ________, Price $ ___________

☐ *Love Lifted Me,* E-1375A

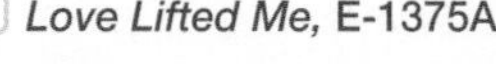

Mark	Price	Mark	Price
UM	$175.00	[fish]	$110.00
▲	$115.00	[cross]	$107.00
[hourglass]	$110.00	[dove]	$107.00
		[olive branch]	$107.00
		[cedar tree]	$100.00
		[flower]	$95.00
		[bow & arrow]	$93.00
		[flame]	$90.00
		[vessel]	$90.00
		[G-clef]	$90.00
		[butterfly]	$85.00

Retired 1993, Issue Price $11.00, '79
One of the Original "21"

Purchased ________, Price $ ___________

☐ *Prayer Changes Things,* E-1375B

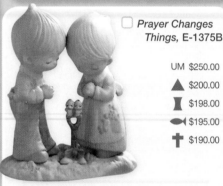

UM	$250.00
▲	$200.00
[hourglass]	$198.00
[fish]	$195.00
[cross]	$190.00

Suspended 1984, Issue Price $11.00, '79
One of the Original "21"

Purchased ________, Price $ ___________

☐ *Love One Another,* E-1376

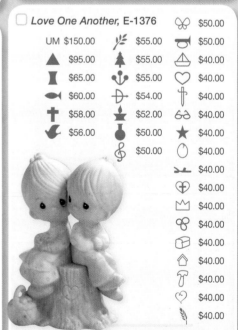

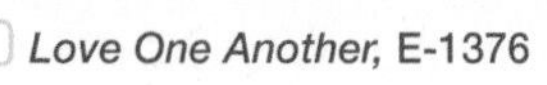

Mark	Price	Mark	Price	Mark	Price
UM	$150.00	[olive branch]	$55.00	[butterfly]	$50.00
▲	$95.00	[cedar tree]	$55.00	[trumpet]	$50.00
[hourglass]	$65.00	[flower]	$55.00	[ship]	$40.00
[fish]	$60.00	[bow & arrow]	$54.00	[heart]	$40.00
[cross]	$58.00	[flame]	$52.00	[sword]	$40.00
[dove]	$56.00	[vessel]	$50.00	[eyeglasses]	$40.00
		[G-clef]	$50.00	★	$40.00
				[egg]	$40.00
				[bird]	$40.00
				[cross in heart]	$40.00
				[crown]	$40.00
				[clover]	$40.00
				[box]	$40.00
				[house]	$40.00
				[mushroom]	$40.00
				[small heart]	$40.00
				[leaf]	$40.00

Open, Issue Price $10.00, '79
One of the Original "21"

Purchased ________, Price $ ___________

☐ ***He Leadeth Me,* E-1377A**

UM $180.00
▲ $135.00
⧗ $115.00
🐟 $115.00
✝ $110.00

Classic variation: the incorrect inspirational title, *He Careth For You,* is on the understamp decal of some Unmarked pieces. This is one of the most difficult to find of all the classic variations. The few known sales are in the $350.00 range. Reintroduced in 1998 with a color change as E-1377R — November 19 on QVC and November 21 at DSRs and Century Circle Retailers.

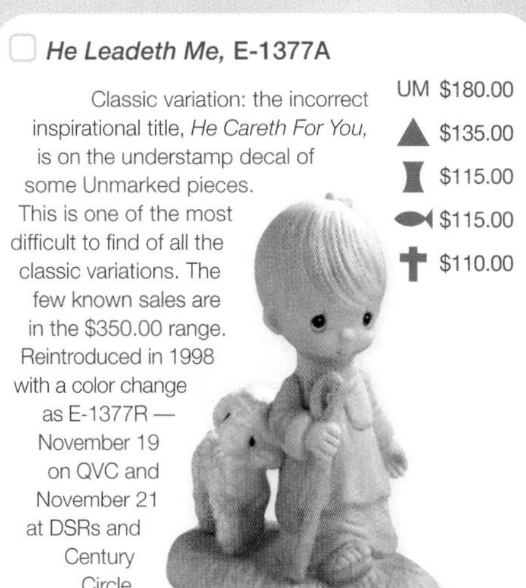

Suspended 1984, Reintroduced 1998, Retired 1998, Issue Price $9.00, '79
One of the Original "21"

Purchased ________, Price $ ____________

☐ ***He Careth For You,* E-1377B**

UM $200.00
▲ $155.00
⧗ $135.00
🐟 $115.00
✝ $110.00

Classic variation: The incorrect inspiration title, *He Leadeth Me,* is on the understamp decal of some Unmarked pieces. This is a more difficult variation to find than the variation of E-1377A. Known sale at $600.00.

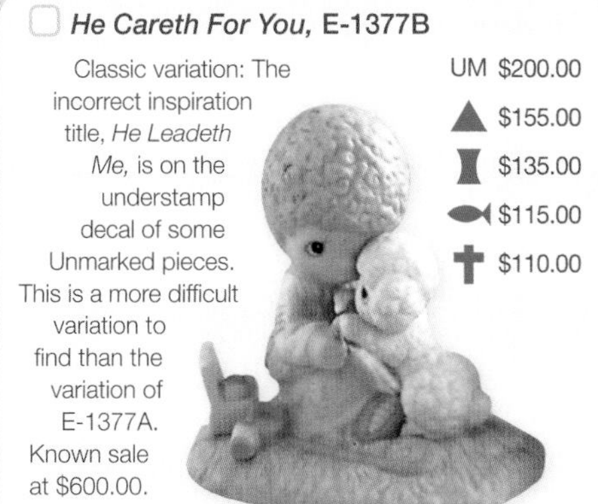

Suspended 1984, Issue Price $9.00, '79
One of the Original "21"

Purchased ________, Price $ ____________

☐ ***He Leadeth Me,* E-1377R**

👓 $55.00

Brought back with a color change for 11/21/98 *Turn Back The Clock Event Celebration.* Retired after the event.

Retired 1998, Issue Price $9.00, '98

Purchased ________, Price $ ____________

☐ ***God Loveth A Cheerful Giver,* E-1378**

UM $750.00

Retired 1981, Issue Price $15.00, '79
One of the Original "21"

Purchased ________, Price $ ____________

☐ ***Love Is Kind,* E-1379A**

UM $175.00
▲ $125.00
⧗ $115.00
🐟 $110.00
✝ $100.00

Suspended 1984, Reintroduced 1998, Retired 1998, Issue Price $8.00, '79
One of the Original "21"

Purchased ________, Price $ ____________

☐ ***God Understands,* E-1379B**

UM $150.00
▲ $125.00
⧗ $115.00
🐟 $112.00
✝ $105.00

Suspended 1984, Issue Price $8.00, '79
One of the Original "21"

Purchased ________

Price $ ________

☐ ***God Understands,* E-1379BR**

⋈ $45.00

Retired 2001, Issue Price $19.50, '01
Back To School Event

Purchased ________

Price $____________

☐ ***Love Is Kind,* E-1379R**

👓 $70.00

Piece Retired immediately after event. Color change for reintroduction. Precious Moments Twentieth Anniversary understamp.

Retired 1998, Issue Price $8.00, '98
Turn Back The Clock Event Celebration

Purchased ________, Price $ ____________

☐ ***O, How I Love Jesus,* E-1380B**

UM $180.00
▲ $160.00
⧗ $145.00
🐟 $140.00
✝ $130.00

Retired 1984, Issue Price $8.00, '79
One of the Original "21"

Purchased ________

Price $ ____________

☐ ***His Burden Is Light,* E-1380G**

UM $185.00
▲ $165.00
⧗ $150.00
🐟 $145.00
✝ $135.00

Retired 1984, Issue Price $8.00, '79
One of the Original "21"

Purchased ________

Price $________

☐ ***Jesus Is The Answer,* E-1381**

UM $215.00
▲ $180.00
⧗ $175.00
🐟 $165.00
✝ $160.00

E-1381 was re-sculpted and reintroduced in April 1992 as E-1381R. E-1381R was subsequently retired in 1996.

Suspended 1984, Reintroduced 1992, Retired 1996, Issue Price $11.50, '79
One of the Original "21"

Purchased ________, Price $ ____________

☐ *Jesus Is The Answer,* E-1381R

$100.00
$85.00
$83.00
$80.00
$78.00

Retired 1996, Issue Price $55.00, '92
St. Jude Children's Research Hospital Exclusive

Purchased ________, Price $ ____________

☐ *We Have Seen His Star,* E-2010

UM $175.00
$145.00
$135.00
$125.00
$105.00

Suspended 1984, Issue Price $8.00, '79
One of the Original "21"

Purchased ____________

Price $ ____________

☐ *Come Let Us Adore Him,* E-2011

UM $375.00

This piece has been found with one air hole in the bottom instead of two.

Retired 1981, Issue Price $10.00, '79
One of the Original "21"

Purchased ______

Price $__________

☐ *Jesus Is Born,* E-2012

UM $200.00
$175.00
$170.00
$160.00
$155.00

Suspended 1984, Issue Price $12.00, '79
One of the Original "21"

Purchased ________, Price $ ____________

☐ *Unto Us A Child Is Born,* E-2013

UM $195.00
$175.00
$170.00
$160.00
$155.00

Suspended 1984, Issue Price $12.00, '79
One of the Original "21"

Purchased ________, Price $ ____________

☐ *Joy To The World,* E-2343 (Ornament)

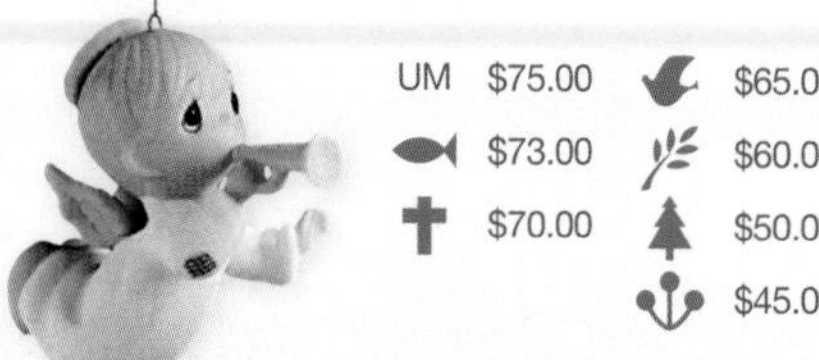

UM $75.00
$73.00
$70.00
$65.00
$60.00
$50.00
$45.00

Suspended 1988, Issue Price $9.00, '82

Purchased ________, Price $ ____________

☐ *Joy To The World,* E-2344 (Candle Climbers)

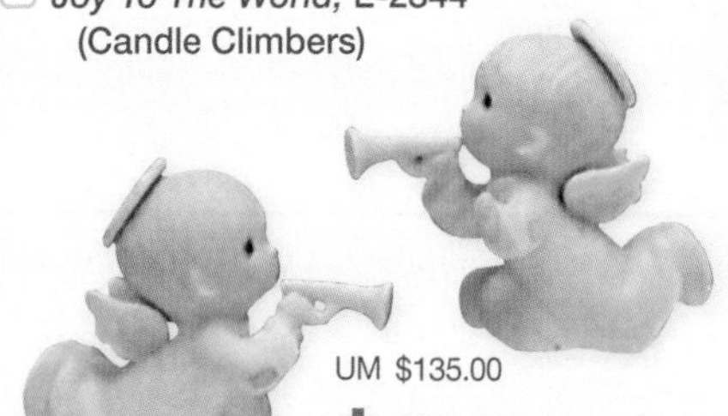

UM $135.00
$125.00
$120.00

Suspended 1985, Issue Price $20.00, '82
Set of 2

Purchased ________, Price $ ____________

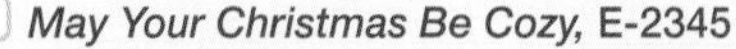

☐ *May Your Christmas Be Cozy,* E-2345

$90.00
$86.00
$78.00

Suspended 1984, Issue Price $23.00, '82

Purchased ________, Price $ ____________

☐ *Let Heaven And Nature Sing,* E-2346 (Musical)

UM $225.00
$180.00
$165.00
$160.00
$158.00
$150.00
$145.00
$140.00
$135.00

Unmarked pieces could have been produced in any of the years of production. Consider Hourglass as the first mark.

Suspended 1989, Issue Price $50.00, '82
Tune: *Joy To The World*

Purchased ________, Price $ ____________

☐ *Let Heaven And Nature Sing,* E-2347 (Plate)

UM $65.00
$62.00
$62.00
$62.00

Limited Ed. 15,000, Issue Price $40.00, '82
Series: *Christmas Collection* — Second Issue, Individually Numbered

Purchased ________, Price $ ____________

☐ *May Your Christmas Be Warm,* E-2348

$180.00
$170.00
$165.00
$160.00
$155.00
$150.00
$145.00

Suspended 1988, Issue Price $30.00, '82

Purchased ________, Price $ ____________

☐ *Tell Me The Story Of Jesus,* E-2349

$160.00
$145.00
$135.00
$125.00

This is a favorite of many collectors and is scarce on the secondary market.

Suspended 1985, Issue Price $30.00, '82

Purchased ________, Price $ ____________

☐ *Dropping In For Christmas,* E-2350

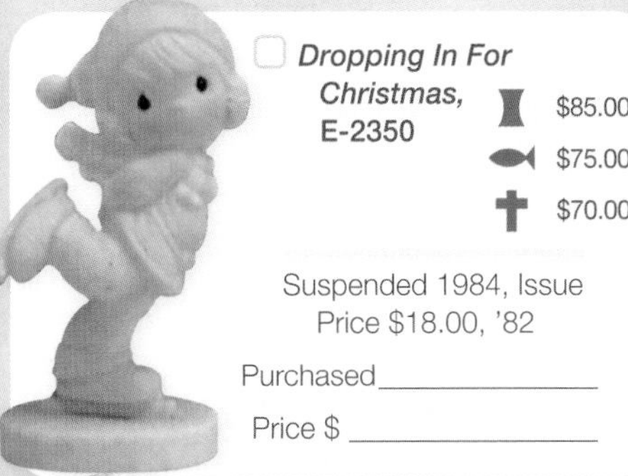

$85.00
$75.00
$70.00

Suspended 1984, Issue Price $18.00, '82

Purchased______________

Price $ ______________

☐ *Holy Smokes,* E-2351

$175.00
$160.00
$150.00
$140.00
$130.00
$120.00

Retired 1987, Issue Price $27.00, '82

Purchased ________, Price $ ____________

☐ *O Come All Ye Faithful,* E-2352 (Musical)

UM $225.00
$185.00
$175.00
$170.00

Suspended 1984, Issue Price $45.00, '82
Tune: *O Come All Ye Faithful*

Purchased ________

Price $ ____________

☐ *O Come All Ye Faithful,* E-2353

$125.00
$115.00
$105.00
$100.00
$95.00

Retired 1986, Issue Price $27.50, '82

Purchased ___________

Price $ ___________

☐ *I'll Play My Drum For Him,* E-2355 (Musical)

$275.00
$265.00
$255.00

Suspended 1984, Issue Price $45.00, '82
Tune: *Little Drummer Boy*

Purchased ________, Price $ ____________

☐ *I'll Play My Drum For Him,* E-2356

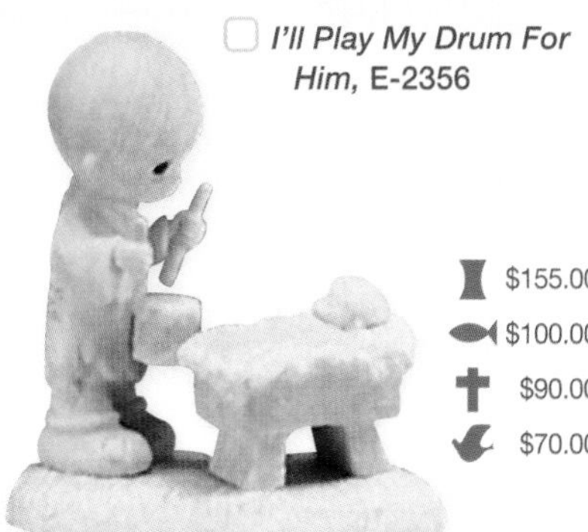

$155.00
$100.00
$90.00
$70.00

Suspended 1985, Issue Price $30.00, '82

Purchased ________, Price $ ____________

☐ *I'll Play My Drum For Him,* E-2357 (Plate)

UM $75.00

Dated Annual 1982, Issue Price $40.00, '82
Series: *Joy Of Christmas* — First Issue

Purchased ________, Price $ ____________

☐ *I'll Play My Drum For Him,* E-2358 (Bell)

UM $75.00

Dated Annual 1982, Issue Price $17.00, '82

Purchased _____________

Price $ _______________

☐ *I'll Play My Drum For Him,* E-2359 (Ornament)

$95.00

Prototypes were dated. The actual production piece was not.

Dated Annual 1982, Issue Price $9.00, '82

Purchased ________, Price $ ____________

☐ *I'll Play My Drum For Him,* E-2360

$60.00	$46.00
$58.00	$44.00
$56.00	$44.00
$54.00	$42.00
$52.00	$42.00
$52.00	$40.00
$50.00	$40.00
$50.00	$38.00
$48.00	$38.00
$46.00	$38.00

Retired 2001, Issue Price $16.00, '82
Nativity Addition

Purchased ________, Price $ ____________

☐ ***Christmas Joy From Head To Toe,*** **E-2361**

$75.00
$70.00
$70.00
$65.00
$60.00

Suspended 1986, Issue Price $25.00, '82

Purchased ________, Price $ ____________

☐ ***Baby's First Christmas,*** **E-2362 (Ornament)**

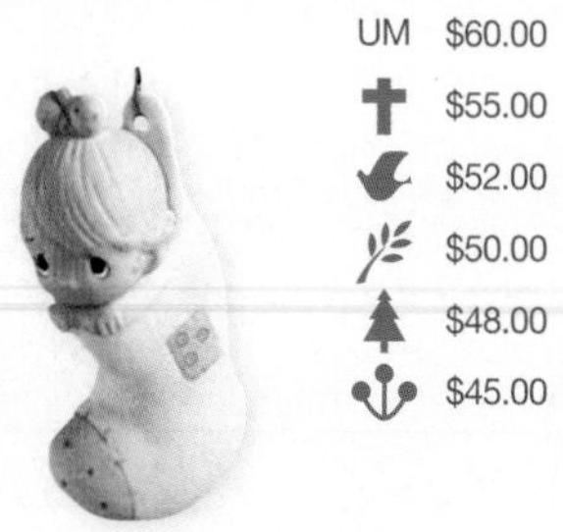

UM $60.00
$55.00
$52.00
$50.00
$48.00
$45.00

Suspended 1988, Issue Price $9.00, '82

Purchased ________, Price $ ____________

☐ ***Camel,*** **E-2363**

$55.00
$52.00
$50.00
$48.00
$48.00
$45.00
$45.00
$45.00
$45.00
$43.00
$43.00
$43.00
$40.00
$40.00
$40.00
$38.00
$38.00
$38.00
$36.00
$36.00
$36.00
$36.00

Retired 2003, Issue Price $20.00, '82
Nativity Addition

Purchased ________, Price $ ____________

☐ ***Goat,*** **E-2364**

UM $73.00
$70.00
$68.00
$65.00
$62.00
$60.00
$60.00
$55.00
$50.00

Suspended 1989, Issue Price $10.00, '82
Nativity Addition

Purchased ________, Price $ ____________

☐ ***The First Noel,*** **E-2365**

UM $90.00
$80.00
$80.00
$75.00

Suspended 1984, Issue Price $16.00, '82
Nativity Addition

Purchased ________, Price $ ____________

☐ ***The First Noel,*** **E-2366**

UM $92.00
$83.00
$80.00
$75.00

Suspended 1984, Issue Price $16.00, '82
Nativity Addition

Purchased ________, Price $ ____________

☐ ***The First Noel,*** **E-2367 (Ornament)**

UM $97.00
$95.00
$85.00
$80.00

Suspended 1984, Issue Price $9.00, '83

Purchased ________, Price $ ____________

☐ ***The First Noel,*** **E-2368 (Ornament)**

$95.00
$85.00
$80.00

Suspended 1984, Issue Price $9.00, '83

Purchased ________, Price $ ____________

☐ ***Dropping In For Christmas,*** **E-2369 (Ornament)**

UM $100.00
$75.00
$73.00
$70.00
$68.00
$65.00

Retired 1986, Issue Price $9.00, '82

Purchased ________, Price $ ____________

☐ ***Unicorn,*** **E-2371 (Ornament)**

UM $125.00
$110.00
$100.00
$98.00
$95.00
$90.00
$85.00

Retired 1988, Issue Price $10.00, '82

Purchased ________, Price $ ____________

☐ ***Baby's First Christmas,*** **E-2372 (Ornament)**

UM $48.00
$46.00
$44.00
$43.00
$38.00

Exists with and without title, *Baby's First Christmas,* in unmarked version. Titled piece is rarer; add $10.00 to value.

Suspended 1985, Issue Price $9.00, '82

Purchased ________, Price $ ____________

☐ *Bundles Of Joy,* E-2374

$165.00 · $135.00 · $130.00 · $125.00 · $120.00 · $115.00 · $110.00 · $105.00 · $100.00 · $95.00 · $90.00 · $85.00

Retired 1993, Issue Price $27.50, '82

Purchased ________, Price $ ___________

☐ *Dropping Over For Christmas,* E-2375

$175.00 · $155.00 · $145.00 · $135.00 · $130.00 · $125.00 · $120.00 · $115.00 · $110.00 · $105.00

Retired 1991, Issue Price $30.00, '82

Purchased ________, Price $ ___________

☐ *Dropping Over For Christmas,* E-2376 (Ornament)

$95.00 · $70.00 · $65.00 · $60.00

Retired 1985, Issue Price $9.00, '82

Purchased ________, Price $ ___________

☐ *Our First Christmas Together,* E-2377

$120.00 · $110.00 · $100.00 · $95.00

Suspended 1985, Issue Price $35.00, '82

Purchased ________, Price $ ___________

☐ *Our First Christmas Together,* E-2378 (Plate)

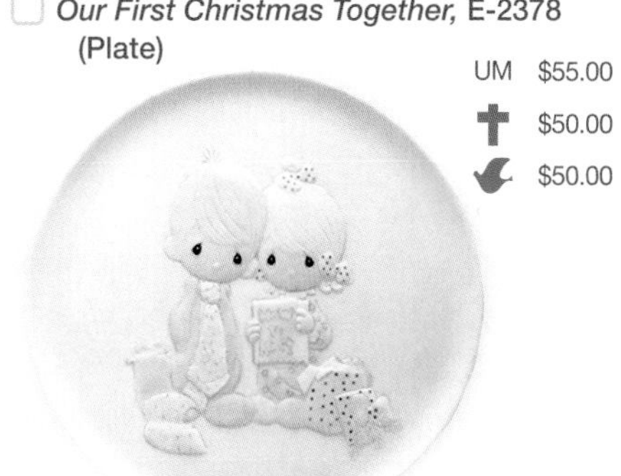

UM $55.00 · $50.00 · $50.00

Suspended 1985, Issue Price $30.00, '82

Purchased ________, Price $ ___________

☐ *Mouse With Cheese,* E-2381 (Ornament)

$130.00 · $110.00 · $105.00

Suspended 1984, Issue Price $9.00, '82

Purchased ________, Price $ ___________

☐ *O Holy Night,* E-2381R

$15.00 · $15.00 · $15.00 · $15.00 · $15.00

Open, Issue Price $15.00, '03
Mini Nativity Addition

Purchased ________, Price $ ___________

☐ *Our First Christmas Together,* E-2385 (Ornament)

$65.00 · $60.00 · $58.00 · $55.00 · $52.00 · $48.00 · $45.00 · $42.00 · $38.00 · $35.00

Suspended 1991, Issue Price $10.00, '82

Purchased ________, Price $ ___________

☐ *Camel, Donkey, And Cow,* E-2386 (Ornaments)

UM $125.00 · $100.00 · $97.00 · $92.00 · $90.00

Unmarked pieces could have been produced in any of the years of production. Mixed sets of Unmarked/Hourglass marks are common.

Suspended 1984, Issue Price $25.00
Set of 3

Purchased ________, Price $ ___________

☐ *House Set And Palm Tree,* E-2387

$225.00 · $185.00 · $180.00 · $175.00 · $170.00 · $170.00 · $170.00 · $165.00 · $165.00 · $165.00 · $160.00 · $160.00 · $160.00 · $155.00 · $155.00 · $155.00 · $150.00 · $150.00 · $150.00 · $150.00 · $145.00 · $145.00 · $140.00 · $140.00

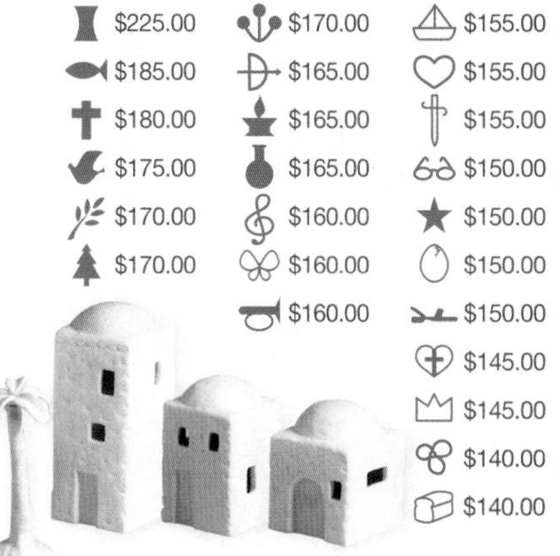

Mini nativity addition. Some Hourglass sets were shipped with the pink house having no mark; add $50.00 to value.

Suspended, Issue Price $45.00, '82
Set of 4, Mini Nativity Addition

Purchased ________, Price $ ___________

☐ *Jesus Is Born,* E-2801

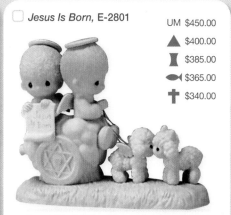

UM $450.00 · $400.00 · $385.00 · $365.00 · $340.00

Suspended 1984, Issue Price $37.50, '80

Purchased ________, Price $ ___________

☐ *Come Let Us Adore Him,* E-2395 (Mini Nativity)

[Hourglass]	$185.00	[Flame]	$155.00	[Star]	$140.00
[Fish]	$180.00	[Vessel]	$150.00	[Egg]	$140.00
[Cross]	$175.00	[G-Clef]	$150.00	[Sandal]	$140.00
[Dove]	$170.00	[Butterfly]	$145.00	[Cross in Heart]	$140.00
[Olive Branch]	$165.00	[Trumpet]	$145.00	[Crown]	$140.00
[Cedar Tree]	$160.00	[Ship]	$140.00	[Three Circles]	$140.00
[Flower]	$160.00	[Heart]	$140.00	[Box]	$140.00
[Bow & Arrow]	$155.00	[Sword]	$140.00	[House]	$140.00
		[Eyeglasses]	$140.00	[Hammer]	$140.00

Classic variation, termed the "Turban Nativity." The shepherd holding a lamb was replaced in some Bow & Arrow sets with a shepherd wearing a turban. "Turban Boy" shepherds were also shipped individually to retailers as replacement pieces, so collectors were sometimes able to add the "Turban Boy" as a twelfth piece to this 11-piece mini nativity set. For the "Turban Nativity" the value is $225.00. The individual "Turban Boy" piece is valued at $95.00. Add $95.00 to the value of the mini nativity if the "Turban Boy" is added as a twelfth piece.

Item number has been changed to #610044.

Open, Issue Price $80.00, '82
Set of 11

Purchased ________, Price $ ___________

☐ *Peace On Earth,* E-2804

UM	$185.00
[Triangle]	$180.00
[Hourglass]	$175.00
[Fish]	$170.00
[Cross]	$165.00

Suspended 1984, Reintroduced 1999, Retired 1999, Issue Price $20.00, '80

Purchased ________, Price $ ___________

☐ *Come Let Us Adore Him,* E-2800 (Nativity)

This set was re-sculpted; the new version is #104000.

UM	$225.00
[Triangle]	$200.00
[Hourglass]	$190.00
[Fish]	$180.00
[Cross]	$175.00
[Dove]	$170.00

Discontinued 1985, Issue Price $60.00, '80, set of 9

Purchased ___________________

Price $_____________________

☐ *Peace On Earth,* E-2804R

[Star] $75.00

This is a revision of E-2804 of the boy angel on globe with teddy bear, which was Suspended in 1984. This version features a girl angel with a cat. The globe also sits square on the base instead of being tilted.

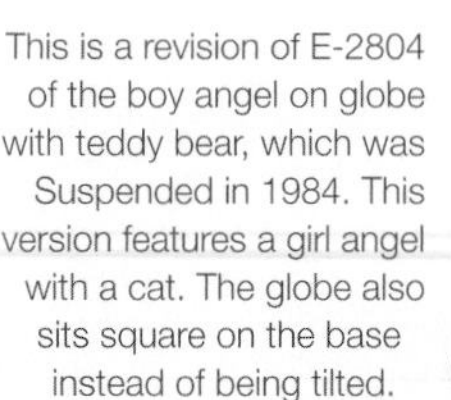

Retired 1999, Issue Price $50.00, '99
Catalog Exclusive

Purchased ________, Price $ ___________

☐ *Christmas Is A Time To Share,* E-2802

UM	$135.00
[Triangle]	$120.00
[Hourglass]	$105.00
[Fish]	$100.00
[Cross]	$90.00
[Dove]	$90.00

Piece was Suspended in 1984, yet exists with the 1985 Dove annual production symbol.

Suspended 1984, Issue Price $20.00, '80

Purchased ________, Price $ ___________

☐ *Crown Him Lord Of All,* E-2803

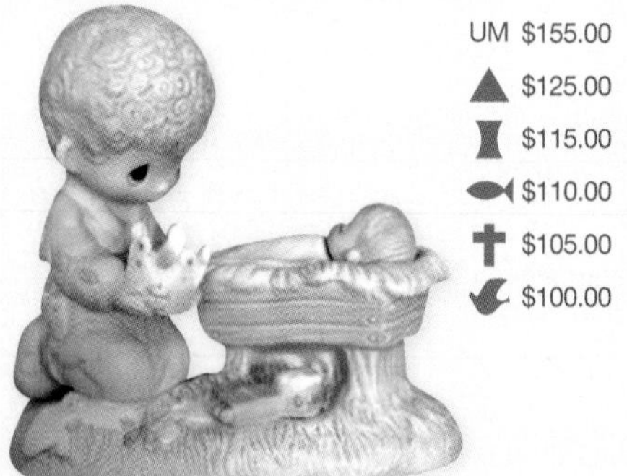

UM	$155.00
[Triangle]	$125.00
[Hourglass]	$115.00
[Fish]	$110.00
[Cross]	$105.00
[Dove]	$100.00

Piece was Suspended in 1984, yet exists with the 1985 Dove annual production symbol.

Suspended 1984, Issue Price $20.00, '80

Purchased ________, Price $ ___________

☐ *Wishing You A Season Filled With Joy,* E-2805

No mark through Cross, only one dog's eye painted. Dove exists with both one and two eyes painted.

UM	$165.00
[Triangle]	$160.00
[Hourglass]	$155.00
[Fish]	$150.00
[Cross]	$140.00
[Dove]	$130.00

Retired 1985, Issue Price $20.00, '80

Purchased ________, Price $ ___________

☐ *Christmas Is A Time To Share,* E-2806 (Musical)

UM $225.00
▲ $200.00
⧗ $190.00
🐟 $180.00
✝ $175.00

Retired 1984, Issue Price $35.00, '80
Tune: *Away In A Manger*

Purchased ________, Price $ ____________

☐ *Crown Him Lord Of All,* E-2807 (Musical)

UM $195.00
▲ $185.00
⧗ $175.00
🐟 $165.00
✝ $155.00

Suspended 1984, Issue Price $35.00, '80
Tune: *O Come All Ye Faithful*

Purchased ________, Price $ ____________

☐ *Unto Us A Child Is Born,* E-2808 (Musical)

UM $170.00
▲ $145.00
⧗ $135.00
🐟 $130.00
✝ $125.00

This piece's first mark was very colorful, unlike those in later years.

Suspended 1984, Issue Price $35.00, '80
Tune: *Jesus Loves Me*

Purchased ________, Price $ ____________

☐ *Jesus Is Born,* E-2809 (Musical)

UM $225.00
▲ $185.00
⧗ $175.00
🐟 $170.00
✝ $165.00
🕊 $160.00

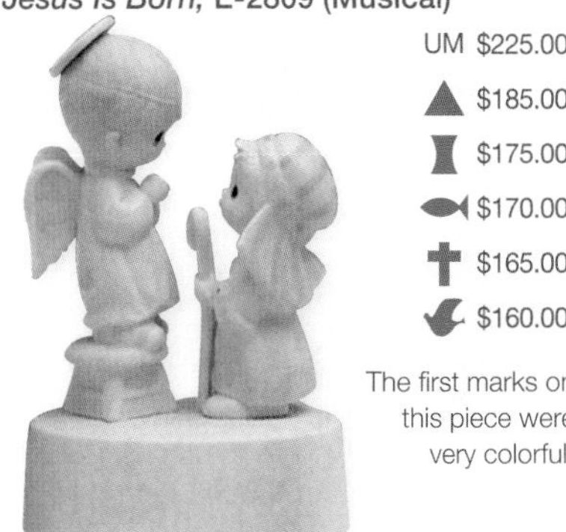

The first marks on this piece were very colorful.

Suspended 1985, Issue Price $35.00, '80
Tune: *Hark! The Herald Angels Sing*

Purchased ________, Price $ ____________

☐ *Come Let Us Adore Him,* E-2810 (Musical)

UM $200.00
▲ $167.00
⧗ $158.00
🐟 $155.00
✝ $152.00
🕊 $149.00
🌿 $145.00
🌲 $142.00
⚓ $139.00
➳ $137.00
🔥 $133.00
🏺 $130.00
𝄞 $130.00
🦋 $130.00

Suspended 1993, Issue Price $45.00, '80
Tune: *Joy To The World*

Purchased ________, Price $ ____________

☐ *You Have Touched So Many Hearts,* E-2821

🐟 $100.00
✝ $95.00
🕊 $90.00
🌿 $85.00
🌲 $83.00
⚓ $80.00
➳ $78.00
🔥 $75.00
🏺 $73.00
𝄞 $70.00
🦋 $68.00
🎺 $65.00
⛵ $63.00
♡ $60.00

Suspended 1996, Issue Price $25.00, '84

Purchased ________, Price $ ____________

☐ *This Is Your Day To Shine,* E-2822

🐟 $195.00
✝ $163.00
🕊 $155.00
🌿 $150.00
🌲 $145.00
⚓ $140.00

Retired 1988, Issue Price $37.50, '84

Purchased ________, Price $ ____________

☐ *To God Be The Glory,* E-2823

🐟 $155.00
✝ $110.00
🕊 $105.00
🌿 $100.00
🌲 $98.00

Suspended 1987, Issue Price $40.00, '84

Purchased ________, Price $ ____________

☐ *To God Be The Glory,* E-2823R

◯ $65.00

The frame was changed to gold and the flowers were changed to roses.

Retired 2000, Issue Price $45.00, '00

Purchased ________, Price $ ____________

To A Very Special Mom, E-2824

$75.00, $65.00, $62.00, $60.00, $58.00, $57.00, $57.00, $53.00, $52.00, $52.00, $50.00, $50.00, $50.00, $50.00, $48.00, $48.00, $48.00, $48.00, $48.00, $48.00

This is a popular piece for Mother's Day.

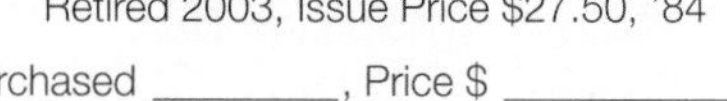

Retired 2003, Issue Price $27.50, '84

Purchased ________, Price $ ____________

To A Very Special Sister, E-2825

$90.00, $75.00, $73.00, $71.00, $70.00, $69.00, $68.00, $67.00, $66.00, $65.00, $63.00, $61.00, $60.00, $60.00, $60.00, $58.00, $58.00, $58.00

Retired 2001, Issue Price $37.50, '84

Purchased ________, Price $ ____________

May Your Birthday Be A Blessing, E-2826

This piece has been found with brown eyes.

$125.00, $115.00, $110.00, $100.00

Suspended 1986, Reintroduced 2000, Retired 2000, Issue Price $37.50, '84

Purchased ________, Price $ ____________

May Your Birthday Be A Blessing, E-2826Q

$95.00

Limited Ed. 25,000, Issue Price $75.00, '00
Individually Numbered
Came with a photo frame

Purchased ________, Price $ ____________

I Get A Kick Out Of You, E-2827

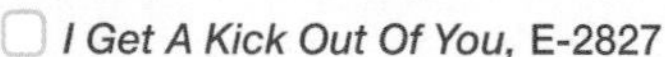

$275.00, $250.00, $225.00, $215.00

Suspended 1986, Issue Price $50.00, '84

Purchased ________, Price $ ____________

Precious Memories, E-2828

$175.00, $155.00, $150.00, $145.00, $140.00, $135.00, $130.00, $125.00, $120.00, $115.00, $110.00, $110.00, $105.00, $105.00, $100.00, $100.00, $100.00

Retired 1999, Issue Price $45.00, '84

Purchased ________, Price $ ____________

I'm Sending You A White Christmas, E-2829

$100.00, $95.00, $90.00, $88.00, $85.00, $80.00, $78.00, $75.00, $70.00, $70.00, $70.00, $70.00, $69.00, $69.00, $69.00, $69.00, $69.00

Retired 2000, Issue Price $37.50, '84

Purchased ________, Price $ ____________

Bridesmaid, E-2831

$45.00, $43.00, $42.00, $41.00, $39.00, $38.00, $36.00, $35.00, $33.00, $31.00, $30.00, $28.00, $27.00, $27.00, $27.00, $26.00, $26.00, $25.00, $25.00, $25.00, $25.00, $25.00, $25.00, $25.00, $25.00, $25.00

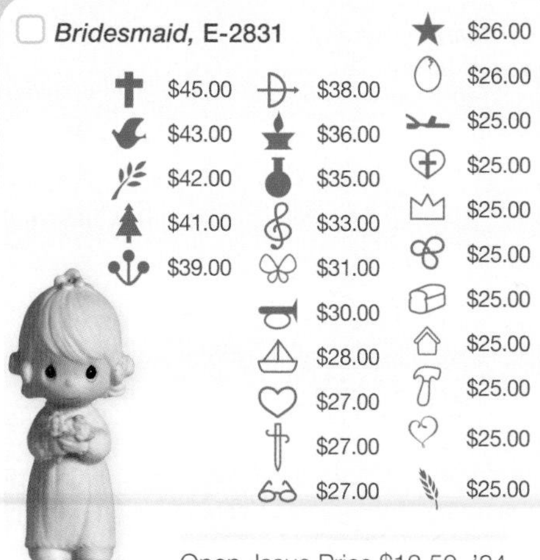

Open, Issue Price $13.50, '84
Series: *Bridal* — First Issue

Purchased ________, Price $ ____________

God Bless The Bride, E-2832

$75.00, $73.00, $71.00, $70.00, $69.00, $68.00, $67.00, $65.00, $65.00, $63.00, $63.00, $62.00, $62.00, $61.00, $61.00, $60.00, $60.00, $59.00, $57.00, $56.00, $55.00, $55.00

Suspended, Issue Price $35.00 '84

Purchased ________, Price $ ____________

Ring Bearer, E-2833

$30.00, $28.00, $27.00, $27.00, $27.00, $26.00, $26.00, $26.00, $25.00, $25.00, $25.00, $25.00, $24.00, $24.00, $24.00, $24.00, $23.00, $22.00, $22.00

Retired 2003, Issue Price $11.00, '85
Series: *Bridal* — Fourth Issue

Purchased ________, Price $ ____________

Sharing Our Joy Together, E-2834

- $85.00
- $70.00
- $68.00
- $65.00
- $60.00
- $58.00

Suspended 1991, Issue Price $31.00, '86

Purchased ________, Price $ ____________

Groom, E-2837

- $40.00
- $37.00
- $35.00
- $35.00
- $32.00
- $32.00
- $30.00
- $30.00
- $30.00
- $30.00
- $30.00
- $30.00
- $30.00
- $30.00
- $30.00
- $30.00
- $30.00
- $30.00
- $30.00
- $30.00
- $30.00
- $30.00
- $30.00
- $30.00
- $30.00

Termed the "No Hands Groom" during the first year of production (Olive Branch), this piece was first produced with no hands. The mold was changed for the subsequent years (Cedar Tree to present) to show the boy's hands.

Open, Issue Price $15.00, '86
Series: *Bridal* — Sixth Issue

Purchased ________, Price $ ____________

Junior Bridesmaid, E-2845

- $35.00
- $32.00
- $30.00
- $29.00
- $28.00
- $27.00
- $27.00
- $25.00
- $25.00
- $25.00
- $25.00
- $25.00
- $25.00
- $25.00
- $25.00
- $25.00
- $25.00
- $25.00
- $25.00
- $25.00
- $25.00
- $25.00
- $25.00
- $25.00

Open, Issue Price $12.50, '86
Series: *Bridal* — Fifth Issue

Purchased ________, Price $ ____________

Flower Girl, E-2835

- $38.00
- $35.00
- $32.00
- $30.00
- $30.00
- $26.00
- $26.00
- $24.00
- $24.00
- $22.00
- $22.00
- $21.00
- $21.00
- $20.00
- $20.00
- $19.00
- $19.00
- $19.00
- $19.00
- $19.00
- $19.00
- $18.50
- $18.50
- $18.50
- $18.50

Open, Issue Price $11.00, '85
Series: *Bridal* — Third Issue

Purchased ________, Price $ ____________

This Is The Day Which The Lord Hath Made, E-2838

- $255.00

Annual 1987, Issue Price $175.00, '87
Series: *Bridal* —
Eighth & Final Issue

Purchased ____________
Price $ ____________

Groomsman, E-2836

- $40.00
- $37.00
- $35.00
- $34.00
- $34.00
- $32.00
- $32.00
- $30.00
- $30.00
- $28.00
- $28.00
- $28.00
- $27.00
- $27.00
- $25.00
- $25.00
- $25.00
- $25.00
- $25.00
- $25.00
- $25.00
- $25.00
- $25.00
- $25.00
- $25.00
- $25.00

Open, Issue Price $13.50, '84
Series: *Bridal* — Third Issue

Purchased ________, Price $ ____________

Baby's First Step, E-2840

- $125.00
- $115.00
- $110.00
- $100.00
- $95.00

Suspended 1988, Issue Price $35.00, '84
Series: *Baby's First* — First Issue

Purchased ________, Price $ ____________

Baby's First Picture, E-2841

- $225.00
- $200.00
- $195.00

Retired 1986, Issue Price $45.00, '84
Series: *Baby's First* — Second Issue

Purchased ________, Price $ ____________

☐ *Bride,* E-2846

$40.00	$30.00
$38.00	$30.00
$36.00	$30.00
$35.00	$30.00
$34.00	$30.00
$33.00	$30.00
$33.00	$30.00
$32.00	$30.00
$32.00	$30.00
$31.00	$30.00
$31.00	$30.00
	$30.00

Open, Issue Price $18.00, '87
Series: *Bridal* — Seventh Issue

Purchased ________, Price $ ____________

☐ *Love Is Kind,* E-2847 (Plate)

UM $65.00
$55.00

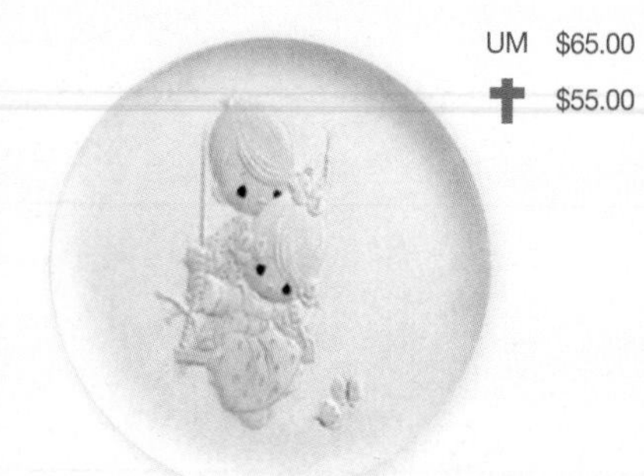

Limited Ed. 15,000, Issue Price $40.00, '84
Series: *Inspired Thoughts* — Fourth Issue
Individually Numbered

Purchased ________, Price $ ____________

☐ *Loving Thy Neighbor,* E-2848 (Plate)

$55.00

This was the first plate with an embossed mark.

Limited Ed. 15,000, Issue Price $40.00, '84
Series: *Mother's Love* — Fourth Issue
Individually Numbered

Purchased ________, Price $ ____________

☐ *Mother Sew Dear,* E-2850 (Doll)

UM $450.00
$450.00
$450.00

Retired 1985, Issue Price $350.00, '84

Purchased ________, Price $ ____________

☐ *Kristy,* E-2851 (Doll)

$250.00
$250.00
$235.00
$225.00
$215.00
$200.00

Suspended 1989, Issue Price $150.00, '84

Purchased ________, Price $ ____________

☐ *Baby Boy Standing,* E-2852A

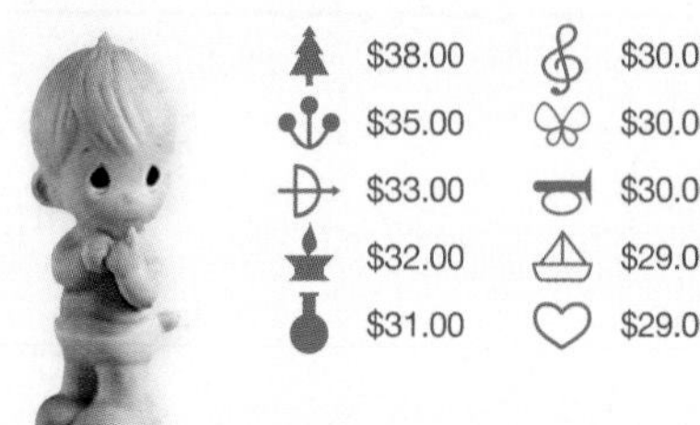

$38.00	$30.00
$35.00	$30.00
$33.00	$30.00
$32.00	$29.00
$31.00	$29.00

Suspended 1996, Issue Price $13.50, '87

Purchased ________, Price $ ____________

☐ *Baby Girl Standing,* E-2852B

$38.00	$30.00
$35.00	$30.00
$33.00	$30.00
$32.00	$29.00
$31.00	$29.00

Suspended 1996, Issue Price $13.50, '87

Purchased ________, Price $ ____________

☐ *Baby Boy Sitting,* E-2852C

$38.00	$30.00
$35.00	$30.00
$33.00	$30.00
$32.00	$29.00
$31.00	$29.00

Suspended 1996, Issue Price $13.50, '87

Purchased ________, Price $ ____________

☐ *Baby Girl Clapping,* E-2852D

$38.00	$30.00
$35.00	$30.00
$33.00	$30.00
$32.00	$29.00
$31.00	$29.00

Suspended 1996, Issue Price $13.50, '87

Purchased ________, Price $ ____________

☐ *Baby Figurines,* E-2852

$250.00	$205.00
$225.00	$200.00

Discontinued 1987, Suspended 1996,
Issue Price $72.00, '84
Set of 6

Purchased ________, Price $ ____________

In 1987, individual item numbers were assigned by Enesco for each figurine in this set of six.

☐ Baby Boy Crawling, E-2852E

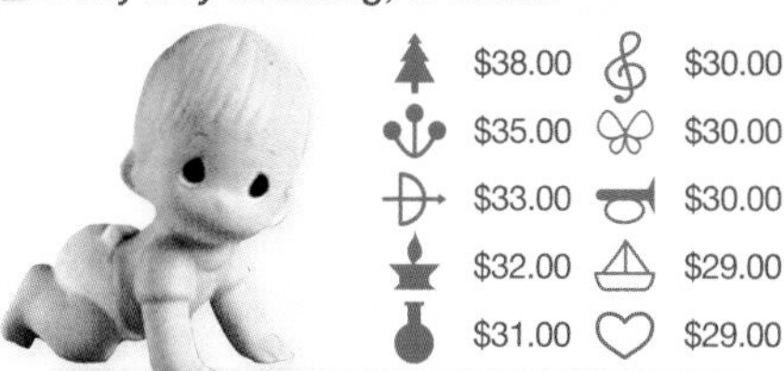

$38.00	$30.00
$35.00	$30.00
$33.00	$30.00
$32.00	$29.00
$31.00	$29.00

Suspended 1996, Issue Price $13.50, '87

Purchased ________, Price $ ____________

☐ Baby Girl Lying Down, E-2852F

$38.00	$30.00
$35.00	$30.00
$33.00	$30.00
$32.00	$29.00
$31.00	$29.00

Suspended 1996, Issue Price $13.50, '87

Purchased ________, Price $ ____________

☐ God Blessed Our Years Together With So Much Love And Happiness, E-2853

$70.00	$62.00	$50.00
$63.00	$58.00	$50.00
$62.00	$58.00	$50.00
	$56.00	$50.00
	$56.00	$50.00
	$54.00	$50.00
	$54.00	$50.00
	$52.00	$50.00
	$52.00	$50.00
	$50.00	$50.00
	$50.00	$50.00
		$50.00

Open, Issue Price $35.00, '84

Purchased ________, Price $ ____________

☐ God Blessed Our Year Together With So Much Love And Happiness, E-2854

Error: Add $75.00 to value if title says "Years."

$75.00	$61.00
$70.00	$60.00
$69.00	$58.00
$68.00	$57.00
$65.00	$56.00
$64.00	$55.00
$63.00	$55.00
$62.00	$55.00
	$55.00

Retired 2000, Issue Price $35.00, '84

Purchased ________, Price $ ____________

☐ God Blessed Our Years Together With So Much Love And Happiness, E-2855

$85.00	$75.00
$80.00	$73.00
	$72.00
	$71.00
	$70.00
$78.00	$69.00
$77.00	$68.00
	$65.00
	$65.00

Suspended 1996, Issue Price $35.00, '84

Purchased ________, Price $ ____________

☐ God Blessed Our Years Together With So Much Love And Happiness, E-2856

$95.00	$88.00
$93.00	$85.00
$90.00	$83.00
	$80.00
	$78.00
	$75.00
	$73.00
	$71.00
	$70.00
	$69.00

Suspended 1996, Issue Price $35.00, '84

Purchased ________, Price $ ____________

☐ God Blessed Our Years Together With So Much Love And Happiness, E-2857

$75.00	$65.00	$61.00
$70.00	$63.00	$60.00
$68.00	$62.00	$58.00
		$58.00
		$58.00
		$56.00
		$56.00
		$56.00
		$55.00
		$55.00
		$54.00
		$53.00

Retired 2001, Issue Price $35.00, '84

Purchased ________, Price $ ____________

☐ God Blessed Our Years Together With So Much Love And Happiness, E-2859

$95.00	$91.00	$87.00
$93.00	$90.00	$85.00
		$83.00
		$80.00
		$78.00
		$76.00
		$75.00
		$73.00
		$72.00

Suspended 1996, Issue Price $35.00, '84

Purchased ________, Price $ ____________

☐ God Blessed Our Years Together With So Much Love And Happiness, E-2860

$95.00	$85.00	$80.00
$90.00	$83.00	$80.00
$88.00	$83.00	$75.00
		$75.00
		$73.00
		$73.00
		$70.00
		$70.00
		$68.00
		$68.00
		$65.00
		$65.00

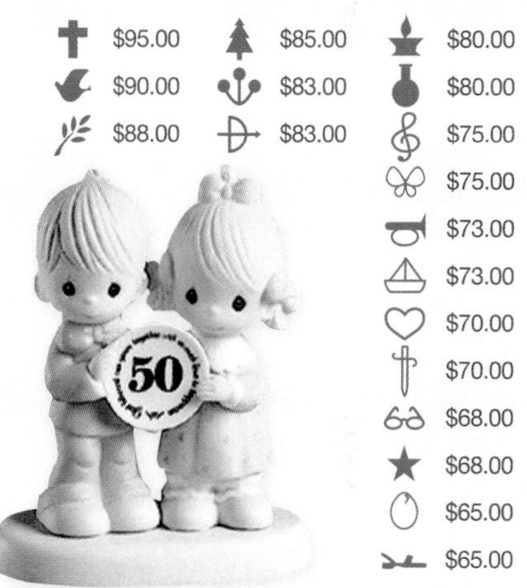

Retired 2001, Issue Price $35.00, '84

Purchased ________, Price $ ____________

☐ Blessed Are The Pure In Heart, E-3104

UM $75.00	$63.00
$70.00	$60.00
$65.00	$58.00
	$55.00
	$55.00
	$50.00
	$50.00
	$48.00
	$45.00

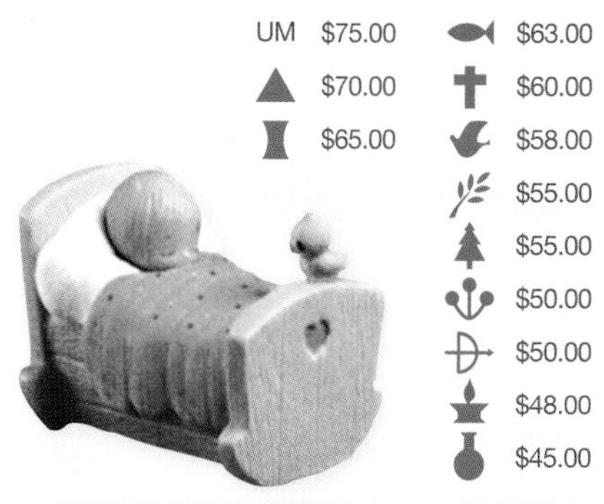

Suspended 1991, Issue Price $9.00, '80

Purchased ________, Price $ ____________

He Watches Over Us All, E-3105

UM	$100.00
▲	$90.00
⧗	$85.00
🐟	$80.00
✝	$75.00

Suspended 1984, Issue Price $11.00, '80

Purchased ________, Price $ ___________

Mother Sew Dear, E-3106

UM	$70.00
▲	$65.00
⧗	$63.00
🐟	$60.00
✝	$58.00
🕊	$58.00
🌿	$53.00
🌲	$53.00
⚘	$50.00
🏹	$50.00
🔥	$45.00
🏺	$45.00
𝄞	$40.00
🦋	$40.00
🎺	$38.00
⛵	$38.00
♡	$35.00
🗡	$35.00
👓	$35.00
★	$35.00
🥚	$35.00
👡	$35.00
💟	$35.00
♔	$35.00

Retired 2003, Issue Price $13.00, '80

Purchased ________, Price $ ___________

Blessed Are The Peacemakers, E-3107

UM	$135.00
▲	$125.00
⧗	$105.00
🐟	$100.00
✝	$90.00
🕊	$85.00

Retired 1985, Issue Price $13.00, '80

Purchased ________, Price $ ___________

The Hand That Rocks The Future, E-3108

UM	$115.00
▲	$100.00
⧗	$95.00
🐟	$85.00
✝	$75.00

Suspended 1984, Issue Price $13.00, '80

Purchased ________, Price $ ___________

The Purr-fect Grandma, E-3109

UM	$80.00
▲	$60.00
⧗	$50.00
🐟	$45.00
✝	$43.00
🕊	$40.00
🌿	$38.00
🌲	$37.00
⚘	$36.00
🏹	$36.00
🔥	$36.00
🏺	$35.00
𝄞	$35.00
🦋	$35.00
🎺	$35.00
⛵	$35.00
♡	$35.00
🗡	$35.00
👓	$35.00
★	$35.00
🥚	$35.00
👡	$35.00
💟	$35.00
♔	$35.00
🍀	$35.00
📦	$35.00
🏠	$35.00
🍄	$35.00
💗	$35.00
🌾	$35.00

Open, Issue Price $13.00, '80

Purchased ________, Price $ ___________

Loving Is Sharing, E-3110B

UM	$155.00
▲	$115.00
⧗	$110.00
🐟	$105.00
✝	$100.00
🕊	$98.00
🌿	$95.00
🌲	$93.00
⚘	$88.00
🏹	$85.00
🔥	$78.00
🏺	$75.00
𝄞	$73.00
🦋	$70.00

Retired 1993, Issue Price $13.00, '80

Purchased ________, Price $ ___________

Loving Is Sharing, E-3110G

UM	$135.00
▲	$85.00
⧗	$83.00
🐟	$80.00
✝	$78.00
🕊	$75.00
🌿	$75.00
🌲	$73.00
⚘	$70.00
🏹	$68.00
🔥	$65.00
🏺	$63.00
𝄞	$60.00
🦋	$55.00
🎺	$53.00
⛵	$50.00
♡	$48.00
🗡	$45.00
👓	$43.00
★	$40.00
🥚	$38.00
👡	$38.00
💟	$35.00
♔	$35.00

Retired 2003, Issue Price $13.00, '80

Purchased ________, Price $ ___________

Be Not Weary In Well Doing, E-3111

Classic Variation: Figurines exist in unmarked versions with an error in the inspirational title on the understamp decal. Instead of *Be Not Weary "In" Well Doing,* they read *Be Not Weary "And" Well Doing.* The black and white boxes in which the pieces were shipped also have the incorrect titles on the labels. Add $175.00 to the value.

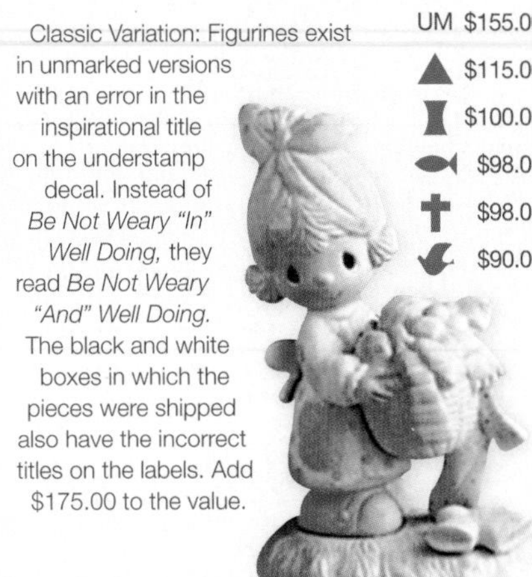

UM	$155.00
▲	$115.00
⧗	$100.00
🐟	$98.00
✝	$98.00
🕊	$90.00

Retired 1985, Issue Price $14.00, '80

Purchased ________, Price $ ___________

God's Speed, E-3112

UM	$155.00
▲	$100.00
⧗	$80.00
🐟	$75.00

Retired 1983, Issue Price $14.00, '80

Purchased ________, Price $ ___________

Thou Art Mine, E-3113

UM $85.00, $60.00, $55.00, $55.00, $53.00, $53.00, $53.00, $52.00, $52.00, $52.00, $51.00, $51.00, $51.00, $51.00, $50.00, $50.00, $50.00, $50.00, $50.00, $48.00, $48.00, $48.00, $45.00, $45.00, $45.00

Retired 2004, Issue Price $16.00, '80

Purchased ________, Price $ ___________

Thee I Love, E-3116

This piece was dark and colorful during its first year of production.

UM $175.00, $105.00, $103.00, $100.00, $95.00, $90.00, $88.00, $85.00, $83.00, $80.00, $78.00, $78.00, $78.00, $75.00, $75.00

Retired 1994, Issue Price $16.50, '80

Purchased ________, Price $ ___________

It's What's Inside That Counts, E-3119

Look for this piece with either the Triangle mark or Unmarked because of the darker colors.

UM $165.00, $135.00, $115.00, $105.00, $100.00

Suspended 1984, Issue Price $13.00, '80

Purchased ________, Price $ ___________

The Lord Bless You And Keep You, E-3114

UM $78.00, $60.00, $55.00, $55.00, $54.00, $54.00, $54.00, $54.00, $53.00, $52.00, $52.00, $52.00, $52.00, $51.00, $51.00, $50.00, $50.00, $50.00, $50.00, $50.00, $50.00, $50.00, $50.00, $50.00, $50.00, $50.00, $50.00, $50.00, $50.00, $50.00, $50.00

Open, Issue Price $16.00, '80

Purchased ________, Price $ ___________

Walking By Faith, E-3117

UM $165.00, $135.00, $133.00, $130.00, $128.00, $125.00, $123.00, $120.00, $118.00, $115.00, $113.00, $110.00, $108.00, $108.00, $105.00, $105.00, $105.00, $103.00, $103.00, $103.00, $100.00

Retired 2000, Issue Price $35.00, '80

Purchased ________, Price $ ___________

To Thee With Love, E-3120

Piece was Suspended in 1986, yet exists with the 1987 Cedar Tree annual production symbol.

UM $125.00, $75.00, $73.00, $70.00, $65.00, $63.00, $60.00, $58.00

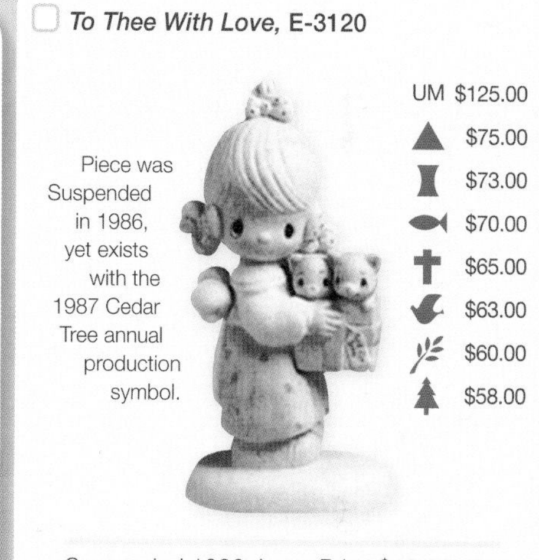

Suspended 1986, Issue Price $13.00, '80

Purchased ________, Price $ ___________

But Love Goes On Forever, E-3115

UM $105.00, $65.00, $55.00, $52.00, $50.00, $50.00, $50.00, $50.00, $48.00, $48.00, $45.00, $45.00, $45.00, $40.00, $40.00, $40.00, $40.00, $40.00, $40.00, $40.00, $40.00, $40.00, $40.00, $40.00, $40.00, $40.00, $40.00, $40.00, $40.00, $40.00

This piece's title is Enesco's logo for the Precious Moments Collection.

Retired 2007, Issue Price $16.50, '80

Purchased ________, Price $ ___________

Eggs Over Easy, E-3118

UM $175.00, $135.00, $105.00, $95.00

Some collectors have said the eggs are missing from their pieces.

Retired 1983, Issue Price $13.00, '80

Purchased ________, Price $ ___________

The Lord Bless You And Keep You, E-4720

UM $55.00, $53.00, $50.00, $45.00, $43.00, $40.00, $38.00, $35.00

Suspended 1987, Issue Price $14.00, '81

Purchased ________, Price $ ___________

☐ *The Lord Bless You And Keep You,* E-4721

UM	$75.00	[Cross]	$47.00	[Sword]	$37.50
▲	$50.00	[Dove]	$46.00	[Eyeglasses]	$37.50
[Hourglass]	$49.00	[Olive Branch]	$45.00	★	$37.50
[Fish]	$48.00	[Cedar Tree]	$44.00	[Egg]	$37.50
		[Flower]	$43.00	[Sandal]	$37.50
		[Bow & Arrow]	$42.00	[Cross in Heart]	$37.50
		[Flame]	$41.00	[Crown]	$37.50
		[Vessel]	$40.00	[Clover]	$37.50
		[G-Clef]	$40.00	[Box]	$37.50
		[Butterfly]	$37.50	[House]	$37.50
		[Trumpet]	$37.50	[Mushroom]	$37.50
		[Ship]	$37.50	[Heart with Tail]	$37.50
		♡	$37.50	[Wheat]	$37.50

Open, Issue Price $14.00, '81

Purchased ________, Price $ ___________

☐ *The Lord Bless You And Keep You,* E-4721B

★ $50.00

Limited Ed., Issue Price $40.00, '00
Came with a version of *Don't Sweat the Small Stuff* by Richard Carlson, PhD

Purchased ________, Price $ ___________

☐ *The Lord Bless You And Keep You,* E-4721D

[Egg]	$38.00	[Box]	$35.00
[Sandal]	$36.00	[House]	$35.00
[Cross in Heart]	$35.00	[Mushroom]	$35.00
[Crown]	$35.00	[Heart with Tail]	$35.00
[Clover]	$35.00	[Wheat]	$35.00

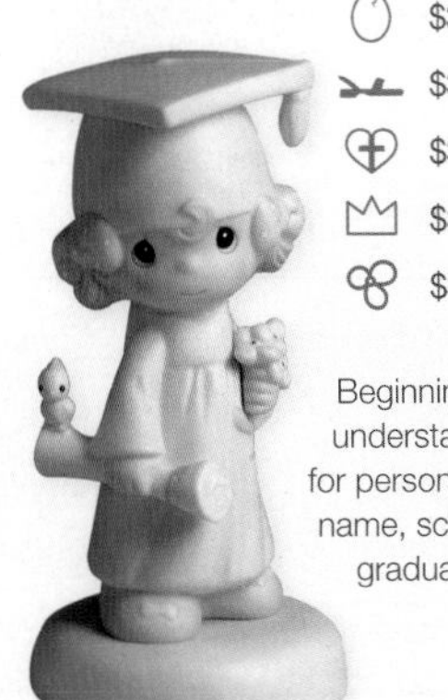

Beginning in 2001, the understamp had a space for personalization with name, school name, and graduation date.

Open, Issue Price $35.00, '00

Purchased ________, Price $ ___________

☐ *The Lord Bless You And Keep You,* E-4721DB

★ $50.00

Limited Ed., Issue Price $40.00, '00
Came with a version of *Don't Sweat the Small Stuff by* Richard Carlson, PhD

Purchased ________, Price $ ___________

☐ *Love Cannot Break A True Friendship,* E-4722

UM	$165.00
▲	$155.00
[Hourglass]	$135.00
[Fish]	$125.00
[Cross]	$115.00
[Dove]	$105.00

Suspended 1985, Issue Price $22.50, '81

Purchased ________, Price $ ___________

☐ *Peace Amid The Storm,* E-4723

UM	$115.00
▲	$105.00
[Hourglass]	$102.00
[Fish]	$100.00
[Cross]	$95.00

Suspended 1984, Issue Price $22.50, '81

Purchased ________, Price $ ___________

☐ *Rejoicing With You,* E-4724

UM	$83.00	[Bow & Arrow]	$60.00	[Eyeglasses]	$55.00
▲	$80.00	[Flame]	$59.00	★	$55.00
[Hourglass]	$78.00	[Vessel]	$58.00	[Egg]	$55.00
[Fish]	$75.00	[G-Clef]	$58.00	[Sandal]	$55.00
[Cross]	$73.00	[Butterfly]	$57.00	[Cross in Heart]	$55.00
[Dove]	$70.00	[Trumpet]	$57.00	[Crown]	$55.00
[Olive Branch]	$67.00	[Ship]	$56.00	[Clover]	$55.00
[Cedar Tree]	$65.00	♡	$56.00	[Box]	$55.00
[Flower]	$62.00	[Sword]	$56.00	[House]	$55.00
				[Mushroom]	$55.00
				[Heart with Tail]	$55.00
				[Wheat]	$55.00

Classic Variation: "No E" or "Bibl Error." During the first years of production the "e" was missing from the word "Bible." Some Hourglass and Fish pieces also have this variation.

Open, Issue Price $25.00, '81

Purchased ________, Price $ ___________

☐ *Peace On Earth,* E-4725

UM	$135.00
▲	$100.00
[Hourglass]	$85.00
[Fish]	$83.00
[Cross]	$80.00

Unmarked and Triangle pieces are very dark and colorful.

Suspended 1984, Issue Price $25.00, '81

Purchased ________, Price $ ___________

☐ *Peace On Earth,* E-4726 (Musical)

UM	$200.00
▲	$175.00
[Hourglass]	$170.00
[Fish]	$165.00
[Cross]	$160.00

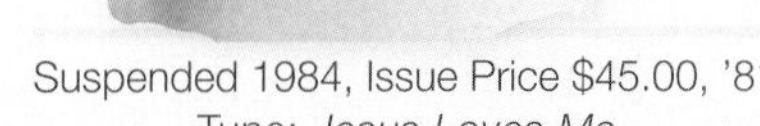

Suspended 1984, Issue Price $45.00, '81
Tune: *Jesus Loves Me*

Purchased ________, Price $ ___________

☐ *Bear Ye One Another's Burdens,* E-5200

UM	$125.00
▲	$100.00
[Hourglass]	$90.00
[Fish]	$85.00
[Cross]	$80.00

Suspended 1984, Issue Price $20.00, '81

Purchased ________, Price $ ___________

☐ *Love Lifted Me,* E-5201

UM	$125.00
▲	$100.00
[Hourglass]	$95.00
[Fish]	$90.00
[Cross]	$85.00

Suspended 1984, Issue Price $25.00, '81

Purchased ________, Price $ ___________

☐ ***Thank You For Coming To My Ade,* E-5202**

UM $175.00
$125.00
$120.00
$118.00
$115.00

Suspended 1984, Issue Price $22.50, '81

Purchased ________, Price $ ____________

☐ ***Let Not The Sun Go Down Upon Your Wrath,* E-5203**

UM $200.00
$150.00
$145.00
$140.00
$135.00

Suspended 1984, Issue Price $22.50, '81

Purchased ________, Price $ ____________

☐ ***The Hand That Rocks The Future,* E-5204 (Musical)**

UM $145.00
$125.00
$120.00
$115.00

$115.00
$113.00
$110.00
$108.00
$105.00
$103.00
$100.00

$98.00
$95.00
$90.00
$88.00
$85.00
$83.00
$80.00
$80.00
$75.00
$75.00
$75.00

Retired 2001, Issue Price $30.00, '81
Tune: *Mozart's Lullaby*

Purchased ________, Price $ ____________

☐ ***My Guardian Angel,* E-5205 (Musical)**

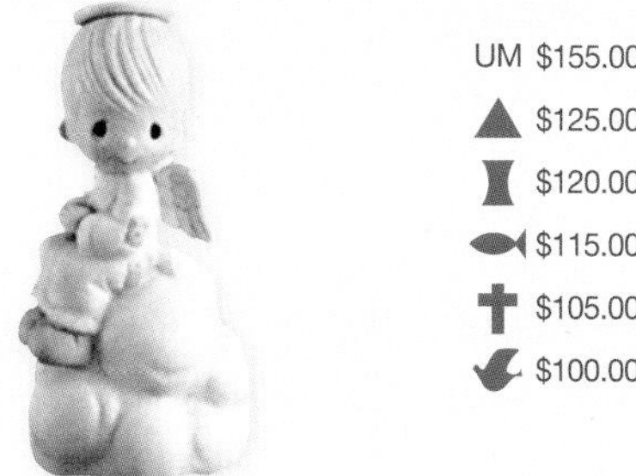

UM $155.00
$125.00
$120.00
$115.00
$105.00
$100.00

Suspended 1985, Issue Price $22.50, '81
Tune: *Brahms' Lullaby*

Purchased ________, Price $ ____________

☐ ***My Guardian Angel,* E-5206 (Musical)**

UM $155.00
$140.00
$135.00
$130.00

$125.00
$120.00
$115.00
$110.00
$105.00

Suspended 1988, Issue Price $22.50, '81
Tune: *Brahms' Lullaby*

Purchased ________, Price $ ____________

☐ ***My Guardian Angel,* E-5207 (Nightlight)**

UM $275.00
$265.00

$260.00
$250.00
$240.00

Suspended 1984, Issue Price $30.00, '81

Purchased ______

Price $ __________

☐ ***Jesus Loves Me,* E-5208 (Bell)**

UM $75.00
$55.00
$53.00

Suspended 1985, Issue Price $15.00, '81

Purchased ____________

Price $ ______________

☐ ***Jesus Loves Me,* E-5209 (Bell)**

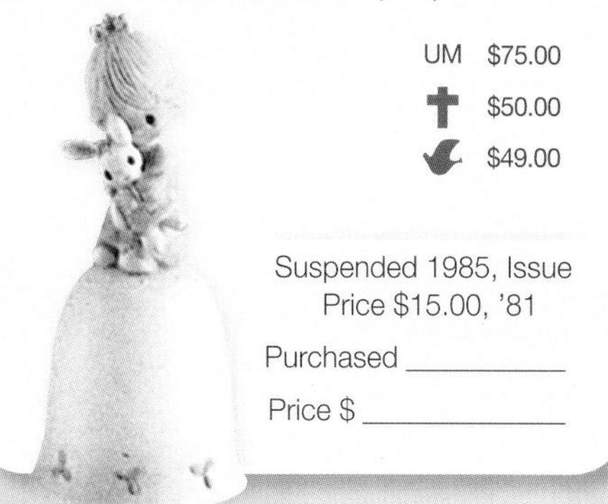

UM $75.00
$50.00
$49.00

Suspended 1985, Issue Price $15.00, '81

Purchased __________

Price $ ______________

☐ ***Prayer Changes Things,* E-5210 (Bell)**

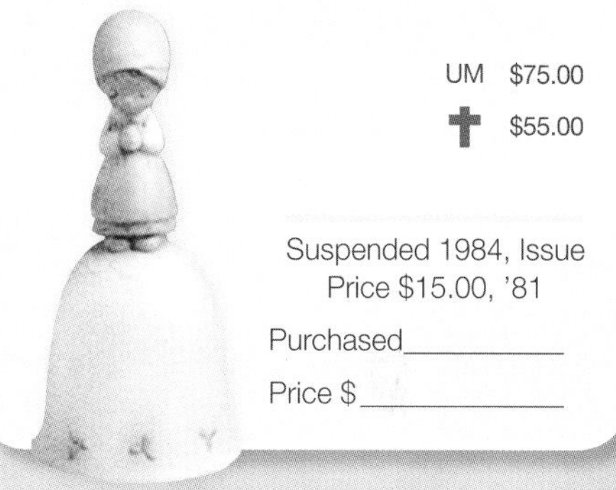

UM $75.00
$55.00

Suspended 1984, Issue Price $15.00, '81

Purchased__________

Price $______________

☐ ***God Understands,* E-5211 (Bell)**

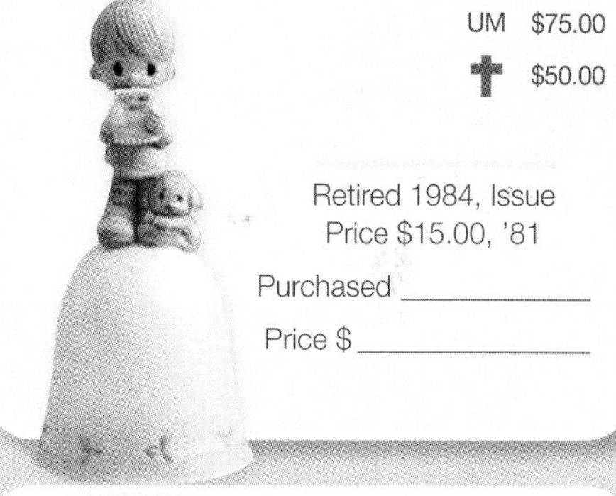

UM $75.00
$50.00

Retired 1984, Issue Price $15.00, '81

Purchased ____________

Price $ ______________

☐ ***To A Special Dad,* E-5212**

UM $105.00
$75.00

$70.00
$67.00
$65.00
$65.00
$63.00

$62.00
$61.00
$60.00
$59.00
$59.00
$58.00
$58.00
$57.00
$57.00
$55.00
$55.00
$50.00

Suspended 1998, Issue Price $20.00, '81

Purchased ________, Price $ ____________

☐ *God Is Love,* E-5213

This piece was re-sculpted in 1985 and reintroduced on 11/28/99 as E-5213R.

UM	$155.00
[Triangle]	$100.00
[Hourglass]	$95.00
[Fish]	$93.00
[Cross]	$90.00
[Dove]	$87.00
[Olive Branch]	$85.00
[Cedar Tree]	$83.00
[Flower]	$80.00
[Bow & Arrow]	$78.00

Suspended 1989, Reintroduced 1999, Retired 1999, Issue Price $17.00, '81

Purchased ________, Price $ ____________

☐ *God Is Love,* E-5213R

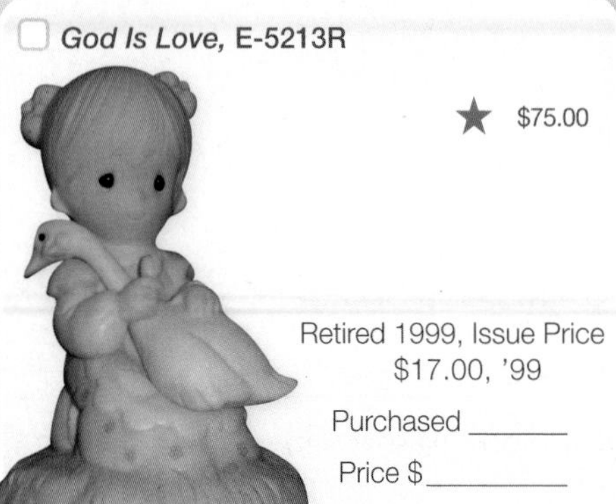

[Star]	$75.00

Retired 1999, Issue Price $17.00, '99

Purchased ______

Price $_________

☐ *Prayer Changes Things,* E-5214

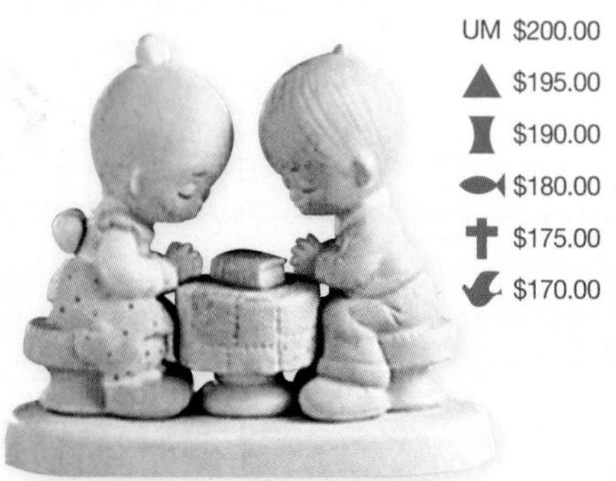

UM	$200.00
[Triangle]	$195.00
[Hourglass]	$190.00
[Fish]	$180.00
[Cross]	$175.00
[Dove]	$170.00

Classic variation: "Backwards Bible." The first production of this figurine had the words "Holy Bible" inscribed on the back cover. Pieces with this error exist in Unmarked and Triangle versions. Reportedly, Unmarked and Triangle pieces also exist where the title is correctly placed, but these may be considered extremely rare. The value for "Backwards Bible" Unmarked is $168.00; "Backwards Bible" with Triangle is $160.00; "Backwards Bible" with Hourglass is $140.00; and correct Hourglass, $140.00. Pieces were Suspended in 1984 yet exist with the 1985 Dove annual production symbol.

Suspended 1984, Issue Price $35.00, '81

Purchased ________, Price $ ____________

☐ *Love One Another,* E-5215 (Plate)

UM	$65.00
[Fish]	$65.00

Limited Ed. 15,000, Issue Price $40.00, '81
Series: *Inspired Thoughts* – First Issue, Individually Numbered

Purchased ________, Price $ ____________

☐ *The Lord Bless You and Keep You,* E-5216 (Plate)

UM	$65.00
[Cross]	$60.00
[Dove]	$58.00
[Olive Branch]	$55.00
[Cedar Tree]	$53.00

Suspended 1987, Issue Price $30.00, '81

Purchased ________, Price $ ____________

☐ *Mother Sew Dear,* E-5217 (Plate)

UM	$65.00

Limited Ed. 15,000, Issue Price $40.00, '81
Series: *Mother's Love* – First Issue, Individually Numbered

Purchased ________, Price $ ____________

☐ *May Your Christmas Be Blessed,* E-5376

In 1984, "Holy Bible" was written on the back of the book, but was omitted in 1985.

[Cross]	$75.00
[Dove]	$70.00
[Olive Branch]	$65.00

Suspended 1986, Issue Price $37.50, '84

Purchased ________, Price $ ____________

☐ *Love Is Kind,* E-5377

[Fish]	$100.00
[Cross]	$95.00
[Dove]	$86.00
[Olive Branch]	$83.00
[Cedar Tree]	$80.00

Retired 1987, Issue Price $27.50, '84

Purchased ________, Price $ ____________

☐ *Joy To The World,* E-5378

[Cross]	$65.00	[Cedar Tree]	$56.00
[Dove]	$60.00	[Flower]	$55.00
[Olive Branch]	$57.00	[Bow & Arrow]	$55.00

Suspended 1989, Issue Price $18.00, '84
Nativity Addition

Purchased ___________

Price $_____________

☐ *Isn't He Precious,* E-5379

		[G-Clef]	$45.00
[Cross]	$55.00	[Butterfly]	$43.00
[Dove]	$53.00	[Trumpet]	$43.00
[Olive Branch]	$50.00	[Ship]	$43.00
[Cedar Tree]	$50.00	[Heart]	$41.00
[Flower]	$48.00	[Sword]	$41.00
[Bow & Arrow]	$48.00	[Eyeglasses]	$38.00
[Flame]	$45.00	[Star]	$38.00
[Vessel]	$45.00	[Egg]	$38.00

With the opening of a new production facility in Indonesia, numerous pieces of unpainted figurines were inadvertently shipped to retailers.

Retired 2000, Issue Price $20.00, '84
Nativity Addition

Purchased ________, Price $ ____________

☐ *A Monarch Is Born,* E-5380

[Cross]	$105.00
[Dove]	$100.00
[Olive Branch]	$98.00

Suspended 1986, Issue Price $33.00, '84

Purchased ________, Price $ ____________

☐ *For God So Loved The World,* E-5382

$155.00
$135.00
$130.00

Suspended 1986, Issue Price $70.00, '84
Deluxe Four-piece Nativity

Purchased ________________

Price $________________

☐ *Joy To The World,* E-5388 (Ornament)

$65.00
$55.00
$53.00
$50.00

Retired 1987, Issue Price $10.00, '84

Purchased ________, Price $ ____________

☐ *His Name Is Jesus,* E-5381

$150.00
$140.00
$135.00
$130.00

Suspended 1987, Issue Price $45.00, '84

Purchased ________, Price $ ____________

☐ *Oh Worship The Lord,* E-5385

$75.00
$70.00
$68.00

Suspended 1986, Issue Price $10.00, '84
Mini Nativity Addition

Purchased ________, Price $ ____________

☐ *Peace On Earth,* E-5389 (Ornament)

$45.00
$43.00
$40.00

Suspended 1986, Issue Price $10.00, '84

Purchased ________, Price $ ____________

☐ *Wishing You A Merry Christmas,* E-5383

$40.00
$40.00

Dated Annual 1984, Issue Price $17.00, '84

Purchased ________________

Price $________________

☐ *Oh Worship The Lord,* E-5386

$78.00
$75.00
$73.00

Suspended 1986, Issue Price $10.00, '84
Mini Nativity Addition

Purchased ________, Price $ ____________

☐ *May God Bless You With A Perfect Holiday Season,* E-5390 (Ornament)

$35.00
$33.00
$30.00
$29.00
$28.00
$27.00

Suspended 1989, Issue Price $10.00, '84

Purchased ________, Price $ ____________

☐ *I'll Play My Drum For Him,* E-5384

$35.00
$33.00
$33.00
$32.00
$31.00
$31.00
$30.00
$29.00
$29.00
$28.00
$28.00
$27.00
$27.00
$26.00
$26.00
$25.00
$25.00
$25.00
$25.00

Retired 2002, Issue Price $10.00, '84
Mini Nativity Addition

Purchased ________, Price $ ____________

☐ *Wishing You A Merry Christmas,* E-5387 (Ornament)

$40.00

Dated Annual 1984, Issue Price $10.00, '84

Purchased ________, Price $ ____________

☐ *Love Is Kind,* E-5391 (Ornament)

$50.00
$40.00
$38.00
$37.00
$36.00
$35.00

Suspended 1989, Issue Price $10.00, '84

Purchased ________, Price $ ____________

☐ ***Blessed Are The Pure In Heart,*** **E-5392 (Ornament)**

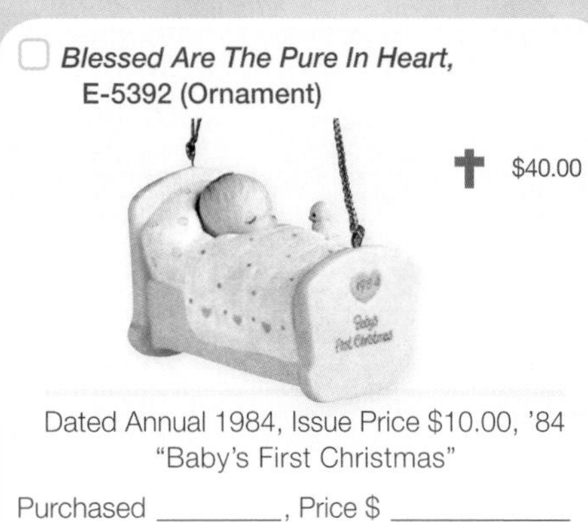

Cross	$40.00

Dated Annual 1984, Issue Price $10.00, '84
"Baby's First Christmas"

Purchased ________, Price $ ___________

☐ ***Wishing You A Merry Christmas,*** **E-5393 (Bell)**

Cross	$50.00

Dated Annual 1984, Issue Price $19.00, '84

Purchased ___________

Price $___________

☐ ***Wishing You A Merry Christmas,*** **E-5394 (Musical)**

UM	$160.00
Cross	$155.00
Dove	$148.00
Olive Branch	$130.00

Suspended 1986, Issue Price $55.00, '84
Tune: *We Wish You A Merry Christmas*

Purchased ________, Price $ ___________

☐ ***Unto Us A Child Is Born,*** **E-5395 (Plate)**

UM	$60.00
Cross	$55.00

Limited Ed. 15,000, Issue Price $40.00, '84
Series: *Christmas Collection* – Fourth Issue, Individually Numbered

Purchased ________, Price $ ___________

☐ ***The Wonder Of Christmas,*** **E-5396 (Plate)**

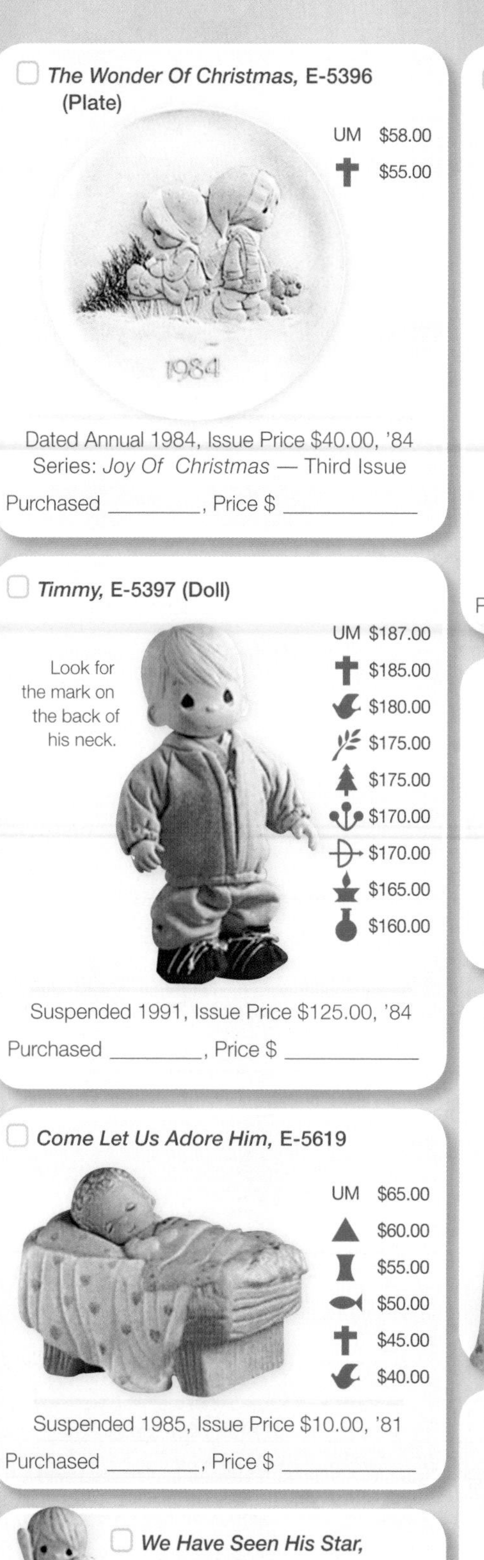

UM	$58.00
Cross	$55.00

Dated Annual 1984, Issue Price $40.00, '84
Series: *Joy Of Christmas* — Third Issue

Purchased ________, Price $ ___________

☐ ***Timmy,*** **E-5397 (Doll)**

Look for the mark on the back of his neck.

UM	$187.00
Cross	$185.00
Dove	$180.00
Olive Branch	$175.00
Cedar Tree	$175.00
Flower	$170.00
Bow & Arrow	$170.00
Flame	$165.00
Vessel	$160.00

Suspended 1991, Issue Price $125.00, '84

Purchased ________, Price $ ___________

☐ ***Come Let Us Adore Him,*** **E-5619**

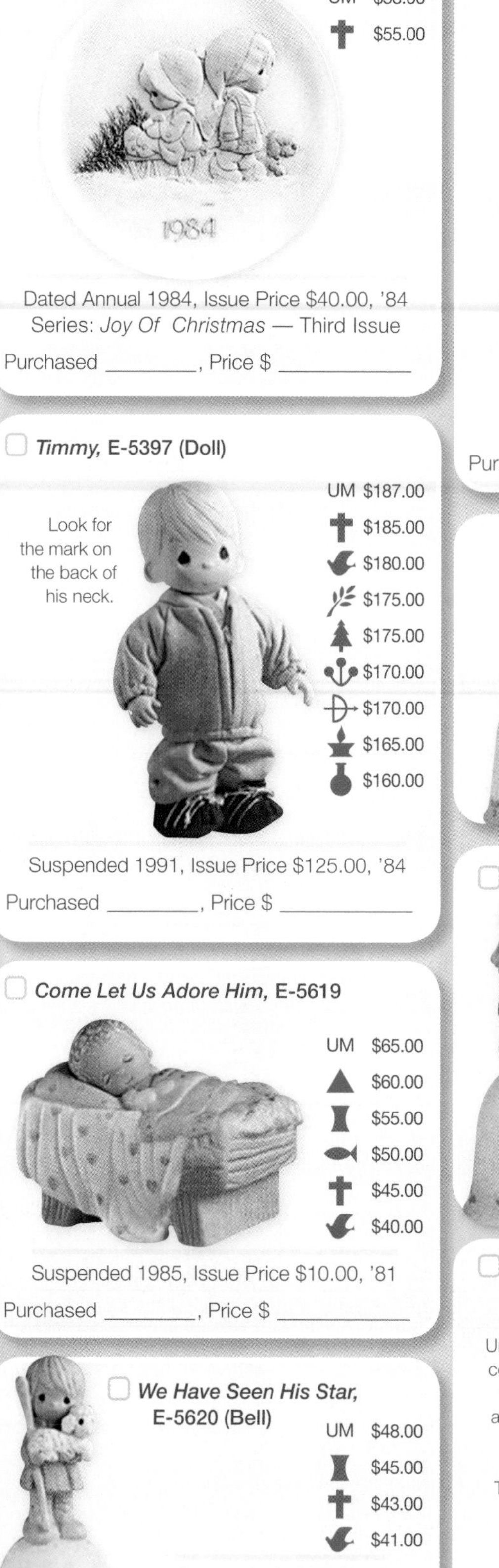

UM	$65.00
Triangle	$60.00
Hourglass	$55.00
Fish	$50.00
Cross	$45.00
Dove	$40.00

Suspended 1985, Issue Price $10.00, '81

Purchased ________, Price $ ___________

☐ ***We Have Seen His Star,*** **E-5620 (Bell)**

UM	$48.00
Hourglass	$45.00
Cross	$43.00
Dove	$41.00

Suspended 1985, Issue Price $15.00, '81

Purchased___________

Price $___________

☐ ***Donkey,*** **E-5621**

UM	$55.00	Flower	$43.00	G-Clef	$40.00
Cross	$45.00	Bow & Arrow	$43.00	Butterfly	$40.00
Dove	$45.00	Flame	$41.00	Trumpet	$38.00
Olive Branch	$45.00	Vessel	$41.00	Ship	$38.00
Cedar Tree	$45.00			Heart	$35.00
				Sword	$35.00
				Eyeglasses	$35.00
				Star	$33.00
				Egg	$33.00
				Sandal	$33.00
				Cross in Heart	$30.00
				Crown	$30.00

Retired 2003, Issue Price $6.00, '81
Nativity Addition

Purchased ________, Price $ ___________

☐ ***Let The Heavens Rejoice,*** **E-5622 (Bell)**

UM	$255.00

Dated Annual 1981, Issue Price $15.00, '81

Purchased___________

Price $___________

☐ ***Jesus Is Born,*** **E-5623 (Bell)**

UM	$75.00
Cross	$65.00

Suspended 1984, Issue Price $15.00, '81

Purchased ___________

Price $___________

☐ ***But Love Goes On Forever,*** **E-5627 (Ornament)**

Unmarked pieces could have been produced in any of the years of production. Consider Triangle as the first mark.

UM	$155.00
Triangle	$125.00
Hourglass	$120.00
Fish	$110.00
Cross	$100.00
Dove	$95.00

Suspended 1985, Issue Price $6.00, '81

Purchased ________, Price $ ___________

They Followed The Star, E-5624

UM	$875.00	[Butterfly]	$300.00
[Triangle]	$500.00	[Trumpet]	$300.00
[Hourglass]	$475.00	[Ship]	$300.00
[Fish]	$450.00	[Heart]	$275.00
[Cross]	$425.00	[Sword]	$275.00
[Dove]	$400.00	[Eyeglasses]	$275.00
[Olive Branch]	$375.00	[Star]	$250.00
[Cedar Tree]	$375.00	[Egg]	$250.00
[Flower]	$350.00	[Sandal]	$225.00
[Bow & Arrow]	$350.00	[Cross in Heart]	$225.00
[Flame]	$325.00	[Crown]	$225.00
[Vessel]	$325.00	[Clover]	$225.00
[G-Clef]	$300.00	[Box]	$225.00
		[House]	$225.00
		[Mushroom]	$225.00

Unmarked pieces could be from any of the years of production. Consider Triangle as the first mark. Mixed sets of Triangle/Hourglass and Hourglass/Fish are common.

Open, Issue Price $130.00, '81
Nativity Addition, Set of 3

Purchased ________, Price $ ___________

Wee Three Kings, E-5634 (Ornaments)

UM	$200.00
[Triangle]	$175.00
[Hourglass]	$165.00
[Fish]	$150.00
[Cross]	$140.00

Unmarked pieces could have been produced in any of the years of production. Consider Triangle as the first mark. Mixed sets of Triangle/Hourglass and Hourglass are common.

Suspended 1984, Issue Price $19.00, '81
Set of 3

Purchased ________, Price $ ___________

But Love Goes On Forever, E-5628 (Ornament)

UM	$175.00
[Triangle]	$145.00
[Hourglass]	$130.00
[Fish]	$125.00
[Cross]	$115.00
[Dove]	$110.00

Unmarked pieces could have been produced in any of the years of production. Consider Triangle as the first mark.

Suspended 1985, Issue Price $6.00, '81

Purchased ________, Price $ ___________

Baby's First Christmas, E-5631 (Ornament)

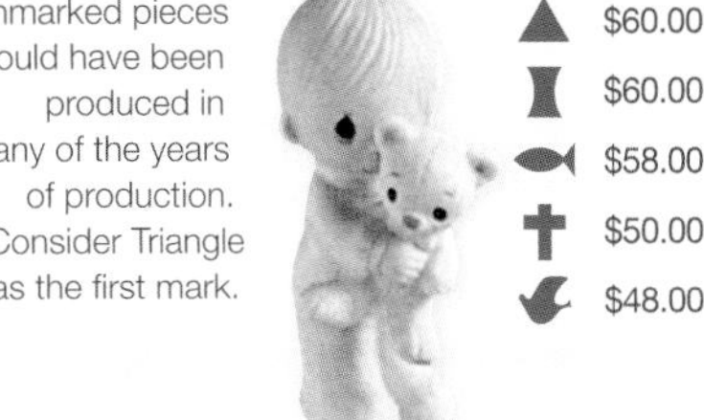

UM	$80.00
[Triangle]	$60.00
[Hourglass]	$60.00
[Fish]	$58.00
[Cross]	$50.00
[Dove]	$48.00

Unmarked pieces could have been produced in any of the years of production. Consider Triangle as the first mark.

Suspended 1985, Issue Price $6.00, '81

Purchased ________, Price $ ___________

Wee Three Kings, E-5635

UM	$165.00	[Flame]	$77.00	[Egg]	$75.00
[Triangle]	$130.00	[Vessel]	$76.00	[Sandal]	$75.00
[Hourglass]	$100.00	[G-Clef]	$75.00	[Cross in Heart]	$75.00
[Fish]	$95.00	[Butterfly]	$75.00	[Crown]	$75.00
[Cross]	$85.00	[Trumpet]	$75.00	[Clover]	$75.00
[Dove]	$83.00	[Ship]	$75.00	[Box]	$75.00
[Olive Branch]	$83.00	[Heart]	$75.00	[House]	$75.00
[Cedar Tree]	$80.00	[Sword]	$75.00	[Mushroom]	$75.00
[Flower]	$79.00	[Eyeglasses]	$75.00	[Heart Swirl]	$75.00
[Bow & Arrow]	$78.00	[Star]	$75.00		

Although scarce, Unmarked pieces could have been produced in any of the years of production. Consider Triangle as the first mark.

Retired 2008, Issue Price $40.00, '81
Nativity Addition, Set of 3

Purchased ________, Price $ ___________

Let The Heavens Rejoice, E-5629 (Ornament)

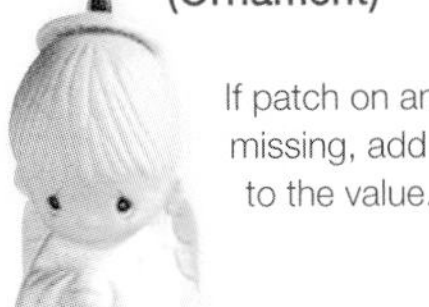

UM	$275.00
[Triangle]	$250.00

If patch on angel is missing, add $30.00 to the value.

Dated Annual 1981,
Issue Price $6.00, '81

Purchased ______________

Price $ ________________

Baby's First Christmas, E-5632 (Ornament)

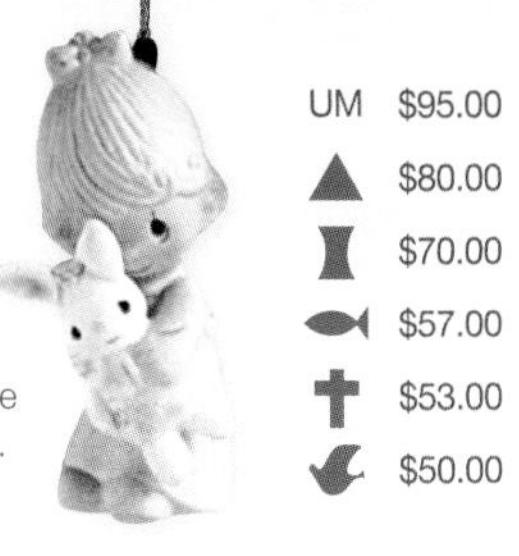

UM	$95.00
[Triangle]	$80.00
[Hourglass]	$70.00
[Fish]	$57.00
[Cross]	$53.00
[Dove]	$50.00

Unmarked pieces could have been produced in any of the years of production. Consider Triangle as the first mark.

Suspended 1985, Issue Price $6.00, '81

Purchased ________, Price $ ___________

Unto Us A Child Is Born, E-5630 (Ornament)

UM	$95.00	[Fish]	$75.00
[Triangle]	$90.00	[Cross]	$73.00
[Hourglass]	$82.00	[Dove]	$70.00

Suspended 1985, Issue Price $6.00, '81

Purchased ________, Price $ ___________

Come Let Us Adore Him, E-5633 (Ornaments)

UM	$200.00	[Triangle]	$175.00	[Fish]	$145.00
		[Hourglass]	$165.00	[Cross]	$135.00

Unmarked pieces could have been produced in any of the years of production. Consider Triangle as the first mark. Mixed sets of Triangle/Hourglass and Hourglass are common.

Suspended 1984, Issue Price $22.00, '81
Set of 4 — Mary, Jesus, Joseph, and Lamb

Purchased ________, Price $ ___________

☐ *Rejoice, O Earth,* E-5636

Mark	Price	Mark	Price	Mark	Price
UM	$103.00	🕊	$88.00	✿	$81.00
▲	$98.00	🌿	$85.00	🏹	$80.00
⧗	$95.00	🌲	$83.00	🕯	$78.00
🐟	$93.00			🏺	$75.00
✝	$90.00			𝄞	$73.00
				🦋	$70.00
				🎺	$68.00
				⛵	$65.00
				♡	$63.00
				🗡	$60.00
				👓	$58.00
				★	$55.00

Unmarked pieces could have been produced in any of the years of production. Consider Triangle as the first mark.

Retired 1999, Issue Price $15.00, '81
Nativity Addition

Purchased ________, Price $ ___________

☐ *Isn't He Wonderful,* E-5639

UM	$90.00
▲	$85.00
⧗	$65.00
🐟	$55.00
✝	$53.00
🕊	$46.00

Unmarked pieces could have been produced in any of the years of production. Consider Triangle as the first mark.

Suspended 1985, Issue Price $12.00, '81
Nativity Addition

Purchased ________, Price $ ___________

☐ *Silent Knight,* E-5642 (Musical)

UM	$600.00
▲	$585.00
⧗	$500.00
🐟	$495.00
✝	$460.00
🕊	$455.00

Unmarked pieces could have been produced in any of the years of production. Consider Triangle as the first mark. Exists in a double mark, Triangle/Hourglass. This is the only musical that does not have a figurine similar to it.

Suspended 1985, Issue Price $45.00, '81
Tune: *Silent Night*

Purchased ________, Price $ ___________

☐ *Isn't He Wonderful,* E-5640

UM	$100.00
▲	$85.00
⧗	$70.00
🐟	$65.00
✝	$63.00
🕊	$60.00

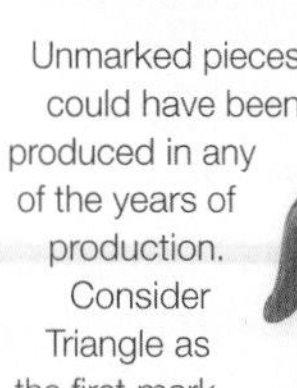

Unmarked pieces could have been produced in any of the years of production. Consider Triangle as the first mark.

Suspended 1985, Issue Price $12.00, '81
Nativity Addition

Purchased ________, Price $ ___________

☐ *The Heavenly Light,* E-5637

Mark	Price	Mark	Price	Mark	Price
UM	$103.00	🐟	$93.00	𝄞	$73.00
▲	$98.00	✝	$90.00	🦋	$70.00
⧗	$95.00	🕊	$88.00	🎺	$68.00
		🌿	$85.00	⛵	$65.00
		🌲	$83.00	♡	$63.00
		✿	$81.00	🗡	$60.00
		🏹	$80.00	👓	$58.00
		🕯	$78.00	★	$55.00
		🏺	$75.00	🥚	$53.00
				👡	$50.00

Unmarked pieces could have been produced in any of the years of production. Consider Triangle as the first mark.

Retired 2001, Issue Price $15.00, '81
Nativity Addition

Purchased ________, Price $ ___________

☐ *They Followed The Star,* E-5641

Mark	Price	Mark	Price	Mark	Price
UM	$325.00	⧗	$290.00	✝	$265.00
▲	$300.00	🐟	$275.00	🕊	$245.00

Unmarked pieces could have been produced in any of the years of production. Consider Triangle as the first mark.

Suspended 1985, Issue Price $75.00, '81
Nativity Addition

Purchased ________, Price $ ___________

☐ *Nativity Wall,* E-5644

UM	$165.00	✿	$128.00	♡	$120.00	🍀	$120.00
▲	$155.00	🏹	$125.00	🗡	$120.00	📦	$120.00
⧗	$153.00	🕯	$123.00	👓	$120.00	⌂	$120.00
🐟	$150.00	🏺	$120.00	★	$120.00	🍄	$120.00
✝	$145.00	𝄞	$120.00	🥚	$120.00	💔	$120.00
🕊	$140.00	🦋	$120.00	👡	$120.00	🌾	$120.00
🌿	$135.00	🎺	$120.00	✚♡	$120.00		
🌲	$130.00	⛵	$120.00	♔	$120.00		

Unmarked pieces could have been produced in any of the years of production. Consider Triangle as the first mark.

Open, Issue Price $60.00, '81
Nativity Addition, two sections of wall

Purchased ________, Price $ ___________

☐ *Cow With Bell,* E-5638

UM	$65.00	🏹	$43.00	⛵	$38.00	👡	$33.00
✝	$50.00	🕯	$43.00	♡	$38.00	✚♡	$33.00
🕊	$48.00	🏺	$40.00	🗡	$35.00	♔	$33.00
🌿	$48.00	𝄞	$40.00	👓	$38.00	🍀	$33.00
🌲	$45.00	🦋	$40.00	★	$33.00	📦	$33.00
✿	$45.00	🎺	$38.00	🥚	$33.00		

Retired, Issue Price $16.00, '84
Nativity Addition

Purchased ________, Price $ ___________

☐ *Rejoice, O Earth,* E-5645 (Musical)

UM	$200.00	✝	$145.00
▲	$175.00	🕊	$140.00
⧗	$150.00	🌿	$135.00
🐟	$145.00	🌲	$130.00
		✿	$125.00

Retired 1988, Issue Price $35.00, '81
Tune: *Joy To The World*

Purchased ___________

Price $ ___________

☐ *Come Let Us Adore Him,* E-5646 (Plate)

UM $65.00

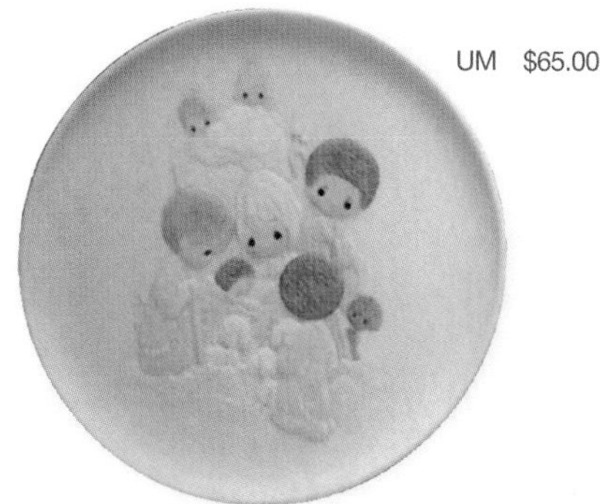

Limited Ed. 15,000, Issue Price $40.00, '81
Series: *Christmas Collection* — First Issue

Purchased ________, Price $ ____________

☐ *But Love Goes On Forever,* E-6118 (Candle Climbers)

UM $135.00
$120.00
$115.00
$113.00
$110.00
$108.00
$105.00

Suspended 1988, Issue Price $14.00, '81
Set of 2

Purchased ________, Price $ ____________

☐ *We Have Seen His Star,* E-6120 (Ornament)

UM $80.00
$73.00
$70.00
$65.00
$60.00

Retired 1984, Issue Price $6.00, '81

Purchased ________, Price $ ____________

☐ *Mikey,* E-6214B (Doll)

UM $250.00 $245.00
$245.00 $235.00
$225.00

Suspended 1985, Issue Price $150.00, '81

Purchased ____________

Price $ ____________

☐ *Debbie,* E-6214G (Doll)

UM $275.00 $265.00
$270.00 $260.00
$255.00

Suspended 1985, Issue Price $150.00, '81

Purchased ________

Price $ ____________

☐ *God Sends The Gift Of His Love,* E-6613

$75.00
$73.00
$69.00
$68.00
$65.00

Suspended 1987, Issue Price $22.50, '84

Purchased ____________

Price $ ____________

☐ *Collection Plaque,* E-6901 (Plaque)

$118.00 $58.00 $51.00
$73.00 $53.00

Found with a double mark, Hourglass/Fish.

Suspended 1986, Issue Price $19.00, '82

Purchased ________, Price $ ____________

☐ *God Is Love, Dear Valentine,* E-7153

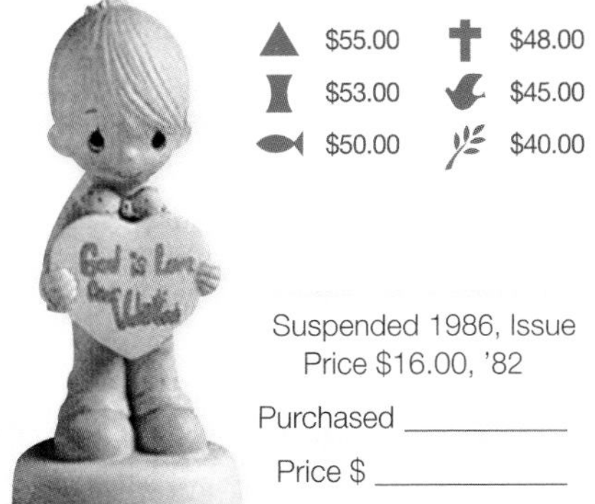

$55.00 $48.00
$53.00 $45.00
$50.00 $40.00

Suspended 1986, Issue Price $16.00, '82

Purchased ____________

Price $ ____________

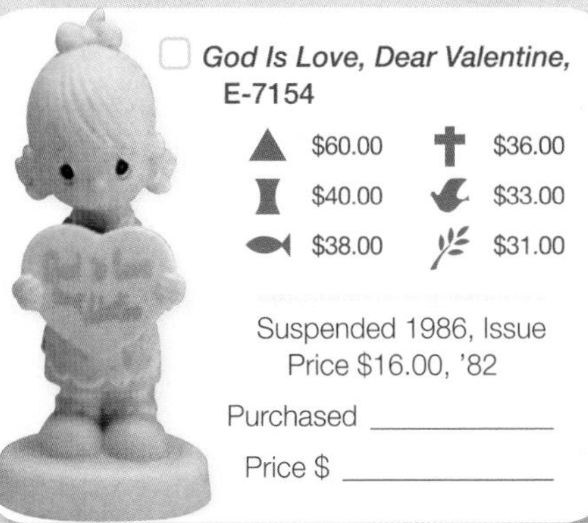

☐ *God Is Love, Dear Valentine,* E-7154

$60.00 $36.00
$40.00 $33.00
$38.00 $31.00

Suspended 1986, Issue Price $16.00, '82

Purchased ____________

Price $ ____________

☐ *Thanking Him For You,* E-7155

$70.00
$55.00
$53.00

Suspended 1984, Issue Price $16.00, '82

Purchased ____________

Price $ ____________

☐ *I Believe In Miracles,* E-7156

See next page for E-7156R.

$90.00
$85.00
$75.00
$70.00

Suspended 1985, Reintroduced 1987, Retired 1992, Issue Price $17.00, '82

Purchased ________, Price $ ____________

☐ *There Is Joy In Serving Jesus,* E-7157

$65.00
$53.00
$50.00
$48.00
$45.00

Retired 1986, Issue Price $17.00, '82

Purchased ________

Price $ ____________

I Believe In Miracles, E-7156R

$80.00
$75.00
$70.00
$65.00
$60.00
$60.00

First introduced in 1982 as E-7156, the original version of this figurine has the boy holding a yellow chick. E-7156 was Suspended in 1985, and in 1987 was resculpted and returned to production as E-7156R. Among the changes made was the addition of the incised "Sam B" on the base of the figurine and a change in the color of the chick, from yellow to blue. The resculpted piece is considerably larger than the original version. During the early part of production in 1987 (Cedar Tree), the molds from the Suspended piece, E-7156, were pulled and used along with the molds for the new Reintroduced piece, E-7156R. Shipments of the figurines crafted from the old Suspended mold but with the new blue painting of the chick were made before the error was discovered. These pieces are the rare version. All rare versions have the Cedar Tree symbol. The values of these rare version pieces are $155.00 each.

Retired 1992, Issue Price $22.50, '87

Purchased ________, Price $ ____________

Love Beareth All Things, E-7158

$62.00
$55.00
$50.00
$49.00
$48.00
$47.00
$46.00
$45.00
$45.00
$45.00
$45.00
$45.00
$45.00
$45.00
$45.00
$45.00
$45.00
$45.00
$45.00
$45.00
$45.00
$45.00
$45.00
$45.00
$45.00
$45.00
$45.00
$45.00
$45.00
$45.00
$45.00

Open, Issue Price $25.00, '82

Purchased ________, Price $ ____________

Lord Give Me Patience, E-7159

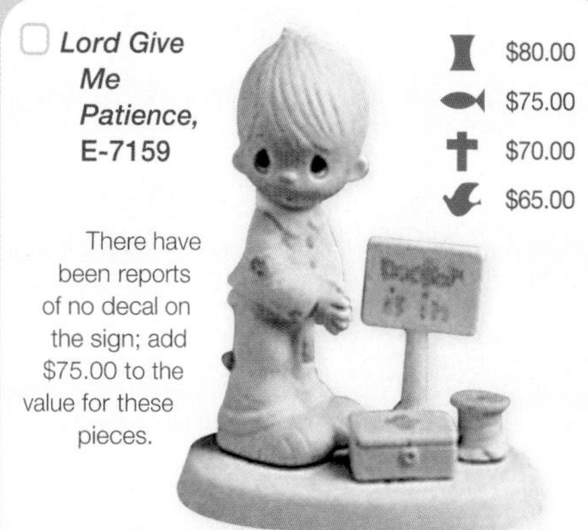

$80.00
$75.00
$70.00
$65.00

There have been reports of no decal on the sign; add $75.00 to the value for these pieces.

Suspended 1985, Issue Price $25.00, '82

Purchased ________, Price $ ____________

The Perfect Grandpa, E-7160

$100.00
$85.00
$83.00
$78.00
$75.00

Suspended 1986, Issue Price $25.00, '82

Purchased ________, Price $ ____________

His Sheep Am I, E-7161

Unmarked pieces could have been produced in any of the years of production. Consider the Hourglass as the first mark.

UM $155.00
$125.00
$115.00
$105.00

Suspended 1984, Issue Price $25.00, '82

Purchased ________, Price $ ____________

Love Is Sharing, E-7162

$165.00
$145.00
$130.00

Suspended 1984, Issue Price $25.00, '82

Purchased ________, Price $ ____________

God Is Watching Over You, E-7163

$145.00
$125.00
$105.00

Suspended 1984, Issue Price $27.50, '82

Purchased ________, Price $ ____________

Bless This House, E-7164

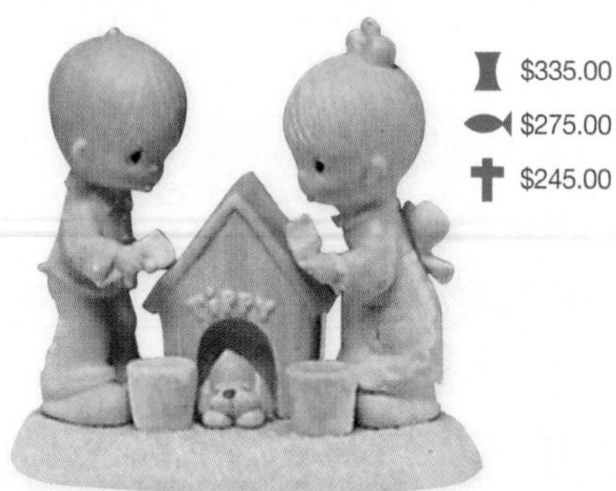

$335.00
$275.00
$245.00

Suspended 1984, Issue Price $45.00, '82

Purchased ________, Price $ ____________

Let The Whole World Know, E-7165

UM $195.00
$170.00
$155.00
$125.00
$115.00
$105.00
$100.00

Unmarked pieces could have been produced in any of the years of production. Consider the Hourglass as the first mark.

Suspended 1987, Issue Price $45.00, '82

Purchased ________, Price $ ____________

☐ *The Lord Bless You And Keep You,* E-7166 (Frame)

$75.00
$70.00
$70.00
$65.00
$63.00
$62.00
$61.00
$60.00
$59.00
$58.00
$57.00
$56.00

Suspended 1993, Issue Price $22.50, '82

Purchased ________, Price $ ____________

☐ *The Lord Bless You And Keep You,* E-7167 (Box)

$75.00
$70.00
$65.00
$60.00

Suspended 1985, Issue Price $22.50, '82

Purchased ________, Price $ ____________

☐ *My Guardian Angel,* E-7168 (Frame)

$88.00
$80.00
$77.00

Suspended 1984, Issue Price $18.00, '82

Purchased ________, Price $ ____________

☐ *My Guardian Angel,* E-7169 (Frame)

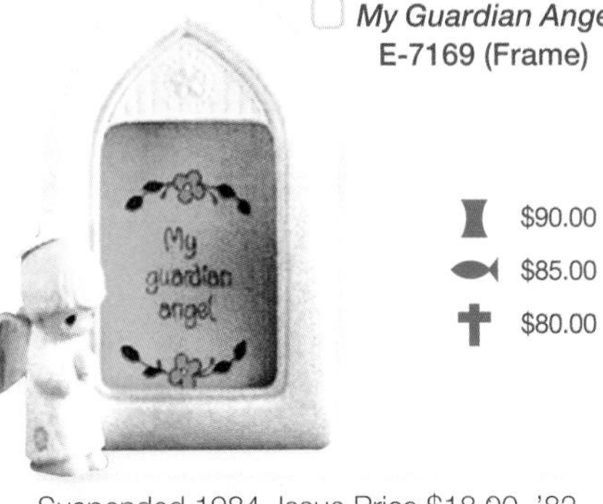

$90.00
$85.00
$80.00

Suspended 1984, Issue Price $18.00, '82

Purchased ________, Price $ ____________

☐ *Jesus Loves Me,* E-7170 (Frame)

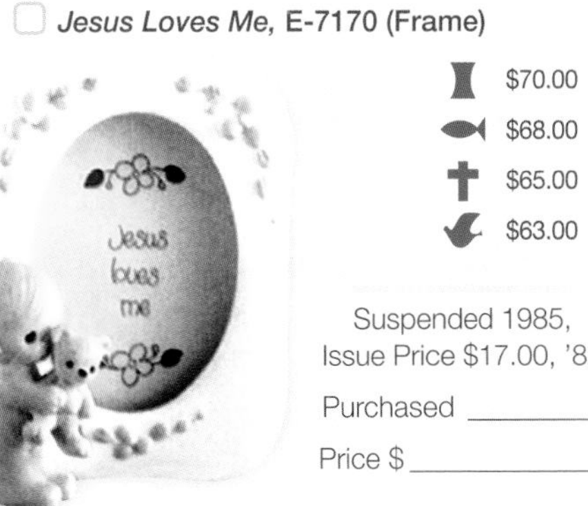

$70.00
$68.00
$65.00
$63.00

Suspended 1985, Issue Price $17.00, '82

Purchased ________

Price $ ____________

☐ *Jesus Loves Me,* E-7171 (Frame)

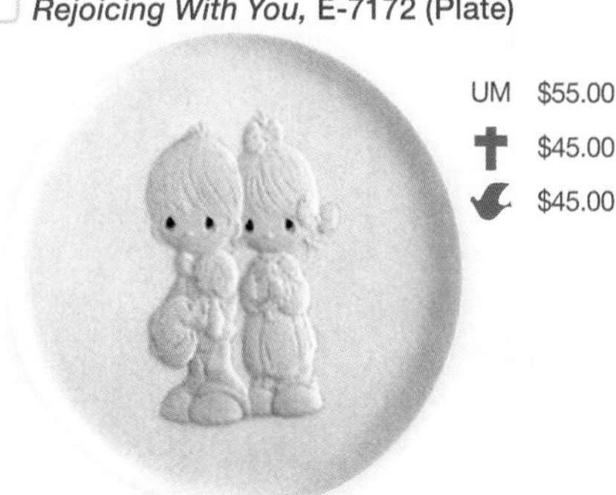

$80.00
$78.00
$75.00
$73.00

Suspended 1985, Issue Price $17.00, '82

Purchased________

Price $____________

☐ *Rejoicing With You,* E-7172 (Plate)

UM $55.00
$45.00
$45.00

Suspended 1985, Issue Price $30.00, '82

Purchased ________, Price $ ____________

☐ *The Purr-fect Grandma,* E-7173 (Plate)

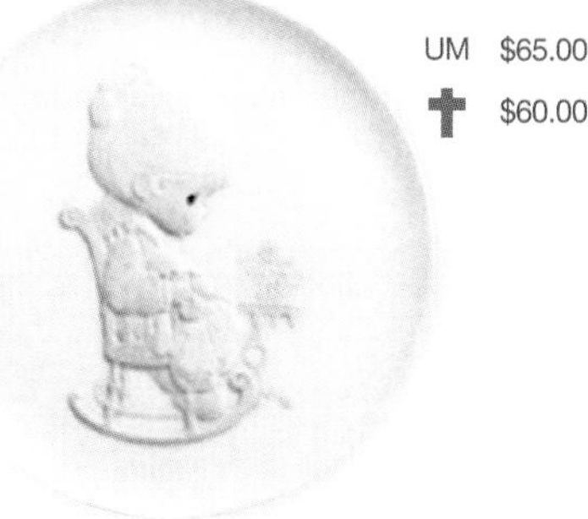

UM $65.00
$60.00

Limited Ed. 15,000, Issue Price $40.00, '82
Series: *Mother's Love* — Second Issue, Individually Numbered

Purchased ________, Price $ ____________

☐ *Make A Joyful Noise,* E-7174 (Plate)

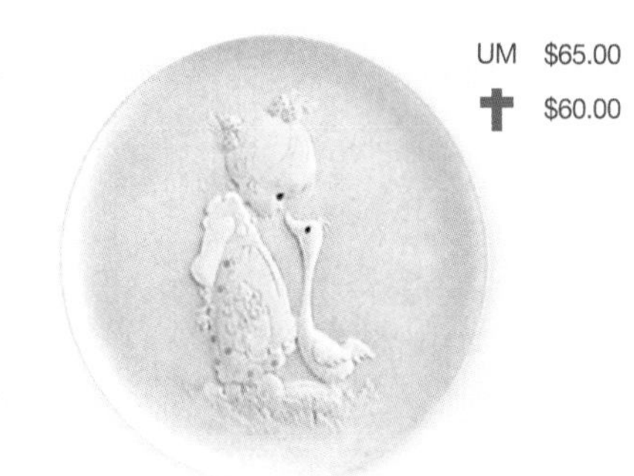

UM $65.00
$60.00

Limited Ed. 15,000, Issue Price $40.00, '82
Series: *Inspired Thoughts* — Second Issue, Individually Numbered

Purchased ________, Price $ ____________

☐ *The Lord Bless You And Keep You,* E-7175 (Bell)

UM $45.00
$40.00
$38.00

Suspended 1985, Issue Price $17.00, '82

Purchased ____________

Price $____________

☐ *The Lord Bless You And Keep You,* E-7176 (Bell)

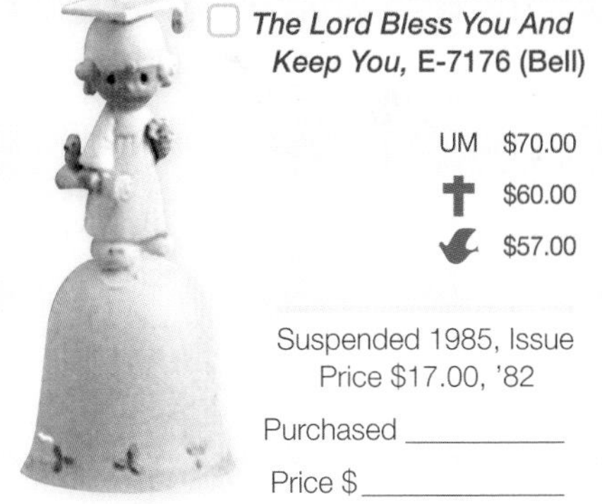

UM $70.00
$60.00
$57.00

Suspended 1985, Issue Price $17.00, '82

Purchased ____________

Price $____________

☐ *The Lord Bless You And Keep You,* E-7177 (Frame)

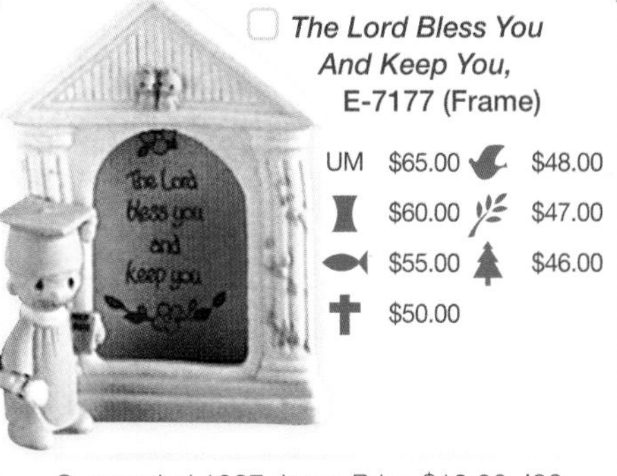

UM $65.00
$60.00
$55.00
$50.00
$48.00
$47.00
$46.00

Suspended 1987, Issue Price $18.00, '82

Purchased ________, Price $ ____________

The Lord Bless You And Keep You, E-7178 (Frame)

UM $73.00
$70.00
$68.00
$65.00
$63.00
$60.00
$55.00

Suspended 1987, Issue Price $18.00, '82

Purchased ________ Price $ ____________

Mother Sew Dear, E-7181 (Bell)

UM $85.00
$65.00
$64.00
$63.00
$62.00
$60.00

Suspended 1988, Issue Price $17.00, '82

Purchased ________, Price $ ____________

The Purr-fect Grandma, E-7184 (Musical)

UM $135.00
$125.00
$123.00
$120.00
$118.00
$115.00
$112.00
$110.00
$108.00
$105.00
$100.00

Suspended 1993, Issue Price $35.00, '82
Tune: *Always In My Heart*

Purchased ________, Price $ ____________

The Lord Bless You And Keep You, E-7179 (Bell)

UM $85.00
$73.00
$71.00
$68.00
$66.00
$61.00
$60.00
$59.00
$58.00
$57.00
$56.00

Suspended 1993, Issue Price $22.50, '82

Purchased ________, Price $ ____________

Mother Sew Dear, E-7182 (Musical)

UM $285.00
$275.00
$270.00
$265.00
$260.00
$255.00
$250.00
$245.00
$240.00
$235.00
$230.00
$225.00
$220.00
$215.00
$210.00
$205.00
$200.00
$200.00
$200.00

Retired 2001, Issue Price $35.00, '82
Tune: *You Light Up My Life*

Purchased ________, Price $ ____________

Love Is Sharing, E-7185 (Musical)

$250.00
$245.00
$235.00
$230.00
$225.00

Retired 1985, Issue Price $40.00, '82
Tune: *School Days*

Purchased ________, Price $ ____________

The Lord Bless You And Keep You, E-7180 (Musical)

UM $285.00
$245.00
$240.00
$240.00
$235.00
$235.00
$225.00
$225.00
$215.00
$215.00
$210.00
$210.00
$205.00
$205.00
$200.00
$200.00
$200.00
$190.00
$190.00

Retired 2001, Issue Price $55.00, '82
Tune: *Wedding March*

Purchased ________, Price $ ____________

The Purr-fect Grandma, E-7183 (Bell)

UM $85.00
$55.00
$52.00
$50.00
$48.00
$47.00

Also exists with ink Cross mark; value, $75.00.

Suspended 1988, Issue Price $17.00, '82

Purchased ________, Price $ ____________

Let The Whole World Know, E-7186 (Musical)

UM $235.00
$225.00
$215.00
$205.00
$200.00
$190.00

Suspended 1986, Issue Price $60.00, '82
Tune: *What A Friend We Have In Jesus*

Purchased ________, Price $ ____________

☐ *Mother Sew Dear,* E-7241 (Frame)

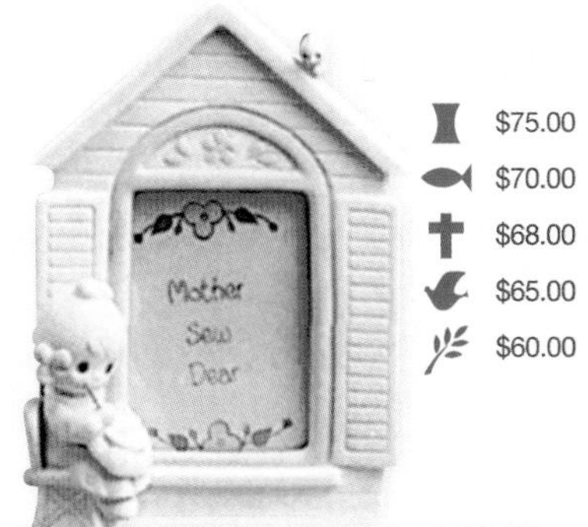

- $75.00
- $70.00
- $68.00
- $65.00
- $60.00

Suspended 1986, Issue Price $18.00, '82

Purchased ________, Price $ ____________

☐ *But Love Goes On Forever,* E-7350 (Retailer's Dome)

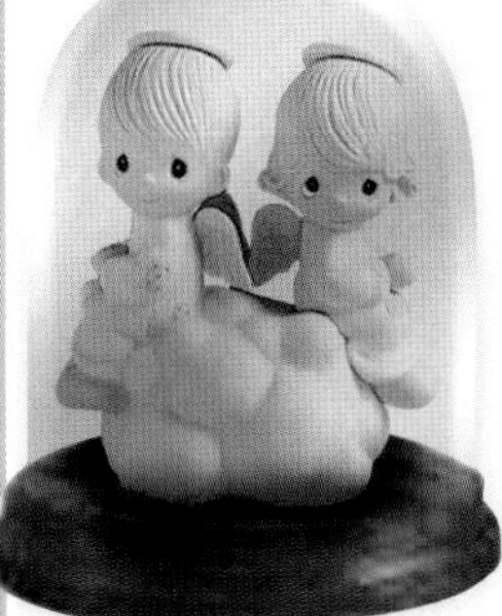

- UM $850.00
- $825.00
- w/out dome $750.00

Special Gift, '84

Purchased ________, Price $ ____________

☐ *Praise The Lord Anyhow,* E-9254

- UM $155.00
- $115.00
- $105.00
- $100.00
- $98.00
- $95.00
- $93.00
- $90.00
- $88.00
- $85.00
- $83.00
- $80.00
- $78.00
- $75.00

Classic variation: "Inked Fish." During 1983, the Fish mark appeared as part of the understamp decal on many pieces. Pieces were also produced that did not have a Fish mark at all – incised or decal. When this occurred we can only speculate that an attempt was made to correct it by actually drawing the Fish mark on the bottom of the piece. This inked symbol can be washed off, creating an unmarked piece. The value for pieces with the erasable inked Fish mark is $182.00.

Retired 1994, Issue Price $35.00, '82

Purchased ________, Price $ ____________

☐ *The Purr-fect Grandma,* E-7242 (Frame)

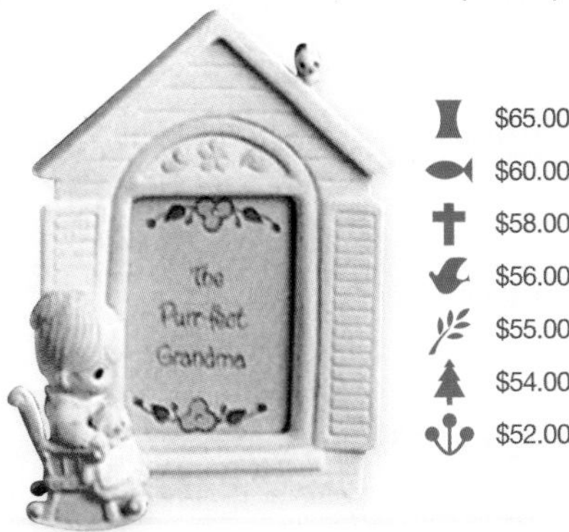

- $65.00
- $60.00
- $58.00
- $56.00
- $55.00
- $54.00
- $52.00

Suspended 1988, Issue Price $18.00, '82

Purchased ________, Price $ ____________

☐ *Love Is Patient,* E-9251

- $105.00
- $75.00
- $70.00

Also exists with Cross decal; value $86.00.

Suspended 1985, Issue Price $35.00, '83

Purchased ________, Price $ ____________

☐ *Bless You Two,* E-9255

- $55.00
- $55.00
- $55.00
- $53.00
- $53.00
- $53.00
- $50.00
- $50.00
- $50.00
- $48.00
- $48.00
- $48.00
- $45.00
- $45.00
- $45.00
- $45.00
- $45.00
- $45.00
- $45.00
- $45.00
- $45.00
- $45.00
- $45.00
- $45.00
- $45.00
- $45.00
- $45.00

Open, Issue Price $21.00, '83

Purchased ________, Price $ ____________

☐ *Cubby,* E-7267B (Doll)

Individually numbered on foot. Comes with certificate of authenticity.

UM $500.00

Limited Ed. 5,000, Issue Price $200.00, '82

Purchased ________

Price $ ____________

☐ *Forgiving Is Forgetting,* E-9252

- $105.00
- $100.00
- $95.00
- $93.00
- $90.00
- $88.00
- $85.00

Suspended 1989, Issue Price $37.50, '83

Purchased ________, Price $ ____________

☐ *Tammy,* E-7267G (Doll)

UM $625.00

Individually numbered on foot. Comes with certificate of authenticity.

Limited Ed. 5,000, Issue Price $300.00, '82

Purchased____________

Price $____________

☐ *The End Is In Sight,* E-9253

- UM $175.00
- $105.00
- $100.00
- $95.00
- $93.00

Unmarked pieces could have been produced in any of the years of production, however it is known many were released in the first year of production.

Suspended 1985, Issue Price $25.00, '83

Purchased ________, Price $ ____________

☐ *The Hand That Rocks The Future,* E-9256 (Plate)

UM $75.00
$75.00

Limited Ed. 15,000, Issue Price $40.00, '83
Series: *Mother's Love* — Third Issue, Individually Numbered

Purchased ________, Price $ ____________

☐ *I Believe In Miracles,* E-9257 (Plate)

UM $75.00
$75.00

Limited Ed. 15,000, Issue Price $40.00, '83
Series: *Inspired Thoughts* — Third Issue, Individually Numbered

Purchased ________, Price $ ____________

☐ *We Are God's Workmanship,* E-9258

$75.00
$73.00
$70.00
$68.00
$65.00
$63.00
$60.00
$58.00
$56.00
$54.00
$52.00
$50.00
$48.00
$45.00
$45.00
$43.00
$43.00
$40.00
$40.00
$40.00

Retired 2001, Issue Price $19.00, '83

Purchased ________, Price $ ____________

☐ *We're In It Together,* E-9259

$115.00
$105.00
$100.00
$95.00
$90.00
$85.00
$80.00
$75.00
$70.00

Suspended 1990, Issue Price $24.00, '83

Purchased ________, Price $ ____________

☐ *God's Promises Are Sure,* E-9260

Also exists with a stamped Fish. This has been a favorite of angel collectors.

$85.00
$80.00
$75.00
$73.00
$70.00

Suspended 1987, Issue Price $30.00, '83
Series: *Heavenly Halos*

Purchased ________, Price $ ____________

☐ *Seek Ye The Lord,* E-9261

Most figurines with the Fish annual production symbol do not have the "h" in the word "he" in the inscription on the graduate's scroll capitalized.

$55.00
$50.00
$48.00
$45.00

Suspended 1986, Issue Price $21.00, '83

Purchased ________, Price $ ____________

☐ *How Can Two Walk Together Except They Agree,* E-9263

$195.00
$175.00
$170.00
$165.00

Suspended 1985, Issue Price $35.00, '83

Purchased ________, Price $ ____________

☐ *Press On,* E-9265

$115.00
$113.00
$110.00
$108.00
$105.00
$103.00
$100.00
$98.00
$95.00
$93.00
$91.00
$89.00
$85.00
$83.00
$80.00
$78.00
$75.00
$70.00

Retired 1999, Issue Price $40.00, '83

Purchased ________, Price $ ____________

☐ *Our Love Is Heaven-Scent,* E-9266 (Box)

Our love is heaven-scent

UM $75.00
$65.00
$60.00
$55.00
$53.00
$50.00
$48.00

Some understamp decals have the title *Somebunny Cares;* add $50.00 for these pieces.

Suspended 1988, Issue Price $13.50, '83

Purchased ________, Price $ ____________

☐ *Seek Ye The Lord,* E-9262

$75.00
$70.00
$68.00
$65.00

Most figurines with the Fish annual production symbol do not have the "h" in the word "he" in the inscription on the graduate's scroll capitalized.

Suspended 1986, Issue Price $21.00, '83

Purchased ________, Price $ ____________

☐ *I'm Falling For Somebunny,* E-9266B (Box)

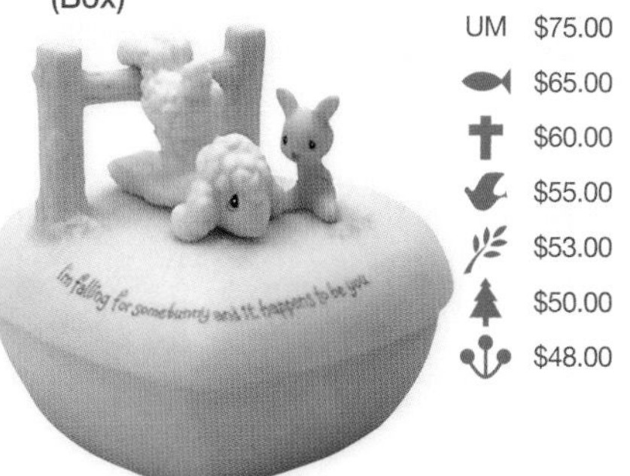

UM $75.00
$65.00
$60.00
$55.00
$53.00
$50.00
$48.00

Some understamp decals have the title *Somebunny Cares;* add $50.00 for these pieces.

Suspended 1988, Issue Price $13.50, '83

Purchased ________, Price $ ____________

☐ *Animal Collection C, Bunny with Carrot,* E-9267C

$28.00
$25.00
$23.00
$21.00

Suspended 1991, Issue Price $8.50, '88

Purchased ________, Price $ ____________

☐ *Animal Collection F, Pig,* E-9267F

$28.00
$25.00
$23.00
$21.00

Suspended 1991, Issue Price $8.50, '88

Purchased ________, Price $ ____________

☐ *Animal Collection,* E-9267

UM $185.00
$165.00
$160.00
$155.00
$150.00
$145.00

Note: The Animal Collection was shipped to retailers in sets of six. Consequently they do not have individual boxes. In 1988, individual Enesco item numbers were assigned to each figurine in the set. Some Cedar Tree symbol pieces have an A-F suffix.

Suspended 1991, Issue Price $39.00, '83
Set of 6

Purchased ________, Price $ ____________

☐ *Nobody's Perfect!* E-9268

$125.00
$115.00
$113.00
$110.00
$108.00
$105.00
$103.00
$100.00
$98.00

Classic variation: "Smiling Dunce." The first Hourglass pieces produced are known as "Smiling Dunces" or "Smiley" and appeared with a smile. An "O" shaped mouth is on the normal piece. The value of the "Smiley" is $495.00.

Retired 1990, Issue Price $21.00, '83

Purchased ________, Price $ ____________

☐ *Let Love Reign,* E-9273

$275.00
$95.00
$88.00
$85.00
$80.00
$75.00

Retired 1987, Issue Price $27.50, '83

Purchased ________, Price $ ____________

☐ *Animal Collection A, Teddy Bear,* E-9267A

$28.00
$25.00
$23.00
$21.00

Suspended 1991, Issue Price $8.50, '88

Purchased ____________

Price $ ____________

☐ *Animal Collection D, Cat with Bowtie,* E-9267D

$28.00
$25.00
$23.00
$21.00

Suspended 1991, Issue Price $8.50, '88

Purchased ________, Price $ ____________

☐ *Animal Collection B, Dog with Slipper,* E-9267B

$28.00
$25.00
$23.00
$21.00

Suspended 1991, Issue Price $8.50, '88

Purchased ________, Price $ ____________

☐ *Animal Collection E, Lamb,* E-9267E

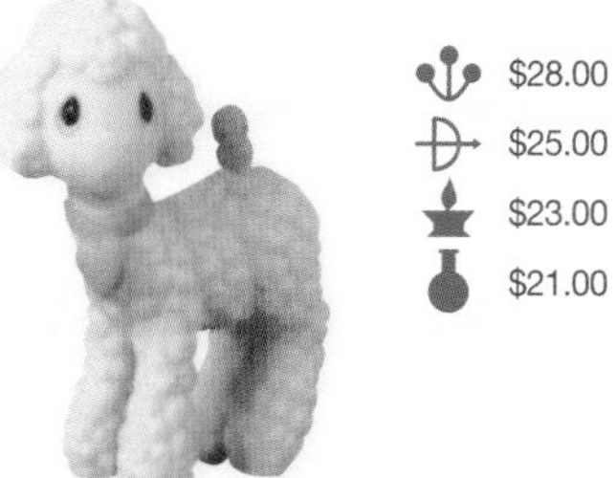

$28.00
$25.00
$23.00
$21.00

Suspended 1991, Issue Price $8.50, '88

Purchased ________, Price $ ____________

☐ *Taste And See That The Lord Is Good,* E-9274

$95.00
$90.00
$85.00
$80.00

Retired 1986, Issue Price $22.50, '83
Series: *Heavenly Halos*

Purchased ____________

Price $ ____________

☐ *Jesus Loves Me,* E-9275 (Plate)

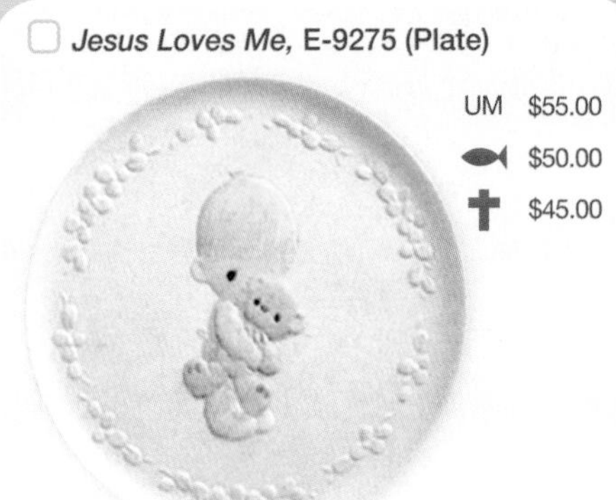

UM	$55.00
Fish	$50.00
Cross	$45.00

Suspended 1984, Issue Price $30.00, '83

Purchased ________, Price $ ____________

☐ *Jesus Loves Me,* E-9280 (Box)

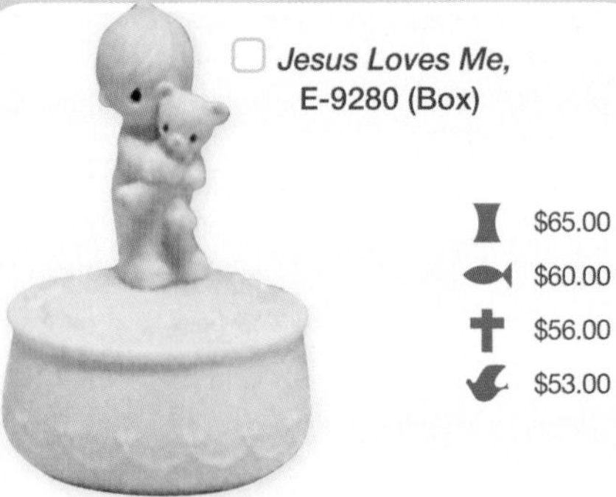

Mark	Price
Hourglass	$65.00
Fish	$60.00
Cross	$56.00
Dove	$53.00

Suspended 1985, Issue Price $17.50, '83

Purchased ________, Price $ ____________

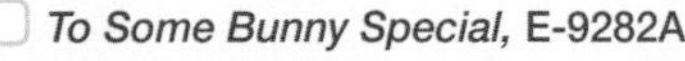

☐ *To Some Bunny Special,* E-9282A

Flower	$55.00
Bow & Arrow	$53.00
Flame	$50.00

Suspended 1990, Issue Price $10.50, '88

Purchased ________

Price $ ____________

☐ *Jesus Loves Me,* E-9276 (Plate)

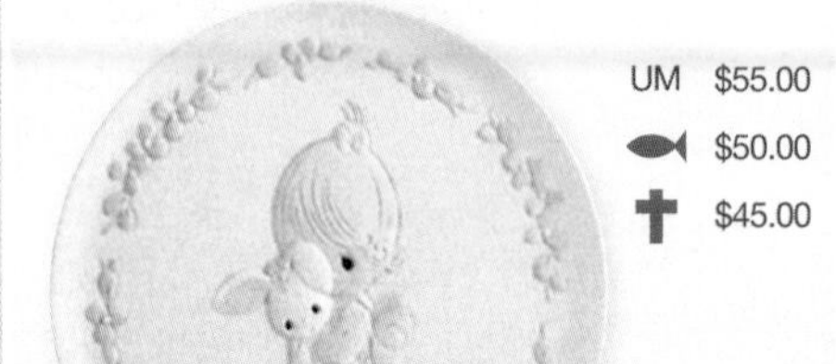

UM	$55.00
Fish	$50.00
Cross	$45.00

Suspended 1984, Issue Price $30.00, '83

Purchased ________, Price $ ____________

☐ *Jesus Loves Me,* E-9281 (Box)

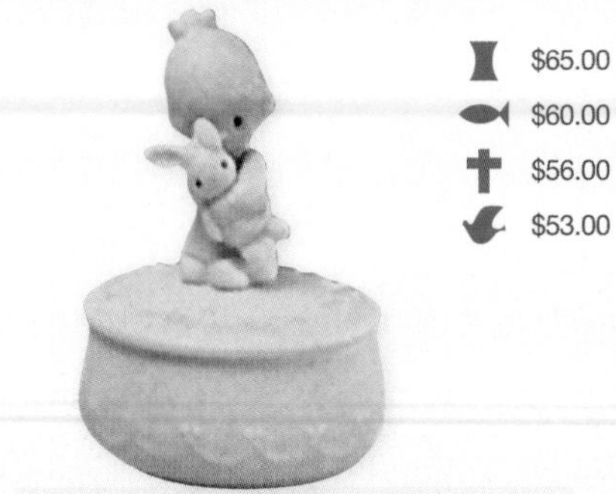

Hourglass	$65.00
Fish	$60.00
Cross	$56.00
Dove	$53.00

Suspended 1985, Issue Price $17.50, '83

Purchased ________, Price $ ____________

☐ *You're Worth Your Weight In Gold,* E-9282

UM	$65.00
Fish	$55.00
Cross	$53.00
Dove	$50.00
Olive Branch	$48.00
Cedar Tree	$45.00

Unmarked pieces could have been produced in any of the years of production. Consider Fish as the first mark. Letter "B" suffix added to item number in 1988.

Suspended 1987, Issue Price $8.00, '83

Purchased ________, Price $ ____________

☐ *Jesus Loves Me,* E-9278

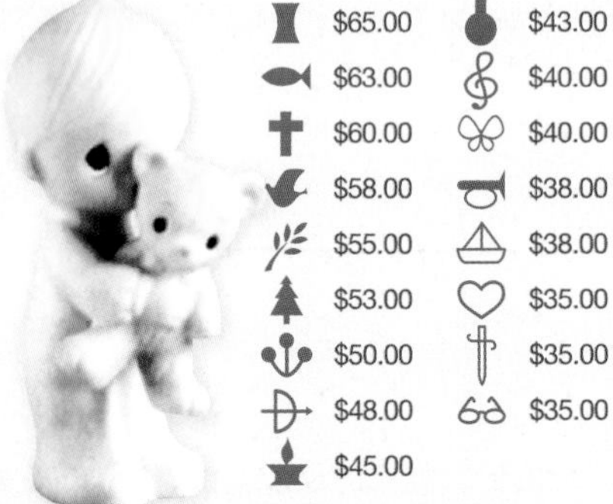

Hourglass	$65.00	Vessel	$43.00
Fish	$63.00	G-Clef	$40.00
Cross	$60.00	Butterfly	$40.00
Dove	$58.00	Trumpet	$38.00
Olive Branch	$55.00	Ship	$38.00
Cedar Tree	$53.00	Heart	$35.00
Flower	$50.00	Sword	$35.00
Bow & Arrow	$48.00	Eyeglasses	$35.00
Flame	$45.00		

Retired 1998, Issue Price $9.00, '83

Purchased ________, Price $ ____________

☐ *To Some Bunny Special,* E-9282

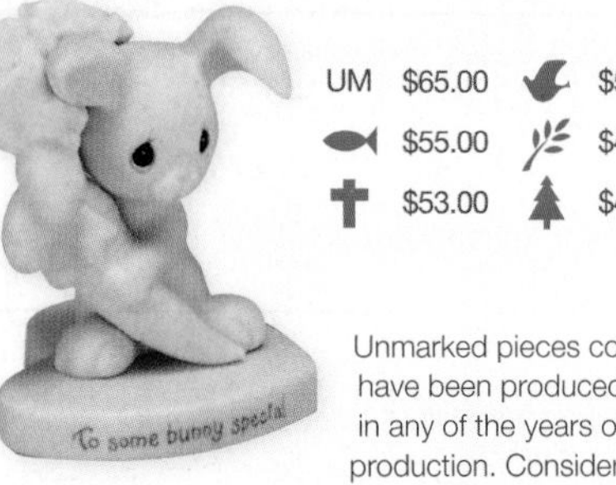

UM	$65.00	Dove	$50.00
Fish	$55.00	Olive Branch	$48.00
Cross	$53.00	Cedar Tree	$45.00

Unmarked pieces could have been produced in any of the years of production. Consider Fish as the first mark. Letter "A" suffix added to item number in 1988.

Suspended 1987, Issue Price $8.00, '83

Purchased ________, Price $ ____________

☐ *You're Worth Your Weight In Gold,* E-9282B

Flower	$55.00
Bow & Arrow	$53.00
Flame	$50.00

Suspended 1990, Issue Price $10.50, '88

Purchased ________

Price $ ____________

☐ *Jesus Loves Me,* E-9279

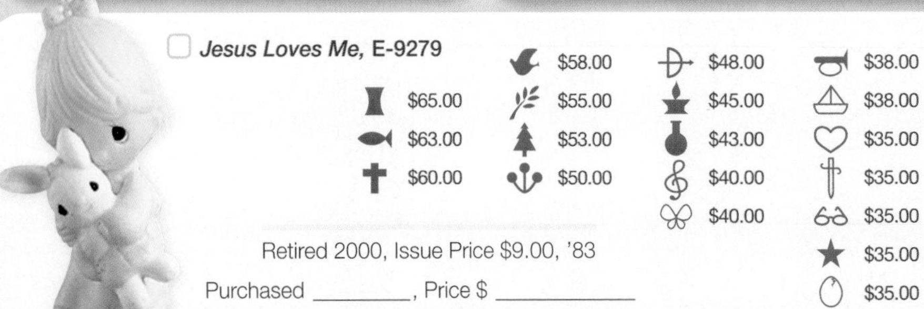

		Dove	$58.00	Bow & Arrow	$48.00	Trumpet	$38.00
Hourglass	$65.00	Olive Branch	$55.00	Flame	$45.00	Ship	$38.00
Fish	$63.00	Cedar Tree	$53.00	Vessel	$43.00	Heart	$35.00
Cross	$60.00	Flower	$50.00	G-Clef	$40.00	Sword	$35.00
				Butterfly	$40.00	Eyeglasses	$35.00
						Star	$35.00
						Egg	$35.00

Retired 2000, Issue Price $9.00, '83

Purchased ________, Price $ ____________

☐ *Especially For Ewe,* E-9282

UM	$65.00
Fish	$55.00
Cross	$53.00
Dove	$50.00
Olive Branch	$48.00
Cedar Tree	$45.00

Unmarked pieces could have been produced in any of the years of production. Consider Fish as the first mark. Letter "C" suffix added to item number in 1988.

Suspended 1987, Issue Price $8.00, '83

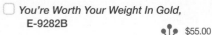

Purchased ________, Price $ ____________

☐ *Especially For Ewe,* E-9282C

⚓	$55.00
Bow & Arrow	$53.00
Candle	$50.00

Suspended 1990, Issue Price $10.50, '88

Purchased ________, Price $ ___________

☐ *Forever Friends,* E-9283A (Box)

Piece was Suspended in 1984, yet exists with the 1985 Dove symbol.

Hourglass	$125.00
Fish	$115.00
Cross	$100.00
Dove	$95.00

Suspended 1984, Issue Price $15.00, '83

Purchased ________, Price $ ___________

☐ *Forever Friends,* E-9283B (Box)

Also exists with decal of Hourglass. Value is $135.00.

Hourglass	$135.00
Fish	$125.00
Cross	$105.00

Suspended 1984, Issue Price $15.00, '83

Purchased ________, Price $ ___________

☐ *If God Be For Us, Who Can Be Against Us?* E-9285

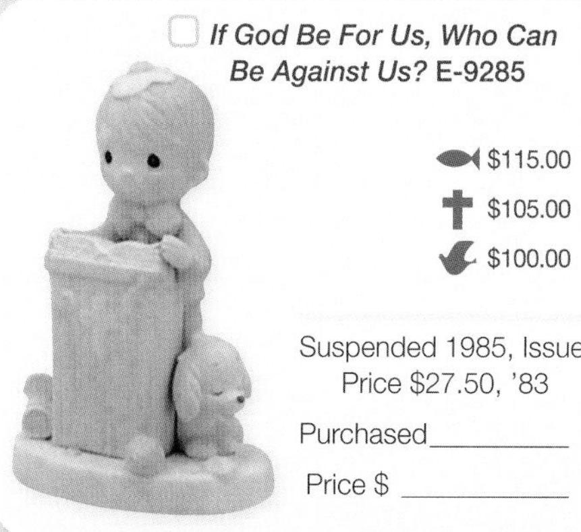

Fish	$115.00
Cross	$105.00
Dove	$100.00

Suspended 1985, Issue Price $27.50, '83

Purchased________

Price $ ___________

☐ *Peace On Earth,* E-9287

Fish	$225.00
Cross	$215.00
Dove	$205.00
Olive Branch	$200.00

Suspended 1986, Reintroduced 1997, Issue Price $37.50, '83

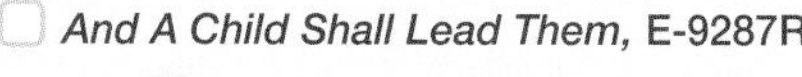

Purchased ________, Price $ ___________

☐ *And A Child Shall Lead Them,* E-9287R

Redesigned and brought back from suspension. Original title was *Peace On Earth.*

Heart	$75.00
Sword	$73.00
Eyeglasses	$72.00
Star	$70.00
Egg	$68.00
Bowl	$65.00
Heart with Cross	$63.00
Crown	$60.00

Retired 2003, Issue Price $50.00, '97

Purchased ________, Price $ ___________

☐ *Sending You A Rainbow,* E-9288

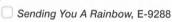

Fish	$125.00	Dove	$105.00
Cross	$115.00	Olive Branch	$100.00

Suspended 1986, Issue Price $22.50, '83

Series: *Heavenly Halos*

Purchased________

Price $___________

☐ *Trust In The Lord,* E-9289

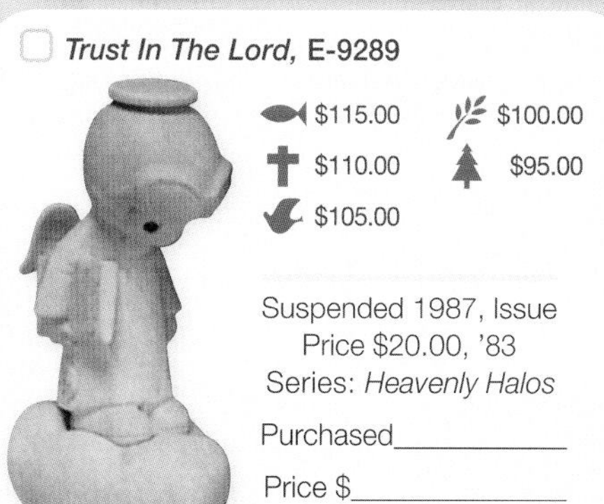

Fish	$115.00	Olive Branch	$100.00
Cross	$110.00	Cedar Tree	$95.00
Dove	$105.00		

Suspended 1987, Issue Price $20.00, '83

Series: *Heavenly Halos*

Purchased___________

Price $___________

☐ *Collecting Life's Most Precious Moments,* 11547 (Medallion)

Crown	$65.00

Available only at the Donald E. Stephens Convention Center through Krause Publications.

Limited Ed. 3,500, Issue Price $33.00, '03

Purchased ________, Price $ ___________

☐ *Love Covers All,* 12009

Cross	$95.00	Olive Branch	$85.00
Dove	$90.00	Cedar Tree	$83.00
		⚓	$80.00
		Bow & Arrow	$78.00
		Candle	$75.00
		Flame	$73.00

Suspended 1991, Issue Price $27.50, '85

Purchased ________, Price $ ___________

☐ *Loving You,* 12017 (Frame)

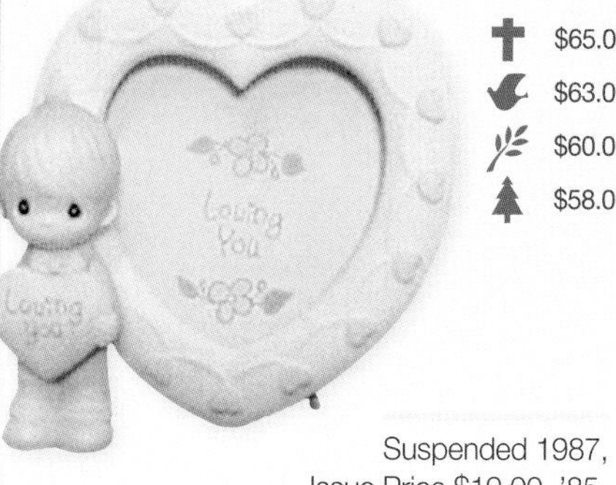

Cross	$65.00
Dove	$63.00
Olive Branch	$60.00
Cedar Tree	$58.00

Suspended 1987, Issue Price $19.00, '85

Purchased ________, Price $ ___________

☐ *Loving You,* 12025 (Frame)

Cross	$65.00
Dove	$63.00
Olive Branch	$60.00
Cedar Tree	$58.00

Suspended 1987, Issue Price $19.00, '85

Purchased ________, Price $ ___________

God's Precious Gift, 12033 (Frame)

$128.00
$125.00
$105.00
$100.00

Suspended 1987, Issue Price $19.00, '85

Purchased ______

Price $ ________

God's Precious Gift, 12041 (Frame)

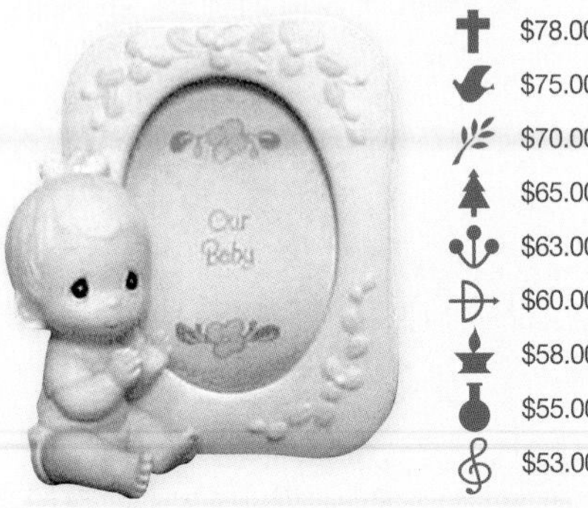

$78.00
$75.00
$70.00
$65.00
$63.00
$60.00
$58.00
$55.00
$53.00

Suspended 1992, Issue Price $19.00, '85

Purchased ________, Price $ ___________

The Voice Of Spring, 12068

$275.00
$275.00

Limited 1985, Issue Price $30.00, '85
Series: *The Four Seasons* — First Issue

Purchased __________

Price $ __________

Summer's Joy, 12076

$175.00
$165.00

Limited 1985, Issue Price $30.00, '85
Series: *The Four Seasons* — Second Issue

Purchased __________

Price $ __________

Autumn's Praise, 12084

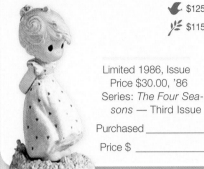

$125.00
$115.00

Limited 1986, Issue Price $30.00, '86
Series: *The Four Seasons* — Third Issue

Purchased __________

Price $ __________

Winter's Song, 12092

$205.00
$175.00

Limited 1986, Issue Price $30.00, '86
Series: *The Four Seasons* — Fourth Issue

Purchased __________

Price $ __________

The Voice Of Spring, 12106 (Plate)

$75.00
$65.00
$60.00

Annual 1985, Issue Price $40.00, '85
Series: *The Four Seasons* — First Issue

Purchased ________, Price $ ___________

Summer's Joy, 12114 (Plate)

$70.00
$60.00

Annual 1985, Issue Price $40.00, '85
Series: *The Four Seasons* — Second Issue

Purchased ________, Price $ ___________

Autumn's Praise, 12122 (Plate)

$70.00
$60.00

Annual 1986, Issue Price $40.00, '86
Series: *The Four Seasons* — Third Issue

Purchased ________, Price $ ___________

Winter's Song, 12130 (Plate)

$70.00
$60.00

Annual 1986, Issue Price $40.00, '86
Series: *The Four Seasons* — Fourth Issue

Purchased ________, Price $ ___________

Part Of Me Wants To Be Good, 12149

$100.00
$95.00
$90.00
$88.00
$85.00
$83.00

Suspended 1989, Issue Price $19.00, '85

Purchased __________

Price $ __________

This Is The Day The Lord Has Made, 12157

$85.00
$73.00
$70.00
$65.00
$60.00

Error: The first pieces were produced with the error "This Is The Day Which The Lord Has Made." The inscription was changed to omit the word "which."

Suspended 1990, Issue Price $20.00, '87

Purchased ________, Price $ ___________

☐ *Lord, Keep My Life In Tune,* 12165 (Musical)

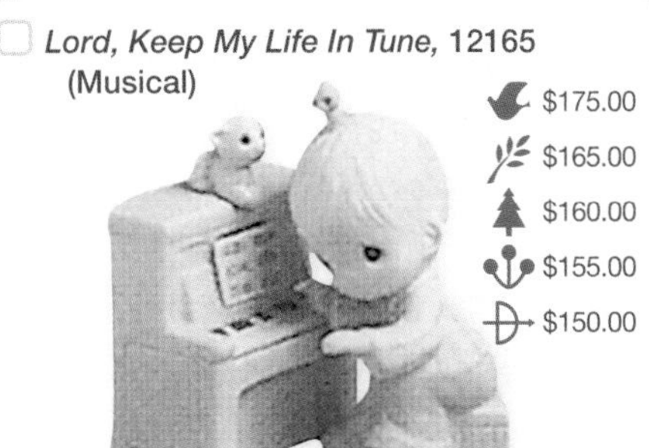

$175.00
$165.00
$160.00
$155.00
$150.00

Suspended 1989, Issue Price $37.50, '85
Tune: *Amazing Grace*
Series: *"Rejoice In The Lord" Band* — Set of 2

Purchased ________, Price $ ___________

☐ *Clown Figurines,* 12238

$175.00 $160.00
$165.00

Classic variation: "Clowns" was misspelled "Crowns" on the understamp decal of some sets. Value for the "Crowns" set of four is $225.00.

Discontinued 1987, Issue Price $54.00, '85
Set of 4 miniatures

Purchased ________, Price $ ___________

☐ *There's A Song In My Heart,* 12173

$75.00 $68.00
$73.00 $65.00
$70.00 $63.00

Suspended 1989, Issue Price $11.00, '85
Series: *"Rejoice In The Lord" Band*

Purchased ________________

Price $ ________________

☐ *Get Into The Habit Of Prayer,* 12203

$60.00
$55.00
$50.00

Suspended 1986, Issue Price $19.00, '85

Purchased ______________

Price $______________

☐ *Baby's First Haircut,* 12211

$185.00
$175.00
$165.00

Suspended 1987, Issue Price $32.50, '85
Series: *Baby's First* — Third Issue

Purchased ________, Price $ ___________

☐ *Clown Figurine,* 12238A

$45.00 $36.00
$40.00 $35.00
$39.00 $34.00
$38.00 $33.00
$37.00 $32.00

Suspended 1996, Issue Price $16.00, '87

Purchased ________, Price $ ___________

☐ *Clown Figurine,* 12238B

$45.00 $36.00
$40.00 $35.00
$39.00 $34.00
$38.00 $33.00
$37.00 $32.00

Suspended 1996, Issue Price $16.00, '87

Purchased ________, Price $ ___________

☐ *Clown Figurine,* 12238C

$45.00 $36.00
$40.00 $35.00
$39.00 $34.00
$38.00 $33.00
$37.00 $32.00

Suspended 1996, Issue Price $16.00, '87

Purchased ________, Price $ ___________

☐ *Clown Figurine,* 12238D

$45.00 $36.00
$40.00 $35.00
$39.00 $34.00
$38.00 $33.00
$37.00 $32.00

Suspended 1996, Issue Price $16.00, '87

Purchased ________, Price $ ___________

☐ *Precious Moments Last Forever,* 12246 (Medallion)

$115.00

This is the first medallion introduced in the Precious Moments collection. It was a gift to new club members.

Annual 1984, Issue Price $10.00, '84
Sharing Season Gift

Purchased ________, Price $ ___________

☐ *Love Covers All,* 12254 (Thimble)

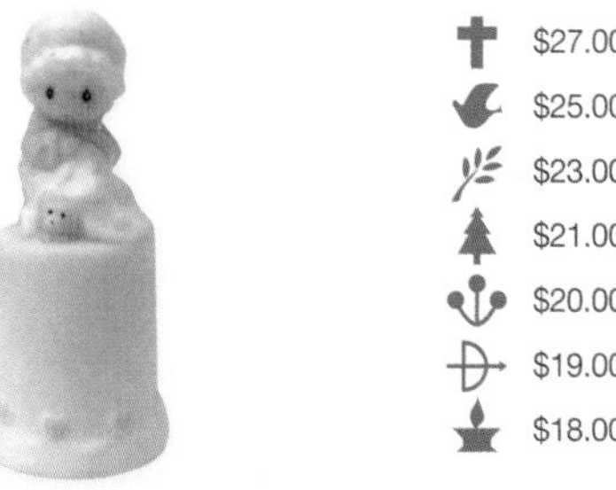

$27.00
$25.00
$23.00
$21.00
$20.00
$19.00
$18.00

Suspended 1990, Issue Price $5.50, '85

Purchased ________, Price $ ___________

I Get A Bang Out Of You, 12262

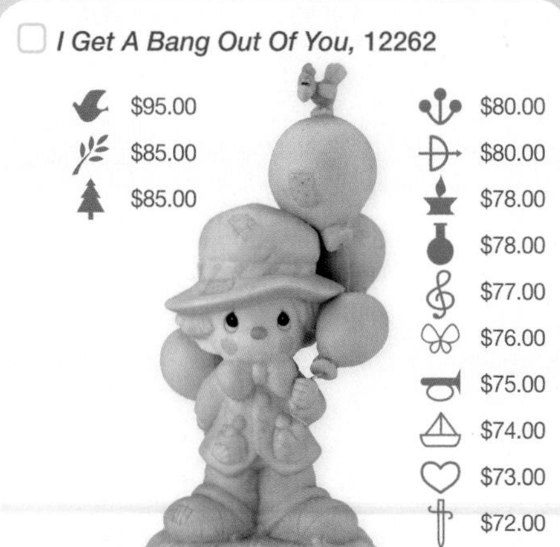

$95.00 · $85.00 · $85.00 · $80.00 · $80.00 · $78.00 · $78.00 · $77.00 · $76.00 · $75.00 · $74.00 · $73.00 · $72.00

Retired 1997, Issue Price $30.00, '85
Series: *Clown* — First Issue

Purchased ________, Price $ ____________

God Bless Our Home, 12319

$90.00 · $85.00 · $85.00 · $83.00 · $83.00 · $80.00 · $80.00 · $78.00 · $78.00 · $75.00 · $75.00 · $73.00 · $73.00 · $70.00

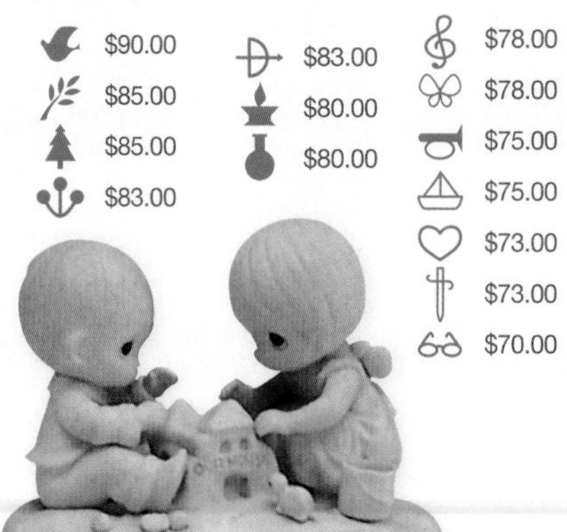

Retired 1998, Issue Price $40.00, '85

Purchased ________, Price $ ____________

Halo, And Merry Christmas, 12351

$225.00 · $200.00 · $195.00 · $190.00

Suspended 1988, Issue Price $40.00, '85

Purchased ________, Price $ ____________

Lord Keep Me On The Ball, 12270

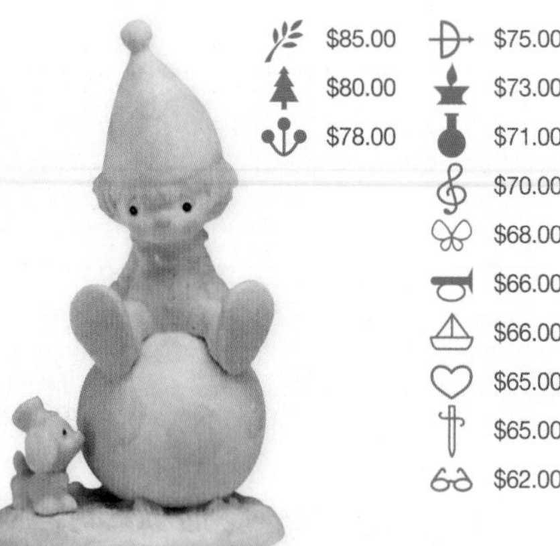

$85.00 · $80.00 · $78.00 · $75.00 · $73.00 · $71.00 · $70.00 · $68.00 · $66.00 · $66.00 · $65.00 · $65.00 · $62.00

Suspended 1998, Issue Price $30.00, '86
Series: *Clown* — Fourth Issue

Purchased ________, Price $ ____________

You Can Fly, 12335

$85.00 · $80.00 · $75.00

Suspended 1988, Issue Price $25.00, '86

Purchased ________, Price $ ____________

Happiness Is The Lord, 12378

$60.00 · $55.00 · $53.00 · $51.00 · $50.00 · $50.00

Suspended 1990, Issue Price $15.00, '85
Series: *"Rejoice In The Lord" Band*

Purchased ____________
Price $ ____________

It Is Better To Give Than To Receive, 12297

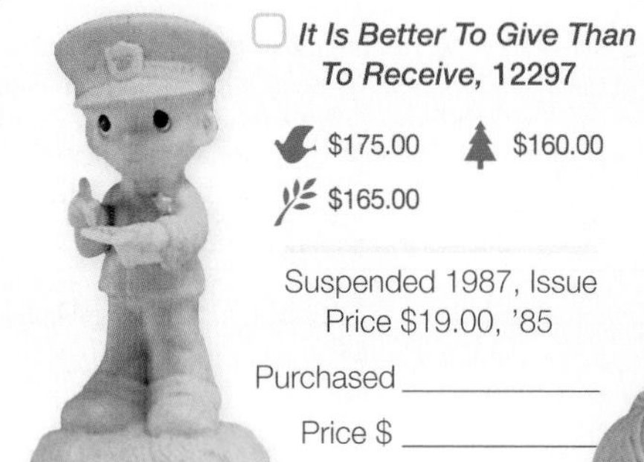

$175.00 · $165.00 · $160.00

Suspended 1987, Issue Price $19.00, '85

Purchased ____________
Price $ ____________

Jesus Is Coming Soon, 12343

$75.00 · $70.00

Suspended 1986, Issue Price $22.50, '85

Purchased ________, Price $ ____________

Lord Give Me A Song, 12386

$55.00 · $50.00 · $47.00 · $45.00 · $44.00 · $42.00

Suspended 1990, Issue Price $15.00, '85
Series: *"Rejoice In The Lord" Band*

Purchased ____________
Price $ ____________

Love Never Fails, 12300

$75.00 · $73.00 · $70.00 · $68.00 · $68.00 · $68.00 · $65.00 · $65.00 · $65.00 · $63.00 · $63.00 · $60.00 · $60.00 · $58.00 · $58.00 · $58.00

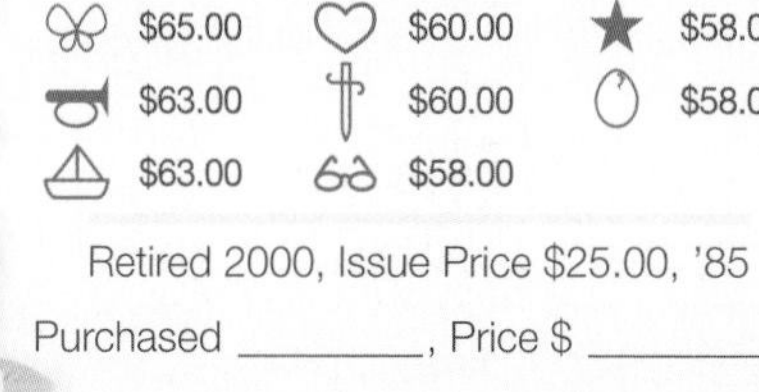

Retired 2000, Issue Price $25.00, '85

Purchased ________, Price $ ____________

He Is My Song, 12394

$65.00 · $63.00 · $63.00 · $60.00 · $58.00 · $55.00

Suspended 1990, Issue Price $17.50, '85
Series: *"Rejoice In The Lord" Band* – Set of 2

Purchased ________, Price $ ____________

☐ *We Saw A Star,* 12408 (Musical)

$145.00 · $135.00 · $125.00

Suspended 1987, Issue Price $50.00, '85
Tune: *Joy To The World* — Set of 3

Purchased ________, Price $ ____________

☐ *Have A Heavenly Christmas,* 12416 (Ornament)

UM $58.00 · $55.00 · $50.00 · $48.00 · $48.00 · $45.00 · $45.00 · $45.00 · $43.00 · $43.00 · $43.00 · $40.00 · $40.00 · $40.00

There are Cedar Tree pieces with two hooks from the Retailer's Wreath, #111465 (see page 142). There are also some ornaments, again from the Retailer's Wreath, that have the inscription "Heaven Bound" upside down.

Suspended 1998, Reintroduced 1998, Retired 1998, Issue Price $12.00, '85

Purchased ________, Price $ ____________

☐ *Have A Heavenly Journey,* 12416R

$55.00

Dated Annual 1998, Issue Price $25.00, '98
Care-A-Van Exclusive

Purchased ________

Price $ ____________

☐ *Aaron,* 12424 (Doll)

$155.00 · $150.00

Suspended 1986, Issue Price $135.00, '85

Purchased ________

Price $ ____________

☐ *Bethany,* 12432 (Doll)

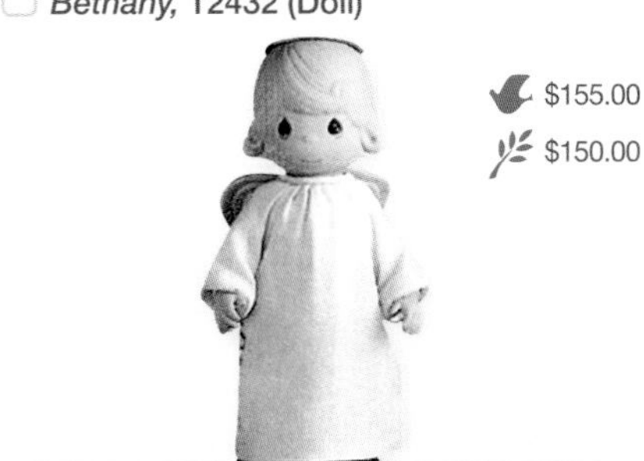

$155.00 · $150.00

Suspended 1986, Issue Price $135.00, '85

Purchased ________, Price $ ____________

☐ *Waddle I Do Without You,* 12459

$95.00 · $93.00 · $90.00 · $88.00 · $85.00

Retired 1989, Issue Price $30.00, '85
Series: *Clown* — Second Issue

Purchased ________, Price $ ____________

☐ *The Lord Will Carry You Through,* 12467

Has been found with the dove mark. It was probably a prototype and came with a "Not for Retail Sale" sticker.

$75.00 · $73.00 · $70.00

Retired 1988, Issue Price $30.00, '86
Series: *Clown* — Third Issue

Purchased ________, Price $ ____________

☐ *P.D.,* 12475 (Doll)

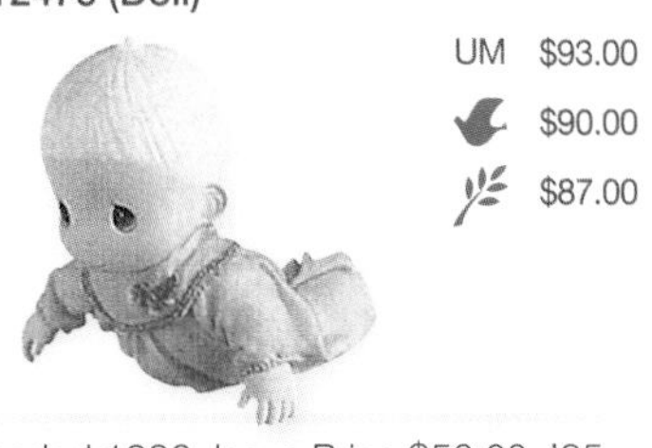

UM $93.00 · $90.00 · $87.00

Suspended 1986, Issue Price $50.00, '85

Purchased ________, Price $ ____________

☐ *Trish,* 12483 (Doll)

UM $93.00 · $90.00 · $87.00

Suspended 1986, Issue Price $50.00, '85

Purchased ________, Price $ ____________

☐ *Angie, The Angel Of Mercy,* 12491 (Doll)

$275.00

Limited Ed. 12,500, Issue Price $160.00, '87
Individually Numbered

Purchased ____________

Price $ ____________

☐ *Lord, Keep My Life In Tune,* 12580 (Musical)

$275.00 · $270.00 · $265.00 · $260.00 · $255.00

Suspended 1990, Issue Price $37.50, '87
Tune: *I'd Like To Teach The World To Sing*
Series: *"Rejoice In The Lord" Band* — Set of 2

Purchased ________, Price $ ____________

☐ *Mother Sew Dear,* 13293 (Thimble)

$35.00 · $30.00 · $28.00 · $26.00 · $25.00 · $25.00 · $23.00 · $23.00 · $22.00 · $22.00 · $20.00 · $20.00 · $19.00 · $19.00 · $18.00 · $18.00

Retired 1999, Issue Price $5.50, '85

Purchased ________, Price $ ____________

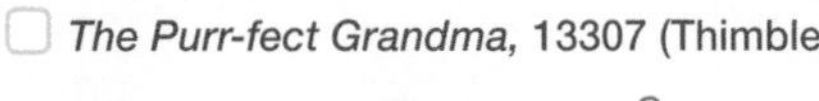

☐ *The Purr-fect Grandma,* 13307 (Thimble)

Dove	$30.00	G-Clef	$22.00
Olive Branch	$28.00	Butterfly	$22.00
Cedar Tree	$26.00	Trumpet	$20.00
Flower	$25.00	Ship	$20.00
Bow & Arrow	$25.00	Heart	$19.00
Flame	$23.00	Sword	$19.00
Vessel	$23.00	Eyeglasses	$18.00
		Star	$18.00

Retired 1999, Issue Price $5.50, '85

Purchased ________, Price $ ____________

☐ *Tell Me The Story Of Jesus,* 15237 (Plate)

Dove $115.00

Dated Annual 1985, Issue Price $40.00, '85
Series: *Joy Of Christmas* — Fourth Issue

Purchased ________, Price $ ____________

☐ *May Your Christmas Be Delightful,* 15482

Dove	$75.00	Flame	$67.00
Olive Branch	$73.00	Vessel	$66.00
Cedar Tree	$70.00	G-Clef	$65.00
Flower	$69.00	Butterfly	$63.00
Bow & Arrow	$68.00	Trumpet	$60.00

Suspended 1994, Issue Price $25.00, '85

Purchased ________, Price $ ____________

☐ *God Sent You Just In Time,* 15504 (Musical)

Dove	$125.00
Olive Branch	$120.00
Cedar Tree	$115.00
Flower	$110.00
Bow & Arrow	$105.00

Retired 1989, Issue Price $45.00, '85
Tune: *We Wish You A Merry Christmas*

Purchased ________, Price $ ____________

☐ *Baby's First Christmas,* 15539

Dove $55.00

Dated Annual 1985, Issue Price $13.00, '85

Purchased ________, Price $ ____________

☐ *Baby's First Christmas,* 15547

Dove $35.00

Dated Annual 1985, Issue Price $13.00, '85

Purchased ________, Price $ ____________

☐ *Honk If You Love Jesus,* 15490

Dove	$50.00	Flame	$40.00	Trumpet	$36.00	Eyeglasses	$33.00
Olive Branch	$48.00	Vessel	$39.00	Ship	$35.00	Star	$33.00
Cedar Tree	$45.00	G-Clef	$38.00	Heart	$34.00	Egg	$30.00
Flower	$43.00	Butterfly	$37.00	Sword	$34.00	Sandal	$30.00
Bow & Arrow	$41.00						

Retired 2001, Issue Price $13.00, '85
Nativity Addition — Set of 2

Purchased ________, Price $ ____________

☐ *God Sent His Love,* 15768 (Ornament)

Dove $35.00

Dated Annual 1985, Issue Price $10.00, '85

Purchased ____________

Price $ ______________

☐ *May You Have The Sweetest Christmas,* 15776

Dove	$70.00	Bow & Arrow	$62.00
Olive Branch	$68.00	Flame	$60.00
Cedar Tree	$65.00	Vessel	$58.00
Flower	$63.00	G-Clef	$55.00

Suspended 1992, Issue Price $17.00, '85
Series: *Family Christmas Scene* — First Issue

Purchased ____________

Price $ ______________

☐ *The Story Of God's Love,* 15784

Dove	$82.00
Olive Branch	$80.00
Cedar Tree	$78.00
Flower	$75.00
Bow & Arrow	$73.00
Flame	$70.00
Vessel	$68.00
G-Clef	$65.00

Suspended 1992, Issue Price $22.50, '85
Series: *Family Christmas Scene* — Second Issue

Purchased ________, Price $ ____________

☐ *Tell Me A Story,* 15792

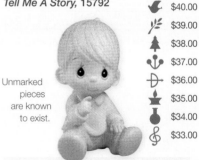

Unmarked pieces are known to exist.

Dove	$40.00
Olive Branch	$39.00
Cedar Tree	$38.00
Flower	$37.00
Bow & Arrow	$36.00
Flame	$35.00
Vessel	$34.00
G-Clef	$33.00

Suspended 1992, Issue Price $10.00, '85
Series: *Family Christmas Scene* — Third Issue

Purchased ________, Price $ ____________

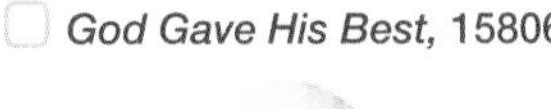

☐ *God Gave His Best,* 15806

$75.00
$60.00
$58.00
$55.00
$53.00
$51.00
$50.00
$49.00

Suspended 1992, Issue Price $13.00, '85
Series: *Family Christmas Scene* — Fourth Issue
Purchased ________, Price $ ____________

☐ *Silent Night,* 15814 (Musical)

$125.00
$120.00
$115.00
$110.00
$105.00
$100.00
$95.00
$93.00

Suspended 1992, Issue Price $37.50, '85
Tune: *Silent Night*
Series: *Family Christmas Scene* — Fifth Issue
Purchased ________, Price $ ____________

☐ *May Your Christmas Be Happy,* 15822 (Ornament)

$55.00
$50.00
$48.00
$45.00
$43.00

Suspended 1989, Issue Price $10.00, '85
Purchased ____________
Price $ ____________

☐ *Happiness Is The Lord,* 15830 (Ornament)

$38.00
$35.00
$33.00
$32.00
$32.00

Suspended 1989, Issue Price $10.00, '85
Purchased ____________
Price $ ____________

☐ *May Your Christmas Be Delightful,* 15849 (Ornament)

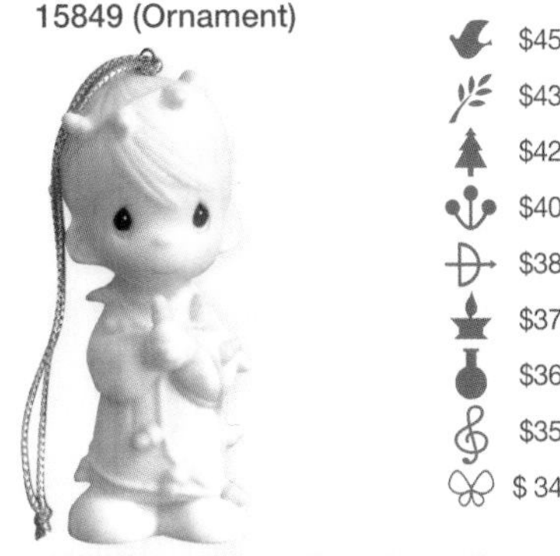

$45.00
$43.00
$42.00
$40.00
$38.00
$37.00
$36.00
$35.00
$ 34.00

Suspended 1993, Reintroduced 1999, Issue Price $10.00, '85
Purchased ________, Price $ ____________

☐ *May Your Christmas Be Delightful,* 15849R (Ornament)

★ $45.00

Limited Ed., Issue Price $20.00, '99
Purchased ________
Price $ ____________

☐ *Honk If You Love Jesus,* 15857 (Ornament)

$40.00
$39.00
$38.00
$37.00
$36.00
$35.00
$34.00
$33.00
$32.00

Suspended 1993, Issue Price $10.00, '85
Purchased ____________
Price $ ____________

☐ *God Sent His Love,* 15865 (Thimble)

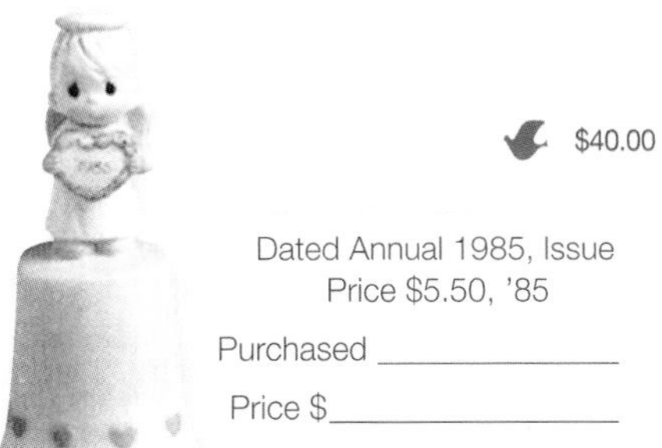

$40.00

Dated Annual 1985, Issue Price $5.50, '85
Purchased ____________
Price $ ____________

☐ *God Sent His Love,* 15873 (Bell)

$40.00

Dated Annual 1985, Issue Price $19.00, '85
Purchased ________, Price $ ____________

☐ *God Sent His Love,* 15881

$50.00

Dated Annual 1985, Issue Price $17.00, '85
Purchased ________, Price $ ____________

☐ *Baby's First Christmas,* 15903 (Ornament)

$35.00

Dated Annual 1985, Issue Price $10.00, '85
Purchased ________, Price $ ____________

☐ *Baby's First Christmas,* 15911 (Ornament)

$35.00

Dated Annual 1985, Issue Price $10.00, '85
Purchased ____________
Price $ ____________

☐ *May Your Birthday Be Warm*, 15938

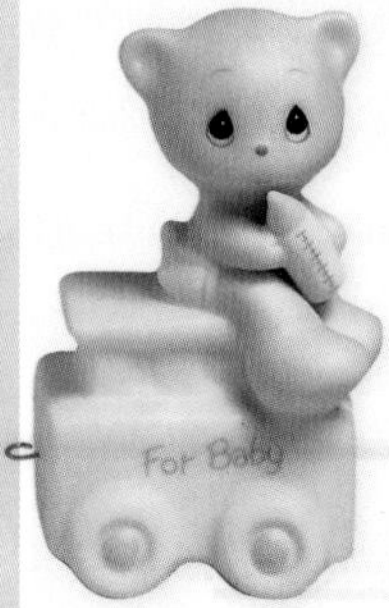

$36.00	$27.00	$18.00
$30.00	$25.00	$18.00
$28.00	$25.00	$18.00
	$23.00	$16.00
	$23.00	$16.00
	$22.00	$16.00
	$21.00	$16.00
	$20.00	$16.00
	$20.00	$16.00
	$20.00	$16.00
	$20.00	$16.00

Open, Issue Price $10.00, '86
Series: *Birthday Circus Train* — Infant

Purchased ________, Price $ ____________

☐ *God Bless You On Your Birthday*, 15962

$45.00	$28.00	$20.00
$40.00	$26.00	$18.50
$35.00	$26.00	$18.50
$30.00	$26.00	$18.50
$28.00	$25.00	$18.50
	$25.00	$18.50
	$23.00	$18.50
	$23.00	$18.50
	$20.00	$18.50
	$20.00	$18.50

Open, Issue Price $11.00, '86
Series: *Birthday Circus Train* — Age 2

Purchased ________, Price $ ____________

☐ *Keep Looking Up*, 15997

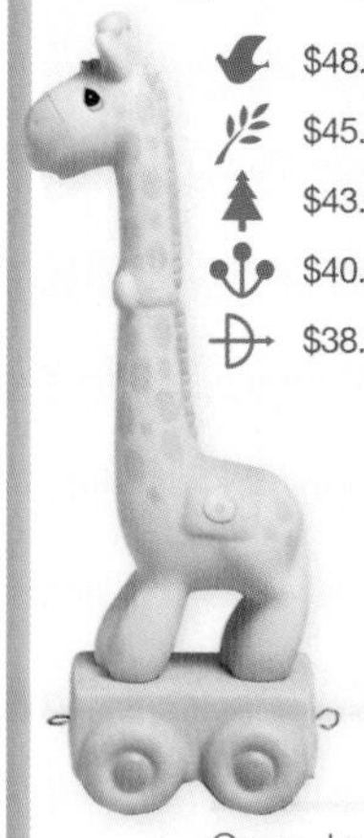

$48.00	$35.00	$28.00
$45.00	$35.00	$26.50
$43.00	$33.00	$26.50
$40.00	$33.00	$26.50
$38.00	$33.00	$26.50
	$30.00	$26.50
	$30.00	$26.50
	$30.00	$26.50
	$28.00	$26.50
	$28.00	$26.50

Open, Issue Price $13.50, '86
Series: *Birthday Circus Train* — Age 6

Purchased ________, Price $ ____________

☐ *Happy Birthday Little Lamb*, 15946

$36.00	$27.00	$18.00
$30.00	$25.00	$18.00
$28.00	$25.00	$18.00
	$23.00	$16.00
	$23.00	$16.00
	$22.00	$16.00
	$21.00	$16.00
	$20.00	$16.00
	$20.00	$16.00
	$20.00	$16.00
	$20.00	$16.00

Open, Issue Price $10.00, '86
Series: *Birthday Circus Train* — Age 1

Purchased ________, Price $ ____________

☐ *May Your Birthday Be Gigantic*, 15970

$45.00	$35.00	$25.00
$40.00	$35.00	$23.00
$38.00	$33.00	$23.00
	$33.00	$21.00
	$30.00	$21.00
	$28.00	$21.00
	$28.00	$21.00
	$28.00	$21.00
	$25.00	$21.00
	$25.00	$21.00
	$25.00	$21.00

Open, Issue Price $12.50, '86
Series: *Birthday Circus Train* — Age 4

Purchased ________, Price $ ____________

☐ *Bless The Days Of Our Youth*, 16004

$55.00	$48.00	$35.00
$53.00	$46.00	$34.00
$50.00	$45.00	$30.00
	$43.00	$28.00
	$40.00	$26.50
	$40.00	$26.50
	$40.00	$26.50
	$39.00	$26.50
	$38.00	$26.50
	$37.00	$26.50
	$36.00	$26.50

Open, Issue Price $15.00, '86
Series: *Birthday Circus Train*

Purchased ________, Price $ ____________

☐ *Heaven Bless Your Special Day*, 15954

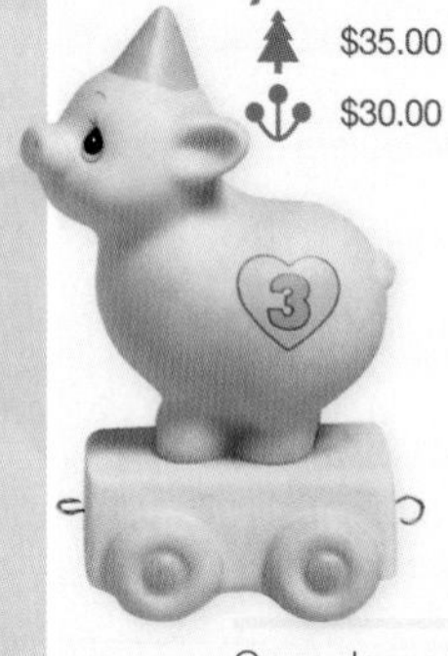

$45.00	$28.00	$20.00
$40.00	$28.00	$18.50
$35.00	$26.00	$18.50
$30.00	$26.00	$18.50
	$26.00	$18.50
	$25.00	$18.50
	$25.00	$18.50
	$23.00	$18.50
	$23.00	$18.50
	$20.00	$18.50
	$20.00	

Open, Issue Price $11.00, '86
Series: *Birthday Circus Train* — Age 3

Purchased ________, Price $ ____________

☐ *This Day Is Something To Roar About*, 15989

$48.00	$40.00	$28.00
$45.00	$38.00	$28.00
$43.00	$35.00	$26.50
	$35.00	$26.50
	$33.00	$26.50
	$33.00	$26.50
	$33.00	$26.50
	$30.00	$26.50
	$30.00	$26.50
	$30.00	$26.50
	$28.00	$26.50

Open, Issue Price $13.50, '86
Series: *Birthday Circus Train* — Age 5

Purchased ________, Price $ ____________

☐ *Baby's First Trip*, 16012

$355.00
$325.00
$300.00
$295.00

Suspended 1989, Issue Price $32.50, '86
Series: *Baby's First* — Fourth Issue

Purchased ________, Price $ ____________

☐ *God Bless You With Rainbows*, 16020 (Nightlight)

$155.00
$150.00
$145.00
$140.00
$135.00

Suspended 1989, Issue Price $45.00, '86

Purchased ________, Price $ ____________

☐ *To My Favorite Paw*, 100021

$100.00
$85.00
$80.00
$75.00

Suspended 1988, Issue Price $22.50, '86

Purchased ________, Price $ ____________

☐ *To My Deer Friend*, 100048

$125.00
$95.00
$93.00
$90.00
$85.00
$83.00
$80.00
$78.00
$75.00
$75.00
$73.00
$70.00
$68.00
$65.00
$65.00
$63.00
$63.00
$60.00

Retired 2003, Issue Price $33.00, '87

Purchased ________, Price $ ____________

☐ *Sending My Love*, 100056

$75.00
$70.00
$65.00
$60.00
$59.00
$58.00
$47.00

Suspended 1991, Issue Price $22.50, '86

Series: *Heavenly Halos*

Purchased ____________

Price $ ______________

☐ *O Worship The Lord*, 100064

$60.00
$58.00
$55.00
$53.00
$53.00
$53.00
$50.00
$50.00
$50.00
$48.00
$48.00
$48.00
$45.00
$45.00
$45.00
$45.00
$45.00
$40.00
$40.00
$40.00
$40.00
$40.00
$40.00
$40.00
$40.00

Open, Issue Price $24.00, '86

Purchased ________, Price $ ____________

☐ *To My Forever Friend*, 100072

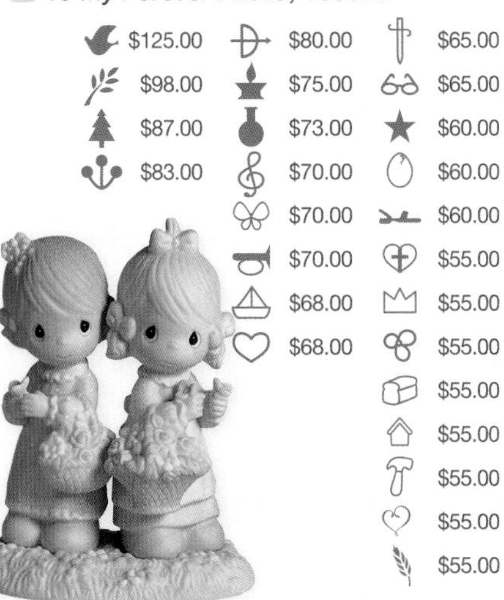

$125.00
$98.00
$87.00
$83.00
$80.00
$75.00
$73.00
$70.00
$70.00
$70.00
$68.00
$68.00
$65.00
$65.00
$60.00
$60.00
$60.00
$55.00
$55.00
$55.00
$55.00
$55.00
$55.00
$55.00
$55.00

Open, Issue Price $33.00, '86

Purchased ________, Price $ ____________

☐ *He's The Healer Of Broken Hearts*, 100080

$125.00
$120.00
$115.00
$110.00
$105.00
$103.00
$100.00
$98.00
$95.00
$93.00
$90.00
$90.00
$85.00
$85.00

Retired 1999, Issue Price $33.00, '87

Purchased ________, Price $ ____________

☐ *Make Me A Blessing*, 100102

$135.00
$125.00
$115.00
$110.00
$105.00

Retired 1990, Issue Price $35.00, '87

Purchased ________, Price $ ____________

☐ *Lord, I'm Coming Home*, 100110

$125.00
$120.00
$118.00
$115.00
$113.00
$110.00
$108.00
$105.00
$103.00
$100.00
$95.00
$95.00
$90.00
$88.00
$85.00
$83.00
$80.00
$78.00
$75.00

Retired 2003, Issue Price $22.50, '86

Purchased ________, Price $ ____________

☐ *Lord Keep Me On My Toes*, 100129

$90.00
$85.00
$80.00
$75.00

Retired 1988, Issue Price $22.50, '86

Purchased ________, Price $ ____________

☐ ***The Joy Of The Lord Is My Strength,*** 100137

$120.00, $110.00, $95.00, $85.00, $80.00, $75.00, $73.00

$70.00, $70.00, $70.00

$68.00, $68.00, $65.00, $65.00, $65.00, $55.00, $55.00, $55.00, $55.00, $55.00

Suspended 2004, Issue Price $35.00, '86

Purchased ________, Price $ ____________

☐ ***God Bless The Day We Found You,*** 100145

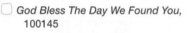

$125.00, $115.00, $110.00, $105.00, $100.00

Suspended 1990, Reintroduced 1995, Issue Price $40.00, '86

Purchased ________, Price $ ____________

☐ ***God Bless The Day We Found You,*** 100145R

$100.00, $95.00, $90.00, $88.00, $85.00, $83.00, $80.00, $78.00, $75.00

Redesigned and brought back from Suspension with the original title.

Retired 2002, Issue Price $60.00, '95

Purchased ________, Price $ ____________

☐ ***God Bless The Day We Found You,*** 100153

$115.00, $110.00, $105.00, $100.00, $95.00

Suspended 1990, Reintroduced 1995, Issue Price $40.00, '86

Purchased ________, Price $ ____________

☐ ***God Bless The Day We Found You,*** 100153R

$110.00, $108.00, $105.00, $103.00, $100.00, $98.00, $95.00, $93.00, $90.00

Redesigned and brought back from Suspension with the original title.

Retired 2002, Issue Price $60.00, '95

Purchased ________, Price $ ____________

☐ ***Serving The Lord,*** 100161

$75.00, $70.00, $68.00

$65.00, $63.00, $60.00

Suspended 1990, Issue Price $19.00, '86

Purchased ____________

Price $ ____________

☐ ***The Spirit Is Willing, But The Flesh Is Weak,*** 100196

$85.00, $80.00, $78.00, $75.00, $73.00

Retired 1991, Issue Price $19.00, '87

Purchased ________, Price $ ____________

☐ ***The Lord Giveth, And The Lord Taketh Away,*** 100226

$135.00, $115.00, $113.00, $110.00

$108.00, $105.00, $103.00, $100.00, $98.00

Retired 1995, Issue Price $33.50, '87

Purchased ________, Price $ ____________

☐ ***Friends Never Drift Apart,*** 100250

$103.00, $100.00, $97.00

$95.00, $93.00, $90.00

$88.00, $85.00, $85.00, $85.00, $83.00, $83.00, $80.00, $80.00, $78.00, $78.00

Retired 2000, Issue Price $35.00, '86

Purchased ________, Price $ ____________

☐ ***I'm A Possibility,*** 100188

$125.00, $115.00, $110.00, $105.00

$100.00, $95.00, $90.00, $85.00

Retired 1993, Issue Price $22.00, '86

Purchased ________, Price $ ____________

☐ *Help Lord, I'm In A Spot*, 100269

$93.00
$90.00
$89.00
$87.00

Retired 1989, Issue Price $18.50, '86

Purchased ________, Price $ ___________

☐ *He Cleansed My Soul*, 100277

$60.00 $45.00 $40.00
$55.00 $44.00 $40.00
$50.00 $40.00 $40.00
$40.00 $40.00
$40.00 $40.00
$40.00 $40.00
$40.00 $40.00
$40.00
$40.00
$40.00
$40.00
$40.00
$40.00
$40.00

Has been found with the Bible inscription missing.

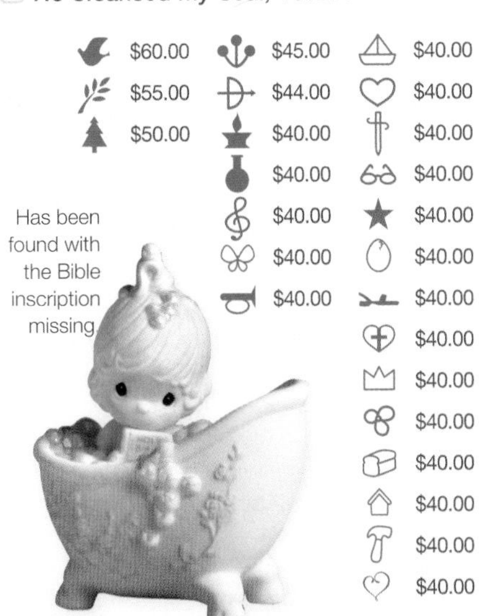

Retired 2008, Issue Price $24.00, '86

Purchased ________, Price $ ___________

☐ *Heaven Bless You*, 100285 (Musical)

$155.00
$125.00
$123.00
$120.00
$115.00
$113.00
$110.00
$108.00
$105.00

Suspended 1993, Issue Price $45.00, '86
Tune: *Brahms' Lullaby*

Purchased ________, Price $ ___________

☐ *Serving The Lord*, 100293

$80.00 $67.00
$75.00 $60.00
$70.00 $45.00

Suspended 1990, Issue Price $19.00, '86

Purchased_______________

Price $ _______________

☐ *Bong Bong*, 100455 (Doll)

$375.00

Individually numbered on foot. Includes certificate of authenticity.

Limited Ed. 12,000, Issue Price $150.00, '86

Purchased ________, Price $ ___________

☐ *Candy*, 100463 (Doll)

$375.00

Individually numbered on foot. Includes certificate of authenticity.

Limited Ed. 12,000, Issue Price $150.00, '86

Purchased ________, Price $ ___________

☐ *God Bless Our Family*, 100498

$105.00 $100.00 $88.00
$95.00 $85.00
$85.00
$83.00
$83.00
$80.00
$80.00
$78.00
$78.00
$75.00

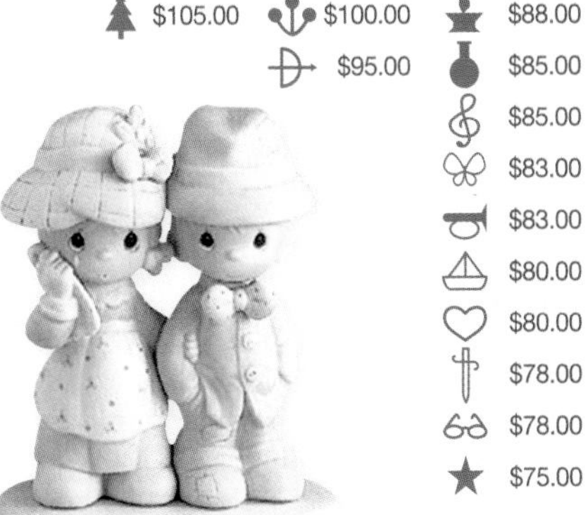

Retired 1999, Issue Price $35.00, '87

Purchased ________, Price $ ___________

☐ *God Bless Our Family*, 100501

$95.00 $93.00 $78.00
$80.00 $75.00
$75.00
$70.00
$70.00
$68.00
$68.00
$65.00
$65.00
$65.00

Retired 1999, Issue Price $35.00, '87

Purchased ________, Price $ ___________

☐ *Scent From Above*, 100528

$85.00 $78.00
$83.00 $75.00
$80.00 $73.00

Retired 1991, Issue Price $19.00, '87

Purchased___________

Price $ ___________

☐ *I Picked A Special Mom*, 100536

$105.00
$100.00

Limited 1987, Issue Price $37.50, '87

Purchased ________, Price $ ___________

☐ *Brotherly Love*, 100544

$115.00
$105.00
$103.00
$100.00

Suspended 1989, Issue Price $37.00, '86

Purchased ________, Price $ ___________

☐ *God Is Love, Dear Valentine,* 100625 (Thimble)

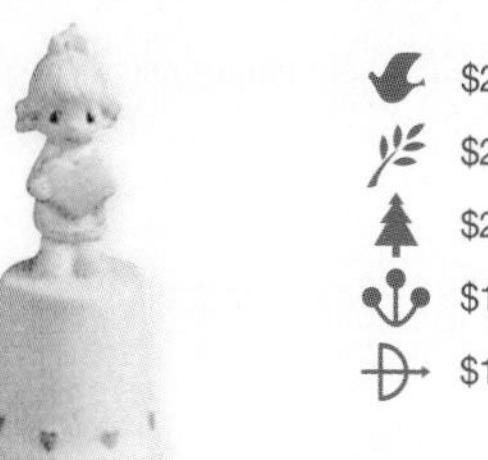

$25.00
$23.00
$20.00
$18.00
$17.00

Suspended 1989, Issue Price $5.50, '86

Purchased ________, Price $ ___________

☐ *The Lord Bless You And Keep You,* 100633 (Thimble)

$25.00
$25.00
$23.00
$23.00
$20.00
$20.00
$18.00

Suspended 1991, Issue Price $5.50, '86

Purchased ________, Price $ ___________

☐ *Four Seasons,* 100641 (Thimbles)

$195.00 $155.00

Annual 1986, Issue Price $20.00, '86
Set of 4

Purchased ________, Price $ ___________

☐ *Clowns,* 100668 (Thimbles)

$75.00
$73.00
$70.00

Suspended 1988, Issue Price $11.00, '86
Set of 2

Purchased ________, Price $ ___________

☐ *Cherishing Each Special Moment,* 101233

$60.00
$55.00
$50.00
$50.00
$50.00
$50.00
$50.00
$50.00
$50.00

Open, Issue Price $50.00, '02
Series: *Motherhood* — Third and Final Issue

Purchased ________, Price $ ___________

☐ *A Penny A Kiss, A Penny A Hug,* 101234

$65.00
$65.00

Limited Ed., Issue Price $35.00, '01
Authorized Retailer Event, 3/2/01

Purchased ________, Price $ ___________

☐ *A Penny A Kiss, A Penny A Hug,* 101234C

Limited Ed., '02 $75.00
Canadian Event Exclusive

Purchased ________, Price $ ___________

☐ *So You Finally Met Your Match, Congratulations,* 101493

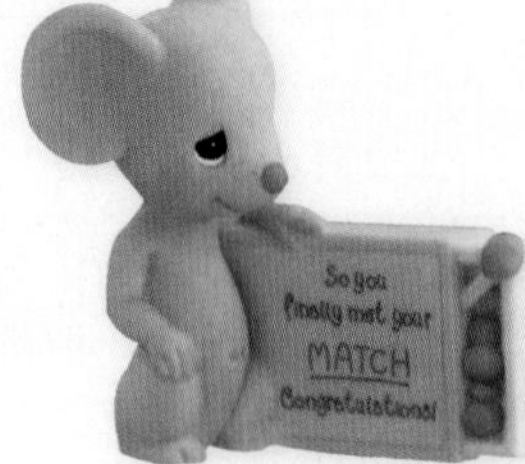

$25.00
$23.00
$20.00
$20.00
$20.00
$20.00
$20.00

Open, Issue Price $20.00, '02
Series: *Animal Affections*

Purchased ________, Price $ ___________

☐ *You Are A Real Cool Mommy!* 101495

$25.00 $20.00
$23.00 $20.00
$20.00 $20.00
$20.00

Open, Issue Price $16.00, '02
Series: *Animal Affections*

Purchased ___________

Price $ ___________

☐ *Rats, I Missed Your Birthday,* 101496

$25.00
$20.00
$20.00
$20.00
$20.00
$20.00
$20.00

Open, Issue Price $20.00, '02
Series: *Animal Affections*

Purchased ________, Price $ ___________

☐ *It's What's Inside That Counts,* 101497

$38.00 $35.00
$35.00 $35.00
$35.00 $35.00
$35.00 $35.00

Open, Issue Price $35.00, '02

Purchased ___________

Price $___________

☐ *You're An All Star Graduate,* 101498

$32.00 $30.00
$32.00 $30.00
$32.00 $30.00
$30.00 $30.00
$30.00

Open, Issue Price $25.00, '02

Purchased ___________

Price $___________

☐ *You're An All Star Graduate,* 101499

$32.00 $30.00
$32.00 $30.00
$32.00 $30.00
$30.00 $30.00
$30.00

Open, Issue Price $25.00, '02

Purchased ____________

Price $ ____________

☐ *The Sweetest Baby Boy,* 101500

$20.00 $20.00
$20.00 $20.00
$20.00
$20.00
$20.00
$20.00

Open, Issue Price $17.50, '02

Purchased _____

Price $_________

☐ *The Sweetest Baby Girl,* 101501

$20.00 $20.00
$20.00 $20.00
$20.00
$20.00
$20.00
$20.00

Open, Issue Price $17.50, '02

Purchased ________, Price $ ____________

☐ *I'm A Big Sister,* 101502

$22.00 $20.00
$20.00 $20.00
$20.00

Suspended 2005, Issue Price $20.00, '02

Purchased____________

Price $____________

☐ *I'm A Big Brother,* 101503

$22.00 $20.00
$20.00 $20.00
$20.00

Suspended 2005, Issue Price $20.00, '02

Purchased _________

Price $ ___________

☐ *Precious Grandma,* 101504

$27.00
$25.00
$25.00
$25.00
$25.00
$25.00
$25.00
$25.00
$25.00

Open, Issue Price $25.00, '02

Purchased ________, Price $ ___________

☐ *Precious Grandpa,* 101505

$27.00
$25.00
$25.00
$25.00
$25.00
$25.00
$25.00
$25.00
$25.00

Open, Issue Price $25.00, '02

Purchased ________, Price $ ____________

☐ *My Love Spills Over For You Mom,* 101513

Comes with "Pampered Mom Coupon Book," designed to be personalized

$45.00
$40.00

Retired 2002, Issue Price $35.00, '02

Purchased __________

Price $ ___________

☐ *Loads Of Love For My Mommy,* 101514

$45.00
$40.00

Comes with "Pampered Mom Coupon Book," designed to be personalized

Retired 2002, Issue Price $35.00, '02

Purchased ________

Price $ __________

☐ *January — Snowdrop, "Pure And Gentle,"* 101515

$45.00 $40.00 $40.00
$43.00 $40.00 $40.00
$40.00 $40.00 $40.00

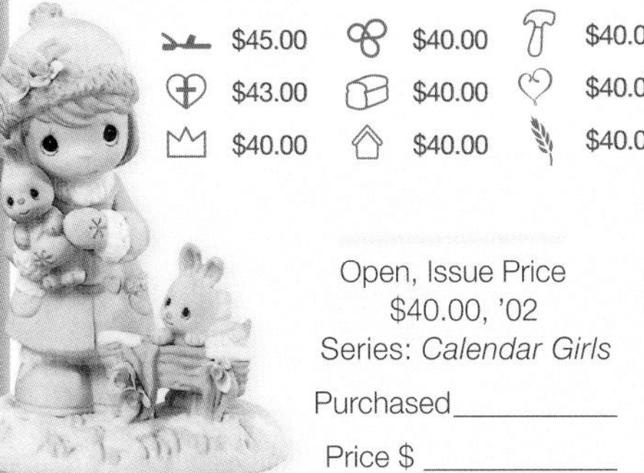

Open, Issue Price $40.00, '02

Series: *Calendar Girls*

Purchased__________

Price $ ___________

☐ *February — Carnation, "Bold And Brave,"* 101517

$45.00 $40.00
$43.00 $40.00
$40.00 $40.00
$40.00 $40.00
$40.00

Open, Issue Price $40.00, '02

Series: *Calendar Girls*

Purchased __________

Price $ ___________

☐ *March — Violet, "Modest,"* 101518

$45.00 $40.00
$43.00 $40.00
$40.00 $40.00
$40.00 $40.00
$40.00

Open, Issue Price $40.00, '02

Series: *Calendar Girls*

Purchased ________

Price $ __________

☐ *April — Lily, "Virtuous,"* 101519

$45.00 · $43.00 · $40.00 · $40.00 · $40.00 · $40.00 · $40.00 · $40.00 · $40.00

Open, Issue Price $40.00, '02
Series: *Calendar Girls*

Purchased ________, Price $ ____________

☐ *May — Hawthorne, "Bright And Hopeful,"* 101520

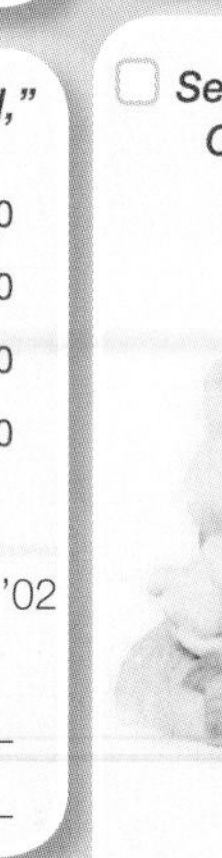

$45.00 · $43.00 · $40.00 · $40.00 · $40.00 · $40.00 · $40.00 · $40.00 · $40.00

Open, Issue Price $40.00, '02
Series: *Calendar Girls*

Purchased____________

Price $ ____________

☐ *June — Rose, "Beautiful,"* 101521

$45.00 · $43.00 · $40.00 · $40.00 · $40.00 · $40.00 · $40.00 · $40.00 · $40.00

Open, Issue Price $40.00, '02
Series: *Calendar Girls*

Purchased ________, Price $ ____________

☐ *July — Daisy, "Wide-Eyed And Innocent,"* 101522

$45.00 · $43.00 · $40.00 · $40.00 · $40.00 · $40.00 · $40.00 · $40.00 · $40.00

Open, Issue Price $40.00, '02
Series: *Calendar Girls*

Purchased ________

Price $ ________

☐ *August — Poppy, "Peaceful,"* 101523

$45.00 · $43.00 · $40.00 · $40.00 · $40.00 · $40.00 · $40.00 · $40.00 · $40.00

Open, Issue Price $40.00, '02
Series: *Calendar Girls*

Purchased ________, Price $ ____________

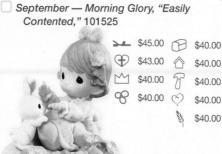

☐ *September — Morning Glory, "Easily Contented,"* 101525

$45.00 · $43.00 · $40.00 · $40.00 · $40.00 · $40.00 · $40.00 · $40.00 · $40.00

Open, Issue Price $40.00, '02
Series: *Calendar Girls*

Purchased ________, Price $ ____________

☐ *October — Cosmos, "Ambitious,"* 101526

$45.00 · $43.00 · $40.00 · $40.00 · $40.00 · $40.00 · $40.00 · $40.00 · $40.00

Open, Issue Price $40.00, '02
Series: *Calendar Girls*

Purchased ________, Price $ ____________

☐ *November — Chrysanthemum, "Sassy And Cheerful,"* 101527

$45.00 · $43.00 · $40.00 · $40.00 · $40.00 · $40.00 · $40.00 · $40.00 · $40.00

Open, Issue Price $40.00, '02
Series: *Calendar Girls*

Purchased ________

Price $__________

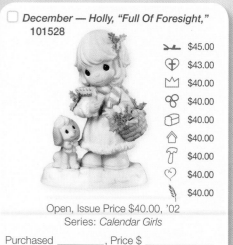

☐ *December — Holly, "Full Of Foresight,"* 101528

$45.00 · $43.00 · $40.00 · $40.00 · $40.00 · $40.00 · $40.00 · $40.00 · $40.00

Open, Issue Price $40.00, '02
Series: *Calendar Girls*

Purchased ________, Price $ ____________

☐ *Friends Are Never Far Behind,* 101543

$125.00

Limited Ed. 5,000, Issue Price $45.00, '02
Series: *Smiles Forever* — Fifth Issue

Purchased ________, Price $ ____________

☐ *Love Is On Its Way,* 101544

$165.00 · $155.00

Limited Ed. 5,000, Issue Price $30.00, '02
Series: *Smiles Forever* — First Issue

Purchased ____________

Price $____________

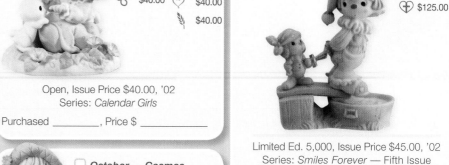

☐ *Lord, Help Me Clean Up My Act,* 101545

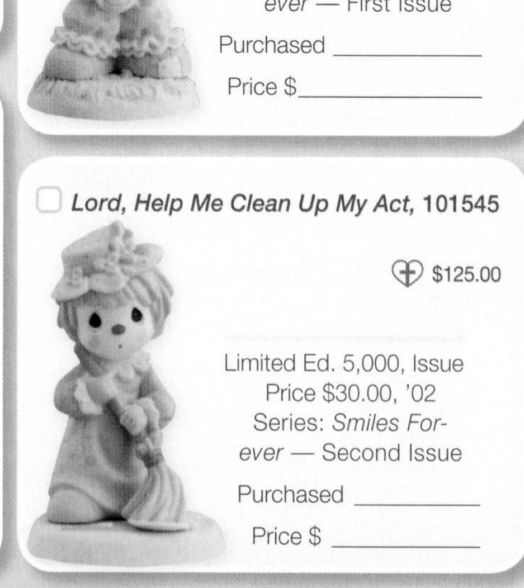

$125.00

Limited Ed. 5,000, Issue Price $30.00, '02
Series: *Smiles Forever* — Second Issue

Purchased ____________

Price $ ____________

Our Love Is Heaven Scent, 101546

$125.00

Limited Ed. 5,000, Issue Price $30.00, '02
Series: *Smiles Forever* — Fourth Issue

Purchased ________
Price $ ________

Life Never Smelled So Sweet, 101547

$125.00

Limited Ed. 5,000, Issue Price $30.00, '02
Series: *Smiles Forever* — Third Issue

Purchased ________
Price $ ________

Planting The Seeds Of Love, 101548

$175.00

Limited Ed. 7,500, Issue Price $99.50, '02
CCR Exclusive

Purchased ________, Price $ ________

Precious Moments In Paradise, 101549

$60.00

Limited Ed., Issue Price $45.00, '02
CCR Exclusive

Purchased ________, Price $ ________

A Beary Warm Aloha! 101550 (Ornament)

$25.00

Limited Ed., Issue Price $15.00, '02
CCR Exclusive

Purchased ________, Price $ ________

Home, Home On The Range, 101551

2002 Precious Moments Club Event Exclusive (Dallas)

$300.00
$300.00

Limited Ed., Gift, '02

Purchased ________, Price $ ________

Where The Deer And The Antelope Play, 101552

$45.00
$43.00
$40.00

Retired 2004, Issue Price $28.00, '02

Purchased ________, Price $ ________

Nurses Are Blessed With Patients, 101554

UM $25.00
$20.00
$20.00

Open, Issue Price $20.00, '02
Series: *Little Moments*

Purchased ________, Price $ ________

Dew Remember Me, 101555

$50.00
$48.00

Limited Ed. 5,000, Issue Price $40.00, '02
Syndicated Catalog Exclusive

Purchased ________, Price $ ________

Our First Christmas Together, 101702 (Musical)

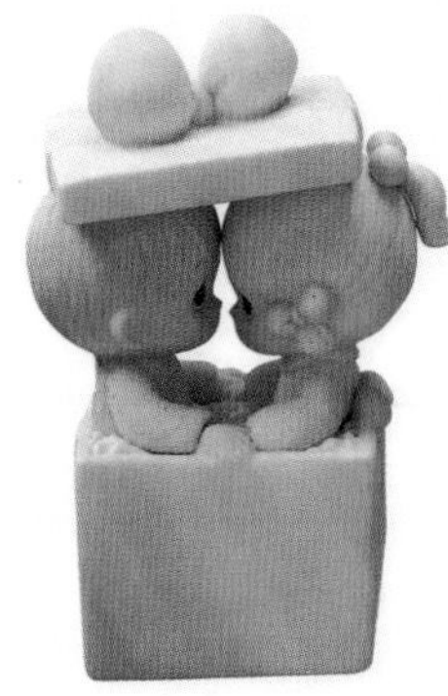

$125.00
$120.00
$115.00
$110.00
$105.00
$100.00
$95.00

Retired 1992, Issue Price $50.00, '86
Tune: *We Wish You A Merry Christmas*

Purchased ________, Price $ ________

☐ ***No Tears Past The Gate*, 101826**

$115.00 $90.00 $85.00
$105.00 $90.00 $85.00
$100.00 $88.00 $83.00
$95.00 $88.00 $80.00
$80.00
$78.00
$75.00
$75.00
$75.00
$75.00
$75.00

Suspended 2005, Issue Price $40.00, '87
Purchased ________, Price $ ____________

☐ ***I'm Sending You A White Christmas*, 101834 (Plate)**

$65.00

Dated Annual 1986, Issue Price $45.00, '86
Series: *Christmas Love* — First Issue
Purchased ________, Price $ ____________

☐ ***Smile Along The Way*, 101842**

$205.00
$175.00
$168.00
$165.00
$163.00
$160.00

Retired 1991, Issue Price $30.00, '87
Purchased ________, Price $ ____________

☐ ***Lord, Help Us Keep Our Act Together*, 101850**

$155.00 $125.00
$145.00 $115.00
$135.00 $105.00
$100.00

Retired 1992, Issue Price $35.00, '87
Purchased ______________
Price $ ________________

☐ ***O Worship The Lord*, 102229**

$75.00 $63.00
$73.00 $60.00
$70.00 $60.00
$68.00 $60.00
$68.00 $58.00
$65.00 $58.00
$65.00 $55.00
$63.00 $55.00
$63.00 $53.00
$53.00

Retired 2003, Issue Price $24.00, '86
Purchased ________, Price $ ____________

☐ ***Connie*, 102253 (Doll)**

$305.00

Limited Ed. 7,500, Issue Price $160.00, '86
Individually Numbered
Purchased __________
Price $ ____________

☐ ***Shepherd Of Love*, 102261**

$40.00 $33.00 $25.00
$38.00 $33.00 $25.00
$35.00 $33.00 $25.00
$35.00 $30.00 $20.00
$35.00 $30.00 $20.00
$30.00 $20.00
$30.00 $20.00

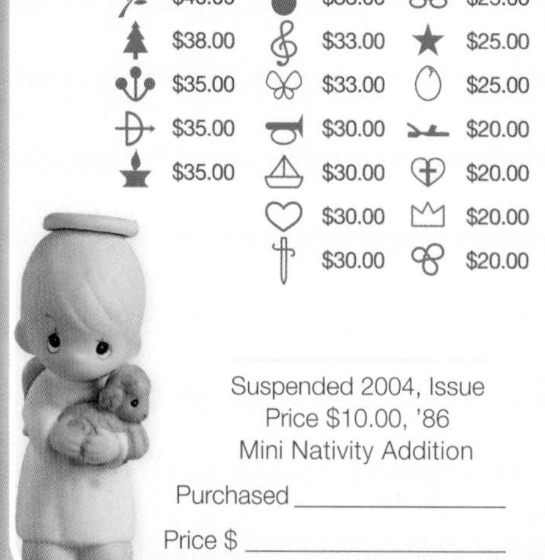

Suspended 2004, Issue Price $10.00, '86
Mini Nativity Addition
Purchased ______________
Price $ ________________

☐ ***Shepherd Of Love*, 102288 (Ornament)**

$50.00
$48.00
$46.00
$44.00
$43.00
$42.00
$41.00
$40.00

Suspended 1993, Issue Price $10.00, '86
Purchased ________, Price $ ____________

☐ ***Mini Animals*, 102296**

$45.00 $38.00 $35.00
$40.00 $36.00 $34.00
$33.00

Suspended 1992, Issue Price $13.50, '86
Mini Nativity Addition
Set of 3 — Sheep, Bunny, and Turtle
Purchased ________, Price $ ____________

☐ ***Wishing You A Cozy Christmas*, 102318 (Bell)**

$35.00

Dated Annual 1986, Issue Price $20.00, '86
Purchased ___________
Price $ _____________

☐ ***Wishing You A Cozy Christmas*, 102326 (Ornament)**

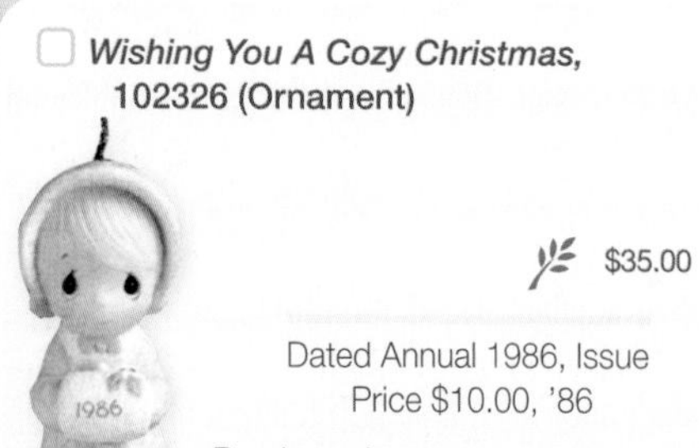

$35.00

Dated Annual 1986, Issue Price $10.00, '86
Purchased ______________
Price $ ________________

☐ *Wishing You A Cozy Christmas,* 102334 (Thimble)

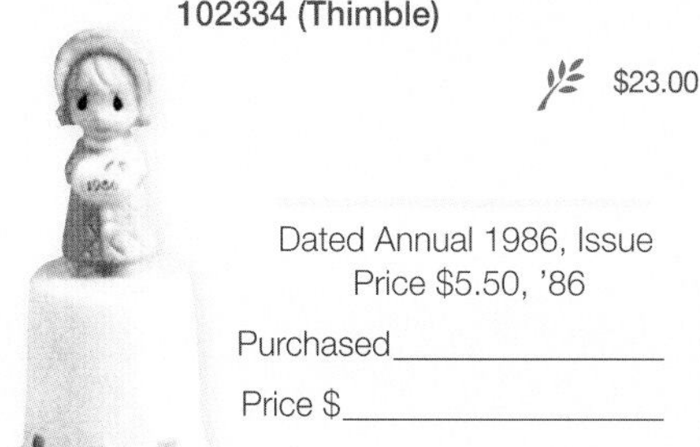

$23.00

Dated Annual 1986, Issue Price $5.50, '86

Purchased________________

Price $________________

☐ *Wishing You A Cozy Christmas,* 102342

$38.00

Dated Annual 1986, Issue Price $18.00, '86

Purchased________________

Price $________________

☐ *Our First Christmas Together,* 102350 (Ornament)

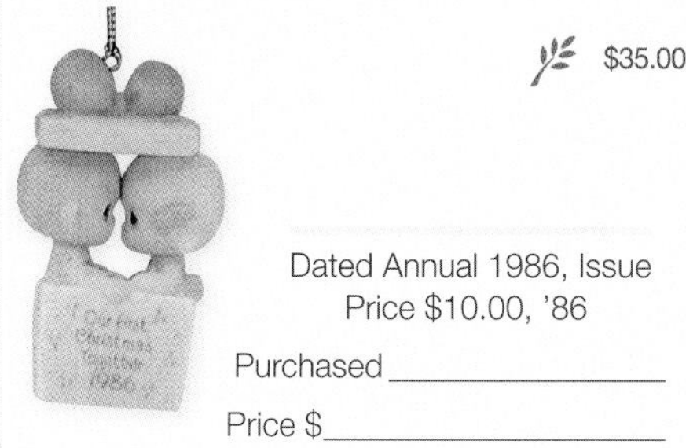

$35.00

Dated Annual 1986, Issue Price $10.00, '86

Purchased________________

Price $________________

☐ *Wedding Arch,* 102369

$75.00
$73.00
$70.00
$68.00
$65.00
$63.00
$60.00

Suspended 1992, Issue Price $22.50, '86

Purchased ________, Price $ ____________

☐ *Trust And Obey,* 102377 (Ornament)

$45.00	$38.00
$43.00	$35.00
$43.00	$35.00
$40.00	$35.00
$40.00	$33.00
$40.00	$33.00
$38.00	$30.00
$38.00	$30.00
	$30.00

Retired 2001, Issue Price $10.00, '86

Purchased ________, Price $ ____________

☐ *Love Rescued Me,* 102385 (Ornament)

$45.00	$38.00
$43.00	$35.00
$43.00	$35.00
$40.00	$35.00
$40.00	$33.00
$40.00	$33.00
$38.00	$30.00
$38.00	$30.00

Retired 2001, Issue Price $10.00, '86

Purchased ________, Price $ ____________

☐ *Love Rescued Me,* 102393

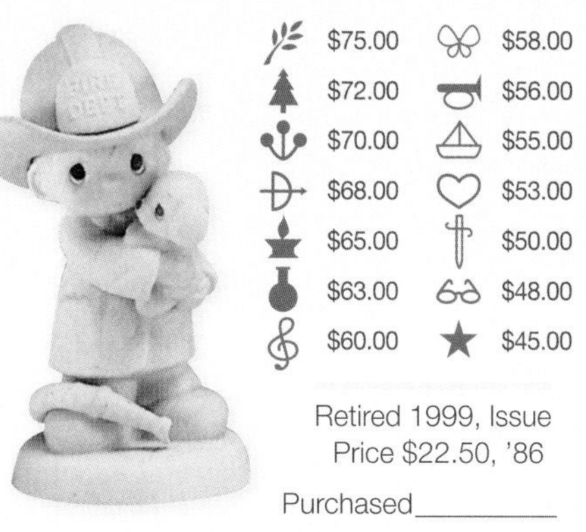

$75.00	$58.00
$72.00	$56.00
$70.00	$55.00
$68.00	$53.00
$65.00	$50.00
$63.00	$48.00
$60.00	$45.00

Retired 1999, Issue Price $22.50, '86

Purchased________

Price $____________

☐ *It's A Perfect Boy,* 102415 (Ornament)

$45.00
$43.00
$40.00
$38.00

Suspended 1989, Issue Price $10.00, '86

Purchased ________, Price $ ____________

☐ *Lord, Keep Me On My Toes,* 102423 (Ornament)

$55.00
$53.00
$50.00
$48.00
$45.00

Retired 1990, Issue Price $10.00, '86

Purchased ________, Price $ ____________

☐ *Serve With A Smile,* 102431 (Ornament)

$45.00
$43.00
$40.00

Suspended 1988, Issue Price $10.00, '86

Purchased ________, Price $ ____________

☐ *Angel Of Mercy,* 102407 (Ornament)

$75.00	$65.00	$60.00	$55.00
$73.00	$63.00	$58.00	$53.00
$70.00	$63.00	$58.00	$53.00
$68.00	$60.00	$55.00	$50.00
$65.00	$60.00	$55.00	$50.00

Suspended 2005, Issue Price $10.00, '86

Purchased ________, Price $ ____________

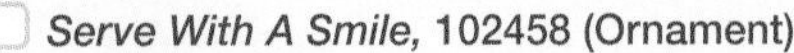

☐ ***Serve With A Smile*, 102458 (Ornament)**

$40.00
$38.00
$35.00

Suspended 1988, Issue Price $10.00, '86

Purchased ________

Price $ ________

☐ ***Sharing Our Christmas Together*, 102490**

$90.00
$85.00
$80.00

Suspended 1988, Issue Price $37.00, '86

Purchased ________, Price $ ________

☐ ***There's Sno-One Quite Like You*, 102726**

UM $20.00

Open, Issue Price $20.00, '02
Series: *Little Moment*

Purchased ________

Price $ ________

☐ ***Reindeer*, 102466 (Ornament)**

First ornament in the Birthday Collection. Left off the retailer order form, they were in the stores and gone before the collectors knew about them.

$180.00
$175.00

Dated Annual 1986, Issue Price $11.00, '86
Series: *Birthday Collection*

Purchased ________, Price $ ________

☐ ***Baby's First Christmas*, 102504 (Ornament)**

$33.00

Dated Annual 1986, Issue Price $10.00, '86

Purchased ________

Price $ ________

☐ ***We Are All Precious In His Sight*, 102903**

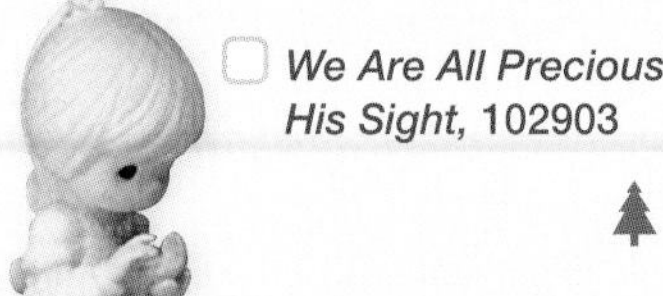

$73.00

Annual 1987, Issue Price $30.00, '87

Purchased ________

Price $ ________

☐ ***Mom, You're A Sweetheart*, 102913**

UM $38.00
$35.00

Limited Ed., Issue Price $19.99, '02
Avon Exclusive

Purchased ________

Price $ ________

☐ ***Rocking Horse*, 102474 (Ornament)**

$48.00
$45.00
$45.00
$43.00
$43.00
$40.00

Suspended 1991, Issue Price $10.00, '86

Purchased ________, Price $ ________

☐ ***Baby's First Christmas*, 102512 (Ornament)**

$33.00

Dated Annual 1986, Issue Price $10.00, '86

Purchased ________

Price $ ________

☐ ***God Bless America*, 102938**

$85.00

Annual 1986, Reintroduced 2001, Issue Price $30.00, '86
Series: *America Forever*

Purchased ________

Price $ ________

☐ ***Angel Of Mercy*, 102482**

$65.00
$60.00
$58.00
$55.00
$53.00
$50.00
$48.00
$45.00
$45.00
$43.00
$43.00
$40.00
$40.00
$38.00
$38.00
$37.50
$37.50
$37.50
$37.50
$37.50
$37.50
$37.50
$37.50
$37.50

Open, Issue Price $20.00, '86

Purchased ________, Price $ ________

☐ ***Let's Keep In Touch*, 102520 (Musical)**

$155.00
$153.00
$150.00
$147.00
$144.00
$140.00
$138.00
$135.00
$133.00
$130.00
$128.00
$125.00
$123.00
$120.00

Retired 1999, Issue Price $65.00, '86
Tune: *Be A Clown*

Purchased ________, Price $ ________

☐ ***God Bless America*, 102938R**

$65.00
$63.00
$60.00
$58.00

This piece features a second mark, the 4 Star Flag. A portion of the proceeds went to benefit the victims of September 11th and the Precious Moments September 11th Relief Fund.

Retired 2004, Issue Price $40.00, '02
Series: *America Forever*

Purchased ________, Price $ ________

☐ *My Peace I Give Unto Thee*, 102954 (Plate)

$65.00

Dated Annual 1987, Issue Price $45.00, '87
Series: *Christmas Love* — Second Issue

Purchased ________, Price $ ___________

☐ *It's The Birthday Of A King*, 102962

$50.00 $45.00
$48.00 $43.00

Suspended 1989, Issue Price $19.00, '86
Nativity Addition

Purchased ___________

Price $ ______________

☐ *I Would Be Sunk Without You*, 102970

$65.00 $47.00
$63.00 $46.00
$60.00 $45.00
$58.00 $44.00
$55.00 $43.00
$53.00 $42.00
$50.00 $41.00
$48.00 $40.00

Retired 2002, Issue Price $15.00, '87

Purchased ________, Price $ ___________

☐ *We Belong To The Lord*, 103004

$275.00
Without Bible $250.00

The Damien-Dutton Society for Leprosy Aid operates two gift shops and all of the profits go back to this charity. This figurine was a special edition produced for and sold by the Damien-Dutton Society. Comes with a leatherbound Bible.

Special Piece, Issue Price $50.00, '86
Damien-Dutton Piece

Purchased ________, Price $ ___________

☐ *Living Each Day With Love*, 103175

$70.00
$65.00

Limited Ed. 7,500, Issue Price $49.95, '02
Series: *Rose Petal*
GoCollect.com/CCR Exclusive

Purchased ________, Price $ ___________

☐ *You Are The Rose In My Bouquet*, 103176

$70.00
$65.00

Limited Ed. 7,500, Issue Price $40.00, '02
Series: *Rose Petal* — First Issue
GoCollect.com/CCR Exclusive

Purchased ________, Price $ ___________

☐ *A Smile Is Cherished In The Heart*, 103177

$65.00
$60.00

Out of Production, Issue Price $40.00, '02
Series: *Rose Petal*
GoCollect.com/CCR Exclusive

Purchased ________, Price $ ___________

☐ *Hang Onto Your Happiness*, 103178

$30.00 $25.00
$25.00 $25.00
$25.00 $25.00
$25.00 $25.00

Open, Issue Price $16.00, '03
Japanese Exclusive

Purchased ________, Price $ ___________

☐ *We Are The Sheep Of His Pasture*, 103180

$30.00 $25.00
$25.00 $25.00
$25.00 $25.00
$25.00 $25.00

Open, Issue Price $16.00, '03
Japanese Exclusive

Purchased _______

Price $___________

☐ *New Beginning*, 103181

$30.00 $25.00 $25.00
$25.00 $25.00 $25.00
$25.00 $25.00

Open, Issue Price $16.00, '03
Japanese Exclusive

Purchased ___________

Price $ ___________

☐ *Good Fortune Is Just Around The Corner*, 103182

$30.00 $25.00 $25.00
$25.00 $25.00 $25.00
$25.00 $25.00

Open, Issue Price $16.00, '03
Japanese Exclusive

Purchased___________

Price $ ___________

☐ ***Life Is No Boar With You,* 103183**

$30.00 $25.00 $25.00
$25.00 $25.00 $25.00
$25.00 $25.00

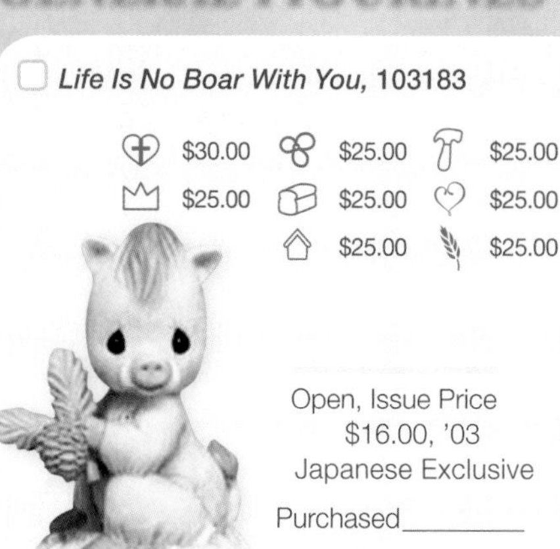

Open, Issue Price $16.00, '03
Japanese Exclusive

Purchased ________

Price $ __________

☐ ***I'm Bouncing With Joy,* 103188**

$30.00 $25.00
$25.00 $25.00
$25.00 $25.00
$25.00 $25.00

Open, Issue Price $16.00, '03
Japanese Exclusive

Purchased __________

Price $ ___________

☐ ***With This Ring I…,* 104019**

$95.00 $75.00 $70.00
$90.00 $73.00 $68.00
$85.00 $73.00 $68.00
$80.00 $70.00 $68.00
$70.00 $68.00
$70.00 $65.00
$65.00
$65.00
$65.00
$65.00
$65.00
$65.00
$65.00

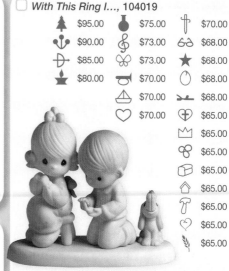

Open, Issue Price $65.00, '87

Purchased ________, Price $ ___________

☐ ***Life's Blessings Are Bountiful,* 103184**

$30.00 $25.00 $25.00
$25.00 $25.00 $25.00
$25.00 $25.00

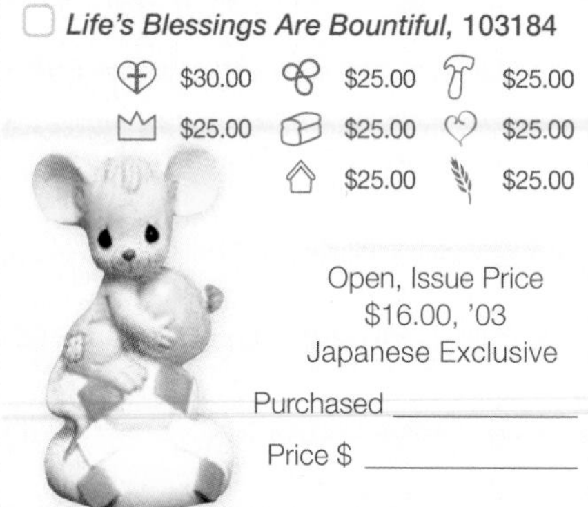

Open, Issue Price $16.00, '03
Japanese Exclusive

Purchased ____________

Price $ ______________

☐ ***My Love Will Never Let You Go,* 103497**

$65.00 $50.00
$63.00 $50.00
$60.00 $50.00
$58.00 $50.00
$55.00 $49.00
$53.00 $48.00
$53.00 $48.00
$52.00 $45.00
$52.00 $45.00

Retired 2004, Issue Price $25.00, '87

Purchased ________, Price $ ___________

☐ ***Love Is The Glue That Mends,* 104027**

$95.00 $85.00
$90.00 $80.00

Suspended 1990, Issue Price $33.50, '87

Purchased ___________

Price $ ________

☐ ***Ringing In A Year Of Good Health,* 103185**

$30.00 $25.00 $25.00
$25.00 $25.00 $25.00
$25.00
$25.00

Open, Issue Price $16.00, '03
Japanese Exclusive

Purchased ________, Price $ ___________

☐ ***I Believe In The Old Rugged Cross,* 103632**

$65.00 $53.00 $49.00 $47.00 $45.00
$63.00 $53.00 $49.00 $47.00 $45.00
$60.00 $50.00 $48.00 $45.00 $45.00
$58.00 $50.00
$55.00 $50.00
$53.00

Retired 2004, Issue Price $25.00, '86

Purchased ________, Price $ ___________

☐ ***Strength Comes From Within,* 103186**

$30.00 $25.00 $25.00
$25.00 $25.00
$25.00 $25.00
$25.00

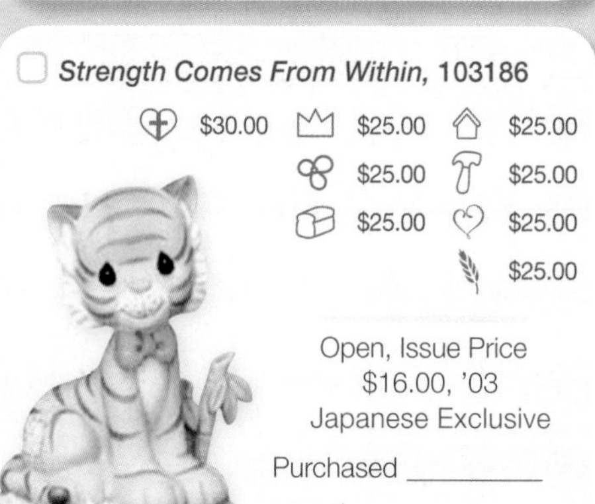

Open, Issue Price $16.00, '03
Japanese Exclusive

Purchased __________

Price $ ___________

☐ ***Come Let Us Adore Him,* 104000**

$185.00 $160.00 $150.00
$180.00 $158.00 $150.00
$175.00 $158.00 $145.00
$170.00 $155.00 $145.00
$168.00 $155.00 $140.00
$165.00 $155.00 $140.00
$152.00 $140.00
$152.00 $140.00

Item number has been changed to 610043.

Open, Issue Price $95.00, '86
Nativity Set of 9 with Cassette

Purchased ________, Price $ ___________

Cheers To The Leader, 104035

Tree	$88.00	G-Clef	$75.00
Anchor	$85.00	Butterfly	$73.00
Bow & Arrow	$83.00	Trumpet	$70.00
Candle	$80.00	Boat	$68.00
Flame	$78.00	Heart	$65.00
		Sword	$63.00

Retired 1997, Issue Price $22.50, '87

Purchased ________, Price $ ____________

May Your Holidays Sparkle With Joy, 104202

Heart/Cross $53.00

Dated Annual 2002, Issue Price $35.00, '02

Purchased ___________

Price $___________

May Your Holidays Sparkle With Joy, 104203 (Ornament)

Heart/Cross $28.00

Dated Annual 2002, Issue Price $20.00, '02

Purchased ___________

Price $ ______________

Baby's First Christmas, 104204 (Ornament)

Heart/Cross $28.00

Dated Annual 2002, Issue Price $20.00, '02

Purchased ____________

Price $ ________________

Baby's First Christmas, 104206 (Ornament)

Heart/Cross $28.00

Dated Annual 2002, Issue Price $20.00, '02

Purchased ________________

Price $ ___________________

Our First Christmas Together, 104207 (Ornament)

Heart/Cross $35.00

Dated Annual 2002, Issue Price $25.00, '02

Purchased ____________

Price $______________

Home Sweet Home, 104208 (Ornament)

Heart/Cross $40.00

Dated Annual 2002, Issue Price $30.00, '02

Purchased ___________

Price $ ____________

There's Sno-One Like You, 104209 (Ornament)

Heart/Cross $40.00

Dated Annual 2002, Issue Price $19.00, '02

Series: *Birthday Collection*

Purchased____________

Price $ _______________

Jesus Is Born, 104210

Heart/Cross	$45.00	Box	$40.00
Crown	$43.00	House	$40.00
Clover	$40.00	Hammer	$40.00

Out of Production, Issue Price $40.00, '03

Nativity Addition

Purchased__________

Price $___________

Hark, The Harold Angel Sings, 104211

Heart/Cross	$25.00	Box	$20.00
Crown	$23.00	House	$20.00
Clover	$20.00	Hammer	$20.00

Open, Issue Price $20.00, '02

Mini Nativity Addition

Purchased ___________

Price $______________

You Are My Christmas Special, 104215

Heart/Cross $125.00

Annual 2002, Issue Price $100.00, '02

Purchased ________, Price $ ____________

...And To All A Good Night, 104217

Heart/Cross	$65.00
Crown	$60.00

Retired 2003, Issue Price $55.00, '02

Series: *Christmas Remembered* — Third Issue

Purchased ________, Price $ ___________

Merry Christ-Miss, 104218

Heart/Cross	$38.00
Crown	$35.00
Clover	$35.00

Suspended, Issue Price $35.00, '02

Purchased_______________

Price $_________________

☐ *Friends Share A Special Bond,* 104219

$48.00
$45.00
$45.00
$45.00
$45.00
$45.00

Open, Issue Price $45.00, '02

Purchased ________, Price $ ___________

☐ *You're O.K. Buy Me,* 104267

$43.00 $37.50
$40.00 $37.50
$37.50 $37.50
$37.50 $37.50

Open, Issue Price $37.50, '02

Purchased ______

Price $___________

☐ *Your Love Is Just So Comforting,* 104268

$38.00
$35.00
$35.00

Suspended 2004, Issue Price $35.00, '02

Purchased ________, Price $ ___________

☐ *I'm So Lucky To Have You As A Daughter,* 104269

$37.00 $35.00
$35.00 $35.00
$35.00 $35.00

Open, Issue Price $35.00, '02

Purchased_________

Price $___________

☐ *I Get A Cluck Out Of You,* 104270

$55.00
$53.00
$50.00

Retired 2004, Issue Price $40.00, '02
Series: *Country Lane Collection*

Purchased ________, Price $ ___________

☐ *Owl Always Be There For You,* 104271

$28.00
$27.00
$25.00
$25.00

Suspended 2005, Issue Price $25.00, '02

Purchased ________, Price $ ___________

☐ *You Cane Count On Me,* 104273

$50.00

Limited Ed. 9,000, Issue Price $35.00, '02
GCC Fall Exclusive

Purchased ___________

Price $ ___________

☐ *You Cane Count On Me,* 104274 (Ornament)

$45.00

Limited Ed. 6,000, Issue Price $20.00, '02
GCC Fall Exclusive

Purchased ___________

Price $ ___________

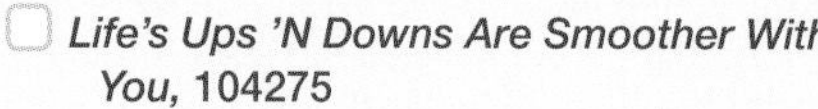

☐ *Life's Ups 'N Downs Are Smoother With You,* 104275

$40.00

Comes with tart burner, tea light candle, and bayberry-scented tart.

Limited Ed., Issue Price $30.00, '03
Gift To Go

Purchased ________, Price $ ___________

☐ *Twogether We Can Move Mountains,* 104276

$80.00 $80.00 $80.00
$80.00 $80.00 $80.00
$80.00 $80.00

Open, Issue Price $80.00, '02
Boys & Girls Club Commemorative

Purchased ________, Price $ ___________

☐ *A Journey Of Hope,* 104277

$45.00
$45.00

Limited 2004, Issue Price $45.00, '04
(Breast Cancer Awareness Benefits NABCO)

Purchased ________, Price $ ___________

His Love Is Reflected In You, 104279

$90.00
$90.00

Limited Ed., Issue Price $85.00, '03

Purchased ________, Price $ ___________

Carry A Song In Your Heart, 104281

$50.00

Limited Ed. 8,500, Issue Price $35.00, '02
CCR & DSR Exclusive

Purchased ________, Price $ ___________

Hugs Can Tame The Wildest Heart, 104282

$65.00

Limited Ed. 8,500, Issue Price $35.00, '02
CCR & DSR Exclusive

Purchased ________, Price $ ___________

A Mother's Love Is From Above, 104311

$45.00
$40.00
$40.00

Suspended 2004, Issue Price $40.00, '03
Series: *Motherhood*

Purchased ________, Price $ ___________

A Mother's Love Is From Above, 104311C

$70.00 $65.00

Limited Ed., Issue Price $40.00, '02
Series: *Motherhood*
Carlton Card Early Release

Purchased ________, Price $ ___________

Happy Days Are Here Again, 104396

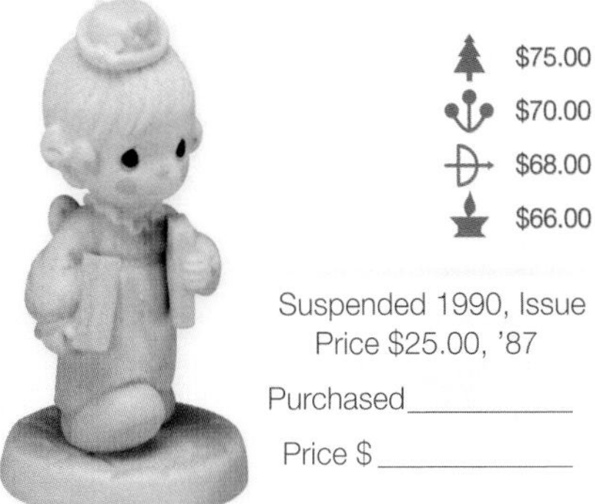

$75.00
$70.00
$68.00
$66.00

Suspended 1990, Issue Price $25.00, '87

Purchased___________

Price $ ___________

Friends To The End, 104418

UM $60.00
$58.00
$55.00
$53.00
$50.00
$48.00
$45.00

Suspended 1993, Issue Price $15.00, '88

Purchased ________, Price $ ___________

Bear The Good News Of Christmas, 104515 (Ornament)

$40.00

Dated Annual 1987,
Issue Price $11.00, '87
Series: *Birthday Collection*

Purchased ___________

Price $ ___________

Come Let Us Adore Him, 104523

$1,000.00

Dealers Only Promotional Pieces,
Issue Price $400.00, '88
Nativity With Backdrop & Video — Set of 9

Purchased ________, Price $ ___________

Jesus Loves Me, 104531

$1,750.00 $1,700.00

Limited Ed. 1,000, Issue Price $500.00, '88
Easter Seals, Lily Understamp
Individually Numbered

Purchased___________

Price $ ___________

Lots Of Good Things Are Coming Your Way, 104778

$65.00

Limited Ed., Issue Price $45.00, '03
Kirlin's Exclusive

Purchased ________, Price $ ___________

☐ *Lots Of Good Things Are Coming Your Way,* 104780 (Ornament)

$35.00

Limited Ed., Issue Price $20.00, '03
Kirlin's Exclusive

Purchased__________
Price $____________

☐ *There's Sno-One Quite Like You,* 104781

UM $40.00

Limited Ed., Issue Price $25.00, '02
Gift To Go
Series: *Little Moments*

Purchased__________
Price $ ___________

☐ *Bakin' The Holidays Even Sweeter,* 104782

UM $30.00
$25.00

Limited Ed., Issue Price $20.00, '03
Kirlin's Hallmark Exclusive
Series: *Little Moments*

Purchased __________
Price $____________

☐ *The True Spirit Of Christmas Guides The Way,* 104784

$155.00

Limited Ed. 5,000, Issue Price $125.00, '02
DSR Exclusive

Purchased ________, Price $ ___________

☐ *No One's Sweeter Than Mom,* 104785 (Ornament)

$22.00 $18.50
$20.00 $18.50
$18.50 $18.50

Open, Issue Price $18.50, '02
Series: *Family Ornament*, Mom

Purchased ___________
Price $ _____________

☐ *Papas Make The Season Bright,* 104786 (Ornament)

$22.00 $18.50
$20.00 $18.50
$18.50 $18.50

Open, Issue Price $18.50, '02
Series: *Family Ornament,* Dad

Purchased __________
Price $ _____________

☐ *Making The Holidays Special,* 104788 (Ornament)

$18.50
$22.00 $20.00 $18.50
$18.50 $18.50
$18.50 $18.50

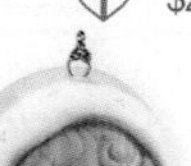

Open, Issue Price $18.50, '02
Series: *Family Ornament,* Grandma

Purchased ___________
Price $ ____________

☐ *Delivering Lots Of Love,* 104789 (Ornament)

$22.00 $18.50
$20.00 $18.50
$18.50 $18.50
$18.50 $18.50

Open, Issue Price $18.50, '02
Series: *Family Ornament,* Grandpa

Purchased ________, Price $ ___________

☐ *Bringing Bouquets Of Love,* 104790 (Ornament)

$25.00
$30.00 $23.00
$28.00 $23.00

Suspended, Issue Price $20.00, '02
Series: *Family Ornament,* Daughter

Purchased____________
Price $ _____________

☐ *Packed With Love,* 104791 (Ornament)

$30.00 $25.00
$28.00 $23.00
$23.00

Suspended, Issue Price $18.50, '02
Series: *Family Ornament,* Son

Purchased____________
Price $ _____________

☐ *Overflowing With Holiday Joy,* 104792 (Ornament)

$30.00 $25.00
$28.00 $23.00

Suspended, Issue Price $18.50, '02
Series: *Family Ornament,* Toddler Daughter

Purchased ___________
Price $____________

☐ *Holiday Surprises Come In All Sizes,* 104793 (Ornament)

$22.00 $18.50
$20.00 $18.50
$18.50 $18.50

Suspended, Issue Price $18.50, '02
Series: *Family Ornament*, Toddler Son

Purchased ___________
Price $ ____________

☐ *Hooked On the Holidays,* 104794 (Ornament)

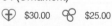

$30.00 $25.00
$28.00 $23.00

Suspended, Issue Price $18.50, '02
Series: *Family Ornament,* Dog

Purchased___________
Price $_____________

☐ *Hanging Out For The Holidays,* 104796 (Ornament)

$30.00 $25.00
$28.00 $23.00

Suspended, Issue Price $18.50, '02
Series: *Family Ornament,* Cat

Purchased ____________
Price $ ____________

☐ *I Trust In The Lord For My Strength,* 104798

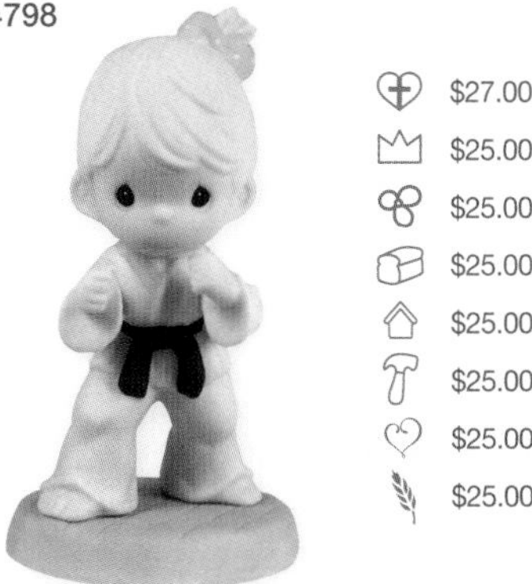

$27.00
$25.00
$25.00
$25.00
$25.00
$25.00
$25.00
$25.00

Open, Issue Price $25.00, '02
Purchased ________, Price $ ____________

☐ *I'd Jump Through Hoops For You,* 104799

$27.00 $25.00
$25.00 $25.00
$25.00 $25.00
$25.00 $25.00

Open, Issue Price $25.00, '02
Purchased ________, Price $ ____________

☐ *You're A Perfect 10,* 104800

$27.00 $25.00
$25.00 $25.00
$25.00 $25.00

Open, Issue Price $25.00, '02
Purchased ________, Price $ ____________

☐ *You're A Perfect Match,* 104801

$27.00 $25.00
$25.00 $25.00
$25.00 $25.00
$25.00 $25.00

Open, Issue Price $25.00, '02
Purchased ________, Price $ ____________

☐ *Your Spirit Is An Inspiration,* 104802

$25.00
$25.00
$27.00 $25.00
$25.00 $25.00
$25.00 $25.00

Open, Issue Price $25.00, '02
Purchased ____________
Price $ ____________

☐ *Serving Up Fun,* 104803

$27.00 $25.00
$25.00 $25.00
$25.00 $25.00
$25.00 $25.00

Open, Issue Price $25.00, '02
Purchased ____________
Price $ ____________

☐ *A Tub Full Of Love,* 104817

$65.00 $58.00
$63.00 $55.00
$60.00 $53.00
$51.00
$50.00
$48.00
$45.00
$45.00
$45.00

Suspended 1998, Issue Price $22.50, '87
Purchased ________, Price $ ____________

☐ *Sitting Pretty,* 104825

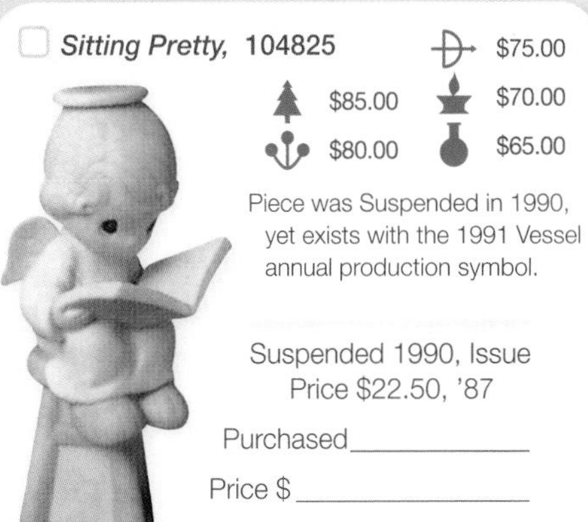

$75.00
$85.00 $70.00
$80.00 $65.00

Piece was Suspended in 1990, yet exists with the 1991 Vessel annual production symbol.

Suspended 1990, Issue Price $22.50, '87
Purchased ____________
Price $ ____________

☐ *Mom, You're A Sweetheart,* 104850

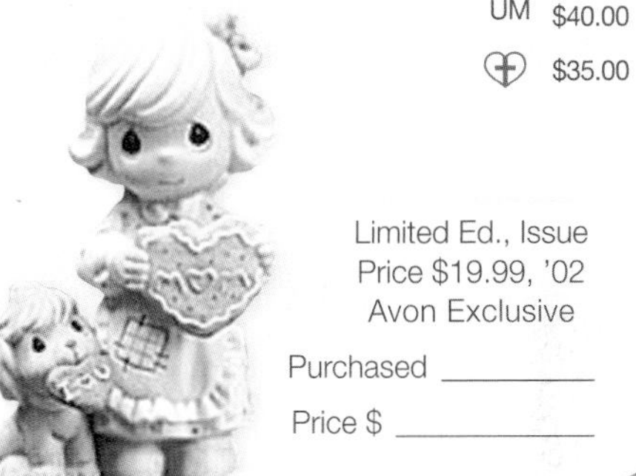

UM $40.00
$35.00

Limited Ed., Issue Price $19.99, '02
Avon Exclusive
Purchased ____________
Price $ ____________

☐ *Have I Got News For You,* 105635

$70.00
$65.00
$60.00
$58.00
$55.00

Suspended 1991, Issue Price $22.50, '87
Nativity Addition
Purchased ________, Price $ ____________

☐ *Something's Missing When You're Not Around,* 105643

$78.00
$70.00
$68.00
$65.00

Suspended 1991, Issue Price $32.50, '88
Purchased ________, Price $ ____________

To Tell The Tooth You're Special, 105813

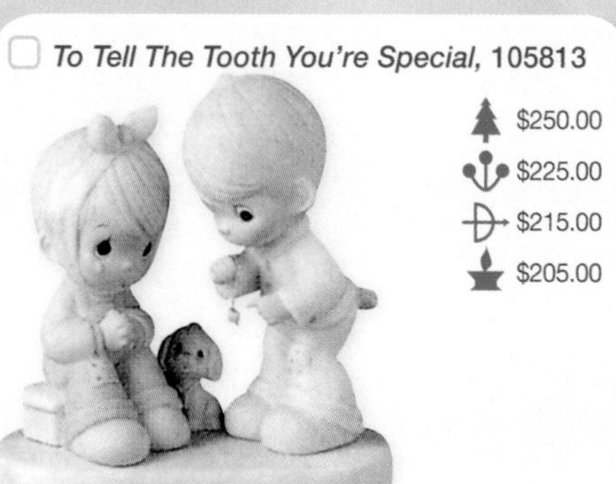

$250.00
$225.00
$215.00
$205.00

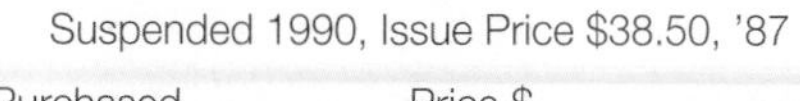

Suspended 1990, Issue Price $38.50, '87

Purchased ________, Price $ ___________

Hallelujah Country, 105821

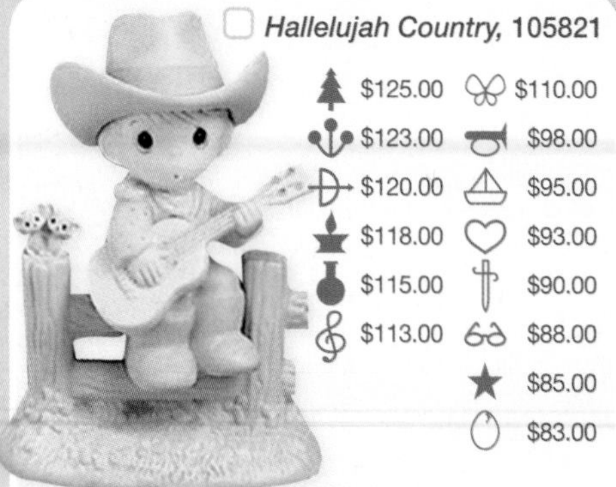

$125.00 $110.00
$123.00 $98.00
$120.00 $95.00
$118.00 $93.00
$115.00 $90.00
$113.00 $88.00
$85.00
$83.00

Retired 2000, Issue Price $35.00, '88

Purchased ________, Price $ ___________

Showers Of Blessings, 105945

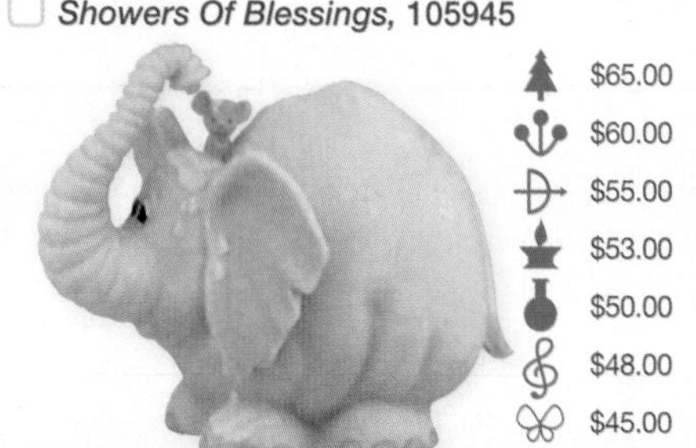

$65.00
$60.00
$55.00
$53.00
$50.00
$48.00
$45.00

Retired 1993, Issue Price $16.00, '87
Series: *Birthday Collection*

Purchased ________, Price $ ___________

Brighten Someone's Day, 105953

$40.00 $35.00
$37.00 $33.00
$31.00
$30.00
$28.00

Suspended 1993, Issue Price $12.50, '88
Series: *Birthday Collection*

Purchased ________, Price $ ___________

The Heart Of The Home Is Love, 106109

UM $90.00
$88.00

Limited Ed. 1,300, Issue Price $35.00, '02
Chapel Exclusive
2002 Licensee Event Exclusive

Purchased ________________

Price $________________

We're Pulling For You, 106151

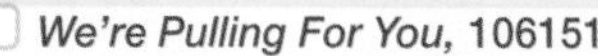

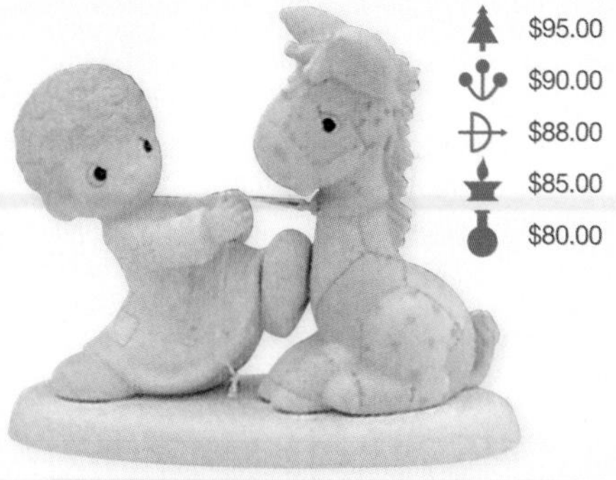

$95.00
$90.00
$88.00
$85.00
$80.00

Suspended 1991, Issue Price $40.00, '87

Purchased ________, Price $ ___________

God Bless You Graduate, 106194

$60.00 $40.00
$55.00 $40.00
$50.00 $38.00
$48.00 $38.00
$45.00 $38.00
$45.00 $38.00
$43.00 $35.00
$40.00 $35.00
$40.00 $35.00
$40.00 $35.00
$40.00 $35.00

Open, Issue Price $20.00, '86

Purchased ________, Price $ ___________

Lord, Help Me Make The Grade, 106216

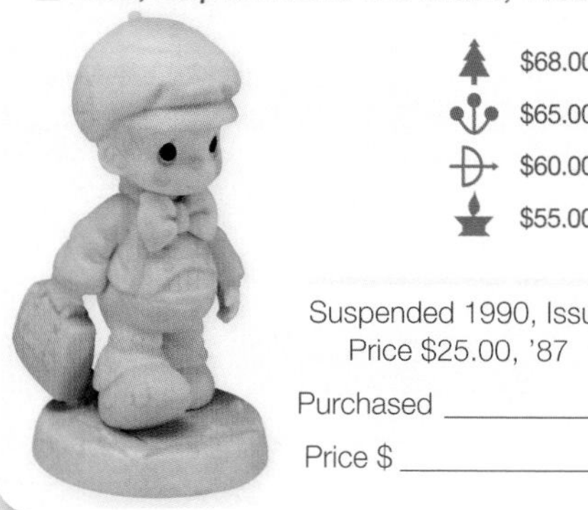

$68.00
$65.00
$60.00
$55.00

Suspended 1990, Issue Price $25.00, '87

Purchased ___________

Price $ ___________

God Shed His Grace On Thee, 106632

$90.00
$85.00
$85.00

Limited Ed., Issue Price $60.00, '02

Purchased ________

Price $___________

Stand Beside Her And Guide Her, 106671

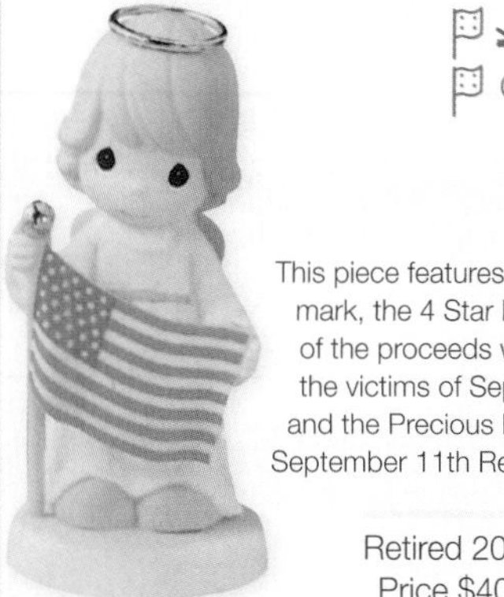

$55.00
$53.00

This piece features a second mark, the 4 Star Flag. A portion of the proceeds went to benefit the victims of September 11th and the Precious Moments September 11th Relief Fund.

Retired 2004, Issue Price $40.00, '01
Series: *America Forever*

Purchased________, Price $ ___________

Congratulations, Princess, 106208

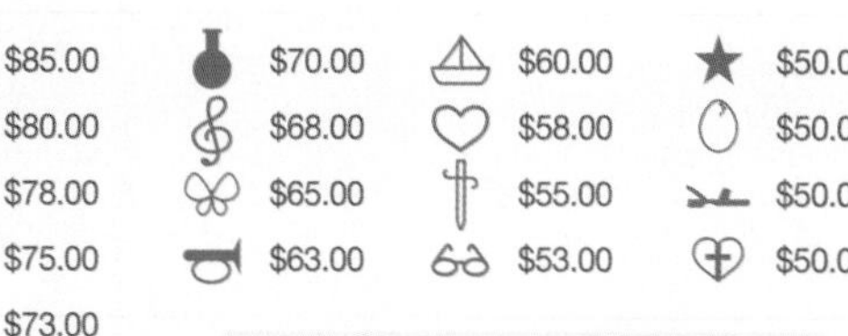

$85.00 $70.00 $60.00 $50.00
$80.00 $68.00 $58.00 $50.00
$78.00 $65.00 $55.00 $50.00
$75.00 $63.00 $53.00 $50.00
$73.00

Retired 2002, Issue Price $20.00, '86

Purchased ________, Price $ ___________

Land Of The Free, Home Of The Brave, 106672

UM $75.00

Limited Ed. 1,100, Issue Price $35.00, '03
2003 Licensee Show And Collectors' Event Piece

Purchased __________

Price $ __________

They Followed The Star, 108243

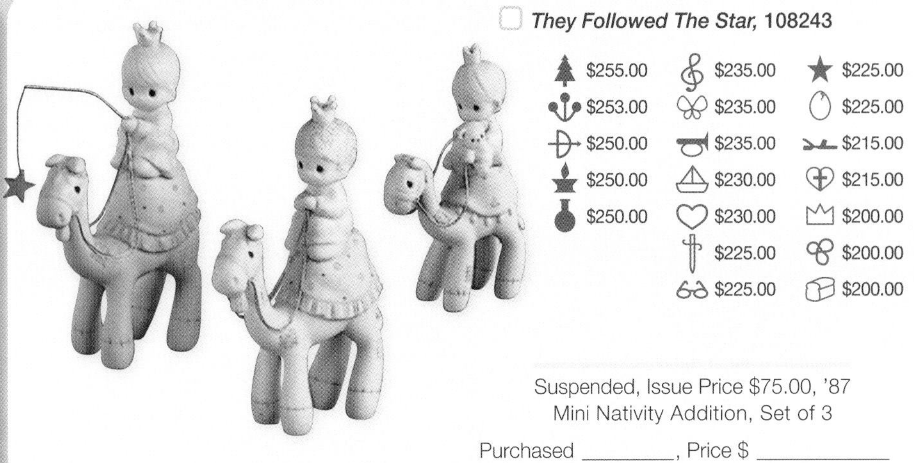

$255.00
$253.00
$250.00
$250.00
$250.00
$235.00
$235.00
$235.00
$230.00
$230.00
$225.00
$225.00
$225.00
$225.00
$215.00
$215.00
$200.00
$200.00
$200.00

Suspended, Issue Price $75.00, '87
Mini Nativity Addition, Set of 3

Purchased ________, Price $ __________

Heaven Bless Your Togetherness, 106755

$155.00
$150.00
$148.00
$148.00
$145.00
$145.00
$143.00
$143.00
$140.00
$140.00
$140.00
$135.00
$130.00

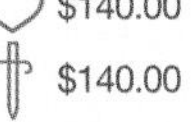

Retired 1999, Issue Price $65.00, '88

Purchased ________, Price $ __________

Puppy Love Is From Above, 106798

$105.00
$103.00
$100.00
$98.00
$95.00
$93.00
$90.00
$88.00
$85.00

Retired 1995, Issue Price $45.00, '88

Purchased ________, Price $ __________

Sew In Love, 106844

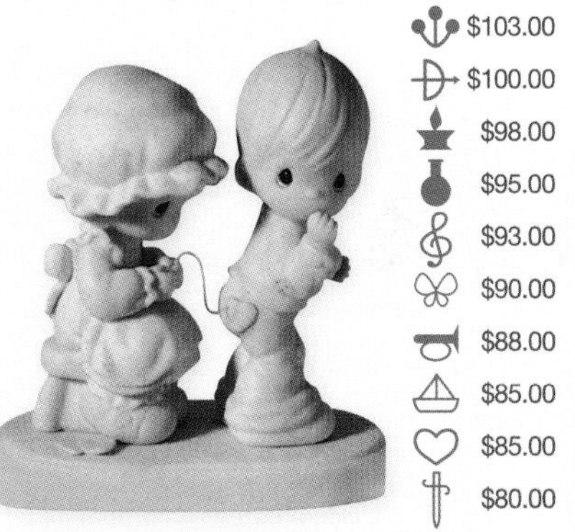

$105.00
$103.00
$100.00
$98.00
$95.00
$93.00
$90.00
$88.00
$85.00
$85.00
$80.00

Retired 1997, Issue Price $45.00, '88

Purchased ________, Price $ __________

Precious Memories, 106763

$80.00
$75.00
$73.00
$70.00
$68.00
$65.00
$63.00
$60.00
$60.00
$60.00
$55.00
$55.00
$55.00
$55.00
$55.00
$55.00
$55.00
$55.00
$55.00
$55.00
$55.00

Open, Issue Price $37.50, '88

Purchased ________, Price $ __________

Happy Birthday Poppy, 106836

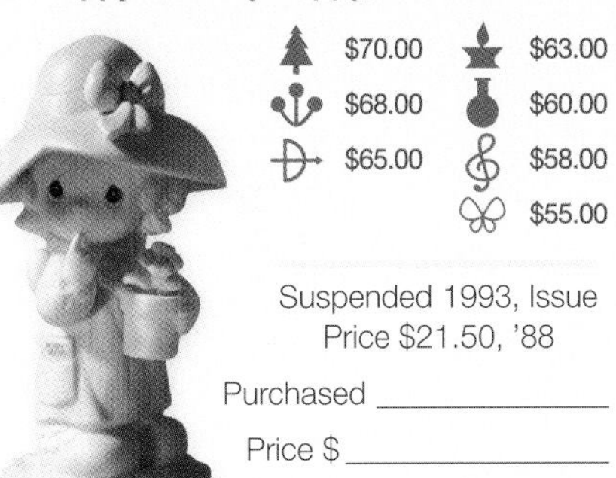

$70.00
$68.00
$65.00
$63.00
$60.00
$58.00
$55.00

Suspended 1993, Issue Price $21.50, '88

Purchased __________

Price $ __________

Your Love Fills My Heart, 108522

$65.00
$65.00

Limited Ed., Issue Price $50.00, '03

Purchased __________

Price $ __________

He Walks With Me, 107999

$135.00
$130.00

Annual 1987, Issue Price $25.00, '87
Easter Seals Commemorative, Lily Understamp

Purchased __________

Price $ __________

☐ *Overflowing With Love*, 108523

$25.00 $25.00
$25.00 $25.00
$25.00 $25.00

Open, Issue Price $25.00, '03

Purchased ____________

Price $ ____________

☐ *My Most Precious Mom-ents Are With You (Mom)*, 108528

$40.00 $40.00 $40.00
$40.00 $40.00 $40.00
$40.00 $40.00

Open, Issue Price $40.00, '03

Purchased ____________

Price $ ____________

☐ *Wishing You A Birthday Fit For A Princess*, 108534

$25.00 $25.00
$25.00 $25.00
$25.00 $25.00
$25.00 $25.00

Open, Issue Price $25.00, '03

Purchased ____________

Price $ ____________

☐ *Alleluiah, He Is Risen*, 108525

$40.00
$40.00
$40.00
$40.00
$40.00
$40.00
$40.00
$40.00

Open, Issue Price $40.00, '03

Purchased ________, Price $ ____________

☐ *Collecting Life's Most Precious Moments*, 108531

$65.00
$63.00

Limited Ed., Issue Price $50.00, '03
25th Anniversary Commemorative

Purchased ________, Price $ ____________

☐ *I-rish You Lots Of Luck*, 108535

$30.00 $30.00
$30.00 $30.00
$30.00 $30.00

Open, Issue Price $30.00, '03

Purchased ____________

Price $ ____________

☐ *Family's Fur-ever*, 108526

$35.00 $35.00
$35.00 $35.00
$35.00 $35.00
$35.00 $35.00

Open, Issue Price $35.00, '03

Purchased ____________

Price $ ____________

☐ *Collecting Life's Most Precious Moments*, 108532 (Ornament)

$45.00
$45.00

Limited Ed., Issue Price $25.00, '03
25th Anniversary Commemorative

Purchased ____________

Price $ ____________

☐ *Grounds For A Great Friendship*, 108536

$50.00
$50.00
$50.00
$50.00
$50.00
$50.00

Open, Issue Price $50.00, '03

Purchased ________, Price $ ____________

☐ *Adopting A Life Of Love*, 108527

$50.00
$50.00
$50.00
$50.00
$50.00
$50.00

Open, Issue Price $50.00, '03

Purchased ________, Price $ ____________

☐ *Just For Your Knowledge, I'll Miss You At College*, 108533

$40.00
$40.00
$40.00
$40.00
$40.00
$40.00
$40.00
$40.00

Open, Issue Price $40.00, '03

Purchased ________, Price $ ____________

☐ *Friends Always Deserve Special Treatment*, 108538

$50.00
$50.00
$50.00
$50.00
$50.00
$50.00
$50.00
$50.00

Open, Issue Price $50.00, '03

Purchased ________, Price $ ____________

I'm So Glad I Spotted You As A Friend, 108539

$25.00 $25.00
$25.00 $25.00
$25.00 $25.00
$25.00 $25.00

Open, Issue Price $25.00, '03

Purchased ____________

Price $____________

Marching Ahead To Another 25 Years Of Precious Moments, 108544

$375.00

Limited Ed. 5,000,
Issue Price $325.00, '03
Precious Moments
25th Anniversary
CCR Exclusive

Purchased ____________

Price $____________

May Your Faith Grow With Daily Care, 108540

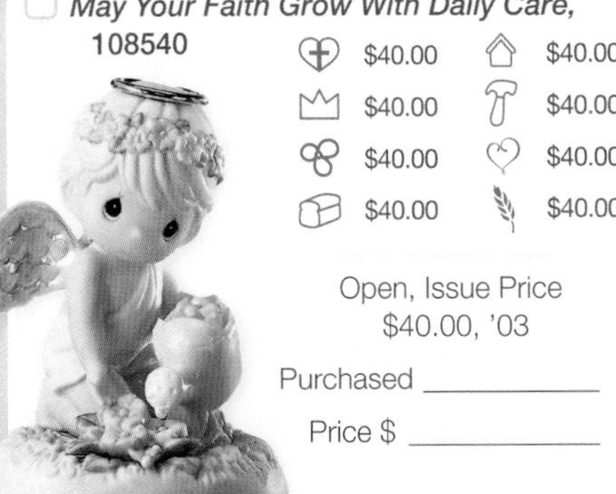

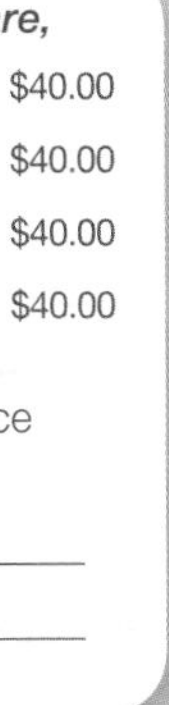

$40.00 $40.00
$40.00 $40.00
$40.00 $40.00
$40.00 $40.00

Open, Issue Price $40.00, '03

Purchased ____________

Price $ ____________

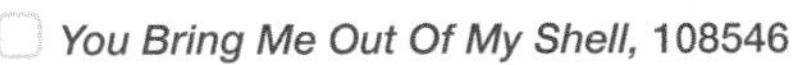

You Bring Me Out Of My Shell, 108546

$45.00
$45.00
$45.00
$45.00
$45.00
$45.00
$45.00

Open, Issue Price $45.00, '03
Series: *Sea Of Friendship*

Purchased ________, Price $ ____________

I'd Be Lost Without You, 108592

$80.00
$80.00

Limited Ed. 7,500, Issue Price $45.00, '03
Series: *Endangered Species* — Third Issue

Purchased ________, Price $ ____________

Forever In Our Hearts, 108541

$35.00 $35.00
$35.00 $35.00
$35.00 $35.00
$35.00 $35.00

Open, Issue Price $35.00, '03

Purchased ____________

Price $____________

Water I Do Without You? 108547

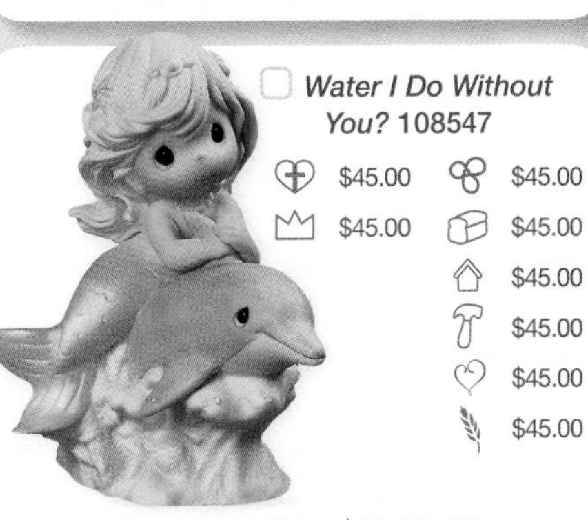

$45.00 $45.00
$45.00 $45.00
$45.00
$45.00
$45.00
$45.00

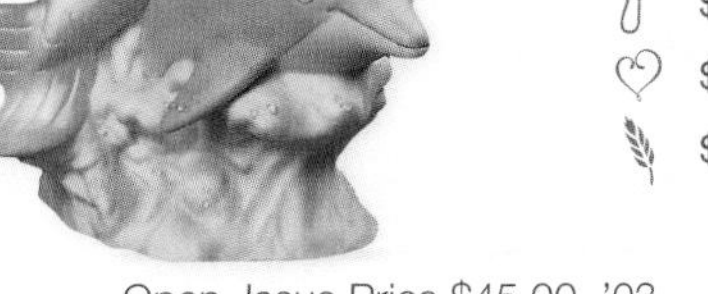

Open, Issue Price $45.00, '03
Series: Sea Of Friendship

Purchased ________, Price $ ____________

Have You Herd How Much I Love You? 108593

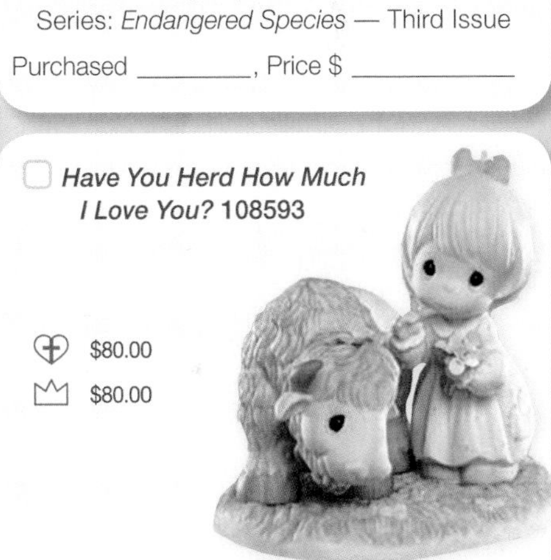

$80.00
$80.00

Limited Ed. 7,500, Issue Price $45.00, '03
Series: *Endangered Species* — Sixth Issue

Purchased ________, Price $ ____________

Simple Pleasures Are Life's True Treasures, 108542

$80.00
$80.00

Limited Ed. 5,000, Issue Price $75.00, '02

Purchased ________, Price $ ____________

I'm Filled With Love For You, 108548

$45.00 $45.00
$45.00 $45.00
$45.00 $45.00
$45.00

Open, Issue Price $45.00, '03
Series: *Sea Of Friendship*

Purchased ________, Price $ ____________

Stay With Me A Whale, 108595

$80.00
$80.00

Limited Ed. 7,500, Issue Price $45.00, '03
Series: *Endangered Species* — First Issue

Purchased ________, Price $ ____________

☐ ***Everything's Better When Shared Together,* 108597**

$80.00
$80.00

Limited Ed. 7,500, Issue Price $45.00, '03
Series: *Endangered Species* — Second Issue
Purchased ________, Price $ ___________

☐ ***Head And Shoulders Above The Rest,* 108598**

$80.00
$80.00

Limited Ed. 7,500, Issue Price $45.00, '03
Series: *Endangered Species* — Fourth Issue
Purchased ________, Price $ ___________

☐ ***Together Fur-Ever,* 108600**

$80.00
$80.00

Limited Ed. 7,500, Issue Price $45.00, '03
Series: *Endangered Species* — Fifth Issue
Purchased ________, Price $ ___________

☐ ***Love Is The True Reward,* 108603**

$45.00
$43.00

Limited Ed. 3,500, Issue Price $37.50, '03
GCC Exclusive
Purchased ___________
Price $___________

☐ ***I Love You Knight And Day,* 108604**

$40.00
$38.00

Comes with votive holder.

Retired 2003, Issue Price $25.00, '03
Purchased ________, Price $ ___________

☐ ***Mom Hits A Home Run Every Day,* 108606**

$175.00

Precious Moments Day at Wrigley Field, May 12, 2002.

Limited Ed. 10,000, '02
Purchased ________, Price $ ___________

☐ ***Gotta Hula-ta Love For You,* 108608**

$40.00
$40.00
$40.00
$40.00

Limited Ed., Issue Price $35.00, '04
Hawaii Exclusive
Purchased___________
Price $ ___________

☐ ***The Greatest Gift Is A Friend,* 109231**

$75.00
$73.00
$70.00
$68.00
$65.00
$63.00
$60.00
$58.00
$55.00
$55.00
$55.00
$53.00
$53.00

Retired 1999, Issue Price $30.00, '87
Purchased ________, Price $ ___________

☐ ***Baby's First Christmas,* 109401 (Ornament)**

$45.00

Dated Annual 1987, Issue Price $12.00, '87
Purchased ___________
Price $ ___________

☐ ***Thanks For A Quarter Century Of Loving, Caring And Sharing,* 108602**

$125.00
$125.00

Limited Ed., Issue Price $100.00, '02
Precious Moments 25th Anniversary
CCR Exclusive
Purchased ________, Price $ ___________

☐ ***Baby's First Christmas,* 109428 (Ornament)**

$45.00

Dated Annual 1987, Issue Price $12.00, '87
Purchased ___________
Price $___________

☐ ***Isn't Eight Just Great,* 109460**

$45.00
$43.00
$40.00
$38.00
$35.00
$35.00
$35.00
$33.00
$33.00
$33.00
$30.00
$30.00
$26.50
$26.50
$26.50
$26.50
$26.50
$26.50
$26.50
$26.50
$26.50
$26.50
$26.50

Open, Issue Price $18.50, '88
Series: *Birthday Circus Train* — Age 8

Purchased ________, Price $ ____________

There were reports of sets having two fathers or mothers instead of one of each. This does not increase the value.

☐ ***We Gather Together To Ask The Lord's Blessing,* 109762**

$355.00
$345.00
$340.00
$335.00
$330.00
$325.00
$320.00
$315.00
$310.00

Retired 1995, Issue Price $130.00, '87
Family Thanksgiving Set, Set of 6 plus cassette

Purchased ________, Price $ ____________

☐ ***Wishing You Grr-eatness,* 109479**

$45.00
$43.00
$40.00
$38.00
$35.00
$35.00
$35.00
$33.00
$33.00
$33.00
$30.00
$30.00
$26.50
$26.50
$26.50
$26.50
$26.50
$26.50
$26.50
$26.50
$26.50
$26.50
$26.50

Open, Issue Price $18.50, '88
Series: *Birthday Circus Train* — Age 7

Purchased ________, Price $ ____________

☐ ***Believe The Impossible,* 109487R**

$75.00
$70.00

Limited Ed., Issue Price $45.00, '00
Care-A-Van Exclusive

Purchased ________, Price $ ____________

☐ ***Wishing You A Yummy Christmas,* 109754**

$85.00
$83.00
$80.00
$78.00
$75.00
$73.00
$70.00
$68.00

Suspended 1994, Issue Price $35.00, '87

Purchased ________, Price $ ____________

☐ ***Happiness Divine,* 109584**

$105.00
$100.00
$95.00
$90.00
$85.00

Retired 1992, Issue Price $25.00, '88

Purchased ______________

Price $______________

☐ ***Love Is The Best Gift Of All,* 109770 (Ornament)**

$50.00

Dated Annual 1987, Issue Price $11.00, '87

Purchased ________, Price $ ____________

☐ ***Believe The Impossible,* 109487**

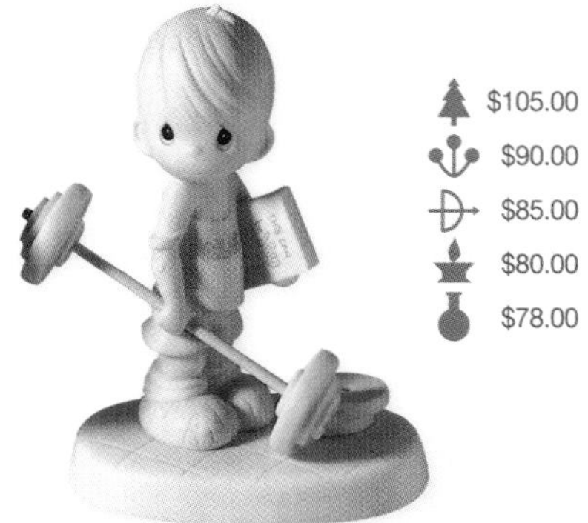

$105.00
$90.00
$85.00
$80.00
$78.00

Suspended 1991, Issue Price $35.00, '88

Purchased ________, Price $ ____________

☐ ***Peace On Earth,* 109746 (Musical)**

$180.00
$175.00
$173.00
$170.00
$168.00
$165.00
$160.00

Suspended 1993, Issue Price $100.00, '88
Tune: *Hark! The Herald Angels Sing*

Purchased ________, Price $ ____________

☐ ***Meowie Christmas,* 109800**

$75.00
$73.00
$70.00
$68.00
$65.00
$63.00
$60.00
$58.00
$55.00
$53.00
$50.00
$48.00
$45.00

Retired 2000, Issue Price $30.00, '88

Purchased ________, Price $ ____________

Oh What Fun It Is To Ride, 109819

$175.00 · $170.00 · $165.00 · $160.00 · $155.00 · $153.00 · $150.00 · $148.00 · $145.00 · $145.00 · $145.00 · $145.00

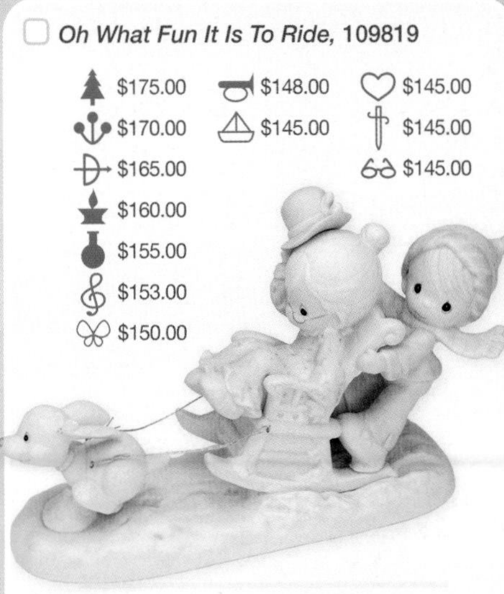

Retired 1998, Issue Price $85.00, '87

Purchased ________, Price $ ____________

Love Is The Best Gift Of All, 109835 (Bell)

$35.00

Dated Annual 1987, Issue Price $22.50, '87

Purchased __________

Price $__________

Love Is The Best Gift Of All, 109843 (Thimble)

$40.00

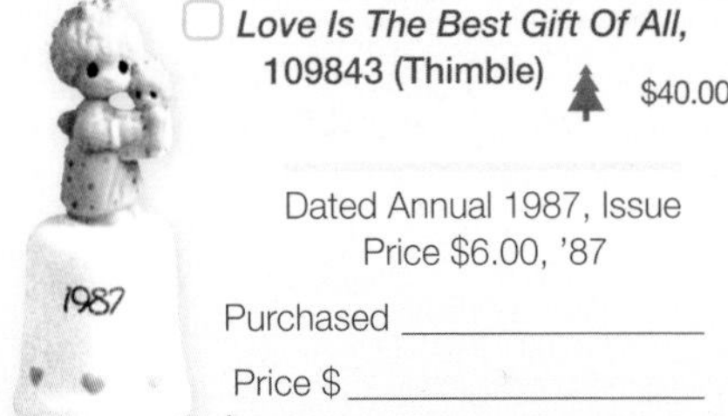

Dated Annual 1987, Issue Price $6.00, '87

Purchased ______________

Price $______________

Wishing You A Happy Easter, 109886

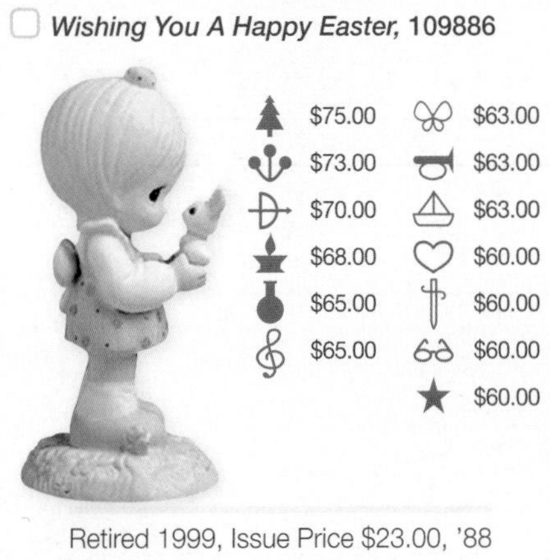

$75.00 · $73.00 · $70.00 · $68.00 · $65.00 · $65.00 · $63.00 · $63.00 · $63.00 · $60.00 · $60.00 · $60.00 · $60.00

Retired 1999, Issue Price $23.00, '88

Purchased ________, Price $ ____________

Wishing You A Basket Full Of Blessings, 109924

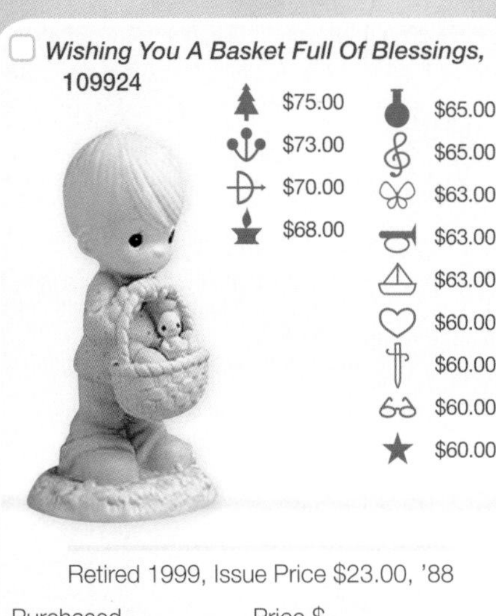

$75.00 · $73.00 · $70.00 · $68.00 · $65.00 · $65.00 · $63.00 · $63.00 · $63.00 · $60.00 · $60.00 · $60.00 · $60.00

Retired 1999, Issue Price $23.00, '88

Purchased ________, Price $ ____________

Sending You My Love, 109967

$80.00 · $78.00 · $75.00 · $75.00 · $73.00 · $73.00 · $70.00 · $70.00 · $68.00 · $68.00 · $65.00 · $65.00 · $65.00 · $65.00

Retired 2000, Issue Price $35.00, '88

Series: *Heavenly Halos*

Purchased ________, Price $ ____________

Mommy, I Love You, 109975

$55.00 · $53.00 · $50.00 · $48.00 · $48.00 · $48.00 · $45.00 · $45.00 · $45.00 · $43.00 · $43.00 · $43.00 · $40.00 · $40.00 · $40.00 · $40.00 · $40.00

Retired 2003, Issue Price $30.00, '87

Purchased ________, Price $ ____________

January, 109983

$105.00 · $100.00 · $95.00 · $93.00 · $90.00 · $88.00 · $85.00 · $83.00 · $80.00 · $80.00 · $78.00 · $78.00 · $75.00 · $75.00 · $70.00 · $70.00

Retired 2002, Issue Price $37.50, '88

Series: *Calendar Girls*

Purchased ________, Price $ ____________

February, 109991

$85.00 · $80.00 · $78.00 · $75.00 · $73.00 · $70.00 · $68.00 · $65.00 · $63.00 · $60.00 · $58.00 · $55.00 · $53.00 · $53.00 · $50.00 · $50.00

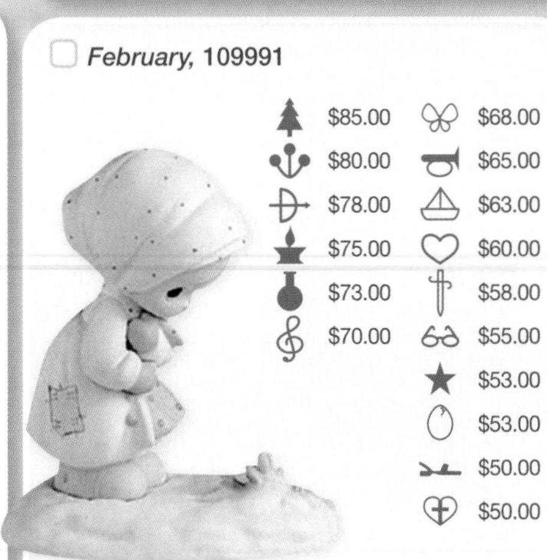

Retired 2002, Issue Price $27.50, '88

Series: *Calendar Girls*

Purchased ________, Price $ ____________

March, 110019

$85.00 · $80.00 · $78.00 · $75.00 · $73.00 · $70.00 · $68.00 · $65.00 · $63.00 · $60.00 · $58.00 · $55.00 · $53.00 · $53.00 · $50.00 · $50.00

Retired 2002, Issue Price $37.50, '88

Series: *Calendar Girls*

Purchased ________, Price $ ____________

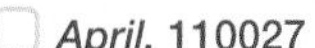

☐ *April*, 110027

$135.00 $125.00 $120.00 $115.00 $110.00 $105.00 $95.00 $90.00
$85.00 $80.00 $75.00 $70.00 $65.00 $60.00 $55.00 $55.00

Retired 2002, Issue Price $30.00, '88
Series: *Calendar Girls*

Purchased ________, Price $ ___________

☐ *May*, 110035

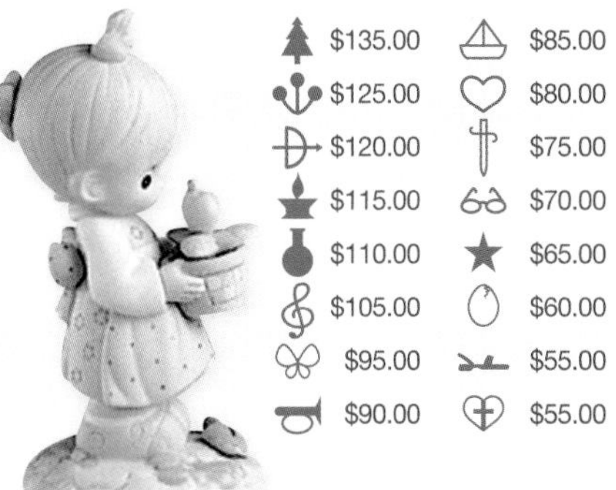

$135.00 $125.00 $120.00 $115.00 $110.00 $105.00 $95.00 $90.00
$85.00 $80.00 $75.00 $70.00 $65.00 $60.00 $55.00 $55.00

Retired 2002, Issue Price $25.00, '88
Series: *Calendar Girls*

Purchased ________, Price $ ___________

☐ *June*, 110043

$140.00 $130.00 $125.00
$120.00 $115.00 $110.00
$105.00 $100.00 $95.00 $90.00 $85.00 $80.00 $75.00 $70.00 $65.00 $60.00

Retired 2002, Issue Price $40.00, '88
Series: *Calendar Girls*

Purchased ________, Price $ ___________

☐ *July*, 110051

$95.00
$90.00 $87.00 $85.00 $83.00 $80.00
$75.00 $73.00 $70.00 $70.00 $68.00 $68.00 $65.00 $65.00 $65.00 $65.00

Retired 2002, Issue Price $35.00, '88
Series: *Calendar Girls*

Purchased ________, Price $ ___________

☐ *August*, 110078

$95.00 $90.00
$87.00 $85.00 $83.00 $80.00 $75.00 $73.00
$70.00 $70.00 $68.00 $68.00 $65.00 $65.00 $65.00 $65.00

Retired 2002, Issue Price $40.00, '88
Series: *Calendar Girls*

Purchased ________, Price $ ___________

☐ *September*, 110086

$95.00 $90.00 $87.00 $85.00 $83.00 $80.00 $75.00 $73.00
$70.00 $70.00 $68.00 $68.00 $65.00 $65.00 $65.00 $65.00

Retired 2002, Issue Price $27.50, '88
Series: *Calendar Girls*

Purchased ________, Price $ ___________

☐ *October*, 110094

$95.00 $90.00 $87.00 $85.00 $83.00 $80.00
$75.00
$73.00 $70.00 $70.00 $68.00 $68.00 $65.00 $65.00 $65.00 $65.00

Retired 2002, Issue Price $35.00, '88
Series: *Calendar Girls*

Purchased ________, Price $ ___________

☐ *November*, 110108

$115.00 $105.00 $100.00 $95.00 $90.00
$85.00
$80.00 $75.00 $70.00 $65.00 $60.00 $55.00 $55.00 $50.00 $50.00

Retired 2002, Issue Price $32.50, '88
Series: *Calendar Girls*

Purchased ________, Price $ ___________

☐ *December*, 110116

$100.00 $95.00 $90.00 $85.00 $83.00 $80.00
$78.00 $75.00 $70.00 $65.00 $63.00 $60.00 $58.00 $55.00 $53.00

Retired 2002, Issue Price $27.50, '88
Series: *Calendar Girls*

Purchased ________, Price $ ___________

☐ ***Precious Moments From The Beginning*, 110238**

$200.00
$200.00

Limited Ed., Issue Price $175.00, '03
25th Anniversary Celebration CCR Exclusive

Purchased ____________

Price $ ____________

☐ ***I Love You A Bushel And A Peck*, 110265**

$20.00 $20.00 $20.00 $20.00
$20.00 $20.00

Open, Issue Price $20.00, '03
Series: *Animal Affections*

Purchased ______

Price $ ______

☐ ***God Loveth A Cheerful Giver*, 110239 (Ornament)**

$25.00

Limited, Issue Price $25.00, '03
25th Anniversary Celebration
CCR Exclusive

Purchased ________, Price $ ________

☐ ***It's Down Hill All The Way, Congratulations*, 110261**

$20.00 $20.00
$20.00 $20.00
$20.00
$20.00

Open, Issue Price $20.00, '03
Series: *Animal Affections*

Purchased ________, Price $ ________

☐ ***A Chip Off The Old Block*, 110266**

$20.00 $20.00 $20.00
$20.00 $20.00
$20.00

Open, Issue Price $20.00, '03
Series: *Animal Affections*

Purchased ________

Price $ ________

☐ ***A Mother's Love Is Beyond Measure*, 110267**

$45.00
$45.00

Retired 2003, Issue Price $27.50, '03

Purchased ________

Price $ ________

☐ ***Celebrating 25 Years Of Sunshine & Smiles*, 110254**

$165.00

Given to those who went on the 25th Anniversary Cruise to the Carribbean in May '03
Limited Ed., SRP: Gift

Purchased ________, Price $ ________

☐ ***Are You Lonesome Tonight?* 110262**

$20.00 $20.00
$20.00 $20.00
$20.00 $20.00

Open, Issue Price $20.00, '03
Series: Animal Affections

Purchased ______

Price $ ______

☐ ***My Heart Belongs To You*, 110268**

$155.00
$155.00

First "mature" or "elongated" figurine to feature both boy and girl.

Limited Ed., Issue Price $125.00, '03

Purchased ________, Price $ ________

☐ ***I Just Go Bats Over You*, 110260**

$20.00 $20.00
$20.00 $20.00
$20.00
$20.00

Out of Production, Issue Price $20.00, '03
Series: Animal Affections

Purchased ________, Price $ ________

☐ ***Remember To Reach For The Stars*, 110263**

$20.00
$20.00
$20.00
$20.00
$20.00
$20.00

Open, Issue Price $20.00, '03
Series: Animal Affections

Purchased ________

Price $ ________

☐ ***Friendship Is Always A Sweet Surprise*, 110269**

$45.00
$45.00

Limited Ed., Issue Price $35.00, '02
Carlton Cards Exclusive

Purchased ________

Price $ ________

Reisen In Deutschland, 110270 (Medallion)

UM $450.00

This piece was given to members who went to Germany in 2002.

Open, Gift, '02
Germany Tour Exclusive — May 2002

Purchased ________, Price $ ___________

4-H The Power Of YOUth, 110271

UM $45.00
$40.00
$40.00

Limited Ed., Issue Price $30.00, '02
Chapel Exclusive,
4-H Commemorative

Purchased ___________
Price $ ___________

Love Is A Heavenly Song, 110367

$125.00
$125.00
$125.00
$125.00
$125.00
$125.00

Open, Issue Price $125.00, '03
Easter Seals Exclusive
Series: *Heaven's Grace* — Second Issue

Purchased ________, Price $ ___________

Wish You Were Hare, 110447

$40.00
$40.00
$40.00

Suspended 2004, Issue Price $40.00, '03

Purchased ___________
Price $ ___________

Love Is The Best Gift Of All, 110930

$40.00

Dated Annual 1987,
Issue Price $22.50, '87

Purchased___________
Price $ ___________

I'm A Possibility, 111120 (Ornament)

$45.00 $40.00
$43.00 $38.00

Suspended 1990, Issue Price $11.00, '87

Purchased___________
Price $ ___________

Faith Takes The Plunge, 111155

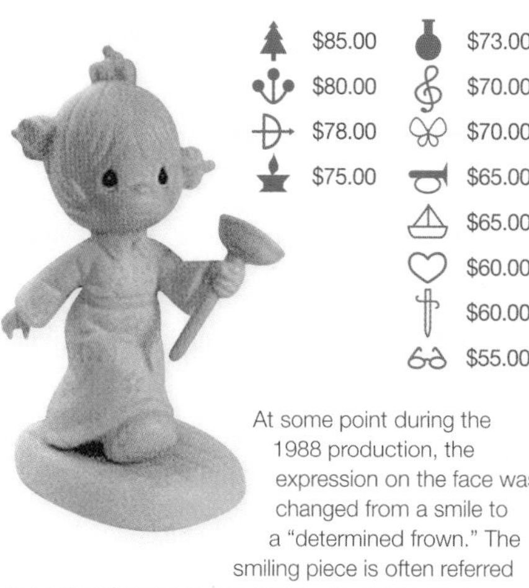

$85.00 $73.00
$80.00 $70.00
$78.00 $70.00
$75.00 $65.00
$65.00
$60.00
$60.00
$55.00

At some point during the 1988 production, the expression on the face was changed from a smile to a "determined frown." The smiling piece is often referred to as the "Smiling Plunger." Value for Cedar Tree Smiling is $50.00. Flower Smiling is valued at $48.00.

Suspended 1998, Issue Price $27.50, '88

Purchased ________, Price $ ___________

'Tis The Season, 111163

$70.00 $58.00
$68.00 $55.00
$65.00 $53.00
$60.00 $50.00
$48.00

Suspended 1996, Issue Price $27.50, '88

Purchased___________
Price $ ___________

O Come, Let Us Adore Him, 111333

$275.00
$265.00
$255.00
$245.00
$235.00

Suspended 1991, Issue Price $200.00, '87
Large (9") Nativity, Set of 4

Purchased ________, Price $ ___________

Ma-Holo-Day Wishes For You, 111413

UM $55.00
$50.00

2002 Collector's Weekend, December 6 – 8.

Limited Ed. 1,200, Issue Price $35.00, '02
Chapel Exclusive

Purchased ________, Price $ ___________

Retailer's Wreath, 111465

$225.00

On some wreaths, the *Have a Heavenly Christmas* ornament has the inscription "Heaven Bound" upside down. The value for the wreath with this error is $200.00.

Promotional Item, Issue Price $150.00, '87

Purchased ________, Price $ ___________

☐ *You're Worth Waiting On,* **111749**

UM $35.00 · $35.00 · $35.00 · $35.00 · $35.00

Open, Issue Price $35.00, '03
Chapel Exclusive

Purchased ____________
Price $______________

☐ *Everybody's Grandmother,* **111752**

UM $50.00 · $50.00 · $50.00 · $50.00 · $50.00

Open, Issue Price $50.00, '03
Chapel Exclusive

Purchased ________, Price $ ____________

☐ *Heather (If You Could Only See Heaven),* **111753**

UM $50.00 · $45.00 · $45.00 · $45.00 · $45.00 · $45.00 · $45.00

Open, Issue Price $45.00, '03
Chapel Exclusive

Purchased _________
Price $ __________

☐ *Fairytales Can Come True,* **111754**

UM $100.00 · $100.00 · $100.00

Out of Production, Issue Price $100.00, '03
Chapel Exclusive

Purchased ________, Price $ ____________

☐ *Every Precious Moment Needs A Smile,* **111757**

UM $35.00 · $35.00 · $35.00 · $35.00 · $35.00

Open, Issue Price $35.00, '03
Chapel Exclusive

Purchased ________, Price $ ____________

☐ *Holding Him Close To My Heart,* **111760**

UM $30.00 · $30.00 · $30.00 · $30.00 · $30.00

Open, Issue Price $30.00, '03
Chapel Exclusive

Purchased __________
Price $____________

☐ *Holding Him Close To My Heart,* **111762 (Ornament)**

UM $20.00 · $20.00 · $20.00 · $20.00 · $20.00 · $20.00

Open, Issue Price $20.00, '03
Chapel Exclusive

Purchased ____________
Price $ ______________

☐ *Welcome And God Bless You,* **111765 (Plaque)**

UM $45.00

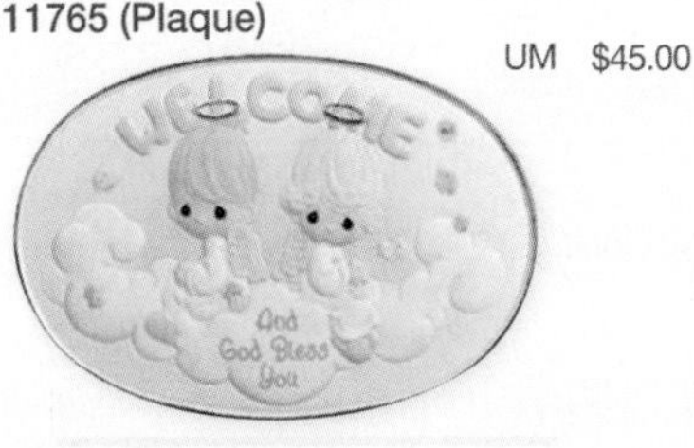

Open, Issue Price $45.00, '03
Chapel Exclusive

Purchased ________, Price $ ____________

☐ *Mommy's Little Angel (Brunette),* **111869**

$25.00 · $25.00 · $25.00

Suspended 2004, Issue Price $25.00, '03

Purchased ____________
Price $ ____________

☐ *Mommy's Little Angel (Blonde),* **111870**

$25.00 · $25.00 · $25.00

Suspended 2004, Issue Price $25.00, '03

Purchased____________
Price $____________

☐ *A Time To Wish You A Merry Christmas,* **111895**

$50.00 · $50.00 · $50.00 · $50.00 · $50.00

Open, Issue Price $50.00, '04

Purchased ________, Price $ ____________

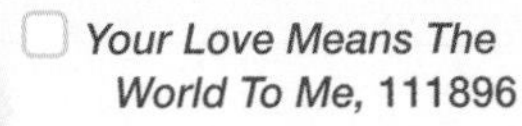

☐ *Your Love Means The World To Me,* **111896**

$45.00 · $37.50 · $35.00

Limited Ed., Issue Price $50.00, '04

Purchased __________
Price $ ____________

With A Little Help From Above, 111897

$50.00
$50.00

2004 Signing Event Exclusive.

Limited Ed., Issue Price $50.00, '04

Purchased ________, Price $ ____________

Mommy, I Love You, 112143

$80.00
$70.00
$65.00
$60.00
$58.00
$55.00
$53.00
$50.00
$50.00
$48.00
$48.00
$45.00
$45.00
$40.00
$40.00

Retired 2001, Issue Price $22.50, '88

Purchased ________, Price $ ____________

Waddle I Do Without You, 112364 (Ornament)

$45.00
$43.00
$40.00
$38.00
$35.00
$35.00
$35.00
$33.00
$33.00
$33.00
$30.00
$30.00
$28.00

Retired 1999, Issue Price $11.00, '87

Purchased ________, Price $ ____________

Simple Pleasures Make Holiday Treasures, 111898

$125.00

Limited 2003, Issue Price $125.00, '03
Set of 5

Purchased ________, Price $ ____________

A Tub Full Of Love, 112313

$75.00
$73.00
$73.00
$70.00
$70.00
$65.00
$65.00
$63.00
$63.00
$63.00
$60.00
$60.00
$60.00
$58.00
$58.00
$58.00
$58.00
$58.00
$58.00

Suspended, Issue Price $22.50, '87

Purchased ________, Price $ ____________

I'm Sending You A White Christmas, 112372 (Ornament)

UM $38.00
$35.00
$33.00
$30.00
$28.00
$25.00
$23.00

Suspended 1992, Issue Price $11.00, '87

Purchased ____________

Price $ ____________

Retailer's Wreath Bell, 112348 (Ornament)

$75.00

Promotional Item, '87

Purchased ____________

Price $ ____________

He Cleansed My Soul, 112380 (Ornament)

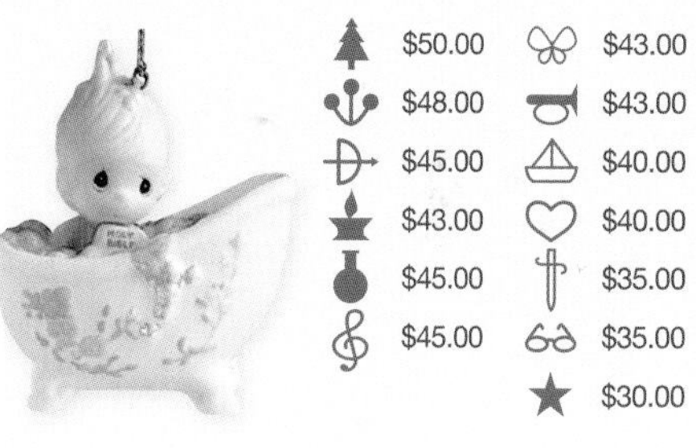

$50.00
$48.00
$45.00
$43.00
$45.00
$45.00
$43.00
$43.00
$40.00
$40.00
$35.00
$35.00
$30.00

Retired 1999, Issue Price $12.00, '87

Purchased ________, Price $ ____________

The Lord Bless You And Keep You, 111904

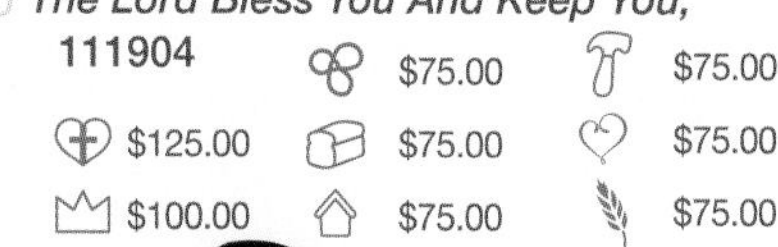

$75.00
$125.00
$100.00
$75.00
$75.00
$75.00
$75.00
$75.00
$75.00

Open, Issue Price $70.00, '03
Japanese Exclusive, Set of 5

Purchased ________, Price $ ____________

You Have Touched So Many Hearts, 112356 (Ornament)

$45.00
$40.00
$38.00
$35.00
$35.00
$35.00
$33.00
$33.00
$30.00
$30.00
$30.00

Retired 1997, Issue Price $11.00, '87

Purchased ________, Price $ ____________

Our First Christmas Together, 112399 (Ornament)

$35.00

Dated Annual 1987, Issue Price $11.00, '87

Purchased ________, Price $ ____________

☐ *I'm Sending You A White Christmas*, 112402 (Musical)

$155.00
$150.00
$148.00
$143.00
$140.00
$138.00
$135.00

Retired 1993, Issue Price $55.00, '87
Tune: *White Christmas*
Purchased ________, Price $ ____________

☐ *You Have Touched So Many Hearts*, 112577 (Musical)

$125.00
$120.00
$115.00
$113.00
$110.00
$108.00
$105.00
$100.00
$98.00
$95.00

Suspended 1996, Issue Price $50.00, '88
Tune: *Everybody Loves Somebody*
Purchased ________, Price $ ____________

☐ *Icy Good Times Ahead*, 112839

$45.00

Dated Annual 2003, Issue Price $35.00, '03
Purchased ____________
Price $____________

☐ *Icy Good Times Ahead*, 112840 (Ornament)

$30.00

Dated Annual 2003, Issue Price $20.00, '03
Purchased____________
Price $ ____________

☐ *Our First Christmas Together*, 112841 (Ornament)

$35.00

Dated Annual 2003, Issue Price $25.00, '03
Purchased ____________
Price $____________

☐ *Baby's First Christmas*, 112842 (Ornament)

$30.00

Dated Annual 2003, Issue Price $20.00, '03
Purchased ____________
Price $ ____________

☐ *Baby's First Christmas*, 112843 (Ornament)

$30.00

Dated Annual 2003, Issue Price $20.00, '03
Purchased ____________
Price $ ____________

☐ *A Nurse's Care Is The Best Medicine*, 112845

$30.00 $30.00
$30.00 $30.00
$30.00

Open, Issue Price $30.00, '03
Purchased ____________
Price $ ____________

☐ *Everyday Hero*, 112857

$30.00 $30.00
$30.00 $30.00
$30.00 $30.00
$30.00

Open, Issue Price $30.00, '03
Purchased ____________
Price $ ____________

☐ *Take A Note, You're Great!* 112858

$30.00 $30.00
$30.00 $30.00
$30.00 $30.00
$30.00

Open, Issue Price $30.00, '03
Purchased____________
Price $ ____________

☐ *Coach, You're A Real Sport*, 112859

$30.00 $30.00
$30.00 $30.00
$30.00

Open, Issue Price $30.00, '03
Purchased ____________
Price $ ____________

☐ *Teacher, You're A Precious Work Of Art*, 112861

$30.00 $30.00
$30.00 $30.00
$30.00 $30.00
$30.00

Open, Issue Price $30.00, '03
Purchased ____________
Price $ ____________

☐ *It's Only Gauze I Care*, 112862

$30.00
$30.00
$30.00
$30.00
$30.00

Open, Issue Price $30.00, '03
Purchased ________, Price $ ____________

Bearing Gifts Of Great Joy, 112863

$35.00 $35.00
$35.00 $35.00
$35.00

Open, Issue Price $35.00, '03
Nativity Addition

Purchased ____________

Price $ ____________

I Can't Give You Anything But Love, 112864

$30.00 $30.00
$30.00 $30.00
$30.00

Open, Issue Price $30.00, '03

Purchased ____________

Price $ ____________

To A Niece With A Bubbly Personality, 112870

$30.00 $30.00
$30.00 $30.00
$30.00 $30.00
$30.00

Open, Issue Price $25.00, '03

Purchased ____________

Price $ ____________

Squashed With Love, 112874

$45.00
$45.00
$45.00
$45.00
$45.00
$45.00
$45.00

Open, Issue Price $45.00, '03

Purchased ________, Price $ ____________

I-cy Potential In You, 112875 (Ornament)

$35.00
$35.00

Dated Annual 2003, Issue Price $30.00, '03

Purchased ____________

Price $ ____________

May The Holidays Keep You Bright Eyed And Bushy Tailed, 112876 (Ornament)

$25.00

Dated Annual 2003, Issue Price $20.00, '03
Series: *Birthday Collection*

Purchased ____________

Price $ ____________

God Rest Ye Merry Gentlemen, 112878

$75.00
$70.00
$70.00

Retired 2004, Issue Price $55.00, '03
Series: *Christmas Remembered*

Purchased ________, Price $ ____________

May Your Heart Be Filled With Christmas Joy, 112880

$50.00
$50.00
$50.00
$50.00
$50.00

Open, Issue Price $50.00, '03
Series: *Christmas Remembered* — 4th Edition

Purchased ________, Price $ ____________

Warmest Wishes For The Holidays, 112881

$50.00
$50.00
$50.00
$50.00
$50.00

Out of Production, Issue Price $50.00, '03

Purchased ________, Price $ ____________

You're A Gem Of A Friend, 112882

$37.50
$37.50 $37.50
$37.50 $37.50
$37.50 $37.50

Open, Issue Price $37.50, '03

Purchased ____________

Price $ ____________

Joy Is The Music Of Angels, 112966

$125.00 $125.00
$125.00 $125.00
$125.00 $125.00

Open, Issue Price $125.00, '03
Easter Seals — Series: *Heaven's Grace* — 3rd Edition

Purchased ____________

Price $ ____________

Hope Is A Gentle Melody, 112967

$135.00
$125.00
$125.00
$125.00
$125.00

Open, Issue Price $125.00, '04
Easter Seals
Series: *Heaven's Grace* — 4th Edition

Purchased ____________

Price $ ____________

☐ *Happiness Is A Song From Heaven*, 112969

$125.00
$125.00
$125.00
$125.00

Open, Issue Price $125.00, '04 Easter Seals — Series: *Heaven's Grace* — 5th Edition

Purchased ________, Price $ ____________

☐ *Mom, I Always Have A Ball With You*, 112995

$100.00
$95.00

Figurine given at "Precious Moments Day," May 5, 2003, at Wrigley Field, Chicago, Illinois.

Limited Ed. 10,000, Gift, '03

Purchased ________, Price $ ____________

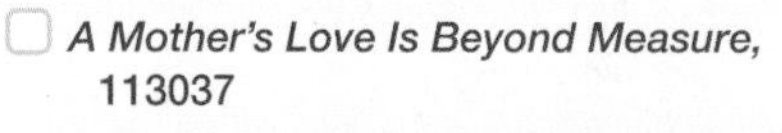

☐ *A Mother's Love Is Beyond Measure*, 113037

$45.00
$40.00

Retired 2003, Issue Price $30.00, '03 Gift Set

Purchased ________, Price $ ____________

☐ *A Mother's Story Is One Of Love*, 113369

$45.00 $45.00
$45.00 $45.00

Limited 2003, Issue Price $40.00

Purchased ________, Price $ ____________

☐ *A Mother's Story Is One Of Love*, 113369C

$45.00
$45.00

Limited Ed., Issue Price $40.00, '03 Carlton Cards Early Release

Purchased ________

Price $__________

☐ *I Love You Forever And Always*, 113944

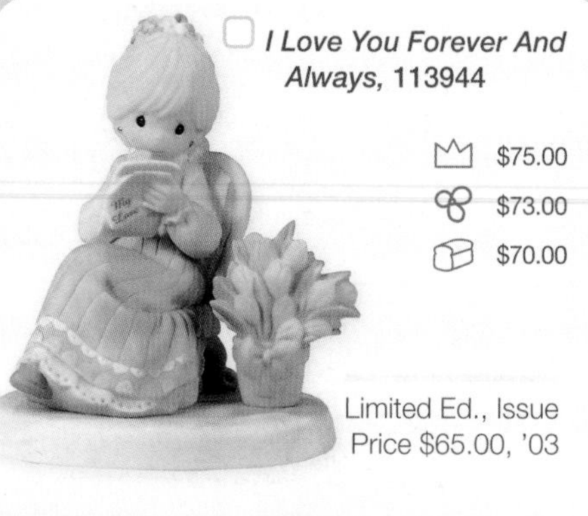

$75.00
$73.00
$70.00

Limited Ed., Issue Price $65.00, '03

Purchased ________, Price $ ____________

☐ *You Have A Certain Glow About You*, 113945

$32.50 $32.50
$32.50 $32.50
$32.50 $32.50
$32.50

Open, Issue Price $32.50, '03

Purchased__________

Price $__________

☐ *Hold On To Your Faith*, 113946

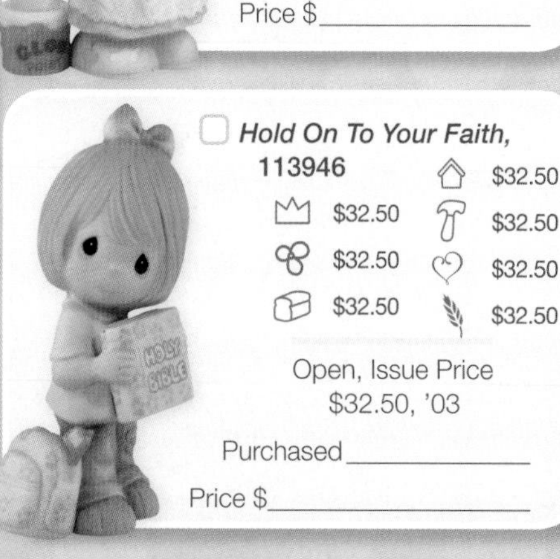

$32.50 $32.50
$32.50 $32.50
$32.50 $32.50
$32.50

Open, Issue Price $32.50, '03

Purchased__________

Price $__________

☐ *Hold On To Your Faith*, 113947

$32.50
$32.50
$32.50
$32.50
$32.50
$32.50
$32.50

Open, Issue Price $32.50, '03

Purchased ________, Price $ ____________

☐ *This Little Light Of Mine, I'm Gonna Let It Shine*, 113949

$32.50 $32.50
$32.50 $32.50
$32.50 $32.50
$32.50

Open, Issue Price $32.50, '03

Purchased __________

Price $ __________

☐ *To My Forever Friend*, 113956 (Ornament)

$45.00 $35.00
$40.00 $34.00
$39.00 $33.00
$38.00 $32.00
$37.00 $31.00
$36.00 $30.00

Retired 1999, Issue Price $16.00, '88

Purchased ________, Price $ ____________

☐ *A Child Is A Gift Of God*, 113962

$45.00
$45.00
$45.00
$45.00
$45.00
$45.00
$45.00

Open, Issue Price $45.00, '03

Purchased ________, Price $ ____________

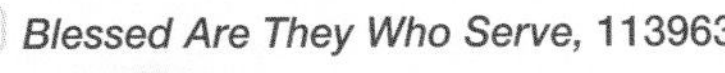

☐ *Blessed Are They Who Serve,* 113963

$30.00 $30.00
$30.00 $30.00
$30.00 $30.00
$30.00

Open, Issue Price $30.00, '03

Purchased ___________

Price $ ___________

☐ *Smile Along The Way,* 113964 (Ornament)

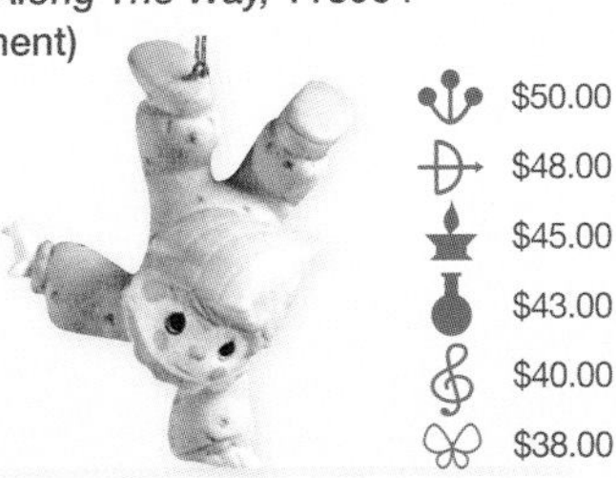

$50.00
$48.00
$45.00
$43.00
$40.00
$38.00

Suspended 1993, Issue Price $15.00, '88

Purchased ________, Price $ ___________

☐ *You Shall Receive A Crown Of Glory,* 113965

$45.00
$43.00
$40.00

Retired 2005, Issue Price $35.00, '03

Purchased ________, Price $ ___________

☐ *His Blessings Are Without Measure,* 113966

$50.00
$48.00
$45.00

Retired 2005, Issue Price $40.00, '03

Purchased ________

Price $ ________

☐ *God Sent You Just In Time,* 113972 (Ornament)

$45.00 $40.00
$43.00 $38.00

Suspended 1991, Issue Price $13.50, '88

Purchased ___________

Price $ ___________

☐ *Rejoice, O Earth,* 113980 (Ornament)

$50.00 $45.00
$48.00 $43.00

Retired 1991, Issue Price $13.50, '88

Purchased ___________

Price $ ___________

☐ *Glad We See Eye To Eye,* 113991

$27.50
$27.50
$27.50
$27.50
$27.50
$27.50
$27.50

Open, Issue Price $27.50, '03

Purchased ________, Price $ ___________

☐ *Cheers To The Leader,* 113999 (Ornament)

$40.00 $37.00
$39.00 $35.00

Suspended 1991, Issue Price $13.50, '88

Purchased ___________

Price $ ___________

☐ *My Love Will Never Let You Go,* 114006 (Ornament)

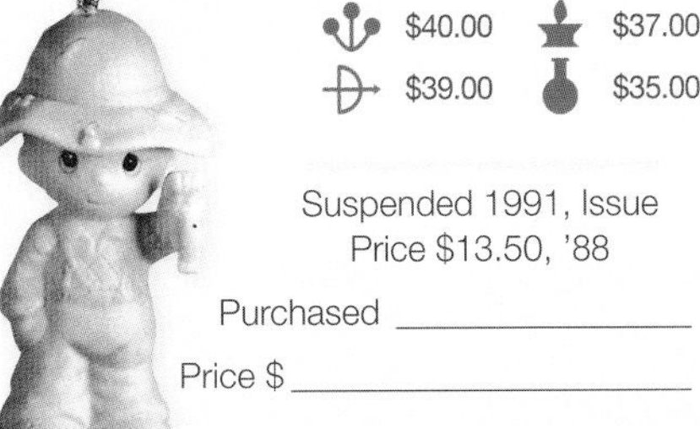

$40.00 $37.00
$39.00 $35.00

Suspended 1991, Issue Price $13.50, '88

Purchased ___________

Price $ ___________

☐ *If The Shoe Fits, Buy It!* 114010

$40.00
$40.00 $40.00
$40.00 $40.00
$40.00 $40.00

Open, Issue Price $40.00, '03

Purchased ___________

Price $ ___________

☐ *I'm Sorry,* 114011

$30.00
$30.00
$30.00
$30.00
$30.00
$30.00
$30.00

Open, Issue Price $30.00, '03

Purchased ________, Price $ ___________

☐ *No Rest For The Weary,* 114012

$35.00 $35.00
$35.00 $35.00
$35.00 $35.00
$35.00

Open, Issue Price $35.00, '03

Purchased ________

Price $ ________

☐ *You Are The Sunshine Of My Life,* 114013

$35.00
$35.00
$35.00
$35.00
$35.00
$35.00
$35.00

Open, Issue Price $35.00, '03

Purchased ________, Price $ ___________

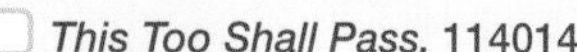

This Too Shall Pass, 114014

$75.00 · $70.00 · $65.00 · $63.00 · $60.00 · $58.00 · $55.00 · $53.00 · $50.00 · $48.00 · $45.00 · $43.00 · $43.00

Retired 1999, Issue Price $23.00, '88

Purchased ________, Price $ ___________

You're Due For A Lifetime Of Happiness, 114015

$37.50 · $37.50 · $37.50 · $37.50 · $37.50 · $37.50 · $37.50

Open, Issue Price $37.50, '03

Purchased ________, Price $ ___________

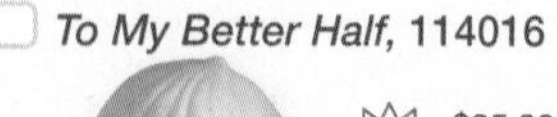

To My Better Half, 114016

$35.00 · $35.00 · $35.00 · $35.00 · $35.00 · $35.00 · $35.00

Open, Issue Price $35.00, '03

Purchased___________

Price $ ____________

Our Love Is Built On A Strong Foundation, 114017

$35.00 · $35.00 · $35.00 · $35.00 · $35.00 · $35.00 · $35.00

Open, Issue Price $35.00, '03

Purchased ___________

Price $___________

Dear Friend, My Love For You Will Never Fade Away, 114018

$60.00 · $60.00 · $60.00 · $60.00 · $60.00

Open, Issue Price $60.00, '03

Purchased ________, Price $ ___________

Friends Of A Feather Shop Together, 114019

$55.00 · $55.00 · $55.00 · $55.00 · $55.00 · $35.00 · $35.00

Open, Issue Price $55.00, '03

Purchased ________, Price $ ___________

Let's Always Preserve Our Friendship, 114020

$37.50 · $37.50 · $37.50 · $37.50 · $37.50 · $37.50 · $37.50

Open, Issue Price $37.50, '03

Purchased ___________

Price $ ___________

Happy Birthday To Our Love, 114021

$50.00 · $50.00 · $50.00 · $50.00 · $50.00 · $50.00 · $50.00

Open, Issue Price $50.00, '03

Purchased ________, Price $ ___________

The Good Lord Has Blessed Us Tenfold, 114022

$265.00 · $255.00

Limited 1988, Issue Price $90.00, '88

Tenth Anniversary Commemorative

Purchased ________, Price $ ___________

Nothing Is Stronger Than Our Love, 114023

$30.00 · $30.00

Limited 2004, Issue Price $30.00, '03

Purchased ________, Price $ ___________

You Arrr A Treasure To Me, 114026

$75.00 · $70.00 · $70.00

Limited Ed., Issue Price $50.00, '03

2004 Event Exlcusive

Purchased ________, Price $ ___________

Hope Blooms In A Garden Of Glory, 114027

$55.00
$55.00

Limited Ed. 7,500, Issue Price $45.00, '03
Series: *Spring Is In Bloom*

Purchased ____________
Price $____________

Kindness Of Spirit Knows No Bounds, 114028

$55.00
$55.00

Limited Ed. 7,500, Issue Price $45.00, '03
Series: *Spring Is In Bloom*

Purchased ____________
Price $ ____________

Humble Prayers Make Hearts Bloom, 114029

$55.00
$55.00

Limited Ed. 7,500, Issue Price $45.00, '03
Series: *Spring Is In Bloom*

Purchased ________, Price $ ____________

Dreams Bloom With A Seed Of Faith, 114031

$55.00
$55.00

Limited Ed. 7,500, Issue Price $45.00, '03
Series: *Spring Is In Bloom*

Purchased ________, Price $ ____________

I Love You More Every Day, 114032

$35.00 $35.00
$35.00 $35.00
$35.00 $35.00
$35.00

Open, Issue Price $35.00, '03

Purchased ____________
Price $____________

Friends Make Life More Fun, 114918

$100.00
$100.00
$100.00

Retired 2005, Issue Price $80.00, '03
Boys & Girls Club Commemorative

Purchased ________, Price $ ____________

I Will Never Leaf You, 114958

$40.00 $40.00
$40.00 $40.00
$40.00

Open, Issue Price $40.00, '05

Purchased ____________
Price $ ____________

You Are My Main Event! 115231

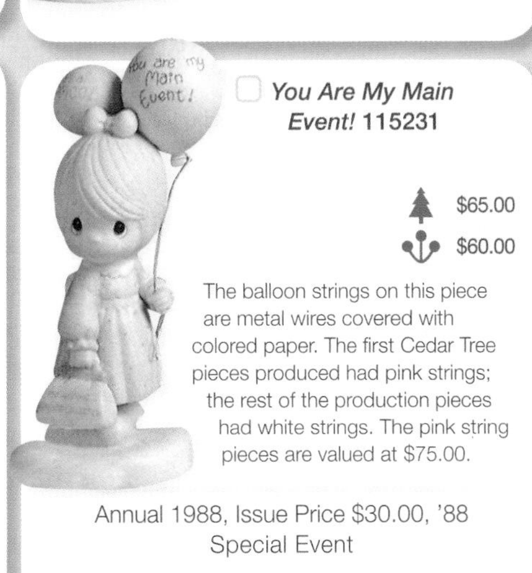

$65.00
$60.00

The balloon strings on this piece are metal wires covered with colored paper. The first Cedar Tree pieces produced had pink strings; the rest of the production pieces had white strings. The pink string pieces are valued at $75.00.

Annual 1988, Issue Price $30.00, '88
Special Event

Purchased ________, Price $ ____________

Your Love Reigns Forever In My Heart, 115248

UM 50.00 $45.00
$45.00 $45.00
$45.00 $45.00

Open, Issue Price $45.00, '03
Chapel Exclusive

Purchased ____________
Price $____________

Celebrating 25 Years Of Sunshine And Smiles, 115272 (Medallion)

$250.00

Given to those who went on the 25th Anniversary Cruise to the Caribbean in May 2003.

Limited Ed. 2003, Issue Price Gift, '03

Purchased ________, Price $ ____________

Some Bunny's Sleeping, 115274

$40.00
$38.00
$35.00
$34.00
$33.00
$32.00
$31.00
$30.00
$29.00

Suspended 1996, Issue Price $15.00, '88
Nativity Addition

Purchased ________, Price $ ____________

Baby's First Christmas, 115282 (Ornament)

$35.00

Dated Annual 1988, Issue Price $15.00, '88

Purchased ________, Price $ ____________

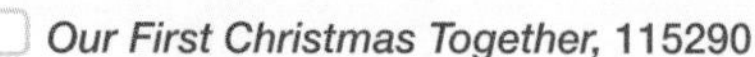

☐ *Our First Christmas Together,* 115290

$90.00
$85.00
$80.00
$75.00

Suspended 1991, Issue Price $50.00, '88

Purchased ________, Price $ ___________

☐ *Time To Wish You A Merry Christmas,* 115304 (Bell)

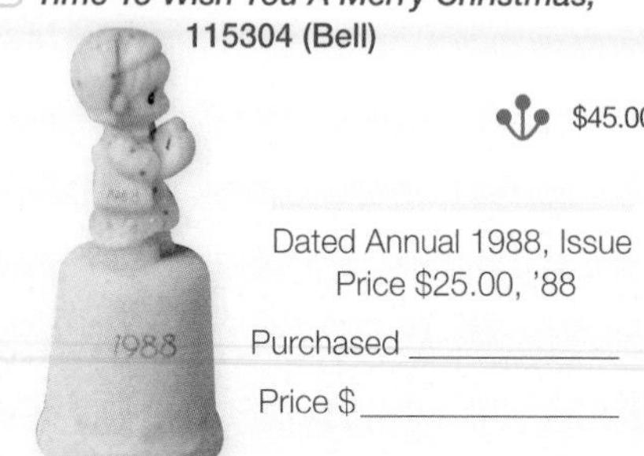

$45.00

Dated Annual 1988, Issue Price $25.00, '88

Purchased ___________

Price $ ______________

☐ *Time To Wish You A Merry Christmas,* 115312 (Thimble)

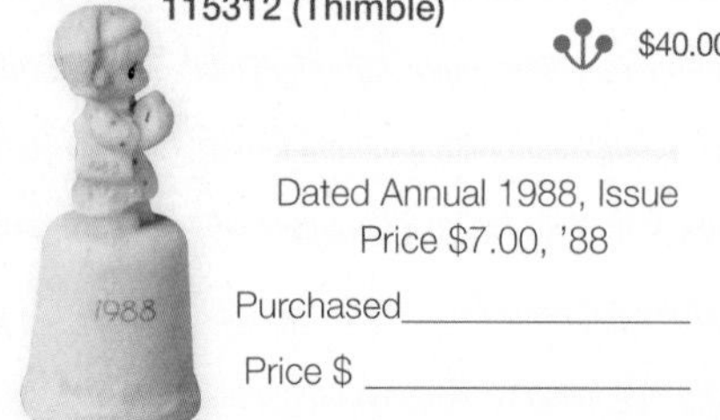

$40.00

Dated Annual 1988, Issue Price $7.00, '88

Purchased ______________

Price $ ________________

☐ *Time To Wish You A Merry Christmas,* 115320 (Ornament)

$55.00

Dated Annual 1988, Issue Price $13.00, '88

Purchased ___________

Price $ _______________

☐ *Time To Wish You A Merry Christmas,* 115339

$60.00

Dated Annual 1988, Issue Price $24.00, '88

Purchased ___________

Price $ ________________

☐ *Collecting Life's Most Precious Moments,* 115476 (Medallion)

$100.00

4-H Commemorative Precious Moments 25th Anniversary Exclusive

Limited Ed. 3,500, Issue Price $65.00, '03

Purchased ________, Price $ ____________

☐ *Blessed Are They That Overcome,* 115479

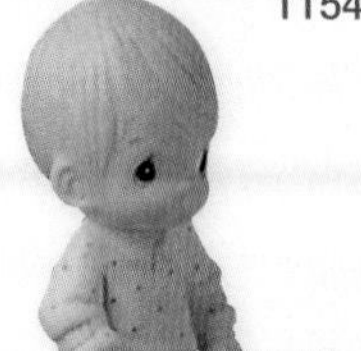

$40.00
$35.00

Easter Seals Lily missing on all decals.

Limited, Issue Price $45.00, '03

Purchased ________, Price $ ___________

☐ *You Are Such A Heavenly Host,* 115625

$50.00

Limited Ed. 5,000, Issue Price $37.50, '03 2003 Fall Catalog Exclusive

Purchased __________

Price $ ______________

☐ *Let's Sea Where This Friendship Takes Us,* 115654

$45.00
$45.00
$45.00

Retired, Issue Price $45.00, '04 Series: *Sea Of Friendship* — Fourth Series

Purchased______________

Price $ ________________

☐ *La Quinceañera,* 115871

$45.00
$45.00
$45.00
$45.00
$45.00

Open, Issue Price $27.50, '88

Purchased_______

Price $ __________

☐ *I Picked You As My Friend,* 115873

$40.00

Limited Ed., Issue Price $40.00, '03 Carlton Cards Retail Exclusive

Purchased ________, Price $ ___________

☐ *Love From The First Impression — Boy,* 115898

Includes a coupon book that can be personalized.

$30.00
$30.00
$30.00
$30.00
$30.00
$30.00
$30.00

Open, Issue Price $30.00, '04

Purchased ________, Price $ ___________

☐ *Love From The First Impression — Girl,* 115899

Includes a coupon book that can be personalized.

$30.00
$30.00
$30.00
$30.00
$30.00

Open, Issue Price $30.00, '04

Purchased ________, Price $ ___________

Mommy & Me — Boy, 115900

$27.50 $27.50 $27.50
$27.50 $27.50
$27.50 $27.50

Open, Issue Price $25.00, '04

Purchased ______________

Price $ ______________

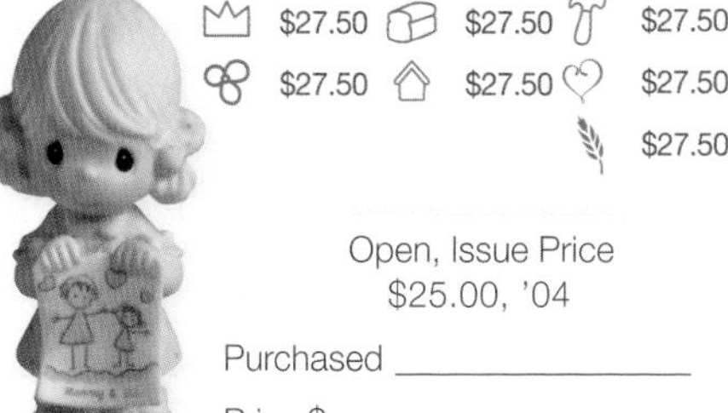

Mommy & Me — Girl, 115901

$27.50 $27.50 $27.50
$27.50 $27.50 $27.50
$27.50

Open, Issue Price $25.00, '04

Purchased ______________

Price $ ______________

Grandma & Me — Boy, 115902

$27.50 $27.50 $27.50
$27.50 $27.50 $27.50
$27.50

Open, Issue Price $25.00, '04

Purchased ______________

Price $ ______________

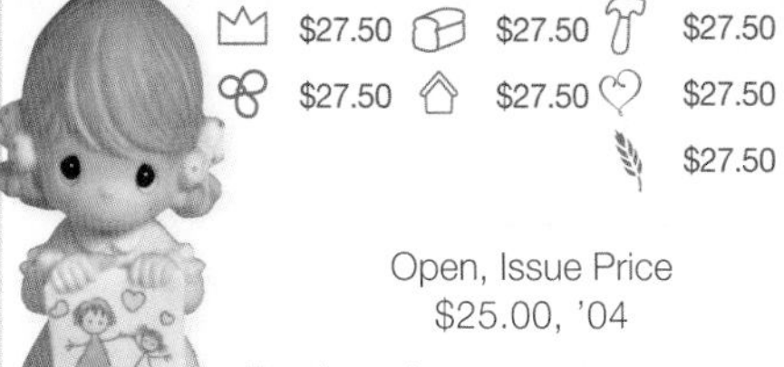

Grandma & Me — Girl, 115903

$27.50 $27.50 $27.50
$27.50 $27.50 $27.50
$27.50

Open, Issue Price $25.00, '04

Purchased ______________

Price $ ______________

Godmother & Me — Boy, 115904

$25.00 $25.00
$25.00 $25.00
$25.00 $27.50
$27.50

Open, Issue Price $25.00, '04

Purchased ______________

Price $ ______________

Godmother & Me — Girl, 115905

$27.50 $27.50 $27.50
$27.50 $27.50 $27.50
$27.50

Open, Issue Price $25.00, '04

Purchased ______________

Price $ ______________

Like Father, Like Son, 115906

$60.00
$55.00
$55.00
$55.00
$55.00
$55.00
$55.00

Open, Issue Price $55.00, '04

Purchased ________, Price $ ________

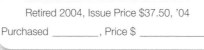

How Do You Spell Mom, 115907

$27.50 $27.50

Retired 2004, Issue Price $37.50, '04

Purchased ________, Price $ ________

Our Love Was Meant To Be, 115909

$50.00
$50.00
$50.00
$50.00
$50.00
$50.00
$50.00

Open, Issue Price $50.00, '04

Purchased ________, Price $ ________

A Whole Year Filled With Special Moments — First Anniversary, 115910

$50.00
$50.00
$50.00
$50.00
$50.00
$50.00
$50.00

Open, Issue Price $50.00, '04

Purchased ________, Price $ ________

Our Love Still Sparkles In Your Eyes — 25th Anniversary, 115911

$50.00
$50.00
$50.00
$50.00
$50.00
$50.00
$50.00

Open, Issue Price $50.00, '04

Purchased ________, Price $ ________

We Share A Love Forever Young — 50th Anniversary, 115912

$50.00
$50.00 $50.00
$50.00
$50.00
$50.00
$50.00

Open, Issue Price $50.00, '04

Purchased ________

Price $ ________

Orange You The Sweetest Thing, 115913

$45.00
$40.00

Limited Ed. 7,500, Issue Price $37.50, '04

Series: *Fruitful Delights*

Purchased ________

Price $ ________

☐ *You're A-peeling To Me,* 115914

$45.00
$40.00

Limited Ed. 7,500, Issue Price $37.50, '04
Series: *Fruitful Delights*

Purchased__________
Price $__________

☐ *You Are The Apple Of My Eye,* 115915

$45.00
$40.00

Limited Ed. 7,500, Issue Price $37.50, '04
Series: *Fruitful Delights*

Purchased__________
Price $__________

☐ *You Are The Apple Of My Eye,* 115915Y

Error: Has yellow apple. Correct piece has red apple.

$90.00

Limited Ed., Issue Price $37.50, '04
Series: *Fruitful Delights*

Purchased __________
Price $ __________

☐ *You're Pear-fectly Sweet,* 115917

$45.00
$40.00

Limited Ed. 7,500, Issue Price $37.50, '04
Series: *Fruitful Delights*

Purchased__________
Price $__________

☐ *You're Just Peachy,* 115918

$45.00
$40.00

Limited Ed. 7,500, Issue Price $37.50, '04
Series: *Fruitful Delights*

Purchased__________
Price $ __________

☐ *Girls Rule,* 115919

$35.00
$35.00
$35.00
$35.00
$35.00
$35.00
$35.00

Open, Issue Price $35.00, '04

Purchased ________, Price $ __________

☐ *Sixteen…Sweet!* 115920

$37.50
$37.50
$37.50
$37.50
$37.50
$37.50
$37.50

Open, Issue Price $37.50, '04

Purchased__________
Price $__________

☐ *A Bright And Shining Moment,* 115921

$35.00
$35.00

Limited Ed., Issue Price $35.00, '04
CCR & DSR Event Piece

Purchased__________
Price $__________

☐ *May Love Blossom Around You,* 115922

$150.00
$150.00
$150.00

Limited Ed. 3,500, Issue Price $150.00, '04

Purchased ________, Price $ __________

☐ *A Special Moment Just For You,* 115923

$45.00 $45.00

Limited Ed., Issue Price $45.00, '04
CCR Exclusive

Purchased__________
Price $__________

☐ *May Love Blossom Around You,* 115925 (Ornament)

$20.00
$20.00

Limited Ed., Issue Price $35.00, '04
CCR Exclusive

Purchased ________, Price $ __________

☐ *Happiness Is Being A Mom,* 115926

$50.00 $50.00
$50.00 $50.00
$50.00

Limited Ed., Issue Price $50.00, '05

Purchased __________
Price $__________

☐ *Happiness Is Being A Mom,* 115926C

$50.00 $50.00

Limited Ed., Issue Price $50.00, '04
Carlton Cards and American Greetings Early Release

Purchased ________, Price $ __________

☐ *Sprinkled With Kindness,* **115927**

$37.50
$37.50

Limited Ed., Issue Price $37.50, '03
GCC Catalog Exclusive

Purchased ________, Price $ ___________

☐ *A Basket Full Of Blessings,* **116267**

UM $35.00
$35.00
$35.00
$35.00
$35.00
$35.00

Received free with application for Precious Moments Platinum Plus credit card.

Limited Ed., Gift, '05

Purchased ________, Price $ ___________

☐ *A Mother's Love Brings Sweet Serenity,* **116269**

$30.00
$30.00
$30.00
$30.00

Open, Issue Price $30.00, '04
Hallmark Exclusive

Purchased ________, Price $ ___________

☐ *Express Who You Are And You'll Be A Star,* **116611**

$35.00
$35.00

Limited Ed., Issue Price $35.00, '04
2004 Authorized Dealer Exclusive

Purchased ________, Price $ ___________

☐ *Friends Let You Be You,* **116612**

$50.00
$50.00

Limited Ed., Issue Price $30.00, '04
2004 *PM Rocks* Tour Exclusive

Purchased __________

Price $ ___________

☐ *Christmas Around The World,* **116710**

UM $60.00
$60.00

Limited Ed. 1,100, Issue Price $35.00, '03
2003 Christmas Event

Purchased __________

Price $ ______________

☐ *Praise Him With The Sound Of The Trumpet,* **116712**

UM $40.00
$37.50
$37.50
$37.50
$37.50
$37.50
$37.50

Open, Issue Price $37.50, '04
Chapel Exclusive

Purchased__________

Price $___________

☐ *It's Your Birthday, Live It Large,* **116945**

$26.50
$26.50
$26.50
$26.50
$26.50
$26.50
$26.50

Open, Issue Price $25.00, '03
Series: *Birthday Train* — Age 14

Purchased ________, Price $ ___________

☐ *It's Your Birthday, Go Bananas,* **116946**

$26.50
$26.50
$26.50
$26.50
$26.50
$26.50
$26.50

Open, Issue Price $25.00, '03
Series: *Birthday Train* — Age 15

Purchased ________, Price $ ___________

☐ *16 And Feline Fine,* **116948**

$26.50
$26.50
$26.50
$26.50
$26.50
$26.50
$26.50

Open, Issue Price $25.00, '03
Series: *Birthday Train* — Age 16

Purchased ________, Price $ ___________

☐ *A Banner Of Hope, A Symbol Of Pride,* **117581**

$40.00
$40.00
$40.00
$40.00
$40.00

Open, Issue Price $40.00, '05

Purchased_________

Price $___________

S'Mitten With The Christmas Spirit, 117784 (Ornament)

UM $30.00
$25.00

Dated Annual 2004, Issue Price $24.00, '04

Purchased ________

Price $ ________

S'Mitten With The Christmas Spirit, 117785

$40.00

Dated Annual 2004, Issue Price $35.00, '04

Purchased ________, Price $ ________

Our First Christmas Together, 117786 (Ornament)

$30.00

Dated Annual 2004, Issue Price $25.00, '04

Purchased ________

Price $________

Baby's First Christmas — Boy, 117787 (Ornament)

$25.00

Dated Annual 2004, Issue Price $20.00, '04

Purchased ________

Price $________

Baby's First Christmas — Girl, 117788 (Ornament)

$25.00

Dated Annual 2004, Issue Price $20.00, '04

Purchased ________

Price $ ________

Thoughts Of You Are So Heartwarming, 117789 (Ornament)

$33.00

Dated Annual 2004, Issue Price $30.00, '04

Purchased ________

Price $ ________

Bea-ver-y Good This Year, 117790 (Ornament)

$25.00

Dated Annual 2004, Issue Price $20.00, '04

Purchased________

Price $ ________

Wise Men Still Seek Him, 117791

$20.00
$20.00
$20.00
$20.00
$20.00
$20.00

Open, Issue Price $20.00, '04
Mini Nativity Addition

Purchased ________, Price $ ________

Tidings Of Comforter & Joy, 117792

$50.00
$50.00
$50.00
$50.00
$50.00
$50.00

Open, Issue Price $50.00, '04

Purchased ________, Price $ ________

Bringing You The Gift Of Peace, 117793

$50.00
$50.00

Limited Ed. 10,000, Issue Price $45.00, '04
Series: *Heavenly Angels*

Purchased ________

Price $ ________

Simple Joys Put A Song In Your Heart, 117794

$50.00
$50.00

Limited Ed. 10,000, Issue Price $45.00, '04
Series: *Heavenly Angels*

Purchased________

Price $ ________

All Wrapped Up With Love, 117795

$50.00
$50.00

Limited Ed. 10,000, Issue Price $45.00, '04
Series: *Heavenly Angels*

Purchased________

Price $ ________

A Little Help Goes A Long Way, 117796

$45.00
$45.00
$45.00
$45.00
$45.00
$45.00

Open, Issue Price $45.00, '04

Purchased ________, Price $ ________

I'm Gonna Stick With You, 117797

$40.00
$40.00
$40.00
$40.00
$40.00
$40.00

Open, Issue Price $40.00, '04

Purchased ________, Price $ ___________

Remember, We're In It Together, 117800

$55.00
$55.00
$55.00
$55.00
$55.00
$55.00

Open, Issue Price $50.00, '04

Purchased ________, Price $ ___________

The World Is A Stage Featuring Precious Moments, 118259 (Musical)

$600.00

Limited Ed. 1,000, Issue Price $125.00, '03
25th Anniversary QVC Exclusive

Purchased ________, Price $ ___________

T'was The Night Before Christmas, 117798

$125.00
$125.00

Limited Ed., Issue Price $125.00, '04
Set of 4

Purchased ________, Price $ ___________

A Grandma's Love Is One Size Fits All, 117801

$35.00 $35.00
$35.00 $35.00
$35.00 $35.00

Open, Issue Price
$35.00, '04

Purchased ___________

Price $ ___________

Beautiful And Blushing, My Baby's Now A Bride, 117802

$55.00
$55.00
$55.00
$55.00
$55.00
$55.00

Open, Issue Price $50.00, '04

Purchased ________, Price $ ___________

Crown Him King Of Kings, 118262

$32.50 $32.50
$32.50 $32.50
$32.50 $32.50

Open, Issue Price
$32.50, '04
Nativity Addition

Purchased ___________

Price $ ___________

Crown Him King Of Kings, 118263

$32.50 $32.50
$32.50 $32.50
$32.50 $32.50

Open, Issue Price $32.50, '04
Nativity Addition

Purchased ________, Price $ ___________

Dance To Your Own Beat, 117799

$32.50 $32.50
$32.50 $32.50
$32.50 $32.50

Open, Issue Price
$30.00, '04

Purchased ___________

Price $___________

There's Snow Place Like Home, 118129

$40.00
$40.00

Limited Ed., Issue
Price $40.00, '04
Special Issue and Limited Edition First Quarter Exclusive

Purchased ___________

Price $___________

Crown Him King Of Kings, 118264

$32.50 $32.50 $32.50
$32.50 $32.50
$32.50

Open, Issue Price
$32.50, '04
Nativity Addition

Purchased ________, Price $ ___________

Note To Self: Take Time For Me, 118266

$37.50 $37.50
$37.50 $37.50
$37.50 $37.50

Open, Issue Price
$37.50, '04

Purchased ________

Price $ ________

Happy Hula Days, 118267 (Ornament)

$20.00 $20.00
$20.00 $20.00

Open, Issue Price
$20.00, '04

Purchased ________

Price $________

Wishing You A Heavenly Holiday, 118301

$50.00
$50.00
$50.00
$50.00
$50.00

Also issued in 2005 as a Carlton Card Exclusive, with Bread mark and value of $50.00.

Open, Issue Price $50.00, '06

Purchased ________, Price $ ________

Nature Provides Us With Such Sweet Pleasures, 118302

$45.00

Limited Ed., Issue Price $45.00, '04
Canadian Exclusive

Purchased ________, Price $ ________

You Make My Heart Soar, 118316

$35.00
$35.00

Limited, Issue Price $35.00, '04
2004 Special Issue

Purchased ________, Price $ ________

I'm There For You Rain Or Shine, 118361

$32.50 $32.50
$32.50 $32.50
$32.50 $32.50
$32.50

Open, Issue Price $32.50, '04

Purchased ________

Price $ ________

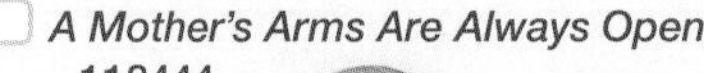

A Mother's Arms Are Always Open, 118444

$50.00
$50.00
$50.00
$50.00
$50.00
$50.00
$50.00

Open, Issue Price $50.00, '04

Purchased ________, Price $ ________

Loving, 118872

Three-piece set with Caring and Sharing.

$55.00
$55.00

Limited Ed. 3,500, Issue Price $55.00, '03
eBay Exclusive

Purchased ________, Price $ ________

Caring, 118873

Three-piece set with Loving and Sharing.

$55.00
$55.00

Limited Ed. 3,500, Issue Price $45.00, '04
DS & CCR Exclusive

Purchased ________, Price $ ________

Sharing, 118874

$55.00
$55.00

Three-piece set with Loving and Caring.

Limited Ed. 3,500, Issue Price $40.00, '04
DS & CCR Exclusive

Purchased ________, Price $ ________

Bringing You My Heart, 118728

$50.00 $50.00

Retired, Issue Price $50.00, '04

Purchased ________, Price $ ________

Friendship Has No Limits, 118875

UM $35.00 | $35.00
$35.00 | $35.00

Gift from credit card company with approval.

Limited Ed., Gift, '03

Purchased________

Price $ ________

Our Friendship's In The Bag, 119094

$30.00 | $30.00
$30.00 | $30.00
$30.00 | $30.00

Open, Issue Price $30.00, '04

Purchased________

Price $ ________

May Your Dreams Be Warm & Fuzzy, 119374

Comes with an 11 oz. cocoa mug.

$35.00
$35.00
$35.00
$35.00
$35.00
$35.00

Open, Issue Price $35.00, '04
Set of 2

Purchased ________, Price $ ________

Birthday Train Frame, 119424

$20.00 | $20.00
$20.00 | $20.00
$20.00 | $20.00
$20.00

Open, Issue Price $20.00, '04
Series: *Birthday Train*

Purchased ________

Price $________

You've Made An Impression On Me, 119434

$37.50 | $37.50
$37.50 | $37.50
$37.50 | $37.50

Open, Issue Price $37.50, '04

Purchased________

Price $ ________

Sisters In Purple, 119435

$40.00 | $40.00
$40.00 | $40.00
$40.00 | $40.00

Open, Issue Price $40.00, '04

Purchased______

Price $ ________

Mom, No One Measures Up To You, 119436

$35.00
$35.00
$35.00

Hallmark/ Kirlin's Exclusive

Limited Ed., Issue Price $35.00, '04

Purchased ________

Price $ ________

Take My Hand, 119460

$45.00
$45.00
$45.00
$45.00

Includes "Pop Tab" keeper box.

Limited Ed., Issue Price $40.00, '05
Ronald McDonald House Charities

Purchased ________, Price $ ________

Heavenly Angels, 119559

$225.00 | $225.00

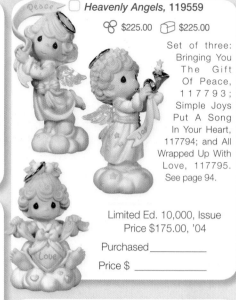

Set of three: Bringing You The Gift Of Peace, 117793; Simple Joys Put A Song In Your Heart, 117794; and All Wrapped Up With Love, 117795. See page 94.

Limited Ed. 10,000, Issue Price $175.00, '04

Purchased________

Price $ ________

You Are Always Here, 119642

UM $65.00
$60.00
$55.00
$45.00
$45.00
$45.00
$45.00

Retired, Issue Price $45.00, '04
Chapel Exclusive

Purchased ________, Price $ ________

Uphold His Name, 119643

UM $30.00 | $30.00
$30.00 | $30.00
$30.00 | $30.00
$30.00

Open, Issue Price $30.00, '04
Chapel Exclusive

Purchased ________

Price $ ________

Saving Sweet Memories, 119836

Only available 12/01/04 on eBay.

$50.00

Limited Ed. 2,500, Issue Price $40.00, '04
eBay Exclusive

Purchased ________

Price $ ________

Messenger Of Love, 119837

$20.00 $20.00
$20.00 $20.00

Open, Issue Price $20.00, '04

Purchased ____________

Price $ ______________

Messenger Of Love, 119838

$20.00 $20.00
$20.00 $20.00

Open, Issue Price $20.00, '04

Purchased ____________

Price $ ______________

Uphold His Name, 119839 (Ornament)

$20.00
UM $20.00 $20.00
$20.00 $20.00
$20.00 $20.00

Open, Issue Price $20.00, '04

Purchased ____________

Price $______________

We're All Cut From The Same Cloth, 119840

UM $75.00

Limited Ed. 1,100, Issue Price $35.00, '04
Chapel Exclusive, 2004 Licensee Summer Event

Purchased ________, Price $ ___________

Throwing A Holiday Wish Your Way, 119841

UM $60.00

Limited Ed. 1,100, Issue Price $35.00, '04
2004 Chapel Christmas Event

Purchased ________, Price $ ___________

Baby (Boy Standing), 119916

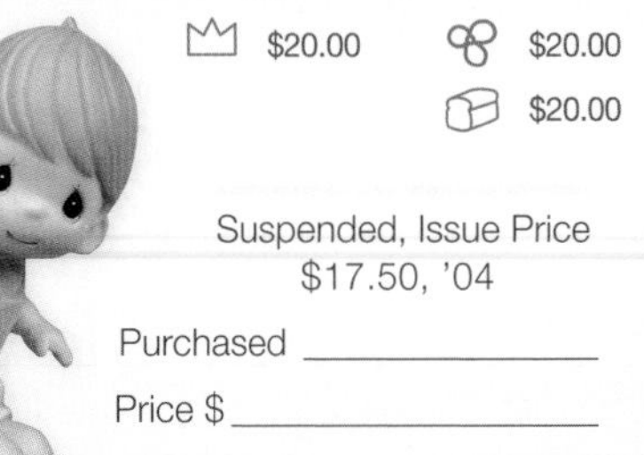

$20.00 $20.00
$20.00

Suspended, Issue Price $17.50, '04

Purchased ______________

Price $______________

Baby (Boy Kneeling), 119917

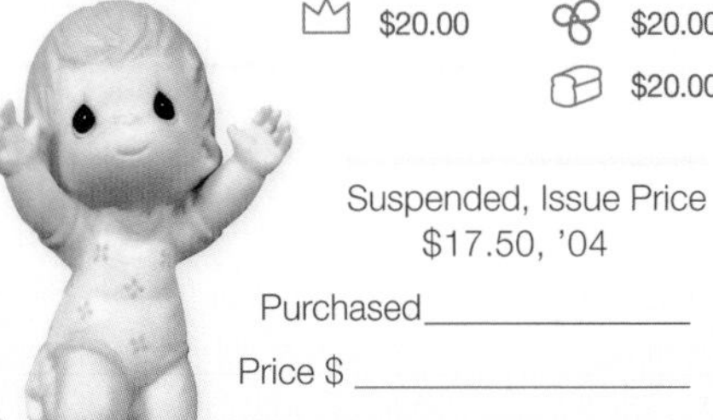

$20.00 $20.00
$20.00

Suspended, Issue Price $17.50, '04

Purchased______________

Price $ ______________

Baby (Girl Sitting), 119918

$20.00 $20.00
$20.00

Suspended, Issue Price $17.50, '04

Purchased__________

Price $ __________

Baby (Girl Standing), 119919

$20.00 $20.00
$20.00

Suspended, Issue Price $17.50, '04

Purchased ________, Price $ ___________

Baby (Boy Crawling), 119920

$20.00 $20.00
$20.00

Suspended, Issue Price $17.50, '04

Purchased ________, Price $ ___________

Baby (Girl Crawling), 119921

$20.00 $20.00
$20.00

Suspended, Issue Price $17.50, '04

Purchased __________

Price $__________

You Have The Sweetest Smile, 120007

$32.50
$32.50

Limited Ed., Issue Price $32.50, '04

Purchased ________, Price $ ___________

Mom, Thanks For Always Supporting Our Team, 120008

$110.00
$95.00

Special gift for Precious Moments Day, May 9, 2004, at Wrigley Field.

Limited Ed. 10,000, Gift, '04
Boys & Girls Club of America

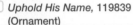

Purchased ________, Price $ ___________

My Last One For You, 120104

$40.00
$40.00

Special Issue, Issue Price $37.50, '04

Purchased ________, Price $ ____________

Purse-suit Of Happiness, 120105

$37.50 $37.50
$37.00 $37.00
$37.50 $37.50

Open, Issue Price $37.50, '04

Purchased ____________

Price $ ____________

Love Is The Color Of Rainbows, 120106

$95.00
$95.00

One Year of Production, Issue Price $50.00, '04

Purchased ________

Price $___________

There's More To Life Than Nine To Five, 120107

$40.00
$40.00
$40.00
$40.00

Open, Issue Price $40.00, '04

Purchased___________

Price $ ___________

Tossing A Little Luck Your Way, 120108

$35.00 $35.00
$35.00 $35.00
$35.00 $35.00

Open, Issue Price $35.00, '04

Purchased _______

Price $ ___________

Just A Little Paws For A Warm Welcome, 120109

$25.00
$25.00
$25.00
$25.00
$25.00
$25.00

Open, Issue Price $25.00, '04

Purchased ________, Price $ ____________

Blessed With A Miracle, 120110

$55.00
$55.00
$55.00
$55.00
$55.00
$55.00

Open, Issue Price $55.00, '04

Purchased ________, Price $ ____________

"Stressed" Is "Desserts" Spelled Backwards, 120112

$35.00 $35.00
$35.00 $35.00
$35.00 $35.00

Open, Issue Price $35.00, '04

Purchased ____________

Price $____________

Wishing You The Sweetest Birthday, 120113

$35.00 $35.00
$35.00 $35.00
$35.00 $35.00

Open, Issue Price $35.00, '04

Purchased ____________

Price $ ____________

Safely Home, 120114

$42.50
$42.50
$42.50
$42.50
$42.50
$42.50

Open, Issue Price $40.00, '04

Purchased ________, Price $ ____________

On A Wing And A Prayer, 120115

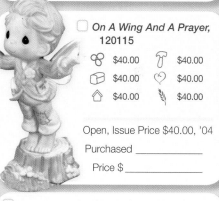

$40.00 $40.00
$40.00 $40.00
$40.00 $40.00

Open, Issue Price $40.00, '04

Purchased ____________

Price $ ____________

Open Your Eyes To All His Blessings, 120116

$40.00
$40.00
$40.00
$40.00
$40.00
$40.00

Open, Issue Price $40.00, '04

Purchased ________, Price $ ____________

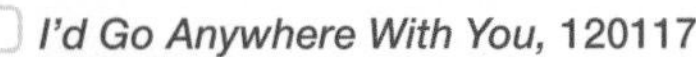

☐ *I'd Go Anywhere With You,* 120117

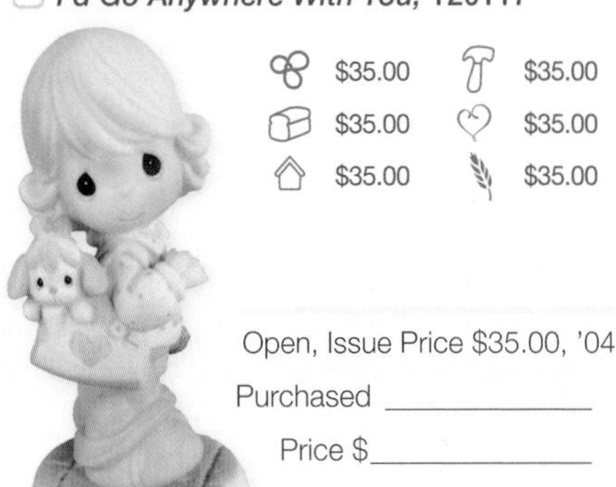

$35.00 $35.00
$35.00 $35.00
$35.00 $35.00

Open, Issue Price $35.00, '04
Purchased ____________
Price $____________

☐ *You Bet Your Boots I Love You,* 120121

$35.00
$35.00

Gift set includes porcelain boot vase.

Retired, Issue Price $30.00, '04
Purchased ________, Price $ ____________

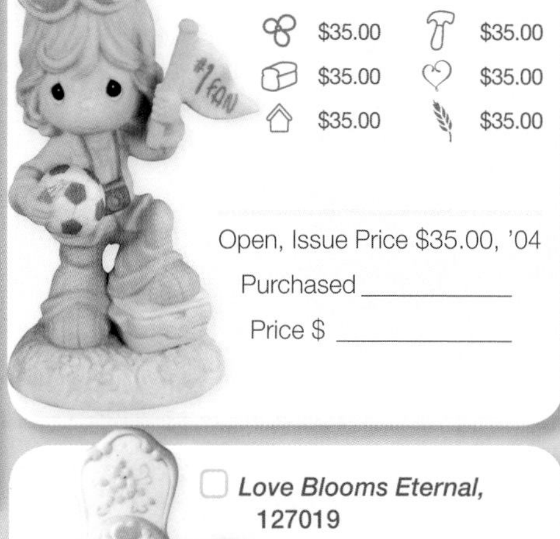

☐ *Always On The Ball,* 120124

$35.00 $35.00
$35.00 $35.00
$35.00 $35.00

Open, Issue Price $35.00, '04
Purchased ____________
Price $ ____________

☐ *I Am Me!* 120118

$32.50 $32.50
$32.50 $32.50
$32.50 $32.50

Open, Issue Price $32.50, '04
Purchased ____________
Price $ ____________

☐ *I've Got A Crush On You,* 120122

$30.00 $30.00
$30.00 $30.00
$30.00 $30.00

Open, Issue Price $30.00, '04
Purchased ________
Price $ ________

☐ *Love Blooms Eternal,* 127019

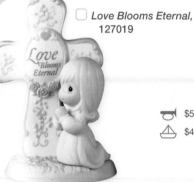

$50.00
$45.00

Dated Annual 1995, Issue Price $35.00, '95
Series: *Dated Cross* — First Issue
Purchased ________, Price $ ____________

☐ *Our Friendship Has Always Been Write On,* 120119

$30.00
$30.00

Comes with a diary.

Open, Issue Price $25.00, '04
Purchased ________, Price $ ____________

☐ *Sharing Fun And Games Together,* 120123

$85.00
$85.00
$85.00
$85.00

Annual 2004, Issue Price $80.00, '04
Boys & Girls Club of America Commemorative
Purchased ________, Price $ ____________

☐ *Congratulations, You Earned Your Stripes,* 127809

$35.00
$30.00
$28.00
$25.00
$25.00
$20.00
$20.00
$20.00

Retired 2002, Issue Price $15.00, '95
Series: *Two By Two*
Purchased ________, Price $ ____________

☐ *Love Grows Where You Plant It,* 120120

$32.50
$32.50
$32.50
$32.50
$32.50
$32.50

Open, Issue Price $32.50, '04
Purchased ________, Price $ ____________

☐ *He Shall Lead The Children Into The 21st Century,* 127930

★ $350.00

Available exclusively at the Enesco "A Toast To 2000" Millennium Event held at 4,500 retail locations across the country on 10/29/99. Two artists' proofs (127930A) were sold through silent auction at each location to benefit breast cancer awareness. These were marked with a star and are valued at $1,000.00.

Limited Ed. 1999, Issue Price $160.00, '99
Set of 5
Purchased ______
Price $ ______

An Event Showered With Love, ☐ 128295A, ☐ 128295B, ☐ 128295C, ☐ 128295D (Ornament)

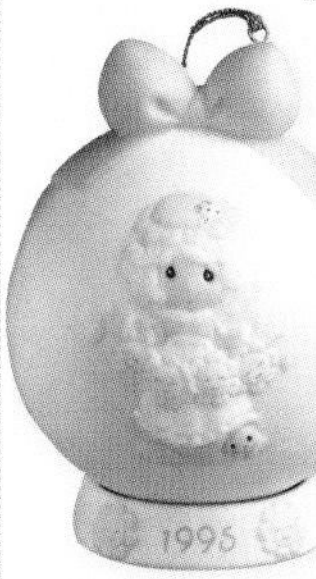

$110.00

Dated Annual 1994, Issue Price $30.00, '94
Regional Event — Wisconsin, New York, Texas, and California
Approximately 1,000 each distributed

Purchased ________, Price $ ____________

☐ *Dreams Really Do Come True,* 128309

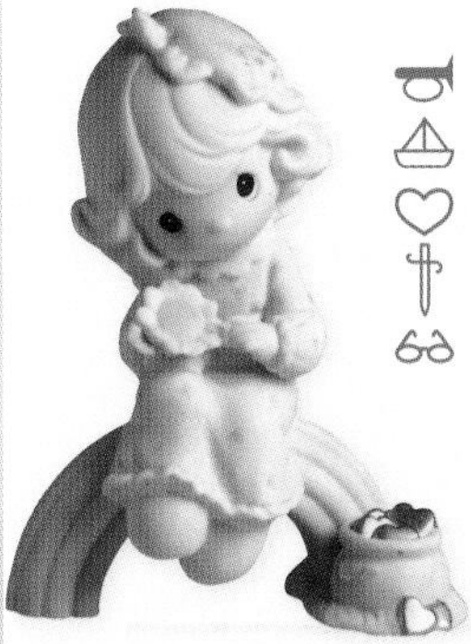

$70.00
$65.00
$63.00
$60.00
$58.00
$50.00
$48.00
$45.00
$45.00
$43.00
$43.00
$43.00

Suspended, Issue Price $37.50, '95

Purchased ________, Price $ ____________

☐ *Another Year And More Grey Hares,* 128686

$45.00
$43.00
$40.00
$38.00
$35.00
$35.00
$33.00
$33.00
$30.00
$30.00

Retired 2003, Issue Price $17.50, '95
Series: *Birthday Collection*

Purchased ________, Price $ ____________

☐ *Happy Hula Days,* 128694

$35.00
$35.00
$35.00
$35.00
$35.00
$35.00
$35.00
$35.00
$35.00
$35.00
$35.00
$35.00
$35.00
$35.00
$35.00

Open, Issue Price $30.00, '95

Purchased ____________________

Price $ ______________________

☐ *Owl Be Home For Christmas,* 128708 (Ornament)

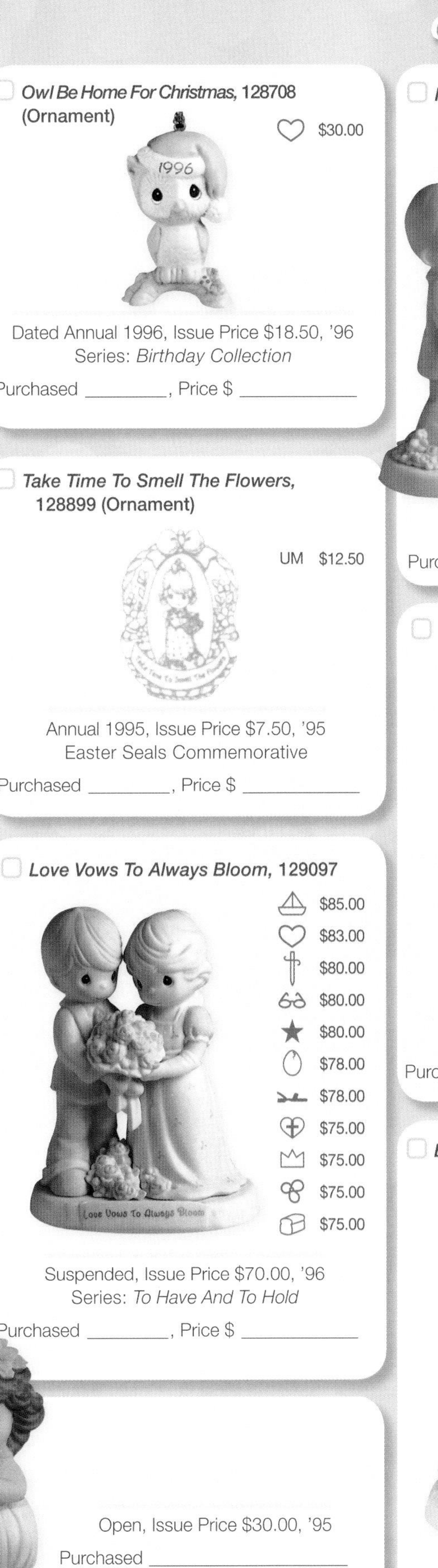

$30.00

Dated Annual 1996, Issue Price $18.50, '96
Series: *Birthday Collection*

Purchased ________, Price $ ____________

☐ *Take Time To Smell The Flowers,* 128899 (Ornament)

UM $12.50

Annual 1995, Issue Price $7.50, '95
Easter Seals Commemorative

Purchased ________, Price $ ____________

☐ *Love Vows To Always Bloom,* 129097

$85.00
$83.00
$80.00
$80.00
$80.00
$78.00
$78.00
$75.00
$75.00
$75.00
$75.00

Suspended, Issue Price $70.00, '96
Series: *To Have And To Hold*

Purchased ________, Price $ ____________

☐ *I Give You My Love Forever True,* 129100

$85.00
$83.00
$80.00
$80.00
$78.00
$78.00
$78.00
$75.00
$75.00
$75.00
$75.00
$75.00
$75.00
$75.00
$75.00
$75.00

Open, Issue Price $70.00, '95

Purchased ________, Price $ ____________

☐ *He Graces The Earth With Abundance,* 129119

$65.00
$63.00
$60.00
$58.00
$55.00
$55.00

Retired 2004, Issue Price $50.00, '99
Series: *New Four Seasons — Fall*

Purchased ________, Price $ ____________

☐ *Beside The Still Waters,* 129127

$75.00
$73.00
$70.00
$68.00
$65.00
$65.00

Retired 2004, Issue Price $50.00, '00
Series: *New Four Seasons — Summer*

Purchased ________, Price $ ____________

☐ ***He Covers The Earth With His Glory*, 129135**

- ★ $65.00
- [egg] $60.00
- [bow & arrow] $58.00
- [heart with cross] $58.00
- [crown] $55.00
- [clover] $55.00

Retired 2004, Issue Price $50.00, '00
Series: *New Four Seasons — Winter*

Purchased ________, Price $ ___________

☐ ***The Beauty Of God Blooms Forever*, 129143**

- ★ $65.00
- [egg] $60.00
- [bow & arrow] $58.00
- [heart with cross] $58.00
- [crown] $55.00
- [clover] $55.00

Retired 2004, Issue Price $50.00, '00
Series: *New Four Seasons — Spring*

Purchased ________, Price $ ___________

☐ ***He Hath Made Everything Beautiful In His Time*, 129151 (Plate)**

- [ship] $55.00

He Hath Made Every Thing Beautiful in His Time
1995

Dated Annual 1995, Issue Price $50.00, '95
Series: Mother's Day — Second Issue

Purchased ________, Price $ ___________

☐ ***Grandpa's Island*, 129259**

- [ship] $225.00
- [heart] $223.00
- [sword] $220.00
- [glasses] $218.00
- ★ $215.00
- [egg] $210.00
- [bow & arrow] $205.00
- [heart with cross] $200.00

Suspended 2002, Issue Price $100.00, '95
Chapel Exclusive

Purchased ________, Price $ ___________

☐ ***Lighting The Way To A Happy Holiday*, 129267**

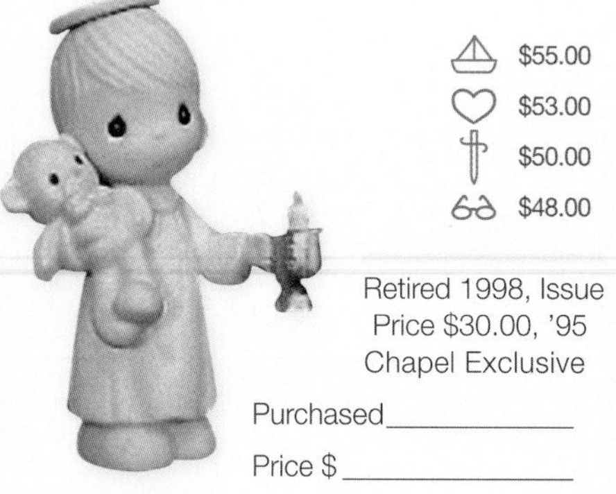

- [ship] $55.00
- [heart] $53.00
- [sword] $50.00
- [glasses] $48.00

Retired 1998, Issue Price $30.00, '95
Chapel Exclusive

Purchased___________

Price $ ___________

☐ ***Lighting The Way To A Happy Holiday*, 129275 (Ornament)**

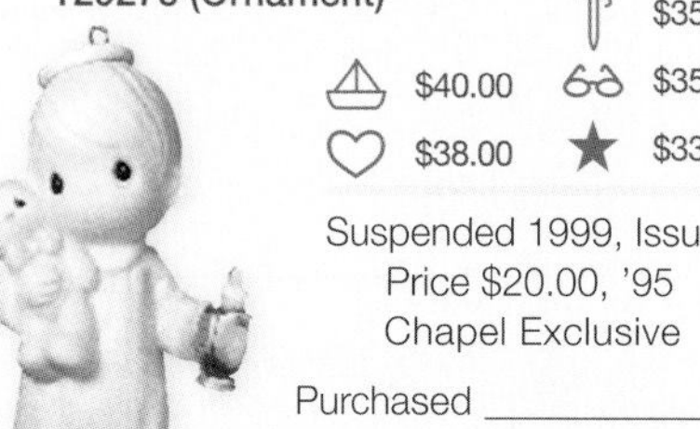

- [ship] $40.00
- [heart] $38.00
- [sword] $35.00
- [glasses] $35.00
- ★ $33.00

Suspended 1999, Issue Price $20.00, '95
Chapel Exclusive

Purchased ___________

Price $ ___________

☐ ***Love Letters In The Sand*, 129488**

- [heart] $75.00
- [sword] $70.00
- [glasses] $68.00
- ★ $65.00
- [egg] $60.00
- [bow & arrow] $55.00
- [heart with cross] $50.00

Retired 2002, Issue Price $35.00, '97

Purchased ________, Price $ ___________

☐ ***Gone But Never Forgotten*, 135976**

- UM $55.00
- [bow & arrow] $53.00
- [heart with cross] $50.00
- [crown] $50.00
- [clover] $50.00
- [box] $50.00
- [house] $50.00
- [hammer] $50.00

Open, Issue Price $50.00, '00
Chapel Exclusive

Purchased ________, Price $ ___________

☐ ***He Is My Salvation*, 135984**

NEED KNOWS NO SEASON
Sharing Is...

- ★ $60.00
- [egg] $58.00

A portion of the proceeds from the sales of this figurine was donated to the Salvation Army.

Retired 2004, Issue Price $45.00, '00

Purchased ________, Price $ ___________

☐ ***Heaven Must Have Sent You*, 135992**

- UM $80.00
- [sword] $78.00
- [glasses] $75.00
- ★ $73.00
- [egg] $70.00
- [bow & arrow] $68.00
- [heart with cross] $65.00

Suspended 2002, Issue Price $45.00, '96
Chapel Exclusive

Purchased ________, Price $ ___________

Going To The Chapel, 136018

UM	$45.00
[Bow]	$40.00
[Cross in Heart]	$35.00
[Crown]	$35.00
[Clover]	$30.00
[Box]	$30.00
[House]	$30.00
[Mushroom]	$30.00

Open, Issue Price $25.00, '02
Chapel Exclusive

Purchased ________, Price $ ____________

It's A Girl, 136204B

[Cross in Heart]	$25.00	[House]	$25.00
[Crown]	$25.00	[Mushroom]	$25.00
[Clover]	$25.00	[Heart Sprout]	$25.00
[Box]	$25.00	[Wheat]	$25.00

Open, Issue Price $22.50, '02
Series: *Growing In Grace* (Brunette)

Purchased ____________

Price $____________

Age 3, 136220

[Boat]	$35.00	[Bow]	$25.00
[Heart]	$32.00	[Cross in Heart]	$25.00
[Cross]	$30.00	[Crown]	$25.00
[Glasses]	$28.00	[Clover]	$25.00
[Star]	$25.00	[Box]	$25.00
[Egg]	$25.00	[House]	$25.00
		[Mushroom]	$25.00
		[Heart Sprout]	$25.00
		[Wheat]	$25.00

Open, Issue Price $25.00, '95
Series: *Growing In Grace* (Blonde)

Purchased ________, Price $ ____________

Age 1, 136190

[Boat]	$35.00	[Egg]	$25.00
[Heart]	$32.00	[Bow]	$25.00
[Cross]	$30.00	[Cross in Heart]	$25.00
[Glasses]	$28.00	[Crown]	$25.00
[Star]	$25.00	[Clover]	$25.00
		[Box]	$25.00
		[House]	$25.00
		[Mushroom]	$25.00
		[Heart Sprout]	$25.00
		[Wheat]	$25.00

Open, Issue Price $25.00, '95
Series: *Growing In Grace* (Blonde)

Purchased ________, Price $ ____________

Age 2, 136212

[Boat]	$35.00	[Bow]	$25.00
[Heart]	$32.00	[Cross in Heart]	$25.00
[Cross]	$30.00	[Crown]	$25.00
[Glasses]	$28.00	[Clover]	$25.00
[Star]	$25.00	[Box]	$25.00
[Egg]	$25.00	[House]	$25.00
		[Mushroom]	$25.00
		[Heart Sprout]	$25.00
		[Wheat]	$25.00

Open, Issue Price $25.00, '95
Series: *Growing In Grace* (Blonde)

Purchased ________, Price $ ____________

Age 3, 136220B

[Cross in Heart]	$25.00
[Crown]	$25.00
[Clover]	$25.00
[Box]	$25.00
[House]	$25.00
[Mushroom]	$25.00
[Heart Sprout]	$25.00
[Wheat]	$25.00

Open, Issue Price $25.00, '02
Series: *Growing In Grace* (Brunette)

Purchased ________, Price $ ____________

Age 1, 136190B

[Cross in Heart]	$25.00
[Crown]	$25.00
[Clover]	$25.00
[Box]	$25.00
[House]	$25.00
[Mushroom]	$25.00
[Heart Sprout]	$25.00
[Wheat]	$25.00

Open, Issue Price $25.00, '02
Series: *Growing In Grace* (Brunette)

Purchased ________, Price $ ____________

Age 2, 136212B

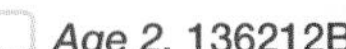

[Cross in Heart]	$25.00
[Crown]	$25.00
[Clover]	$25.00
[Box]	$25.00
[House]	$25.00
[Mushroom]	$25.00
[Heart Sprout]	$25.00
[Wheat]	$25.00

Open, Issue Price $25.00, '02
Series: *Growing In Grace* (Brunette)

Purchased ________, Price $ ____________

Age 4, 136239

[Boat]	$35.00	[Star]	$30.00
[Heart]	$32.00	[Egg]	$30.00
[Cross]	$30.00	[Bow]	$30.00
[Glasses]	$30.00	[Cross in Heart]	$30.00
		[Crown]	$30.00
		[Clover]	$30.00
		[Box]	$30.00
		[House]	$30.00
		[Mushroom]	$30.00
		[Heart Sprout]	$30.00
		[Wheat]	$30.00

Open, Issue Price $27.50, '95
Series: *Growing In Grace* (Blonde)

Purchased ________, Price $ ____________

It's A Girl, 136204

[Boat]	$35.00	[Star]	$25.00	[Crown]	$25.00	[Mushroom]	$25.00
[Heart]	$32.00	[Egg]	$25.00	[Clover]	$25.00	[Heart Sprout]	$25.00
[Cross]	$30.00	[Bow]	$25.00	[Box]	$25.00	[Wheat]	$25.00
[Glasses]	$28.00	[Cross in Heart]	$25.00	[House]	$25.00		

Open, Issue Price $22.50, '95
Series: *Growing In Grace* (Blonde)

Purchased________, Price $ ____________

Age 4, 136239B

$30.00
$30.00
$30.00
$30.00
$30.00
$30.00
$30.00
$30.00

Open, Issue Price $27.50, '95
Series: *Growing In Grace* (Brunette)

Purchased ________, Price $ ____________

Age 6, 136255B

$30.00
$30.00
$30.00
$30.00
$30.00
$30.00
$30.00
$30.00

Open, Issue Price $30.00, '95
Series: *Growing In Grace* (Brunette)

Purchased ________, Price $ ____________

***You Will Always Be Our Hero*, 136271**

$55.00
$50.00

Annual 1995, Issue Price $40.00, '95
Celebrating 50th Anniversary of WWII

Purchased ________, Price $ ____________

Age 5, 136247

$35.00
$32.00
$30.00
$30.00
$30.00
$30.00
$30.00
$30.00
$30.00
$30.00
$30.00
$30.00
$30.00
$30.00
$30.00
$30.00

Open, Issue Price $27.50, '95
Series: *Growing In Grace* (Blonde)

Purchased ________, Price $ ____________

Age 16, 136263

$55.00
$50.00
$48.00
$45.00
$45.00
$45.00
$45.00
$45.00
$45.00
$45.00
$45.00
$45.00
$45.00
$45.00
$45.00
$45.00

Open, Issue Price $45.00, '95
Series: *Growing In Grace* (Blonde)

Purchased ________, Price $ ____________

***Love Makes The World Go 'Round*, 139475**

$450.00

Limited Ed. 15,000, Issue Price $200.00, '95
Century Circle Exclusive
Individually Numbered

Purchased ________, Price $ ____________

Age 5, 136247B

$30.00
$30.00
$30.00
$30.00
$30.00
$30.00
$30.00
$30.00

Open, Issue Price $27.50, '95
Series: *Growing In Grace* (Brunette)

Purchased ____________

Price $ ____________

Age 16, 136263B

$45.00
$45.00
$45.00
$45.00
$45.00
$45.00
$45.00
$45.00

Open, Issue Price $45.00, '95
Series: *Growing In Grace* (Brunette)

Purchased ________, Price $ ____________

***Where Would I Be Without You*, 139491**

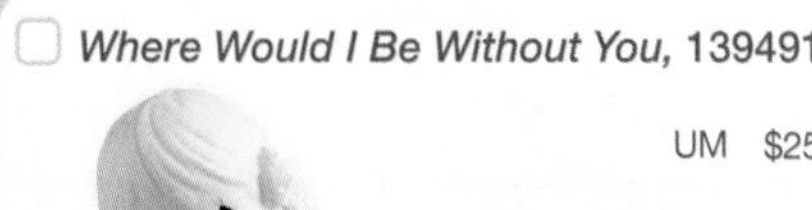

UM $25.00

Open, Issue Price $20.00, '97
Series: *Little Moments*

Purchased ____________

Price $ ____________

Age 6, 136255

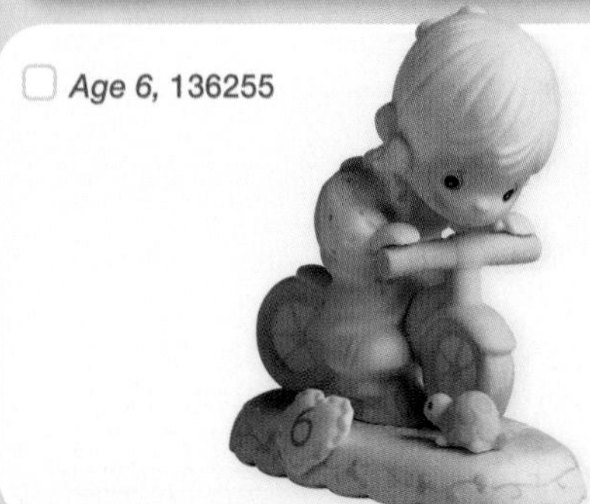

$35.00
$32.00
$30.00
$30.00
$30.00
$30.00
$30.00
$30.00
$30.00
$30.00
$30.00
$30.00
$30.00
$30.00
$30.00

Open, Issue Price $30.00, '95
Series: *Growing In Grace* (Blonde)

Purchased ________, Price $ ____________

***All Things Grow With Love*, 139505**

UM $25.00

Open, Issue Price $20.00, '97
Series: *Little Moments*

Purchased ____________

Price $ ____________

☐ ***You're The Berry Best,*** **139513**

UM $25.00

Open, Issue Price 20.00, '97
Series: *Little Moments*

Purchased ____________

Price $ ____________

☐ ***You Make The World A Sweeter Place,*** **139521**

UM $25.00

Open, Issue Price $20.00, '97
Series: *Little Moments*

Purchased ____________

Price $ ____________

☐ ***You're Forever In My Heart,*** **139548**

UM $25.00

Open, Issue Price $20.00, '97
Series: *Little Moments*

Purchased ________, Price $ ____________

☐ ***Birthday Wishes With Hugs And Kisses,*** **139556**

UM $25.00

Open, Issue Price $20.00, '97
Series: *Little Moments*

Purchased ____________

Price $ ____________

☐ ***You Make My Spirit Soar,*** **139564**

UM $25.00

Open, Issue Price $20.00, '97
Series: *Little Moments*

Purchased ____________

Price $ ____________

☐ ***He Covers The Earth With His Beauty,*** **142654**

△ $48.00

Dated Annual 1995, Issue Price $30.00, '95

Purchased ________, Price $ ____________

☐ ***He Covers The Earth With His Beauty,*** **142662 (Ornament)**

UM $35.00

△ $33.00

Dated Annual 1995, Issue Price $17.00, '95

Purchased ________, Price $ ____________

☐ ***He Covers The Earth With His Beauty,*** **142670 (Plate)**

△ $65.00

Dated Annual 1995, Issue Price $50.00, '95
Series: *The Beauty Of Christmas*
Second Issue

Purchased ________, Price $ ____________

☐ ***He Covers The Earth With His Beauty,*** **142689 (Ornament)**

△ $45.00

Dated Annual 1995, Issue Price $30.00, '95

Purchased ____________

Price $ ____________

☐ ***Our First Christmas Together,*** **142700 (Ornament)**

△ $30.00

Dated Annual 1995, Issue Price $18.50, '95

Purchased ________, Price $ ____________

☐ ***Baby's First Christmas,*** **142719 (Ornament)**

△ $28.00

Dated Annual 1995, Issue Price $17.50, '95

Purchased ________, Price $ ____________

☐ ***Baby's First Christmas,*** **142727 (Ornament)**

△ $28.00

Dated Annual 1995, Issue Price $17.50, '95

Purchased ________, Price $ ____________

☐ *Come Let Us Adore Him,* 142735

$55.00 $50.00 $50.00 $50.00
$53.00 $50.00 $50.00 $50.00
$50.00 $50.00 $50.00 $50.00
$50.00
$50.00

Retired 2008, Issue Price $50.00, '95
Three-piece Nativity Starter Set with Booklet

Purchased ________, Price $ ___________

☐ *Joy From Head To Mistletoe,* 150126 (Ornament)

$28.00 $21.00
$25.00 $21.00
$25.00 $20.00
$23.00 $20.00
$23.00 $19.00

Suspended, Issue Price $17.00, '95

Purchased ________, Price $ ___________

☐ *Come Let Us Adore Him,* 142743

$40.00 $35.00 $35.00
$38.00 $35.00 $35.00
$35.00
$35.00
$35.00
$35.00
$35.00
$35.00
$35.00
$35.00

Retired 2008, Issue Price $35.00, '95
Mini Figurines, 2¾" tall, Set of 3

Purchased ________, Price $ ___________

☐ *I'll Give Him My Heart,* 150088

$80.00
$78.00
$75.00
$70.00

Retired 1998, Issue Price $40.00, '95

Purchased ________, Price $ ___________

☐ *Merry Chrismoose,* 150134 (Ornament)

$35.00

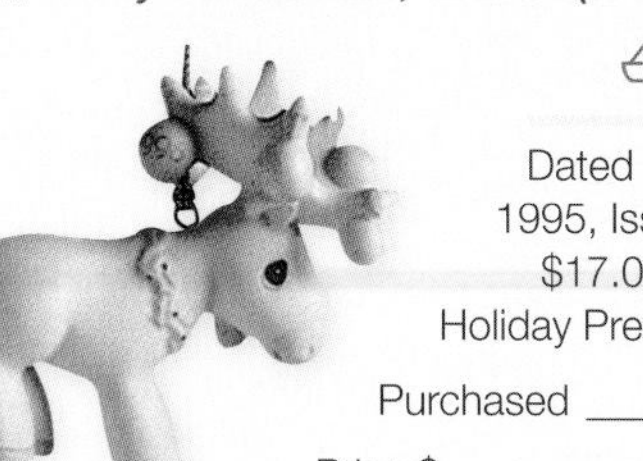

Dated Annual 1995, Issue Price $17.00, '95
Holiday Preview Event

Purchased ________

Price $___________

☐ *You're "A" Number One In My Book, Teacher,* 150142 (Ornament)

$35.00
$33.00
$30.00
$28.00
$25.00
$25.00
$25.00
$25.00

Retired 2002, Issue Price $17.00, '95

Purchased ________, Price $ ___________

☐ *Making A Trail To Bethlehem,* 142751

$40.00 $35.00
$38.00 $35.00

Retired 1998, Issue Price $30.00, '95
Nativity Addition

Purchased ___________

Price $ ___________

☐ *Soot Yourself To A Merry Christmas,* 150096

$75.00
$73.00
$70.00
$68.00
$65.00

Retired 1999, Issue Price $35.00, '95

Purchased ________, Price $ ___________

☐ *Train Station,* 150150 (Nightlight)

$175.00
$165.00
$160.00

Retired 1997, Issue Price $100.00, '95
Series: *Sugar Town*

Purchased ________, Price $ ___________

☐ *Sailabration Cruise,* 150061

$525.00

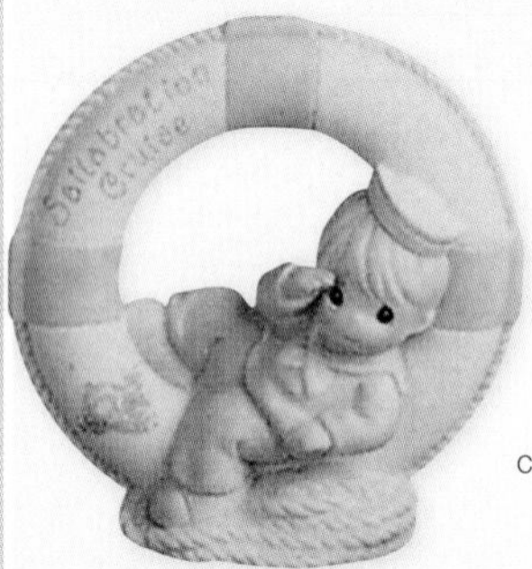

This piece was given to those who went on a Precious Moments cruise in 1995.

Limited Ed., 1995, Gift, '95

Purchased ________, Price $ ___________

☐ *Making Spirits Bright,* 150118

$75.00
$73.00
$70.00
$68.00
$25.00

Retired 1998, Issue Price $37.50, '95

Purchased ________

Price $ ___________

☐ ***Sam*, 150169**

△ $45.00

Annual 1995, Issue Price $20.00, '95
Series: *Sugar Town*

Purchased ________

Price $ ________

☐ ***Fire Hydrant*, 150215**

♡ $17.00
△ $19.00 † $15.00

Retired 1997, Issue Price $5.00, '95
Series: *Sugar Town*

Purchased ________

Price $ ________

☐ ***Even The Heavens Shall Praise Him*, 150312**

👓 $155.00

Limited Ed. 15,000, Issue Price $125.00, '98
CCR Exclusive

Purchased _____

Price $ _____

☐ ***Railroad Crossing Sign*, 150177**

△ $22.00
♡ $20.00
† $18.00

Retired 1997, Issue Price $12.00, '95
Series: *Sugar Town*

Purchased ________

Price $ ________

☐ ***Bird Bath*, 150223**

♡ $18.00
△ $20.00 † $15.00

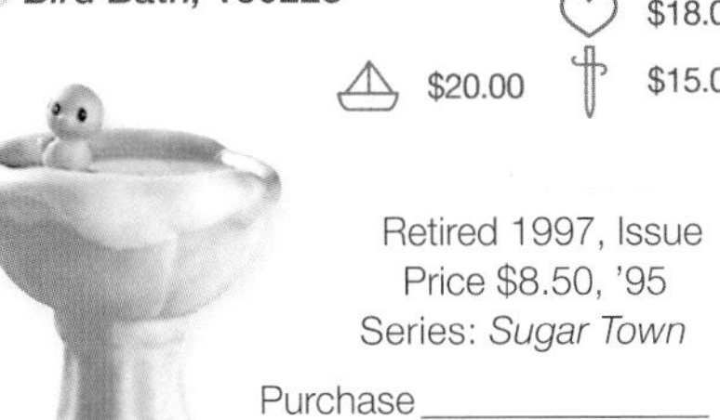

Retired 1997, Issue Price $8.50, '95
Series: *Sugar Town*

Purchase ________

Price $ ________

☐ ***Joy To The World*, 150320 (Ornament)**

△ $40.00 † $35.00
♡ $38.00 👓 $35.00
★ $35.00

Retired 1999, Issue Price $20.00, '95

Purchased ________

Price $ ________

☐ ***Luggage Cart*, 150185**

△ $28.00
♡ $25.00
† $20.00

Retired 1997, Issue Price $13.00, '95
Series: *Sugar Town*

Purchased ________

Price $ ________

☐ ***God Bless Our Home*, 150231 (Ornament)**

△ $60.00

Issued in Sugar Town boxes.

Out Of Production, Issue Price $19.95, '95
Series: *Sugar Town*

Purchased ________, Price $ ________

☐ ***Sugar Town Enhancement Set*, 152269**

△ $75.00 ♡ $73.00
† $70.00

Retired 1997, Issue Price $45.00, '95
Series: *Sugar Town,* Set of 5
(Fire Hydrant, Bench, Bus Stop Sign, Bird Bath, and Street Sign)

Purchased ________, Price $ ________

☐ ***Bus Stop Sign*, 150207**

△ $20.00
♡ $18.00
† $15.00

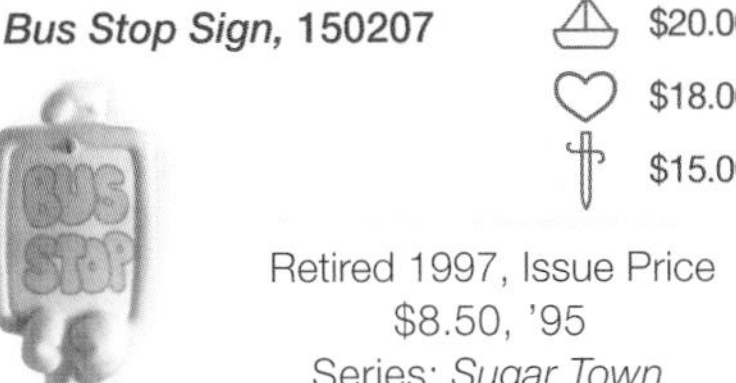

Retired 1997, Issue Price $8.50, '95
Series: *Sugar Town*

Purchased ________

Price $ ________

☐ ***Sugar Town Chapel*, 150304 (Lighted Plate)**

UM $100.00

LImited 1996, Issue Price $90.00, '96
Series: *Sugar Town*

Purchased ______

Price $ ______

☐ ***Train Station Set*, 150193**

△ $325.00 † $305.00
♡ $315.00

Retired 1997, Issue Price $190.00, '95
Series: *Sugar Town,* Set of 6
(Train Station, Railroad Crossing Sign, Luggage Cart, Sam, Tammy & Debbie, and Donny)

Purchased ________

Price $ ________

☐ ***He Loves Me*, 152277**

△ $575.00
♡ $550.00

Limited Ed. 2,000, Issue Price $500.00, '96
Easter Seals, Lily Understamp
Individually Numbered

Purchased ________

Price $ ________

☐ ***Sugar Town Express*, 152595 (Musical)**

UM $100.00

Retired 1997, Issue Price $75.00, '95
Series: *Sugar Town*, Set of 3 plus track
Tunes: *Jingle Bells, We Wish You A Merry Christmas*, and *Santa Claus Is Coming To Town*

Purchased ________, Price $ ____________

☐ ***You Are Always There For Me*, 163627**

Mark	Price	Mark	Price
		👓	$70.00
⛵	$75.00	★	$68.00
♡	$73.00	⬯	$65.00
†	$70.00	➳	$65.00
		✚♡	$65.00
		♕	$65.00

Retired 2003, Issue Price $50.00, '96

Purchased ________, Price $ ____________

☐ ***You Can Always Count On Me*, 152579 (Ornament)**

UM $25.00

Annual 1996, Issue Price $6.50, '96
Easter Seals Commemorative

Purchased ________, Price $ ____________

☐ ***You Are Always There For Me*, 163597**

♡	$75.00
†	$73.00
👓	$70.00
★	$68.00
⬯	$65.00
➳	$63.00

Retired 2001, Issue Price $50.00, '97

Purchased ________, Price $ ____________

☐ ***You Are Always There For Me*, 163635**

♡	$55.00
†	$53.00
👓	$50.00
★	$50.00
⬯	$50.00
➳	$50.00
✚♡	$50.00
♕	$50.00
✿	$50.00
⬡	$50.00

Out of Production, Issue Price $50.00, '96

Purchased ________, Price $ ____________

☐ ***Joy To The World*, 153338 (Ornament)**

Mark	Price	Mark	Price
♡	$43.00	👓	$38.00
†	$40.00	★	$35.00

Retired 1999, Issue Price $20.00, '96

Purchased ____________

Price $ ____________

☐ ***You Are Always There For Me*, 163600**

Mark	Price	Mark	Price
⛵	$60.00	†	$55.00
♡	$55.00	👓	$55.00
		★	$55.00
		⬯	$55.00
		➳	$55.00
		✚♡	$50.00
		♕	$50.00
		✿	$50.00

Suspended 2004, Issue Price $50.00, '96

Purchased ________, Price $ ____________

☐ ***Baby Girl Personalized*, 163651G**

⛵ $40.00

Limited, Issue Price $25.00, '95

Purchased ____________

Price $ ____________

***An Event Filled With Sunshine And Smiles*, ☐ 160334A, ☐ 160334B, ☐ 160334C, ☐ 160334D, ☐ 160334E, ☐ 160334F, ☐ 160334G, ☐ 160334H (Ornament)**

⛵ $78.00

Dated Annual 1995, Issue Price $35.00, '95
Regional Event — Illinois, California, New Jersey, Missouri, Maryland, Florida, Ohio, and Canada

Purchased ________, Price $ ____________

☐ ***You Are Always There For Me*, 163619**

♡	$60.00
†	$55.00
👓	$55.00
★	$55.00
⬯	$55.00
➳	$55.00
✚♡	$50.00
♕	$50.00
✿	$50.00

Suspended, Issue Price $50.00, '97

Purchased ________, Price $ ____________

☐ ***Baby Boy Personalized*, 163651B**

⛵ $40.00

LImited, Issue Price $25.00, '95

Purchased ____________

Price $____________

☐ *Birthday Personalized,* 163686E

$50.00
$48.50
$45.00

Discontinued 1997, Issue Price $42.50, '95

Purchased ________

Price $ ______________

☐ *I'd Goat Anywhere With You,* 163694

$33.00
$31.00
$30.00
$29.00
$28.00
$25.00
$23.00
$20.00

Retired 2002, Issue Price $10.00, '96
Series: *Two By Two*

Purchased ________, Price $ ____________

☐ *Jennifer,* 163708

$40.00
$38.00

Suspended 1996, Issue Price $20.00, '96
Series: *Sammy's Circus*, Set of 2

Purchased ________, Price $ ____________

☐ *Of All The Mothers I Have Known, There's None As Precious As My Own,* 163716 (Plate)

$45.00
$45.00

Dated Annual 1996, Issue Price $37.50, '96
Series: *Mother's Day* — Third Issue

Purchased ________, Price $ ____________

☐ *Blessed Are They With A Caring Heart,* 163724

$65.00

Limited Ed., Issue Price $55.00, '99
Century Circle Exclusive

Purchased ________, Price $ ____________

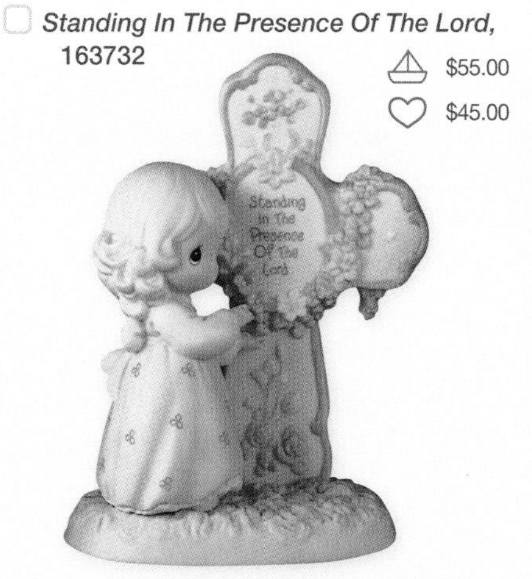

☐ *Standing In The Presence Of The Lord,* 163732

$55.00
$45.00

Dated Annual 1996, Issue Price $37.50, '96
Series: *Dated Cross* — Second Issue

Purchased ________, Price $ ____________

☐ *Age 7,* 163740

$48.00
$45.00
$43.00
$40.00
$40.00
$38.00
$35.00
$35.00
$35.00
$35.00
$35.00
$35.00
$35.00
$35.00
$35.00

Open, Issue Price $32.50, '96
Series: *Growing In Grace* (Blonde)

Purchased ________, Price $ ____________

☐ *Age 7,* 163740B

$35.00
$35.00
$35.00
$35.00
$35.00
$35.00
$35.00
$35.00

Open, Issue Price $32.50, '02
Series: *Growing In Grace* (Brunette)

Purchased ________, Price $ ____________

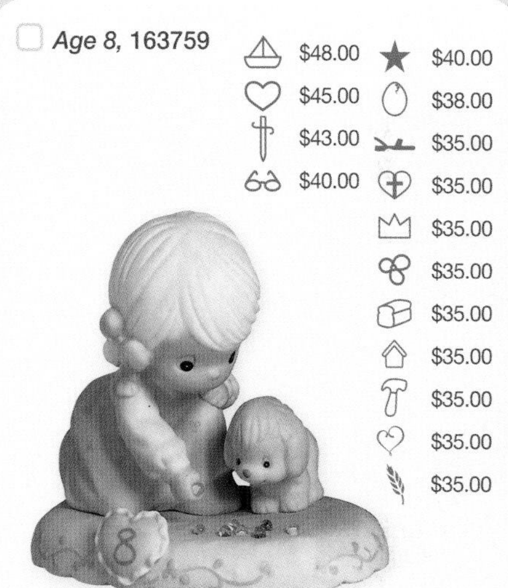

☐ *Age 8,* 163759

$48.00
$45.00
$43.00
$40.00
$40.00
$38.00
$35.00
$35.00
$35.00
$35.00
$35.00
$35.00
$35.00
$35.00
$35.00

Open, Issue Price $32.50, '96
Series: *Growing In Grace* (Blonde)

Purchased ________, Price $ ____________

☐ *Age 8,* 163759B

$35.00
$35.00
$35.00
$35.00
$35.00
$35.00
$35.00
$35.00

Open, Issue Price $32.50, '02
Series: *Growing In Grace* (Brunette)

Purchased ________, Price $ ____________

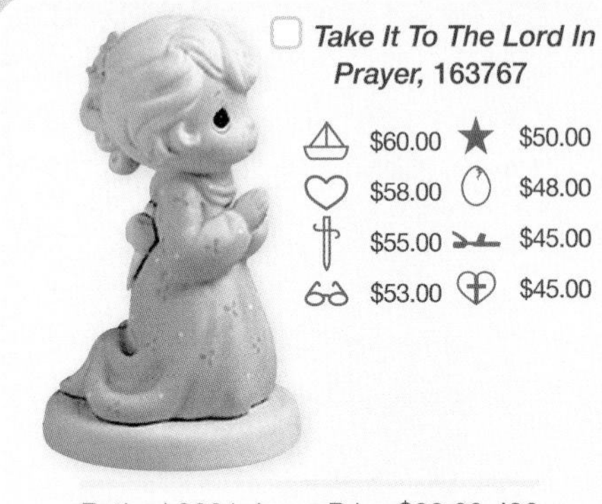

☐ *Take It To The Lord In Prayer*, 163767

$60.00 $50.00
$58.00 $48.00
$55.00 $45.00
$53.00 $45.00

Retired 2001, Issue Price $30.00, '96

Purchased ________, Price $ ___________

☐ *The Sun Is Always Shining Somewhere*, 163775

$65.00
$60.00
$55.00
$53.00
$50.00

Retired 1999, Issue Price $37.50, '96

Purchased __________

Price $ ___________

☐ *A Year Of Blessings*, 163783

$85.00 $75.00
$83.00 $75.00
$80.00 $75.00
$78.00 $75.00
$75.00 $75.00
$75.00 $75.00
$75.00
$75.00
$75.00

Open, Issue Price $70.00, '96
Series: *To Have And To Hold*

Purchased ________, Price $ ___________

☐ *Ten Years Heart To Heart*, 163805

$85.00 $80.00
$83.00 $78.00
$75.00
$75.00
$75.00
$75.00
$75.00
$75.00
$75.00
$75.00
$75.00
$75.00

Open, Issue Price $70.00, '96
Series: *To Have And To Hold*

Purchased ________, Price $ ___________

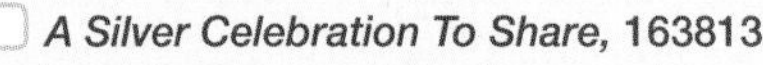

☐ *A Silver Celebration To Share*, 163813

$85.00 $80.00
$83.00 $78.00
$75.00
$75.00
$75.00
$75.00
$75.00
$75.00
$75.00
$75.00
$75.00
$75.00

Open, Issue Price $70.00, '96
Series: *To Have And To Hold*

Purchased ________, Price $ ___________

☐ *Each Hour Is Precious With You*, 163791

$85.00 $75.00 $75.00
$83.00 $75.00 $75.00
$80.00 $75.00 $75.00
$78.00 $75.00 $75.00
$75.00 $75.00 $75.00

Open, Issue Price $70.00, '96
Series: *To Have And To Hold*

Purchased ________, Price $ ___________

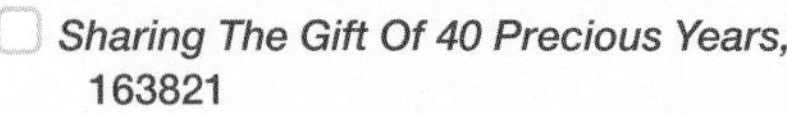

☐ *Sharing The Gift Of 40 Precious Years*, 163821

$85.00 $78.00
$83.00 $75.00
$80.00 $75.00
$75.00
$75.00
$75.00
$75.00
$75.00
$75.00
$75.00
$75.00
$75.00

Open, Issue Price $70.00, '96
Series: *To Have And To Hold*

Purchased ________, Price $ ___________

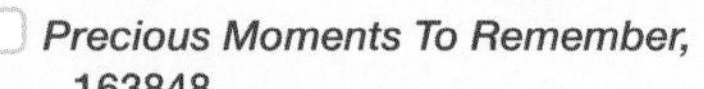

☐ *Precious Moments To Remember*, 163848

$85.00 $80.00 $75.00
$83.00 $78.00 $75.00
$75.00
$75.00
$75.00
$75.00
$75.00
$75.00
$75.00
$75.00
$75.00

Open, Issue Price $70.00, '96
Series: *To Have And To Hold*

Purchased ________, Price $ ___________

☐ *Sowing Seeds Of Kindness*, 163856

$50.00 $47.00
$49.00 $47.00
$48.00 $45.00
$45.00
$45.00
$43.00
$43.00

Retired 2004, Issue Price $37.50, '96
Series: *Growing In God's Garden Of Love*
First Issue

Purchased ________, Price $ ___________

☐ *Hallelujah Hoedown*, 163864

△ $85.00
♡ $80.00

Annual 1996, Issue Price $32.50, '96
Spring Celebration

Purchased ________, Price $ ____________

☐ *His Presence Is Felt In The Chapel*, 163872

UM $55.00
† $50.00
ꝏ $48.00

Retired 1998, Issue Price $25.00, '96
Chapel Exclusive

Purchased ________, Price $ ____________

☐ *His Presence Is Felt In The Chapel*, 163880 (Ornament)

UM $32.00
† $27.00

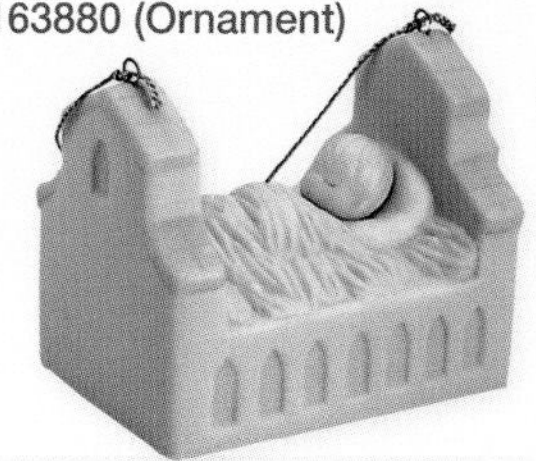

Suspended 1997, Issue Price $17.50, '96
Chapel Exclusive

Purchased ________, Price $ ____________

☐ *It May Be Greener, But It's Just As Hard To Cut*, 163899

△ $65.00 ꝏ $55.00
♡ $60.00 ★ $53.00
† $58.00 ◯ $50.00
⋈ $50.00

Retired 2001, Issue Price $37.50, '96

Purchased____________

Price $ ____________

☐ *God's Love Is Reflected In You*, 175277

♡ $255.00

Limited Ed. 15,000, Issue Price $150.00, '96
Century Circle Exclusive
Individually Numbered

Purchased ________, Price $ ____________

☐ *Some Plant, Some Water, But God Giveth The Increase*, 176958

♡ $55.00 ◯ $51.00
† $54.00 ⋈ $50.00
ꝏ $53.00 ♡+ $50.00
★ $52.00 ♔ $50.00
✿ $50.00

Retired 2004, Issue Price $37.50, '96
Series: *Growing In God's Garden of Love* — Second Issue

Purchased ________, Price $ ____________

☐ *A Perfect Display Of 15 Happy Years*, 177083 (Medallion)

△ $425.00

This Medallion was given to the attendees of the 1995 Local Club Chapter Convention. This is the fifth in the collection.

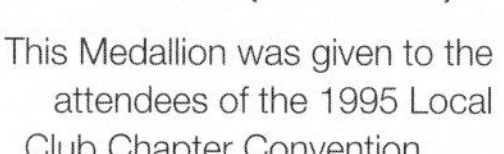

Convention Gift, '95

Purchased ________, Price $ ____________

☐ *Peace On Earth*, 177091 (Ornament)

UM $38.00

Limited Ed. 15,000, Issue Price $25.00, '95
Century Circle Exclusive

Purchased ____________

Price $ ____________

☐ *Peace On Earth...Anyway*, 183342

♡ $48.00
† $48.00

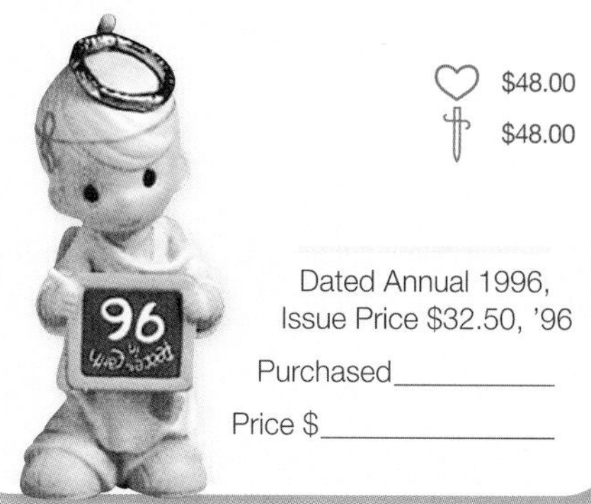

Dated Annual 1996, Issue Price $32.50, '96

Purchased____________

Price $____________

☐ *Peace On Earth...Anyway*, 183350 (Ornament)

♡ $43.00
† $40.00

Dated Annual 1996, Issue Price $30.00, '96

Purchased ________, Price $ ____________

☐ *Peace On Earth...Anyway*, 183369 (Ornament)

♡ $25.00
† $25.00

Dated Annual 1996, Issue Price $18.50, '96

Purchased ____________

Price $ ____________

☐ *Peace On Earth...Anyway*, 183377 (Plate)

♡ $60.00
† $60.00

Dated Annual 1996, Issue Price $50.00, '96
Series: *Beauty Of Christmas* — Third Issue

Purchased ________, Price $ ____________

Angels On Earth, 183776

$65.00
$63.00
$60.00
$58.00
$55.00
$55.00

Retired 2001, Issue Price $40.00, '96

Purchased ________, Price $ ____________

Snowbunny Loves You Like I Do, 183792

$45.00
$43.00
$42.00
$41.00
$40.00
$38.00

Retired 2001, Issue Price $18.50, '96

Purchased ________

Price $ ____________

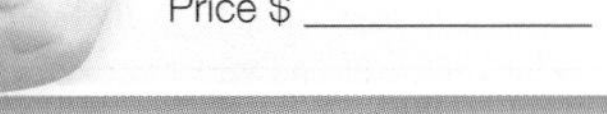

The Most Precious Gift Of All, 183814

$55.00
$53.00
$52.00
$51.00
$50.00
$50.00

Retired 2001, Issue Price $37.50, '97
Pink dress

Purchased ________, Price $ ____________

The Most Precious Gift Of All, 183814S

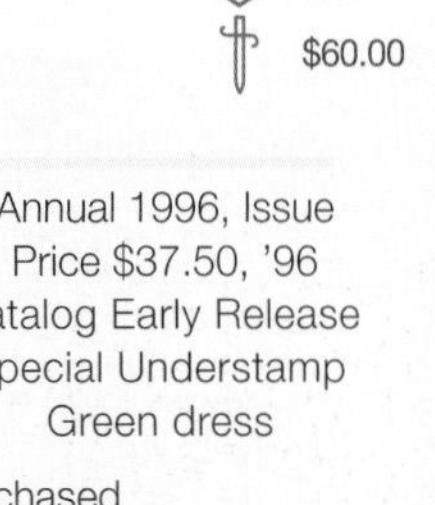

$60.00
$60.00

Annual 1996, Issue Price $37.50, '96
Catalog Early Release
Special Understamp
Green dress

Purchased ________

Price $____________

Sing In Excelsis Deo, 183830 (Tree Topper)

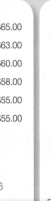

$165.00
$160.00
$155.00
$150.00

Retired 1999, Issue Price $125.00, '96

Purchased ________, Price $ ____________

You're Just Too Sweet To Be Scary, 183849

$75.00
$70.00
$68.00
$68.00
$65.00
$65.00
$65.00
$65.00

Retired 2004, Issue Price $55.00, '97

Purchased ________, Price $ ____________

Color Your World With Thanksgiving, 183857

$85.00
$83.00
$70.00

Retired 1998, Issue Price $50.00, '96

Purchased ________, Price $ ____________

Age 9, 183865B

$30.00 $30.00
$30.00 $30.00
$30.00 $30.00
$30.00 $30.00

Open, Issue Price $30.00, '02
Series: *Growing In Grace* (Brunette)

Purchased ____________

Price $ ____________

Age 10, 183873

$45.00
$43.00
$40.00
$40.00

$40.00
$40.00
$40.00
$40.00
$40.00
$40.00
$40.00
$40.00
$30.00
$30.00

Open, Issue Price $35.00, '96
Series: *Growing In Grace* (Blonde)

Purchased ________, Price $ ____________

Age 10, 183873B

$40.00
$40.00
$40.00
$40.00
$40.00
$40.00
$40.00
$40.00

Open, Issue Price $35.00, '02
Series: *Growing In Grace* (Brunette)

Purchased ________, Price $ ____________

Age 9, 183865

$35.00
$33.00
$30.00

$30.00
$30.00
$30.00

$30.00
$30.00
$30.00
$30.00

$30.00
$30.00
$30.00
$30.00

Open, Issue Price $30.00, '96
Series: *Growing In Grace* (Blonde)

Purchased ________, Price $ ____________

☐ *God's Precious Gift*, 183881 (Ornament)

Heart	$30.00	Sandal	$25.00
Sword	$29.00	Cross in Heart	$25.00
Eyeglasses	$28.00	Crown	$25.00
Star	$27.00	Clover	$25.00
Egg	$26.00	(mark)	$100.00
		(mark)	$100.00

This piece is all white.

Suspended 2004, Issue Price $20.00, '96

Purchased ________, Price $ ____________

☐ *When The Skating's Ruff, Try Prayer*, 183903 (Ornament)

Heart	$20.00	Sandal	$18.50
Sword	$19.00	Cross in Heart	$18.50
Eyeglasses	$18.50	Crown	$18.50
Star	$18.50	Clover	$18.50
Egg	$18.50	Cube	$18.50

Suspended, Issue Price $18.50, '96

Purchased ________, Price $ ____________

☐ *Our First Christmas Together*, 183911 (Ornament)

Heart $30.00

Dated Annual 1996, Issue Price $22.50, '96

Purchased__________

Price $____________

☐ *Baby's First Christmas (Girl)*, 183938 (Ornament)

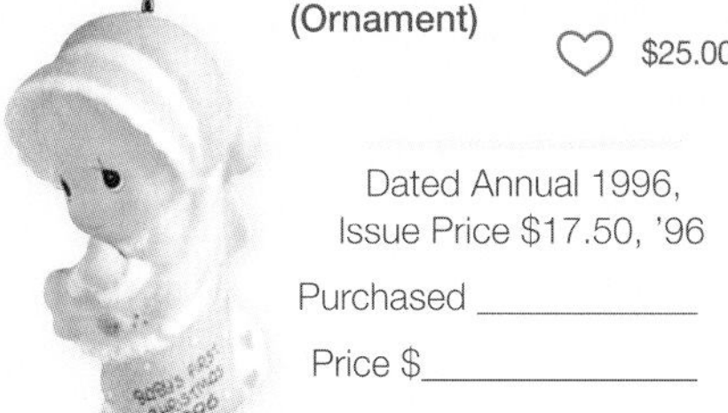

Heart $25.00

Dated Annual 1996, Issue Price $17.50, '96

Purchased ___________

Price $____________

☐ *Baby's First Christmas (Boy)*, 183946 (Ornament)

Heart $25.00

Dated Annual 1996, Issue Price $17.50, '96

Purchased ___________

Price $ ______________

☐ *Shepherd With Lambs*, 183954

Heart	$45.00	Egg	$40.00
Sword	$43.00	Sandal	$40.00
Eyeglasses	$40.00	Cross in Heart	$40.00
Star	$40.00	Crown	$40.00
		Clover	$40.00
		Cube	$40.00
		House	$40.00
		Hammer	$40.00

Open, Issue Price $40.00, '96
Nativity Addition, Set of 3

Purchased ________, Price $ ____________

☐ *Shepherd With Lambs*, 183962

Heart	$55.00	Cross in Heart	$40.00
Sword	$53.00	Crown	$40.00
Eyeglasses	$50.00	Clover	$40.00
Star	$48.00	Cube	$40.00
Egg	$45.00	House	$40.00
Sandal	$43.00	Hammer	$40.00

Open, Issue Price $40.00, '97
Nativity Addition, Set of 3

Purchased ________, Price $ ____________

☐ *Making A Trail To Bethlehem*, 184004

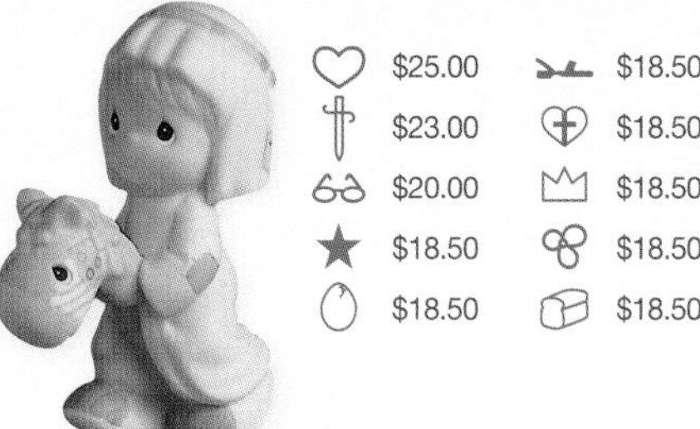

Heart	$25.00	Sandal	$18.50
Sword	$23.00	Cross in Heart	$18.50
Eyeglasses	$20.00	Crown	$18.50
Star	$18.50	Clover	$18.50
Egg	$18.50	Cube	$18.50

Out of Production, Issue Price $18.50, '96
Mini Nativity Addition

Purchased ________, Price $ ____________

☐ *Sugar Town Skating Sign*, 184020

Heart $28.00
Sword $28.00

Limited Ed., Issue Price $15.00, '96
Series: *Sugar Town*

Purchased______________

Price $ ______________

☐ *Sugar Town Tree*, 184039 (Lighted)

Heart $85.00
Sword $80.00

Retired 1997, Issue Price $45.00, '96
Series: *Sugar Town*

Purchased __________

Price $ ___________

☐ *Sugar Town Skating Pond*, 184047

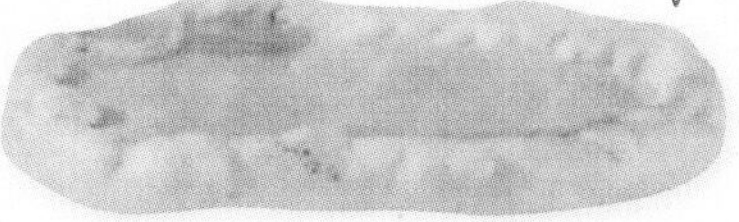

Ship $65.00
Heart $65.00
Sword $60.00

Retired 1997, Issue Price $40.00, '96
Series: *Sugar Town*

Purchased ________, Price $ ____________

☐ *Mazie*, 184055

Ship $40.00
Heart $38.00
Sword $35.00

Retired 1997, Issue Price $18.50, '96
Series: *Sugar Town*

Purchased_____________

Price $ ______________

☐ *All Sing His Praises*, 184012

Heart	$45.00	Eyeglasses	$42.00	Egg	$40.00	Crown	$35.00
Sword	$43.00	Star	$40.00	Sandal	$38.00	Clover	$35.00
				Cross in Heart	$38.00	Cube	$35.00

Suspended, Issue Price $32.50, '96
Nativity Addition

Purchased ________, Price $ ____________

☐ ***Cocoa*, 184063**

$20.00
$17.00
$15.00

Retired 1997, Issue Price $7.50, '96
Series: *Sugar Town*

Purchased ________, Price $ ____________

☐ ***Leroy*, 184071**

$40.00
$40.00
$38.00

Retired 1997, Issue Price $18.50, '96
Series: *Sugar Town*

Purchased ________
Price $ __________

☐ ***Hank And Sharon*, 184098**

$40.00
$40.00
$38.00

Retired 1997, Issue Price $25.00, '96
Series: *Sugar Town*

Purchased _______
Price $ _________

☐ ***Train Station*, 184101**
(Ornament)

$35.00
$35.00
$35.00

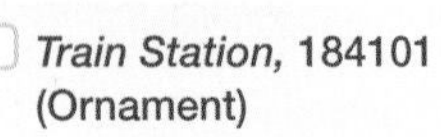

Limited Ed., Issue Price $18.50, '96
Series: *Sugar Town*

Purchased _______
Price $ _________

☐ ***Flagpole*, 184136**

$27.00
$25.00
$23.00

Retired 1997, Issue Price $15.00, '96
Series: *Sugar Town*

Purchased ________
Price $__________

☐ ***Sugar Town Skating Pond Set*, 184128**

$285.00
$275.00
$265.00

Retired 1997, Issue Price $184.50, '97
Series: *Sugar Town*, Set of 7
(Warming Hut, Mazie, Hank And Sharon, Leroy, Cocoa, Sugar Town Skating Sign, and Sugar Town Skating Pond)

Purchased ________________
Price $__________________

☐ ***Hot Cocoa Stand*, 184144**

$27.00
$25.00
$23.00

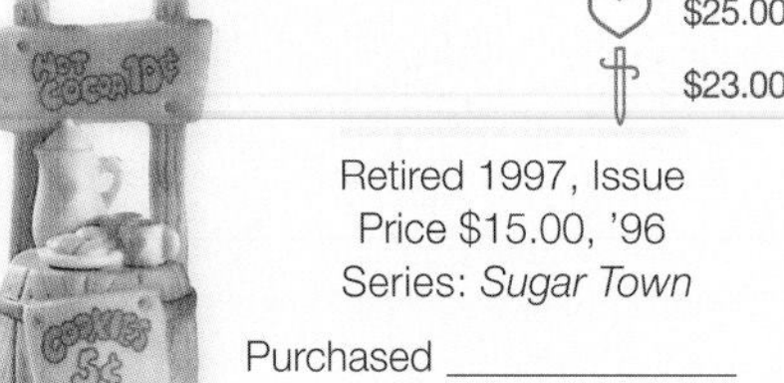

Retired 1997, Issue Price $15.00, '96
Series: *Sugar Town*

Purchased ___________
Price $ ____________

☐ ***Bonfire*, 184152**

$24.00
$22.00
$20.00

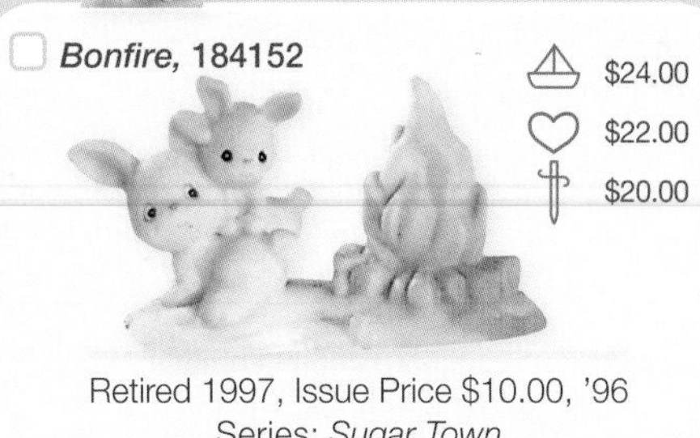

Retired 1997, Issue Price $10.00, '96
Series: *Sugar Town*

Purchased ________, Price $ ___________

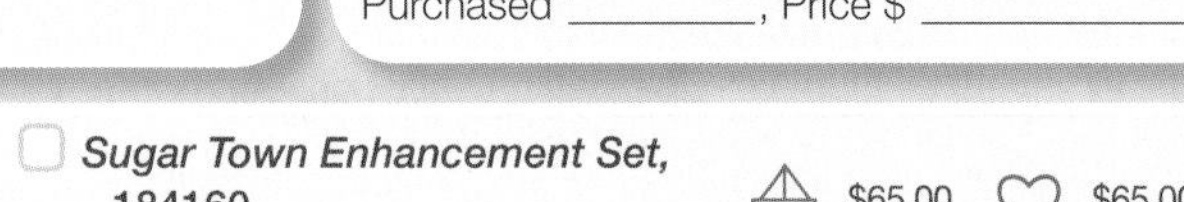

☐ ***Sugar Town Enhancement Set*, 184160**

$65.00
$65.00
$65.00

Retired 1997, Issue Price $40.00, '96
Series: *Sugar Town*, Set of 3 (Hot Cocoa Stand, Flagpole, and Bonfire)

Purchased ________ , Price $_________

☐ ***Train Station Set*, 184179**

$265.00
$260.00
$255.00

Retired 1997, Issue Price $170.00, '96
Series: *Sugar Town*, Set of 6 (Train Station, Donny, Luggage Cart, Tammy and Debbie, Railroad Crossing Sign, and Sam)

Purchased ________, Price $ ___________

☐ *Doctor's Office Set,* 184187

$270.00
$265.00
$260.00
$255.00

Retired 1997, Issue Price $170.00, '96
Series: *Sugar Town*, Set of 6 (Doctor's Office, Sugar and Her Doghouse, Jan, Dr. Sam Sugar, Leon and Evelyn Mae, and Free Christmas Puppies)

Purchased ____________

Price $ ______________

☐ *Warm Hands, Warm Heart, Warm Wishes,* 191353

UM $135.00
$125.00

Limited Ed. 1,200, Issue Price $45.00, '01
Chapel Exclusive, 2001 Christmas Event

Purchased ________, Price $ ___________

☐ *Sam's House Set,* 184195

$265.00
$260.00
$255.00
$250.00
$240.00

Retired 1997, Issue Price $170.00, '93
Series: *Sugar Town,* Set of 6
(Sam's House, Fence, Sam's Car, Sammy, Katy Lynne, and Dusty)

Purchased ________, Price $ ___________

☐ *Warming Hut,* 192341 (Nightlight)

$95.00
$95.00
$93.00

Retired 1997, Issue Price $60.00, '96
Series: *Sugar Town*

Purchased ________, Price $ ___________

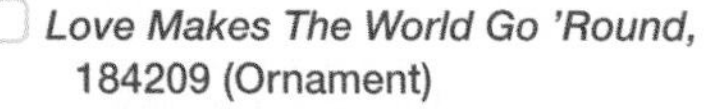

☐ *Love Makes The World Go 'Round,* 184209 (Ornament)

$55.00

Limited Ed. 19 96, Issue Price $22.50, '96
Century Circle Exclusive

Purchased ___________

Price $ ______________

☐ *May The Sun Always Shine On You,* 184217

$65.00

Limited Ed., Issue Price $37.50, '96
Century Circle Event Exclusive

Purchased ________

Price $ __________

☐ *Give Ability A Chance,* 192368

$40.00
$38.00

None of these pieces have the Easter Seals Lily on them.

Annual 1997, Issue Price $30.00, '97
Easter Seals Commemorative

Purchased ________, Price $ ___________

☐ *Winter Wishes Warm The Heart,* 184241 (Ornament)

UM $38.00

Limited Ed., Issue Price $20.00, '00
Avon Exclusive

Purchased ________

Price $ ____________

☐ *A Bouquet From God's Garden Of Love,* 184268

$55.00 $52.00 $50.00
$53.00 $50.00 $50.00
$50.00

Retired 2001, Issue Price $37.50, '97
Series: *Growing In God's Garden Of Love*
Third Issue

Purchased ________, Price $ ___________

☐ *Love Is Universal*, 192376

[Heart] $550.00
[Sword] $540.00

Limited Ed. 2,000, Issue Price $500.00, '97
Easter Seals — Lily Understamp
Individually Numbered

Purchased ________, Price $ ____________

☐ *Give Ability A Chance*, 192384 (Ornament)

UM $10.00

Dated Annual 1997,
Issue Price $6.00, '96
Easter Seals
Commemorative

Purchased________

Price $ ____________

☐ *Passenger Car*, 192406

UM $40.00

Dated Annual 1996, Issue Price $27.50, '96
Series: *Sugar Town*

Purchased ________, Price $ ____________

☐ *You Are A Lifesaver To Me*, 204854

[Heart] $55.00
[Sword] $53.00
[Eyeglasses] $50.00
[Star] $48.00
[Egg] $45.00

Retired 2000, Issue
Price $35.00, '97

Purchased ____________

Price $ ________________

☐ *The Lord Is Our Chief Inspiration*, 204862

UM $75.00
[Sword] $73.00
[Eyeglasses] $71.00
[Star] $70.00
[Egg] $68.00
[Bow & Arrow] $65.00
[Flower] $63.00
[Crown] $60.00
[Clover] $60.00

Retired 2003, Issue Price $45.00, '96
Chapel Exclusive

Purchased ________, Price $ ____________

☐ *The Lord Is Our Chief Inspiration*, 204870

UM $335.00
[Sword] $300.00

Limited Ed., Issue Price $250.00, '96
Chapel Exclusive, One Year of Production

Purchased ________, Price $ ____________

☐ *Coleenia*, 204889

UM $65.00
[Sword] $60.00
[Eyeglasses] $58.00
[Star] $58.00
[Egg] $55.00
[Bow & Arrow] $55.00
[Flower] $55.00

Retired 2002, Issue
Price $32.50, '96
Chapel Exclusive

Purchased ____________

Price $ ____________

☐ *The Most Precious Gift Of Them All*, 212520 (Ornament)

[Heart] $40.00

Annual 1996, Issue
Price $20.00, '96
Catalog Exclusive

Purchased __________

Price $ ______________

☐ *This World Is Not My Home (I'm Just A Passin' Thru)*, 212547

UM $135.00
[Eyeglasses] $130.00
[Star] $125.00

Gospel cassette
tape was
included with
this figurine.

Retired 1999, Issue Price $85.00, '97
Chapel Exclusive
Honors Albert E. Brumley

Purchased ________, Price $ ____________

Your Precious Spirit Comes Shining Through,
☐ 212563, ☐ 212563A, ☐ 212563B

[Heart] $155.00
[Sword] $155.00

Dated Annual 1996, Issue Price $35.00, '96
Regional Event — Knoxville, Indianapolis, and Minneapolis

Purchased ________, Price $ ____________

☐ *Sugar Town Accessories*, 212725

UM $25.00

Retired 1997, Issue
Price $20.00, '97
Series: *Sugar Town*,
Set of 8 (3 Trees,
2 Bushes, Fence,
Wreath, and Garland)

Purchased ____________

Price $______________

Shepherd And Sheep, **213616**

$45.00 $40.00
$43.00 $38.00
$41.00 $38.00
$35.00
$35.00
$35.00

Suspended, Issue Price $22.50, '97
Mini Nativity Addition, Set of 2

Purchased ________, Price $ ____________

Wee Three Kings, **213624**

$95.00 $93.00 $90.00
$88.00
$85.00
$83.00
$80.00
$78.00
$75.00
$75.00

Suspended, Issue Price $55.00, '96
Mini Nativity Addition, Set of 3

Purchased ________, Price $ ____________

A Mother's Story Is One Of Love, **220226**

$40.00
$40.00

Open,
Issue Price
$40.00, '02
Carlton Cards
Exclusive

Purchased ________, Price $ ____________

Always In His Care, **225290 (Ornament)**

UM $15.00

Ornament is shaped like the Easter Seals Lily.

Dated Annual 1990,
Issue Price $8.00, '90
Easter Seals Commemorative

Purchased ________________

Price $ ____________________

The Enesco Precious Moments Collection, **230448 (Plaque)** UM $15.00

Open, Issue Price $15.00, '88

Purchased ________, Price $ ____________

Sharing A Gift Of Love, **233196 (Ornament)** UM $15.00

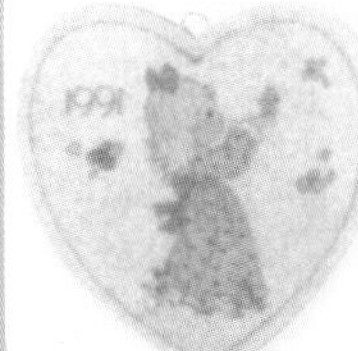

Dated Annual 1991,
Issue Price $8.00, '91
Easter Seals
Commemorative

Purchased__________

Price $ ____________

A Universal Love, **238899 (Ornament)**

UM $15.00

Annual 1992, Issue Price $8.00, '92
Easter Seals Commemorative

Purchased ________, Price $ ____________

Special Times With Mom Create Memories Of A Lifetime, **239260**

$55.00

Limited Ed., Issue Price $50.00, '05
Carlton Cards Exclusive

Purchased ________, Price $ ____________

You Make My Heart Shine, **244265**

$35.00

Limited Ed., Issue
Price $35.00, '06
Early Release, Carlton
Cards Exclusive

Purchased __________

Price $ __________

It Is No Secret What God Can Do, **244570 (Ornament)**

UM $12.00

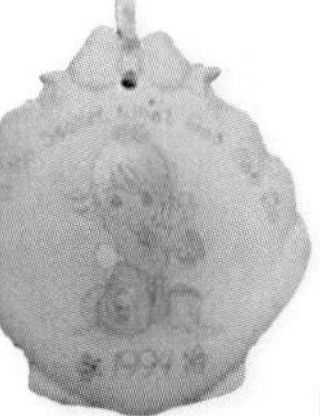

Dated Annual 1994, Issue
Price $6.50, '94
Easter Seals
Commemorative

Purchased __________

Price $ ____________

You're My Number One Friend, **250112 (Ornament)**

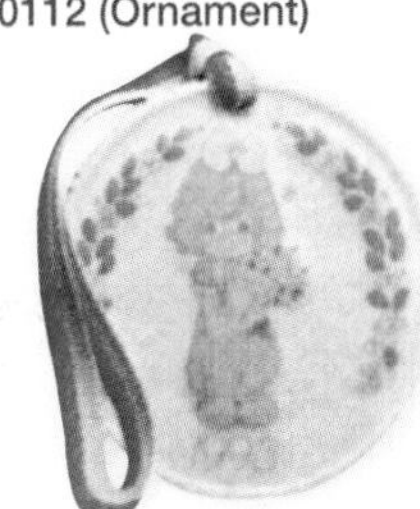

UM $15.00

Dated Annual 1993, Issue Price $8.00, '93
Easter Seals Commemorative

Purchased ________, Price $ ____________

Lead Me To Calvary, **260916**

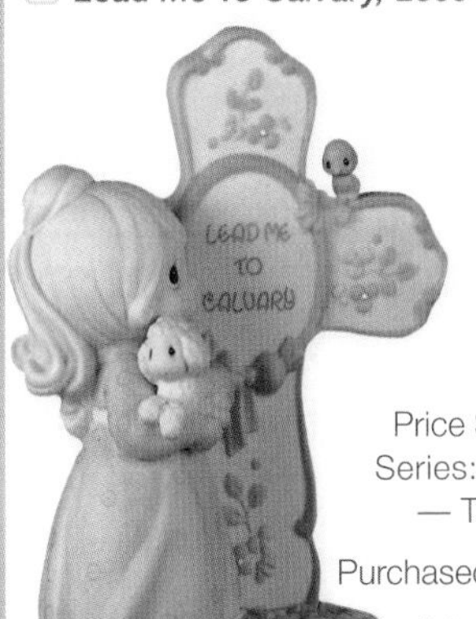

$50.00
$48.00

Dated Annual
1997, Issue
Price $37.50, '97
Series: *Dated Cross*
— Third Issue

Purchased__________

Price $ __________

☐ **Age 11, 260924**

$43.00 $40.00
$45.00 $40.00 $40.00
$40.00 $40.00
$40.00 $40.00
$40.00 $40.00
$40.00 $40.00
$40.00

Open, Issue Price $37.50, '97
Series: *Growing In Grace* (Blonde)

Purchased ________, Price $ ___________

☐ **From The Time I Spotted You I Knew (Know) We'd Be Friends, 260940**

The "Know" error occurred on all Heart marks and the first production run of the Sword marks.

$55.00 $45.00
$50.00 $40.00
$35.00

Retired 2000, Issue Price $20.00, '97
Series: *Birthday Collection*

Purchased ________, Price $ ___________

☐ **You Have Touched So Many Hearts (Brunette), 261084B**

$60.00
$55.00
$50.00
$48.00

Suspended 2004, Issue Price $40.00, '01

Purchased___________

Price $ ___________

☐ **Age 11, 260924B**

$40.00
$40.00 $40.00
$40.00 $40.00
$40.00 $40.00
$40.00

Open, Issue Price $37.50, '02
Series: *Growing In Grace* (Brunette)

Purchased _____

Price $ ________

☐ **Friends From The Very Beginning, 261068**

$75.00
$73.00
$71.00
$69.00
$65.00

Retired 2000, Issue Price $50.00, '97

Purchased ________, Price $ ___________

☐ **Lettuce Pray, 261122**

$35.00
$33.00
$32.00
$31.00

Retired 1999, Issue Price $17.50, '97

Purchased ________, Price $ ___________

☐ **Age 12, 260932**

$40.00 $40.00
$45.00 $40.00 $40.00
$43.00 $40.00 $40.00
$40.00 $40.00
$40.00 $40.00
$40.00 $40.00

Open, Issue Price $37.50, '97
Series: *Growing In Grace* (Blonde)

Purchased ________

Price $ ___________

☐ **You Have Touched So Many Hearts (Blonde), 261084**

$44.00
$55.00 $43.00
$53.00 $40.00
$50.00 $40.00
$48.00 $40.00
$45.00 $40.00
$40.00

Open, Issue Price $37.50, '97

Purchased _________

Price $ ___________

☐ **Have You Any Room For Jesus, 261130**

$65.00 $60.00 $53.00
$63.00 $55.00 $50.00
$50.00

Error: Spelling of "Biowling" found on some of the pieces with Heart marks; value is $95.00.

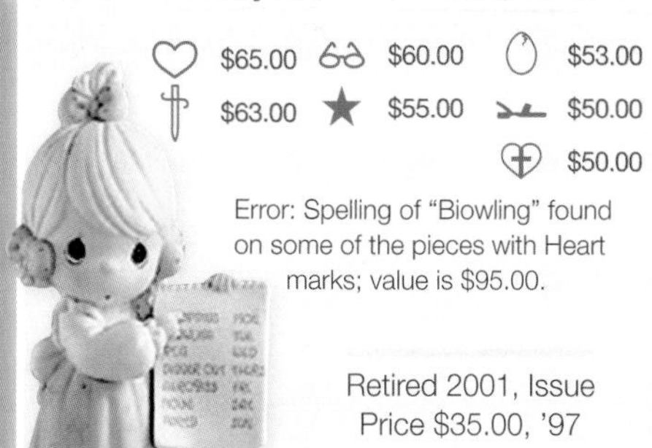

Retired 2001, Issue Price $35.00, '97

Purchased___________

Price $ _______________

☐ **Age 12, 260932B**

$40.00 $40.00
$40.00 $40.00
$40.00
$40.00
$40.00
$40.00

Open, Issue Price $37.50, '02
Series: *Growing In Grace* (Brunette)

Purchased ________, Price $ ___________

☐ **Hogs And Kisses, 261106**

Open, Issue Price $50.00, '99
Series: *Country Lane Collection*

Purchased ________, Price $ ________

$60.00 $50.00
$57.00 $50.00
$55.00 $50.00
$53.00 $50.00
$50.00 $50.00

☐ **Hogs And Kisses, 261106S**

Limited Ed. 1,500, Gift, '98
Chapel Understamp, Swap 'N Sell Weekend
Series: *Country Lane Collection*

UM $175.00

Purchased ________, Price $ ___________

☐ *Say I Do*, 261149

$65.00 $65.00 $65.00
$65.00 $65.00 $65.00
$65.00
$65.00
$65.00
$65.00
$65.00
$65.00
$65.00
$65.00

Open, Issue Price $55.00, '97

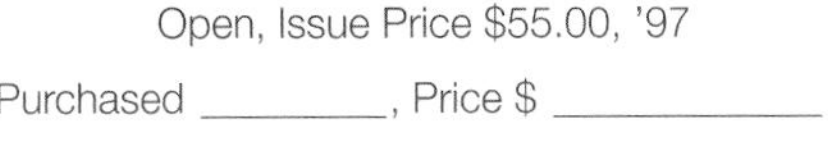

Purchased ________, Price $ ____________

☐ *We All Have Our Bad Hair Days*, 261157

$48.00 $45.00
$45.00 $43.00
$45.00 $43.00
$40.00

Retired 2002, Issue Price $35.00, '97

Purchased __________

Price $ __________

☐ *Bless Your Little Tutu*, 261173

UM $30.00

Open, Issue Price $20.00, '97
Series: *Sports — Little Moments*

Purchased ____________

Price $ ____________

☐ *January*, 261203

UM $20.00

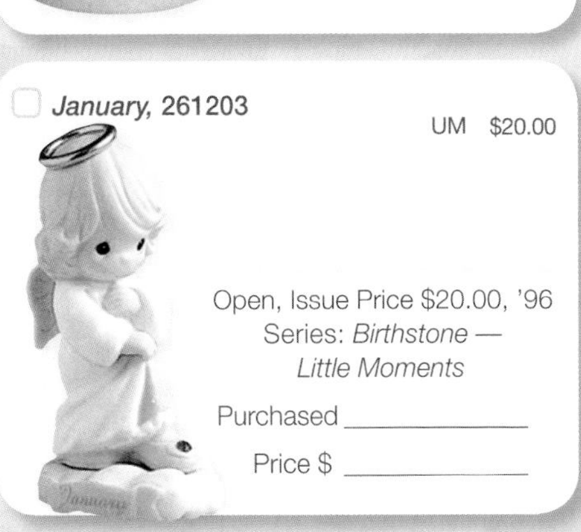

Open, Issue Price $20.00, '96
Series: *Birthstone — Little Moments*

Purchased ____________

Price $ ____________

☐ *May*, 261211

UM $20.00

Open, Issue Price $20.00, '96
Series: Birthstone — Little Moments

Purchased ____________

Price $ ____________

☐ *September*, 261238

UM $20.00

Open, Issue Price $20.00, '96
Series: *Birthstone — Little Moments*

Purchased ____________

Price $ ____________

☐ *February*, 261246

UM $20.00

Open, Issue Price $20.00, '96
Series: *Birthstone — Little Moments*

Purchased ____________

Price $____________

☐ *June*, 261254

UM $20.00

Open, Issue Price $20.00, '96
Series: *Birthstone — Little Moments*

Purchased ____________

Price $____________

☐ *October*, 261262

UM $20.00

Open, Issue Price $20.00, '96
Series: *Birthstone — Little Moments*

Purchased ____________

Price $____________

☐ *March*, 261270

UM $20.00

Open, Issue Price $20.00, '96
Series: *Birthstone — Little Moments*

Purchased ____________

Price $ ____________

☐ *July*, 261289

UM $20.00

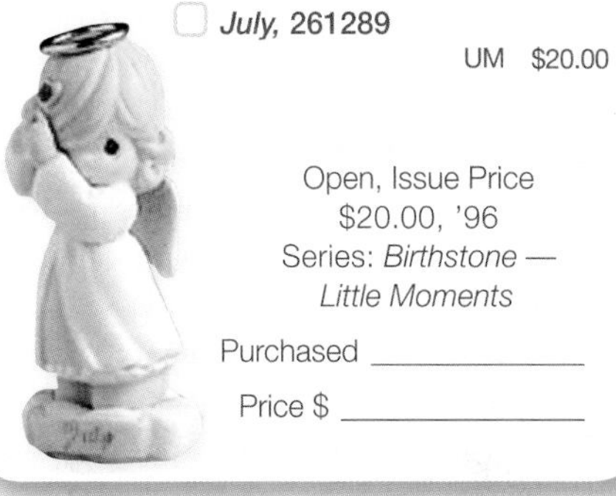

Open, Issue Price $20.00, '96
Series: *Birthstone — Little Moments*

Purchased ____________

Price $ ____________

☐ *November*, 261297

UM $20.00

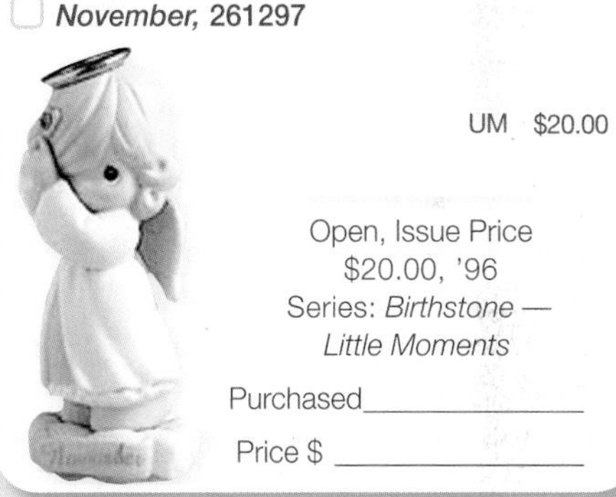

Open, Issue Price $20.00, '96
Series: *Birthstone — Little Moments*

Purchased____________

Price $ ____________

☐ *April*, 261300

UM $20.00

Open, Issue Price $20.00, '96
Series: *Birthstone — Little Moments*

Purchased ____________

Price $ ____________

☐ *August*, 261319

UM $20.00

Open, Issue Price $20.00, '96
Series: *Birthstone — Little Moments*

Purchased ____________

Price $ ____________

☐ *December*, 261327

UM $20.00

Open, Issue Price $20.00, '96
Series: *Birthstone — Little Moments*

Purchased ____________

Price $ ____________

☐ *We're So Hoppy You're Here*, 261351

$58.00
$55.00

Annual 1997, Issue Price $32.50, '97 Spring Celebration Event (April 26, 1997)

Purchased ________, Price $ ____________

☐ *We're So Hoppy You're Here*, 261351

$58.00
$55.00

Annual 1997, Issue Price $32.50, '97 Spring Celebration Event (April 26, 1997)

Purchased ________, Price $ ____________

☐ *Happiness To The Core*, 261378

$55.00
$50.00

Annual 1997, Issue Price $37.50, '97 Catalog Exclusive

Purchased ______

Price $ ________

☐ *Blessed Are Thou Amongst Women*, 261556

This piece has been found double marked with both Eyeglasses and Star.

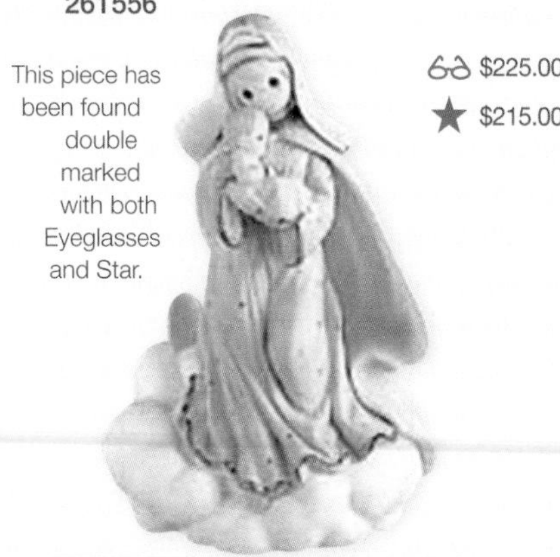

$225.00
$215.00

Annual 1999, Issue Price $175.00, '99
1998 Fall Show Exclusive

Purchased ________, Price $ ____________

☐ *The Lord Is The Hope Of Our Future*, 261564

This piece was paired with a copy of the book *Chicken Soup for the Soul* as a limited edition graduation promotion (261564B) in 2000. Issue price was $45.00; value (Egg mark) is $50.00.

$45.00 $45.00
$45.00 $45.00
$45.00
$45.00
$45.00
$45.00
$45.00
$45.00
$45.00
$45.00
$45.00
$45.00

Open, Issue Price $40.00, '97

Purchased ________, Price $ ____________

☐ *The Lord Is The Hope Of Our Future*, 261564L

This piece was paired with a copy of the book *Chicken Soup for the Soul* as a limited edition graduation promotion (261564G) in 2000. Issue price was $45.00; value (Egg mark) is $50.00.

$45.00
$45.00
$45.00
$45.00
$45.00
$45.00
$45.00
$45.00
$45.00
$45.00

Open, Issue Price $40.00, '00

Purchased ________, Price $ ____________

☐ *We Have The Sweetest Times Together*, 261580

$135.00
$130.00

Limited Ed. 10,000, Issue Price $100.00, '01

Purchased ________, Price $ ____________

☐ *In God's Beautiful Garden Of Love*, 261599 (Ornament)

$70.00

Limited Ed., Issue Price $50.00, '97
Century Circle Exclusive

Purchased____________

Price $____________

☐ *Crown Him Lord Of All*, 261602

UM $45.00 $35.00 $35.00
$35.00 $35.00
$35.00
$35.00
$35.00
$35.00
$35.00

Open, Issue Price $45.00, '97
Chapel Exclusive

Purchased ________, Price $ ____________

☐ *Crown Him Lord Of All*, 261610 (Ornament)

$28.00
UM $35.00 $25.00
$30.00 $25.00
$25.00
$25.00
$25.00
$25.00
$25.00
$25.00

Open, Issue Price $35.00, '97
Chapel Exclusive

Purchased ________, Price $ ____________

☐ *In God's Beautiful Garden Of Love*, 261629

[Heart] $200.00
[Cross] $200.00

Limited Ed. 15,000, Issue Price $150.00, '97
Century Circle Exclusive

Purchased ______
Price $__________

☐ *Sweet Sixteen*, 266841 (Medallion)

[Heart] $375.00

Given to attendees of the 1996 Local Club Chapter Convention. Sixth medallion in the collection.

Convention Gift, '96

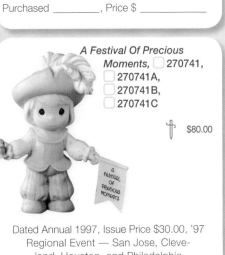

Purchased ________, Price $ ____________

A Festival Of Precious Moments, ☐ 270741, ☐ 270741A, ☐ 270741B, ☐ 270741C

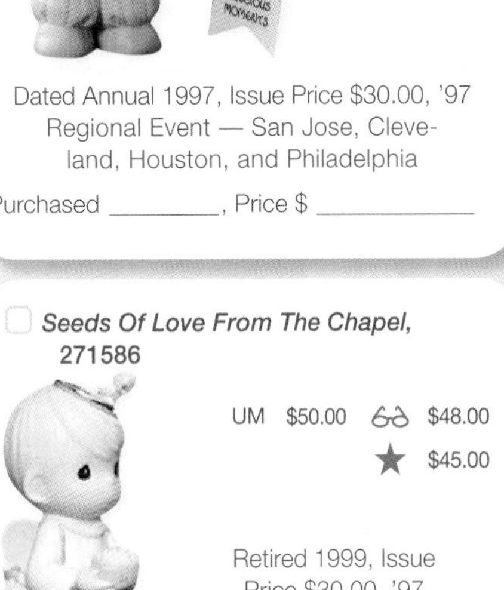

[Cross] $80.00

Dated Annual 1997, Issue Price $30.00, '97
Regional Event — San Jose, Cleveland, Houston, and Philadelphia

Purchased ________, Price $ ____________

☐ *Seeds Of Love From The Chapel*, 271586

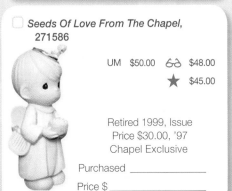

UM $50.00 [Glasses] $48.00
[Star] $45.00

Retired 1999, Issue Price $30.00, '97
Chapel Exclusive

Purchased ______________
Price $________________

☐ *Good Friends Are Forever*, 272422

[Heart] $45.00
[Cross] $43.00
[Glasses] $42.00
[Star] $41.00
[Flame] $41.00
[Bow & Arrow] $40.00
[Cross in Heart] $40.00
[Crown] $40.00
[Flower] $40.00

Retired 2004, Issue Price $30.00, '97
Series: *Baby Classics*

Purchased ________, Price $ ___________

☐ *We Are God's Workmanship*, 272434

[Heart] $38.00
[Cross] $35.00
[Glasses] $33.00
[Star] $33.00
[Flame] $30.00
[Bow & Arrow] $30.00
[Cross in Heart] $30.00
[Crown] $30.00
[Flower] $30.00

Retired 2004, Issue Price $25.00, '97
Series: *Baby Classics*

Purchased ________, Price $ ___________

☐ *Make A Joyful Noise*, 272450

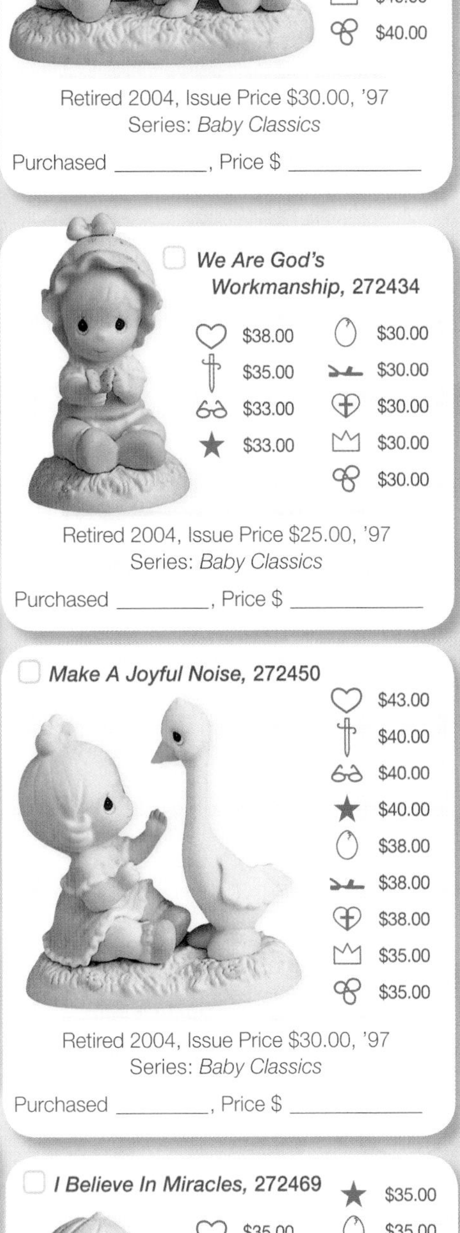

[Heart] $43.00
[Cross] $40.00
[Glasses] $40.00
[Star] $40.00
[Flame] $38.00
[Bow & Arrow] $38.00
[Cross in Heart] $38.00
[Crown] $35.00
[Flower] $35.00

Retired 2004, Issue Price $30.00, '97
Series: *Baby Classics*

Purchased ________, Price $ ___________

☐ *I Believe In Miracles*, 272469

[Heart] $35.00
[Cross] $33.00
[Glasses] $33.00
[Star] $35.00
[Flame] $35.00
[Bow & Arrow] $35.00
[Cross in Heart] $35.00

Retired 2002, Issue Price $25.00, '97
Series: *Baby Classics*

Purchased ________
Price $ ___________

☐ *God Loveth A Cheerful Giver*, 272477

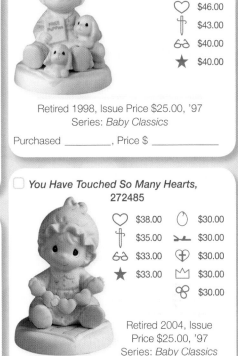

[Heart] $46.00
[Cross] $43.00
[Glasses] $40.00
[Star] $40.00

Retired 1998, Issue Price $25.00, '97
Series: *Baby Classics*

Purchased ________, Price $ ____________

☐ *You Have Touched So Many Hearts*, 272485

[Heart] $38.00
[Cross] $35.00
[Glasses] $33.00
[Star] $33.00
[Flame] $30.00
[Bow & Arrow] $30.00
[Cross in Heart] $30.00
[Crown] $30.00
[Flower] $30.00

Retired 2004, Issue Price $25.00, '97
Series: *Baby Classics*

Purchased ________ Price $ ____________

☐ *Love Is Sharing*, 272493

[Heart] $38.00
[Cross] $35.00
[Glasses] $33.00
[Star] $33.00
[Flame] $30.00
[Bow & Arrow] $30.00
[Cross in Heart] $30.00

Retired 2002, Issue Price $25.00, '97
Series: *Baby Classics*

Purchased ________, Price $ ____________

☐ *Love One Another*, 272507

[Heart] $45.00
[Cross] $43.00
[Glasses] $42.00
[Star] $42.00
[Flame] $41.00
[Bow & Arrow] $41.00
[Cross in Heart] $40.00
[Crown] $40.00
[Flower] $40.00

Retired 2004, Issue Price $30.00, '97
Series: *Baby Classics*

Purchased ________, Price $ ____________

☐ *Happy Birthday Jesus,* 272523

[cross] $40.00, [glasses] $38.00, [star] $36.00, [egg] $35.00, [bow] $35.00, [heart-cross] $35.00, [crown] $35.00, [clover] $35.00, [box] $35.00, [house] $35.00, [hammer] $35.00

Openn, Issue Price $35.00, '97

Purchased ________

Price $____________

☐ *Sharing The Light Of Love,* 272531

[cross] $45.00, [glasses] $43.00, [star] $40.00, [egg] $38.00, [bow] $35.00, [heart-cross] $35.00, [crown] $35.00, [clover] $35.00, [box] $35.00

Retired 10/15/05, Issue Price $35.00, '97

Purchased ________

Price $____________

☐ *I Think You're Just Divine,* 272558

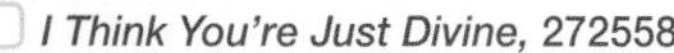

[cross] $55.00, [glasses] $53.00, [star] $53.00, [egg] $50.00, [bow] $50.00

First production pieces have the logo missing from the understamp. Also known as *Holy Cow.*

Retired 2001, Issue Price $40.00, '97

Purchased ________, Price $ ____________

☐ *Joy To The World,* 272566 (Ornament)

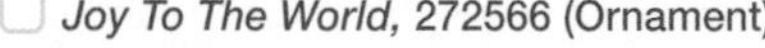

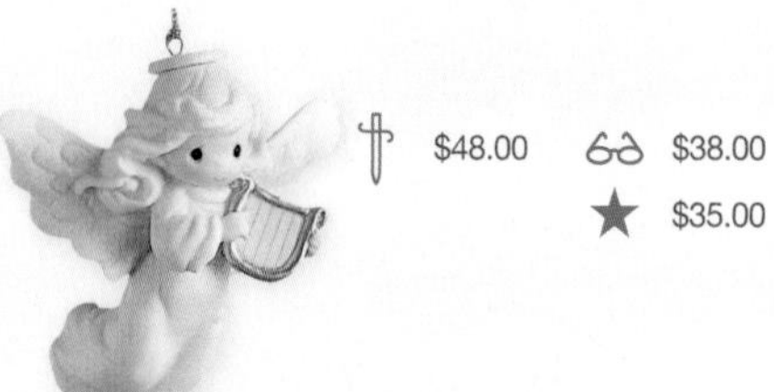

[cross] $48.00, [glasses] $38.00, [star] $35.00

Retired 1999, Issue Price $20.00, '97

Purchased ________, Price $ ____________

☐ *Enhancement Set For Large Nativity,* 272582

[cross] $68.00, [glasses] $65.00, [star] $63.00, [egg] $60.00, [bow] $60.00, [heart-cross] $60.00, [crown] $60.00, [clover] $60.00, [box] $60.00, [house] $60.00, [hammer] $60.00

Out of Production, Issue Price $60.00, '97

Nativity Addition, Set of 4

Purchased ________, Price $ ____________

☐ *I'm Dreaming Of A White Christmas,* 272590

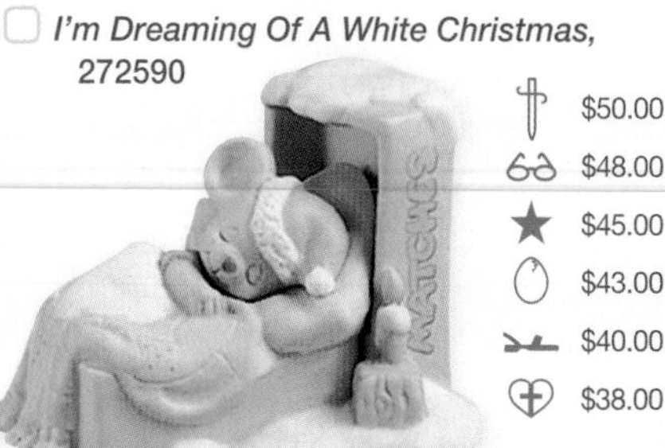

[cross] $50.00, [glasses] $48.00, [star] $45.00, [egg] $43.00, [bow] $40.00, [heart-cross] $38.00

Retired 2002, Issue Price $25.00, '97

Purchased ________, Price $ ____________

☐ *You Will Always Be A Winner To Me (Boy),* 272612

UM $20.00

Open, Issue Price $20.00, '97

Series: *Sports — Little Moments*

Purchased ________

Price $____________

☐ *It's Ruff To Always Be Cheery,* 272639

UM $20.00

Open, Issue Price $20.00, '97

Series: *Sports — Little Moments*

Purchased ________, Price $ ____________

☐ *Age 13,* 272647

[cross] $45.00, [glasses] $43.00, [star] $40.00, [egg] $40.00, [bow] $40.00, [heart-cross] $40.00, [crown] $40.00, [clover] $40.00, [box] $40.00, [house] $40.00, [hammer] $40.00, [heart] $40.00, [wheat] $40.00

Open, Issue Price $40.00, '97

Series: *Growing In Grace* (Blonde)

Purchased ________, Price $ ____________

☐ *Age 13,* 272647B

[heart-cross] $40.00, [crown] $40.00, [clover] $40.00, [box] $40.00, [house] $40.00, [hammer] $40.00, [heart] $40.00, [wheat] $40.00

Open, Issue Price $40.00, '02

Series: *Growing In Grace* (Brunette)

Purchased ________, Price $ ____________

☐ *Age 14,* 272655

[cross] $40.00, [glasses] $38.00, [star] $37.00, [egg] $35.00, [bow] $35.00, [heart-cross] $35.00, [crown] $35.00, [clover] $35.00, [box] $35.00, [house] $35.00, [hammer] $35.00, [heart] $35.00, [wheat] $35.00

Open, Issue Price $35.00, '97

Series: *Growing In Grace* (Blonde)

Purchased ________, Price $ ____________

☐ *Age 14,* 272655B

[heart-cross] $35.00, [crown] $35.00, [clover] $35.00, [box] $35.00, [house] $35.00, [hammer] $35.00

Open, Issue Price $35.00, '02

Series: *Growing In Grace* (Brunette)

Purchased ________

Price $____________

☐ *Age 15*, 272663

†	$45.00	crown	$40.00
eyeglasses	$40.00	clover	$40.00
★	$40.00	box	$40.00
egg	$40.00	house	$40.00
bow & arrow	$40.00	hammer	$40.00
heart	$40.00	heart	$40.00
		wheat	$40.00

Open, Issue Price $40.00, '97
Series: *Growing In Grace* (Blonde)

Purchased ________, Price $ ____________

☐ *Age 15*, 272663B

heart	$40.00	house	$40.00
crown	$40.00	hammer	$40.00
clover	$40.00	heart	$40.00
box	$40.00	wheat	$40.00

Open, Issue Price $40.00, '02
Series: *Growing In Grace* (Brunette)

Purchased ________, Price $ ____________

☐ *Cane You Join Us For A Merry Christmas*, 272671

† $45.00

Dated Annual 1997, Issue Price $30.00, '97

Purchased ________, Price $ ____________

☐ *Cane You Join Us For A Merry Christmas*, 272698 (Ornament)

† $33.00

Dated Annual 1997, Issue Price $18.50, '97

Purchased ______________

Price $ ______________

☐ *Cane You Join Us For A Merry Christmas*, 272701 (Plate)

† $60.00

Dated Annual 1997, Issue Price $50.00, '97
Series: *Beauty Of Christmas* — Fourth Issue

Purchased ________, Price $ ____________

☐ *Cane You Join Us For A Merry Christmas*, 272728 (Ornament)

† $38.00

Dated Annual 1997, Issue Price $30.00, '97

Purchased__________

Price $__________

☐ *Our First Christmas Together*, 272736 (Ornament)

† $30.00

Dated Annual 1997, Issue Price $20.00, '97

Purchased______________

Price $ ______________

☐ *Baby's First Christmas (Girl)*, 272744 (Ornament)

† $30.00

Dated Annual 1997, Issue Price $18.50, '97

Purchased ______________

Price $______________

☐ *Baby's First Christmas (Boy)*, 272752 (Ornament)

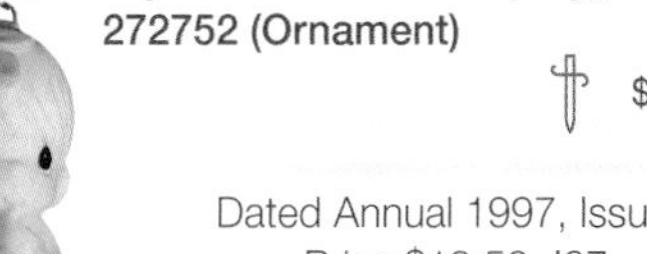

† $30.00

Dated Annual 1997, Issue Price $18.50, '97

Purchased ______________

Price $ ______________

☐ *Slow Down For The Holidays*, 272760 (Ornament)

† $30.00

Dated Annual 1997, Issue Price $18.50, '97
Series: *Birthday Collection*

Purchased __________ Price $ ____________

☐ *And You Shall See A Star*, 272787

†	$55.00
eyeglasses	$50.00
★	$48.00
egg	$45.00
bow & arrow	$45.00

Retired 2001, Issue Price $32.50, '97
Nativity Addition

Purchased ________, Price $ ____________

☐ *Schoolhouse*, 272795 (Nightlight)

† $155.00

American Flag version. Also came with Canadian flag, #272795C.

Retired 1997, Issue Price $80.00, '97
Series: *Sugar Town*

Purchased ________, Price $ ____________

☐ *Chuck*, 272809

† $45.00

Dated Annual 1997, Issue Price $22.50, '97
Series: *Sugar Town*

Purchased ________, Price $ ____________

Aunt Cleo, 272817

† $30.00

Retired 1997, Issue Price $18.50, '97
Series: *Sugar Town*

Purchased ________

Price $ ________

Schoolhouse Collector's Set, 272876

† $255.00

Dated Annual 1997, Issue Price $183.50, '97
Series: *Sugar Town,* Set of 6
(Schoolhouse, Chuck, Aunt Cleo, Aunt Bulah and Uncle Sam, Merry-Go-Round, and Heather)

Purchased ________, Price $ ________

Schoolhouse came in American flag and Canadian flag versions.

Aunt Bulah And Uncle Sam, 272825

† $45.00

Retired 1997, Issue Price $22.50, '97
Series: *Sugar Town*

Purchased ________

Price $ ________

Heather, 272833

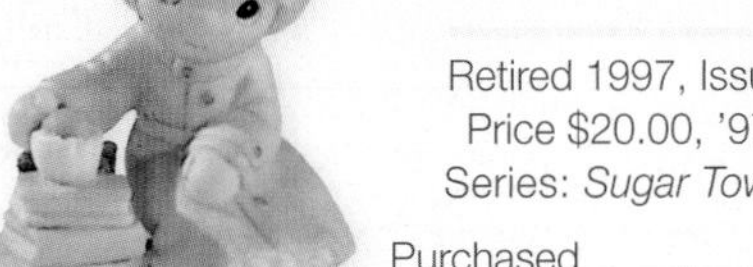

† $35.00

Retired 1997, Issue Price $20.00, '97
Series: *Sugar Town*

Purchased ________

Price $ ________

Merry-Go-Round, 272841

† $35.00

Retired 1997, Issue Price $20.00, '97
Series: *Sugar Town*

Purchased ________, Price $ ________

Puppies On Sled, 272892 (Ornament)

† $28.00 ★ $26.00
👓 $27.00 ◯ $25.00
⋈ $25.00
♡ $25.00

Retired 2002, Issue Price $18.50, '97

Purchased ________, Price $ ________

Bike Rack, 272906

† $25.00

Retired 1997, Issue Price $15.00, '97
Series: *Sugar Town*

Purchased ________, Price $ ________

Garbage Can, 272914

† $27.00

Retired 1997, Issue Price $20.00, '97
Series: *Sugar Town*

Purchased ________

Price $ ________

Somebody Cares, 272922 (Ornament)

† $12.00

Annual 1998, Issue Price $6.50, '98
Easter Seals Commemorative

Purchased ________

Price $ ________

Pack Your Trunk For The Holidays, 272949 (Ornament)

† $30.00

LImited 1,050, Issue Price $20.00, '97
Holiday Preview Event

Purchased ________

Price $ ________

Sugar Town Skating Pond Collector's Set, 272930

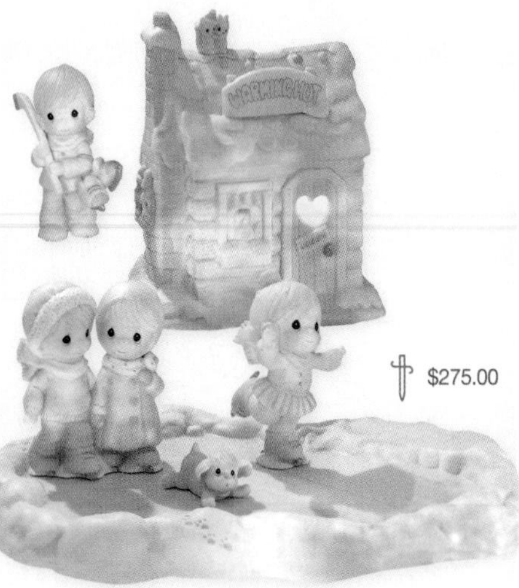

† $275.00

Retired 1997, Issue Price $169.50, '97
Series: *Sugar Town,* Set of 6
(Warming Hut, Hank And Sharon, Cocoa, Mazie, Leroy, and Sugar Town Skating Pond)

Purchased ________, Price $ ________

My Love Will Keep You Warm, 272957

👓 $45.00 ♔ $37.50
★ $42.00 ✿ $37.50
◯ $40.00 ▢ $37.50
⋈ $38.00 ⌂ $37.50
♡ $37.50 ⚒ $37.50

Open, Issue Price $37.50, '98

Purchased ________, Price $ ________

☐ ***My Love Will Keep You Warm*, 272957S**

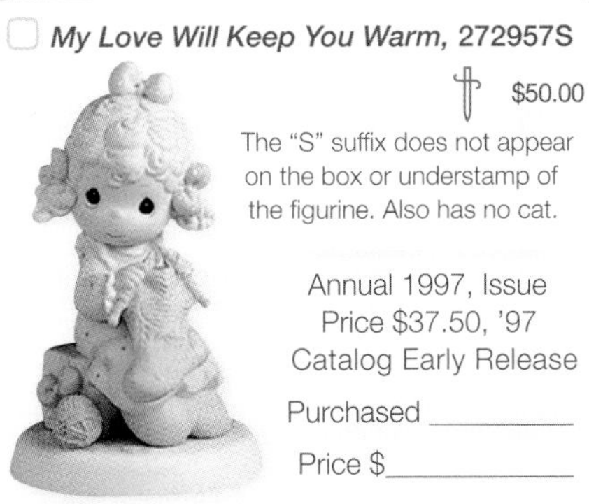

† $50.00

The "S" suffix does not appear on the box or understamp of the figurine. Also has no cat.

Annual 1997, Issue Price $37.50, '97 Catalog Early Release

Purchased ________

Price $__________

☐ ***My Love Will Keep You Warm*, 272965 (Ornament)**

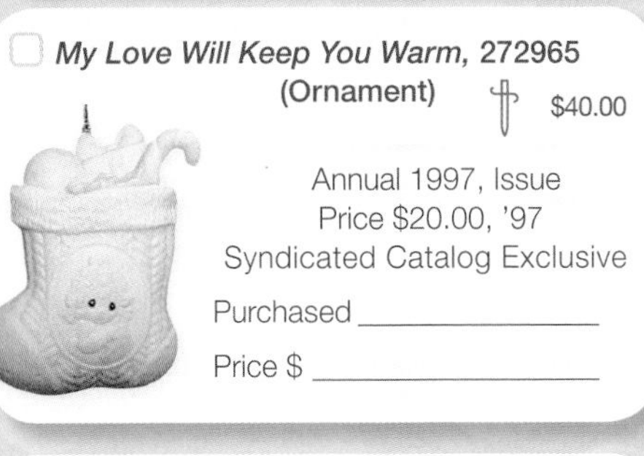

† $40.00

Annual 1997, Issue Price $20.00, '97 Syndicated Catalog Exclusive

Purchased ______________

Price $ ________________

☐ ***Love Grows Here*, 272981**

† $650.00
👓 $600.00

Limited Ed. 2,000, Issue Price $500.00, '98 Easter Seals Commemorative Lily Understamp Individually Numbered

Purchased __________

Price $ _____________

☐ ***Cargo Car*, 273007**

† $38.00

Dated Annual 1997, Issue Price $27.50, '97 Series: *Sugar Town*

Purchased ________, Price $ ___________

☐ ***Animal Additions*, 279323**

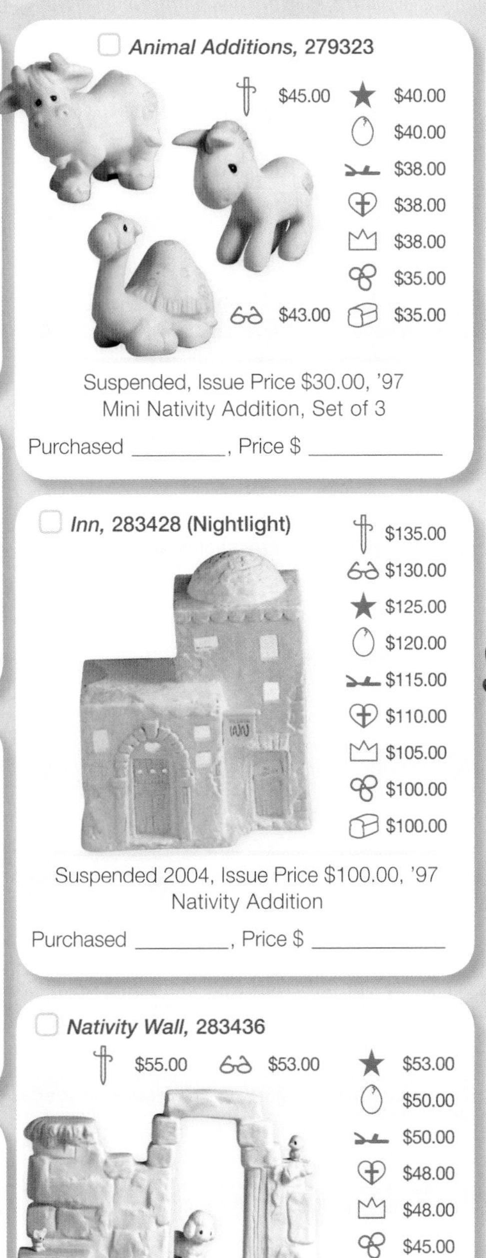

† $45.00
★ $40.00
⬯ $40.00
⋈ $38.00
♡ $38.00
♕ $38.00
✤ $35.00
👓 $43.00
⬡ $35.00

Suspended, Issue Price $30.00, '97 Mini Nativity Addition, Set of 3

Purchased ________, Price $ ___________

☐ ***Inn*, 283428 (Nightlight)**

† $135.00
👓 $130.00
★ $125.00
⬯ $120.00
⋈ $115.00
♡ $110.00
♕ $105.00
✤ $100.00
⬡ $100.00

Suspended 2004, Issue Price $100.00, '97 Nativity Addition

Purchased ________, Price $ ___________

☐ ***Nativity Wall*, 283436**

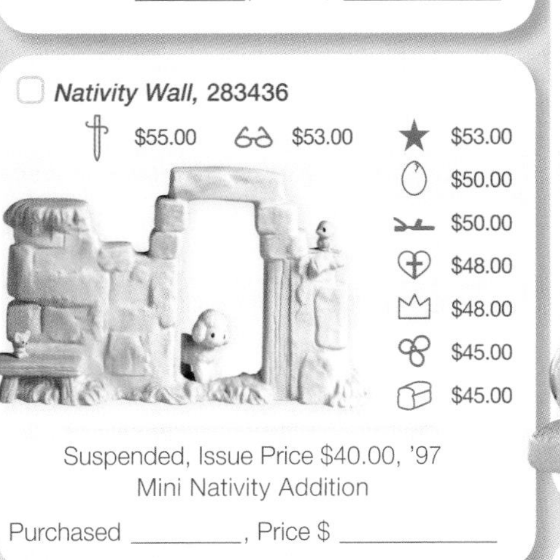

† $55.00
👓 $53.00
★ $53.00
⬯ $50.00
⋈ $50.00
♡ $48.00
♕ $48.00
✤ $45.00
⬡ $45.00

Suspended, Issue Price $40.00, '97 Mini Nativity Addition

Purchased ________, Price $ ___________

☐ ***Sugar Town Enhancement Set*, 273015**

† $53.00

Retired 1997, Issue Price $43.50, '97 Series: *Sugar Town*, Set of 3 (Bike Rack, Bunnies Caroling, and Garbage Can)

Purchased ________, Price $ ___________

☐ ***For An Angel You're So Down To Earth*, 283444**

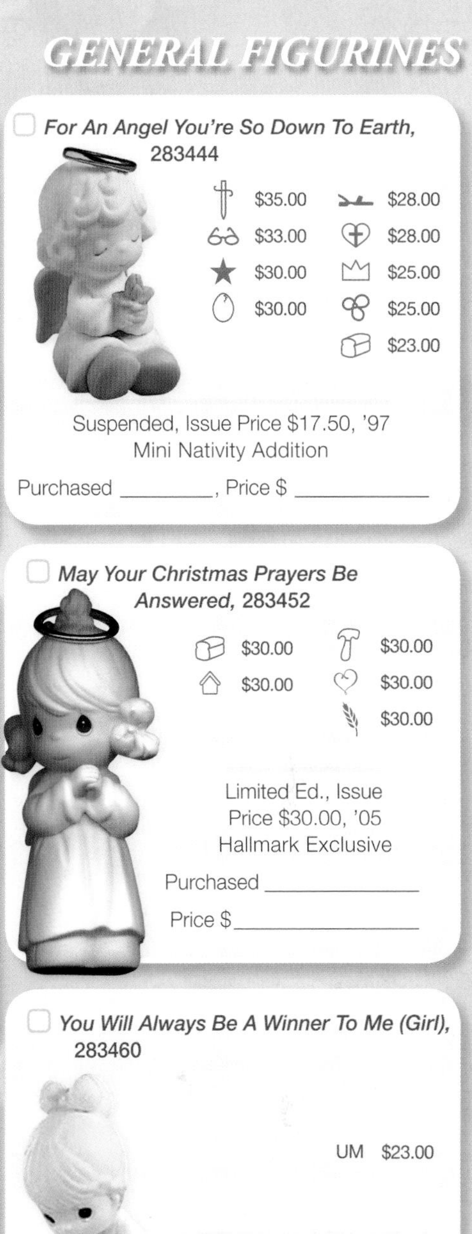

† $35.00
⋈ $28.00
👓 $33.00
♡ $28.00
★ $30.00
♕ $25.00
⬯ $30.00
✤ $25.00
⬡ $23.00

Suspended, Issue Price $17.50, '97 Mini Nativity Addition

Purchased ________, Price $ ___________

☐ ***May Your Christmas Prayers Be Answered*, 283452**

⬡ $30.00
⚲ $30.00
⌂ $30.00
♥ $30.00
❦ $30.00

Limited Ed., Issue Price $30.00, '05 Hallmark Exclusive

Purchased ___________

Price $______________

☐ ***You Will Always Be A Winner To Me (Girl)*, 283460**

UM $23.00

Open, Issue Price $20.00, '97 Series: *Sports — Little Moments*

Purchased __________

Price $ __________

☐ ***Cats With Kitten*, 291293**

† $22.00
★ $19.00
⬯ $18.50
👓 $20.00
⋈ $18.50
♡ $18.50
♕ $18.50
✤ $18.50
⬡ $18.50

Out of Production, Issue Price $18.50, '97 Mini Nativity Addition

Purchased ________, Price $ ___________

☐ **Nativity Well, 292753**

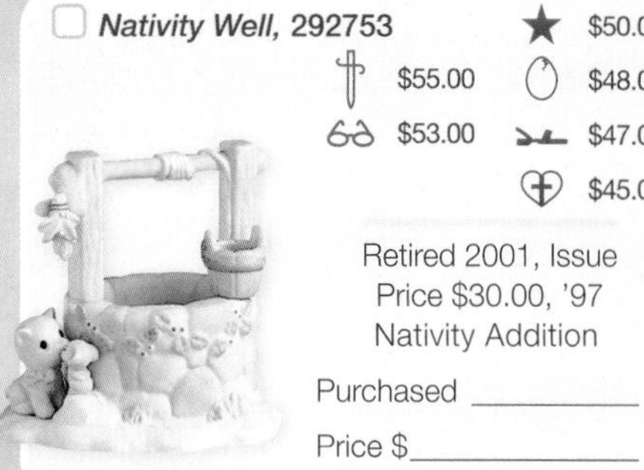

- [Sword] $55.00
- [Eyeglasses] $53.00
- ★ $50.00
- [Egg] $48.00
- [Bow & Arrow] $47.00
- [Heart] $45.00

Retired 2001, Issue Price $30.00, '97
Nativity Addition

Purchased __________

Price $__________

☐ ***Under His Wings I Am Safely Abiding*, 306835**

- [Sword] $55.00
- [Eyeglasses] $50.00

Dated Annual 1998, Issue Price $40.00, '98
Series: *Dated Cross* — Fourth Issue

Purchased ________, Price $ __________

☐ ***20 Years And The Vision's Still The Same*, 306843**

- [Eyeglasses] $55.00

Dated Annual 1998, Issue Price $55.00, '98
Commemorates Twentieth Anniversary Of Precious Moments

Purchased ________, Price $ __________

☐ ***20 Years And The Vision's Still The Same*, 306843**

- [Sword] $70.00
- [Eyeglasses] $55.00

Purchased ________, Price $ __________

☐ ***Friendship Hits The Spot*, 306916**

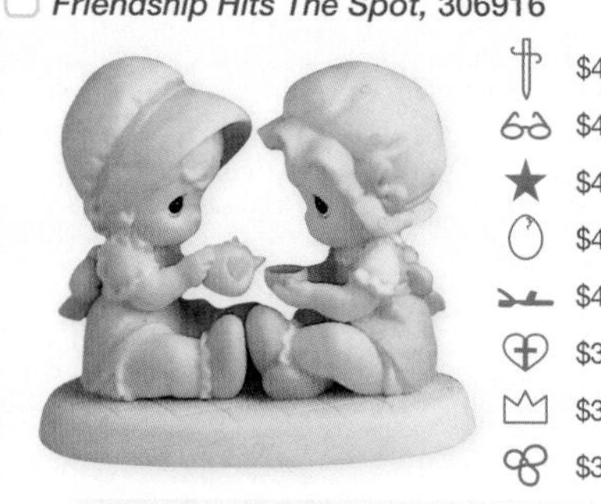

- [Sword] $45.00
- [Eyeglasses] $43.00
- ★ $42.00
- [Egg] $40.00
- [Bow & Arrow] $40.00
- [Heart] $38.00
- [Crown] $35.00
- [Clover] $35.00

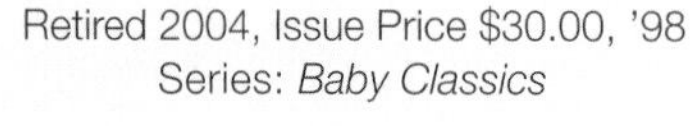

Retired 2004, Issue Price $30.00, '98
Series: *Baby Classics*

Purchased ________, Price $ __________

☐ ***Loving You Dear Valentine*, 306932**

- [Sword] $35.00
- [Eyeglasses] $33.00
- ★ $30.00
- [Egg] $30.00
- [Bow & Arrow] $30.00
- [Heart] $30.00

Retired 2002, Issue Price $25.00, '98
Series: *Baby Classics*

Purchased __________

Price $__________

☐ ***He Cleansed My Soul*, 306940**

- [Sword] $40.00
- [Eyeglasses] $38.00
- ★ $37.00
- [Egg] $35.00
- [Bow & Arrow] $35.00
- [Heart] $35.00
- [Crown] $35.00
- [Clover] $35.00

Retired 2004, Issue Price $25.00, '98
Series: *Baby Classics*

Purchased ________, Price $ __________

☐ ***For The Sweetest Tu-lips In Town*, 306959**

- [Sword] $40.00
- [Eyeglasses] $38.00
- ★ $37.50
- [Egg] $37.50
- [Bow & Arrow] $37.50
- [Heart] $35.00
- [Crown] $37.50
- [Clover] $37.50
- [Box] $37.50
- [House] $37.50
- [Mushroom] $37.50
- [Heart outline] $37.50
- [Wheat] $37.50

Open, Issue Price $35.00, '98

Purchased __________

Price $__________

☐ ***For The Sweetest Tu-lips In Town*, 306959B**

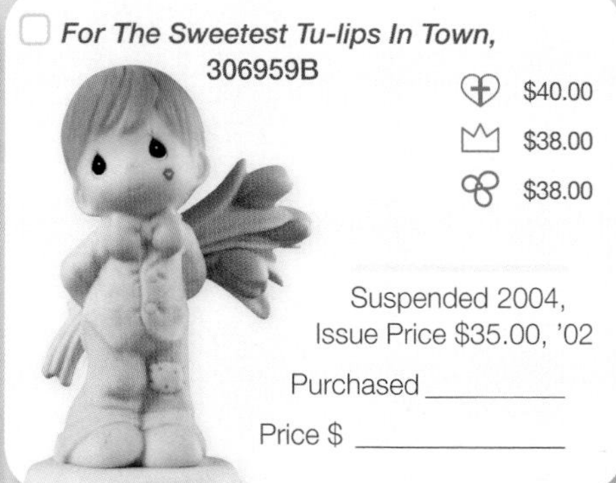

- [Heart] $40.00
- [Crown] $38.00
- [Clover] $38.00

Suspended 2004, Issue Price $35.00, '02

Purchased __________

Price $ __________

☐ ***You Are Always On My Mind*, 306967**

- [Sword] $58.00
- [Eyeglasses] $55.00
- ★ $53.00
- [Egg] $50.00

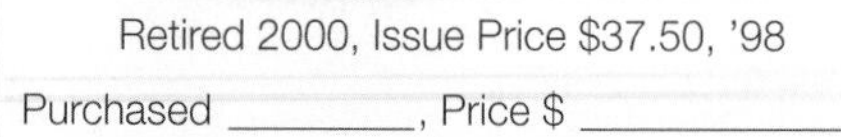

Retired 2000, Issue Price $37.50, '98

Purchased ________, Price $ __________

☐ ***Missum You*, 306991**

- [Sword] $65.00
- [Eyeglasses] $63.00
- ★ $60.00
- [Egg] $58.00
- [Bow & Arrow] $55.00
- [Heart] $55.00

Retired 2001, Issue Price $45.00, '98

Purchased ________, Price $ __________

☐ ***Charity Begins In The Heart*, 307009**

- [Sword] $75.00
- [Eyeglasses] $73.00

Retired 1998, Issue Price $50.00, '98
Series: *Always Victorian* — First Issue

Purchased __________

Price $__________

☐ *You're Just As Sweet As Pie,* 307017

Mark	Value
Eyeglasses	$68.00
★	$65.00
Egg	$63.00
Bow & Arrow	$60.00

Retired 2001, Issue Price $45.00, '98
Series: *Country Lane Collection*

Purchased ________, Price $ ____________

☐ *I'll Never Tire Of You,* 307068

Mark	Value
Eyeglasses	$80.00
★	$75.00

Retired 1999, Issue Price $50.00, '98
Series: *Country Lane Collection*

Purchased ________, Price $ ____________

☐ *Holiday Wishes, Sweety Pie,* 312444

UM $30.00

Came with miniature cinnamon potpourri pie.

Limited Ed., Issue Price $20.00, '97
Series: *Little Moments,* Set of 2

Purchased ________, Price $ ____________

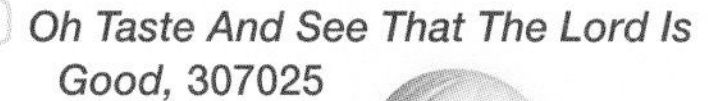

☐ *Oh Taste And See That The Lord Is Good,* 307025

Mark	Value
Eyeglasses	$75.00
★	$73.00
Egg	$70.00
Bow & Arrow	$68.00

Retired 2001, Issue Price $55.00, '98
Series: *Country Lane Collection*

Purchased ________, Price $ ____________

☐ *Peas Pass The Carrots,* 307076

Mark	Value
Eyeglasses	$55.00
★	$53.00
Egg	$50.00

Retired 2000, Issue Price $35.00, '98
Series: *Country Lane Collection*

Purchased ________, Price $ ____________

☐ *You're Just Perfect In My Book,* 320560

UM $25.00

Open, Issue Price $25.00, '98
Series: *Professionals — Little Moments*

Purchased ________, Price $ ____________

☐ *Fork Over Those Blessings To Others,* 307033

Mark	Value
Eyeglasses	$75.00
★	$73.00
Egg	$70.00
Bow & Arrow	$68.00
Heart	$68.00
Crown	$65.00
Flower	$65.00

Retired 2004, Issue Price $45.00, '98
Series: *Country Lane Collection*

Purchased ________, Price $ ____________

☐ *Bringing In The Sheaves,* 307084 (Musical)

Mark	Value
UM	$425.00
Cross	$415.00
Eyeglasses	$410.00

Limited Ed. 12,000, Issue Price $90.00, '98
Series: *Country Lane Collection*
Tune: *Bringing In The Sheaves*

Purchased ________, Price $ ____________

☐ *Loving Is Caring,* 320579

UM $20.00

Open, Issue Price $20.00, '98
Series: *Professionals — Little Moments*

Purchased ____________

Price $____________

☐ *Nobody Likes To Be Dumped,* 307041

Mark	Value
Eyeglasses	$105.00
★	$100.00

Retired 1999, Issue Price $65.00, '98
Series: *Country Lane Collection*

Purchased ________, Price $ ____________

☐ *Loving Is Caring,* 320595

UM $20.00

Open, Issue Price $20.00, '98
Series: *Professionals — Little Moments*

Purchased____________

Price $ ____________

☐ *You Set My Heart Ablaze,* 320625

UM $20.00

Open, Issue Price $20.00, '98
Series: *Professionals — Little Moments*

Purchased ____________
Price $ ____________

☐ *Just The Facts... You're Terrific,* 320668

UM $20.00

Open, Issue Price $20.00, '98
Series: *Professionals — Little Moments*

Purchased ____________
Price $ ____________

☐ *You Have Such A Special Way Of Caring Each And Every Day,* 320706

UM $25.00

Open, Issue Price $25.00, '98
Series: *Professionals — Little Moments*

Purchased ____________
Price $ ____________

☐ *What Would I Do Without You,* 320714

UM $25.00

Open, Issue Price $25.00, '98
Series: *Professionals — Little Moments*

Purchased ____________
Price $ ____________

☐ *Wait Patiently On The Lord,* 325279

○ $48.00 ♡ $43.00
⋈ $45.00 ♔ $40.00
✿ $40.00

Retired 2004, Issue Price $30.00, '01

Purchased ____________
Price $ ____________

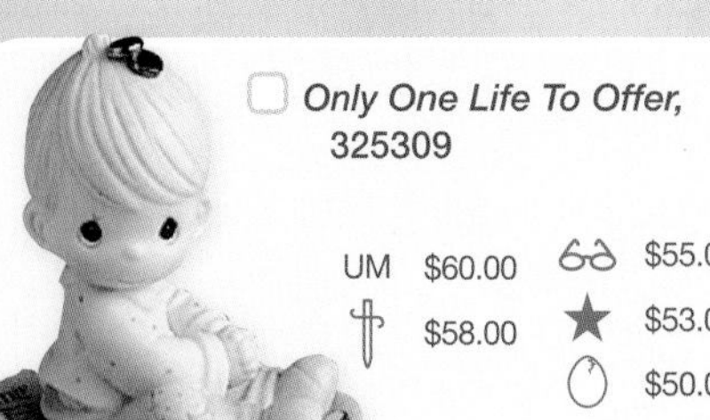

☐ *Only One Life To Offer,* 325309

UM $60.00 👓 $55.00
† $58.00 ★ $53.00
○ $50.00
⋈ $48.00
♡ $48.00

Retired 2001, Issue Price $35.00, '98

Purchased ________, Price $ ____________

☐ *The Good Lord Will Always Uphold Us,* 325325

† $75.00 ○ $68.00
👓 $73.00 ⋈ $55.00
★ $70.00 ♡ $55.00

Retired 2001, Issue Price $50.00, '98

Purchased ____________
Price $ ____________

☐ *By Grace We Have Communion With God,* 325333C

○ $105.00

Piece is a bible holder and comes with a New Testament Bible.

Annual 2000, Issue Price $75.00, '00
Show Special

Purchased ________, Price $ ____________

☐ *There Are Two Sides To Every Story,* 325368

UM $32.00
† $30.00
👓 $28.00
★ $25.00
○ $23.00
⋈ $20.00
♡ $20.00

Retired 2001, Issue Price $15.00, '98

Purchased ________, Price $ ____________

☐ *Life Can Be A Jungle,* 325457

UM $58.00
👓 $55.00

Annual 1998, Issue Price $37.50, '98
10/31/98 Jungle Jamboree DSR Event Piece

Purchased ____________
Price $ ____________

☐ *Mom You Always Make Our House A Home,* 325465

† $55.00
👓 $50.00

Limited Ed., Issue Price $37.50, '98
Catalog Exclusive

Purchased ____________
Price $ ____________

☐ *Mom, You're My Special-Tea,* 325473

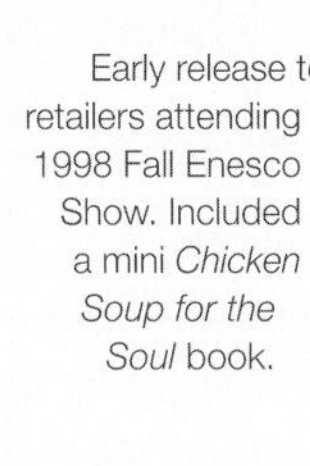

Early release to retailers attending 1998 Fall Enesco Show. Included a mini *Chicken Soup for the Soul* book.

👓 $45.00
★ $43.00

Retired 1999, Issue Price $25.00, '99
Mother's Day 1999

Purchased ________, Price $ ____________

☐ *Home Is Where The Heart Is,* 325481

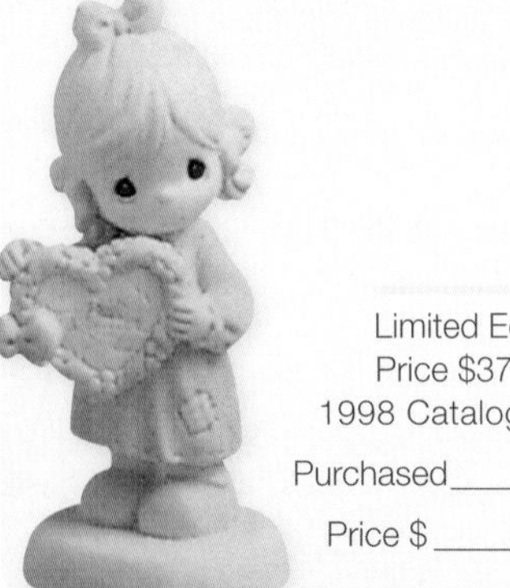

† $63.00
👓 $60.00

Limited Ed., Issue Price $37.50, '98
1998 Catalog Exclusive

Purchased ____________
Price $ ____________

☐ ***Marvelous Grace,*** 325503

[eyeglasses]	$65.00

Limited Ed., Issue Price $50.00, '98 Century Circle Exclusive

Purchased ________, Price $ ____________

☐ ***Our Future Is Looking Much Brighter,*** 325511

[eyeglasses]	$475.00

Given to those on the 1998 Precious Moments Cruise.

Dated Annual 1998, Gift, '98 Cruise Piece

Purchased ________, Price $ ____________

☐ ***Well, Blow Me Down It's Yer Birthday,*** 325538

UM	$75.00
[sword]	$70.00
[eyeglasses]	$68.00
[star]	$65.00
[egg]	$63.00
[bow]	$60.00
[heart]	$60.00

Retired 2001, Issue Price $50.00, '98

Purchased ________, Price $ ____________

☐ ***Garnet — Color Of Boldness (January),*** 335533 (Hinged Box)

[eyeglasses]	$30.00	[heart]	$25.00
[star]	$28.00	[crown]	$25.00
[egg]	$25.00	[clover]	$25.00
[bow]	$25.00	[cube]	$25.00

Out of Production, Issue Price $25.00, '98

Series: *Birthstone Collection*

Purchased ________, Price $ ____________

☐ ***Amethyst — Color Of Faith (February),*** 335541 (Hinged Box)

[eyeglasses]	$30.00	[heart]	$25.00
[star]	$28.00	[crown]	$25.00
[egg]	$25.00	[clover]	$25.00
[bow]	$25.00	[cube]	$25.00

Out of Production, Issue Price $25.00, '98

Series: *Birthstone Collection*

Purchased ________, Price $ ____________

☐ ***Aquamarine — Color Of Kindness (March),*** 335568 (Hinged Box)

[eyeglasses]	$30.00	[heart]	$25.00
[star]	$28.00	[crown]	$25.00
[egg]	$25.00	[clover]	$25.00
[bow]	$25.00	[cube]	$25.00

Out of Production, Issue Price $25.00, '98

Series: *Birthstone Collection*

Purchased ________, Price $ ____________

☐ ***Diamond — Color Of Purity (April),*** 335576 (Hinged Box)

[eyeglasses]	$30.00	[heart]	$25.00
[star]	$28.00	[crown]	$25.00
[egg]	$25.00	[clover]	$25.00
[bow]	$25.00	[cube]	$25.00

Out of Production, Issue Price $25.00, '98

Series: *Birthstone Collection*

Purchased ________, Price $ ____________

☐ ***Emerald — Color Of Patience (May),*** 335584 (Hinged Box)

[eyeglasses]	$30.00	[heart]	$25.00
[star]	$28.00	[crown]	$25.00
[egg]	$25.00	[clover]	$25.00
[bow]	$25.00	[cube]	$25.00

Out of Production, Issue Price $25.00, '98

Series: *Birthstone Collection*

Purchased ________, Price $ ____________

☐ ***Pearl — Color Of Love (June),*** 335592 (Hinged Box)

[eyeglasses]	$30.00	[heart]	$25.00
[star]	$28.00	[crown]	$25.00
[egg]	$25.00	[clover]	$25.00
[bow]	$25.00	[cube]	$25.00

Out of Production, Issue Price $25.00, '98

Series: *Birthstone Collection*

Purchased ____________

Price $____________

☐ ***Ruby — Color Of Joy (July),*** 335606 (Hinged Box)

[eyeglasses]	$30.00	[heart]	$25.00
[star]	$28.00	[crown]	$25.00
[egg]	$25.00	[clover]	$25.00
[bow]	$25.00	[cube]	$25.00

Out of Production, Issue Price $25.00, '98

Series: *Birthstone Collection*

Purchased ________, Price $ ____________

☐ ***Peridot — Color Of Pride (August),*** 335614 (Hinged Box)

[eyeglasses]	$30.00	[heart]	$25.00
[star]	$28.00	[crown]	$25.00
[egg]	$25.00	[clover]	$25.00
[bow]	$25.00	[cube]	$25.00

Out of Production, Issue Price $25.00, '98

Series: *Birthstone Collection*

Purchased ________, Price $ ____________

☐ ***Sapphire — Color Of Confidence (September),*** 335622 (Hinged Box)

Mark	Price	Mark	Price
[eyeglasses]	$30.00	[heart]	$25.00
[star]	$28.00	[crown]	$25.00
[egg]	$25.00	[clover]	$25.00
[bow]	$25.00	[cube]	$25.00

Out of Production, Issue Price $25.00, '98

Series: *Birthstone Collection*

Purchased ________, Price $ ____________

☐ *Opal — Color Of Happiness (October),* 335657 (Hinged Box)

[eyeglasses]	$30.00	[heart]	$25.00
★	$28.00	[crown]	$25.00
[egg]	$25.00	[clover]	$25.00
[bow and arrow]	$25.00	[box]	$25.00

Out of Production, Issue Price $25.00, '98
Series: *Birthstone Collection*

Purchased ______________

Price $__________________

☐ *Topaz — Color Of Truth (November),* 335665 (Hinged Box)

[eyeglasses]	$30.00	[heart]	$25.00
★	$28.00	[crown]	$25.00
[egg]	$25.00	[clover]	$25.00
[bow and arrow]	$25.00	[box]	$25.00

Out of Production, Issue Price $25.00, '98
Series: *Birthstone Collection*

Purchased______________

Price $ ________________

☐ *Turquoise — Color Of Loyalty (December),* 335673 (Hinged Box)

[eyeglasses]	$30.00	[heart]	$25.00
★	$28.00	[crown]	$25.00
[egg]	$25.00	[clover]	$25.00
[bow and arrow]	$25.00	[box]	$25.00

Out of Production, Issue Price $25.00, '98
Series: *Birthstone Collection*

Purchased ______________

Price $ ________________

☐ *I'm Gonna Let It Shine,* 349852

UM	$60.00
[egg]	$55.00
[bow and arrow]	$53.00
[heart]	$50.00
[crown]	$50.00
[clover]	$50.00
[box]	$50.00

Retired 2004, Issue Price $50.00, '99
Chapel Exclusive

Purchased ________, Price $ ___________

☐ *A Prayer Warrior's Faith Can Move Mountains,* 354406

UM	$65.00
★	$60.00
[egg]	$58.00
[bow and arrow]	$55.00
[heart]	$55.00

Retired 2002, Issue Price $45.00, '98
Chapel Exclusive

Purchased ___________

Price $______________

☐ *A Prayer Warrior's Faith Can Move Mountains,* 354414

UM $275.00

Limited Ed., Issue Price $250.00, '98
Chapel Exclusive, One Year Production

Purchased ________, Price $ ___________

☐ *Safe In Mom's Arms,* 357949

[house] $35.00

Limited Ed., Issue Price $35.00, '06
American Greetings/ Carlton Cards Exclusive

Purchased___________

Price $_____________

☐ *Catch Ya Later,* 358959

UM	$25.00
[heart]	$25.00
[crown]	$25.00
[clover]	$25.00
[box]	$25.00
[house]	$25.00
[symbol]	$25.00

Open, Issue Price $25.00, '03

Purchased ________, Price $ ___________

☐ *Thank You For The Time We Share,* 384836

UM $45.00

Limited Ed., Issue Price $22.00, '97
Avon Exclusive
Series: *Little Moments*

Purchased ______________

Price $ ________________

☐ *Fountain Of Angels,* 384844

UM	$55.00
★	$53.00
[egg]	$50.00
[bow and arrow]	$48.00
[heart]	$45.00
[crown]	$45.00
[clover]	$45.00
[box]	$45.00
[house]	$45.00
[symbol]	$45.00

Out of Production, Issue Price $45.00, '98
Chapel Exclusive

Purchased ________, Price $ ___________

☐ *Many Years Of Blessing You,* 384887

[cross]	$85.00
[eyeglasses]	$80.00

Sent to 61 retailers from 2/15/98 to 4/1/98. Remainders available to retailers who attended Oct. '98 Enesco Show.

Limited Ed., Issue Price $60.00, '98
Commemorates Kirlin Hallmark Fiftieth Anniversary

Purchased ________, Price $ ___________

☐ *The Voice Of Spring,* 408735 (Musical)

[flame]	$250.00
[vessel]	$250.00

Two Year Collectible, Issue Price $200.00, '90
Series: *The Four Seasons,* Tune: *April Love*

Purchased ___________

Price $ _____________

☐ *Summer's Joy,* 408743 (Musical)

$250.00
$250.00

Two Year Collectible, Issue Price $200.00, '90
Series: *The Four Seasons*
Tune: *You Are My Sunshine*

Purchased ____________
Price $ ______________

☐ *Summer's Joy,* 408794 (Doll)

$200.00
$200.00

Two Year Collectible, Issue Price $150.00, '90
Series: *The Four Seasons*

Purchased ________
Price $ ____________

☐ *May You Have An Old Fashioned Christmas,* 417785 (Doll)

$200.00
$200.00
$200.00

Two Year Collectible, Issue Price $150.00, '91

Purchased ________
Price $ ___________

☐ *Autumn's Praise,* 408751 (Musical)

$250.00
$250.00

Two Year Collectible, Issue Price $200.00, '90
Series: *The Four Seasons*
Tune: *Autumn Leaves*

Purchased ____________
Price $______________

☐ *Autumn's Praise,* 408808 (Doll)

$200.00
$200.00

Two Year Collectible, Issue Price $150.00, '90
Series: *The Four Seasons*

Purchased__________
Price $____________

☐ *You Have Touched So Many Hearts,* 422282 (Musical)

$235.00
$235.00
$235.00

Two Year Collectible, Issue Price $175.00, '91
Tune: *Everybody Loves Somebody*

Purchased ____________
Price $ ______________

☐ *Winter's Song,* 408778 (Musical)

$250.00
$250.00

Two Year Collectible, Issue Price $200.00, '90
Series: *The Four Seasons*
Tune: *Through The Eyes Of Love*

Purchased ________, Price $ ____________

☐ *Winter's Song,* 408816 (Doll)

$200.00
$200.00

Two Year Collectible, Issue Price $150.00, '90
Series: *The Four Seasons*

Purchased ________, Price $ ____________

☐ *You Have Touched So Many Hearts,* 427527 (Doll)

$155.00
$155.00
$155.00

Two Year Collectible, Issue Price $90.00, '91

Purchased ________, Price $ ____________

☐ *The Voice Of Spring,* 408786 (Doll)

$200.00
$200.00

Two Year Collectible, Issue Price $150.00, '90
Series: *The Four Seasons*

Purchased ________, Price $ ____________

☐ *May You Have An Old Fashioned Christmas,* 417777 (Musical)

$250.00
$250.00
$250.00

Two Year Collectible, Issue Price $200.00, '91
Tune: *Have Yourself A Merry Christmas*

Purchased ________, Price $ ____________

☐ *The Eyes Of The Lord Are Upon You (Boy),* 429570 (Musical)

$100.00
$95.00
$90.00
$88.00
$85.00

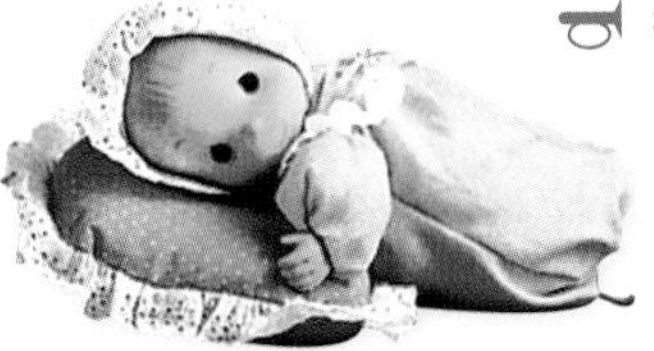

Suspended 1994, Issue Price $65.00, '91
Tune: *Brahms' Lullaby*

Purchased ________, Price $ ____________

☐ ***The Eyes Of The Lord Are Upon You (Girl),*** **429589 (Musical)**

$100.00
$95.00
$90.00
$88.00
$85.00

Suspended, 1994, Issue Price $65.00, '91
Tune: *Brahms' Lullaby*

Purchased ________, Price $ ___________

☐ ***20 Years And The Vision's Still The Same,*** **451312 (Ornament)**

$30.00

Limited Ed., Issue Price $22.50, '98
Commemorates Twentieth Anniversary of Precious Moments

Purchased ________, Price $ ___________

☐ ***Feed My Lambs,*** **453722**

UM $75.00
$70.00
$69.00
$69.00
$68.00
$68.00
$67.50
$67.50
$67.50
$67.50
$67.50
$67.50

Open, Issue Price $67.50, '98
Chapel Exclusive
Shepherd Of The Hills Exclusive

Purchased ________, Price $ ___________

☐ ***I'm Sending You A Merry Christmas,*** **455601**

$45.00

Dated Annual 1998, Issue Price $30.00, '98

Purchased ________, Price $ ___________

☐ ***I'm Sending You A Merry Christmas,*** **455628 (Ornament)**

$35.00

Dated Annual 1998, Issue Price $18.50, '98

Purchased ___________

Price $ ___________

☐ ***Our First Christmas Together,*** **455636 (Ornament)**

$30.00

Dated Annual 1998, Issue Price $25.00, '98

Purchased ________, Price $ ___________

☐ ***Baby's First Christmas (Girl),*** **455644 (Ornament)**

$25.00

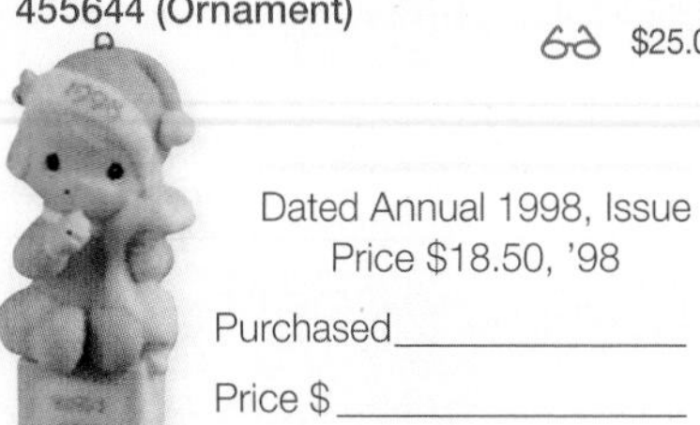

Dated Annual 1998, Issue Price $18.50, '98

Purchased___________

Price $___________

☐ ***Baby's First Christmas (Boy),*** **455652 (Ornament)**

$25.00

Dated Annual 1998, Issue Price $18.50, '98

Purchased ___________

Price $ ___________

☐ ***I'll Be Dog-ged It's That Season Again,*** **455660 (Ornament)**

$25.00

Dated Annual 1998, Issue Price $18.50, '98
Series: *Birthday Collection*

Purchased ________, Price $ ___________

☐ ***Mornin' Pumpkin,*** **455687**

$60.00
$55.00

Retired 1999, Issue Price $45.00, '98

Purchased ________, Price $ ___________

☐ ***Praise God From Whom All Blessings Flow,*** **455695**

$63.00
$60.00
$58.00
$55.00
$55.00

Retired 2001, Issue Price $40.00, '98

Purchased ________, Price $ ___________

☐ ***Praise The Lord And Dosie-Do,*** **455733**

$75.00
$73.00
$70.00
$68.00
$65.00
$63.00
$60.00

Retired 2004, Issue Price $50.00, '98

Purchased ________, Price $ ___________

☐ ***Peas On Earth,*** **455768**

$65.00
$60.00
$55.00
$50.00

Retired 2001, Issue Price $32.50, '98

Purchased ________

Price $___________

☐ *I'm Just Nutty About The Holidays,* 455776 (Ornament)

$28.00
$25.00
$23.00
$22.00
$21.00

Retired 2002, Issue Price $17.50, '98

Purchased ________, Price $ ____________

☐ *Alaska Once More, How's Yer Christmas?* 455784

$40.00
$38.00
$35.00
$35.00
$35.00
$35.00
$35.00

Suspended, Issue Price $35.00, '98

Purchased ________, Price $ ____________

☐ *You Can Always Fudge A Little During The Season,* 455792

$40.00 $35.00
$38.00 $35.00
$35.00 $35.00
$35.00 $35.00

Suspended 2004, Issue Price $35.00, '98

Purchased____________

Price $____________

☐ *Things Are Poppin' At Our House This Christmas,* 455806

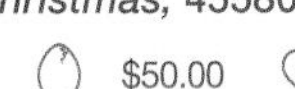

$50.00 $45.00
$48.00 $45.00
$45.00

Suspended, Issue Price $45.00, '00

Purchased ____________

Price $ ____________

☐ *Wishing You A Yummy Christmas,* 455814

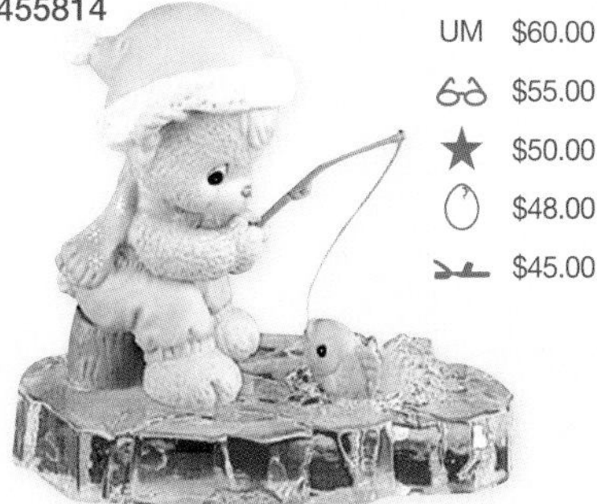

UM $60.00
$55.00
$50.00
$48.00
$45.00

Retired 2001, Issue Price $30.00, '98

Purchased ________, Price $ ____________

☐ *I Saw Mommy Kissing Santa Claus,* 455822

$85.00
$83.00
$80.00
$78.00
$75.00
$74.00
$73.00
$70.00

Suspended, Issue Price $65.00, '98

Purchased ________, Price $ ____________

☐ *Warmest Wishes For The Holidays,* 455830

$80.00

One Year Production, Issue Price $50.00, '98

Purchased _____

Price $ ________

☐ *Warmest Wishes For The Holidays,* 455830

$75.00
$70.00
$68.00
$65.00

Retired 2001, Issue Price $50.00, '99

Purchased ________, Price $ ____________

☐ *Time For A Holy Holiday,* 455849

$55.00 $48.00
$50.00 $45.00

Retired 2001, Issue Price $35.00, '98

Purchased____________

Price $ ____________

☐ *Wishing You A Moo-ie Christmas,* 455865

$85.00
$80.00
$78.00
$75.00
$73.00
$70.00
$68.00

Retired 2004, Issue Price $60.00, '99
Series: Country Lane Collection

Purchased ________, Price $ ____________

☐ *Have A Cozy Country Christmas,* 455873

$58.00 $55.00
$53.00
$50.00
$50.00
$50.00
$50.00
$50.00
$50.00
$50.00
$50.00

Open, Issue Price $50.00, '98

Purchased ________, Price $ ____________

☐ *Friends Are Forever, Sew Bee It,* 455903

$85.00
$83.00
$80.00
$78.00
$75.00

Retired 2002, Issue Price $60.00, '98

Purchased ________, Price $ ____________

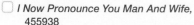

I Now Pronounce You Man And Wife, 455938

$35.00 · $33.00 · $31.00 · $30.00 · $30.00 · $30.00 · $30.00

Suspended, Issue Price $30.00, '98

Purchased ________

Price $________

My True Love Gave To Me, 455989 (Ornament)

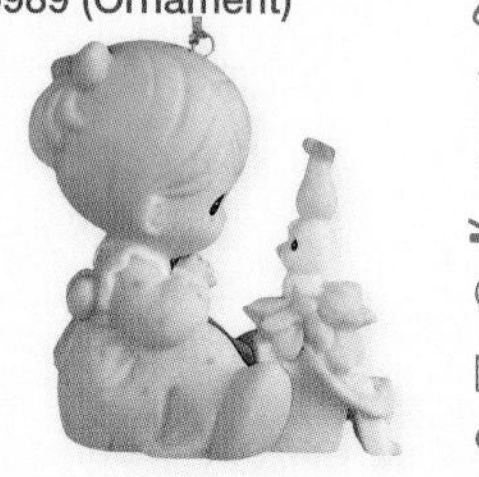

$25.00 · $23.00 · $22.00 · $20.00 · $20.00 · $20.00 · $20.00

Suspended 11/04/04, Issue Price $20.00, '98
Series: *12 Days Of Christmas* — Day 1

Purchased ________, Price $ ________

The Golden Rings Of Friendship, 456020 (Ornament)

$25.00 · $23.00 · $22.00 · $20.00 · $20.00 · $20.00

Suspended 11/04/04, Issue Price $20.00, '98
Series: *12 Days Of Christmas* — Day 5

Purchased ________, Price $ ________

The Light Of The World Is Jesus, 455954

$35.00 · $33.00 · $31.00 · $30.00 · $30.00 · $30.00 · $30.00 · $30.00 · $30.00 · $30.00

Open, Issue Price $30.00, '98
Nativity Addition

Purchased ________, Price $ ________

We're Two Of A Kind, 455997 (Ornament)

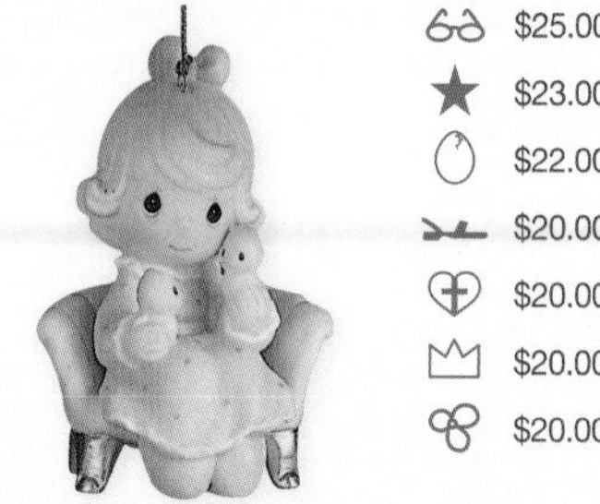

$25.00 · $23.00 · $22.00 · $20.00 · $20.00 · $20.00 · $20.00

Suspended 11/04/04, Issue Price $20.00, '98
Series: *12 Days Of Christmas* — Day 2

Purchased ________, Price $ ________

Hatching The Perfect Holiday, 456039 (Ornament)

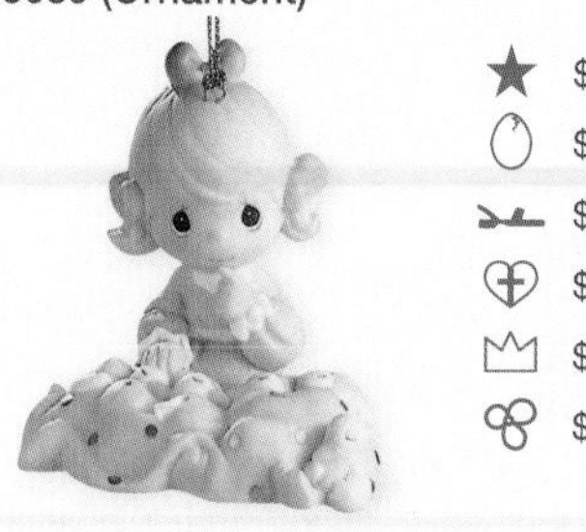

$25.00 · $23.00 · $22.00 · $20.00 · $20.00 · $20.00

Suspended 11/04/04, Issue Price $20.00, '98
Series: *12 Days Of Christmas* — Day 6

Purchased ________, Price $ ________

Hang On To That Holiday Feeling, 455962

$35.00 · $33.00 · $30.00 · $30.00

Retired 2001, Issue Price $17.50, '98
Mini Nativity Addition

Purchased ________

Price $ ________

Saying "Oui" To Our Love, 456004 (Ornament)

$25.00 · $23.00 · $22.00 · $20.00 · $20.00 · $20.00 · $20.00

Suspended 11/04/04, Issue Price $20.00, '98
Series: *12 Days Of Christmas* — Day 3

Purchased ________, Price $ ________

Swimming Into Your Heart, 456047 (Ornament)

$25.00 · $23.00 · $22.00 · $20.00 · $20.00 · $20.00

Suspended 11/04/04, Issue Price $20.00, '98
Series: *12 Days Of Christmas* — Day 7

Purchased ________, Price $ ________

Flight Into Egypt, 455970

Offered to retailers who attended the 1998 Spring Fling Show.

$100.00

Annual 1998, Issue Price $75.00, '98
Complements Large Nativity, Set of 2

Purchased ________, Price $ ________

Ringing In The Season, 456012 (Ornament)

$25.00 · $23.00 · $22.00 · $20.00 · $20.00 · $20.00 · $20.00

Suspended 11/04/04, Issue Price $20.00, '98
Series: *12 Days Of Christmas* — Day 4

Purchased ________, Price $ ________

Eight Mice A Milking, 456055 (Ornament)

$25.00 · $23.00 · $22.00 · $20.00 · $20.00 · $20.00

Suspended 11/04/04, Issue Price $20.00, '98
Series: *12 Days Of Christmas* — Day 8

Purchased ________, Price $ ________

☐ *Nine Ladies Dancing With Joy,* 456063 (Ornament)

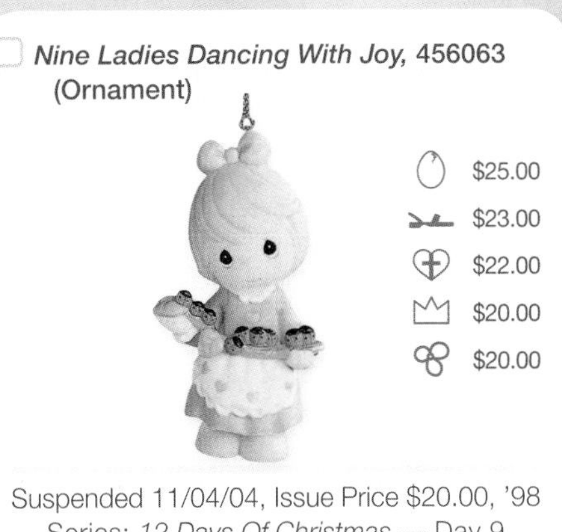

$25.00
$23.00
$22.00
$20.00
$20.00

Suspended 11/04/04, Issue Price $20.00, '98
Series: *12 Days Of Christmas* — Day 9

Purchased ________, Price $ ___________

☐ *Leaping Into The Holidays,* 456071 (Ornament)

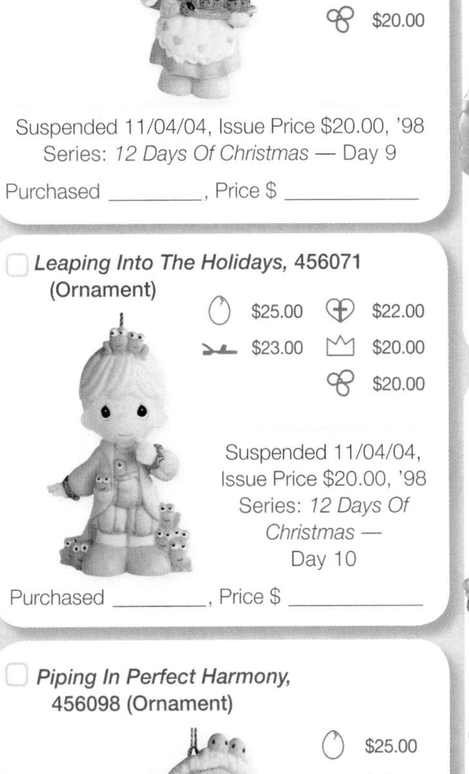

$25.00 $22.00
$23.00 $20.00
$20.00

Suspended 11/04/04, Issue Price $20.00, '98
Series: *12 Days Of Christmas* — Day 10

Purchased ________, Price $ ___________

☐ *Piping In Perfect Harmony,* 456098 (Ornament)

$25.00
$23.00
$22.00
$20.00
$20.00

Suspended 11/04/04, Issue Price $20.00, '98
Series: *12 Days Of Christmas* — Day 11

Purchased ________, Price $ ___________

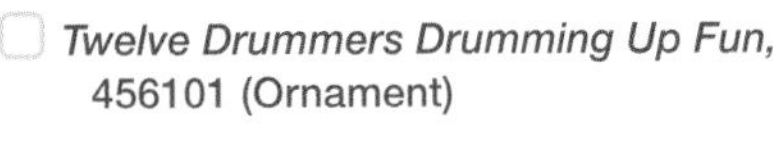

☐ *Twelve Drummers Drumming Up Fun,* 456101 (Ornament)

$25.00
$23.00
$22.00
$20.00
$20.00

Suspended 11/04/04, Issue Price $20.00, '98
Series: *12 Days Of Christmas* — Day 12

Purchased ________, Price $ ___________

☐ *Sugar Town Post Office Collector's Set,* 456217

$310.00
$305.00

Limited Ed., Issue Price $250.00, '98
Series: *Sugar Town,* Lighted, Set of 7 (Post Office, girl with lights, girl with goose, girl mailing snowball, boy with ice cream, postman in car, girl pushing sleigh of puppies)

Purchased ________, Price $ ___________

☐ *God Loveth A Cheerful Giver,* 456225

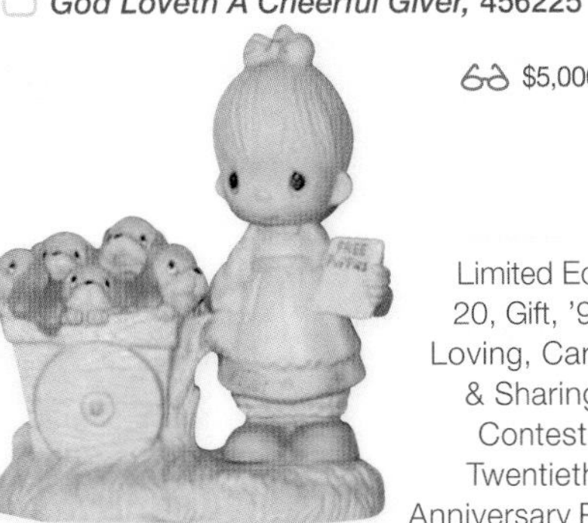

$5,000.00

Limited Ed. 20, Gift, '98
Loving, Caring & Sharing Contest Twentieth Anniversary Piece

Purchased ________, Price $ ___________

☐ *How Can Two Work Together Except They Agree,* 456268 (Ornament)

$35.00
$30.00

Limited Ed., Issue Price $25.00, '98
Care-A-Van Exclusive

Purchased ________
Price $ ___________

☐ *You Have Mastered The Art Of Caring,* 456276

$55.00

Limited Ed., Issue Price $40.00, '98
Fall Syndicated Catalog

Purchased ________, Price $ ___________

☐ *Heaven Bless You Easter Seal,* 456314

$45.00
★ $43.00

Annual 1999, Issue Price $35.00, '99
Easter Seals Commemorative, Lily Understamp

Purchased ________, Price $ ___________

☐ *Sharing Our Time Is So Precious,* 456349

★ $165.00

Limited Ed. 15,000, Issue Price $110.00, '99
CCR Exclusive
Individually Numbered

Purchased ________, Price $ ___________

☐ *You Are A Dutch-ess To Me (Holland)*, 456373

UM $20.00

Open, Issue Price $20.00, '98
Series: *International — Little Moments*

Purchased ________
Price $ ________

☐ *Hola, Amigo! (Mexico)*, 456454

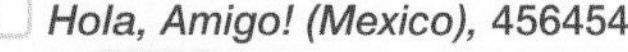

UM $20.00

Open, Issue Price $20.00, '98
Series: *International — Little Moments*

Purchased ________
Price $ ________

☐ *Our Friendship Is Always In Bloom (Japan)*, 456926

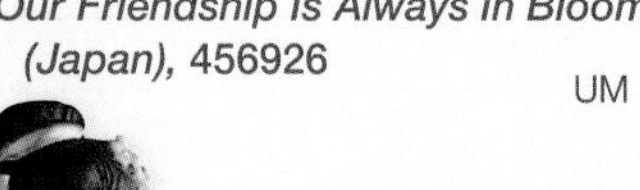

UM $20.00

Open, Issue Price $20.00, '98
Series: *International — Little Moments*

Purchased ________
Price $ ________

☐ *Life Is A Fiesta (Spain)*, 456381

UM $20.00

Open, Issue Price $20.00, '98
Series: *International — Little Moments*

Purchased ________
Price $ ________

☐ *Afri-can Be There For You, I Will Be (Kenya)*, 456462

UM $20.00

Open, Issue Price $20.00, '98
Series: *International — Little Moments*

Purchased ________
Price $ ________

☐ *My Love Will Stand Guard Over You (England)*, 456934

UM $20.00

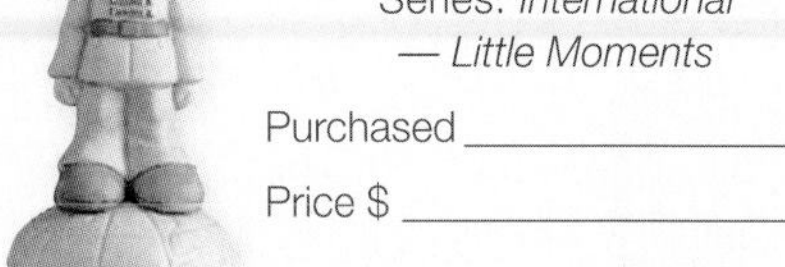

Open, Issue Price $20.00, '98
Series: *International — Little Moments*

Purchased ________
Price $ ________

☐ *Don't Rome Too Far From Home (Italy)*, 456403

UM $20.00

Open, Issue Price $20.00, '98
Series: *International — Little Moments*

Purchased ________
Price $ ________

☐ *I'd Travel The Highlands To Be With You (Scotland)*, 456470

UM $20.00

Open, Issue Price $20.00, '98
Series: *International — Little Moments*

Purchased ________
Price $ ________

☐ *I'm Sending You A Merry Christmas*, 469327 (Plate)

$60.00

Dated Annual 1998, Issue Price $50.00, '98
Series: *Wonder Of Christmas*

Purchased ________, Price $ ________

☐ *You Can't Beat The Red, White And Blue (United States)*, 456411

UM $20.00

Open, Issue Price $20.00, '98
Series: *International — Little Moments*

Purchased ________
Price $ ________

☐ *Sure Would Love To Squeeze You (Germany)*, 456896

UM $20.00

Open, Issue Price $20.00, '98
Series: *International — Little Moments*

Purchased ________
Price $ ________

☐ *May Your Christmas Be Warm*, 470279 (Ornament)

$25.00 $15.00
★ $22.00 $15.00
$20.00 $15.00
$18.00 $15.00

Open, Issue Price $15.00, '98
Series: *Birthday Circus Train*

Purchased ________, Price $ ________

☐ *Love's Russian Into My Heart (Russia)*, 456446

UM $20.00

Open, Issue Price $20.00, '98
Series: *International — Little Moments*

Purchased ________
Price $ ________

☐ *You Are My Amour (France)*, 456918

UM $20.00

Open, Issue Price $20.00, '98
Series: *International — Little Moments*

Purchased ________
Price $ ________

☐ *We Are All Precious In His Sight,* 475068

UM	$600.00
[Eyeglasses]	$575.00
[Star]	$550.00

Limited Ed. 1,500, Issue Price $500.00, '99
Easter Seals, Lily Understamp
Individually Numbered

Purchased ________, Price $ ____________

☐ *Heaven Bless You Easter Seal,* 475076 (Ornament)

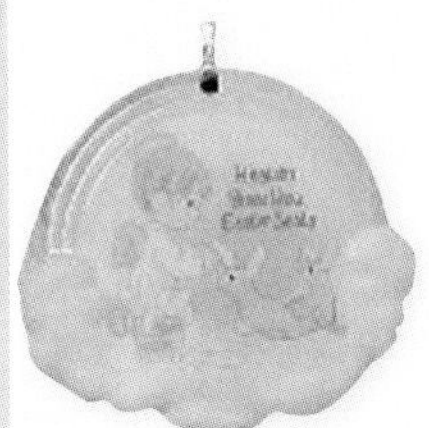

UM	$7.00

Open, Issue Price $5.00, '02

Purchased ________

Price $ ___________

☐ *Even The Heavens Shall Praise Him,* 475084 (Ornament)

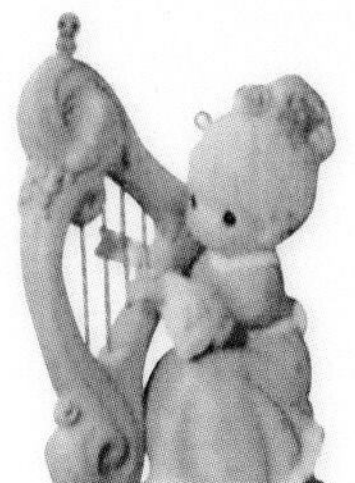

[Eyeglasses]	$42.00

Annual 1998, Issue Price $30.00, '98
Century Circle Exclusive

Purchased ___________

Price $ ___________

☐ *Toy Maker,* 475092

Memorial to Pat Carson's father.

UM	$65.00
[Star]	$63.00
[Egg]	$62.00
[Sword]	$61.00
[Cross in Heart]	$60.00
[Crown]	$60.00
[Clover]	$60.00
[Box]	$60.00
[House]	$60.00
[Mushroom]	$60.00

Open, Issue Price $40.00, '98
Chapel Exclusive

Purchased ________, Price $ ____________

☐ *Toy Maker,* 475106 (Ornament)

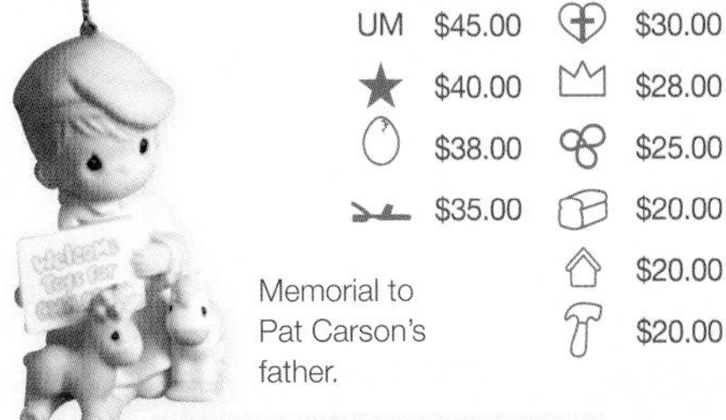

Memorial to Pat Carson's father.

UM	$45.00	[Cross in Heart]	$30.00
[Star]	$40.00	[Crown]	$28.00
[Egg]	$38.00	[Clover]	$25.00
[Sword]	$35.00	[Box]	$20.00
		[House]	$20.00
		[Mushroom]	$20.00

Open, Issue Price $20.00, '98
Chapel Exclusive

Purchased ________, Price $ ____________

☐ *On Our Way To A Special Day,* 481602

[Eyeglasses]	$35.00	[Clover]	$28.00
[Star]	$33.00	[Box]	$28.00
[Egg]	$33.00	[House]	$28.00
[Sword]	$30.00	[Mushroom]	$28.00
[Cross in Heart]	$30.00	[Heart]	$28.00
[Crown]	$28.00	[Wheat]	$28.00

Open, Issue Price $17.50, '99
Japan and CCR Exclusive

Purchased ________, Price $ ____________

☐ *On Our Way To A Special Day,* 481610

[Eyeglasses]	$25.00	[Egg]	$20.00	[Box]	$17.50
[Star]	$22.00	[Sword]	$17.50	[House]	$17.50
		[Cross in Heart]	$17.50	[Mushroom]	$17.50
		[Crown]	$17.50	[Heart]	$17.50
		[Clover]	$17.50	[Wheat]	$17.50

Open, Issue Price $17.50, '99
Japan and CCR Exclusive

Purchased___________

Price $ ___________

☐ *Shiny New And Ready For School,* 481629

[Eyeglasses]	$45.00	[Egg]	$40.00	[Box]	$20.00
[Star]	$43.00	[Sword]	$37.50	[House]	$20.00
		[Cross in Heart]	$35.00	[Mushroom]	$20.00
		[Crown]	$30.00	[Heart]	$20.00
		[Clover]	$25.00	[Wheat]	$20.00

Open, Issue Price $20.00, '99
Japan and CCR Exclusive

Purchased___________

Price $___________

☐ *Shiny New And Ready For School,* 481637

[Eyeglasses]	$45.00	[Egg]	$40.00	[Box]	$20.00
[Star]	$43.00	[Sword]	$37.50	[House]	$20.00
		[Cross in Heart]	$35.00	[Mushroom]	$20.00
		[Crown]	$30.00	[Heart]	$20.00
		[Clover]	$25.00	[Wheat]	$20.00

Open, Issue Price $20.00, '99
Japan and CCR Exclusive

Purchased ___________

Price $ ___________

☐ *Growing In Wisdom,* 481645

[Eyeglasses]	$45.00	[Clover]	$22.50
[Star]	$40.00	[Box]	$22.50
[Egg]	$38.00	[House]	$22.50
[Sword]	$35.00	[Mushroom]	$22.50
[Cross in Heart]	$30.00	[Heart]	$22.50
[Crown]	$25.00	[Wheat]	$22.50

Open, Issue Price $22.50, '99
Japan and CCR Exclusive

Purchased ________, Price $ ____________

☐ *Growing In Wisdom,* 481653

[Eyeglasses]	$45.00	[Cross in Heart]	$30.00	[House]	$22.50
[Star]	$40.00	[Crown]	$25.00	[Mushroom]	$22.50
[Egg]	$38.00	[Clover]	$22.50	[Heart]	$22.50
[Sword]	$35.00	[Box]	$22.50	[Wheat]	$22.50

Open, Issue Price $22.50, '99
Japan and CCR Exclusive

Purchased___________

Price $ ___________

☐ *All Girls Are Beautiful,* 481661

[Eyeglasses]	$100.00	[Sword]	$80.00	[Clover]	$60.00	[Mushroom]	$60.00
[Star]	$90.00	[Cross in Heart]	$75.00	[Box]	$60.00	[Heart]	$60.00
[Egg]	$85.00	[Crown]	$60.00	[House]	$60.00	[Wheat]	$60.00

Open, Issue Price $60.00, '99
Japan and CCR Exclusive
Set of 5 (Emperor, Empress, and 3 Flower Arrangements)

Purchased ________, Price $ ____________

☐ *Make Me Strong,* 481688

[eyeglasses]	$100.00	[cross in heart]	$75.00	[house]	$60.00
[star]	$90.00	[crown]	$70.00	[mushroom]	$60.00
[egg]	$85.00	[clover]	$60.00	[heart]	$60.00
[sandal]	$80.00	[box]	$60.00	[wheat]	$60.00

Open, Issue Price $60.00, '99
Japan and CCR Exclusive
Set of 4
(Samurai, Helmet, Bow, and Arrows)

Purchased ________, Price $ ____________

☐ *What Better To Give Than Yourself,* 487988

[eyeglasses]	$45.00
[star]	$43.00
[egg]	$40.00
[sandal]	$38.00
[cross in heart]	$35.00

Retired 2002, Issue Price $30.00, '99

Purchased ____________

Price $ ______________

☐ *Love Is The Key,* 482242

[eyeglasses]	$55.00
[star]	$50.00

Limited Ed., Issue Price $30.00, '98
Avon Exclusive

Purchased ____________

Price $ ______________

☐ *You're My Honey Bee,* 487929

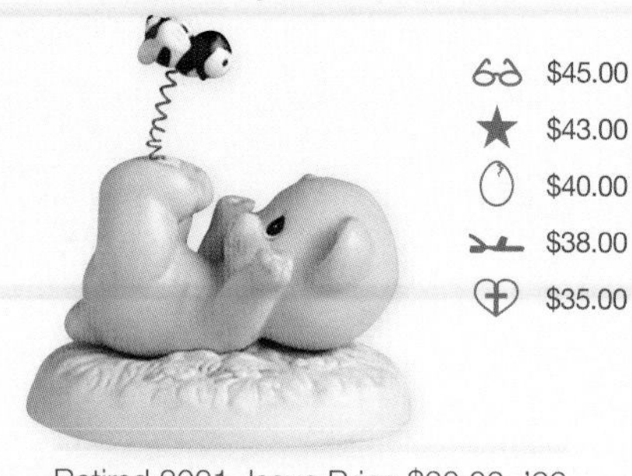

[eyeglasses]	$45.00
[star]	$43.00
[egg]	$40.00
[sandal]	$38.00
[cross in heart]	$35.00

Retired 2001, Issue Price $20.00, '99

Purchased ________, Price $ ____________

☐ *Take Your Time It's Your Birthday,* 488003

[eyeglasses]	$30.00	[clover]	$26.50
[star]	$28.00	[box]	$26.50
[egg]	$26.50	[house]	$26.50
[sandal]	$26.50	[mushroom]	$26.50
[cross in heart]	$26.50	[heart]	$26.50
[crown]	$26.50	[wheat]	$26.50

Open, Issue Price $25.00, '99
Series: *Birthday Circus Train* — Age 11

Purchased ________, Price $ ____________

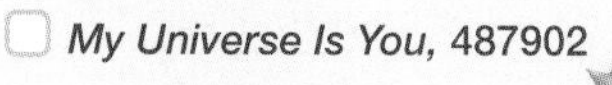

☐ *My Universe Is You,* 487902

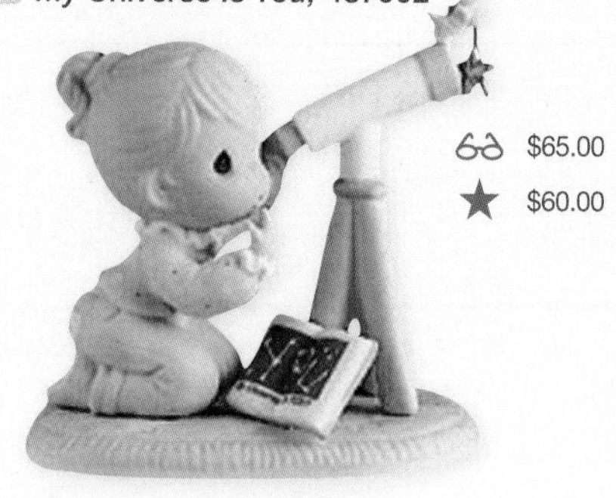

[eyeglasses]	$65.00
[star]	$60.00

Retired 1999, Issue Price $45.00, '99

Purchased ________, Price $ ____________

☐ *Jesus Is My Lighthouse,* 487945 (Lighted)

[eyeglasses]	$105.00
[star]	$100.00

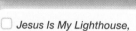

Limited Ed., Issue Price $75.00, '99

Purchased ________

Price $ __________

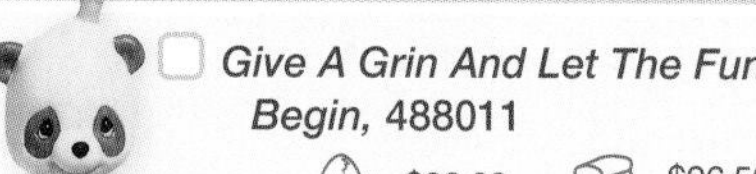

☐ *Give A Grin And Let The Fun Begin,* 488011

[egg]	$28.00	[box]	$26.50
[sandal]	$27.00	[house]	$26.50
[cross in heart]	$26.50	[mushroom]	$25.00
[crown]	$26.50	[heart]	$26.50
[clover]	$26.50	[wheat]	$26.50

Open, Issue Price $25.00, '00
Series: *Birthday Circus Train* — Age 12

Purchased ________, Price $ ____________

☐ *Believe It Or Knot I Luv You,* 487910

[eyeglasses]	$45.00	[cross in heart]	$35.00
[star]	$40.00	[crown]	$35.00
[egg]	$35.00	[clover]	$35.00
[sandal]	$35.00	[box]	$35.00
		[house]	$35.00
		[mushroom]	$35.00
		[heart]	$35.00
		[wheat]	$35.00

Open, Issue Price $35.00, '99

Purchased ________, Price $ ____________

☐ *You Can Always Count On Me,* 487953

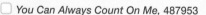

[eyeglasses]	$50.00	[egg]	$45.00
[star]	$48.00	[sandal]	$43.00
		[cross in heart]	$40.00

Retired 2002, Issue Price $35.00, '99

Purchased____________

Price $ ______________

☐ *You Mean The Moose To Me,* 488038

[egg]	$28.00	[box]	$26.50
[sandal]	$27.00	[house]	$26.50
[cross in heart]	$26.50	[mushroom]	$25.00
[crown]	$26.50	[heart]	$26.50
[clover]	$26.50	[wheat]	$26.50

Open, Issue Price $25.00, '00
Series: *Birthday Circus Train* — Age 13

Purchased ________, Price $ ____________

Mom, You've Given Me So Much, 488046

$45.00
$40.00
$40.00
$35.00
$35.00
$35.00
$35.00
$35.00
$35.00
$35.00
$35.00
$35.00

Open, Issue Price $35.00, '99

Purchased ________, Price $ ___________

Confirmed In The Lord, 488178

$40.00 $30.00
$35.00 $30.00
$30.00 $30.00
$30.00 $30.00
$30.00 $30.00
$30.00 $30.00

Open, Issue Price $30.00, '99

Purchased ________, Price $ ___________

Hope Is Revealed Through God's Word, 488259

$88.00

Annual, Issue Price $70.00, '98
Series: *Always Victorian,* Second Issue

Purchased ___________

Price $___________

You Just Can't Replace A Good Friendship, 488054

$45.00 $35.00
$40.00 $35.00
$40.00 $35.00
$35.00
$35.00
$35.00
$35.00
$35.00
$35.00

Open, Issue Price $35.00, '99

Purchased ________, Price $ ___________

You'll Always Be Daddy's Little Girl, 488224

$55.00
$50.00
$50.00
$50.00
$50.00
$50.00
$50.00
$50.00

Open, Issue Price $50.00, '00

Purchased ________, Price $ ___________

Jonah And The Whale, 488283

UM $25.00

Open, Issue Price $25.00, '99
Series: *Bible Stories — Little Moments*

Purchased ________, Price $ ___________

Dedicated To God, 488232

$45.00 $35.00
$40.00 $35.00
$35.00 $35.00
$35.00
$35.00
$35.00
$35.00
$35.00

Open, Issue Price $35.00, '99

Purchased ________, Price $ ___________

Daniel And The Lion's Den, 488291

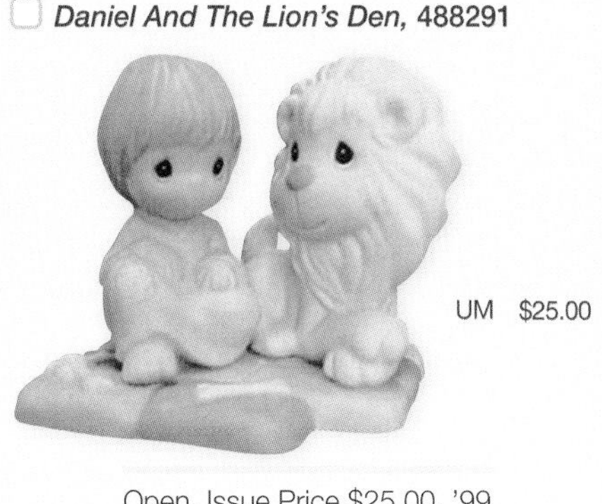

UM $25.00

Open, Issue Price $25.00, '99
Series: *Bible Stories — Little Moments*

Purchased ________, Price $ ___________

He'll Carry Me Through, 488089

$65.00
$63.00
$60.00
$58.00
$55.00

Retired 2004, Issue Price $45.00, '00

Purchased ________, Price $ ___________

A Very Special Bond, 488240

$85.00 $78.00 $75.00
$83.00 $75.00 $75.00
$80.00 $75.00 $75.00
$80.00 $75.00 $75.00

Open, Issue Price $70.00, '99

Purchased ________, Price $ ___________

☐ ***Joseph's Special Coat,* 488305**

UM $25.00

Open, Issue Price $25.00, '99
Series: *Bible Stories — Little Moments*
Purchased ________, Price $ ____________

☐ ***You Can't Take It With You,* 488321**

[Eyeglasses]	$45.00
[Star]	$43.00
[Egg]	$40.00
[Bow & Arrow]	$38.00
[Heart]	$35.00
[Crown]	$33.00
[Flower]	$30.00

Retired 2004, Issue Price $25.00, '99
Purchased ________, Price $ ____________

☐ ***Holiday Surprises Come In All Sizes,* 488348**

[Crown]	$35.00
[Flower]	$30.00
[Cube]	$30.00
[House]	$30.00
[Hammer]	$30.00

Open, Issue Price $30.00, '04
Purchased ________, Price $ ____________

☐ ***Always Listen To Your Heart,* 488356**

[Eyeglasses]	$35.00
[Star]	$33.00
[Egg]	$30.00
[Bow & Arrow]	$30.00
[Heart]	$28.00
[Crown]	$28.00
[Flower]	$28.00
[Cube]	$28.00

Suspended 2005, Issue Price $25.00, '99
Purchased ________, Price $ ____________

☐ ***Purr-fect Friends,* 488364**

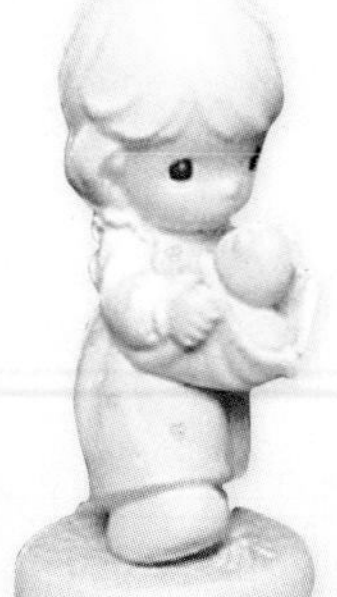

[Star] $475.00

Annual 1999, Issue Price $25.00, '99
Parade of Gifts Exclusive
Purchased ____________
Price $ ____________

☐ ***You Count,* 488372**

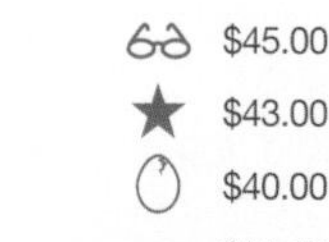

[Eyeglasses]	$45.00
[Star]	$43.00
[Egg]	$40.00
[Bow & Arrow]	$38.00
[Heart]	$35.00
[Crown]	$35.00
[Flower]	$35.00

Retired 2004, Issue Price $25.00, '99
Purchased ________, Price $ ____________

☐ ***Jesus Loves Me,* 488380 (Hinged Box)**

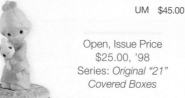

UM $45.00

Open, Issue Price $25.00, '98
Series: *Original "21" Covered Boxes*
Purchased ____________
Price $ ____________

☐ ***Jesus Loves Me,* 488399 (Hinged Box)**

UM $45.00

Open, Issue Price $25.00, '98
Series: *Original "21" Covered Boxes*
Purchased ____________
Price $ ____________

☐ ***Make A Joyful Noise,* 488402 (Hinged Box)**

UM $45.00

Open, Issue Price $25.00, '98
Series: *Original "21" Covered Boxes*
Purchased ____________
Price $ ____________

☐ ***Love One Another,* 488410 (Hinged Box)**

UM $45.00

Open, Issue Price $25.00, '98
Series: *Original "21" Covered Boxes*
Purchased ____________
Price $____________

☐ ***His Burden Is Light,* 488429 (Hinged Box)**

UM $45.00

Open, Issue Price $25.00, '98
Series: *Original "21" Covered Boxes*
Purchased ____________
Price $____________

☐ ***Jesus Is The Light,* 488437 (Hinged Box)**

UM $45.00

Open, Issue Price $25.00, '98
Series: *Original "21" Covered Boxes*
Purchased ____________
Price $ ____________

☐ ***Give Your Whole Heart,*** 490245

★ $35.00
$33.00

Annual 2000, Issue Price $30.00, '00 Easter Seals Commemorative

Purchased ________

Price $ ________

☐ ***God Knows Our Ups And Downs,*** 490318

★ $45.00
$43.00
$40.00
$38.00
$35.00
$35.00

Retired 2004, Issue Price $30.00, '99

Purchased ________, Price $ ________

☐ ***You Oughta Be In Pictures,*** 490327

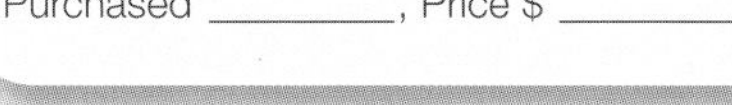

★ $50.00

Annual 1999, Issue Price $32.50, '99 DSR Event Figurine 5/22/99

Purchased ________

Price $ ________

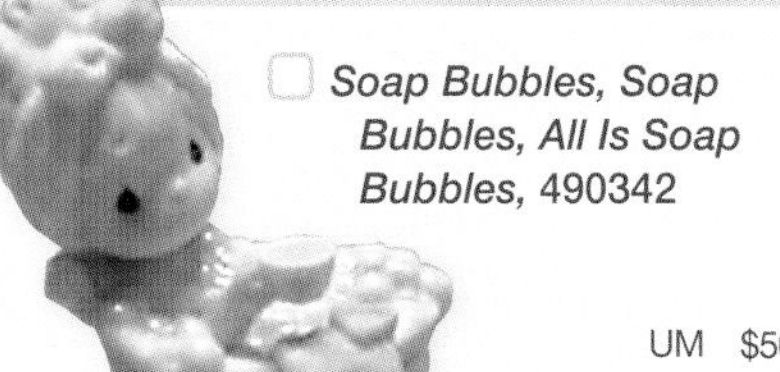

☐ ***Soap Bubbles, Soap Bubbles, All Is Soap Bubbles,*** 490342

UM $50.00

Limited Ed., Issue Price $20.00, '99
Series: *Little Moments — Avon Exclusive*

Purchased ________, Price $ ________

☐ ***World's Greatest Student (Boy),*** 491586

UM $20.00

Open, Issue Price $20.00, '99
Series: *Trophies — Little Moments*

Purchased ________

Price $ ________

☐ ***World's Sweetest Girl,*** 491594

UM $20.00

Open, Issue Price $20.00, '99
Series: *Trophies — Little Moments*

Purchased ________

Price $ ________

☐ ***World's Best Helper (Girl),*** 491608

UM $20.00

Open, Issue Price $20.00, '99
Series: *Trophies — Little Moments*

Purchased ________

Price $ ________

☐ ***World's Greatest Student (Girl),*** 491616

UM $20.00

Open, Issue Price $20.00, '99
Series: *Trophies — Little Moments*

Purchased ________

Price $ ________

☐ ***You're No. 1 (Girl),*** 491624

UM $20.00

Open, Issue Price $20.00, '99
Series: *Trophies — Little Moments*

Purchased ________

Price $ ________

☐ ***You're No. 1 (Boy),*** 491640

UM $20.00

Open, Issue Price $20.00, '99
Series: *Trophies — Little Moments*

Purchased ________

Price $ ________

☐ ***You Always Stand Behind Me,*** 492140

$60.00 | ★ $55.00 | $50.00 | $50.00 | $50.00
$50.00 | $50.00 | $50.00 | $50.00 | $50.00 | $50.00 | $50.00

Open, Issue Price $50.00, '99

Purchased ________, Price $ ________

☐ ***Goose Girl,*** 493627 (Medallion)

UM $600.00

Presented to those who toured the Taiwan facility in 1987. "Heart with Flowers" decal on back, also reported with Bow and Arrow decal. The PM Collector's Club logo of the kids on the cloud.

Limited Ed. 25, Gift, '87
1987 Orient Tour Exclusive

Purchased ________, Price $ ________

☐ ***Goose Girl,*** 495298 (Medallion)

Presented to those who atended the Dealer Tour of the Orient. Back says "Precious Moments Collectors' Club Tour of the Orient March 1990.

$600.00

Limited Ed. 25,Gift, '90
1990 Orient Tour Exclusive

Purchased ________, Price $ ________

☐ ***Goose Girl,*** 495301 (Medallion)

Back reads "Commemorating the Enesco Precious Moments Collectors' Club Tour of the Orient, April 1990."

UM $600.00

Limited Ed. 25, Gift, '90
1990 Orient Tour Medallion

Purchased ________, Price $ ________

☐ ***Have Faith In God*, 505153**

$75.00
$70.00
$68.00

Retired 2002, Issue Price $50.00, '00
Series: *Always Victorian* — Third Issue

Purchased __________

Price $__________

☐ ***Our First Christmas Together*, 520233 (Ornament)**

$28.00

Dated Annual 1988, Issue Price $13.00, '88

Purchased __________

Price $ __________

☐ ***Baby's First Christmas*, 520241 (Ornament)**

$28.00

Dated Annual 1988, Issue Price $15.00, '88

Purchased ________, Price $ __________

☐ ***You Are My Gift Come True*, 520276 (Ornament)**

$28.00

Dated Annual 1988, Issue Price $12.50, '88
Tenth Anniversary Commemorative

Purchased __________

Price $ __________

☐ ***Merry Christmas, Deer*, 520284 (Plate)**

$65.00

Dated Annual 1988, Issue Price $50.00, '88
Series: *Christmas Love* — Third Issue

Purchased ________, Price $ __________

☐ ***Hang On For The Holly Days*, 520292 (Ornament)**

$40.00
$40.00

Dated Annual 1988, Issue Price $13.00, '88
Series: *Birthday Collection*

Purchased ________, Price $ __________

☐ ***Make A Joyful Noise*, 520322**

$825.00

Limited Ed. 1,500, Issue Price $500.00, '89
Easter Seals — Lily Understamp
Individually Numbered

Purchased __________

Price $__________

☐ ***Jesus The Savior Is Born*, 520357**

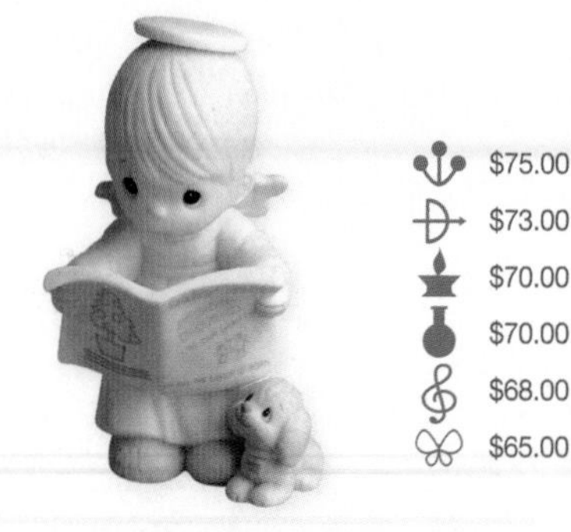

$75.00
$73.00
$70.00
$70.00
$68.00
$65.00

Suspended 1993, Issue Price $25.00, '88
Nativity Addition

Purchased ________, Price $ __________

☐ ***Hippo Holly Days*, 520403 (Ornament)**

$28.00

Dated Annual 1995, Issue Price $17.00, '95
Series: *Birthday Collection*

Purchased __________

Price $ __________

☐ ***Rejoice, O Earth*, 520268**

$35.00	$23.00	$18.50	$18.50
$30.00	$20.00	$18.50	$18.50
$28.00	$20.00	$18.50	$18.50
$25.00	$18.50	$18.50	$18.50
$24.00	$18.50	$18.50	$18.50
		$18.50	$18.50

Open, Issue Price $13.00, '88
Mini Nativity Addition

Purchased ________, Price $ __________

☐ ***I'm Nuts About You*, 520411 (Ornament)**

$28.00

Dated Annual 1992, Issue Price $16.00, '92
Series: *Birthday Collection*

Purchased ________, Price $ __________

☐ *Sno-Bunny Falls For You Like I Do,* 520438 (Ornament)

$35.00

Dated Annual 1991, Issue Price $15.00, '91
Series: *Birthday Collection*

Purchased ____________
Price $ ______________

☐ *Sno-Ball Without You,* 520446 (Ornament)

UM $25.00
$25.00

Dated Annual 2001, Issue Price $19.00, '01
Series: *Birthday Collection*

Purchased ____________
Price $______________

☐ *Happy Holidaze,* 520454 (Ornament)

$30.00 $25.00
$28.00 $25.00
$25.00

Retired 2002, Issue Price $17.50, '98

Purchased ____________
Price $ ______________

☐ *Christmas Is Ruff Without You,* 520462 (Ornament)

$40.00
$38.00

Dated Annual 1989, Issue Price $13.00, '89
Series: *Birthday Collection*

Purchased____________
Price $______________

☐ *Take A Bow Cuz You're My Christmas Star,* 520470 (Ornament)

$28.00

Annual 1994, Issue Price $16.00, '94
Holiday Preview Event

Purchased ____________
Price $ ______________

☐ *Slow Down And Enjoy The Holidays,* 520489 (Ornament)

$35.00

Dated Annual 1993, Issue Price $16.00, '93
Series: *Birthday Collection*

Purchased ________
Price $ ___________

☐ *Wishing You A Purr-fect Holiday,* 520497 (Ornament)

$38.00

Dated Annual 1990, Issue Price $15.00, '90
Series: *Birthday Collection*

Purchased ____________
Price $______________

☐ *The Lord Turned My Life Around,* 520535

$70.00
$68.00
$65.00
$63.00
$60.00

Suspended 1996, Issue Price $35.00, '92

Purchased ________, Price $ ____________

☐ *In The Spotlight Of His Grace,* 520543

$75.00
$73.00
$70.00
$68.00
$65.00
$63.00

Suspended 1996, Issue Price $35.00, '91

Purchased ________, Price $ ____________

☐ *Lord, Turn My Life Around,* 520551

$75.00
$73.00
$70.00
$68.00
$65.00
$63.00
$60.00
$58.00

Suspended 1996, Issue Price $35.00, '90

Purchased ________, Price $ ____________

☐ *You Deserve An Ovation,* 520578

$75.00 $65.00
$73.00 $63.00
$70.00 $60.00
$68.00 $60.00
$58.00
$58.00
$55.00
$55.00
$55.00
$55.00

Suspended 2004, Issue Price $35.00, '92

Purchased ________, Price $ ____________

☐ *My Heart Is Exposed With Love,* 520624

$105.00 $95.00 $90.00
$100.00 $93.00 $88.00
$98.00 $93.00 $88.00
$95.00 $90.00 $85.00

Retired 1999, Issue Price $45.00, '89

Purchased ________, Price $ ____________

☐ *A Friend Is Someone Who Cares,* 520632

$105.00 · $103.00 · $100.00 · $98.00 · $95.00 · $93.00 · $90.00 · $90.00

Retired 1995, Issue Price $30.00, '89

Purchased ________, Price $ ____________

☐ *I'm So Glad You Fluttered Into My Life,* 520640

$375.00 · $365.00 · $355.00 · $345.00

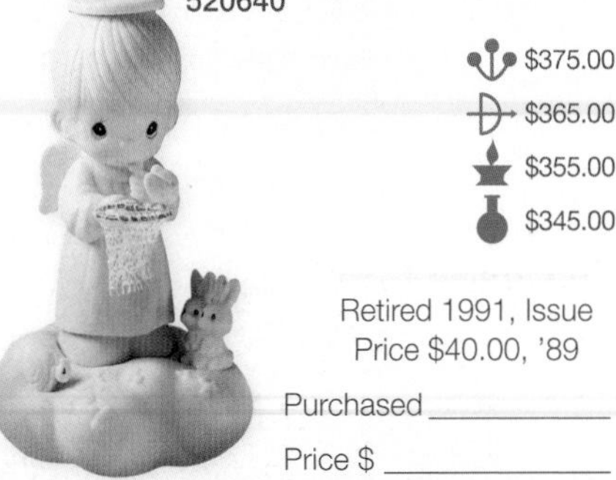

Retired 1991, Issue Price $40.00, '89

Purchased ____________

Price $ ______________

☐ *Wishing You A Happy Bear Hug,* 520659

$60.00 · $55.00 · $50.00

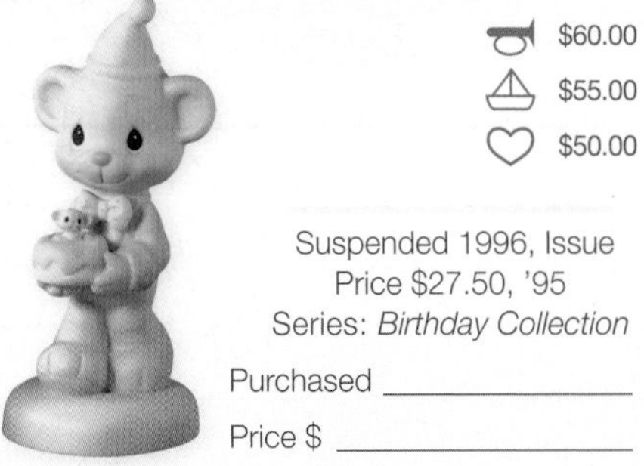

Suspended 1996, Issue Price $27.50, '95

Series: *Birthday Collection*

Purchased ______________

Price $ ________________

☐ *Egg-specially For You,* 520667

$105.00 · $103.00 · $100.00 · $98.00 · $98.00 · $95.00 · $95.00 · $90.00 · $90.00 · $88.00 · $88.00 · $88.00

Retired 1999, Issue Price $45.00, '89

Purchased ________, Price $ ____________

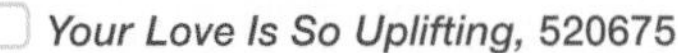

☐ *Your Love Is So Uplifting,* 520675

$125.00 · $123.00 · $120.00 · $118.00 · $115.00 · $113.00 · $110.00 · $105.00 · $103.00 · $100.00 · $100.00

Retired 1998, Issue Price $60.00, '89

Purchased ________, Price $ ____________

☐ *Sending You Showers Of Blessings,* 520683

$125.00 · $123.00 · $120.00 · $118.00 · $115.00

Retired 1992, Issue Price $32.50, '89

Purchased ________

Price $ ___________

☐ *Lord, Keep My Life In Balance,* 520691 (Musical)

$105.00 · $100.00 · $95.00

Suspended 1993, Issue Price $60.00, '91

Tune: *Music Box Dancer*

Purchased ________, Price $ ____________

☐ *Baby's First Pet,* 520705

$95.00 · $93.00 · $90.00 · $88.00 · $85.00 · $83.00 · $80.00

Suspended 1994, Issue Price $45.00, '89

Series: *Baby's First* — Fifth Issue

Purchased ________, Price $ ____________

☐ *Just A Line To Wish You A Happy Day,* 520721

$125.00 · $120.00 · $115.00 · $110.00 · $105.00 · $100.00 · $98.00 · $95.00 · $93.00

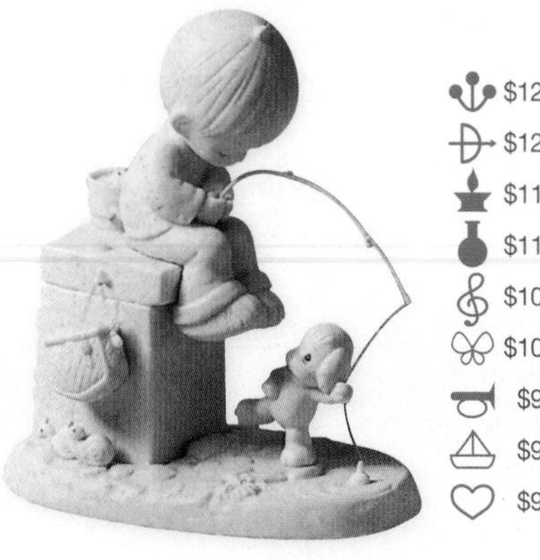

Suspended 1996, Issue Price $65.00, '89

Purchased ________, Price $ ____________

☐ *Friendship Hits The Spot,* 520748

Errors: Misspelled "Freindship" on boxes and figurines in Trumpet and Ship marks. Several have been found with tables missing.

$110.00 · $108.00 · $105.00 · $103.00 · $100.00 · $100.00 · $98.00 · $98.00 · $95.00 · $95.00 · $93.00 · $93.00 · $93.00

Retired 2000, Issue Price $55.00, '89

Purchased ________, Price $ ____________

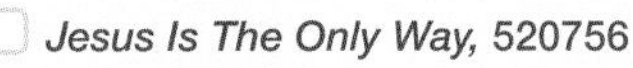

Jesus Is The Only Way, 520756

[Flower]	$95.00	[Vessel]	$88.00
[Bow & Arrow]	$93.00	[G-Clef]	$85.00
[Flame]	$90.00	[Butterfly]	$83.00

Suspended 1993, Issue Price $40.00, '89

Purchased ________ Price $____________

Someday My Love, 520799

[Flower]	$98.00
[Bow & Arrow]	$95.00
[Flame]	$93.00
[Vessel]	$90.00
[G-Clef]	$88.00

Retired 1992, Issue Price $40.00, '89

Purchased ________, Price $ ____________

You Are My Number One, 520829

[Flower]	$55.00	[Butterfly]	$40.00
[Bow & Arrow]	$50.00	[Trumpet]	$40.00
[Flame]	$48.00	[Ship]	$40.00
[Vessel]	$45.00	[Heart]	$38.00
[G-Clef]	$43.00	[Sword]	$38.00
		[Eyeglasses]	$38.00

Suspended 1998, Issue Price $25.00, '89

Purchased____________

Price $ ____________

Puppy Love, 520764

[Flower]	$45.00	[G-Clef]	$38.00
[Bow & Arrow]	$42.00	[Butterfly]	$38.00
[Flame]	$40.00	[Trumpet]	$35.00
[Vessel]	$40.00	[Ship]	$35.00
		[Heart]	$35.00
		[Sword]	$33.00
		[Eyeglasses]	$33.00
		[Star]	$33.00

Retired 02/14/99, Issue Price $12.50, '89

Purchased ________, Price $ ____________

My Days Are Blue Without You, 520802

[Flower]	$125.00	[Flame]	$115.00
[Bow & Arrow]	$120.00	[Vessel]	$110.00

Exists with three variations of the mouth — smiling, frowning, and open. Value for smiling with Flower mark, $125.00; smiling with Bow & Arrow mark, $115.00.

Suspended 1991, Issue Price $65.00, '89

Purchased ________, Price $ ____________

The Lord Is Your Light To Happiness, 520837

		[Vessel]	$65.00	[Ship]	$65.00
[Flower]	$75.00	[G-Clef]	$65.00	[Heart]	$65.00
[Bow & Arrow]	$72.00	[Butterfly]	$65.00	[Sword]	$65.00
[Flame]	$68.00	[Trumpet]	$65.00	[Eyeglasses]	$65.00
				[Star]	$65.00
				[Egg]	$65.00
				[Sandal]	$65.00
				[Cross in Heart]	$65.00
				[Crown]	$65.00
				[Clover]	$65.00
				[Box]	$65.00

Suspended 2004, Issue Price $50.00, '89

Purchased ________, Price $ ____________

Many Moons In Same Canoe, Blessum You, 520772

[Flower]	$275.00
[Bow & Arrow]	$250.00
[Flame]	$250.00

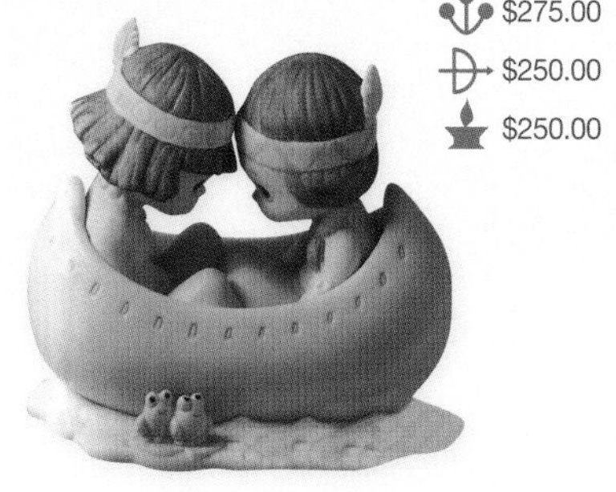

Retired 1990, Issue Price $50.00, '89

Purchased ________, Price $ ____________

We Need A Good Friend Through The Ruff Times, 520810

[Flower]	$65.00
[Bow & Arrow]	$63.00
[Flame]	$60.00
[Vessel]	$58.00

Suspended 1991, Issue Price $35.00, '89

Purchased ________, Price $ ____________

Wishing You A Perfect Choice, 520845

[Flower]	$83.00	[G-Clef]	$75.00	[Sword]	$75.00
[Bow & Arrow]	$80.00	[Butterfly]	$75.00	[Eyeglasses]	$75.00
[Flame]	$78.00	[Trumpet]	$75.00	[Star]	$75.00
[Vessel]	$75.00	[Ship]	$75.00	[Egg]	$75.00
		[Heart]	$75.00	[Sandal]	$75.00
				[Cross in Heart]	$75.00
				[Crown]	$75.00
				[Clover]	$75.00
				[Box]	$75.00
				[House]	$75.00
				[Hammer]	$75.00
				[Heart]	$75.00
				[Wheat]	$75.00

Open, Issue Price $55.00, '89

Purchased ________, Price $ ____________

Wishing You Roads Of Happiness, 520780

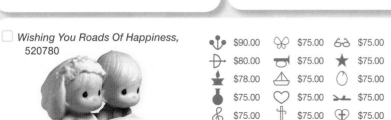

[Flower]	$90.00	[Butterfly]	$75.00	[Eyeglasses]	$75.00	[Clover]	$75.00
[Bow & Arrow]	$80.00	[Trumpet]	$75.00	[Star]	$75.00	[Box]	$75.00
[Flame]	$78.00	[Ship]	$75.00	[Egg]	$75.00	[House]	$75.00
[Vessel]	$75.00	[Heart]	$75.00	[Sandal]	$75.00	[Hammer]	$75.00
[G-Clef]	$75.00	[Sword]	$75.00	[Cross in Heart]	$75.00	[Heart]	$75.00
				[Crown]	$75.00	[Wheat]	$75.00

Open, Issue Price $60.00, '89

Purchased ________, Price $ ____________

☐ *I Belong To The Lord*, 520853

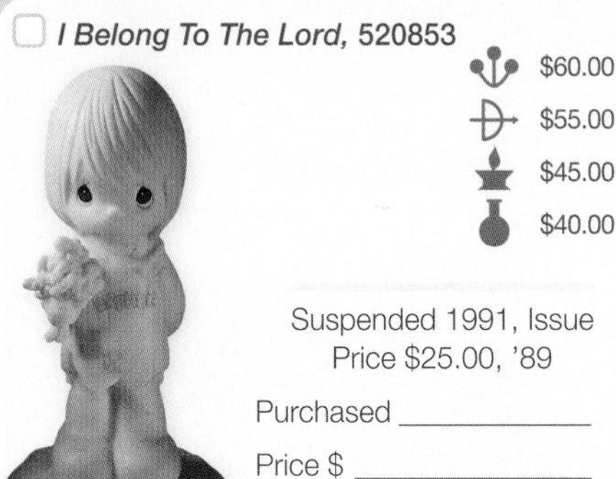

$60.00
$55.00
$45.00
$40.00

Suspended 1991, Issue Price $25.00, '89

Purchased ____________

Price $ ______________

☐ *Sharing Begins In The Heart*, 520861

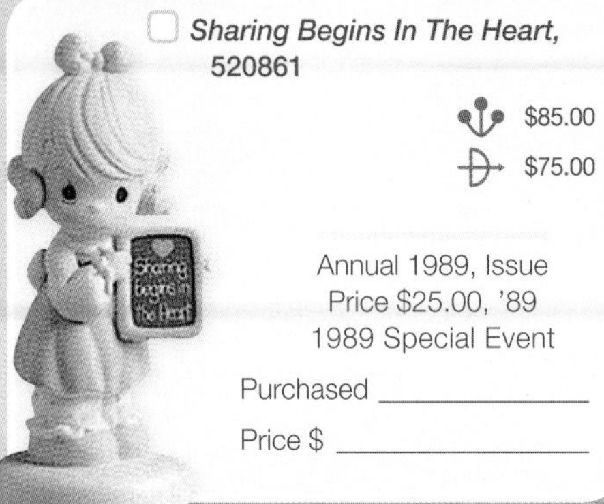
Sharing begins in The Heart

$85.00
$75.00

Annual 1989, Issue Price $25.00, '89
1989 Special Event

Purchased ____________

Price $ ______________

☐ *Blessed Be The Tie That Binds*, 520918

$60.00
$55.00
$50.00
$50.00
$50.00
$50.00
$50.00
$50.00
$50.00

Open, Issue Price $50.00, '99

Purchased ________, Price $ ____________

☐ *Heaven Bless You*, 520934

$135.00
$133.00
$130.00
$125.00
$120.00
$115.00
$110.00
$105.00
$100.00
$95.00
$90.00
$85.00
$80.00
$80.00

Retired 2001, Issue Price $35.00, '90

Purchased ________, Price $ ____________

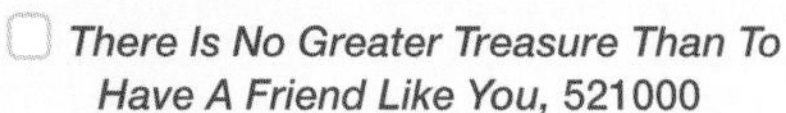

☐ *There Is No Greater Treasure Than To Have A Friend Like You*, 521000

$85.00
$80.00
$75.00
$70.00
$65.00
$60.00
$60.00

Retired 1998, Issue Price $30.00, '93

Purchased ____________

Price $ ______________

☐ *To My Favorite Fan*, 521043

$55.00
$53.00
$50.00
$48.00
$45.00

Suspended 1993, Issue Price $16.00, '90
Series: *Birthday Collection*

Purchased ________, Price $ ____________

☐ *Merry Christmas, Little Lamb*, 521078 (Ornament)

$25.00
$23.00
$20.00
$20.00
$20.00
$20.00

Suspended 2003, Issue Price $15.00, '98
Series: *Birthday Circus Train* — Age 1

Purchased ________, Price $ ____________

☐ *Heaven Bless Your Special Christmas*, 521086 (Ornament)

$25.00
$23.00
$20.00
$20.00
$20.00
$20.00

Suspended 2003, Issue Price $15.00, '98
Series: *Birthday Circus Train* — Age 3

Purchased ________, Price $ ____________

☐ *God Bless You This Christmas*, 521094 (Ornament)

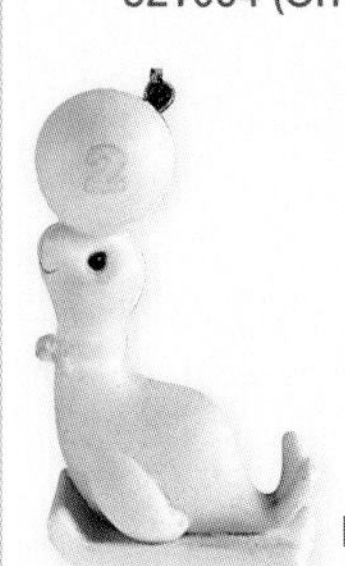

$25.00
$23.00
$20.00
$20.00
$20.00
$20.00

Suspended 2003, Issue Price $15.00, '98
Series: *Birthday Circus Train — Age 2*

Purchased ____________

Price $ ______________

☐ *May Your Christmas Be Gigantic*, 521108 (Ornament)

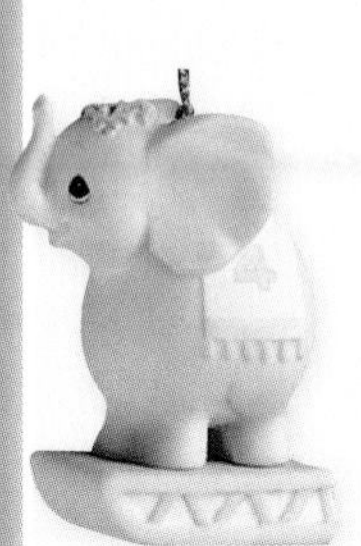

$25.00
$23.00
$20.00
$20.00
$20.00
$20.00

Suspended 2003, Issue Price $15.00, '98
Series: *Birthday Circus Train* — Age 4

Purchased ____________

Price $ ______________

☐ *Christmas Is Something To Roar About*, 521116 (Ornament)

$25.00
$23.00
$20.00
$20.00
$20.00
$20.00

Suspended 2003, Issue Price $15.00, '98
Series: *Birthday Circus Train* — Age 5

Purchased ____________

Price $ ______________

☐ *Christmas Keeps Looking Up*, 521124 (Ornament)

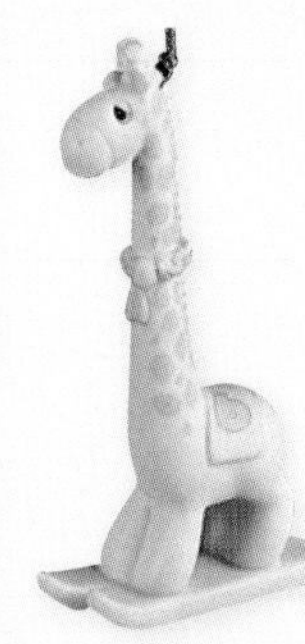

$25.00
$23.00
$20.00
$20.00
$20.00
$20.00

Suspended 2003, Issue Price $15.00, '98
Series: *Birthday Circus Train* — Age 6

Purchased ____________

Price $ ______________

☐ ***Hello World*, 521175**

$45.00, $43.00, $40.00, $38.00, $38.00, $35.00, $35.00, $33.00, $33.00, $30.00, $30.00, $30.00

Retired 1999, Issue Price $13.50, '89
Series: *Birthday Collection*

Purchased ________, Price $ ___________

☐ ***That's What Friends Are For*, 521183**

$85.00, $83.00, $80.00, $78.00, $78.00, $75.00, $75.00, $73.00, $73.00, $70.00, $70.00

Retired 2000, Issue Price $45.00, '90

Purchased ________, Price $ ___________

☐ ***Lord, Spare Me*, 521191**

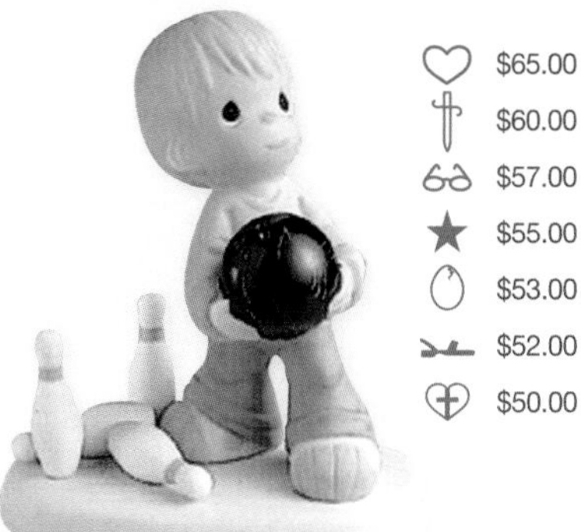

$65.00, $60.00, $57.00, $55.00, $53.00, $52.00, $50.00

Retired 2001, Issue Price $37.50, '97

Purchased ________, Price $ ___________

☐ ***The Fruit Of The Spirit Is Love*, 521213**

$65.00, $63.00, $60.00, $58.00, $55.00, $53.00, $50.00

Retired 1999, Issue Price $30.00, '93

Purchased ___________

Price $ ___________

☐ ***Enter His Court With Thanksgiving*, 521221**

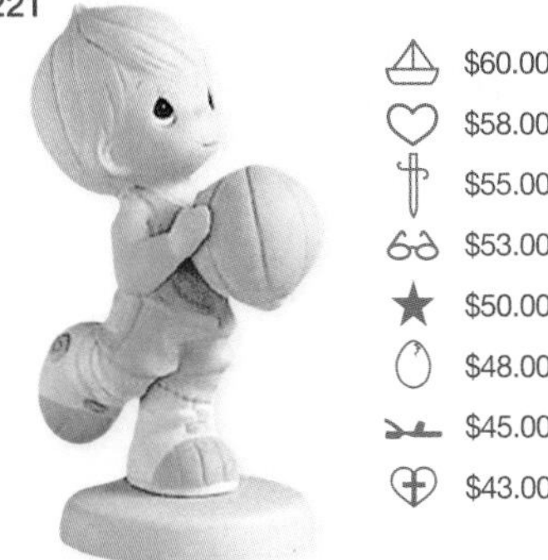

$60.00, $58.00, $55.00, $53.00, $50.00, $48.00, $45.00, $43.00

Retired 2002, Issue Price $35.00, '96

Purchased ________, Price $ ___________

☐ ***Take Heed When You Stand*, 521272**

Limited Ship mark figurines offered to retailers at Fall 1998 Enesco show.

$87.00, $85.00, $83.00, $80.00, $78.00

Suspended 1994, Issue Price $55.00, '91

Purchased ________, Price $ ___________

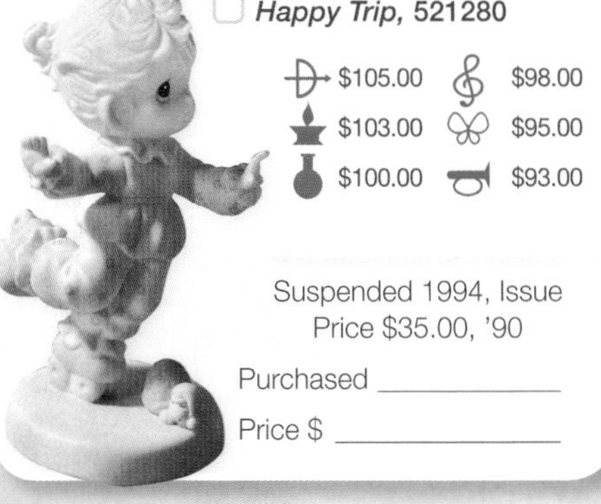

☐ ***Happy Trip*, 521280**

$105.00, $103.00, $100.00, $98.00, $95.00, $93.00

Suspended 1994, Issue Price $35.00, '90

Purchased ___________

Price $ ___________

☐ ***Hug One Another*, 521299**

$105.00, $103.00, $100.00, $98.00, $95.00, $93.00

Retired 1995, Issue Price $45.00, '91

Purchased ________, Price $ ___________

☐ ***May All Your Christmases Be White*, 521302 (Ornament)**

$45.00, $43.00, $40.00, $38.00, $35.00, $33.00

Retired 1999, Issue Price $13.50, '89

Purchased ___________

Price $ ___________

☐ ***May All Your Christmases Be White*, 521302R (Ornament)**

$33.00

Limited Ed., Issue Price $20.00, '99
Limited To One Year Production

Purchased ________, Price $ ___________

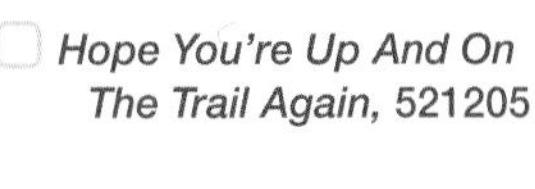

☐ ***Hope You're Up And On The Trail Again*, 521205**

$70.00, $65.00, $63.00, $60.00, $58.00

Suspended 1993, Issue Price $35.00, '90

Purchased ________, Price $ ___________

☐ ***Yield Not To Temptation*, 521310**

$65.00, $50.00, $55.00, $53.00, $50.00

Suspended 1993, Issue Price $27.50, '90

Purchased ___________

Price $ ___________

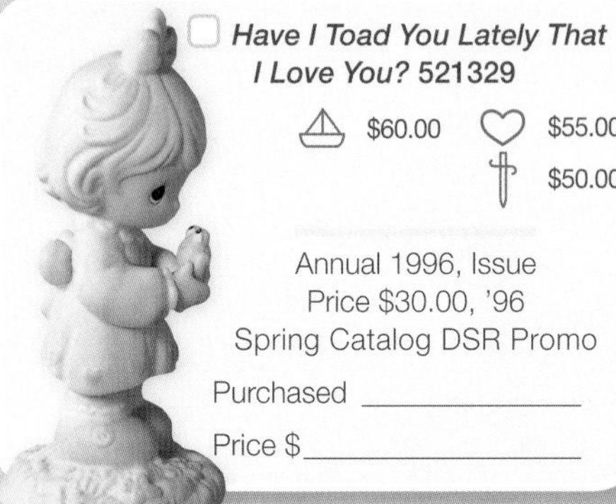

☐ **_Have I Toad You Lately That I Love You? 521329_**

$60.00
$55.00
$50.00

Annual 1996, Issue Price $30.00, '96
Spring Catalog DSR Promo

Purchased ____________

Price $______________

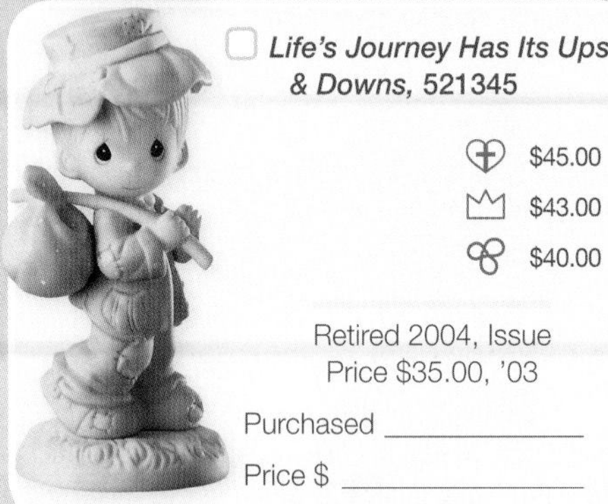

☐ **_Life's Journey Has Its Ups & Downs, 521345_**

$45.00
$43.00
$40.00

Retired 2004, Issue Price $35.00, '03

Purchased ____________

Price $ ____________

☐ **_Heaven Must Have Sent You, 521388_**

$95.00
$93.00
$90.00
$88.00
$85.00

Retired 2001, Issue Price $60.00, '98
Series: _Birthday Collection_

Purchased ________, Price $ ___________

☐ **_Faith Is A Victory, 521396_**

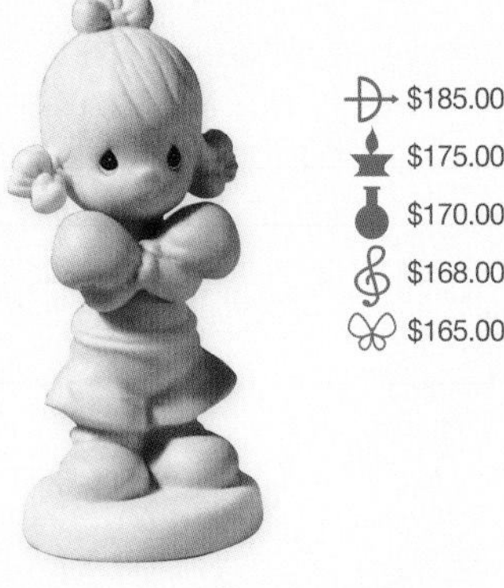

$185.00
$175.00
$170.00
$168.00
$165.00

Retired 1993, Issue Price $25.00, '90

Purchased ________, Price $ ___________

☐ **_I'll Never Stop Loving You, 521418_**

$85.00
$83.00
$80.00
$78.00
$75.00
$73.00
$70.00
$68.00

Retired 1996, Issue Price $37.50, '90

Purchased ________, Price $ ___________

☐ **_To A Very Special Mom And Dad, 521434_**

$60.00
$58.00
$55.00

Suspended 1993, Issue Price $35.00, '91

Purchased ___________

Price $_____________

☐ **_Lord, Help Me Stick To My Job, 521450_**

$85.00
$83.00
$80.00
$78.00
$75.00
$73.00
$70.00
$68.00
$65.00

Retired 1997, Issue Price $30.00, '90

Purchased ________, Price $ ___________

☐ **_I'll Weight For You, 521469_**

$45.00
$40.00

Annual 2000, Issue Price $30.00, '00
Spring Catalog Syndicated Exclusive

Purchased ___________

Price $_____________

☐ **_Tell It To Jesus, 521477_**

$75.00
$70.00
$68.00
$65.00
$63.00

$63.00
$60.00
$60.00
$58.00
$58.00
$55.00
$55.00
$55.00
$55.00
$55.00

Retired 2003, Issue Price $35.00, '89

Purchased ________, Price $ ___________

☐ **_There's A Light At The End Of The Tunnel, 521485_**

$95.00
$90.00
$88.00
$85.00
$83.00
$80.00

Suspended 1996, Issue Price $55.00, '91

Purchased ________, Price $ ___________

☐ **_A Special Delivery, 521493_**

$45.00
$43.00
$40.00
$38.00
$38.00
$35.00
$35.00
$35.00
$35.00
$35.00
$35.00
$35.00
$35.00
$35.00
$35.00
$35.00
$35.00
$35.00
$35.00

Open, Issue Price $30.00, '91

Purchased ________, Price $ ___________

☐ *The Light Of The World Is Jesus,* 521507 (Musical)

$105.00, $100.00, $98.00, $95.00, $93.00, $90.00, $88.00, $85.00, $85.00, $85.00, $85.00

Retired 1999, Issue Price $60.00, '89
Tune: *White Christmas*

Purchased _______

Price $ _________

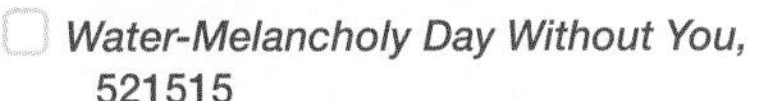

☐ *Water-Melancholy Day Without You,* 521515

$65.00, $63.00, $60.00, $58.00, $55.00, $53.00

Retired 2002, Issue Price $35.00, '98

Purchased_______

Price $_________

☐ *Our First Christmas Together,* 521558 (Ornament)

$38.00

Dated Annual 1989, Issue Price $17.50, '89

Purchased _______, Price $ _________

☐ *Glide Through The Holidays,* 521566 (Ornament)

$48.00, $43.00, $40.00

Retired 1992, Issue Price $13.50, '90

Purchased _________

Price $ _________

☐ *Dashing Through The Snow,* 521574 (Ornament)

$38.00, $35.00, $33.00, $31.00, $30.00

Suspended 1994, Issue Price $15.00, '90

Purchased _________

Price $_________

☐ *Don't Let The Holidays Get You Down,* 521590 (Ornament)

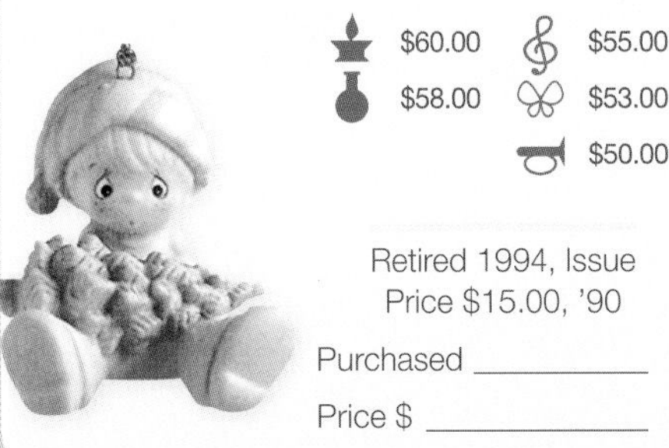

$60.00, $58.00, $55.00, $53.00, $50.00

Retired 1994, Issue Price $15.00, '90

Purchased _________

Price $ _________

☐ *Hope You're Over The Hump,* 521671

$45.00, $43.00, $40.00, $38.00

Suspended 1996, Issue Price $17.50, '93
Series: *Birthday Collection*

Purchased _______, Price $ _________

☐ *Thumb-Body Loves You,* 521698

$95.00, $90.00, $85.00, $80.00, $78.00, $75.00, $75.00

Suspended 1996, Issue Price $55.00, '91

Purchased _______, Price $ _________

☐ *Shoot For The Stars And You'll Never Strike Out,* 521701

$75.00, $73.00, $70.00, $65.00, $60.00, $60.00, $60.00, $60.00, $60.00, $60.00, $60.00, $60.00, $60.00

Open, Issue Price $60.00, '96
Boys & Girls Club Of America Commemorative

Purchased _______, Price $ _________

☐ *My Love Blooms For You,* 521728

$65.00, $63.00, $60.00, $58.00, $55.00, $53.00, $50.00, $50.00, $50.00, $50.00, $50.00, $50.00, $50.00, $50.00, $50.00

Open, Issue Price $50.00, '96

Purchased _______, Price $ _________

☐ *Sweep All Your Worries Away,* 521779

This figurine has been found with the dog missing; values increase by $75.00.

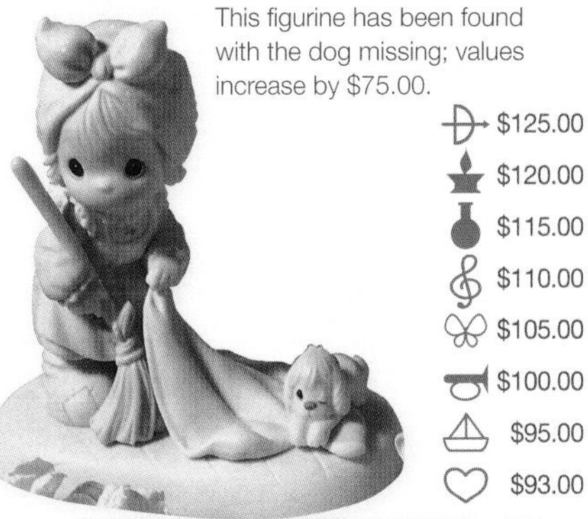

$125.00, $120.00, $115.00, $110.00, $105.00, $100.00, $95.00, $93.00

Retired 1996, Issue Price $40.00, '90

Purchased _______, Price $ _________

☐ *Good Friends Are Forever,* 521817

$95.00 $90.00 $85.00
$93.00 $88.00 $85.00
$88.00 $80.00
$80.00
$75.00
$75.00
$73.00
$73.00
$70.00
$70.00

Retired 2003, Issue Price $50.00, '90

Purchased ________, Price $ ____________

☐ *May Your Birthday Be Mammoth,* 521825

$26.50 $26.50
$30.00 $26.50 $26.50
$28.00 $26.50 $26.50
$26.50 $26.50
$26.50 $26.50
$26.50 $26.50
$26.50
$26.50
$26.50
$26.50

Open, Issue Price $25.00, '92

Series: *Birthday Circus Train* — Age 10

Purchased ________, Price $ ____________

☐ *Being Nine Is Just Divine,* 521833

$30.00 $26.50 $26.50
$28.00 $26.50 $26.50
$26.50 $26.50
$26.50 $26.50
$26.50 $26.50
$26.50
$26.50
$26.50
$26.50
$26.50
$26.50

Open, Issue Price $25.00, '92

Series: *Birthday Circus Train* — Age 9

Purchased ________, Price $ ____________

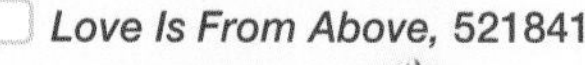

☐ *Love Is From Above,* 521841

$85.00
$80.00
$75.00
$75.00
$70.00
$70.00
$70.00
$70.00

Suspended 1996, Issue Price $45.00, '90

Purchased ________, Price $ ____________

☐ *The Greatest Of These Is Love,* 521868

$55.00
$40.00
$38.00

Suspended 1991, Issue Price $27.50, '89

Purchased ____________

Price $ ____________

☐ *Pizza On Earth,* 521884

$75.00
$70.00
$68.00
$65.00
$63.00

Retired 2001, Issue Price $55.00, '97

Purchased ________, Price $ ____________

☐ *Easter's On Its Way,* 521892

$105.00 $100.00
$103.00 $98.00
$95.00
$93.00
$90.00
$88.00
$85.00
$83.00
$80.00

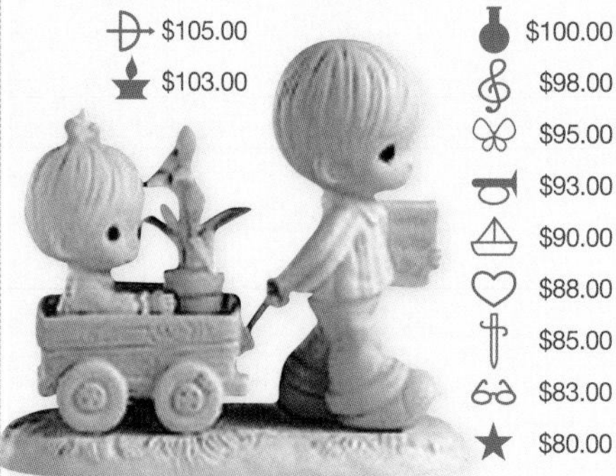

Retired 1999, Issue Price $60.00, '90

Purchased ________, Price $ ____________

☐ *Hoppy Easter, Friend,* 521906

$65.00 $58.00 $50.00
$63.00 $55.00 $50.00
$60.00 $53.00 $50.00
$50.00

Retired 1999, Issue Price $40.00, '91

Purchased ________, Price $ ____________

☐ *Perfect Harmony,* 521914

$85.00
$83.00
$80.00
$78.00
$75.00
$73.00

Retired 1999, Issue Price $55.00, '94

Purchased ________, Price $ ____________

☐ *Safe In The Arms Of Jesus,* 521922

$50.00 $35.00 $35.00
$48.00 $35.00 $35.00
$45.00 $35.00 $35.00
$43.00 $35.00 $35.00
$40.00 $35.00 $35.00
$35.00 $35.00
$35.00

Open, Issue Price $30.00, '93

Child Evangelism Fellowship Piece

Purchased ________, Price $ ____________

☐ *Wishing You A Cozy Season, 521949*

$70.00 $63.00
$68.00 $60.00
$65.00

Suspended 1993, Issue Price $42.50, '89

Purchased ______

Price $__________

☐ *High Hopes, 521957*

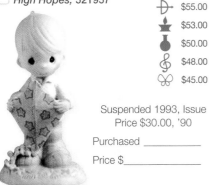

$55.00
$53.00
$50.00
$48.00
$45.00

Suspended 1993, Issue Price $30.00, '90

Purchased ___________

Price $_______________

☐ *To A Special Mum, 521965*

$65.00 $55.00
$63.00 $55.00
$60.00 $55.00
$58.00 $50.00
$58.00 $50.00

Retired 1999, Issue Price $30.00 '91

Purchased ___________

Price $_______________

☐ *Caught Up In Sweet Thoughts Of You, 521973*

$45.00 $43.00
$43.00 $38.00
$38.00
$35.00
$35.00
$35.00

Suspended, Issue Price $30.00, '99

Purchased__________

Price $ ___________

☐ *Marching To The Beat Of Freedom's Drum, 521981*

$75.00 $63.00
$73.00 $60.00
$71.00 $58.00
$68.00 $55.00
$65.00 $50.00

Retired 2004, Issue Price $35.00, '96

Purchased___________

Price $_____________

☐ *To The Apple Of God's Eye, 522015*

$55.00 $48.00
$53.00 $45.00
$50.00 $43.00
$40.00

Retired 1999, Issue Price $32.50, '93

Purchased ___________

Price $______________

☐ *May Your Life Be Blessed With Touchdowns, 522023*

$85.00 $80.00 $75.00
$83.00 $78.00 $73.00
$70.00
$68.00
$65.00
$63.00

Retired 1998, Issue Price $45.00, '89

Purchased ________, Price $ ______________

☐ *Thank You, Lord, For Everything, 522031*

$100.00
$98.00
$95.00
$93.00
$90.00

Suspended 1993, Issue Price $60.00, '89

Purchased ________, Price $ ____________

☐ *Now I Lay Me Down To Sleep, 522058*

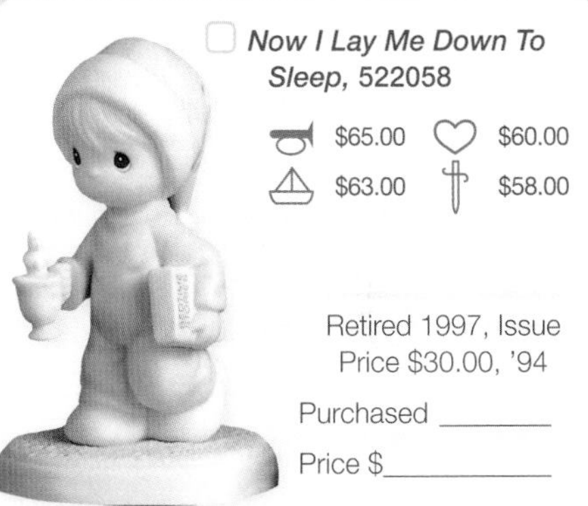

$65.00 $60.00
$63.00 $58.00

Retired 1997, Issue Price $30.00, '94

Purchased ________

Price $__________

☐ *May Your World Be Trimmed With Joy, 522082*

$95.00
$90.00
$85.00
$80.00
$78.00
$75.00

Suspended 1996, Issue Price $55.00, '91

Purchased ________, Price $ ____________

☐ *There Shall Be Showers Of Blessings, 522090*

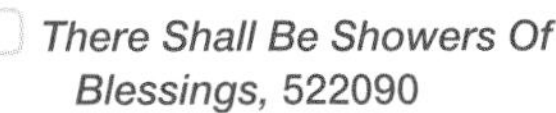

$95.00 $86.00
$92.00 $86.00
$90.00 $84.00
$88.00 $84.00
$88.00 $82.00
$82.00

Retired 1999, Issue Price $60.00, '90

Purchased ______________________

Price $__________________________

It's No Yolk When I Say I Love You, 522104

$105.00
$100.00
$95.00
$90.00

Suspended 1994, Issue Price $60.00, '92

Purchased ________, Price $ ___________

Bon Voyage! 522201

$140.00 $133.00 $125.00
$138.00 $130.00 $123.00
$135.00 $128.00 $120.00

Suspended 1996, Issue Price $75.00, '89

Purchased ________, Price $ ___________

Do Not Open 'Til Christmas, 522244 (Musical)

$140.00
$135.00
$125.00

Suspended 1994, Issue Price $75.00, '92
Tune: *Toyland*

Purchased ________, Price $ ___________

A Reflection Of His Love, 522279

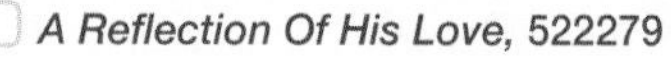

$108.00 $98.00
$105.00 $95.00
$93.00
$90.00
$88.00
$85.00
$83.00
$80.00

Retired 1999, Issue Price $50.00, '91

Purchased ________, Price $ ___________

Don't Let The Holidays Get You Down, 522112

$125.00
$120.00
$115.00
$110.00
$105.00

Retired 1993, Issue Price $42.50, '89

Purchased ________, Price $ ___________

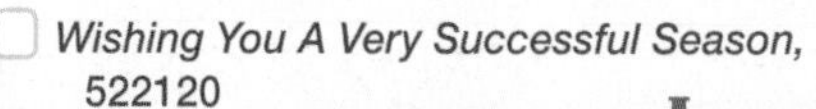

Wishing You A Very Successful Season, 522120

$115.00
$113.00

$110.00
$108.00
$105.00
$103.00
$100.00
$98.00
$97.00
$95.00
$93.00

Retired 1999, Issue Price $60.00, '89

Purchased ________, Price $ ___________

He Is The Star Of The Morning, 522252

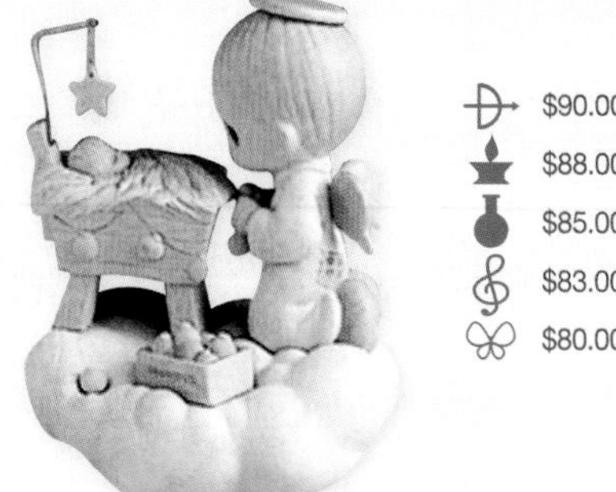

$90.00
$88.00
$85.00
$83.00
$80.00

Suspended 1993, Issue Price $55.00, '89

Purchased ________, Price $ ___________

Thinking Of You Is What I Really Like To Do, 522287

$60.00
$58.00
$55.00
$53.00
$50.00
$48.00
$45.00
$43.00

Suspended 1996, Issue Price $30.00, '90

Purchased ________, Price $ ___________

I Will Make You Fishers Of Men, 522139

$65.00
$60.00

Limited Ed., Issue Price $50.00, '02
Precious Moments 25th Anniversary

Purchased ________, Price $ ___________

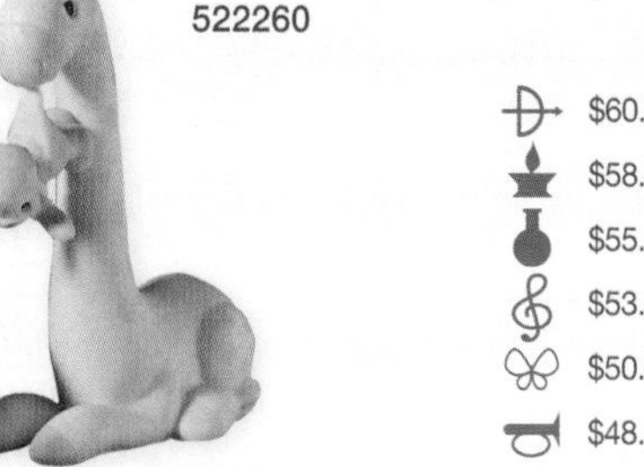

To Be With You Is Uplifting, 522260

$60.00
$58.00
$55.00
$53.00
$50.00
$48.00

Retired 1994, Issue Price $20.00, '89
Series: *Birthday Collection*

Purchased ________, Price $ ___________

Merry Christmas, Deer, 522317

$125.00
$120.00
$118.00
$115.00
$110.00
$105.00
$98.00
$95.00
$93.00

Retired 1997, Issue Price $50.00, '89

Purchased ________, Price $ ___________

☐ *Somebody Cares,* 522325

$65.00
$60.00

Annual 1998, Issue Price $40.00, '98 Easter Seals Commemorative Lily Understamp

Purchased ________, Price $ ____________

☐ *Sweeter As The Years Go By,* 522333

$95.00
$90.00
$85.00

Retired 1998, Issue Price $60.00, '96

Purchased ________, Price $ ____________

☐ *His Love Will Shine On You,* 522376

$60.00
$58.00

Annual 1989, Issue Price $30.00, '89 Easter Seals Commemorative, Lily Understamp

Purchased__________

Price $__________

☐ *Oh Holy Night,* 522546

$53.00

Dated Annual 1989, Issue Price $25.00, '89

Purchased__________

Price $__________

☐ *Oh Holy Night,* 522554 (Thimble)

$28.00

Dated Annual 1989, Issue Price $7.50, '89

Purchased ____________

Price $ ____________

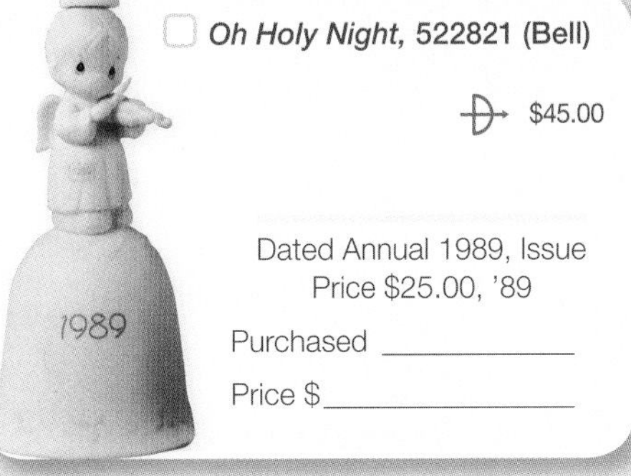

☐ *Oh Holy Night,* 522821 (Bell)

$45.00

Dated Annual 1989, Issue Price $25.00, '89

Purchased ____________

Price $____________

☐ *Oh Holy Night,* 522848 (Ornament)

$38.00 $38.00

Dated Annual 1989, Issue Price $13.50, '89

Purchased ____________

Price $____________

☐ *Have A Beary Merry Christmas,* 522856

$55.00 $52.00
$53.00 $50.00

Suspended 1992, Issue Price $15.00, '89 Series: *Family Christmas Scene* — Sixth Issue

Purchased ____________

Price $ ____________

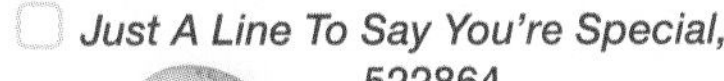

☐ *Just A Line To Say You're Special,* 522864

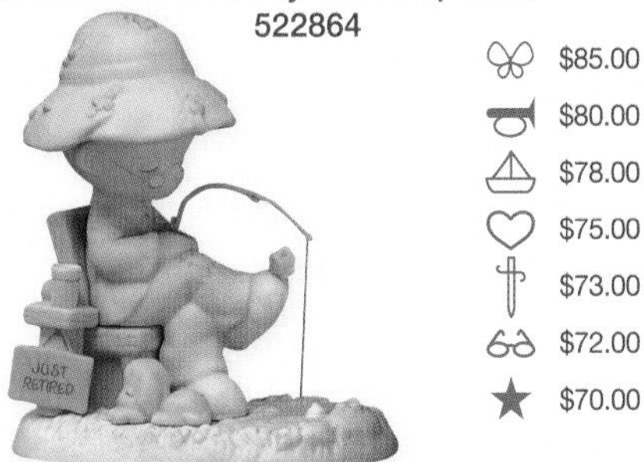

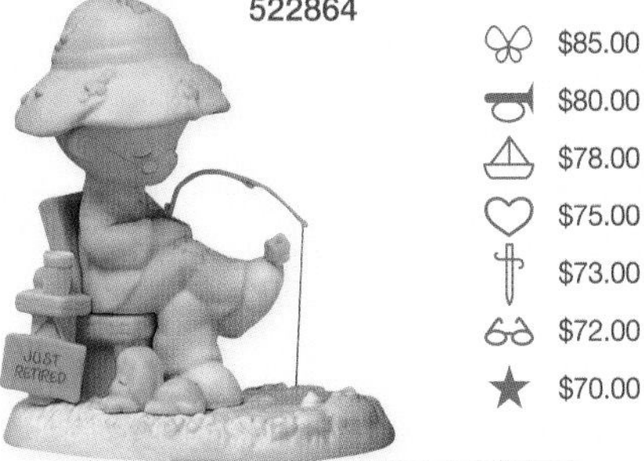

$85.00
$80.00
$78.00
$75.00
$73.00
$72.00
$70.00

Retired 1999, Issue Price $45.00, '95

Purchased ________, Price $ ____________

☐ *On My Way To A Perfect Day,* 522872

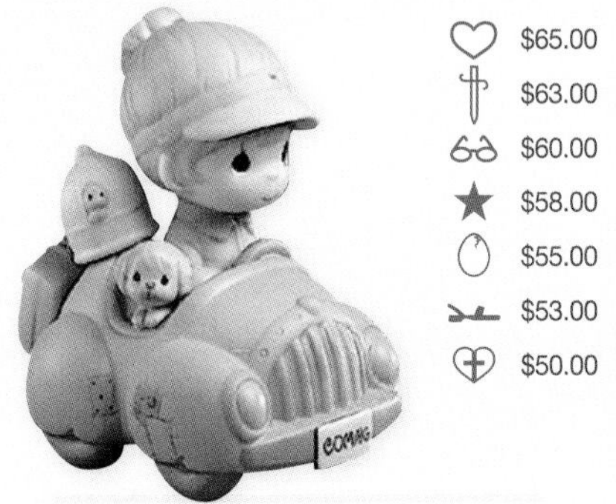

$65.00
$63.00
$60.00
$58.00
$55.00
$53.00
$50.00

Retired 2002, Issue Price $45.00, '97

Purchased ________, Price $ ____________

☐ *Make A Joyful Noise,* 522910 (Ornament)

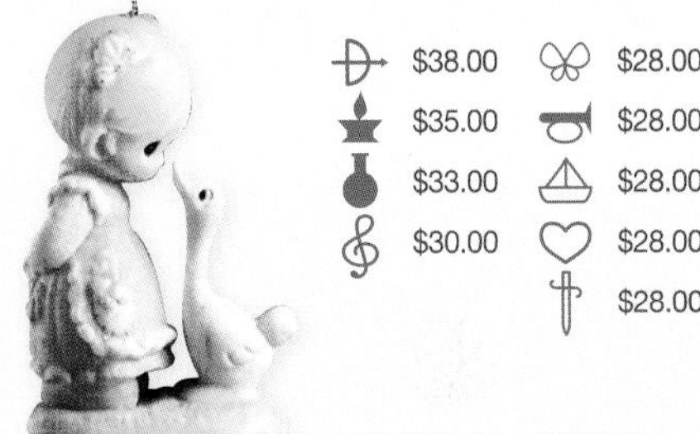

$38.00 $28.00
$35.00 $28.00
$33.00 $28.00
$30.00 $28.00
$28.00

Suspended 1996, Issue Price $15.00, '89

Purchased ________, Price $ ____________

☐ *Love One Another,* 522929 (Ornament)

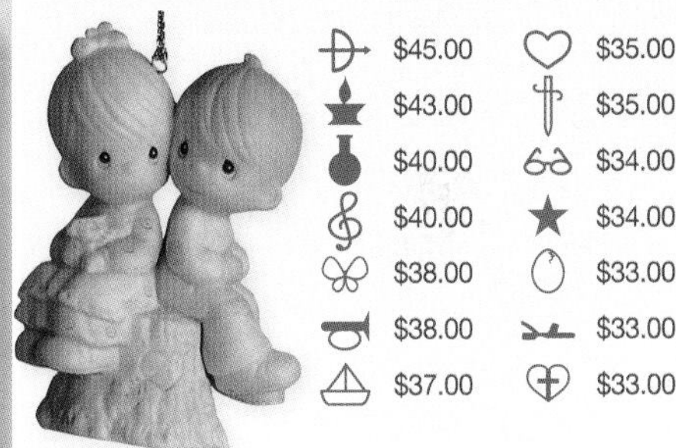

$45.00 $35.00
$43.00 $35.00
$40.00 $34.00
$40.00 $34.00
$38.00 $33.00
$38.00 $33.00
$37.00 $33.00

Retired 2001, Issue Price $17.50, '89

Purchased ________, Price $ ____________

☐ *Friends Never Drift Apart,* 522937 (Ornament)

$45.00
$43.00
$40.00
$38.00
$36.00
$35.00

Retired 1995, Issue Price $17.50, '90

Purchased ________, Price $ ____________

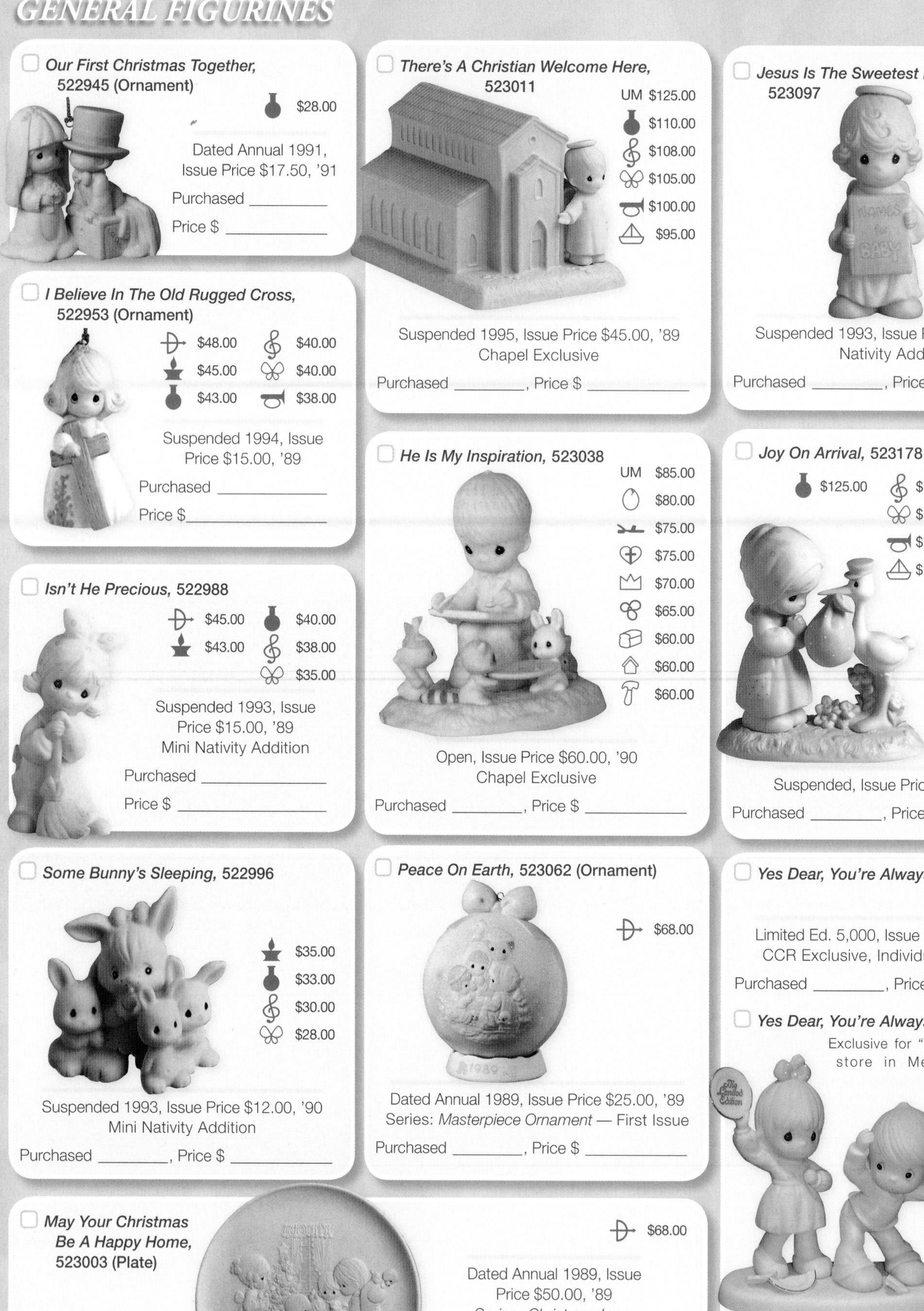

☐ ***Our First Christmas Together,*** **522945 (Ornament)**

$28.00

Dated Annual 1991, Issue Price $17.50, '91

Purchased ________

Price $ ____________

☐ ***There's A Christian Welcome Here,*** **523011**

UM $125.00
$110.00
$108.00
$105.00
$100.00
$95.00

Suspended 1995, Issue Price $45.00, '89
Chapel Exclusive

Purchased ________, Price $ ____________

☐ ***Jesus Is The Sweetest Name I Know,*** **523097**

$60.00
$58.00
$55.00
$53.00
$50.00

Suspended 1993, Issue Price $22.50, '89
Nativity Addition

Purchased ________, Price $ ____________

☐ ***I Believe In The Old Rugged Cross,*** **522953 (Ornament)**

$48.00 $40.00
$45.00 $40.00
$43.00 $38.00

Suspended 1994, Issue Price $15.00, '89

Purchased ____________

Price $____________

☐ ***He Is My Inspiration,*** **523038**

UM $85.00
$80.00
$75.00
$75.00
$70.00
$65.00
$60.00
$60.00
$60.00

Open, Issue Price $60.00, '90
Chapel Exclusive

Purchased ________, Price $ ____________

☐ ***Joy On Arrival,*** **523178**

$125.00 $123.00 $108.00
$120.00 $105.00
$115.00 $100.00
$110.00 $95.00
$93.00
$90.00
$88.00
$85.00
$83.00
$80.00

Suspended, Issue Price $50.00, '91

Purchased ________, Price $ ____________

☐ ***Isn't He Precious,*** **522988**

$45.00 $40.00
$43.00 $38.00
$35.00

Suspended 1993, Issue Price $15.00, '89
Mini Nativity Addition

Purchased ____________

Price $ ____________

☐ ***Some Bunny's Sleeping,*** **522996**

$35.00
$33.00
$30.00
$28.00

Suspended 1993, Issue Price $12.00, '90
Mini Nativity Addition

Purchased ________, Price $ ____________

☐ ***Peace On Earth,*** **523062 (Ornament)**

$68.00

Dated Annual 1989, Issue Price $25.00, '89
Series: *Masterpiece Ornament* — First Issue

Purchased ________, Price $ ____________

☐ ***Yes Dear, You're Always Right,*** **523186**

$75.00

Limited Ed. 5,000, Issue Price $60.00, '99
CCR Exclusive, Individually Numbered

Purchased ________, Price $ ____________

☐ ***Yes Dear, You're Always Right,*** **523186E**

Exclusive for "The Limited Edition" store in Merrick, New York. Understamp reads "Premiere Edition of 500," and plate in girl's hand has "The Limited Edition" on it.

$155.00

Limited Ed. 500, Issue Price $60.00, '99
Store Exclusive

Purchased ________, Price $ ____________

☐ ***May Your Christmas Be A Happy Home,*** **523003 (Plate)**

$68.00

Dated Annual 1989, Issue Price $50.00, '89
Series: *Christmas Love* — Fourth Issue

Purchased ____________

Price $ ____________

☐ *Baby's First Christmas*, 523194 (Ornament)

$35.00

Dated Annual 1989, Issue Price $15.00, '89

Purchased ___________

Price $ ______________

☐ *Baby's First Christmas*, 523208 (Ornament)

 $35.00

Dated Annual 1989, Issue Price $15.00, '89

Purchased ___________

Price $ ______________

☐ *Happy Trails Is Trusting Jesus*, 523224 (Ornament)

$38.00 $34.00
$35.00 $33.00

Suspended 1994, Issue Price $15.00, '91

Purchased ___________

Price $ ______________

☐ *You Have Touched So Many Hearts*, 523283

$675.00
$625.00

Limited Ed. 2,000, Issue Price $500.00, '90
Easter Seals, Lily Understamp
Individually Numbered

Purchased ___________

Price $ ______________

☐ *Blessed Are The Merciful, For They Shall Obtain Mercy*, 523291 (Wall Hanging)

UM $125.00
$125.00

Limited Ed., Issue Price $55.00, '94
Series: *Beatitudes* — Fifth Issue,
One Year Production
Chapel Exclusive, Chapel Window Collection, Individually Numbered

Purchased ________, Price $ ____________

☐ *He Leads Me Beside The Still Waters*, 523305 (Wall Hanging)

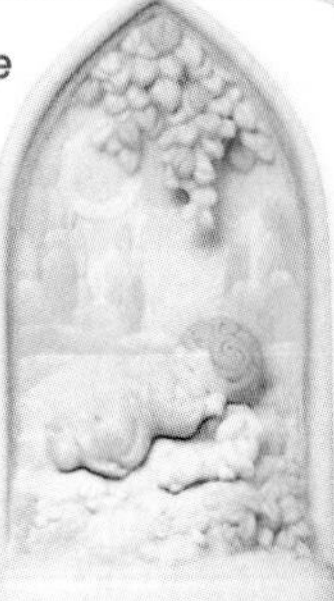

UM $75.00
$75.00

Limited Ed. 7,500, Issue Price $55.00, '97
Series: *23rd Psalm Collection* — Second Issue
Chapel Exclusive, Individually Numbered

Purchased ________, Price $ ____________

☐ *Blessed Are The Meek, For They Shall Inherit The Earth*, 523313 (Wall Hanging)

UM $110.00
$105.00

Limited Ed., Issue Price $55.00, '93
Series: *Beatitudes* — Third Issue,
One Year Production
Chapel Exclusive, Chapel Window Collection, Individually Numbered

Purchased ________, Price $ ____________

☐ *Blessed Are They That Hunger And Thirst For Righteousness*, 523321 (Wall Hanging)

UM $125.00
 $125.00

Limited Ed., Issue Price $55.00, '93
Series: *Beatitudes* — Fourth Issue, One Year Production
Chapel Exclusive, Chapel Window Collection, Individually Numbered

Purchased ________, Price $ ____________

☐ *Blessed Are The Peacemakers, For They Shall Be Called Sons Of God*, 523348 (Wall Hanging)

UM $125.00
$125.00
$125.00

Limited Ed., Issue Price $55.00, 95
Series: *Beatitudes* — Seventh & Final Issue
One Year Production
Chapel Exclusive, Chapel Window Collection, Individually Numbered

Purchased ________, Price $ ____________

☐ *I Will Fear No Evil*, 523356 (Wall Hanging)

UM $125.00
$125.00

Limited Ed. 7,500, Issue Price $55.00, '98
Series: *23rd Psalm Collection* — Fourth Issue
Chapel Exclusive, Individually Numbered

Purchased ________, Price $ ____________

☐ *He Restores My Soul*, 523364 (Wall Hanging)

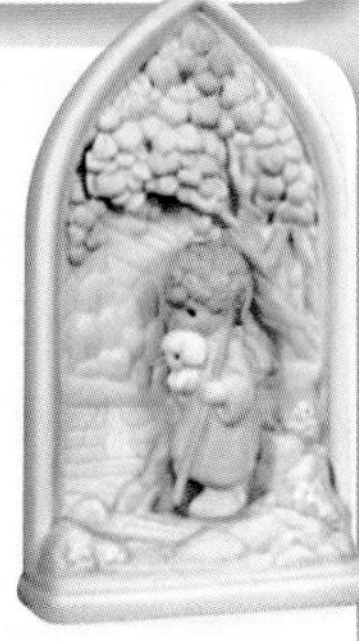

UM $95.00
$95.00

Limited Ed. 7,500, Issue Price $55.00, '98
Series: *23rd Psalm Collection* — Third Issue
Chapel Exclusive, Individually Numbered

Purchased ________, Price $ ____________

☐ *You Prepare A Table Before Me*, 523372 (Wall Hanging)

UM $95.00  $95.00

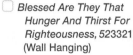

Limited Ed. 7,500, Issue Price $55.00, '98
Series: *23rd Psalm Collection* — Fifth Issue
Chapel Exclusive, Individually Numbered

Purchased ________, Price $ ____________

☐ ***Blessed Are They That Mourn, For They Shall Be Comforted,*** **523380 (Wall Hanging)**

UM $100.00
$95.00
$95.00

Limited Ed., Issue Price $55.00, '92
Series: *Beatitudes* — Second Issue, One Year Production
Chapel Exclusive, Chapel Window Collection, Individually Numbered

Purchased ________, Price $ ___________

☐ ***And I Will Dwell In The House Of The Lord Forever,*** **523410 (Wall Hanging)**

UM $95.00
$95.00

Limited Ed. 7,500, Issue Price $55.00, '98
Series: *23rd Psalm Collection* — Seventh Issue
Chapel Exclusive, Individually Numbered

Purchased ________, Price $ ___________

☐ ***The Good Lord Always Delivers,*** **523453**

$45.00
$43.00
$40.00
$38.00
$35.00
$35.00
$34.00
$33.00
$33.00
$31.00
$31.00
$30.00
$30.00
$30.00
$30.00
$30.00
$30.00
$30.00
$30.00
$30.00
$30.00

Open, Issue Price $27.50, '90
(Blonde)

Purchased ________, Price $ ___________

☐ ***Blessed Are The Pure In Heart, For They Shall See God,*** **523399 (Wall Hanging)**

UM $100.00
$95.00

Limited Ed., Issue Price $55.00, '94
Series: *Beatitudes* — Sixth Issue, One Year Production
Chapel Exclusive, Chapel Window Collection, Individually Numbered

Purchased ________, Price $ ___________

☐ ***You Anoint My Head With Oil,*** **523429 (Wall Hanging)**

UM $95.00
$95.00

Limited Ed. 7,500, Issue Price $55.00, '98
Series: *23rd Psalm Collection* — Sixth Issue
Chapel Exclusive, Individually Numbered

Purchased ________, Price $ ___________

☐ ***The Good Lord Always Delivers,*** **523453B**

$30.00
$30.00
$30.00
$30.00

Suspended 2005, Issue Price $27.50, '90
(Brunette)

Purchased ________, Price $ ___________

☐ ***The Lord Is My Shepherd, I Shall Not Want,*** **523402 (Wall Hanging)**

UM $95.00
$95.00

Limited Ed. 7,500, Issue Price $55.00, '97
Series: *23rd Psalm Collection* — First Issue
Chapel Exclusive, Individually Numbered

Purchased ________, Price $ ___________

☐ ***Blessed Are The Poor In Spirit, For Theirs Is The Kingdom Of Heaven,*** **523437 (Wall Hanging)**

UM $140.00
$135.00

Limited Ed., Issue Price $55.00, '92
Series: *Beatitudes* — First Issue, One Year Production
Chapel Exclusive, Chapel Window Collection, Individually Numbered

Purchased ________, Price $ ___________

☐ ***This Day Has Been Made In Heaven,*** **523496**

$53.00
$50.00
$48.00
$45.00
$45.00
$43.00
$43.00
$40.00
$40.00
$38.00
$38.00
$37.50
$37.50
$37.50
$37.50
$37.50
$37.50
$37.50
$37.50
$37.50
$37.50
$37.50

Open, Issue Price $30.00, '90

Purchased ________, Price $ ___________

☐ *God Is Love, Dear Valentine,* 523518

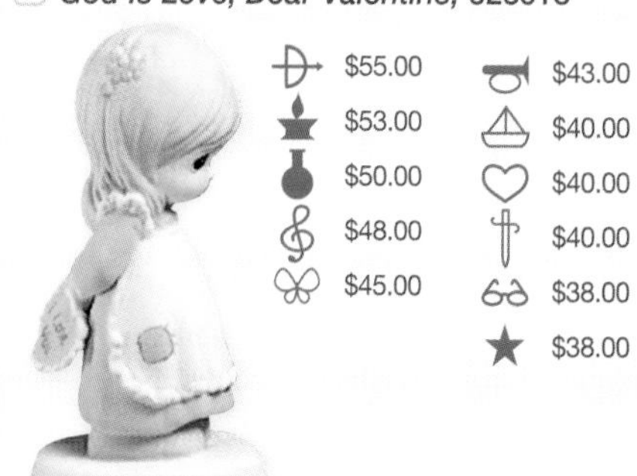

$55.00
$53.00
$50.00
$48.00
$45.00
$43.00
$40.00
$40.00
$40.00
$38.00
$38.00

Retired 1999, Issue Price $27.50, '90

Purchased ________, Price $ ___________

☐ *I'm A Precious Moments Fan,* 523526

$65.00
$60.00

Annual 1990, Issue Price $30.00, '90
Special Event

Purchased___________

Price $ ___________

☐ *I Will Cherish The Old Rugged Cross,* 523534 (Egg)

$40.00
$35.00

Dated Annual 1991, Issue Price $27.50, '91
Set of 2, Series: *Eggs* — First Issue

Purchased ________

Price $ ___________

☐ *You Are The Type I Love,* 523542

$65.00
$63.00
$63.00
$60.00
$60.00
$60.00
$58.00
$58.00
$58.00
$55.00
$55.00
$55.00

Retired 2002, Issue Price $40.00, '92

Purchased ________, Price $ ___________

☐ *He Is Our Shelter From The Storm,* 523550

$95.00
$93.00
$90.00
$88.00
$88.00
$85.00
$85.00
$83.00

Retired 2004, Issue Price $75.00, '98
Boys & Girls Club of America Commemorative

Purchased ________, Price $ ___________

☐ *I Will Always Love You,* 523569

$75.00
$73.00

Limited Ed., Issue Price $45.00, '01
2001 Spring Catalog Exclusive

Purchased ________, Price $ ___________

☐ *The Lord Will Provide,* 523593

$75.00
$73.00

Annual 1993, Issue Price $40.00, '93

Purchased___________

Price $___________

☐ *A Friend Like You Is Heaven-Scent,* 523607

$45.00
$45.00
$45.00
$45.00
$45.00

Open, Issue Price $45.00, '05
Carlton Cards Exclusive

Purchased ________, Price $ ___________

☐ *Good News Is So Uplifting,* 523615

$105.00
$103.00
$100.00
$98.00
$95.00
$93.00
$90.00
$88.00
$85.00

Retired 1999, Issue Price $60.00, '91

Purchased ________, Price $ ___________

☐ *I'm So Glad That God Has Blessed Me With A Friend Like You,* 523623

$105.00
$100.00
$95.00
$90.00

Retired 1995, Issue Price $50.00, '93

Purchased ________, Price $ ___________

☐ *I Will Always Be Thinking Of You,* 523631

$75.00
$73.00
$70.00
$68.00

Retired 1996, Issue Price $45.00, '94

Purchased ________, Price $ ___________

☐ *This Day Has Been Made In Heaven,* 523682 (Musical)

$108.00
$105.00
$100.00
$98.00
$95.00
$95.00
$93.00
$93.00
$90.00
$90.00
$85.00
$85.00
$80.00

Retired 2003, Issue Price $60.00, '92
Tune: *Amazing Grace*

Purchased ________, Price $ ____________

☐ *Just Poppin' In To Say Halo!* 523755

$85.00
$83.00
$80.00
$78.00
$75.00
$70.00

Retired 1999, Issue Price $45.00, '94

Purchased ________, Price $ ____________

☐ *Baby's First Christmas,* 523798 (Ornament)

$30.00

Dated Annual 1990, Issue Price $15.00, '90

Purchased____________

Price $______________

☐ *Wishing You A Yummy Christmas,* 523801 (Plate)

$65.00

Dated Annual 1990, Issue Price $50.00, '90
Series: *Christmas Blessings* — First Issue

Purchased ________, Price $ ____________

☐ *May Your Christmas Be A Happy Home,* 523704 (Ornament)

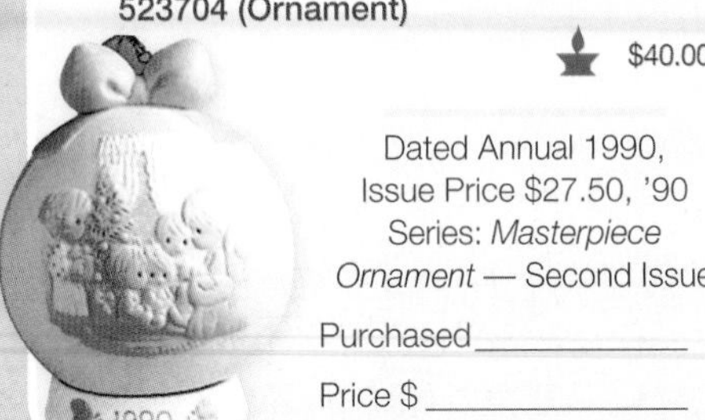

$40.00

Dated Annual 1990,
Issue Price $27.50, '90
Series: *Masterpiece Ornament* — Second Issue

Purchased____________

Price $______________

☐ *I Can't Spell Success Without You,* 523763

$135.00
$115.00
$110.00
$105.00
$100.00

Suspended 1994, Issue Price $40.00, '91

Purchased ________, Price $ ____________

☐ *Time Heals,* 523739

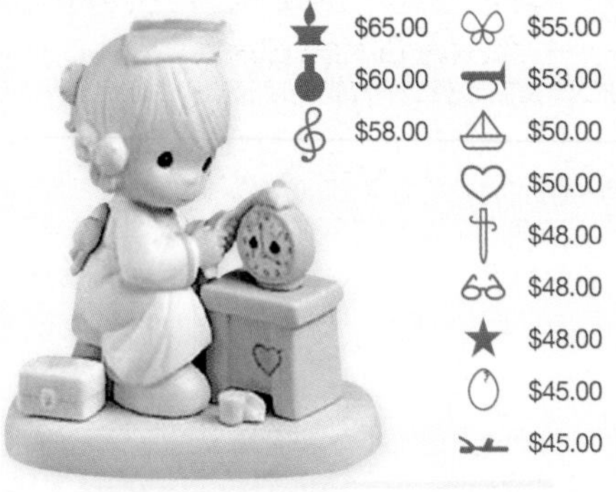

$65.00
$60.00
$58.00
$55.00
$53.00
$50.00
$50.00
$48.00
$48.00
$48.00
$45.00
$45.00

Retired 2001, Issue Price $37.50, '90

Purchased ________, Price $ ____________

☐ *Baby's First Christmas,* 523771 (Ornament)

$30.00

Dated Annual 1990,
Issue Price $15.00, '90

Purchased __________

Price $ ____________

☐ *Once Upon A Holy Night,* 523828 (Bell)

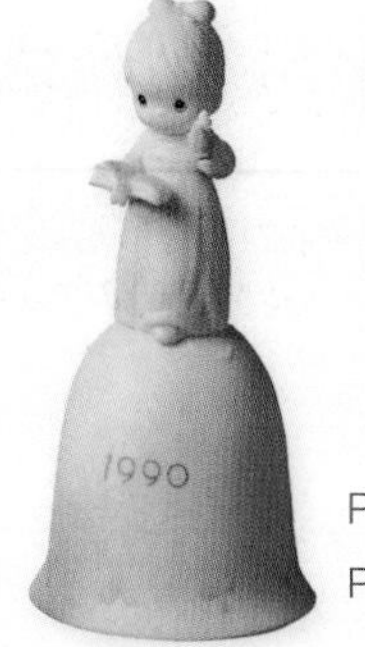

$45.00

Dated Annual 1990,
Issue Price $25.00, '90

Purchased __________

Price $ ____________

☐ *Blessings From Above,* 523747

$125.00
$115.00
$110.00
$105.00
$100.00

Retired 1994, Issue Price $45.00, '90

Purchased ________, Price $ ____________

☐ *Once Upon A Holy Night,* 523836

$55.00

Dated Annual 1990, Issue Price $25.00, '90

Purchased____________

Price $______________

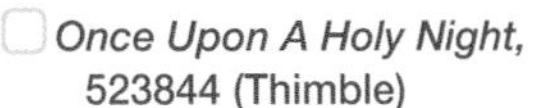

Once Upon A Holy Night, 523844 (Thimble)

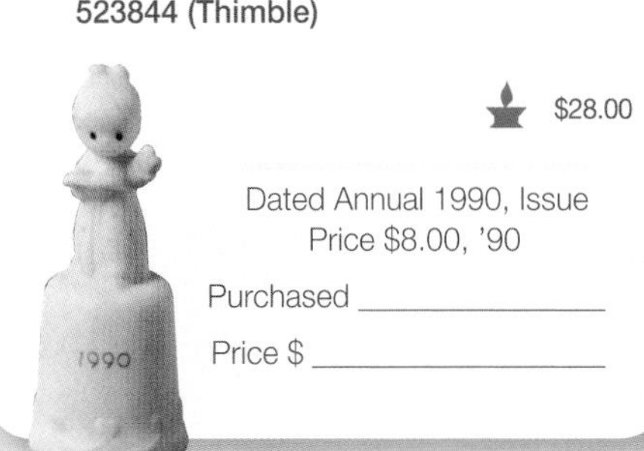

$28.00

Dated Annual 1990, Issue Price $8.00, '90

Purchased ____________

Price $ ____________

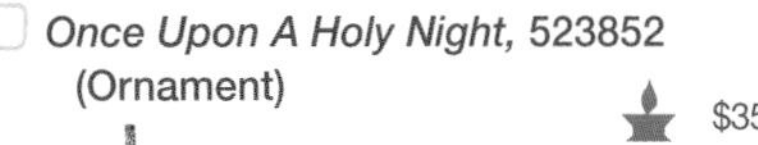

Once Upon A Holy Night, 523852 (Ornament)

$35.00

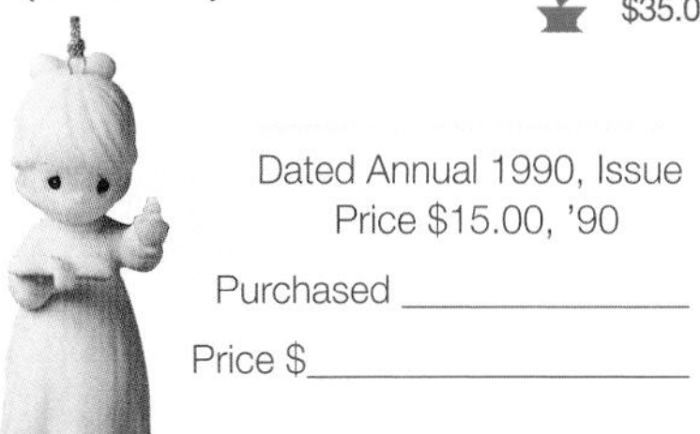

Dated Annual 1990, Issue Price $15.00, '90

Purchased ____________

Price $____________

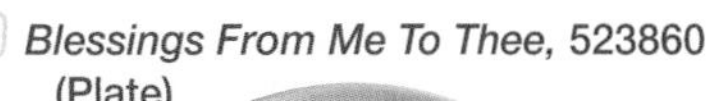

Blessings From Me To Thee, 523860 (Plate)

$65.00

Dated Annual 1991, Issue Price $50.00, '91
Series: *Christmas Blessings* — Second Issue

Purchased ________, Price $ ____________

We Are God's Workmanship, 523879

$725.00
$700.00

Limited Ed. 2,000, Issue Price $500.00, '91
Easter Seals, Lily Understamp
Individually Numbered

Purchased ________, Price $ ____________

Love Never Leaves A Mother's Arms, 523941

$50.00 | $43.00
$47.00 | $40.00
$45.00 | $40.00
$45.00 | $40.00
$43.00 | $40.00
$40.00
$40.00
$40.00
$40.00
$40.00

Open, Issue Price $40.00, '96

Purchased ________, Price $ ____________

You're The Best Friend On The Block, 524018

$65.00
$63.00
$63.00
$60.00
$60.00

Suspended 2005, Issue Price $50.00, '02

Purchased ________, Price $ ____________

Life's Filled With Little Surprises, 524034

UM $30.00

Limited Ed., Issue Price $22.50, '00
Series: *Little Moments*
Hallmark Gold Crown Exclusive

Purchased ________, Price $ ____________

Baby's First Birthday, 524069

$35.00 | $25.00
$33.00 | $25.00
$30.00 | $25.00
$28.00 | $25.00
$25.00 | $25.00
$25.00 | $25.00
$25.00

Suspended 2004, Issue Price $25.00, '93
Series: *Baby's First* — Eighth & Final Issue

Purchased ________, Price $ ____________

Baby's First Meal, 524077

$65.00
$63.00
$60.00
$58.00
$55.00
$55.00
$53.00
$53.00
$50.00

Retired 1999, Issue Price $35.00, '91
Series: *Baby's First* — Sixth Issue

Purchased ________, Price $ ____________

My Warmest Thoughts Are You, 524085

$135.00
$130.00
$125.00
$120.00
$115.00
$110.00

Retired 1996, Issue Price $55.00, '92

Purchased ________, Price $ ____________

Missing You, 524107

$55.00 | $48.00
$53.00 | $45.00
$50.00 | $40.00
$40.00

Open, Issue Price $40.00, '01

Purchased ____________

Price $ ____________

☐ *Sharing Our Christmas Together,* 524115

$95.00
$95.00
$95.00
$95.00

Open, Issue Price $125.00, '04
Purchased ________, Price $ ___________

☐ *Good Friends Are For Always,* 524123

$65.00 $58.00
$63.00 $58.00
$60.00 $55.00
$60.00 $50.00
$45.00

Retired 1999, Issue Price $27.50, '91
Purchased ___________
Price $ ___________

☐ *Good Friends Are For Always,* 524131 (Ornament)

$38.00 $30.00
$35.00 $28.00
$33.00 $28.00

Retired 1997, Issue Price $15.00, '92
Purchased ________, Price $ ___________

☐ *Lord, Teach Us To Pray,* 524158

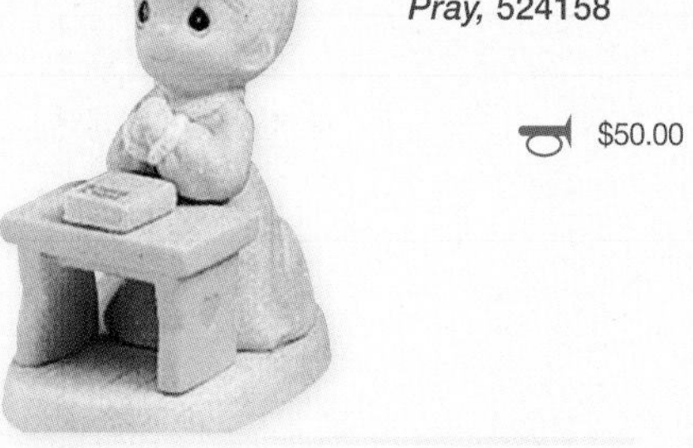

$50.00

Annual 1994, Issue Price $35.00, '94
National Day Of Prayer
Purchased ________, Price $ ___________

☐ *May Your Christmas Be Merry,* 524166

$50.00

Dated Annual 1991, Issue Price $27.50, '91
Purchased ________, Price $ ___________

☐ *May Your Christmas Be Merry,* 524174 (Ornament)

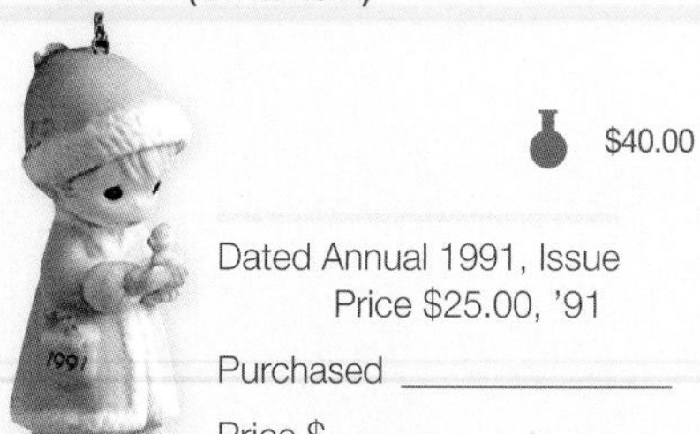

$40.00

Dated Annual 1991, Issue Price $25.00, '91
Purchased ___________
Price $ ___________

☐ *May Your Christmas Be Merry,* 524182 (Bell)

$38.00

Dated Annual 1991, Issue Price $25.00, '91
Purchased ___________
Price $ ___________

☐ *May Your Christmas Be Merry,* 524190 (Thimble)

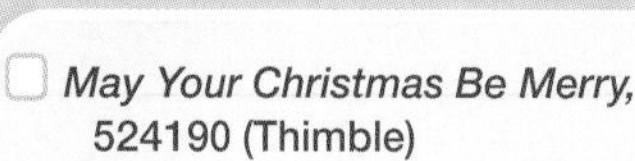

$28.00

Dated Annual 1991, Issue Price $8.00, '91
Purchased ___________
Price $ ___________

☐ *Love Is Color Blind,* 524204

$60.00

One Year of Production, Issue Price $60.00, '98
Boys & Girls Club of America Commemorative
Purchased ________, Price $ ___________

☐ *Love Is Color Blind,* 524204

$75.00
$73.00
$73.00
$70.00
$70.00
$68.00
$68.00

Retired 2004, Issue Price $60.00, '99
Boys & Girls Club of America Commemorative
Purchased ________, Price $ ___________

☐ *Walk In The Sonshine,* 524212

$55.00 $50.00
$53.00 $48.00
$52.00 $47.00
$51.00 $45.00

Retired 2001, Issue Price $35.00, '95
Purchased ___________
Price $ ___________

☐ *He Loves Me,* 524263

$60.00
$55.00

Annual 1991, Issue Price $35.00, '91
Purchased ___________
Price $ ___________

Friendship Grows When You Plant A Seed, 524271

$125.00
$115.00
$110.00
$105.00

Retired 1994, Issue Price $40.00, '92

Purchased ________, Price $ ___________

May Your Every Wish Come True, 524298

$70.00 $53.00
$68.00 $50.00
$65.00 $50.00
$63.00 $50.00
$60.00 $50.00
$58.00 $50.00
$55.00 $50.00
$50.00
$50.00

Open, Issue Price $50.00, '93

Purchased ________, Price $ ___________

May Your Birthday Be A Blessing, 524301

$50.00 $45.00 $35.00
$48.00 $45.00 $35.00
$43.00 $35.00
$40.00 $35.00
$40.00 $35.00
$38.00 $35.00
$36.00 $35.00
$35.00 $35.00
$35.00 $35.00

Open, Issue Price $30.00, '91 (Blonde)

Purchased ________, Price $ ___________

May Your Birthday Be A Blessing, 524301B

$38.00 $37.50
$37.50 $37.50
$37.50 $37.50

Suspended 2005, Issue Price $35.00, '02 (Brunette)

Purchased ________, Price $ ___________

Our Friendship Is Soda-licious, 524336

$105.00
$103.00
$100.00
$98.00
$95.00
$93.00
$90.00
$85.00

Retired 1999, Issue Price $65.00, '93

Purchased ________, Price $ ___________

What The World Needs Now, 524352

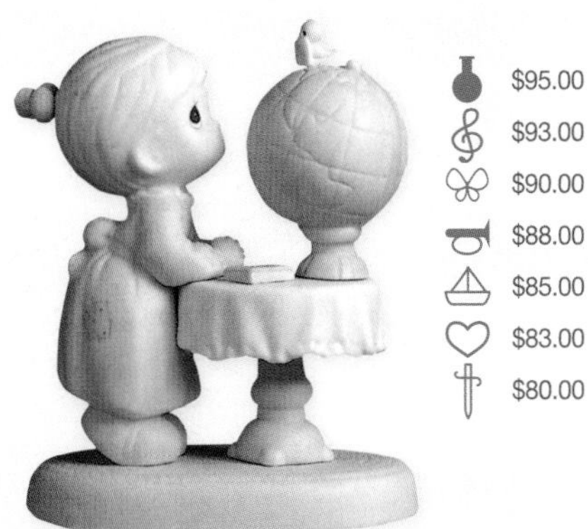

$95.00
$93.00
$90.00
$88.00
$85.00
$83.00
$80.00

Retired 1997, Issue Price $50.00, '92

Purchased ________, Price $ ___________

Something Precious From Above, 524360

$65.00
$63.00
$60.00
$58.00
$55.00
$55.00
$55.00
$55.00
$55.00

Suspended 2004, Issue Price $50.00, '97

Purchased ________, Price $ ___________

So Glad I Picked You As A Friend, 524379

$60.00
$55.00

Annual 1994, Issue Price $40.00, '94
DSR Spring Catalog Exclusive

Purchased ________, Price $ ___________

Take Time To Smell The Flowers, 524387

$55.00 $50.00

Annual 1995, Issue Price $30.00, '95
Easter Seals Commemorative Lily Understamp

Purchased ___________

Price $ ___________

You Are Such A Purr-fect Friend, 524395

$50.00 $35.00
$45.00 $35.00
$43.00 $35.00
$40.00 $35.00
$38.00 $35.00
$36.00 $35.00
$35.00 $35.00
$35.00 $35.00

Open, Issue Price $35.00, '93

Purchased ________, Price $ ___________

Be Fruitful And Multiply, 524409

$60.00 $50.00
$58.00 $50.00
$55.00 $50.00
$50.00 $50.00
$50.00

Open, Issue Price $50.00, '99

Purchased ________, Price $ ___________

May Only Good Things Come Your Way, 524425

$65.00 · $53.00 · $63.00 · $50.00 · $60.00 · $48.00 · $58.00 · $45.00 · $55.00 · $45.00

Retired 1998, Issue Price $30.00, '91

Purchased ________, Price $ ____________

Sealed With A Kiss, 524441

$110.00 · $105.00 · $100.00 · $95.00 · $90.00

Retired 1996, Issue Price $50.00, '93

Purchased ________, Price $ ____________

A Special Chime For Jesus, 524468

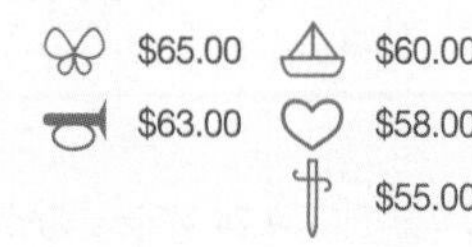

$65.00 · $60.00 · $63.00 · $58.00 · $55.00

Retired 1997, Issue Price $32.50, '93

Purchased ____________

Price $ ______________

God Cared Enough To Send His Best, 524476

$105.00 · $100.00 · $95.00

Retired 1996, Issue Price $50.00, '94

Purchased ________, Price $ ____________

Not A Creature Was Stirring, 524484

$50.00 · $48.00 · $45.00 · $43.00 · $40.00

Suspended 1994, Issue Price $17.00, '90
Series: *Birthday Collection*, Set of 2

Purchased ________, Price $ ____________

Can't Be Without You, 524492

$45.00 · $43.00 · $40.00 · $38.00 · $35.00 · $33.00 · $30.00 · $30.00 · $30.00

Retired 1999, Issue Price $16.00, '91
Series: *Birthday Collection*

Purchased ________, Price $ ____________

Oinky Birthday, 524506

$40.00 · $38.00 · $40.00 · $35.00 · $38.00 · $35.00 · $30.00

Retired 1999, Issue Price $13.50, '94
Series: *Birthday Collection*

Purchased ________, Price $ ____________

Always In His Care, 524522

$65.00 · $55.00

Limited Ed., Issue Price $30.00, '90
Easter Seals Commemorative Lily Understamp

Purchased ____________

Price $ ______________

Happy Birthday Dear Jesus, 524875

$55.00 · $50.00 · $48.00 · $45.00

Suspended 1993, Issue Price $13.50, '90
Nativity Addition

Purchased ________, Price $ ____________

Christmas Fireplace, 524883

$75.00 · $70.00 · $65.00

Suspended 1992, Issue Price $37.50, '90
Series: *Family Christmas Scene*

Purchased ________, Price $ ____________

It's So Uplifting To Have A Friend Like You, 524905

$75.00 · $65.00 · $73.00 · $63.00 · $70.00 · $60.00 · $68.00 · $58.00

Retired 1999, Issue Price $40.00, '92

Purchased ____________

Price $ ______________

We're Going To Miss You, 524913

$105.00 · $103.00 · $98.00 · $100.00 · $95.00 · $93.00 · $90.00 · $85.00 · $83.00 · $80.00 · $78.00 · $75.00 · $75.00

Retired 2001, Issue Price $50.00, '90

Purchased ________, Price $ ____________

☐ *Angels We Have Heard On High,* 524921

There have been many reports of the African-American angel's hand not being painted.

$105.00
$103.00
$100.00
$95.00
$93.00
$90.00

Retired 1996, Issue Price $60.00, '91

Purchased ________, Price $ ___________

☐ *It's A Perfect Boy,* 525286

$35.00
$33.00
$33.00
$30.00
$30.00
$28.00
$28.00
$25.00
$25.00

Retired 1999, Issue Price $16.50, '91
Mini Nativity Addition

Purchased ________, Price $ ___________

☐ *Ring Those Christmas Bells,* 525898

$185.00
$175.00
$165.00
$160.00
$155.00

Retired 1996, Issue Price $95.00, '92

Purchased ________, Price $ ___________

☐ *Good Friends Are Forever,* 525049

$675.00

Only collectors who attended the 1990 "Good Friends Are Forever" Special Event with a friend had the opportunity to be included in a drawing for this special Rosebud decal understamp figurine. Last known sale of this piece was $625.00.

Annual
1990, Special Event

Purchased ________, Price $ ___________

☐ *May Your Future Be Blessed,* 525316

$55.00
$53.00
$50.00
$48.00
$45.00
$44.00
$42.00
$40.00
$40.00
$40.00
$40.00
$40.00
$40.00
$40.00
$40.00
$40.00
$40.00
$40.00

Open, Issue Price $35.00, '93

Purchased ________, Price $ ___________

☐ *We All Need A Friend Through The Ruff Times,* 525901

$50.00
$48.00
$45.00
$45.00
$45.00

Suspended 2004, Issue Price $45.00, '01

Purchased ________, Price $ ___________

☐ *Bundles Of Joy,* 525057 (Ornament)

$33.00

Annual 1990, Issue Price $15.00, '90

Purchased ___________

Price $___________

☐ *Our First Christmas Together,* 525324 (Ornament)

$30.00

Dated Annual 1990, Issue Price $17.50, '90

Purchased ________

Price $________

☐ *Let's Put The Pieces Together,* 525928

$70.00
$65.00
$63.00
$60.00
$60.00
$60.00
$60.00
$60.00
$60.00
$60.00
$60.00
$60.00
$60.00

Open, Issue Price $60.00, '98

Purchased ________, Price $ ___________

☐ *Tubby's First Christmas,* 525278

$20.00
$18.00
$18.00
$18.00
$15.00
$15.00
$15.00
$15.00

Retired 1999, Issue Price $10.00, '92
Mini Nativity Addition

Purchased ________, Price $ ___________

☐ *Lord, Keep Me On My Toes,* 525332 (Ornament)

$33.00
$30.00
$30.00
$30.00
$28.00
$28.00
$25.00
$25.00
$25.00
$25.00
$25.00

Retired 2001, Issue Price $15.00, '92

Purchased ________, Price $ ___________

☐ ***Lord, I'm In It Again, 525944***

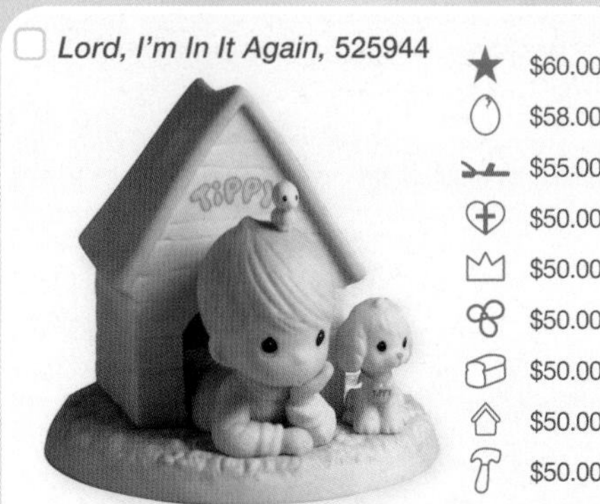

$60.00
$58.00
$55.00
$50.00
$50.00
$50.00
$50.00
$50.00
$50.00

Suspended 2004 Price $50.00, '99

Purchased ________, Price $ ___________

☐ ***All About Heaven, 525952***

$28.00 $23.00
$25.00 $20.00

Open, Issue Price $20.00, '01
Mini Nativity Addition

Purchased ___________

Price $ ___________

☐ ***We Are God's Workmanship, 525960 (Egg)***

$40.00
$38.00

Dated Annual 1992, Issue Price $27.50, '92
Set of 2, Series: *Eggs* — Second Issue

Purchased ________, Price $ ___________

☐ ***You Are Such A Purr-fect Friend, 526010***

$725.00
$700.00

Limited Ed. 2,000, Issue Price $500.00, '92
Easter Seals, Lily Understamp
Individually Numbered

Easter Seals

Purchased ________, Price $ ___________

☐ ***A Prince Of A Guy, 526037***

$55.00 $48.00
$53.00 $45.00
$50.00 $43.00

Retired 2000, Issue Price $35.00, '95

Purchased___________

Price $ ___________

☐ ***A Prince Of A Guy, 526037S***

$38.00

Limited Ed., Issue Price $35.00, '95
1995 Fall Catalog Exclusive

Purchased ________, Price $ ___________

☐ ***Pretty As A Princess, 526053***

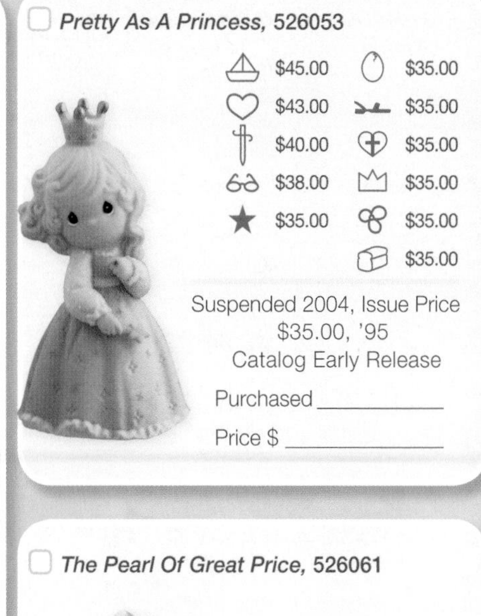

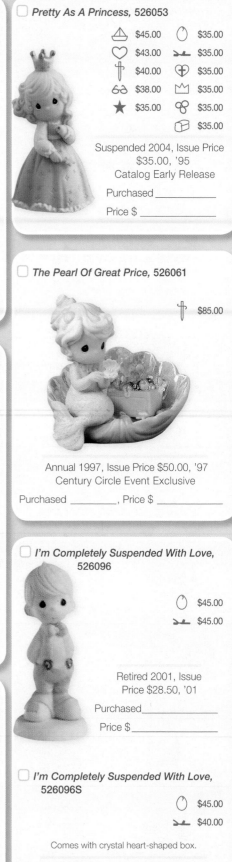

$45.00 $35.00
$43.00 $35.00
$40.00 $35.00
$38.00 $35.00
$35.00 $35.00
$35.00

Suspended 2004, Issue Price $35.00, '95
Catalog Early Release

Purchased ___________

Price $ ___________

☐ ***The Pearl Of Great Price, 526061***

$85.00

Annual 1997, Issue Price $50.00, '97
Century Circle Event Exclusive

Purchased ________, Price $ ___________

☐ ***I'm Completely Suspended With Love, 526096***

$45.00
$45.00

Retired 2001, Issue Price $28.50, '01

Purchased___________

Price $___________

☐ ***I'm Completely Suspended With Love, 526096S***

$45.00
$40.00

Comes with crystal heart-shaped box.

Retired 2001, Issue Price $28.50, '01

Purchased ________, Price $ ___________

☐ ***Going Home, 525979***

$100.00 $90.00 $80.00
$98.00 $88.00 $78.00
$95.00 $85.00 $78.00
$93.00 $83.00 $78.00
$80.00 $75.00

Has been found with "Heaven Bound" missing from license plate.

Retired 2004, Issue Price $60.00, '92
Philip Butcher Memorial Figurine

Purchased ________, Price $ ___________

☐ *I Would Be Lost Without You, 526142*

$55.00
$53.00
$50.00
$48.00
$48.00
$45.00
$45.00
$43.00
$43.00

Retired 1999, Issue Price $27.50, '92

Purchased ____________

Price $ ____________

☐ *Friends To The Very End, 526150*

$85.00
$83.00
$80.00
$78.00
$75.00

Retired 1997, Issue Price $40.00, '94

Purchased ________, Price $ ____________

☐ *You Are My Happiness, 526185*

$85.00
$83.00

Limited Ed., Issue Price $37.50, '92

Purchased ________

Price $____________

☐ *You Suit Me To A Tee, 526193*

$65.00
$63.00
$60.00
$58.00
$55.00
$53.00

Retired 1999, Issue Price $35.00, '94

Purchased ________, Price $ ____________

☐ *Sharing Sweet Moments Together, 526487*

$65.00
$63.00
$60.00
$58.00
$55.00
$53.00
$50.00

Retired 1999, Issue Price $45.00, '94

Purchased ________, Price $ ____________

☐ *Bless Those Who Serve Their Country — Navy, 526568*

UM $175.00
$165.00
$160.00

Suspended 1992, Issue Price $32.50, '91

Purchased ________, Price $ ____________

☐ *Bless Those Who Serve Their Country — Army, 526576*

$60.00
$58.00

Suspended 1992, Issue Price $32.50, '91

Purchased ____________

Price $ ____________

☐ *Bless Those Who Serve Their Country — Air Force, 526584*

$60.00
$58.00

Suspended 1992, Issue Price $32.50, '91

Purchased ____________

Price $ ____________

☐ *You Can Always Count On Me, 526827*

$60.00
$58.00

Annual 1996, Issue Price $30.00, '96
Easter Seals Commemorative
Lily Understamp

Purchased ________, Price $ ____________

☐ *The Lord Is With You, 526835*

$45.00
$43.00
$40.00
$38.00
$35.00

Retired 1999, Issue Price $27.50, '96

Purchased ____________

Price $ ____________

☐ *He's Got The Whole World In His Hands, 526886*

$650.00
$625.00

Limited Ed. 2,000, Issue Price $500.00, '95
Easter Seals,
Lily Understamp
Individually
Numbered

Purchased____________

Price $____________

☐ *Wishing You Were Here, 526916* (Musical)

$175.00
$170.00
$165.00
$160.00
$155.00
$150.00
$145.00

Retired 1998, Issue Price $100.00, '93
Tune: *When You Wish Upon A Star*

Purchased ________, Price $ ____________

☐ ***How Can I Ever Forget You*, 526924**

$45.00 | $33.00
$43.00 | $33.00
$40.00 | $30.00
$38.00 | $30.00
$35.00 | $25.00
$35.00 | $25.00

Retired 2001, Issue Price $15.00, '91
Series: *Birthday Collection*

Purchased ________, Price $ ____________

☐ ***May Your Christmas Be Merry*, 526940 (Ornament)**

$50.00

Dated Annual 1991, Issue Price $30.00, '91
Series: *Masterpiece Ornament* — Third Issue
Set of 2

Purchased ________
Price $____________

☐ ***We Have Come From Afar*, 526959**

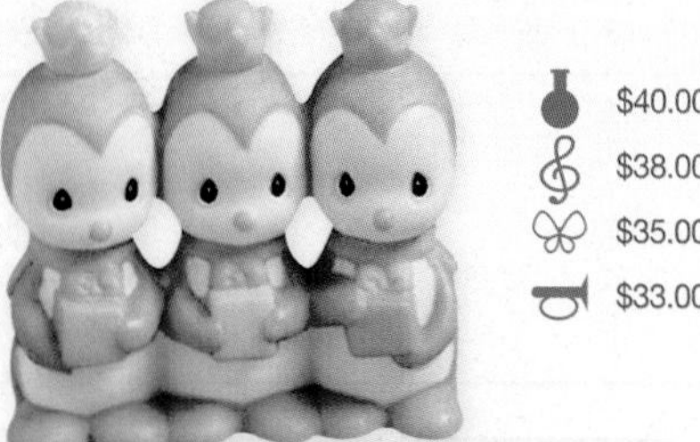

$40.00
$38.00
$35.00
$33.00

Suspended 1994, Issue Price $17.50, '91
Nativity Addition

Purchased ________, Price $ ____________

☐ ***Baby's First Christmas*, 527084 (Ornament)**

$30.00

Dated Annual 1991, Issue Price $15.00, '91

Purchased ____________
Price $____________

☐ ***Baby's First Christmas*, 527092 (Ornament)**

$30.00

Dated Annual 1991, Issue Price $15.00, '91

Purchased ____________
Price $____________

☐ ***He Is Not Here For He Is Risen As He Said*, 527106**

UM $115.00 | $80.00 | $73.00
$100.00 | $75.00 | $70.00
$85.00 | | $68.00
$65.00
$63.00
$60.00
$60.00
$60.00
$60.00
$60.00

Open, Issue Price $60.00, '93
Chapel Exclusive

Purchased ________, Price $ ____________

☐ ***Sharing A Gift Of Love*, 527114**

$75.00
$70.00

Annual 1991, Issue Price $30.00, '91
Easter Seals Commemorative Lily Understamp

Purchased ____________
Price $____________

☐ ***You Can Always Bring A Friend*, 527122**

$70.00
$65.00

Annual 1991, Issue Price $27.50, '91
Special Event

Purchased ____________
Price $ ____________

☐ ***The Good Lord Always Delivers*, 527165 (Ornament)**

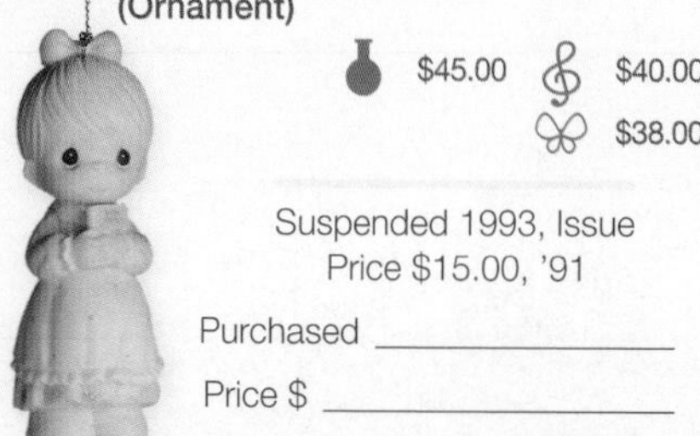

$45.00 | $40.00
$38.00

Suspended 1993, Issue Price $15.00, '91

Purchased ____________
Price $ ____________

☐ ***A Universal Love*, 527173**

$125.00
$120.00

Annual 1992, Issue Price $32.50, '92
Easter Seals Commemorative Lily Understamp

Purchased ____________
Price $____________

☐ ***Share In The Warmth Of Christmas*, 527211 (Ornament)**

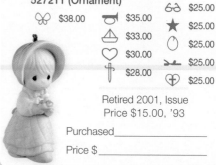

$38.00 | $35.00 | $25.00
$33.00 | $25.00
$30.00 | $25.00
$28.00 | $25.00
$25.00

Retired 2001, Issue Price $15.00, '93

Purchased____________
Price $____________

☐ ***Baby's First Word*, 527238**

$60.00 | $50.00
$58.00 | $48.00
$55.00 | $45.00
$53.00 | $43.00

Retired 1999, Issue Price $25.00, '92
Series: *Baby's First* — Seventh Issue

Purchased ____________
Price $ ____________

☐ ***Let's Be Friends*, 527270**

$50.00
$45.00
$43.00
$40.00
$38.00
$35.00

Retired 1996, Issue Price $15.00, '92
Series: *Birthday Collection*

Purchased ________, Price $ ____________

☐ *Bless Those Who Serve Their Country — Girl Soldier*, 527289

$65.00
$60.00

Suspended 1992, Issue Price $32.50, '91

Purchased ________, Price $ ____________

☐ *Bless Those Who Serve Their Country — African-American Soldier*, 527297

$65.00
$60.00

Suspended 1992, Issue Price $32.50, '91

Purchased ____________

Price $ ______________

☐ *An Event Worth Wading For*, 527319

$65.00
$60.00

Annual 1992, Issue Price $32.50, '92
Special Event

Purchased ________, Price $ ____________

☐ *Onward Christmas Soldiers*, 527327 (Ornament)

$40.00
$38.00
$35.00
$33.00
$30.00
$30.00
$28.00
$28.00
$28.00

Retired 2001, Issue Price $16.00, '94

Purchased ______________

Price $ ______________

☐ *Bless-um You*, 527335

$65.00
$63.00
$60.00
$58.00
$55.00
$53.00
$50.00

Retired 1998, Issue Price $35.00, '93

Purchased ________, Price $ ____________

☐ *Happy Birdie*, 527343

$45.00
$43.00
$40.00
$38.00
$35.00

Suspended 1996, Issue Price $16.00, '92
Series: *Birthday Collection*

Purchased ________, Price $ ____________

☐ *You Are My Favorite Star*, 527378

$125.00
$120.00
$115.00
$110.00
$105.00
$100.00

Retired 1997, Issue Price $60.00, '92

Purchased ________, Price $ ____________

☐ *Baby's First Christmas (Girl)*, 527475 (Ornament)

$35.00

Dated Annual 1992, Issue Price $15.00, '92

Purchased______________

Price $______________

☐ *Baby's First Christmas (Boy)*, 527483 (Ornament)

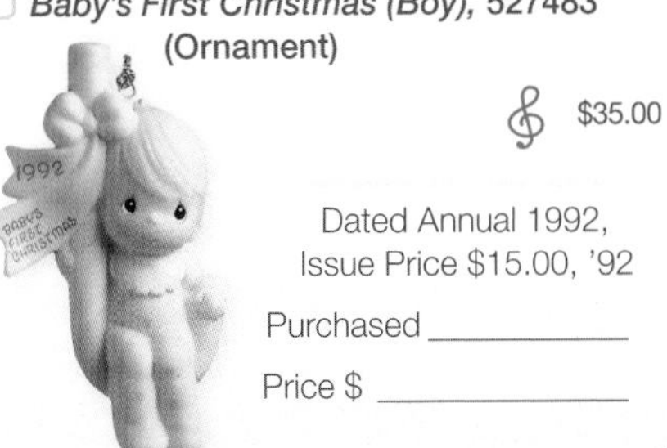

$35.00

Dated Annual 1992, Issue Price $15.00, '92

Purchased ____________

Price $ ____________

☐ *Bless Those Who Serve Their Country — Marine*, 527521

$85.00
$80.00

Suspended 1992, Issue Price $32.50, '91

Purchased ________, Price $ ____________

☐ *Bring The Little Ones To Jesus*, 527556

$145.00
$143.00
$140.00
$138.00
$135.00
$130.00
$128.00
$125.00
$125.00
$123.00
$123.00
$120.00
$120.00

Retired 2003, Issue Price $90.00, '92
Child Evangelism Fellowship

Purchased ________, Price $ ____________

☐ *God Bless The USA*, 527564

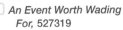

$65.00
$60.00

Annual 1992, Issue Price $32.50, '92

Purchased ____________

Price $____________

Tied Up For The Holidays, 527580

- $70.00
- $65.00
- $60.00
- $58.00

Suspended 1996, Issue Price $40.00, '93

Purchased ________, Price $ ____________

Bringing You A Merry Christmas, 527599

- $115.00
- $110.00
- $105.00

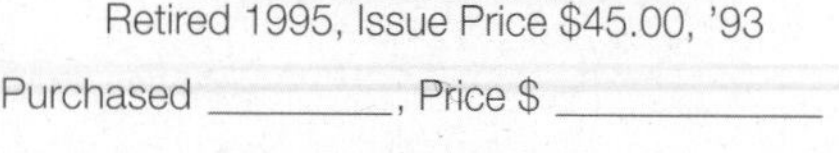

Retired 1995, Issue Price $45.00, '93

Purchased ________, Price $ ____________

Wishing You A Ho, Ho, Ho, 527629

- $75.00
- $73.00
- $70.00
- $68.00
- $68.00
- $65.00
- $65.00
- $63.00
- $63.00
- $60.00
- $60.00

Retired 2001, Issue Price $40.00, '92

Purchased ________, Price $ ____________

Waiting For A Merry Christmas, 527637

- $95.00

Retired 2000, Issue Price $65.00, '00

Purchased ________, Price $ ____________

You Have Touched So Many Hearts, 527661

- $50.00
- $48.00
- $45.00
- $43.00
- $40.00
- $40.00

Suspended 1996, Issue Price $35.00, '91
DSR Exclusive

Purchased ________, Price $ ____________

But The Greatest Of These Is Love, 527688

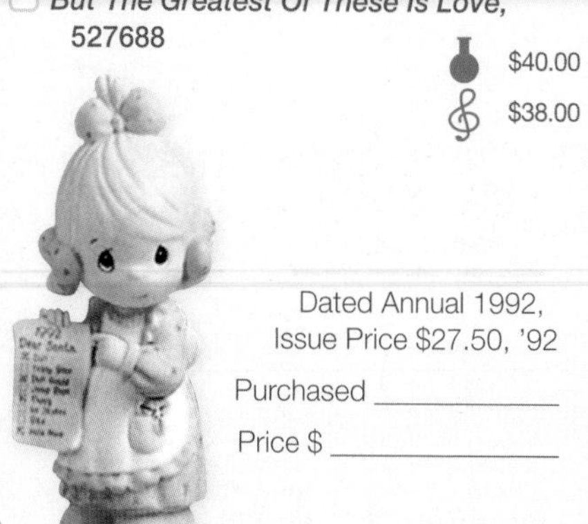

- $40.00
- $38.00

Dated Annual 1992, Issue Price $27.50, '92

Purchased ____________

Price $ ____________

But The Greatest Of These Is Love, 527696 (Ornament)

- $38.00

Dated Annual 1992, Issue Price $15.00, '92

Purchased ____________

Price $____________

But The Greatest Of These Is Love, 527718 (Thimble)

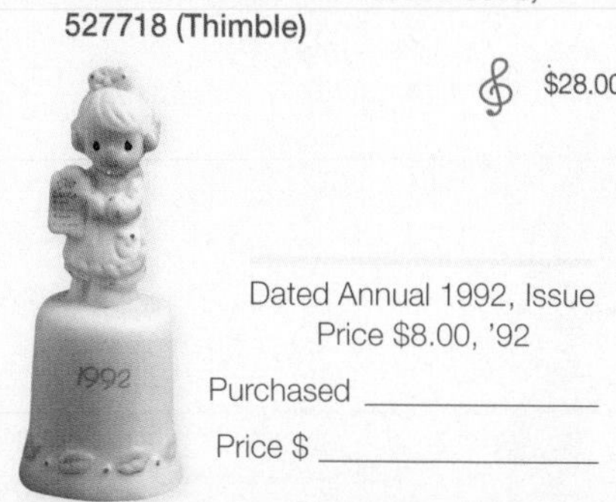

- $28.00

Dated Annual 1992, Issue Price $8.00, '92

Purchased ____________

Price $ ____________

But The Greatest Of These Is Love, 527726 (Bell)

- $38.00

Dated Annual 1992, Issue Price $25.00, '92

Purchased____________

Price $ ____________

But The Greatest Of These Is Love, 527734 (Ornament)

- $48.00

Dated Annual 1992, Issue Price $30.00, '92
Series: *Masterpiece Ornament* — Fourth Issue
Set of 2

Purchased ________, Price $ ____________

But The Greatest Of These Is Love, 527742 (Plate)

- $65.00

Dated Annual 1992, Issue Price $50.00, '92
Series: *Christmas Blessings* — Third Issue

Purchased ________, Price $ ____________

Wishing You A Comfy Christmas, 527750

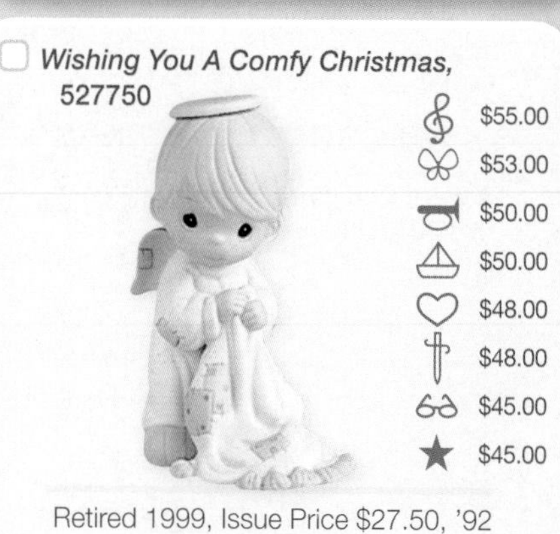

- $55.00
- $53.00
- $50.00
- $50.00
- $48.00
- $48.00
- $45.00
- $45.00

Retired 1999, Issue Price $27.50, '92
Nativity Addition

Purchased ________, Price $ ____________

☐ *I Only Have Arms For You,* 527769

$35.00
$33.00
$30.00
$28.00
$25.00
$23.00
$23.00

Retired 1998, Issue Price $15.00, '93
Series: *Birthday Collection*

Purchased ________, Price $ ___________

☐ *This Land Is Our Land,* 527777

$48.00

Annual 1992, Issue Price $35.00, '92

Purchased ______

Price $ ___________

☐ *There's A Christian Welcome Here,* 528021 (Ornament)

UM $45.00
$43.00
$40.00
$38.00
$35.00
$35.00

Suspended 1997, Issue Price $22.50, '92
Chapel Exclusive

Purchased ________, Price $ ___________

☐ *Free Christmas Puppies,* 528064

$45.00
$43.00
$40.00
$38.00

Retired 1997, Issue Price $12.50, '94
Series: *Sugar Town*

Purchased ________, Price $ ___________

☐ *Nativity Cart,* 528072

$45.00 $38.00
$43.00 $35.00
$40.00 $35.00
$38.00 $33.00

Retired 2001, Issue Price $18.50, '94
Nativity Addition

Purchased ________, Price $ ___________

☐ *Follow Your Heart,* 528080

There have been reports of the decal being on backwards.

$70.00
$60.00

Annual 1995, Issue Price $30.00, '95
Spring Celebration Event

Purchased ___________

Price $ ___________

☐ *Markie,* 528099

$38.00 $30.00
$35.00 $28.00

Suspended 1996, Issue Price $18.50, '94
Series: *Sammy's Circus*

Purchased___________

Price $ ___________

☐ *He Came As The Gift Of God's Love,* 528129

$35.00 $30.00
$40.00 $33.00 $30.00
$38.00 $30.00 $30.00
$30.00

Open, Issue Price $30.00, '99
Nativity, Set of 4

Purchased ________, Price $ ___________

☐ *Have I Got News For You,* 528137

$40.00 $35.00
$38.00 $33.00
$35.00 $33.00

Retired 1999, Issue Price $16.00, '94
Mini Nativity Addition

Purchased ___________

Price $ ___________

☐ *Circus Tent,* 528196 (Nightlight)

$125.00 $110.00
$115.00 $105.00

Suspended 1996, Issue Price $90.00, '94
Series: *Sammy's Circus*

Purchased ________, Price $ ___________

☐ *Sending You A White Christmas,* 528218 (Ornament)

$38.00 $30.00
$35.00 $30.00
$35.00 $28.00
$33.00 $25.00
$25.00

Retired 2001, Issue Price $16.00, '94

Purchased___________

Price $ ___________

☐ *Bringing You A Merry Christmas,* 528226 (Ornament)

$33.00 $28.00
$30.00 $25.00
$23.00

Suspended 1998, Issue Price $16.00, '94

Purchased___________

Price $ ___________

☐ ***I'm Sending My Love Your Way*, 528609**

$75.00
$70.00

Annual 1995, Issue Price $40.00, '95
Spring Catalog DSR Promo

Purchased ____________
Price $ ____________

☐ ***Make A Joyful Noise*, 528617**

$43.00
$40.00

Dated Annual 1993, Issue Price $27.50, '93
Set of 2, Series: *Eggs*

Purchased ________, Price $ ____________

☐ ***To A Very Special Sister*, 528633**

$115.00
$105.00
$103.00
$100.00
$98.00
$95.00
$93.00
$90.00
$90.00

Retired 2002, Issue Price $60.00, '94

Purchased ________, Price $ ____________

☐ ***Sammy*, 528668**

$43.00
$40.00
$38.00
$35.00
$33.00

Retired 1997, Issue Price $17.00, '93
Series: *Sugar Town*

Purchased ________, Price $ ____________

☐ ***Alive With The Spirit Of The Season*, 528676 (Ornament)**

$20.00
$20.00

Suspended 2004, Issue Price $20.00, '04
Series: *The Legend Of The Christmas Tree*

Purchased ____________
Price $____________

☐ ***Evergreen Tree*, 528684**

$48.00
$43.00
$40.00

Retired 1994, Issue Price $15.00, '92
Series: *Sugar Town*

Purchased ____________
Price $ ____________

☐ ***It's So Uplifting To Have A Friend Like You*, 528846 (Ornament)**

$33.00
$30.00
$28.00
$25.00
$25.00
$23.00
$23.00

Retired 1999, Issue Price $16.00, '93

Purchased ____________
Price $____________

☐ ***America, You're Beautiful*, 528862**

$65.00
$60.00

Annual 1993, Issue Price $35.00, '93
National Day of Prayer

Purchased ________, Price $ ____________

☐ ***America, You're Beautiful*, 528862R**

$50.00
$45.00

A portion of the proceeds from the sales of this figurine benefited the September 11th Relief Fund.

Retired 2004, Issue Price $35.00, '01
Series: *America Forever*

Purchased ________, Price $ ____________

☐ ***Our First Christmas Together*, 528870 (Ornament)**

$33.00

Dated Annual 1992, Issue Price $17.50, '92

Purchased ________
Price $ ________

☐ ***Friends Never Drift Apart*, 529079 (Medallion)**

UM $825.00
$800.00

Dated Annual 1993, Gift, '93
Fifteenth Anniversary Cruise Piece

Purchased ________, Price $ ____________

☐ ***15 Years, Tweet Music Together*, 529087 (Medallion)**

UM $110.00
$105.00

Dated Annual 1993, Gift, '93
Fifteenth Anniversary Convention
Orlando Celebration

Purchased ________, Price $ ____________

☐ ***A Reflection Of His Love*, 529095 (Egg)**

$43.00
$40.00

Dated Annual 1994, Issue Price $27.50, '94
Series: *Eggs* — Fourth & Final Issue

Purchased ________, Price $ ____________

☐ ***Jordan*, 529168**

$38.00
$35.00
$30.00

Suspended 1996, Issue Price $20.00, '95
Series: *Sammy's Circus*, Set of 2

Purchased ________, Price $ ____________

☐ ***Dusty*, 529176**

$38.00
$35.00
$30.00
$28.00

Suspended 1996, Issue Price $22.50, '94
Series: *Sammy's Circus*

Purchased ________, Price $ ____________

☐ ***Katie*, 529184**

$38.00
$35.00
$33.00
$30.00

Suspended 1996, Issue Price $17.00, '94
Series: *Sammy's Circus*

Purchased ________, Price $ ____________

☐ ***Tippy*, 529192**

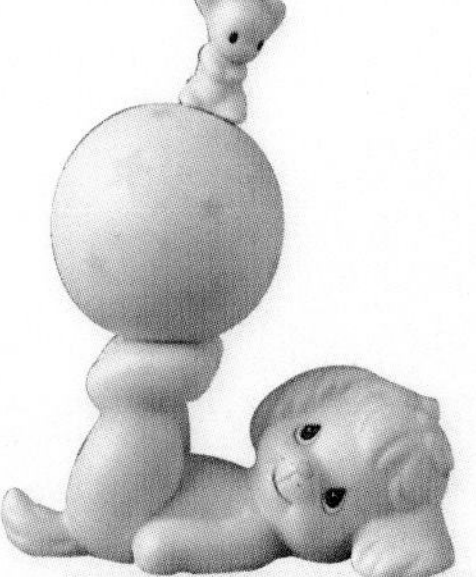

$28.00
$25.00
$23.00
$23.00

Suspended 1996, Issue Price $12.00, '94
Series: *Sammy's Circus*

Purchased ________, Price $ ____________

☐ ***Our First Christmas Together*, 529206 (Ornament)**

$28.00

Dated Annual 1994,
Issue Price $18.50, '94

Purchased__________

Price $____________

☐ ***Collin*, 529214**

$38.00 $33.00
$35.00 $30.00

Suspended 1996, Issue Price $20.00, '94
Series: *Sammy's Circus*

Purchased__________

Price $____________

☐ ***Sammy*, 529222**

$53.00
$48.00

Dated Annual 1994,
Issue Price $20.00, '94
Series: *Sammy's Circus*

Purchased __________

Price $____________

☐ ***My True Love Gave To Me*, 529273**

$65.00
$63.00
$60.00
$58.00
$55.00
$53.00
$53.00

Retired 2002, Issue Price $40.00, '96

Purchased ________, Price $ ____________

☐ ***Dusty*, 529435**

$38.00 $33.00
$35.00 $30.00
$28.00

Retired 1997, Issue
Price $17.00, '93
Series: *Sugar Town*

Purchased ________, Price $ ____________

☐ ***Doctor's Office Set*, 529281**

$350.00
$325.00
$320.00
$315.00
$305.00

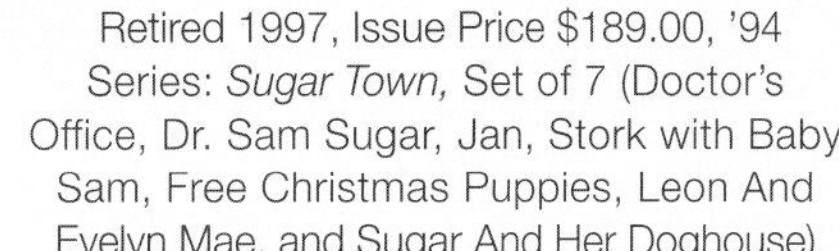

Retired 1997, Issue Price $189.00, '94
Series: *Sugar Town,* Set of 7 (Doctor's Office, Dr. Sam Sugar, Jan, Stork with Baby Sam, Free Christmas Puppies, Leon And Evelyn Mae, and Sugar And Her Doghouse)

Purchased ________, Price $ ____________

☐ ***Sam's Car*, 529443**

$50.00
$45.00
$40.00
$35.00
$30.00

Retired 1997, Issue Price $22.50, '93
Series: *Sugar Town*

Purchased ________, Price $ ___________

☐ ***The Best Gifts Are Loving, Caring and Sharing*, 529451 (Ornament)**

$20.00
$20.00

Suspened 2004, Issue Price $20.00, '04
Series: *The Legend Of Gifts*

Purchased ___________

Price $ ______________

☐ ***Aunt Ruth & Aunt Dorothy*, 529486**

$48.00 $45.00
$43.00

Retired 1994, Issue Price $20.00, '92
Series: *Sugar Town*

Purchased ________, Price $ ___________

☐ ***Philip*, 529494**

$48.00 $45.00
$43.00

Retired 1994, Issue Price $17.00, '92
Series: *Sugar Town*

Purchased ___________

Price $ ______________

☐ ***Nativity*, 529508**

$65.00
$60.00
$55.00

Retired 1994, Issue Price $20.00, '92
Series: *Sugar Town*

Purchased ________, Price $ ___________

☐ ***Grandfather*, 529516**

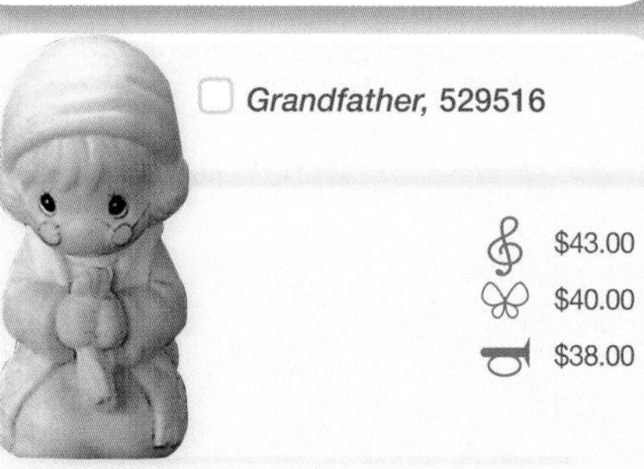

$43.00
$40.00
$38.00

Retired 1994, Issue Price $15.00, '92
Series: *Sugar Town*

Purchased ________, Price $ ___________

☐ ***Katy Lynne*, 529524**

$43.00
$40.00
$38.00
$35.00
$33.00

Retired 1997, Issue Price $20.00, '93
Series: *Sugar Town*

Purchased ________, Price $ ___________

☐ ***Welcome Are Those With Happy Hearts*, 529532 (Ornament)**

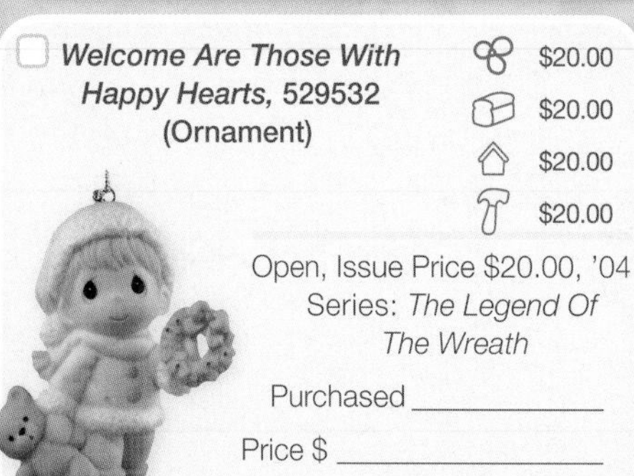

$20.00
$20.00
$20.00
$20.00

Open, Issue Price $20.00, '04
Series: *The Legend Of The Wreath*

Purchased ___________

Price $ ______________

☐ ***Park Bench*, 529540**

$28.00
$25.00
$20.00

Retired 1997, Issue Price $13.00, '95
Series: *Sugar Town*

Purchased ________, Price $ ___________

☐ ***Lamp Post*, 529559**

$25.00 $21.00
$23.00 $20.00

Retired 1997, Issue Price $8.00, '94
Series: *Sugar Town*

Purchased ______________

Price $ ______________

☐ ***Sam Butcher*, 529567**

$205.00

Sign reads: "Established 1992. Population 5 and Growing."

Retired 1995, Issue Price $22.50, '92
Series: *Sugar Town*

Purchased ________, Price $ ___________

☐ ***Sam's House*, 529605 (Nightlight)**

$125.00 $120.00 $110.00
$115.00 $105.00

Retired 1997, Issue Price $80.00, '93
Series: *Sugar Town*

Purchased ________, Price $ ___________

Chapel, 529621 (Nightlight)

$185.00
$180.00
$175.00

Retired 1994, Issue Price $85.00, '92
Series: *Sugar Town*

Purchased ________, Price $ ___________

The Magic Starts With You, 529648 (Ornament)

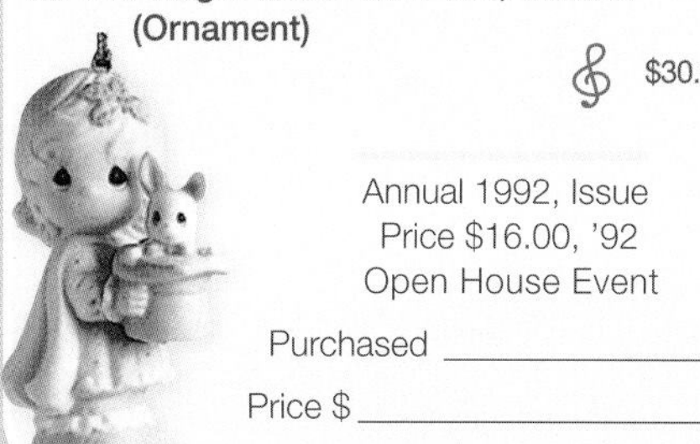

$30.00

Annual 1992, Issue Price $16.00, '92
Open House Event

Purchased ___________
Price $ ___________

Goose Girl, 529672 (Medallion)

UM $600.00

Given to those who attended the annual tour of the Orient.

Limited Ed. 25, Gift, '92
1992 Orient Tour Exclusive

Purchased ________, Price $ ___________

Gather Your Dreams, 529680

$750.00
$720.00

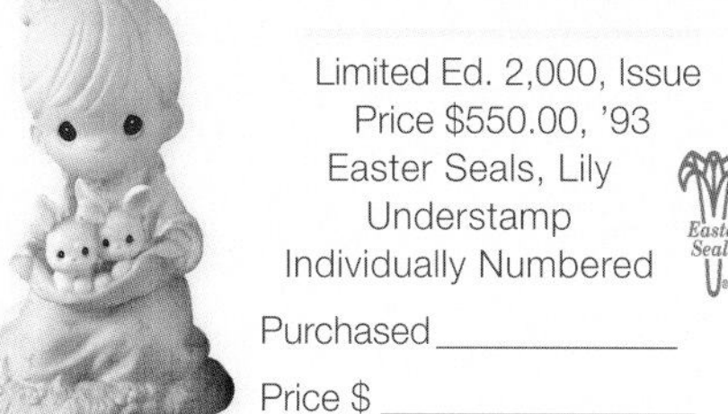

Limited Ed. 2,000, Issue Price $550.00, '93
Easter Seals, Lily Understamp
Individually Numbered

Purchased ___________
Price $ ___________

Stork With Baby Sam, 529788

$60.00

Annual 1994, Issue Price $22.50, '94
Series: *Sugar Town*

Purchased ____
Price $________

Fence, 529796

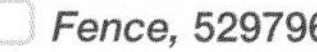

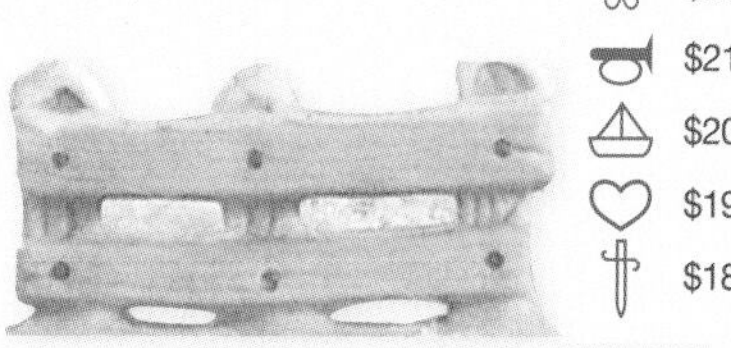

$23.00
$21.00
$20.00
$19.00
$18.00

Retired 1997, Issue Price $10.00, '93
Series: *Sugar Town*

Purchased ________, Price $ ___________

Leon And Evelyn Mae, 529818

$35.00
$33.00
$30.00
$28.00

Retired 1997, Issue Price $20.00, '94
Series: *Sugar Town*

Purchased ________, Price $ ___________

Jan, 529826

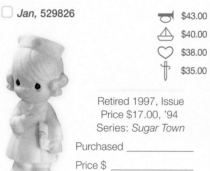

$43.00
$40.00
$38.00
$35.00

Retired 1997, Issue Price $17.00, '94
Series: *Sugar Town*

Purchased ___________
Price $ ___________

Sam Butcher With Sugar Town Population Sign, 529842

$90.00
$85.00

Annual 1993, Issue Price $22.50, '93
Series: *Sugar Town*

Purchased ___________
Price $ ___________

Dr. Sam Sugar, 529850

$35.00
$33.00
$30.00
$28.00

Retired 1997, Issue Price $17.00, '94
Series: *Sugar Town*

Purchased ___________
Price $ ___________

Doctor's Office, 529869 (Nightlight)

$125.00
$115.00
$110.00
$105.00

Retired 1997, Issue Price $80.00, '94
Series: *Sugar Town*

Purchased ________, Price $ ___________

Happiness Is At Our Fingertips, 529931

$85.00
$80.00

Annual 1993, Issue Price $35.00, '93
Catalog Exclusive

Purchased ___________
Price $ ___________

Ring Out The Good News, 529966

$75.00
$70.00
$65.00
$60.00
$55.00
$50.00

Retired 1997, Issue Price $27.50, '93
Nativity Addition

Purchased ________, Price $ ___________

☐ *An Event For All Seasons*, 529974 (Ornament)

$35.00
$30.00

Annual 1993, Issue Price $15.00, '93
Open House Event

Purchased ____________

Price $ ____________

☐ *Noah's Ark*, 530042 (Nightlight)

$225.00 $210.00 $200.00
$220.00 $205.00 $200.00
$215.00 $200.00 $200.00
$200.00

Retired 2002, Issue Price $125.00, '93
Series: *Two By Two*, Set of 3

Purchased ____________

Price $ ____________

☐ *Memories Are Made Of This*, 529982

$60.00
$55.00

Annual 1994, Issue Price $30.00, '94
Special Event

Purchased ____________

Price $ ____________

☐ *Sheep*, 530077

$23.00 $19.00
$21.00 $18.00
$20.00 $17.00
$16.00
$15.00
$15.00
$15.00

Retired 2002, Issue Price $10.00, '93
Series: *Two By Two*

Purchased ________, Price $ ____________

☐ *Bunnies*, 530123

$23.00
$28.00 $21.00
$25.00 $20.00
$18.00
$18.00
$18.00
$18.00
$18.00

Retired 2002, Issue Price $9.00, '93
Series: *Two By Two*

Purchased ________, Price $ ____________

☐ *Wishes For The World*, 530018

$55.00

Annual 1999, Issue Price $35.00, '99
Millennium Event Exclusive

Purchased ________, Price $ ____________

☐ *Pigs*, 530085

$28.00 $21.00
$25.00 $20.00
$18.00
$18.00
$18.00
$18.00
$23.00 $18.00

Retired 2002, Issue Price $12.00, '93
Series: *Two By Two*

Purchased ________, Price $ ____________

☐ *Elephants*, 530131

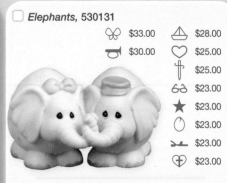

$33.00 $28.00
$30.00 $25.00
$25.00
$23.00
$23.00
$23.00
$23.00
$23.00

Retired 2002, Issue Price $18.00, '93
Series: *Two By Two*

Purchased ________, Price $ ____________

☐ *You're My Number One Friend*, 530026

$55.00
$53.00
$50.00

Annual 1993, Issue Price $30.00, '93
Easter Seals Commemorative Lily Understamp

Purchased ____________

Price $ ____________

☐ *Giraffes*, 530115

$30.00 $22.00
$28.00 $20.00
$25.00 $20.00
$23.00 $20.00
$20.00
$20.00

Retired 2002, Issue Price $16.00, '93
Series: *Two By Two*

Purchased ________, Price $ ____________

☐ *An Event For All Seasons*, 530158

$60.00
$55.00

Annual 1993, Issue Price $30.00, '93
Special Event

Purchased ____________

Price $ ____________

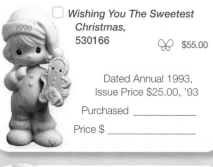

☐ ***Wishing You The Sweetest Christmas,* 530166**

$55.00

Dated Annual 1993, Issue Price $25.00, '93

Purchased ____________

Price $ ________________

☐ ***Wishing You The Sweetest Christmas,* 530174 (Bell)**

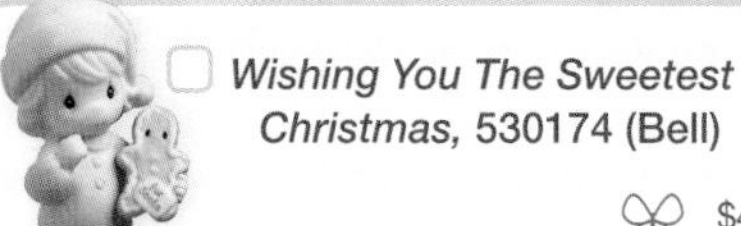

$40.00

Dated Annual 1993, Issue Price $25.00, '93

Purchased ____________

Price $ ____________

☐ ***Wishing You The Sweetest Christmas,* 530182 (Thimble)**

$23.00

Dated Annual 1993, Issue Price $8.00, '93

Purchased ____________

Price $ ____________

☐ ***Wishing You The Sweetest Christmas,* 530190 (Ornament)**

$38.00

Dated Annual 1993, Issue Price $30.00, '93

Series: *Masterpiece Ornament* — Fifth Issue

Purchased ____________

Price $____________

☐ ***Wishing You The Sweetest Christmas,* 530204 (Plate)**

$65.00

Dated Annual 1993, Issue Price $50.00, '93

Series: *Christmas Blessings* — Fourth & Final Issue

Purchased ________, Price $ ____________

☐ ***Wishing You The Sweetest Christmas,* 530212 (Ornament)**

$43.00

Dated Annual 1993, Issue Price $15.00, '93

Purchased ____________

Price $ ________________

☐ ***Baby's First Christmas,* 530255 (Ornament)**

$33.00

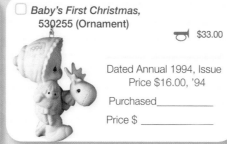

Dated Annual 1994, Issue Price $16.00, '94

Purchased____________

Price $ ____________

☐ ***Baby's First Christmas,* 530263 (Ornament)**

$33.00

Dated Annual 1994, Issue Price $16.00, '94

Purchased ____________

Price $____________

☐ ***You're As Pretty As A Christmas Tree,* 530387 (Ornament)**

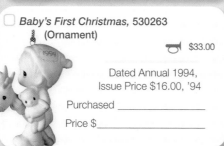

$38.00

Dated Annual 1994, Issue Price $30.00, '94

Series: *Masterpiece Ornament* — Sixth Issue

Purchased ________, Price $ ____________

☐ ***You're As Pretty As A Christmas Tree,* 530395 (Ornament)**

$33.00

Dated Annual 1994, Issue Price $16.00, '94

Purchased____________

Price $ ____________

☐ ***You're As Pretty As A Christmas Tree,* 530409 (Plate)**

$65.00

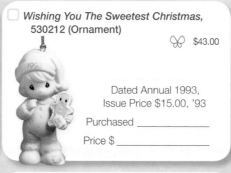

Dated Annual 1994, Issue Price $50.00, '94

Series: *Beauty Of Christmas* — First Issue

Purchased ________, Price $ ____________

☐ ***You're As Pretty As A Christmas Tree,* 530425**

$40.00

Dated Annual 1994, Issue Price $27.50, '94

Purchased____________

Price $____________

☐ ***Doctor's Office,* 530441 (Ornament)**

$28.00

Annual 1995, Issue Price $17.50, '95

Series: *Sugar Town*

Purchased ________, Price $ ____________

☐ ***Sam's House,* 530468 (Ornament)**

$28.00

$28.00

Annual 1994, Issue Price $17.50, '94

Series: *Sugar Town*

Purchased ________, Price $ ____________

☐ ***Chapel,* 530484 (Ornament)**

$28.00 $28.00

Annual 1993, Issue Price $17.50, '93

Series: *Sugar Town*

Purchased ____________

Price $ ____________

Happy Birthday Jesus, 530492

$45.00
$43.00
$40.00
$38.00
$35.00
$35.00
$33.00

Retired 1999, Issue Price $20.00, '93
Mini Nativity Addition

Purchased ________, Price $ ____________

Our First Christmas Together, 530506 (Ornament)

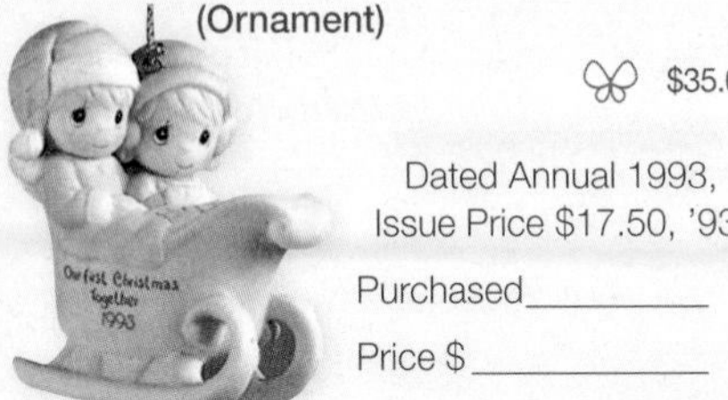

$35.00

Dated Annual 1993,
Issue Price $17.50, '93

Purchased__________

Price $ ____________

Serenity Prayer — Girl, 530697

$65.00
$63.00
$60.00
$58.00
$55.00
$55.00
$53.00
$53.00
$50.00
$50.00
$50.00
$50.00

Retired 2004, Issue Price $35.00, '94

Purchased ________, Price $ ____________

Serenity Prayer — Boy, 530700

$65.00
$63.00
$60.00
$58.00
$55.00
$55.00
$53.00
$53.00
$50.00
$50.00
$50.00

Retired 2003, Issue Price $35.00, '94

Purchased ________, Price $ ____________

15 Happy Years Together, What A Tweet! 530786

$185.00
$155.00

1993 Commemorative figurine. One per dealer, with dome and walnut base display with brass plate and cloisonné 15-year medallion. Value for G-clef with dome, $250.00. Butterfly with dome, $225.00.

Annual 1993, Issue Price $100.00, '93
Fifteenth Anniversary Commemorative

Purchased ________, Price $ ____________

15 Years, Tweet Music Together, 530840 (Ornament)

$35.00
$30.00

Annual 1993, Issue
Price $15.00, '93
Fifteenth Anniversary
Commemorative

Purchased ______________

Price $ ______________

Baby's First Christmas, 530859 (Ornament)

$28.00

Dated Annual 1993, Issue
Price $15.00, '93

Purchased ______________

Price $ ______________

Baby's First Christmas, 530867 (Ornament)

$28.00

Dated Annual 1993,
Issue Price $15.00, '93

Purchased ____________

Price $______________

We Have Come From Afar, 530913

$35.00
$33.00
$33.00
$30.00
$28.00
$28.00
$25.00
$25.00

Retired 2001, Issue Price $12.00, '95
Mini Nativity Addition

Purchased ________, Price $ ____________

I Only Have Ice For You, 530956

$95.00
$90.00
$88.00
$85.00
$80.00

Retired 1999, Issue Price $55.00, '95

Purchased ________, Price $ ____________

Two By Two Collector's Set, 530948

$375.00
$370.00
$365.00
$360.00
$355.00
$350.00
$345.00
$340.00
$335.00
$330.00

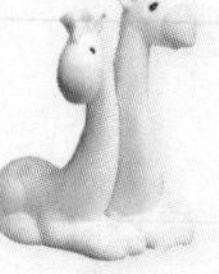

Retired 2002, Issue Price $190.00, '93
Series: *Two By Two*, Set of 8
(Ark, Bunnies, Pigs, Noah, Noah's Wife,
Elephants, Giraffes, and Sheep)

Purchased ________, Price $ ____________

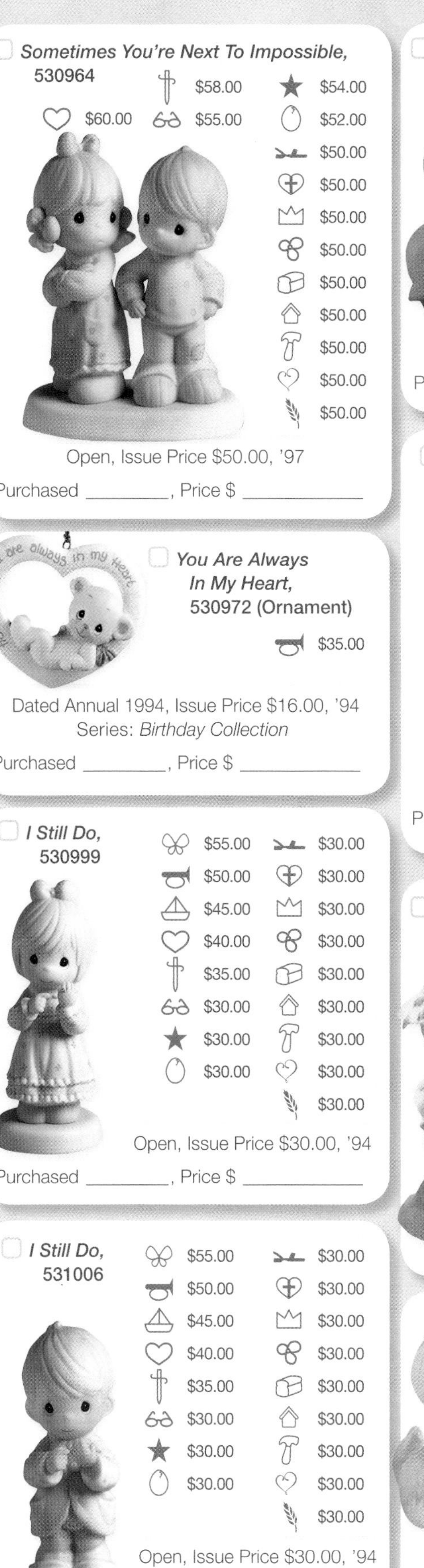

Sometimes You're Next To Impossible, 530964

$58.00 · $54.00 · $60.00 · $55.00 · $52.00 · $50.00 · $50.00 · $50.00 · $50.00 · $50.00 · $50.00 · $50.00 · $50.00 · $50.00

Open, Issue Price $50.00, '97

Purchased ________, Price $ ____________

You Are Always In My Heart, 530972 (Ornament)

$35.00

Dated Annual 1994, Issue Price $16.00, '94
Series: *Birthday Collection*

Purchased ________, Price $ ____________

I Still Do, 530999

$55.00 · $30.00 · $50.00 · $30.00 · $45.00 · $30.00 · $40.00 · $30.00 · $35.00 · $30.00 · $30.00 · $30.00 · $30.00 · $30.00 · $30.00 · $30.00 · $30.00

Open, Issue Price $30.00, '94

Purchased ________, Price $ ____________

I Still Do, 531006

$55.00 · $30.00 · $50.00 · $30.00 · $45.00 · $30.00 · $40.00 · $30.00 · $35.00 · $30.00 · $30.00 · $30.00 · $30.00 · $30.00 · $30.00 · $30.00 · $30.00

Open, Issue Price $30.00, '94

Purchased ____________

Price $ ____________

My World's Upside Down Without You, 531014

$20.00 · $18.00 · $15.00 · $15.00 · $15.00 · $15.00 · $15.00 · $15.00 · $15.00

Suspended 2004, Issue Price $15.00, '98

Purchased ________, Price $ ____________

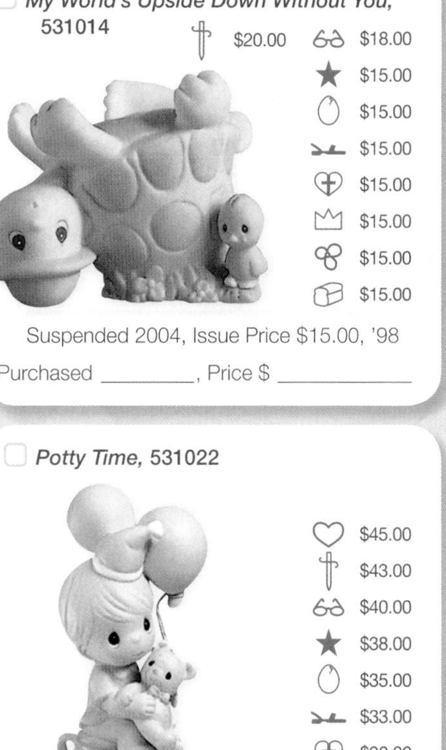

Potty Time, 531022

$45.00 · $43.00 · $40.00 · $38.00 · $35.00 · $33.00 · $30.00

Retired 2001, Issue Price $25.00, '97

Purchased ________, Price $ ____________

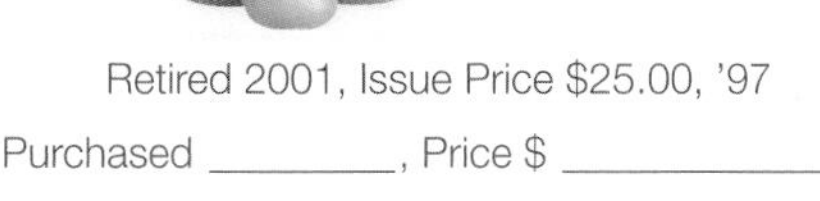

You Are My Once In A Lifetime, 531030

$75.00 · $70.00 · $73.00 · $68.00 · $65.00

Retired 2000, Issue Price $45.00, '98

Purchased ____________

Price $ ____________

I Haven't Seen Much Of You Lately, 531057

$33.00 · $25.00 · $31.00 · $24.00 · $30.00 · $23.00 · $28.00 · $22.00

Retired 2002, Issue Price $13.50, '96
Series: *Birthday Collection*

Purchased ________, Price $ ____________

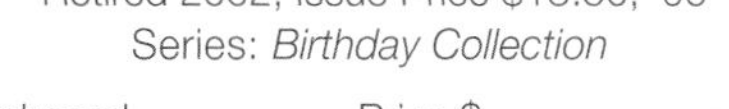

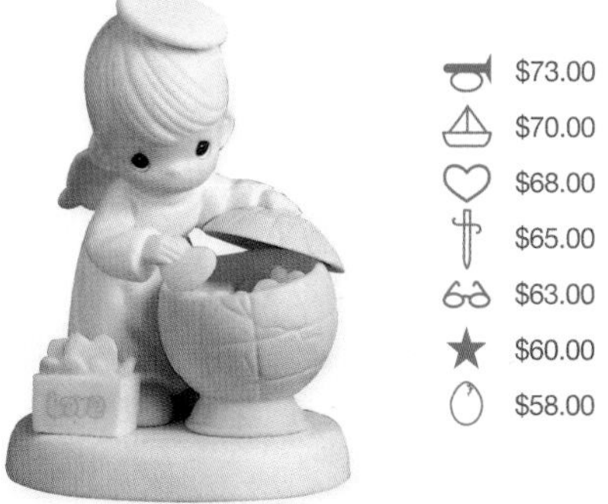

What The World Needs Is Love, 531065

$73.00 · $70.00 · $68.00 · $65.00 · $63.00 · $60.00 · $58.00

Retired 1999, Issue Price $45.00, '95

Purchased ________, Price $ ____________

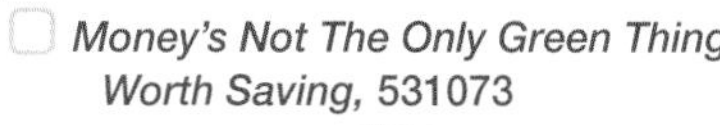

Money's Not The Only Green Thing Worth Saving, 531073

$75.00 · $70.00 · $68.00

Retired 1996, Issue Price $50.00, '94

Purchased ________

Price $ ________

It Is No Secret What God Can Do, 531111

$55.00 · $53.00 · $50.00

Annual 1994, Issue Price $30.00, '94
Easter Seals Commemorative Lily Understamp

Purchased ____________

Price $ ____________

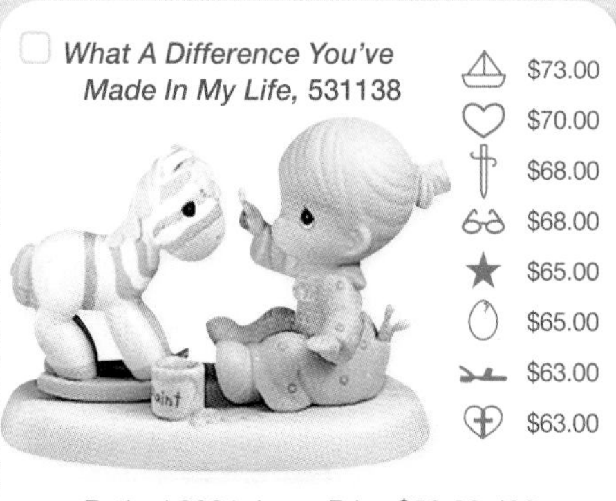

What A Difference You've Made In My Life, 531138

$73.00 · $70.00 · $68.00 · $68.00 · $65.00 · $65.00 · $63.00 · $63.00

Retired 2001, Issue Price $50.00, '96

Purchased ________, Price $ ____________

☐ ***Vaya Con Dios (To Go With God),* 531146**

$55.00 · $46.00
$53.00 · $45.00
$51.00 · $43.00
$50.00 · $40.00
$48.00 · $40.00

Retired 2003, Issue Price $32.50, '95

Purchased ____________

Price $ ____________

☐ ***Bring The Little Ones To Jesus,* 531359 (Plate)**

$65.00
$60.00

Dated Annual 1994, Issue Price $50.00, '94
Child Evangelism Fellowship

Purchased ________, Price $ ____________

☐ ***Our Friendship Goes A Long Way,* 531626**

$85.00
$80.00

Retired 2002, Issue Price $60.00, '02
Series: *Friendship*

Purchased ________, Price $ ____________

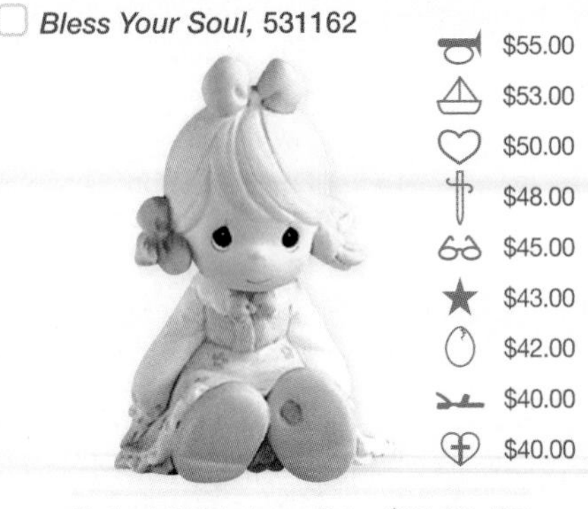

☐ ***Bless Your Soul,* 531162**

$55.00
$53.00
$50.00
$48.00
$45.00
$43.00
$42.00
$40.00
$40.00

Retired 2001, Issue Price $25.00, '95

Purchased ________, Price $ ____________

☐ ***Llamas,* 531375**

$28.00 · $21.00
$25.00 · $20.00
$23.00 · $19.00
$22.00 · $19.00
$19.00

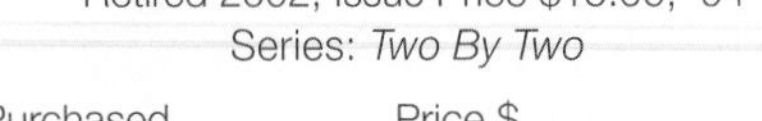

Retired 2002, Issue Price $15.00, '94
Series: *Two By Two*

Purchased ________, Price $ ____________

☐ ***Who's Gonna Fill Your Shoes?* 531634**

$48.00
$45.00
$45.00
$43.00
$40.00
$40.00
$40.00
$40.00
$40.00
$40.00

Suspended 2004, Issue Price $37.50, '97

Purchased ________, Price $ ____________

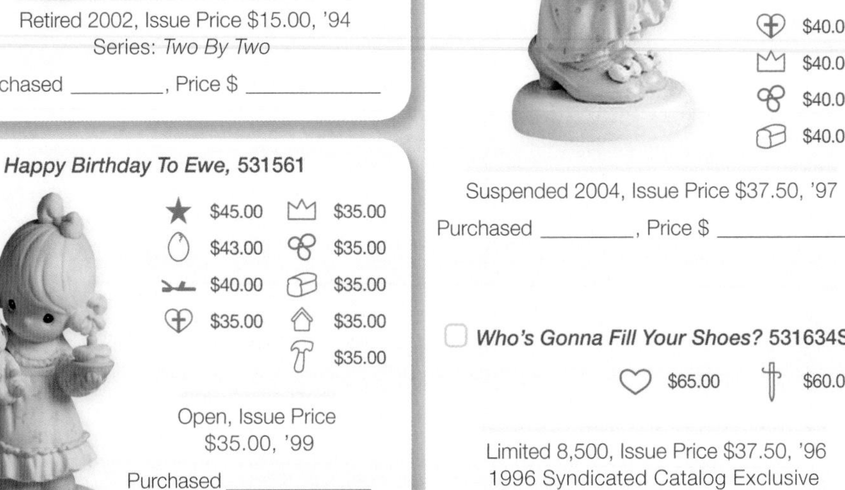

☐ ***Happy Birthday To Ewe,* 531561**

$45.00 · $35.00
$43.00 · $35.00
$40.00 · $35.00
$35.00 · $35.00
$35.00

Open, Issue Price $35.00, '99

Purchased ____________

Price $ ____________

☐ ***Who's Gonna Fill Your Shoes?* 531634S**

$65.00 · $60.00

Limited 8,500, Issue Price $37.50, '96
1996 Syndicated Catalog Exclusive

Purchased ________, Price $ ____________

☐ ***Wishing You A Bear-ie Merry Christmas,* 531200 (Ornament)**

$28.00
$28.00

Dated Annual 1996, Issue Price $17.50, '96
Holiday Preview Event

Purchased ________, Price $ ____________

☐ ***You Are The Rose Of His Creation,* 531243**

$675.00
$625.00

Limited Ed. 2,000, Issue Price $500.00, '94
Easter Seals Commemorative Lily Understamp
Individually Numbered

Purchased ____________

Price $ ____________

☐ ***You Make Such A Lovely Pair,* 531588**

$45.00

Annual 1998, Issue Price $32.50, '98
GCC Fall Exclusive

Purchased ____________

Price $ ____________

☐ ***Surrounded With Joy,* 531677**

UM $55.00 · $50.00 · $40.00
$53.00 · $50.00 · $40.00
$48.00 · $40.00
$45.00 · $40.00
$45.00 · $40.00
$40.00 · $40.00
$40.00

Open, Issue Price $30.00, '93
Chapel Exclusive

Purchased ________, Price $ ____________

☐ *Surrounded With Joy*, 531685 (Ornament)

UM $30.00 $18.00
$28.00 $18.00
$25.00 $18.00
$23.00 $18.00
$20.00 $18.00
$20.00 $18.00
$20.00 $18.00
$18.00

Open, Issue Price $17.50, '93
Chapel Exclusive

Purchased ________, Price $ ____________

☐ *You Deserve A Halo — Thank You*, 531693

$85.00
$83.00
$80.00
$78.00

Retired 1998, Issue Price $55.00, '96

Purchased ________, Price $ ____________

☐ *The Lord Is Counting On You*, 531707

$65.00 $53.00
$60.00 $50.00
$58.00 $50.00
$55.00 $48.00
$48.00

Retired 2002, Issue Price $32.50, '94

Purchased________

Price $___________

☐ *Thinking Of You Is What I Really Like To Do*, 531766 (Plate)

$60.00
$60.00

Dated Annual 1994, Issue Price $50.00, '94
Series: *Mother's Day* — First Issue

Purchased ________, Price $ ____________

☐ *Chapel Set*, 531773

$375.00
$375.00

Retired 1994, Issue Price $189.00, '93
Series: *Sugar Town*, Set of 7
(Chapel, Sam Butcher, Evergreen Tree, Aunt Ruth & Aunt Dorothy, Philip, Grandfather, and Nativity)

Purchased ________, Price $ ____________

☐ *Sam's House Set*, 531774

$375.00

Retired 1997, Issue Price $189.00, '93
Series: *Sugar Town*, Set of 7
(Sam's House, Sam's Car, Dusty, Katy Lynne, Sammy, Fence, and Sam Butcher with Sign)

Purchased ________, Price $ ____________

☐ *Bunnies Caroling*, 531804

$20.00

Retired 1997, Issue Price $10.00, '97
Series: *Sugar Town*

Purchased ___________

Price $ ___________

☐ *Tammy And Debbie*, 531812

$37.00
$35.00
$33.00

Retired 1997, Issue Price $22.50, '95
Series: *Sugar Town*

Purchased ________, Price $ ____________

☐ *Boughs Of Holly To Make You Jolly*, 531820 (Ornament)

$20.00
$20.00

Suspended, Issue Price $20.00, '04
Series: *The Legend Of Holly*

Purchased ___________

Price $___________

☐ *Mailbox*, 531847

$18.00
$17.00
$15.00
$13.00

Retired 1997, Issue Price $5.00, '94
Series: *Sugar Town*

Purchased ________, Price $ ____________

☐ *May Joy Bloom Within You*, 531863 (Ornament)

$20.00
$20.00

Suspended 2004, Issue Price $20.00, '04
Series: *The Legend Of The Poinsettia*

Purchased ___________

Price $___________

Donny, 531871

$40.00
$38.00
$35.00

Retired 1997, Issue Price $22.50, '95
Series: *Sugar Town*

Purchased ________, Price $ ____________

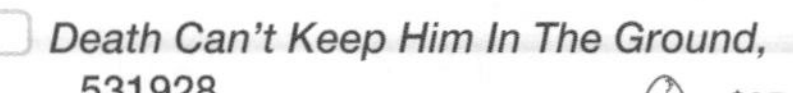

Death Can't Keep Him In The Ground, 531928

UM $45.00
$40.00
$40.00
$40.00
$38.00
$38.00
$35.00
$35.00
$33.00
$33.00
$30.00
$30.00
$30.00
$30.00
$30.00

Open, Issue Price $30.00, '94
Chapel Exclusive

Purchased ________, Price $ ____________

Lord Speak To Me, 531987

$60.00
$58.00
$55.00
$53.00
$53.00
$50.00
$50.00

Retired 2004, Issue Price $45.00, '99

Purchased ________, Price $ ____________

Who's Gonna Fill Your Shoes? 532061

There are pennies in the the loafers.

$65.00
$63.00
$60.00
$58.00
$55.00
$55.00

Retired 2002, Issue Price $37.50, '98
Catalog Early Release

Purchased ________, Price $ ____________

Hallelujah For The Cross, 532002

$55.00
$50.00
$48.00
$45.00
$45.00
$45.00

Retired 1999, Issue Price $35.00, '95

Purchased ____________

Price $____________

Who's Gonna Fill Your Shoes? 532061S

Special Understamp, "1997 Catalog." This piece has no pennies in loafers.

$85.00
$85.00
$80.00

Limited Ed., Issue Price $37.50, '97
Catalog Early Release

Purchased ________, Price $ ____________

Sharing Our Christmas Together, 531944

$45.00
$43.00
$40.00
$40.00
$38.00
$38.00
$38.00

Retired 2003, Issue Price $35.00, '97

Purchased ________, Price $ ____________

Sending You Oceans Of Love, 532010

$65.00
$63.00
$60.00

Retired 1996, Issue Price $35.00, '95

Purchased ________, Price $ ____________

A King Is Born, 532088 (Ornament)

UM $38.00
$35.00

Retired 1995, Issue Price $17.50, '94
Chapel Exclusive

Purchased ____________

Price $ ____________

Dropping In For The Holidays, 531952

$65.00
$63.00
$58.00
$60.00
$55.00

Pink cup has been found with Ship and Heart marks. Blue cup has been found with Trumpet and Ship marks. The decal has been found upside down.

Retired 1998, Issue Price $40.00, '94

Purchased ________, Price $ ____________

I Can't Bear To Let You Go, 532037

$75.00
$70.00
$68.00
$65.00
$63.00
$60.00

Retired 1999, Issue Price $50.00, '95

Purchased ________, Price $ ____________

Lord Help Me To Stay On Course, 532096

$45.00
$45.00
$43.00
$43.00
$40.00
$40.00
$40.00
$38.00
$38.00

Retired 2002, Issue Price $35.00, '95

Purchased ________, Price $ ____________

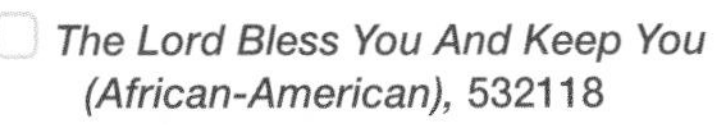

☐ ***The Lord Bless You And Keep You (African-American),*** **532118**

$65.00 · $60.00 · $60.00 · $58.00 · $58.00 · $55.00 · $55.00 · $50.00 · $50.00 · $50.00 · $50.00 · $50.00 · $50.00

Suspended, Issue Price $40.00, '94

Purchased ________, Price $ ___________

☐ ***The Lord Bless You And Keep You (African-American),*** **532126**

$45.00 · $40.00 · $35.00 · $35.00 · $35.00 · $35.00 · $35.00 · $35.00 · $35.00 · $35.00 · $35.00 · $35.00 · $35.00 · $35.00 · $35.00 · $35.00 · $35.00

Open, Issue Price $30.00, '94

Purchased ________, Price $ ___________

☐ ***The Lord Bless You And Keep You (African-American),*** **532134**

$45.00 · $40.00 · $35.00 · $35.00 · $35.00 · $35.00 · $35.00 · $35.00 · $35.00 · $35.00 · $35.00 · $35.00 · $35.00

Suspended, Issue Price $30.00, '94

Purchased ________, Price $ ___________

☐ ***Street Sign,*** **532185**

$23.00 · $21.00 · $20.00

Retired 1997, Issue Price $10.00, '95
Series: *Sugar Town*

Purchased ________, Price $ ___________

☐ ***Remember The Sweetest Of The Season,*** **532193 (Ornament)**

$20.00 · $20.00

Suspended 2004, Issue Price $20.00, '04
Series: *The Legend Of The Candy Cane*

Purchased ______________

Price $ ______________

☐ ***Merry Giftness,*** **532223 (Ornament)**

$28.00

Annual 1999, Issue Price $20.00, '99
DSR Exclusive

Purchased ______________

Price $ ______________

☐ ***Town Square Clock,*** **532908**

$125.00 · $115.00 · $110.00 · $105.00

Retired 1997, Issue Price $80.00, '94
Series: *Sugar Town*

Purchased ________, Price $ ___________

☐ ***Luke 2:10 – 11,*** **532916**

$65.00 · $63.00 · $60.00 · $58.00 · $55.00 · $53.00

Retired 1999, Issue Price $35.00, '94

Purchased ________, Price $ ___________

☐ ***It's Almost Time For Santa,*** **532932**

$90.00

Annual 2001, Issue Price $75.00, '01

Purchased ______

Price $ ________

☐ ***Curved Sidewalk,*** **533149**

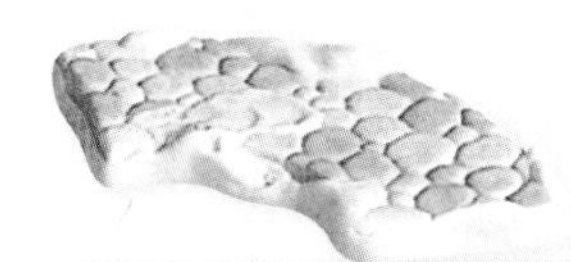

$25.00 · $23.00 · $20.00 · $18.00

Retired 1997, Issue Price $10.00, '94
Series: *Sugar Town*

Purchased ________, Price $ ___________

☐ ***Straight Sidewalk,*** **533157**

$25.00 · $23.00 · $20.00 · $20.00

Retired 1997, Issue Price $10.00, '94
Series: *Sugar Town*

Purchased ________, Price $ ___________

☐ ***Sugar And Her Doghouse,*** **533165**

$33.00 · $28.00 · $30.00 · $25.00

Retired 1997, Issue Price $20.00, '94
Series: *Sugar Town*, Set of 2

Purchased __________

Price $__________

Single Tree, 533173

$33.00 $28.00
$30.00 $25.00

Retired 1997, Issue Price $10.00, '94
Series: *Sugar Town*

Purchased________
Price $________

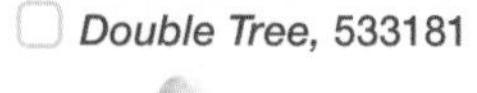

Double Tree, 533181

$38.00
$35.00
$33.00
$30.00

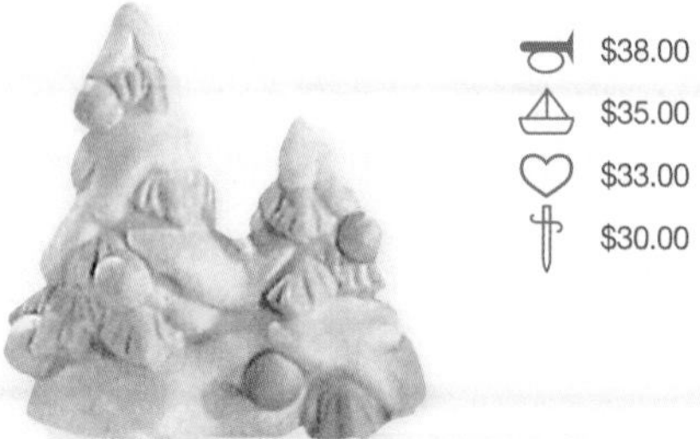

Retired 1997, Issue Price $10.00, '94
Series: *Sugar Town*

Purchased ________, Price $ ________

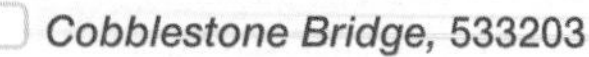

Cobblestone Bridge, 533203

$33.00
$30.00
$28.00
$25.00

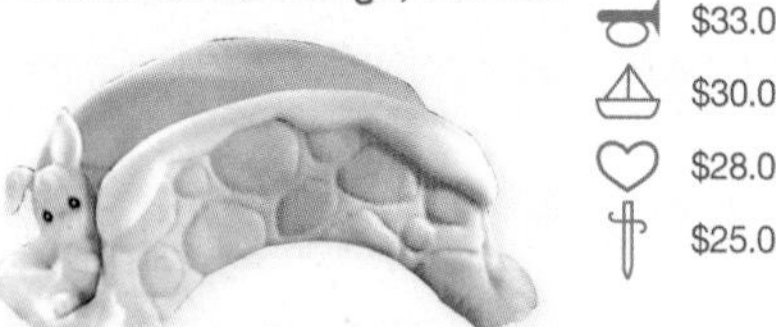

Retired 1997, Issue Price $17.00, '94
Series: *Sugar Town*

Purchased ________, Price $ ________

His Love Will Uphold The World, 539309

Early release to retailers attending the Fall 1998 show.

$205.00
$200.00

Annual 1999, Issue Price $150.00, '99
Precious Moments Millennium Piece

Purchased ________, Price $ ________

Shear Happiness And Hare Cuts, 539910

$65.00
$63.00
$60.00
$58.00
$55.00
$55.00
$55.00

Retired 2004, Issue Price $40.00, '99
Series: *Country Lane Collection*

Purchased ________, Price $ ________

Lord, Police Protect Us, 539953

$60.00 $50.00
$58.00 $48.00
$55.00 $48.00
$53.00 $48.00

Suspended, Issue Price $45.00, '99

Purchased ________, Price $ ________

Sharing Our Winter Wonderland, 539988

$90.00

Annual 1999, Issue Price $75.00, '99

Purchased ________
Price $________

Happy 10th Anniversary, 540013

UM $60.00
$65.00

Annual 1999, Issue Price $45.00, '99
Chapel Exclusive
Tenth Anniversary Commemorative

Purchased________
Price $ ________

Sleep Tight, 542636

UM $65.00
$60.00
$58.00
$55.00
$53.00

Suspended 2003, Issue Price $45.00, '99
Best Western Hotel Exclusive

Purchased ________, Price $ ________

Let's Keep Our Eyes On The Goal, 549975

$55.00
$50.00

Retired 1999, Issue Price $37.50, '98
Canadian Exclusive

Purchased________
Price $ ________

Only You, 550000

$50.00
$50.00
$50.00
$50.00
$50.00

Open, Issue Price $50.00, '06

Purchased ________, Price $ ________

I'll Be Your Shelter In The Storm, 550003

$40.00
$40.00
$40.00
$40.00
$40.00

Open, Issue Price $35.00, '06

Purchased ________
Price $ ________

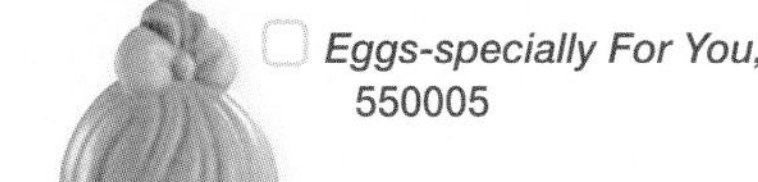

☐ *Eggs-specially For You,* 550005

- $45.00
- $45.00
- $45.00
- $45.00
- $45.00

Open, Issue Price $45.00, '06

Purchased ________, Price $ ___________

☐ *Our Love Can Never Be Broken,* 550010

- $50.00
- $50.00
- $50.00
- $50.00
- $50.00

Open, Issue Price $50.00, '06

Purchased ________, Price $ ___________

☐ *It's In The Book,* 550020

- $45.00
- $45.00
- $45.00
- $45.00
- $45.00

Open, Issue Price $45.00, '06

Purchased ________, Price $ ___________

☐ *My Faith Is In Jesus,* 550007

- $30.00
- $30.00
- $30.00
- $30.00
- $30.00

Open, Issue Price $30.00, '06

Purchased___________

Price $___________

☐ *Moms Are The Greatest Gift Of All,* 550011

- $50.00
- $50.00
- $50.00
- $50.00
- $50.00

Open, Issue Price $45.00, '06

Purchased ________, Price $ ___________

☐ *He Is My Gliding Light,* 550021

Lamp illuminates

- UM $50.00
- $50.00
- $50.00
- $50.00
- $50.00

Open, Issue Price $50.00, '06
Chapel Exclusive

Purchased ________, Price $ ___________

☐ *You Sweep Me Off My Feet,* 550008

- $50.00
- $50.00
- $50.00
- $50.00
- $50.00

Open, Issue Price $50.00, '06

Purchased ________, Price $ ___________

☐ *My Mona Lisa,* 550012

- $45.00
- $45.00

Limited Ed. 10,000, Issue Price $45.00, '06

Purchased ________, Price $ ___________

☐ *Always By Your Side (Girl),* 550022

- $50.00
- $50.00
- $50.00
- $50.00
- $50.00

Open, Issue Price $45.00, '06

Purchased__________

Price $__________

☐ *You Must Be Tickled Pink,* 550009

- $40.00
- $40.00
- $40.00
- $40.00
- $40.00

Open, Issue Price $40.00, '06

Purchased ________, Price $ ___________

☐ *I Always Knew You'd Turn'ip,* 550017

- $25.00
- $25.00
- $25.00
- $25.00
- $25.00

Open, Issue Price $25.00, '05

Purchased ___________

Price $___________

☐ *Always By Your Side (Boy),* 550023

- $50.00
- $50.00
- $50.00
- $50.00
- $50.00

Open, Issue Price $45.00, '06

Purchased ________

Price $ ________

☐ **Her Children Will Rise Up And Call Her Blessed, 550025**

$90.00
$90.00

Limited 2006, Issue Price $90.00, '06

Purchased______

Price $_________

☐ **From This Day Forward, 550027**

$75.00 $75.00
$75.00 $75.00
$75.00

Open, Issue Price $75.00, '06

Purchased ______

Price $_________

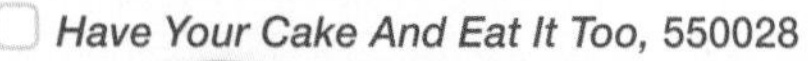

☐ **Have Your Cake And Eat It Too, 550028**

$55.00
$55.00
$55.00
$55.00
$55.00

Open, Issue Price $50.00, '06

Purchased ________, Price $ ____________

☐ **Happily Ever After, 550029**

$60.00
$60.00
$60.00
$60.00
$60.00

Open, Issue Price $55.00, '06

Purchased ________, Price $ ____________

☐ **Your Future Is So Rosy, 550032**

$45.00
$45.00
$45.00
$45.00
$45.00

Open, Issue Price $40.00, '06

Purchased __________

Price $ ____________

☐ **Let Your Gentle Spirit Be Known To All, 550039**

$40.00
$40.00
$40.00
$40.00
$40.00

Open, Issue Price $40.00, '06

Purchased_____

Price $ _______

☐ **I Will Always Care For You, 550041**

$45.00
$45.00
$45.00
$45.00
$45.00

Open, Issue Price $45.00, '06

Purchased ______

Price $ ________

☐ **A Picture's Worth A Thousand Words, 550045**

$40.00
$40.00
$40.00
$40.00
$40.00

Open, Issue Price $40.00, '06

Purchased ________, Price $ ____________

☐ **I Pray The Lord My Soul To Keep, 553867**

UM $30.00

Comes with picture frame.

Dated Annual 2001, Issue Price $22.50, '01
National Children's Day Event Exclusive
Series: *Little Moments*

Purchased ________, Price $ ____________

☐ **I Pray The Lord My Soul To Keep, 553875**

UM $30.00

Comes with picture frame.

Dated Annual 2001, Issue Price $22.50, '01
National Children's Day Event Exclusive
Series: *Little Moments*

Purchased ________, Price $ ____________

☐ **Slide Into The Next Millennium With Joy, 587761**

$55.00
$50.00

Dated Annual 1999, Issue Price $35.00, '99

Purchased ________, Price $ ____________

☐ *Slide Into The Next Millennium With Joy,* 587788 (Ornament)

$33.00
$30.00

Dated Annual 1999, Issue Price $25.00, '99

Purchased ________, Price $ ____________

☐ *Our First Christmas Together,* 587796 (Ornament)

$33.00
$30.00

Dated Annual 1999, Issue Price $25.00, '99

Purchased ________, Price $ ____________

☐ *May Your Wishes For Peace Take Wing,* 587818 (Ornament)

$33.00
$30.00

Dated Annual 1999, Issue Price $20.00, '99

Purchased ____________

Price $ ____________

☐ *Baby's First Christmas (Girl),* 587826 (Ornament)

$28.00
$25.00

Dated Annual 1999, Issue Price $18.50, '99

Purchased ____________

Price $ ____________

☐ *Baby's First Christmas (Boy),* 587834 (Ornament)

$28.00
$25.00

Dated Annual 1999, Issue Price $18.50, '99

Purchased ____________

Price $ ____________

☐ *Eat Ham,* 587842

$45.00
$43.00
$40.00
$40.00
$40.00
$38.00
$38.00
$35.00

Suspended, Issue Price $25.00, '99
Series: *Country Lane Collection*

Purchased ________, Price $ ____________

☐ *You Brighten My Field Of Dreams,* 587850

$75.00
$73.00
$73.00
$70.00
$70.00

Retired 2002, Issue Price $55.00, '99
Series: *Country Lane Collection*

Purchased ________, Price $ ____________

☐ *Witch Way Do You Spell Love?* 587869

$55.00
$53.00
$50.00
$48.00
$45.00

Retired 2002, Issue Price $25.00, '99

Purchased ________

Price $ ____________

☐ *Snow Man Like My Man,* 587877

$75.00
$73.00
$70.00
$68.00
$65.00
$65.00
$60.00
$60.00

Suspended 2005, Issue Price $55.00, '99

Purchased ________, Price $ ____________

☐ *May Your Season Be Jelly And Bright,* 587885

$45.00
$45.00
$43.00
$40.00
$40.00
$40.00
$40.00

Suspended 2004, Issue Price $37.50, '99

Purchased ________, Price $ ____________

☐ *God Loves A Happy Camper,* 587893

$45.00
$45.00
$42.00
$40.00
$40.00
$40.00
$40.00
$40.00
$40.00
$40.00
$40.00

Open, Issue Price $37.50, '99

Purchased ____________

Price $ ____________

☐ *My Life Is A Vacuum Without You,* 587907

$55.00
$53.00
$50.00
$48.00
$45.00
$40.00
$40.00

Suspended 2004, Issue Price $37.50, '99

Purchased ________, Price $ ____________

☐ *RV Haven' Fun Or What*, 587915

[glasses] $75.00
★ $70.00
[egg] $65.00
[sword] $63.00
[heart] $60.00

Retired 2002, Issue Price $45.00, '99

Purchased ________, Price $ ____________

☐ *Thank You Sew Much*, 587923

[glasses] $32.00
★ $30.00
[egg] $30.00
[sword] $30.00
[heart] $30.00
[crown] $30.00
[flower] $30.00
[box] $30.00
[house] $30.00
[mushroom] $30.00
[heart outline] $30.00
[wheat] $30.00

Open, Issue Price $25.00, '99

Purchased ________, Price $ ____________

☐ *May Your Christmas Be Delightful*, 587931 (Ornament)

[glasses] $28.00
★ $28.00

Annual 1999, Issue Price $20.00, '99

Purchased______________

Price $______________

☐ *Pretty As A Princess*, 587958 (Ornament)

[glasses] $28.00
★ $28.00

Annual, 1999, Issue Price $20.00, '99

Purchased ____________

Price $ ____________

☐ *Happy 10th Anniversary*, 588040 (Ornament)

UM $43.00
★ $40.00

Limited Ed., Issue Price $22.50, '99
Tenth Anniversary Commemorative
One Year Production

Purchased ____________

Price $ ____________

☐ *Our Love Will Flow Eternal*, 588059

[sword] $105.00
[heart] $100.00
[crown] $90.00
[flower] $90.00
[box] $90.00
[house] $90.00
[mushroom] $90.00
[heart outline] $90.00

Open, Issue Price $90.00, '99

Purchased ________, Price $ ____________

☐ *Our Love Will Flow Eternal*, 588059C

UM $120.00 [egg] $115.00 [sword] $105.00

Limited Ed., Issue Price $90.00, '99
Chapel Exclusive, Chapel Early Release

Purchased ________, Price $ ____________

☐ *He Is The Bright Morning Star*, 588067

UM $55.00
[egg] $50.00
[sword] $45.00
[heart] $40.00
[crown] $38.00

Retired 2003, Issue Price $30.00, '99
Chapel Exclusive

Purchased ____________

Price $ ____________

☐ *He Is The Bright Morning Star*, 588075 (Ornament)

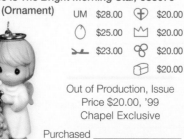

UM $28.00
[egg] $25.00
[sword] $23.00
[heart] $20.00
[crown] $20.00
[flower] $20.00
[box] $20.00

Out of Production, Issue Price $20.00, '99
Chapel Exclusive

Purchased ____________

Price $____________

☐ *Mom, You're A Royal Gem*, 588083

[glasses] $45.00
★ $40.00

Retired 1999, Issue Price $30.00, '99
Avon Exclusive

Purchased ____________

Price $ ____________

☐ *Dear Jon, I Will Never Leave You*, 588091

[glasses] $65.00
★ $60.00
[egg] $60.00
[sword] $58.00
[heart] $58.00
[crown] $55.00
[flower] $53.00
[box] $53.00

Retired 2005, Issue Price $50.00, '99
Series: *Country Lane Collection*

Purchased ________, Price $ ____________

☐ *I'm Proud To Be An American (Army)*, 588105

★ $45.00
[egg] $43.00
[sword] $40.00
[heart] $40.00
[crown] $38.00
[flower] $35.00
[box] $35.00
[house] $35.00
[mushroom] $35.00
[heart outline] $35.00
[wheat] $35.00

Open, Issue Price $32.50, '00

Purchased ________, Price $ ____________

☐ *I'm Proud To Be An American (Marine)*, 588113

★ $45.00
[egg] $43.00
[sword] $40.00
[heart] $40.00
[crown] $38.00
[flower] $35.00
[box] $35.00
[house] $35.00
[mushroom] $35.00
[heart outline] $35.00
[wheat] $35.00

Open, Issue Price $32.50, '00

Purchased ________, Price $ ____________

☐ *I'm Proud To Be An American (Navy),* 588121

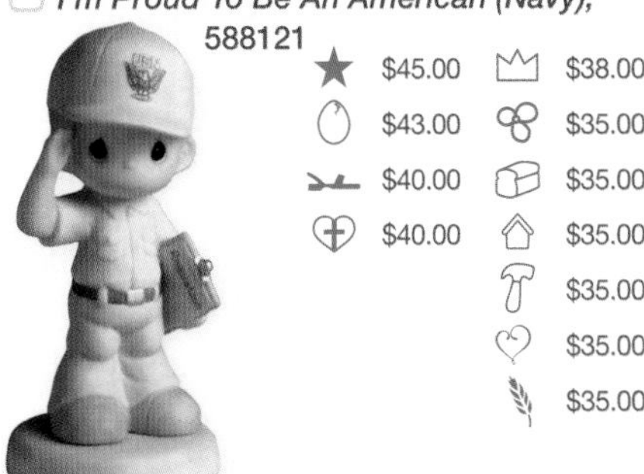

★ $45.00, $43.00, $40.00, $40.00, $38.00, $35.00, $35.00, $35.00, $35.00, $35.00, $35.00

Open, Issue Price $32.50, '00

Purchased ________, Price $ ___________

☐ *I'm Proud To Be An American (Coast Guard),* 588148

$35.00, ★ $45.00, $35.00, $43.00, $35.00, $40.00, $35.00, $40.00, $35.00, $38.00, $35.00

Open, Issue Price $32.50, '00

Purchased ________, Price $ ___________

☐ *I'm Proud To Be An American (Air Force),* 588156

★ $45.00, $43.00, $40.00, $40.00, $38.00, $35.00, $35.00, $35.00, $35.00, $35.00, $35.00

Open, Issue Price $32.50, '00

Purchased ___________

Price $ ___________

☐ *Behold The Lamb Of God,* 588164

★ $65.00, $60.00, $58.00, $55.00, $53.00, $50.00, $50.00

Retired 2002, Issue Price $45.00, '99
Nativity Addition

Purchased ________, Price $ ___________

☐ *A Mother's Love Is Forever,* 590009

$50.00, $50.00, $50.00

Limited Ed., Issue Price $50.00, '06
Hallmark Exclusive

Purchased ________, Price $ ___________

☐ *A Teaspoon Of Friendship Sweetens The Pot,* 590037

$40.00, $40.00, $40.00

Limited Ed., Issue Price $40.00, '06
Hallmark Exclusive

Purchased ___________

Price $___________

☐ *Bisque Ornament Holder,* 603171

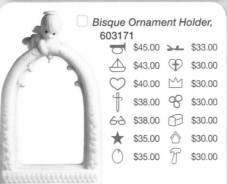

$45.00, $43.00, $40.00, $38.00, $38.00, ★ $35.00, $35.00, $33.00, $30.00, $30.00, $30.00, $30.00, $30.00, $30.00

Out of Production, Issue Price $30.00, '94

Purchased ________, Price $ ___________

☐ *On A Hill Overlooking A Quiet Blue Stream,* 603503

Unmarked version has three verses of poem; Heart version has four verses.

UM $75.00, $70.00, $68.00, $65.00, $63.00

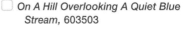

Retired 1998, Issue Price $45.00, '94
Chapel Exclusive

Purchased ________, Price $ ___________

☐ *Nothing Can Dampen The Spirit Of Caring,* 603864

$65.00, $63.00, $60.00, $60.00, $58.00, $55.00, ★ $53.00, $50.00, $50.00, $50.00

Retired 2002, Issue Price $35.00, '94
Series: *Good Samaritan* — First Issue

Purchased ________, Price $ ___________

☐ *Sammy's Circus Set,* 604070

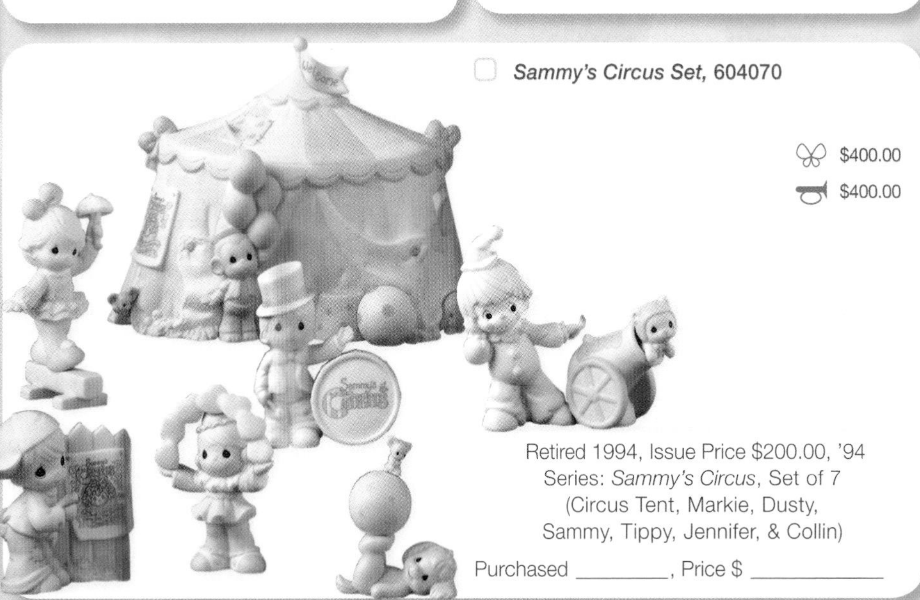

$400.00, $400.00

Retired 1994, Issue Price $200.00, '94
Series: *Sammy's Circus*, Set of 7
(Circus Tent, Markie, Dusty, Sammy, Tippy, Jennifer, & Collin)

Purchased ________, Price $ ___________

May Your Christmas Be Delightful, 604135

$65.00 $58.00
$63.00 $55.00
$60.00 $53.00
$50.00

Retired 2002, Issue Price $40.00, '97
Purchased ________
Price $ ________

A King Is Born, 604151

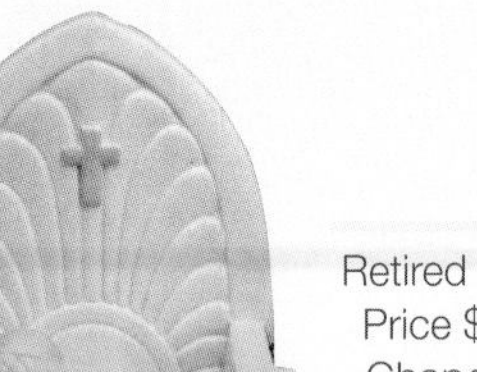

UM $95.00
$90.00

Retired 1995, Issue Price $25.00, '94
Chapel Exclusive
Purchased ______
Price $ ________

A Poppy For You, 604208

$55.00
$50.00
$48.00
$45.00
$40.00

Suspended 1998, Issue Price $35.00, '94
Purchased ________, Price $ ___________

You're As Pretty As A Christmas Tree, 604216 (Bell)

$40.00

Dated Annual 1994, Issue Price $27.50, '94
Purchased ________, Price $ ___________

Ringing In The Season, 610001

$35.00
$35.00

Dated Annual 2006, Issue Price $35.00, '06
Purchased ________, Price $ ___________

Ringing In The Season, 610002 (Ornament)

$20.00
$20.00

Dated Annual 2006, Issue Price $20.00, '06
Purchased ________
Price $ ___________

Ringing In The Season, 610003 (Ornament)

$30.00
$30.00

Dated Annual 2006, Issue Price $30.00, '06
Purchased ________
Price $ ___________

Our First Christmas Together, 610004 (Ornament)

$25.00
$25.00

Dated Annual 2006, Issue Price $25.00, '06
Purchased ________
Price $ ___________

Baby's First Christmas, 610005 (Ornament)

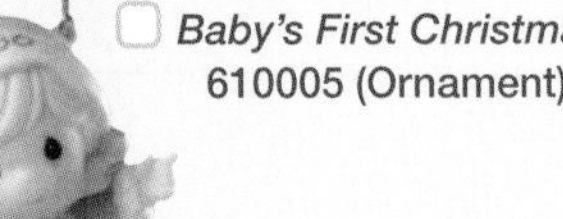

$20.00
$20.00

Dated Annual 2006, Issue Price $20.00, '06
Purchased ___________
Price $ ___________

Baby's First Christmas, 610006 (Ornament)

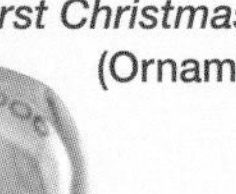

$20.00
$20.00

Dated Annual 2006, Issue Price $20.00, '06
Purchased ___________
Price $ ___________

Wishing "Ewe" Sweet Christmas Dreams, 610007 (Ornament)

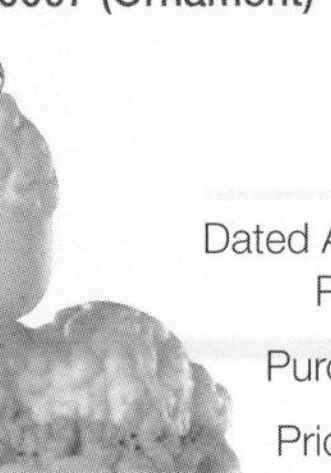

$20.00
$20.00

Dated Annual 2006, Issue Price $20.00, '06
Purchased ________
Price $ ________

Christmas Together, 610008 (Ornament)

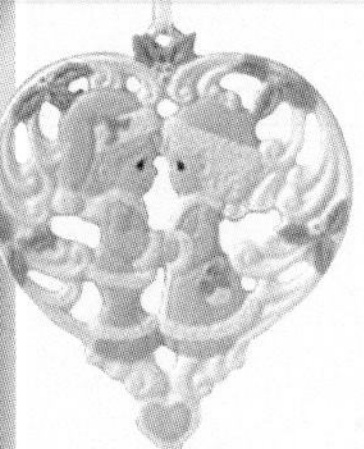

$25.00
$25.00

Dated Annual 2006, Issue Price $25.00, '06
Purchased ___________
Price $ ___________

My True Love Gave To Me, 610011

$50.00
$50.00
$50.00
$50.00
$50.00

Open, Issue Price $50.00, '06
Purchased ________, Price $ ___________

Sleigh Bells Ring, 610012

$75.00 $75.00
$75.00 $75.00
$75.00

Open, Issue Price $75.00, '06
Set of 2

Purchased ________, Price $ ___________

Joy, 610013

$75.00
$75.00
$75.00

Limited Ed. 2,000, Issue Price $75.00, '06

Purchased ________, Price $ ___________

Christmas Is Loving, 610014

$50.00
$50.00
$50.00
$50.00
$50.00

Open, Issue Price $50.00, '06

Purchased ________, Price $ ___________

Christmas Is Caring, 610015

$50.00 $50.00
$50.00 $50.00
$50.00

Open, Issue Price $50.00, '06

Purchased ________, Price $ ___________

Christmas Is Sharing, 610016

$50.00
$50.00
$50.00
$50.00
$50.00

Open, Issue Price $50.00, '06

Purchased ________, Price $ ___________

Guide Us To Thy Perfect Light, 610017

$35.00 $35.00

Limited Ed., Issue Price $35.00, '06

Purchased ___________

Price $ ___________

May Your Christmas Be Filled With Sweet Surprises, 610018

$50.00 $50.00
$50.00 $50.00
$50.00

Open, Issue Price $50.00, '06

Purchased ________, Price $ ___________

Feliz Navidad (Girl), 610019

$30.00
$30.00
$30.00
$30.00
$30.00

Open, Issue Price $30.00, '06

Purchased ___________

Price $ ___________

Feliz Navidad (Boy), 610020

$30.00
$30.00
$30.00
$30.00
$30.00

Open, Issue Price $30.00, '06

Purchased ___________

Price $ ___________

Guide Us To Thy Perfect Light, 610025 (Ornament)

UM $25.00 $25.00

Limited Ed., Issue Price $25.00, '06

Purchased ___________

Price $___________

Christmas Bells Are Ringing, 610026 (Ornament)

$20.00 $20.00
$20.00

Open, Issue Price $20.00, '06

Purchased___________

Price $___________

Trumpet His Arrival, 610027 (Ornament)

$20.00
$20.00 $20.00
$20.00 $20.00

Open, Issue Price $20.00, '06

Purchased ___________

Price $ ___________

☐ *Sing A New Song*, 610028 (Ornament)

$20.00 $20.00
$20.00 $20.00
$20.00

Open, Issue Price $20.00, '06
Purchased ______________
Price $ ______________

☐ *Shall I Play For You*, 610029 (Ornament)

$20.00 $20.00
$20.00 $20.00
$20.00

Open, Issue Price $20.00, '06
Purchased ______________
Price $______________

☐ *Daughter, You Bring Me Joy*, 610030 (Ornament)

$20.00 $20.00
$20.00 $20.00
$20.00

Open, Issue Price $20.00, '06
Purchased______________
Price $______________

☐ *Sister, You're An Angel To Me*, 610031 (Ornament)

$20.00 $20.00
$20.00 $20.00
$20.00

Open, Issue Price $20.00, '06
Purchased______________
Price $ ______________

☐ *Teachers Make The Season Bright*, 610032 (Ornament)

$20.00 $20.00
$20.00 $20.00
$20.00

Open, Issue Price $20.00, '06
Purchased ______________
Price $ ______________

☐ *My Godmother, My Guiding Light*, 610033 (Ornament)

$20.00 $20.00
$20.00 $20.00
$20.00

Open, Issue Price $20.00, '06
Purchased______________
Price $______________

☐ *Nurses Care For The Heart And Soul*, 610034 (Ornament)

$20.00 $20.00
$20.00 $20.00
$20.00

Open, Issue Price $20.00, '06
Purchased ______________
Price $______________

☐ *Grandma, Your Love Keeps Me Warm*, 610035 (Ornament)

$20.00 $20.00
$20.00 $20.00
$20.00

Open, Issue Price $20.00, '06
Purchased ______________
Price $______________

☐ *Visions Of Sugarplums*, 610036

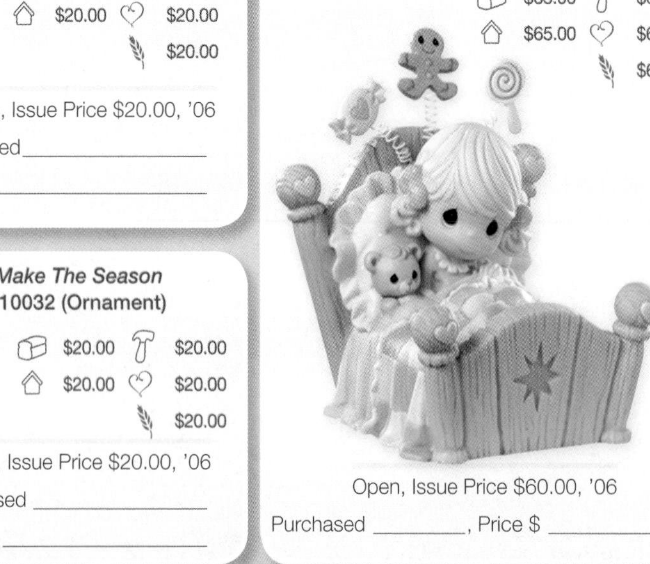

$65.00 $65.00
$65.00 $65.00
$65.00

Open, Issue Price $60.00, '06
Purchased ________, Price $ ____________

☐ *Said The Lamb To The Shepherd Boy*, 610041

$30.00 $30.00
$30.00 $30.00
$30.00

Open, Issue Price $30.00, '06
Purchased ____________
Price $ ____________

☐ *And The Angels Sing*, 610042

$30.00
$30.00
$30.00
$30.00
$30.00

Open, Issue Price $30.00, '06
Purchased ________, Price $ ____________

☐ *Mini Nativity*, 610044

$140.00
$140.00
$140.00

Retired 2008, Issue Price $140.00, '06
Set of 11
Purchased ________, Price $ ____________

☐ *Large Nativity,* 610043

$140.00 $140.00
$140.00 $140.00

Retired 2008, Issue Price $140.00, '06
Set of 9, comes with CD

Purchased ____

Price $_______

☐ *Your Love Gives Me Wings,* 610070

$100.00
$100.00

Limited Ed. 3,000, Issue Price $100.00, '06

Purchased ________, Price $ ___________

☐ *Let Not Your Heart Be Troubled,* 610046

$40.00 $40.00
$40.00 $40.00
$40.00

Open, Issue Price $35.00, '06

Purchased _________

Price $ ___________

☐ *Some Day My Prince Will Come,* 610056

$42.50
$42.50
$42.50
$42.50
$42.50

Open, Issue Price $40.00, '06

Purchased ________, Price $ ___________

☐ *My Dream Boat,* 610071

$100.00
$100.00

Limited Ed. 3,000, Issue Price $100.00, '06

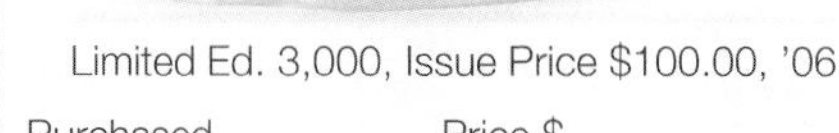

Purchased ________, Price $ ___________

☐ *My Peace I Give Unto Thee,* 610047

$35.00 $35.00
$35.00 $35.00
$35.00

Open, Issue Price $35.00, '06

Purchased ___________

Price $___________

☐ *May Your World Be Filled With Love,* 610058

$50.00
$50.00
$50.00
$50.00
$50.00

Open, Issue Price $50.00, '06

Purchased ________, Price $ ___________

☐ *Rejoice, O Earth,* 617334 (Musical Tree Topper)

$200.00

Annual 1990, Issue Price $125.00, '90
Tune: *Hark! The Herald Angels Sing!*

Purchased ______

Price $_______

☐ *My Cup Runneth Over,* 610051

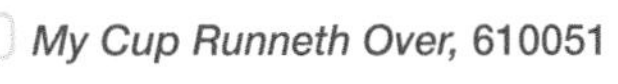

$45.00
$45.00
$45.00
$45.00
$45.00

Open, Issue Price $45.00, '06

Purchased ________, Price $ ___________

☐ *In All Things Give Thanks,* 610068

$45.00
$45.00
$45.00
$45.00
$45.00

Open, Issue Price $45.00, '06

Purchased ________, Price $ ___________

☐ *Moms Always Support Their Cubs,* 619001

$75.00

Given out to the women who attended the 2006 Mother's Day Chicago Cubs baseball game held at Wrigley's Field.

Limited Ed. 11,500, Gift, '06
Chicago Cubs Exclusive

Purchased___________

Price $___________

☐ *Your Friendship Brightens Each Day,* 619002

$42.50
$42.50
$42.50
$42.50

Open, Issue Price $40.00, '06

Purchased ________, Price $ ____________

☐ *Sharing The Joys Of Christmas,* 619005

$40.00

Limited Ed., Issue Price $35.00, '07
Hallmark Exclusive

Purchased ________, Price $ ____________

☐ *How Great Is His Goodness,* 620001

$35.00
$35.00
$35.00
$35.00

Open, Issue Price $35.00, '06

Purchased ________, Price $ ____________

☐ *Your Spirit Glitters From Within,* 620006

$35.00
$35.00
$35.00
$35.00

Open, Issue Price $35.00, '06

Purchased____________

Price $____________

☐ *Kind Hearts Send Showers Of Love,* 620007

$40.00 $40.00
$40.00 $40.00

Open, Issue Price $40.00, '06

Purchased ____________

Price $____________

☐ *You Sparkle With Grace And Charm,* 620008

$35.00 $35.00
$35.00 $35.00

Open, Issue Price $35.00, '06

Purchased ____________

Price $____________

☐ *I Love Thee With An Everlasting Love,* 620011

$55.00
$55.00
$55.00
$55.00

Open, Issue Price $55.00, '06

Purchased ________, Price $ ____________

☐ *In Thy Light Shall We See Light (Girl),* 620016 (Candleholder)

$40.00
$40.00

Open, Issue Price $40.00, '06

Purchased ________, Price $ ____________

☐ *In Thy Light Shall We See Light (Boy),* 620017 (Candleholder)

$40.00
$40.00

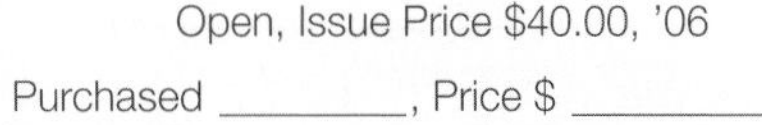

Open, Issue Price $40.00, '06

Purchased ________, Price $ ____________

☐ *Bless You,* 620021

$20.00
$20.00
$20.00
$20.00

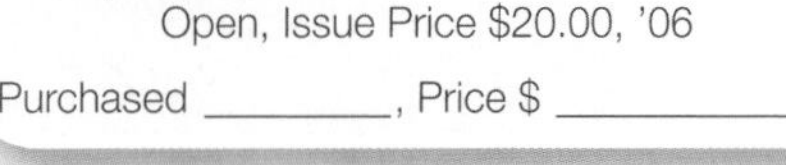

Open, Issue Price $20.00, '06

Purchased ________, Price $ ____________

☐ *Bare Necessities,* 620022

$20.00
$20.00
$20.00
$20.00

Open, Issue Price $20.00, '06

Purchased ________, Price $ ____________

Easy As ABC, 620023

$20.00
$20.00
$20.00
$20.00

Open, Issue Price $20.00, '06

Purchased ________, Price $ ____________

Having A Swell Christmas, 620026

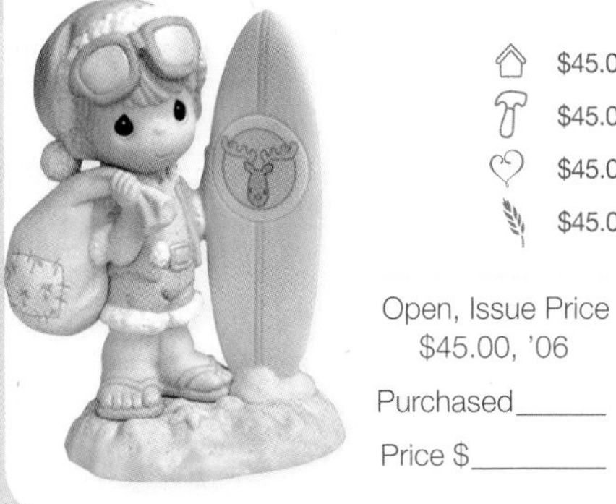

$45.00
$45.00
$45.00
$45.00

Open, Issue Price $45.00, '06

Purchased______

Price $_________

Gloria In Excelsis Deo, 620027

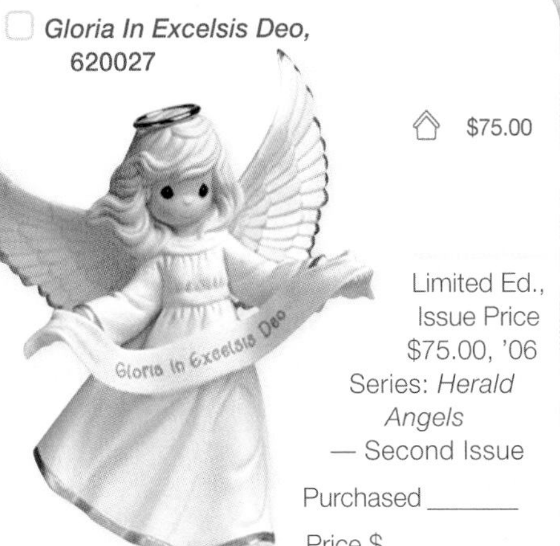

$75.00

Limited Ed., Issue Price $75.00, '06

Series: *Herald Angels* — Second Issue

Purchased ______

Price $ _________

A Dream Is A Wish Your Heart Makes, 620031

$65.00
$65.00

Open, Issue Price $65.00, '06
Disney Showcase Collection

Purchased ________, Price $ ____________

A Dream Is A Wish Your Heart Makes, 620031D

$125.00

First 1,000 were released as 630037D at the Disney Event "A Precious Weekend – World of My Own" held at Disney World Restort on 9/1 – 3/2006. Limited Edition under stamp — The Art of Disney logo.

Limited Ed. 1,000, Issue Price $65.00, '06
Disney Showcase Collection

Purchased ________, Price $ ____________

How Sweet It Is To Be Loved By You, 630001

$50.00
$50.00

Includes a set of four floating message heart candles.

Retired 2/14/07, Issue Price $50.00, '06

Purchased ________, Price $ ____________

Magically Ever After, 620030

$70.00
$70.00
$70.00
$70.00

Open, Issue Price $70.00, '06
Disney Showcase Collection

Purchased ____________________________

Price $_______________________________

Magically Ever After, 620030D

$125.00

First 1,000 were released as 630037D at the Disney Event "A Precious Weekend – World of My Own" held at Disney World Restort on 9/1 – 3/2006. Limited Edition under stamp — The Art of Disney logo.

Limited Ed.1,000, Issue Price $65.00, '06
Disney Showcase Collection

Purchased ________, Price $ ____________

You Melt My Heart, 630002

$30.00
$30.00
$30.00
$30.00

Open, Issue Price $30.00, '06

Purchased ________, Price $ ____________

I'm A Sucker For Your Love, 630003

$40.00
$40.00
$40.00
$40.00

Open, Issue Price $35.00, '06

Purchased____________

Price $_____________

A Tender Touch Helps Love Bloom, 630006

$40.00
$40.00
$40.00
$40.00

Open, Issue Price $40.00, '06
Series: *Seeds of Love* — First Issue

Purchased ________, Price $ ____________

Sow Love To Grow Love, 630007

$30.00
$30.00
$30.00
$30.00

Open, Issue Price $40.00, '06
Series: *Seeds of Love* — Second Issue

Purchased ___________

Price $____________

☐ *Your Love Makes My Heart Bloom,* 630008

$50.00
$50.00
$50.00
$50.00

Open, Issue Price $40.00, '06
Series: *Seeds of Love* — Third Issue
Purchased ________, Price $ ____________

☐ *Flowers And Friendship Are Best When Shared,* 630011

$50.00
$50.00
$50.00
$50.00

Open, Issue Price $50.00, '06
Purchased ______
Price $ _________

☐ *They Call It Puppy Love,* 630012

$40.00
$40.00
$40.00
$40.00

Open, Issue Price $40.00, '06
Purchased ________, Price $ ____________

☐ *Wishing You A Year Filled With Birthday Cheer,* 630016

$35.00
$35.00
$35.00
$35.00

Open, Issue Price $35.00, '06
Purchased _______
Price $ _________

☐ *May Sweetness And Love Shower Down On You!* 630017

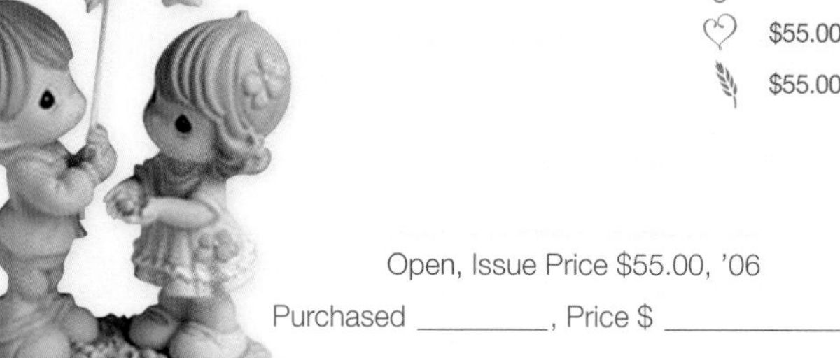

$55.00
$55.00
$55.00
$55.00

Open, Issue Price $55.00, '06
Purchased ________, Price $ ____________

☐ *Count Each Birthday With A Joyful Smile,* 630018

$40.00
$40.00
$40.00
$40.00

Open, Issue Price $40.00, '06
Purchased ________, Price $ ____________

☐ *Bottoms Up,* 630021

$20.00
$20.00
$20.00
$20.00

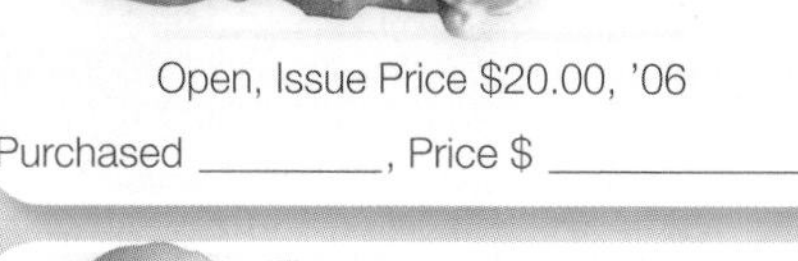

Open, Issue Price $20.00, '06
Purchased ________, Price $ ____________

☐ *Nighty Night,* 630022

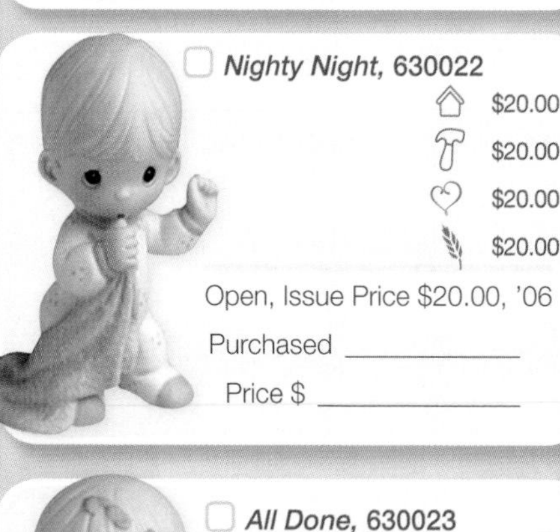

$20.00
$20.00
$20.00
$20.00

Open, Issue Price $20.00, '06
Purchased ___________
Price $ ___________

☐ *All Done,* 630023

$20.00 $20.00
$20.00 $20.00

Open, Issue Price $20.00, '06
Purchased ____________
Price $ ____________

☐ *You Are My Dream Come True,* 630026

$60.00
$60.00
$60.00
$60.00

Open, Issue Price $55.00, '06
Purchased ________, Price $ ____________

☐ *I Found My Love In You,* 630027

$45.00
$45.00
$45.00
$45.00

Open, Issue Price $40.00, '06
Purchased ___________
Price $ ___________

☐ *To Have And To Hold,* 630028

$65.00
$65.00
$65.00
$65.00

Open, Issue Price $60.00, '06
Purchased ________, Price $ ____________

The Wonderful Thing About Tiggers, 630037

$55.00
$55.00
$55.00
$55.00

Open, Issue Price $55.00, '06
Disney Showcase Collection

Purchased ________, Price $ ___________

The Wonderful Thing About Tiggers, 630037D

$75.00

First 1,000 were released as 630037D at the Disney Event "A Precious Weekend – World of My Own" held at Disney World Restort on 9/1 – 3/2006. Limited Edition under stamp — The Art of Disney logo.

Limited Ed., Issue Price $55.00, '06
Disney Showcase Collection

Purchased ________, Price $ ___________

Heigh Ho, It's Off To Play We Go, 630038

$65.00
$65.00
$65.00
$65.00

Open, Issue Price $65.00, '06
Disney Showcase Collection

Purchased ________, Price $ ___________

Part Of Your World, 630039

$60.00
$60.00
$60.00
$60.00

A second version was done for cruise line with her holding a ship.

Open, Issue Price $60.00, '06
Disney Showcase Collection

Purchased ________, Price $ ___________

Life's A Picnic With My Honey, 630040

$120.00
$120.00

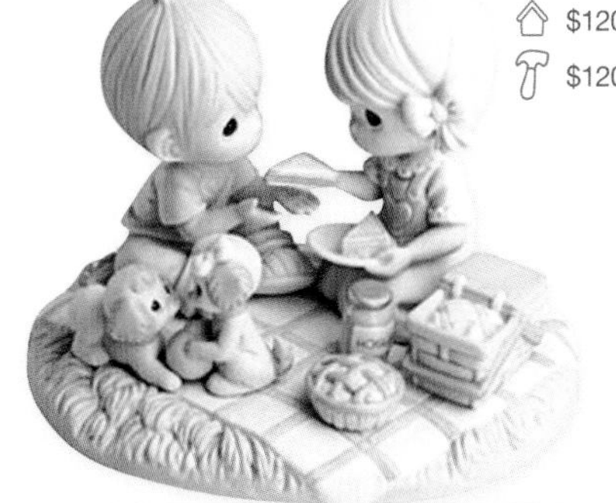

Limited Ed. 3,000, Issue Price $120.00, '06
Century Circle Exclusive

Purchased ________, Price $ ___________

Embraced In Your Love, 630041

$100.00
$100.00

Limited Ed. 3,000, Issue Price $100.00, '06
Century Circle Exclusive

Purchased ________, Price $ ___________

I Pray The Lord My Soul To Keep, 632430

UM $20.00

Open, Issue Price $20.00, '02
Series: *Little Moments*

Purchased ___________
Price $ ___________

I Pray The Lord My Soul To Keep, 632431

UM $20.00

Open, Issue Price $20.00, '02
Series: *Little Moments*

Purchased ___________
Price $ ___________

Baptism Or Christening Frame (Girl), 633001

$25.00 $25.00
$25.00 $25.00

Open, Issue Price $25.00, '06

Purchased ________, Price $ ___________

Baptism Or Christening Frame (Boy), 633002

$25.00 $25.00
$25.00 $25.00

Open, Issue Price $25.00, '06

Purchased ________, Price $ ___________

Jesus Loves Me, 634735

$600.00
$575.00

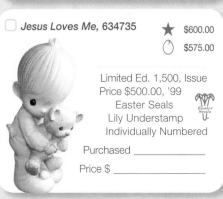

Limited Ed. 1,500, Issue Price $500.00, '99
Easter Seals
Lily Understamp
Individually Numbered

Purchased ___________
Price $ ___________

Give Your Whole Heart, 634751 (Ornament)

UM $15.00
$15.00
$15.00

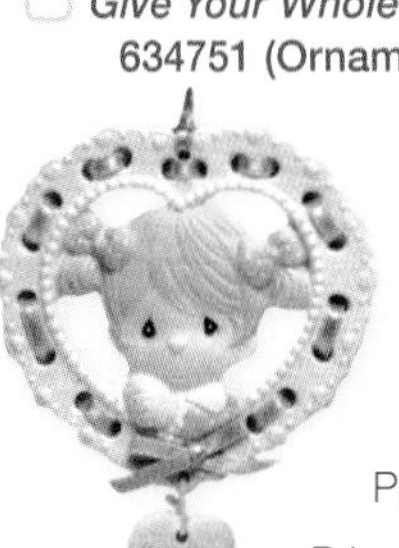

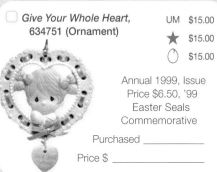

Annual 1999, Issue Price $6.50, '99
Easter Seals
Commemorative

Purchased ___________
Price $ ___________

☐ *Wishing You An Old Fashioned Christmas*, 634778

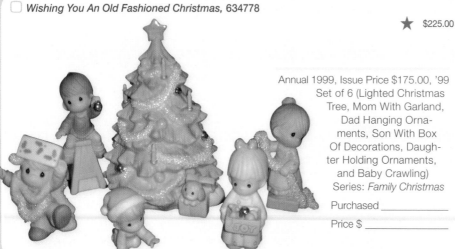

★ $225.00

Annual 1999, Issue Price $175.00, '99
Set of 6 (Lighted Christmas Tree, Mom With Garland, Dad Hanging Ornaments, Son With Box Of Decorations, Daughter Holding Ornaments, and Baby Crawling)
Series: *Family Christmas*

Purchased ____________

Price $ ____________

☐ *I Couldn't Make It Without You*, 635030

Mark	Price
Eyeglasses	$85.00
★	$80.00
Egg	$78.00
Sword	$75.00
Heart	$73.00
Crown	$73.00
Clover	$70.00
Box	$70.00

Limited Ed. 15,000, Issue Price $60.00, '99
Boys & Girls Club of America Commemorative

Purchased ________, Price $ ____________

☐ *Friendship's A Slice Of Life*, 634964

★	$35.00	Heart	$35.00
Egg	$35.00	Crown	$35.00
Sword	$35.00	Clover	$35.00
		Box	$35.00

Suspended 2004, Issue Price $35.00, '99

Purchased ____________

Price $____________

☐ *Scootin' Your Way To A Perfect Day*, 634999

★ $45.00

Dated Annual 1999, Issue Price $25.00, '99
Care-A-Van Exclusive

Purchased ________, Price $ ____________

☐ *Scoopin' Up Some Love*, 635049

Egg $55.00

Chocolate ice cream version.

Limited Ed., Issue Price $35.00, '00
Easter Seals Commemorative
DSR and Century Circle Exclusive

Purchased ________, Price $ ____________

☐ *Reach For The Stars*, 634972

★ $55.00

Annual 1999, Issue Price $35.00, '99
Signing Tour 1999

Purchased ____________

Price $____________

☐ *Hail Mary, Full Of Grace — Madonna II*, 635006

Mark	Price
Crown	$80.00
Clover	$80.00
Box	$80.00

Limited Ed., Issue Price $80.00, '03

Purchased ________, Price $ ____________

☐ *Scoopin' Up Some Love*, 635049

Egg $350.00

Rainbow sherbet version.

Limited Ed., Issue Price $35.00, '00
Easter Seals Commemorative
DSR and Century Circle Exclusive

Purchased ________, Price $ ____________

☐ *Take Time To Smell The Roses*, 634980C

A portion of the proceeds from the sales of this figurine are donated to the United Way.

Mark	Price
★	$55.00
Egg	$55.00

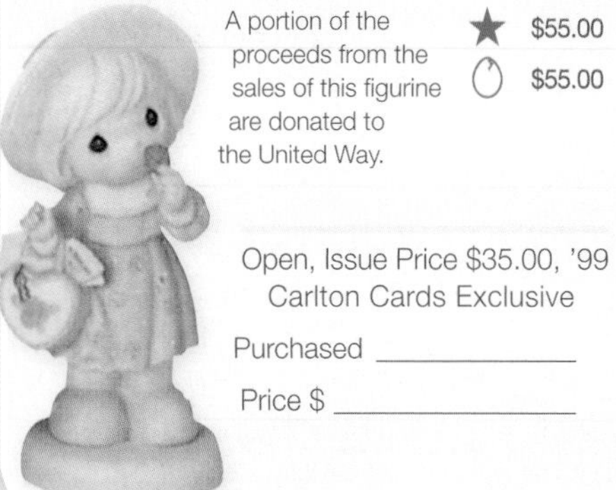

Open, Issue Price $35.00, '99
Carlton Cards Exclusive

Purchased ____________

Price $ ____________

☐ *The Heart Of A Mother Is Reflected In Her Child (Boy),* **640001**

$30.00 $30.00
$30.00 $30.00

Open, Issue Price $30.00, '06
Purchased ___________
Price $ ___________

☐ *The Heart Of A Mother Is Reflected In Her Child (Girl),* **640002**

$30.00 $30.00
$30.00 $30.00

Open, Issue Price $30.00, '06
Purchased ___________
Price $ ___________

☐ *Mom, You Are A Bouquet Of Love And Understanding,* **640003**

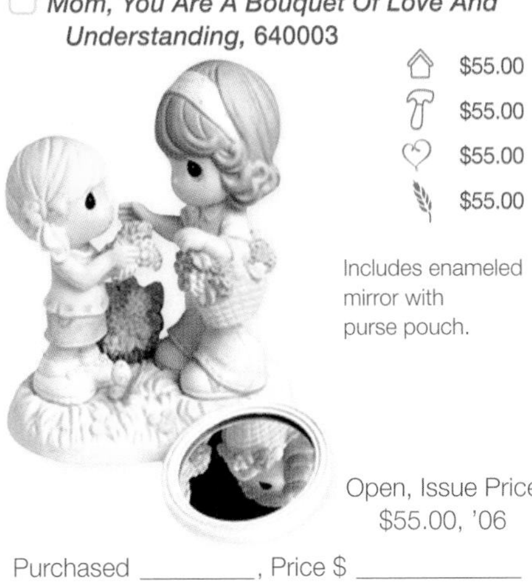

$55.00
$55.00
$55.00
$55.00

Includes enameled mirror with purse pouch.

Open, Issue Price $55.00, '06
Purchased ________, Price $ ___________

☐ *A Mother's Love Grows By Giving,* **640004**

$60.00
$60.00

Retired 2007, Issue Price $60.00, '06
Purchased ___________
Price $___________

☐ *Filled With Wonder And Awe In The Holy Spirit,* **640021**

$40.00 $40.00
$40.00 $40.00

Open, Issue Price $35.00, '06
Purchased ___________
Price $___________

☐ *Do This In Memory Of Me (Girl),* **640022**

$45.00 $45.00
$45.00 $45.00

Open, Issue Price $40.00, '06
Purchased _______
Price $ _______

☐ *Do This In Memory Of Me (Boy),* **640023**

$45.00 $45.00
$45.00 $45.00

Open, Issue Price $40.00, '06
Purchased _______
Price $ _______

☐ *Having A Sister Is Always Having A Friend,* **640031**

$50.00
$50.00
$50.00
$50.00

Open, Issue Price $50.00, '06
Purchased _____
Price $ _____

☐ *A Sister Is A Gift To The Heart And A Friend,* **640032**

$55.00 $55.00
$55.00 $55.00

Open, Issue Price $55.00, '06
Purchased _____
Price $_______

☐ *Sweet Is The Voice Of My Sister,* **640033**

$65.00
$65.00
$65.00
$65.00

Open, Issue Price $60.00, '06
Purchased ________, Price $ ___________

☐ *Dreams Really Do Come True,* **640041**

$65.00
$65.00
$65.00
$65.00

Open, Issue Price $65.00, '06
Disney Showcase Collection
Purchased ________, Price $ ___________

☐ *Follow Your Heart,* **640042**

$65.00
$65.00
$65.00
$65.00

Open, Issue Price $65.00, '06
Disney Showcase Collection
Purchased _____
Price $ _______

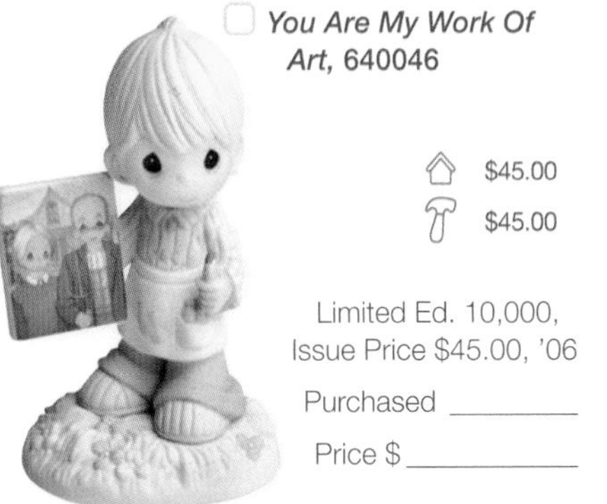

☐ *You Are My Work Of Art,* **640046**

$45.00
$45.00

Limited Ed. 10,000, Issue Price $45.00, '06
Purchased ________
Price $ ________

☐ ***A World Of Possibilities Lies Ahead*, 640047**

$42.50
$42.50
$42.50
$42.50

Open, Issue Price $42.50, '06

Purchased ________, Price $ ____________

☐ ***Life's Beary Precious With You*, 642673**

$45.00 $38.00
$43.00 $35.00
$40.00 $33.00

Suspended 2004, Issue Price $25.00, '01

Purchased ____________

Price $____________

☐ ***You Color Our World With Loving, Caring And Sharing*, 644463**

★ $65.00

Limited Ed., Issue Price $24.00, '99
Tenth Anniversary Chapel Event Exclusive

Purchased ____________

Price $____________

☐ ***You Color Our World With Loving, Caring And Sharing*, 644463C**

UM $50.00 $45.00 $40.00
$48.00 $43.00 $30.00
$48.00 $40.00 $30.00

Open, Issue Price $30.00, '99
Chapel Exclusive

Purchased ________, Price $ ____________

☐ ***Highway To Happiness*, 649457**

UM $23.00

Open, Issue Price $20.00, '99
Series: *Highway To Happiness — Little Moments*

Purchased ______

Price $ __________

☐ ***I'll Never Stop Loving You*, 649465**

UM $23.00

Open, Issue Price $20.00, '99
Series: *Highway To Happiness — Little Moments*

Purchased ____________

Price $____________

☐ ***There's No Wrong Way With You*, 649473**

UM $23.00

Open, Issue Price $20.00, '99
Series: *Highway To Happiness — Little Moments*

Purchased ________, Price $ ____________

☐ ***God's Children At Play*, 649481**

UM $23.00

Open, Issue Price $20.00, '99
Series: *Highway To Happiness — Little Moments*

Purchased ________, Price $ ____________

☐ ***Cross Walk*, 649511**

UM $23.00

Open, Issue Price $20.00, '99
Series: *Highway To Happiness — Little Moments*

Purchased ________, Price $ ____________

☐ ***Go 4 It*, 649538**

UM $23.00

Open, Issue Price $20.00, '99
Series: *Highway To Happiness — Little Moments*

Purchased ________, Price $ ____________

☐ ***Yield To Him*, 649546**

UM $23.00

Open, Issue Price $20.00, '01
Series: *Highway To Happiness — Little Moments*

Purchased ____________

Price $ ____________

☐ ***Let Him Enter Your Heart*, 649554**

UM $23.00

Open, Issue Price $20.00, '01
Series: *Highway To Happiness — Little Moments*

Purchased ____________

Price $____________

Give'em A Brake For Jesus, 649562

UM $23.00

Open, Issue Price $20.00, '01
Series: *Highway To Happiness — Little Moments*

Purchased ___________

Price $ ___________

Hay Good Lookin', 649732

★ $65.00

One Year of Production, Issue Price $45.00, '99
Series: *Country Lane Collection*

Purchased ________, Price $ ___________

Hay Good Lookin', 649732

★ $60.00
[Egg] $58.00
[Bow] $55.00
[Cross in heart] $55.00
[Crown] $53.00
[Flower] $53.00

Retired 2004, Issue Price $45.00, '99
Series: *Country Lane Collection*

Purchased ________, Price $ ___________

Peace In The Valley, 649929

★ $175.00
[Egg] $165.00
[Bow] $160.00

Limited Ed. 12,500, Issue Price $125.00, '99
1999 Enesco Fall Show Exclusive

Purchased ________, Price $ ___________

Ice See In You A Champion, 649937

★ $75.00
[Egg] $73.00
[Bow] $70.00
[Cross in heart] $68.00
[Crown] $65.00
[Flower] $63.00
[Cube] $60.00

Out of Production, Issue Price $37.50, '00
Canadian Exclusive

Purchased ________, Price $ ___________

Ice See In You A Champion, 649937S

★ $85.00
[Egg] $83.00

Limited Ed. 4,800, Issue Price $37.50, '99
Canadian Exclusive
Spring Dating Program

Purchased_________

Price $___________

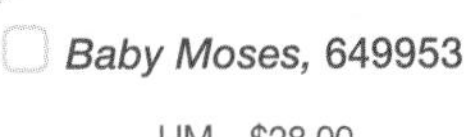

Baby Moses, 649953

UM $28.00

Open, Issue Price $25.00, '00
Series: *Bible Stories — Little Moments*

Purchased ________, Price $ ___________

Ruth & Naomi, 649961

UM $28.00

Open, Issue Price $25.00, '00
Series: *Bible Stories — Little Moments*

Purchased ________, Price $ ___________

The Good Samaritan, 649988

UM $28.00

Open, Issue Price $25.00, '00
Series: *Bible Stories — Little Moments*

Purchased ________, Price $ ___________

The Great Pearl, 649996

UM $28.00

Open, Issue Price $25.00, '00
Series: *Bible Stories — Little Moments*

Purchased ___________

Price $___________

The Sower And The Seed, 650005

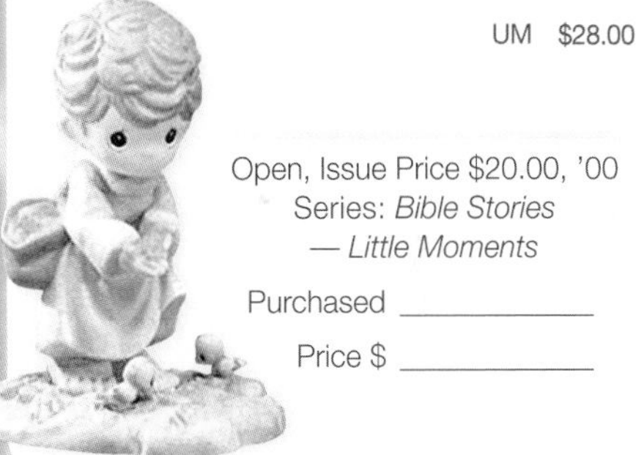

UM $28.00

Open, Issue Price $20.00, '00
Series: *Bible Stories — Little Moments*

Purchased ___________

Price $ ___________

Giving My Heart Freely, 650013

[Egg] $55.00
[Bow] $53.00
[Cross in heart] $50.00
[Crown] $50.00
[Flower] $50.00
[Cube] $50.00

Suspended 2005, Issue Price $40.00, '01

Purchased ________, Price $ ___________

David & Goliath, 650064

UM $28.00

Open, Issue Price $20.00, '01
Series: *Bible Stories — Little Moments*

Purchased ________, Price $ ____________

Peace On Earth, 679259 (Ornament)

★ $43.00

Limited Ed., Issue Price $25.00, '99
GCC Exclusive

Purchased____________

Price $ ______________

I Will Love You All Ways, 679704

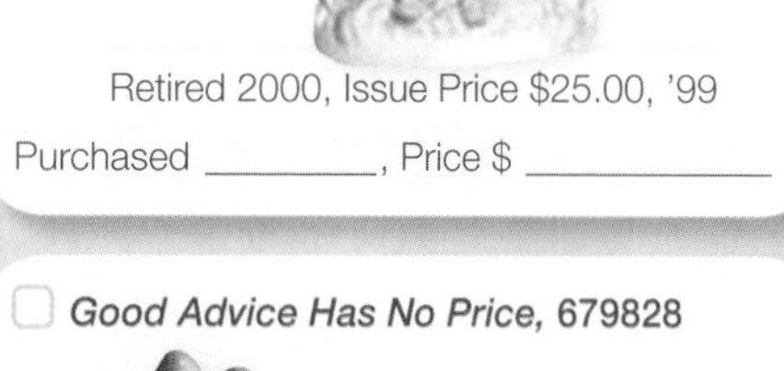

★ $33.00
$30.00

This is a "Gift-to-Go" figurine with a Tender Tail ornament and matching valentine.

Retired 2000, Issue Price $25.00, '99

Purchased ________, Price $ ____________

Good Advice Has No Price, 679828

★ $35.00
$33.00
$30.00
$30.00
$30.00
$30.00
$30.00
$30.00
$30.00
$30.00
$30.00
$30.00

Open, Issue Price $30.00, '99

Purchased ________, Price $ ____________

We Knead You Grandma, 679844

★ $45.00
$43.00
$40.00
$40.00
$40.00
$40.00
$40.00
$40.00
$40.00
$40.00
$40.00

Open, Issue Price $40.00, '99

Purchased ________, Price $ ____________

This Day Has Been Made In Heaven, 679852

★ $35.00
$33.00
$30.00
$30.00
$30.00
$30.00
$30.00
$30.00
$30.00
$30.00
$30.00

Open, Issue Price $30.00, '99

Purchased ____________

Price $______________

Lovingcaringsharing.com, 679860

★ $50.00
$48.00
$45.00
$43.00
$43.00
$40.00
$40.00

Suspended, Issue Price $35.00, '99

Purchased____________

Price $______________

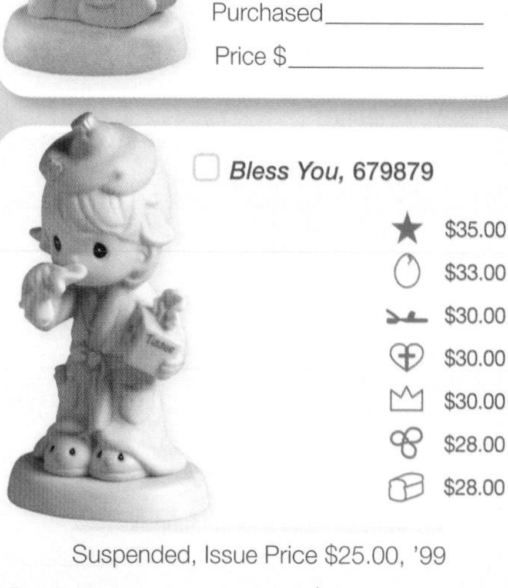

Bless You, 679879

★ $35.00
$33.00
$30.00
$30.00
$30.00
$28.00
$28.00

Suspended, Issue Price $25.00, '99

Purchased ________, Price $ ____________

A Tail Of Love, 679976

★ $30.00
$28.00
$25.00
$25.00
$23.00

Retired 2003, Issue Price $20.00, '99
Series: *Two By Two*

Purchased ________, Price $ ____________

Wishing You A Blow Out Birthday, 680184

★ $40.00
$38.00
$35.00
$35.00
$35.00
$35.00
$35.00
$35.00
$35.00

Open, Issue Price $35.00, '99

Purchased__________

Price $ ____________

Share In The Celebration, 680761 (Medallion)

UM $250.00
★ $250.00

Limited Ed. 1,500, Gift, '99
Chapel Exclusive
Chapel Tenth Anniversary
1999 Licensee Show

Purchased ________, Price $ ____________

Life Is Worth Fighting For (Blonde), 680982

$55.00
$53.00
$50.00
$48.00

Retired 2003, Issue Price $30.00, '00
Breast Cancer Awareness, Benefits NABCO

Purchased ________, Price $ ____________

Life Is Worth Fighting For (Brunette), 680982B

$55.00
$53.00
$50.00
$48.00

Retired 2003, Issue Price $30.00, '00
Breast Cancer Awareness, Benefits NABCO

Purchased ________, Price $ ___________

God Gives Us Memories So That We Might Have Roses In December, 680990

$75.00
$73.00
$70.00
$68.00
$65.00

Retired 2004, Issue Price $45.00, '00
Benefits Compassionate Friends

Purchased ________, Price $ ___________

Precious Moments Will Last Forever, 681008

★ $55.00
$50.00

Limited 2,000, Issue Price $35.00, '99

Purchased ___________

Price $ ___________

His Name Is Jesus, 681032

UM $85.00

Limited Ed. 1,500, Issue Price $40.00, '99
1999 Collector's Christmas Weekend

Purchased___________

Price $ ___________

Let Freedom Ring, 681059

Figurine was also issued as a limited edition show exclusive for Enesco summer shows (681059E); Star mark, $85.00.

★ $65.00
$63.00
$60.00
$58.00
$55.00
$55.00

Retired 2004, Issue Price $45.00, '99

Purchased ________, Price $ ___________

You Complete My Heart, 681067

★ $60.00
$58.00
$55.00
$53.00
$52.00

Suspended 2003, Issue Price $37.50, '99

Purchased ________, Price $ ___________

A Love Like No Other, 681075

★ $50.00
$48.00
$45.00
$45.00
$45.00
$45.00
$45.00
$45.00
$45.00
$45.00
$45.00
$45.00

Open, Issue Price $45.00, '99
Series: *Motherhood* — First Issue

Purchased _________

Price $_________

You Have The Sweetest Heart, 689548

★ $30.00
$28.00
$26.00
$25.00
$25.00
$25.00
$25.00
$25.00
$25.00
$25.00
$25.00

Open, Issue Price $25.00, '99

Purchased ________, Price $ ___________

Take Time 2 Love, 690001

UM $35.00

Limited Ed., Gift, '06
Chapel Exclusive, 2006 Precious Moments Family Reunion

Purchased ___________

Price $ ___________

Life Is Full Of Golden Opportunities, 690002

$35.00
$35.00
$35.00
$35.00

Open, Issue Price $35.00, '06
Japanese Exclusive

Purchased ___________

Price $___________

A World Of My Own, 690003D

$75.00

Available only at Walt Disney World Resort, Orlando, 09/01/2006.

The first 1,000 had a limited edition understamp — $150.00.

Limited Ed., Issue Price $50.00, '06
Disney Showcase Collection

Purchased ________, Price $ ___________

A World Of My Own, 690004D

$75.00

Available only at Disneyland Resort, California, 10/06/2006.

The first 1,000 had a limited edition understamp — $150.00.

Limited Ed., Issue Price $50.00, '06
Disney Showcase Collection

Purchased ________, Price $ ___________

☐ ***Safe In Mother's Arms*, 690005**

$35.00
$35.00

Limited Edition, Issue Price $35.00, '06
American Greetings/ Carlton Cards Early Release

Purchased ___________

Price $___________

☐ ***The Purr-fect Christmas Morning*, 690006**

$35.00 $35.00
$35.00 $35.00

Open, Issue Price $35.00, '07

Purchased ___________

Price $ ___________

☐ ***Mommy's Love Goes With You*, 690007**

UM $50.00
$50.00
$50.00

Open, Issue Price $50.00, '06
Chapel Exclusive Early Release

Purchased ________, Price $ ___________

☐ ***There's Magic In Those Ears*, 690011**

$60.00
$60.00

Limited Ed., Issue Price $55.00, '07
Carlton Cards Exclusive
Disney Showcase Collection

Purchased ________, Price $ ___________

☐ ***There's Magic In Those Ears*, 690011D**

$60.00

Released at the Disney Event "A Precious Weekend – A World of My Own." It has the under stamp — The Art of Disney logo.

Limited Ed., Issue Price $60.00, '07
Disney Showcase Collection

Purchased ________, Price $ ___________

☐ ***The Warmth Of Christmas Comes From The Heart*, 690012**

$50.00
$50.00
$50.00
$50.00

Open, Issue Price $50.00, '06

Purchased ________, Price $ ___________

☐ ***When You Wish Upon A Star*, 690010**

$60.00
$60.00

Limited Ed., Issue Price $60.00, '07
Hallmark Exclusive
Disney Showcase Collection

Purchased ________, Price $ ___________

☐ ***When You Wish Upon A Star*, 690010D**

$60.00

Released at the Disney Event "A Precious Weekend – A World of My Own." It has the under stamp — The Art of Disney logo.

Limited Ed., Issue Price $60.00, '07
Disney Showcase Collection

Purchased ________, Price $ ___________

☐ ***Christmas Morning Is Just The Sweetest*, 690013 (Ornament)**

$20.00 $20.00
$20.00 $20.00

Open, Issue Price $20.00, '07

Purchased ___________

Price $ ___________

☐ ***A New Friend Is A Joy To Find*, 690014 (Ornament)**

$20.00 $20.00
$20.00 $20.00

Open, Issue Price $20.00, '07

Purchased___________

Price $___________

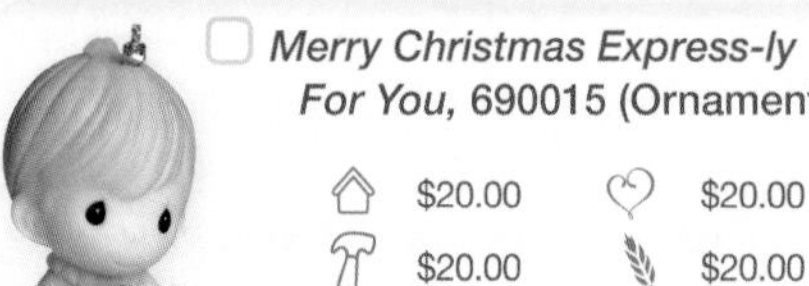

☐ ***Merry Christmas Express-ly For You*, 690015 (Ornament)**

$20.00 $20.00
$20.00 $20.00

Open, Issue Price $20.00, '07

Purchased ___________

Price $ ___________

☐ ***A Dream Is A Wish Your Heart Makes*, 690016 (Ornament)**

$25.00 $25.00
$25.00 $25.00

Open, Issue Price $25.00, '07
Disney Showcase Collection, Kirlin's Exclusive

Purchased ________, Price $ ___________

☐ ***Everything's Better With A Friend*, 690017 (Ornament)**

$25.00 $25.00
$25.00 $25.00

Open, Issue Price $25.00, '07
Disney Showcase Collection
Kirklin's Exclusive

Purchased ________

Price $___________

☐ *Sending All My Love To You*, 690019

$40.00

Comes with heart frame

Limited Ed. 2006, Issue Price $40.00, '06
American Greeting/Carlton Cards Exclusive Early Release

Purchased ________, Price $ ____________

☐ *Thots Of You Bring Out The Best In Me*, 690020

$50.00

Limited Ed., Gift, '06
Precious Thots Exclusive

Purchased ________, Price $ ____________

☐ *Mom You Are Never Too Close For Comfort*, 690021

$40.00
$40.00

Open, Issue Price $40.00, '07
Hallmark Exclusive

Purchased ________, Price $ ____________

☐ *Wrapped In Mom's Love*, 690022

$35.00

Limited Ed., Issue Price $35.00, '07
Early Release/Carlton Cards Exclusive

Purchased ________, Price $ ____________

☐ *Birthday Train Gift Set*, 690024

$50.00
$50.00
$50.00

Set 3 #16004, #119424, and #15938

Open, Issue Price $50.00, '07

Purchased________, Price $ ____________

☐ *A Friend Like You Leads Me To The Sunny Side Of Life*, 690025

$35.00 $35.00
$35.00 $35.00

Open, Issue Price $32.00, '07
Hallmark Exclusive

Purchased ______________

Price $______________

☐ *The Child That's Born On The Sabbath Day...*, 692077

UM $23.00

Open, Issue Price $20.00, '00
Series: *Thought of the Day — Little Moments*

Purchased ____________

Price $____________

☐ *Monday's Child Is Fair Of Face*, 692085

UM $23.00

Open, Issue Price $20.00, '00
Series: *Thought of the Day — Little Moments*

Purchased ____________

Price $____________

☐ *Tuesday's Child Is Full Of Grace*, 692093

UM $23.00

Open, Issue Price $20.00, '00
Series: *Thought of the Day — Little Moments*

Purchased ________, Price $ ____________

☐ *Wednesday's Child Is Full Of Woe*, 692107

UM $23.00

Open, Issue Price $20.00, '00
Series: *Thought of the Day — Little Moments*

Purchased ________, Price $ ____________

☐ *Thursday's Child Has Far To Go*, 692115

UM $23.00

Open, Issue Price $20.00, '00
Series: *Thought of the Day — Little Moments*

Purchased ____________

Price $____________

☐ *Friday's Child Is Loving And Giving,* 692123

UM $23.00

Open, Issue Price $20.00, '00
Series: *Thought of the Day — Little Moments*

Purchased ________, Price $ ____________

☐ *Saturday's Child Works Hard For A Living,* 692131

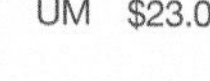

UM $23.00

Open, Issue Price $20.00, '00
Series: *Thought of the Day — Little Moments*

Purchased ____________

Price $ ____________

☐ *Alleluia, He Is Risen,* 692409

★ $45.00
$45.00
$43.00
$43.00
$40.00
$40.00
$35.00

Suspended, Issue Price $30.00, '99

Purchased ____________

Price $ ____________

☐ *Sharing The Season With You,* 702862

UM $60.000
$55.00

Limited Ed., Issue Price $22.50, '01
Series: *Little Moments*, Hallmark Exclusive

Purchased ________, Price $ ____________

☐ *I Will Love You All Ways,* 708158

★ $45.00
$45.00

Gift Set: #679704 Figurine and Tender Tails Bear

Retired 2000, Issue Price $25.00, '99

Purchased ________, Price $ ____________

☐ *Dancing For Joy On Christmas Morning,* 710001

$35.00

Dated 2007, Issue Price $35.00, '07

Purchased ____________

Price $____________

☐ *Dancing For Joy On Christmas Morning,* 710002 (Ornament)

$20.00

Dated 2007, Issue Price $20.00, '07

Purchased ____________

Price $ ____________

☐ *Dancing For Joy On Christmas Morning,* 710003 (Ornament)

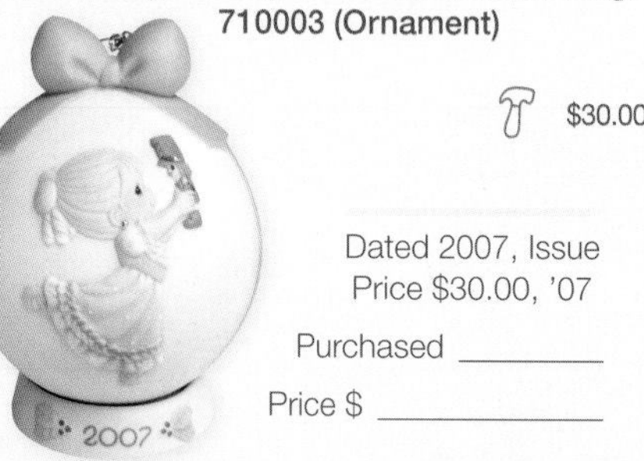

$30.00

Dated 2007, Issue Price $30.00, '07

Purchased ____________

Price $ ____________

☐ *Our First Christmas Together,* 710004 (Ornament)

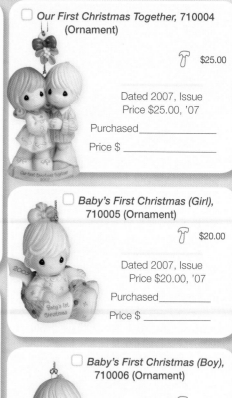

$25.00

Dated 2007, Issue Price $25.00, '07

Purchased____________

Price $ ____________

☐ *Baby's First Christmas (Girl),* 710005 (Ornament)

$20.00

Dated 2007, Issue Price $20.00, '07

Purchased__________

Price $ ____________

☐ *Baby's First Christmas (Boy),* 710006 (Ornament)

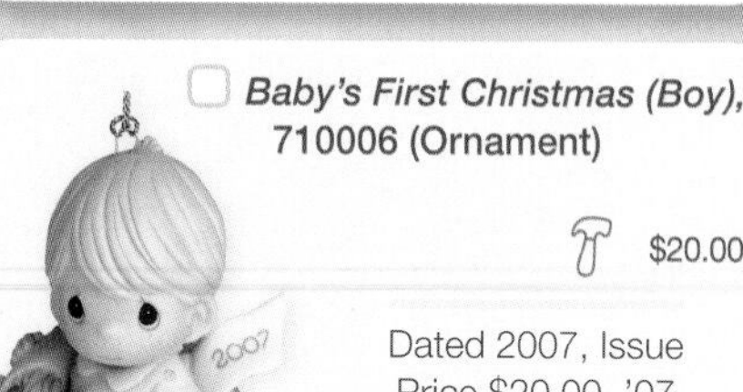

$20.00

Dated 2007, Issue Price $20.00, '07

Purchased __________

Price $____________

☐ *Jump For Joy On Christmas Morning,* 710007 (Ornament)

$20.00

Dated 2007, Issue Price $20.00, '07

Purchased____________

Price $ ____________

☐ *The Wonder Of It All,* 710008

$50.00
$50.00
$50.00

Open, Issue Price $50.00, '07

Purchased ________, Price $ ____________

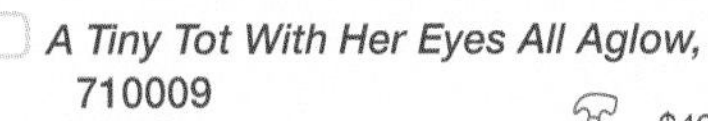

☐ *A Tiny Tot With Her Eyes All Aglow,* 710009

$40.00
$40.00
$40.00

Open, Issue Price $40.00, '07

Purchased ______

Price $________

☐ *The Gift Is In The Giving,* 710010

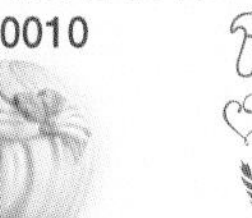

$50.00
$50.00
$50.00

Open, Issue Price $50.00, '07

Purchased ______

Price $________

☐ *A Gift Made With Love,* 710011 (Ornament)

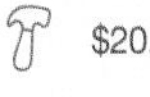

$20.00 $20.00
$20.00

Open, Issue Price $20.00, '07

Purchased____________

Price $______________

☐ *His Eyes How They Twinkled,* 710012 (Ornament)

$20.00 $20.00
$20.00

Open, Issue Price $20.00, '07

Purchased ____________

Price $ ____________

☐ *Let Your Spirit Soar With The Glee Of The Season,* 710016

$40.00
$40.00
$40.00

Open, Issue Price $40.00, '07

Purchased ________, Price $ ___________

☐ *The Fruit Of The Spirit Is Love, Joy, And Peace,* 710017

$50.00
$50.00
$50.00

Open, Issue Price $50.00, '07

Purchased ________, Price $ ___________

☐ *Always Here To Guide And Protect You,* 710018

$60.00
$60.00
$60.00

Dated 2007, Issue Price $60.00, '07

Purchased ________

Price $ ________

☐ *Winter's Such A Ball,* 710019 (Ornament)

$20.00
$20.00
$20.00

Open, Issue Price $20.00, '07

Purchased ________, Price $ ___________

☐ *Warmed By Your Love,* 710020 (Ornament)

$25.00
$25.00
$25.00

Open, Issue Price $25.00, '07

Purchased ________, Price $ ___________

☐ *Clearing A Path To You,* 710021 (Ornament)

$20.00 $20.00
$20.00

Open, Issue Price $20.00, '07

Purchased______________

Price $ ______________

☐ *Deck The Halls,* 710022 (Ornament)

$20.00 $20.00
$20.00

Open, Issue Price $20.00, '07

Purchased__________

Price $ ___________

☐ *Winter Is So Cool,* 710023 (Ornament)

$20.00 $20.00
$20.00

Open, Issue Price $20.00, '07

Purchased__________

Price $ __________

☐ *You're One Of A Kind,* 710024 (Ornament)

$20.00 $20.00
$20.00

Open, Issue Price $20.00, '07

Purchased_______________

Price $ _______________

☐ *I Will Be Glad And Rejoice In You,* 710026

$150.00

Limited Ed 3,000, Issue Price $150.00, '07

Purchased ________, Price $ ___________

☐ *Rock Around The Clock, 710027*

UM $160.00
$155.00

Limited Ed 3,000, Issue Price $100.00, '07

Purchased ________, Price $ ___________

☐ *You Are My Sunshine, 710031*

$40.00
$40.00
$40.00

Open, Issue Price $37.50, '07

Purchased ________, Price $ ___________

☐ *Two Scoops Are Better When Shared With You, 710032*

$45.00
$45.00
$45.00

Open, Issue Price $45.00, '07

Purchased ________, Price $ ___________

☐ *Life Is Sweeter With You, 710033*

$60.00
$60.00
$60.00

Open, Issue Price $60.00, '07

Purchased ______

Price $ _______

☐ *Aren't You Sweet, 710036*

The first 301 were sold at Walt Disney World event June 15 – 16, 2007. Event figurine was to have Art of Disney understamp, however had the Disney Showcase understamp. Those who purchased at the event recieved a Certificate of Authenticity.

$65.00
$65.00
$65.00

Limited Ed., Issue Price $65.00, '07
Disney Showcase Collection

Purchased ________, Price $ ___________

☐ *The Stockings Were Hung By The Chimney With Care, 710037*

The first 319 were sold at Walt Disney World event June 15 – 16, 2007. Event figurine was to have Art of Disney understamp, however had the Disney Showcase understamp. Those who purchased at the event recieved a Certificate of Authenticity.

$70.00
$70.00
$70.00

Limited Ed., Issue Price $70.00, '07
Disney Showcase Collection

Purchased ________, Price $ ___________

☐ *There's Nothin' To It When It Comes To You, 710038*

The first 324 were sold at Walt Disney World event June 15 – 16, 2007. Event figurine was to have Art of Disney understamp, however had the Disney Showcase understamp. Those who purchased at the event recieved a Certificate of Authenticity.

$65.00
$65.00
$65.00

Limited Ed., Issue Price $65.00, '07
Disney Showcase Collection

Purchased ________, Price $ ___________

☐ *Nothing's Sweeter Than Time Together, 710039*

The first 329 were sold at Walt Disney World event June 15 – 16, 2007. Event figurine was to have Art of Disney understamp, however had the Disney Showcase understamp. Those who purchased at the event recieved a Certificate of Authenticity.

$75.00
$75.00
$75.00

Limited Ed., Issue Price $75.00, '07
Disney Showcase Collection

Purchased ________, Price $ ___________

☐ *When They Saw The Star They Were Over-Joyed, 710040*

$35.00
$35.00
$35.00

Open, Issue Price $35.00, '07

Purchased ___________

Price $ ___________

I Bring You News Of Great Joy, 710041

$20.00
$20.00
$20.00

Open, Issue Price $20.00, '07
Purchased ____________
Price $ ______________

Noel, 710042 $75.00 $75.00 $75.00

Open, Issue Price $75.00, '07
Purchased ________, Price $ ___________

Friendship Grows With Sharing, 710046

$20.00
$20.00
$20.00

Open, Issue Price
$20.00, '07
Purchased __________
Price $ ______________

Home Grown Love, 710047

$25.00
$25.00
$25.00

Open, Issue Price $25.00, '07
Purchased ________, Price $ ___________

We Gather Together For Fun And Laughter, 710048

$20.00
$20.00
$20.00

Open, Issue Price $20.00, '07
Purchased ________, Price $ ___________

A Sprinkle On A Sunny Day Is So Refreshing, 710049

$20.00
$20.00
$20.00

Open, Issue Price $20.00, '07
Purchased ________, Price $ __________

The Magic Of The Season, 710050

$70.00
$70.00
$70.00

The first 302 were sold at Walt Disney World event June 15 – 16, 2007. Event figurine was to have Art of Disney understamp, however had the Disney Showcase understamp. Those who purchased at the event recieved a Certificate of Authenticity.

Limited Ed., Issue Price $70.00, '07
Disney Showcase Collection
Purchased ________, Price $ ___________

Old Friends Make The Season Bright, 710051 (Ornament)

$25.00
$25.00
$25.00

Limited Ed., Issue
Price $25.00, '07
Disney Showcase Collection
Purchased ____________
Price $ ______________

Smiles For The Season, 710052 (Ornament)

$25.00

Limited Ed., Issue
Price $25.00, '07
Disney Showcase Collection
Hallmark Exclusive
Purchased ____________
Price $ ______________

Oh Boy! It Must Be Christmas, 710053 (Ornament)

$25.00
$25.00

Limited Ed., Issue
Price $25.00, '07
Disney Showcase Collection
Disney Park Exclusive
Purchased ____________
Price $ ______________

Love And Joy Come To You, 710054 (Ornament)

$25.00
$25.00

Limited Ed., Issue
Price $25.00, '07
Disney Showcase Collection
Carlton Cards Exclusive
Purchased ____________
Price $ ______________

Close Friends Make The Season Special, 710055 (Ornament)

$25.00
$25.00
$25.00

Limited Ed., Issue
Price $25.00, '07
Disney Showcase Collection
Purchased ____________
Price $ ______________

☐ *Making A List And Checking It Twice,* 710056 (Ornament)

$25.00
$25.00
$25.00

Limited Ed., Issue Price $25.00, '07
Disney Showcase Collection

Purchased ______________

Price $ ________________

☐ *Adorn Every Branch With Love,* 710057 (Ornament)

$25.00
$25.00

Limited Ed., Issue Price $25.00, '07
Disney Showcase Collection

Purchased ______________

Price $ ________________

☐ *I'll Be Home For Christmas,* 710058 (Ornament)

$25.00
$25.00
$25.00

Limited Ed., Issue Price $25.00, '07
Disney Showcase Collection

Purchased ______________

Price $ ________________

☐ *Boy With Donald Duck,* 717001 (Frame)

UM $35.00

Open, Issue Price $35.00, '07
Disney Showcase Collection

Purchased ________, Price $ ____________

☐ *Girl With Minnie At The Mantel,* 717002 (Frame)

UM $35.00

Open, Issue Price $35.00, '07
Disney Showcase Collection

Purchased ________, Price $ ____________

☐ *You Make The Grade,* 720001

$40.00
$40.00
$40.00

Open, Issue Price $35.00, '07

Purchased ________, Price $ ____________

☐ *Your Comfort Comes From The Heart,* 720002

$40.00
$40.00
$40.00

Open, Issue Price $35.00, '07

Purchased ________, Price $ ____________

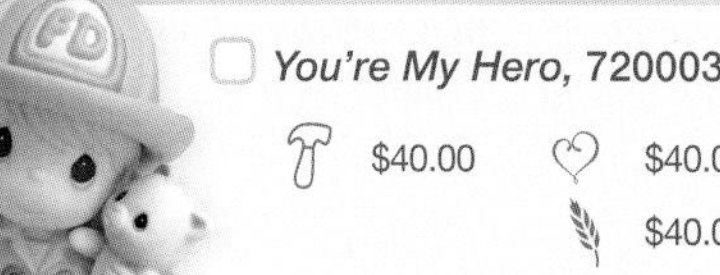

☐ *You're My Hero,* 720003

$40.00 $40.00
$40.00

Open, Issue Price $35.00, '07

Purchased ____________

Price $ ______________

☐ *Godmother, You're An Inspiration To Me,* 720008 (Ornament)

$20.00
$20.00

Open, Issue Price $20.00, '08

Purchased ______________

Price $ ________________

☐ *Teacher, You Are My Shining Star,* 720009 (Ornament)

$20.00
$20.00

Open, Issue Price $20.00, '08

Purchased ______________

Price $ ________________

☐ *Your Friendship Grows Sweeter With Each Day,* 720011

$42.50 $42.50
$42.50

Open, Issue Price $40.00, '07

Purchased ________, Price $ ____________

☐ *Friendship Is A Sweet Journey,* 720012

$50.00 $50.00
$50.00

Open, Issue Price $50.00, '07

Purchased ______

Price $ ________

☐ *Your Friendship Sweetens My Life*, 720013

$60.00
$60.00
$60.00

Open, Issue Price $55.00, '07

Purchased ________, Price $ ___________

☐ *A Friend In Need*, 720017

$60.00 $60.00
$60.00

Limited Ed., Issue Price $60.00, '07 Disney Showcase Collection

Purchased ____

Price $ _______

☐ *You Make The Best Of A Rainy Day*, 720018

$65.00
$65.00
$65.00

Limited Ed., Issue Price $65.00, '07 Disney Showcase Collection

Purchased _____

Price $ ________

☐ *It's So Much More Friendly With Two*, 720019

$70.00
$70.00
$70.00

Limited Ed., Issue Price $70.00, '07 Disney Showcase Collection

Purchased ________

Price $ ___________

☐ *Always Reach For The Stars*, 720020

$50.00
$50.00
$50.00

Limited Ed., Issue Price $50.00, '07 Disney Showcase Collection

Purchased __________

Price $ ___________

☐ *Let Your Heart Give You Joy In The Days Of Your Youth*, 720021

$45.00
$45.00
$45.00

Open, Issue Price $45.00, '07

Purchased ___________

Price $_______________

☐ *Felicidades Quinceañera*, 720022

$45.00
$45.00
$45.00

Open, Issue Price $45.00, '07

Purchased_____________

Price $_______________

☐ *Squeaky Clean*, 723011

$45.00 $45.00
$45.00

Set of 3: Squeaky Clean, Ceramic Ducky soap dish and My First Bath rasin frame

Open, Issue Price $45.00, '07 Gift Set

Purchased ________, Price $ ___________

☐ *Mi Quinceanera*, 724007

$70.00 $70.00
$70.00

Set of 3: #720022 Felicidades Quinceanera Figurine, #724001 Photo Frame, and Porcelain Coverred Box

Open, Issue Price $70.00, '07 Gift Set

Purchased ________, Price $ ___________

☐ *My Sweet Sixteen*, 724008

$70.00 $70.00
$70.00

Set of 3: #720021 Let Your Heart Give You Joy In The Days Of Your Youth figurine, #724003 Photo Frame and Porcelain Covered Box.

Open, Issue Price $70.00, '07 Gift Set

Purchased ________, Price $ ___________

☐ *Puppet Show*, 727001 (Frame)

$35.00

Open, Issue Price $35.00, '07 Disney Showcase Collection

Purchased ________, Price $ ___________

☐ *I'm Proud To Be An American (Army),* 729876

★ $45.00	$35.00
$43.00	$35.00
$40.00	$35.00
$40.00	$35.00
$38.00	$35.00
	$35.00

Open, Issue Price $32.50, '99

Purchased ____________

Price $ ____________

☐ *I'm Proud To Be An American (Air Force),* 729914

★ $45.00	$35.00
$43.00	$35.00
$40.00	$35.00
$40.00	$35.00
$38.00	$35.00
	$35.00

Open, Issue Price $32.50, '99

Purchased ____________

Price $ ____________

☐ *I'm Proud To Be An American (Coast Guard),* 729957

★ $45.00	$35.00
$43.00	$35.00
$40.00	$35.00
$40.00	$35.00
$38.00	$35.00
	$35.00

Open, Issue Price $32.50, '99

Purchased ____________

Price $ ____________

☐ *I'm Proud To Be An American (Marine),* 729884

★ $45.00	$35.00
$43.00	$35.00
$40.00	$35.00
$40.00	$35.00
$38.00	$35.00
	$35.00

Open, Issue Price $32.50, '99

Purchased ____________

Price $ ____________

☐ *I'm Proud To Be An American (Army),* 729922

★ $45.00	$35.00
$43.00	$35.00
$40.00	$35.00
$40.00	$35.00
$38.00	$35.00
	$35.00

Open, Issue Price $32.50, '99

Purchased ____________

Price $ ____________

☐ *I'm Proud To Be An American (Air Force),* 729965

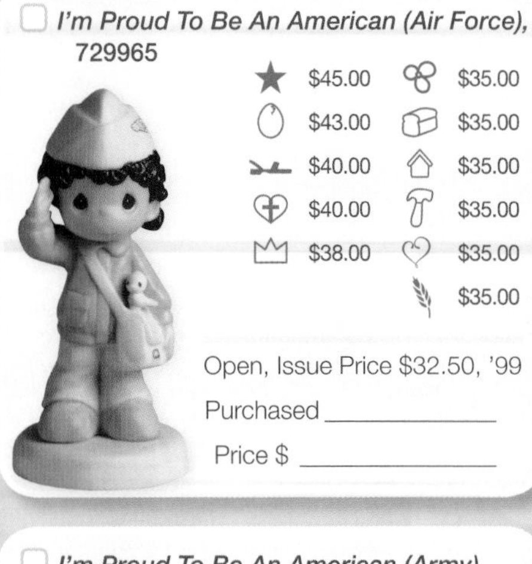

★ $45.00	$35.00
$43.00	$35.00
$40.00	$35.00
$40.00	$35.00
$38.00	$35.00
	$35.00

Open, Issue Price $32.50, '99

Purchased ____________

Price $ ____________

☐ *I'm Proud To Be An American (Navy),* 729892

★ $45.00	$35.00
$43.00	$35.00
$40.00	
$40.00	
$38.00	

Suspended 2005, Issue Price $32.50, '99

Purchased ____________

Price $ ____________

☐ *I'm Proud To Be An American (Marine),* 729930

★ $45.00	$40.00
$43.00	$38.00
$40.00	$35.00
	$35.00

Suspended, Issue Price $32.50, '99

Purchased ____________

Price $ ____________

☐ *I'm Proud To Be An American (Army),* 729973

★ $45.00	$35.00
$43.00	$35.00
$40.00	$35.00
$40.00	$35.00
$38.00	$35.00
	$35.00

Open, Issue Price $32.50, '99

Purchased ____________

Price $ ____________

☐ *I'm Proud To Be An American (Coast Guard),* 729906

★ $45.00	$35.00
$43.00	$35.00
$40.00	$35.00
$40.00	$35.00
$38.00	$35.00
	$35.00

Open, Issue Price $32.50, '99

Purchased ____________

Price $ ____________

☐ *I'm Proud To Be An American (Navy),* 729949

★ $45.00	$35.00
$43.00	$35.00
$40.00	$35.00
$40.00	$35.00
$38.00	$35.00
	$35.00

Open, Issue Price $32.50, '99

Purchased ____________

Price $ ____________

☐ *I Give My Heart To You,* 730001

$35.00
$35.00
$35.00

Open, Issue Price $35.00, '07

Purchased ________, Price $ ____________

You Crafted A Place In My Heart, 730002

$55.00
$55.00

Included heart shaped frame

Retired 2008, Issue Price $50.00, '07
Gift Set

Purchased ________, Price $ ____________

I Fall In Love With You More Each Day, 730006

$50.00
$50.00
$50.00

Open, Issue Price $50.00, '07

Purchased ________, Price $ ____________

It's Never Too Late For Fun With Friends, 730011

$65.00
$65.00
$65.00

Open, Issue Price $65.00, '07
Disney Showcase Collection

Purchased ________, Price $ ____________

Our Hearts Are Interwined With Love, 730003

$50.00
$50.00
$50.00

Open, Issue Price $50.00, '07

Purchased______

Price $________

A Decade of Dreams Come True, 730007

$50.00
$50.00
$50.00

Open, Issue Price $50.00, '07

Purchased _____

Price $ _______

You Make All My Wishes Come True, 730012

$65.00
$65.00
$65.00

Open, Issue Price $65.00, '07
Disney Showcase Collection

Purchased ________, Price $ ____________

Your Love Is A Perfect Fit, 730004

$75.00
$75.00
$75.00

Open, Issue Price $75.00, '07
Disney Showcase Collection

Purchased ________, Price $ ____________

Our Picture Book of Love, 730008

$55.00
$55.00
$55.00

Open, Issue Price $55.00, '07

Purchased ________, Price $ ____________

Discover The Beauty All Around You, 730013

$65.00
$65.00
$65.00

Open, Issue Price $65.00, '07
Disney Showcase Collection

Purchased ___________

Price $___________

Sending All My Love To You, 730005

$40.00
$40.00
$40.00

Open, Issue Price $40.00, '07

Purchased ________, Price $ ____________

I'm Proud To Be An American (Marine), 730009

$45.00 $35.00
$43.00 $35.00
$40.00 $35.00
$40.00 $35.00
$38.00 $35.00
$35.00

Open, Issue Price $32.50, '99

Purchased ___________

Price $ ___________

In The Beginning, 730016

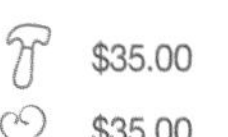

$35.00
$35.00
$35.00

Base says "In The Beginning," Genesis 1:1.

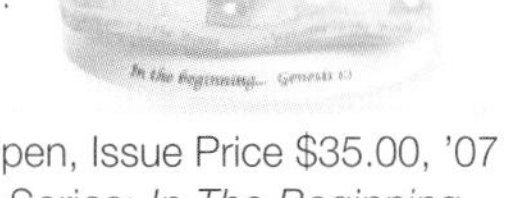

Open, Issue Price $35.00, '07
Series: *In The Beginning*

Purchased ________, Price $ ____________

☐ I'm Proud To Be An American (Navy), 730017

$45.00	$35.00
$43.00	$35.00
$40.00	$35.00
$40.00	$35.00
$38.00	$35.00
	$35.00

Open, Issue Price $32.50, '99

Purchased ______________

Price $ ________________

☐ God Made Heaven And Earth — Age 2, 730018

$35.00
$35.00
$35.00

Base says "God Made Heaven and Earth." Genesis 1:1.

Open, Issue Price $35.00, '07
Series: *In The Beginning*

Purchased ________, Price $ ____________

☐ God Made The Plants And The Trees — Age 3, 730019

$35.00
$35.00
$35.00

Base says "God made the plants and trees." Genesis 1:11.

Open, Issue Price $35, '07
Series: *In The Beginning*

Purchased ________, Price $ ____________

☐ Let There Be Light In The Sky — Age 4, 730020

$35.00
$35.00
$35.00

Base says "Let there light in the sky." Genesis 1:14.

Open, Issue Price $35.00, '07
Series: *In The Beginning*

Purchased ________, Price $ ____________

☐ God Made The Fish And The Birds — Age 5, 730021

$35.00
$35.00
$35.00

Base says "God made the fish and the birds." Genesis 1:21.

Open, Issue Price $35.00 '07
Series: *In The Beginning*

Purchased ________, Price $ ____________

☐ God Made The Animals — Age 6, 730022

Base says "God made the animals.". Genesis 1:124.

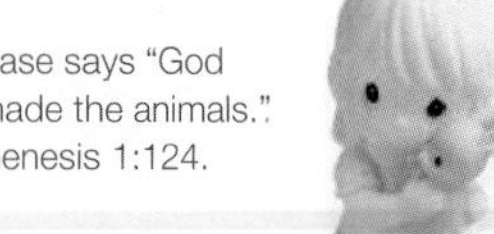

$35.00
$35.00
$35.00

Open, Issue Price $35.00, '07
Series: *In The Beginning*

Purchased ________, Price $ ____________

☐ God Rested — Age 7, 730023

Base says "God rested." Genesis 2:3.

$35.00
$35.00
$35.00

Open, Issue Price $35.00, '07
Series: *In The Beginning*

Purchased ________, Price $ ____________

☐ I'm Proud To Be An American (Coast Guard), 730025

$45.00	$35.00
$43.00	$35.00
$40.00	$35.00
$40.00	$35.00
$38.00	$35.00
	$35.00

Open, Issue Price $32.50, '99

Purchased______________

Price $ ________________

☐ Celebrating The Gift Of Life Now And Forever, 730031

$250.00
$250.00
$250.00

Celebrating Precious Moments 30th Anniversary

Limited 5,030, Issue Price $250.00, '08

Purchased ________, Price $ ____________

☐ Washed Away In Your Love, 730032

$100.00
$100.00

Limited 3,000, Issue Price $100.00, '07

Purchased ________, Price $ ____________

☐ I'm Proud To Be An American (Air Force), 730033

$45.00	$35.00
$43.00	$35.00
$40.00	$35.00
$40.00	$35.00
$38.00	$35.00
	$35.00

Open, Issue Price $32.50, '99

Purchased ______________

Price $ ________________

☐ Grandma, You Insire A Garden Of Dreams, 730034

$50.00
$50.00
$50.00

Open, Issue Price $50.00, '07

Purchased ________, Price $ ____________

☐ *The Path of Love Leads To Grandma,* 730035

$50.00
$50.00
$50.00

Open, Issue Price $50.00, '07

Purchased ________, Price $ ____________

☐ *God Made Night And Day — Age 1,* 730040

$35.00
$35.00
$35.00

Base says "God made night and day." Genesis 1:5.

Open, Issue Price $35.00, '07
Series: *In The Beginning*

Purchased ________, Price $ ____________

☐ *The Future Is In Our Hands,* 730076 (Ornament)

$33.00

Randomly produced with a red cardinal rather than a bluebird.

Dated Annual 2000, Issue Price $19.00, '00

Purchased ________, Price $ ____________

☐ *Make Each Day A Celebration,* 730036

$45.00
$45.00
$45.00

Open, Issue Price $45.00, '07

Purchased ______

Price $ _________

☐ *Gratitude With Attitude,* 730041

$43.00
$43.00
$38.00
$35.00
$35.00
$32.50
$32.50
$32.50

Open, Issue Price $32.50, '01

Purchased ___________

Price $ ____________

☐ *Our First Christmas Together,* 730084 (Ornament)

$33.00

Dated Annual 2000, Issue Price $25.00, '00

Purchased ________, Price $ ____________

☐ *In Seeking Happiness For Others, You Find it For Yourself,* 730037

$45.00
$45.00
$45.00

Open, Issue Price $45.00, '07

Purchased_________

Price $ ___________

☐ *A Garden of Love Blooms In A Grandmother's Heart,* 730042

$40.00
$40.00
$40.00

Open, Issue Price $40.00, '07

Purchased ________, Price $ ____________

☐ *Baby's First Christmas (Girl),* 730092 (Ornament)

$28.00

Dated Annual 2000, Issue Price $19.00, '00

Purchased ________, Price $ ____________

☐ *Rejoice In All You Do,* 730038

$45.00
$45.00
$45.00

Open, Issue Price $45.00, '07

Purchased_____

Price $_________

☐ *The Future Is In Our Hands,* 730068

$50.00

Randomly produced with a red cardinal rather than a bluebird.

Dated Annual 2000, Issue Price $30.00, '00

Purchased__________

Price $ _____________

☐ *Baby's First Christmas (Boy),* 730106 (Ornament)

$28.00

Dated Annual 2000, Issue Price $19.00, '00

Purchased ________, Price $ ____________

☐ ***We're A Family That Sticks Together,* 730114**

$70.00

Limited Ed., Issue Price $40.00, '00
Set of 3

Purchased ________, Price $ ____________

☐ ***Home-Made Of Love,* 730211**

$52.00
$50.00
$48.00
$45.00
$45.00
$45.00

Retired 2005, Issue Price $45.00, '00

Purchased ________, Price $ ____________

☐ ***There's Sno-Boredom With You,* 730122**

$50.00
$48.00
$45.00
$45.00
$45.00
$45.00
$45.00
$45.00

Open, Issue Price $45.00, '00

Purchased ________, Price $ ____________

☐ ***Everything Is Beautiful In Its Own Way,* 730149**

$35.00
$33.00
$30.00
$28.00
$28.00
$28.00

Suspended, Issue Price $25.00, '00

Purchased ________, Price $ ____________

☐ ***I'm A Reflection Of Your Love,* 730238**

UM $45.00

Limited Ed., Issue Price $14.99, '00
Avon Exclusive

Purchased ____________

Price $ ____________

☐ ***Raisin' Cane On The Holidays,* 730130**

$48.00
$45.00
$43.00
$40.00

Suspended 2003, Issue Price $35.00, '00

Purchased____________

Price $ ____________

☐ ***I'll Never Let You Down,* 730165**

$58.00
$55.00
$53.00
$50.00
$50.00
$50.00
$50.00
$50.00
$50.00
$50.00

Open, Issue Price $45.00, '01

Purchased ____________

Price $____________

☐ ***You Have The Beary Best Heart,* 730254**

$55.00
$50.00

Limited Ed., Issue Price $35.00, '01
Authorized Retailer Event 3/10/01
Easter Seals — Lily Understamp

Purchased____________

Price $____________

☐ ***The Peace That Passes Understanding,* 730173**

$160.00
$150.00

Limited Ed. 10,000, Issue Price $100.00, '00
CCR & DSR Exclusive
Set of 7 (Two pilgrims, two Indians, animals, table, and pine tree base which also holds candles)

Purchased ____________

Price $____________

☐ ***The Fun Is Being Together,* 730262**

$250.00
$240.00

Limited Ed. 10,000, Issue Price $200.00, '00
CCR Exclusive, Individually Numbered

Purchased ________, Price $ ____________

Squeaky Clean, 731048

$65.00 | $60.00

Annual 2000, Issue Price $45.00, '00
CCR Event Exclusive

Purchased ________, Price $ ____________

Grandma, I'll Never Outgrow You! 731587

$40.00 | $33.00
$38.00 | $30.00
$35.00 | $30.00

Suspended, Issue Price $25.00, '00
Grandparents' Day Promo

Purchased ________, Price $ ____________

Good Fortune, 731633

★ $35.00 | $25.00
$33.00 | $25.00
$30.00 | $25.00
$28.00 | $25.00
$25.00 | $25.00
$25.00

Open, Issue Price $17.50, '00
Series: *Junishi* — Japanese Exclusive

Purchased ________, Price $ ____________

Take Thyme For Yourself, 731064

$50.00 | $45.00
$48.00 | $43.00
$40.00

Suspended 2004, Issue Price $35.00, '01

Purchased ____________

Price $____________

Grandma, I'll Never Outgrow You! 731595

$40.00 | $33.00
$38.00 | $30.00
$35.00 | $30.00

Suspended, Issue Price $25.00, '00
Grandparents' Day Promo

Purchased ________, Price $ ____________

There Shall Be Fountains Of Blessings, 731668

UM $85.00 | $75.00 | $75.00
$80.00 | $75.00 | $75.00
$75.00

Retired, Issue Price $75.00, '00
Chapel Exclusive

Purchased ________, Price $ ____________

A Collection Of Precious Moments, 731129

★ $35.00 | $28.00
$33.00 | $26.00
$30.00 | $25.00
$25.00

This figurine was part of the Gift Set #745510

Out of Production, Issue Price $25.00, '00

Purchased ____________

Price $ ____________

Everybody Has A Part, 731625

★ $95.00 | $85.00 | $85.00
$93.00 | $85.00 | $85.00
$90.00 | $85.00 | $85.00
$88.00 | $85.00

Open, Issue Price $50.00, '00
Japanese Exclusive, Set of 3

Purchased ________, Price $ ____________

Sharing Sweet Moments Together, 731579

UM $35.00
★ $30.00
$27.50

Limited Ed., Issue Price $20.00, '00
Series: *Little Moments*
2000 Sweetest Day Promo

Purchased ________, Price $ ____________

Our Loss Is Heaven's Gain, 731676

UM $45.00 | $30.00
$43.00 | $30.00
$40.00 | $30.00
$35.00 | $30.00

Open, Issue Price $30.00, '00
Chapel Exclusive

Purchased ________, Price $ ____________

☐ ***Fall Festival*, 732494**

Barn is a nightlight.

$160.00
$158.00
$155.00
$150.00
$150.00
$150.00

Out of Production, Issue Price $150.00, '00
Set of 7

Purchased ____________

Price $ ____________

☐ ***You Color My World With Love*, 740001**

$35.00
$35.00
$35.00

First 2,000 figurines with 2007 Hammer mark.

Open, Issue Price $35.00, '07

Purchased ________, Price $ ____________

☐ ***You Color My World With Love*, 740002**

$35.00
$35.00
$35.00

First 2,000 figurines with 2007 Hammer mark.

Open, Issue Price $35.00, '07

Purchased ________, Price $ ____________

☐ ***You Should Be As Proud As A Peacock — Congratulations*, 733008**

$30.00
$30.00
$27.50
$27.50
$27.50
$27.50
$27.50
$27.50

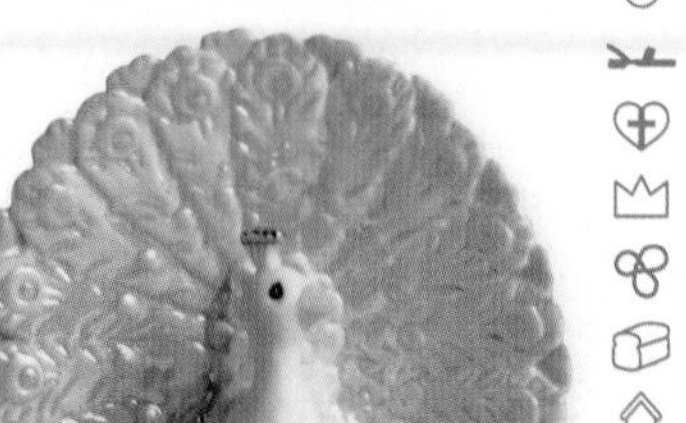

Open, Issue Price $27.50, '00

Purchased ________, Price $ ____________

☐ ***One Good Turn Deserves Another*, 737569 (Ornament)**

$28.00
$25.00
$23.00
$20.00
$20.00
$20.00
$20.00
$20.00

Open, Issue Price $20.00, '00
Series: *Precious Scape*

Purchased ________, Price $ ____________

☐ ***A Mother's Loving Touch Is A Gift From God*, 740003**

$45.00
$45.00

Includes figurine and book: "The love of a Godly mother."

Open, Issue Price $45.00, Gift Set, '07

Purchased ________, Price $ ____________

☐ ***You Have A Special Place In My Heart*, 737534**

$85.00

Limited Ed., Issue Price $55.00, '00
Series: *Christmas Remembered*

Purchased _____

Price $ _______

☐ ***Behold The Lord*, 737607**

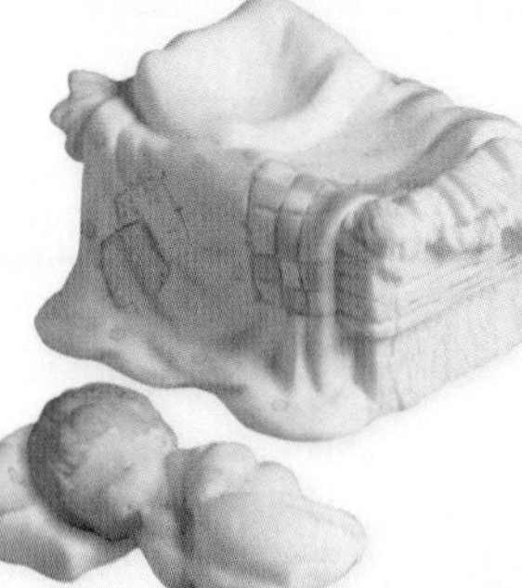

$30.00
$28.00
$25.00
$25.00
$25.00
$25.00
$25.00
$25.00

Open, Issue Price $25.00, '00
Nativity Addition, Set of 3

Purchased ________, Price $ ____________

☐ ***Sure Could Use Less Hustle And Bustle*, 737550**

$55.00
$53.00
$50.00
$48.00
$45.00
$40.00
$40.00
$40.00
$40.00
$40.00

Open, Issue Price $37.50, '00
Series: *Christmas Remembered*

Purchased ____________

Price $ ____________

☐ ***Auntie, You Make Beauty Blossom*, 737623**

$45.00
$43.00
$40.00
$40.00
$40.00
$40.00

Suspended, Issue Price $40.00, '00

Purchased ____________

Price $ ____________

☐ ***Gentle Is A Mother's Love*, 740004**

$70.00
$70.00

Open, Issue Price $70.00, '08

Purchased ____

Price $________

The Simple Bare Neccessities, 740006

$60.00
$60.00
$60.00

First 2,000 figurines with 2007 Hammer mark

Open, Issue Price $60.00, '07
Disney Showcase Collection

Purchased ________, Price $ ____________

With A Smile and A Song, 740007

$75.00
$75.00
$75.00

First 2,000 figurines with 2007 Hammer mark.

Open, Issue Price $75.00, '07
Disney Showcase Collection

Purchased ________, Price $ ____________

Come Along And Sing The Song, 740009

$65.00
$65.00

Open, Issue Price $65.00, '07
Disney Showcase Collection

Purchased ________, Price $ ____________

You Are The Bright Spot Of My Day, 740010

$65.00
$65.00

Open, Issue Price $65.00, '08
Disney Showcase Collection

Purchased ________, Price $ ____________

I know Who Holds The Future, 740011

$50.00
$50.00

Open, Issue Price $50.00, '08
Purchased ____________
Price $ ______________

Your Future Is So Rosy, 740012

Includes figurine and photo frame. (The figurine is different than #740011, which is elongated.)

$55.00
$55.00

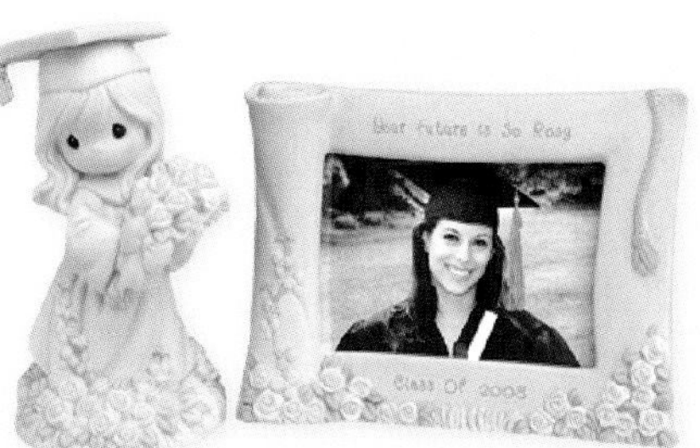

Open, Gift Set, Issue Price $55.00, '08

Purchased ________, Price $ ____________

A World Of Possibilities Lies Ahead, 740013

$42.50
$42.50

Open, Issue Price $42.50, '08
Purchased ____________
Price $______________

Growing In Grace Starter Set – Blonde, 740015

$35.00
$35.00

Includes #740016 figurine and photo frame.

Open, Gift Set, Issue Price $35.00, '08

Purchased ________, Price $ ____________

It's A Girl – Blonde, 740016

$25.00
$25.00

Open, Issue Price $25.00, '08

Purchased ________, Price $ ____________

It's A Girl – Brunette, 740017

$25.00
$25.00

Open, Issue Price $25.00, '08
Purchased _____
Price $ ________

My Soldier, My Hero, 740018

$50.00
$50.00
$50.00

First 2,000 figurines with 2007 Hammer mark.

Open, Issue Price $50.00, '07

Purchased ________, Price $ ____________

Welcome Home My Hero, 740019

$30.00
$30.00
$30.00

Open, Issue Price $30.00, '07

Purchased ________, Price $ ____________

☐ **Welcome Home My Hero, 740020**

$30.00
$30.00
$30.00

Open, Issue Price $30.00, '08

Purchased ________, Price $ __________

☐ **Be Strong and Courageous, 740024**

$35.00
$35.00
$35.00

Open, Issue Price $35.00, '07
Series: *Bible Story Heroes*

Purchased ________, Price $ __________

☐ **Growing In Grace Starter Set — Brunette, 740040**

$35.00
$35.00
$35.00

Includes #740017 figurine and photo frame.

Open, Gift Set, Issue Price $35.00, '07

Purchased ________, Price $ __________

☐ **I Have Set My Rainbow In The Clouds, 740021**

$35.00
$35.00
$35.00

Open, Issue Price $35.00, '07
Series: *Bible Story Heroes*

Purchased ________, Price $ __________

☐ **I Have Spoken To You From Heaven, 740025**

$35.00
$35.00
$35.00

Open, Issue Price $35.00, '07
Series: *Bible Story Heroes*

Purchased ________, Price $ __________

☐ **Do This In Memory Of Me, 740050**

$60.00
$60.00
$60.00

Includes #640022 figurine and cross box.

Open, Gift Set, Issue Price $60.00, '07

Purchased ________, Price $ __________

☐ **The Lord Was With Joseph, 740022**

$35.00
$35.00
$35.00

Open, Issue Price $35.00, '07
Series: *Bible Story Heroes*

Purchased ________, Price $ __________

☐ **The Lord Is My Rock, 740026**

$35.00
$35.00
$35.00

Open, Issue Price $35.00, '07
Series: *Bible Story Heroes*

Purchased ________, Price $ __________

☐ **You're A Real Barbe-cutie, 742872**

$38.00 $35.00
$35.00 $35.00
$35.00 $35.00
$35.00

Open, Issue Price $35.00, '01
Series: *Special Wishes*

Purchased __________

Price $ __________

☐ **How Mighty Are Wonders, 740023**

$35.00
$35.00
$35.00

Open, Issue Price $35.00, '07
Series: *Bible Story Heroes*

Purchased ________, Price $ __________

☐ **They Will Know Us By Our Love, 740031**

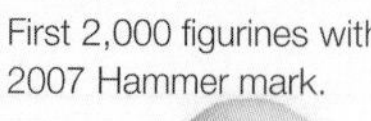

First 2,000 figurines with 2007 Hammer mark.

$50.00
$50.00
$50.00

Open, Issue Price $50.00, '07

Purchased _____

Price $_________

☐ **To The Sweetest Girl In The Cast, 742880**

$40.00 $35.00
$38.00 $35.00
$35.00 $35.00
$35.00 $35.00

Open, Issue Price $35.00, '01

Purchased __________

Price $ __________

☐ You Add Sparkle To My Life, 745413

$45.00

Limited Ed., Issue Price $25.00, '01
Series: *Heavenly Daze* — First Issue
Care-A-Van Exclusive

Purchased ________, Price $ ____________

☐ A Collection Of Precious Moments, 745510

★ $50.00
$48.00

Gift Set came with a copy of the book *Chicken Soup for the Soul*.

Retired 2000, Issue Price $27.00, '99

Purchased ____________
Price $____________

☐ Let Earth Receive Her King, 748382

UM $40.00
$39.00
$38.00
$35.00
$33.00
$32.50

Retired 2004, Issue Price $32.50, '00
Chapel Exclusive

Purchased ________, Price $ ____________

☐ Let Earth Receive Her King, 748390 (Ornament)

UM $27.50
$27.00
$26.00
$25.00
$25.00
$25.00

Out of Production, Issue Price $25.00, '00
Chapel Exclusive

Purchased ________, Price $ ____________

☐ Whale Have Oceans Of Fun, 748412

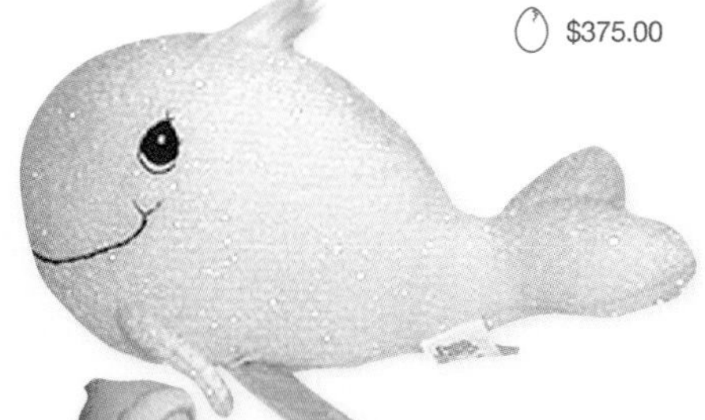

$375.00

Given to those who attended the Precious Moments Cruise to Alaska. June 10 – 17, 2000.

Limited Ed., Gift, '00
2000 Cruise Exclusive

Purchased ________, Price $ ____________

☐ Christmas Street Precious Scape, 750123

For displaying pieces. UM $25.00

Open, Issue Price $25.00, '00
Series: *Precious Scape*

Purchased ____________
Price $____________

☐ Eat Turkey, 763225

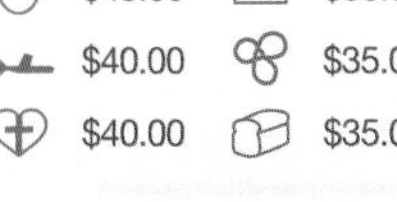

$43.00 $38.00
$40.00 $35.00
$40.00 $35.00

Suspended, Issue Price $25.00, '00
Series: *Country Lane Collection*

Purchased ________
Price $ ____________

☐ You Are Always In My Heart, 768952

$50.00
$48.00

Limited Ed., Issue Price $40.00, '01

Purchased ________, Price $ ____________

☐ You Are Always In My Heart, 768987

$50.00
$48.00

Limited Ed., Issue Price $40.00, '01

Purchased ________, Price $ ____________

☐ May Your Days Be Rosy, 781770

$60.00 $55.00
$58.00 $55.00

Suspended 2004, Issue Price $30.00, '00

Purchased ____________
Price $____________

☐ May Your Days Be Rosy, 781770C

$45.00
$40.00

Limited Ed., Issue Price $30.00, '00
Carlton Cards Exclusive

Purchased ________, Price $ ____________

☐ Sugar Town Enhancement Set, 770272

Series: *Sugar Town*, Set of 7: Double Tree, Lamp Post, Straight Sidewalk, Cobblestone Bridge, Curved Road, Mailbox, and Single Tree.

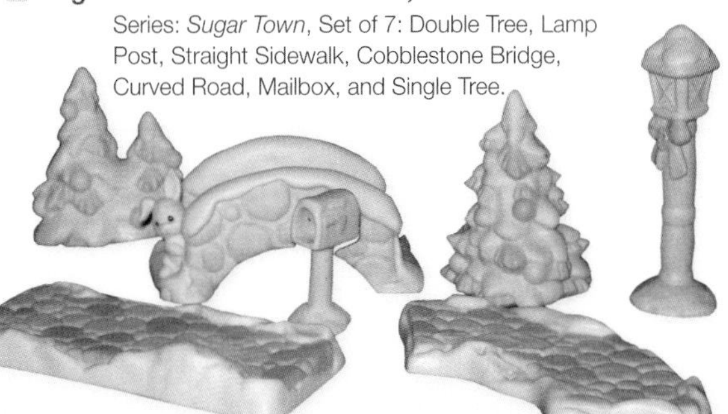

$87.00
$85.00
$83.00
$81.00

Retired 1997, Issue Price $70.00, '94

Purchased ____________
Price $____________

☐ *Mr. Fujioka, 781851*

$60.00

$60.00

Annual 2001, Issue Price $25.00, '01

Purchased ____________

Price $ ______________

☐ *Sharing Sweet Moments Together, 786152*

$30.00

$30.00

Limited Ed., Issue Price $25.00, '00

Purchased ________, Price $ ____________

☐ *Your Love Keeps Me Toasty Warm, 788031*

$55.00

$55.00

Limited Ed., Issue Price $39.95, '00
Winter Syndicated Exclusive

Purchased ________, Price $ ____________

☐ *Christmas Trees Precious Scape, 788171*

UM $45.00

Out of Production, Issue Price $30.00, '00
Set of 3
Series: *Precious Scape*

Purchased ________, Price $ ____________

☐ *Love Wrapped Up With A Bow, 790007*

$35.00

Limited Ed., Issue Price $35.00, '07
Hallmark Exclusive

Purchased ____________

Price $______________

☐ *Where Dreams Come True, 790010*

$135.00

$130.00

First 500 figurines sold at the Walt Disney World event held June 15 – 16, 2007, were pre-signed by Gene Freedman. Those attending the event were later mailed a certificate.

Limited Ed. 1,186, Issue Price $65.00, '07
Disney Theme Park Exclusive

Purchased ________, Price $ ____________

☐ *Get Your Kicks On Route 66, 790011*

UM $400.00

$385.00

Given as part of the 2007 Chapel Family Reunion event package. Pre-signed by Sam.

LImited Ed. 1,000, Issue Price $55.00, '07
Chapel Exclusive

Purchased ________, Price $ ____________

☐ *Nature's Beauty Inspires The Heart and Soul, 790012*

$65.00

Given to those who went on the New England/ Canadian Cruise September 8 – 15, 2007.

Limited Ed., Gift, '07

Purchased ________

Price $____________

☐ *Thankful for The Memories Of Good Times With Friends, 790013*

$65.00

Given to those who went on the New England/ Canadian Cruise September 8 – 15, 2007.

Limited Ed., Gift, '07

Purchased ________, Price $ ____________

☐ *Sharing Of Ourselves Brings A Wealth Of Joy, 790014*

$65.00

Given to those who went on the New England/Canadian Cruise September 8 – 15, 2007.

Limited Ed., Gift, '07

Purchased ________, Price $ ____________

☐ *Spread Your Wings And Fly, 790015D*

$75.00

$75.00

LImited Ed. 1,000, Issue Price $75.00, '07
Disney Theme Park Exclusive

Purchased ________, Price $ ____________

☐ *You are My Cup Of Tea, 790016D*

$75.00

LImited Ed. 1,000, Issue Price $75.00, '08
Disney Theme Park Exclusive

Purchased ____

Price $ _______

☐ ***I Give This Rose As A Token Of My Love,* 790018**

$50.00
$50.00

Open, Issue Price $50.00, '08
Carlton Cards/American Greetings Early Release

Purchased ________, Price $ ___________

☐ ***Rhythm And Flute,* 791091**

$100.00
$90.00
$80.00
$70.00
$60.00
$60.00

Out of Production, Issue Price $80.00, '00
Series: *Girl's Festival* — Set of 5
CCR Exclusive, Japanese Exclusive

Purchased ________, Price $ ___________

☐ ***I Give My Heart To You,* 790019**

$35.00

Came with a heart-shaped frame.

Limited Ed., Issue Price $35.00, '08
Hallmark Exclusive

Purchased ________, Price $ ___________

☐ ***Minnie and Me,* 790022DW**

Released on June 14 and 15, 2008, at Disney World Park signing with Hiko Meada. First 500 pieces sold at Disney World featured the bottom-stamp and debut date.

$70.00
$70.00

Disney Showcase Collection

Limited 500, Issue Price $70.00, '08
Disney Showcase Collection

Purchased ________, Price $ ___________

☐ ***Bringing In Another Grrreat Year,* 791121**

$125.00 $110.00
$115.00 $105.00

Retired, Issue Price $60.00, '00
CCR Exclusive, Japanese Exclusive

Purchased ________, Price $ ___________

☐ ***The Greatest Joy Is Motherhood,* 790021**

$45.00
$45.00

Limited Ed., Issue Price $45.00, '08
Carlton Cards/American Greeting Early Release

Purchased ________, Price $ ___________

☐ ***Minnie and Me,* 790022 DL**

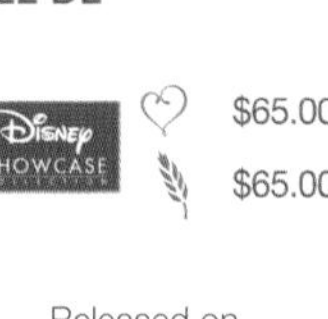

Disney Showcase Collection

$65.00
$65.00

Released on June 7, 2008, at Disney Theme Parks.

Open, Issue Price $65.00, '08
Disney Showcase Collection

Purchased ________, Price $ ___________

☐ ***Courteous Service,* 791113**

$100.00 $60.00
$90.00 $60.00
$80.00
$70.00

Out of Production, Issue Price $60.00, '00
Series: *Girl's Festival* — Set of 3
CCR Exclusive, Japanese Exclusive

Purchased ________, Price $ ___________

☐ ***Different Beats Can Still Come Together,* 791148**

$60.00 $55.00 $55.00
$55.00 $55.00 $55.00
$55.00 $55.00 $55.00

Open, Issue Price $55.00, '01
Set of 3, CCR Exclusive, Japanese Exclusive

Purchased ________, Price $ ___________

☐ *You Are The Queen Of My Heart*, 795151

$60.00

Limited Ed., Issue Price $50.00, '01

Purchased ________

Price $____________

☐ *You Will Always Be Mine*, 795186

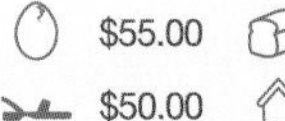

$55.00 $45.00
$50.00 $45.00
$45.00 $45.00
$45.00 $45.00
$45.00

Open, Issue Price $45.00, '01
Set of 2

Purchased ________, Price $ ____________

☐ *You Can't Hide From God*, 795194

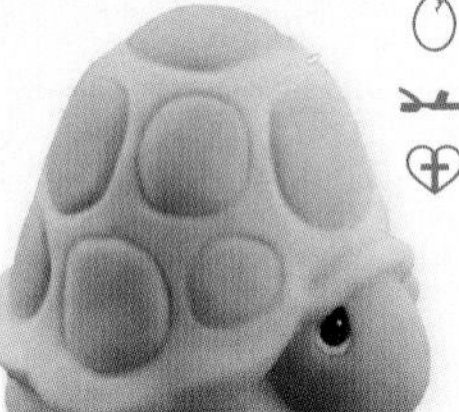

$28.00 $20.00
$25.00 $20.00
$23.00 $20.00

Suspended, Issue Price $18.50, '01

Purchased ________, Price $ ____________

☐ *The Lord Can Dew Anything*, 795208

$50.00 $43.00
$45.00 $40.00
$40.00

Retired 2004, Issue Price $35.00, '01

Purchased ________

Price $ ____________

☐ *Cherish Every Step*, 795224

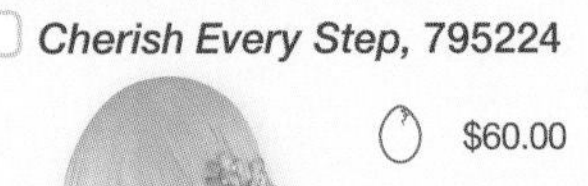

$60.00 $50.00
$55.00 $50.00
$50.00 $50.00
$50.00 $50.00

Open, Issue Price $50.00, '01
Series: *Motherhood*
— Second Issue

Purchased ________

Price $____________

☐ *You're A Dandy Mom And I'm Not Lion*, 795232V

Came with a crystal vase and 15% gift card for FTD.com.

$50.00
$45.00

Retired 2001, Issue Price $27.50, '00

Purchased____________

Price $ ____________

☐ *It's A Banner Day, Congratulations*, 795259

$35.00
$32.50
$32.50
$32.50
$25.00
$25.00
$25.00
$25.00

Open, Issue Price $25.00, '01

Purchased ________, Price $ ____________

☐ *You Are The Wind Beneath My Wings*, 795267

$35.00 $35.00
$35.00 $35.00
$35.00 $35.00

Suspended, Issue Price $35.00, '01

Purchased ____________

Price $ ____________

☐ *You're As Sweet As Apple Pie*, 795275

$48.00
$45.00
$43.00
$38.00
$38.00

Suspended 2004, Issue Price $35.00, '01

Purchased ________, Price $ ____________

☐ *You're A Honey*, 795283

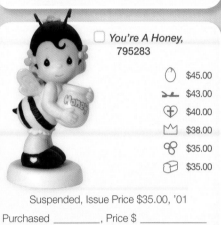

$45.00
$43.00
$40.00
$38.00
$35.00
$35.00

Suspended, Issue Price $35.00, '01

Purchased ________, Price $ ____________

☐ *O-Fish-Aly Friends For A Lifetime*, 795305

$60.00 $55.00
$50.00
$50.00
$50.00
$50.00
$50.00
$50.00

Open, Issue Price $50.00, '01

Purchased ________, Price $ ____________

☐ *Wishing You A Birthday Full Of Surprises*, 795313

$48.00
$48.00
$45.00
$43.00
$43.00
$43.00

Suspended 2005, Issue Price $40.00, '01

Purchased ________, Price $ ____________

☐ *No Bones About It — You're Grrreat,* 795321

$45.00
$40.00
$40.00
$40.00
$40.00

Suspended, Issue Price $40.00, '01
Series: *Special Wishes*

Purchased ________, Price $ ____________

☐ *Groom (African-American),* 795372

$35.00 $30.00
$30.00 $30.00
$30.00 $30.00
$30.00 $30.00
$30.00 $30.00

Open, Issue Price $30.00, '01

Purchased ____________

Price $ ______________

☐ *Groom (Asian),* 795410

$35.00 $30.00
$30.00 $30.00
$30.00 $30.00
$30.00 $30.00
$30.00 $30.00

Open, Issue Price $30.00, '01

Purchased ____________

Price $ ______________

☐ *Blessed With A Loving Godmother,* 795348

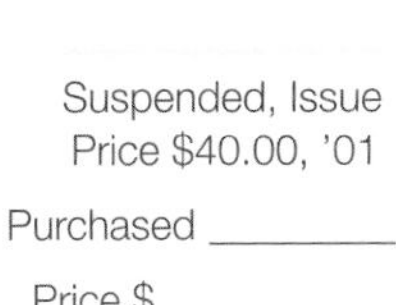

$55.00 $48.00
$53.00 $45.00
$50.00 $43.00

Suspended, Issue Price $40.00, '01

Purchased ________

Price $ _________

☐ *Bride (Hispanic),* 795380

$35.00 $30.00
$30.00 $30.00
$30.00 $30.00
$30.00 $30.00

Suspended 2005, Issue Price $30.00, '01

Purchased ____________

Price $ ______________

☐ *Friendship Grows From The Heart,* 795496

UM $65.00

Limited Ed. 1,500, Issue Price $35.00, '01
2001 Licensee Event Exclusive

Purchased ________

Price $__________

☐ *Life Would Be The Pits Without Friends,* 795356

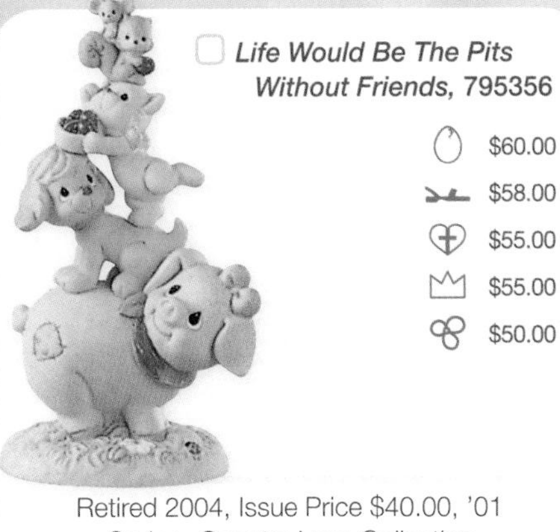

$60.00
$58.00
$55.00
$55.00
$50.00

Retired 2004, Issue Price $40.00, '01
Series: *Country Lane Collection*

Purchased ________, Price $ ____________

☐ *Groom (Hispanic),* 795399

$35.00 $30.00
$30.00 $30.00
$30.00 $30.00
$30.00 $30.00

Suspended 2005, Issue Price $30.00, '01

Purchased ________, Price $ ____________

☐ *On Our Way To The Chapel,* 795518

UM $40.00 $32.50
$35.00 $32.50
$32.50 $32.50
$32.50 $32.50

Open, Issue Price $32.50, '00
Chapel Exclusive

Purchased ____________

Price $ ______________

☐ *Bride (African-American),* 795364

$35.00 $30.00
$30.00 $30.00
$30.00 $30.00
$30.00 $30.00
$30.00 $30.00

Open, Issue Price $30.00, '01

Purchased __________

Price $ ___________

☐ *Bride (Asian),* 795402

$35.00 $30.00
$30.00 $30.00
$30.00 $30.00
$30.00 $30.00
$30.00 $30.00

Open, Issue Price $30.00, '01

Purchased __________

Price $ ___________

☐ *You Tug On My Heart Strings,* 795526

$70.00
$68.00
$65.00
$63.00
$60.00
$60.00
$60.00
$60.00

Annual 2001, Issue Price $60.00, '01
Boys & Girls Club of America Exclusive

Purchased ________, Price $ ____________

Your Love Keeps Me Toasty Warm, 795577 (Ornament)

$40.00
$40.00

Limited Ed. 2000, Issue Price $25.00, '00
GCC Exclusive

Purchased ____________
Price $ ____________

Konnichiwa Friends, 796581

$85.00

Gift to those who attended one of the five regional events in 2001. The event locations and dates were 8/25/01 Columbus, OH; 9/8/01 Oakland, CA; 10/2001 Valley Forge, PA; 11/07/01 Des Moines, IA; and 12/01/01 Savannah, GA.

Limited Ed., Gift, '02
2001 Regional Event Exclusive

Purchased ________, Price $ ____________

You're Just Too Thweet, 797693 (Box)

$25.00
$22.50
$22.50
$22.50

Out of Production, Issue Price $22.50, '02

Purchased ________, Price $ ____________

Grandma, I'll Never Outgrow You! 798223

$38.00
$35.00

Limited Ed., Issue Price $25.00, '00

Purchased ________, Price $ ____________

Grandma, I'll Never Outgrow You! 798231

$38.00
$35.00

Limited Ed., Issue Price $25.00, '00

Purchased ____________
Price $ ____________

I'll Give You The World, 798290 (Hinged Box)

$16.00
$15.00

Limited Ed., Issue Price $12.50, '00
Catalog Exclusive

Purchased ________, Price $ ____________

Your Love Keeps Me Toasty Warm, 800813 (Ornament)

$38.00

Annual 2000, Issue Price $25.00, '00

Purchased ________, Price $ ____________

I Give You My Heart, 801313

$50.00
$45.00

Also issued in 2000 as a limited edition Carlton Cards Early Release (801313C); Egg mark, $55.00, Sandal mark, $50.00.

Limited Ed., Issue Price $30.00, '01
CCR Exclusive

Purchased ________, Price $ ____________

Sweetheart Safari, 802484 (Medallion)

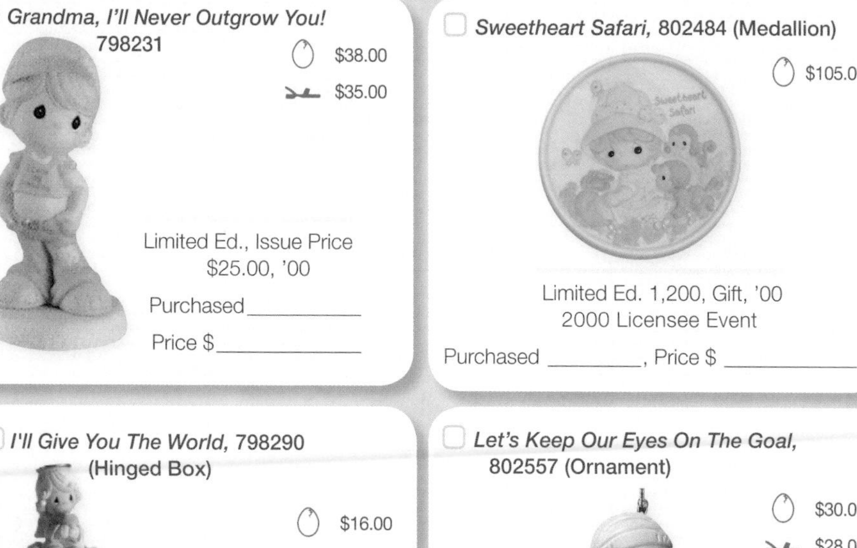

$105.00

Limited Ed. 1,200, Gift, '00
2000 Licensee Event

Purchased ________, Price $ ____________

Let's Keep Our Eyes On The Goal, 802557 (Ornament)

$30.00
$28.00

Limited Ed., Issue Price $20.00, '01
Canadian Exclusive

Purchased ________, Price $ ____________

Ready In The "Nick" Of Time, 804088

UM $275.00
$250.00

Limited Ed. 1,500, Issue Price $45.00, '00
2000 Christmas Event

Purchased ________, Price $ ____________

A Godchild Close To My Heart, 804096

$40.00
$37.50
$35.00
$32.50
$30.00
$27.50
$27.50
$27.50
$27.50
$27.50

Open, Issue Price $25.00, '01

Purchased ________, Price $ ____________

Happy Anniversary, 804444

$35.00

$35.00

Llmited Ed. 2003,
Issue Price $35.00, '03
DSR & CCR Exclusive
One day only,
June 21, 2003

Purchased ________

Price $ ________

Blessings Of Peace To You, 810001

$35.00

$35.00

Annual 2008, Issue
Price $35.00, '08

Purchased ________

Price $________

Blessings Of Peace To You, 810002
(Ornament)

$20.00

$20.00

Annual 2008, Issue
Price $20.00, '08

Purchased ________

Price $ ________

Blessings Of Peace To You, 810003
(Ornament)

$30.00

$30.00

Annual 2008, Issue
Price $30.00, '08

Purchased ________

Price $________

Our First Christmas Together, 810004
(Ornament)

$25.00

$25.00

Annual 2008, Issue
Price $25.00, '08

Purchased ________

Price $ ________

Baby's First Christmas — Girl, 810005
(Ornament)

$20.00

$20.00

Annual 2008, Issue
Price $20.00, '08

Purchased________

Price $________

Baby's First Christmas — Boy, 810006
(Ornament)

$20.00

$20.00

Annual 2008, Issue
Price $20.00, '08

Purchased________

Price $________

Peace Be Within You, 810007
(Ornament)

$25.00

$25.00

Annual 2008, Issue
Price $25.00, '08

Purchased ________

Price $ ________

Your Love Warms My Heart, 810008

$125.00

$125.00

Limited Ed. 5,000, Issue Price $125.00, '08

Purchased ________, Price $ ________

Born The King Of Angels, 810009
(Ornament)

$25.00

$25.00

Open, Issue Price
$25.00, '08

Purchased ________

Price $ ________

Come Let Us Adore Him, 810011

$150.00

$150.00

Open, Issue Price $150.00, '08
Set of 9

Purchased ________, Price $ ________

Come Let Us Adore Him, 810012

$60.00

$60.00

Open, Issue Price $60.00, '08
Set of 3

Purchased ________, Price $ ________

Come Let Us Adore Him, 810013
(Mini)

$150.00

$150.00

Open, Issue Price $150.00, '08
Set of 11

Purchased ________, Price $ ________

Come Let Us Adore Him, 810014
(Mini)

$40.00

$40.00

Open, Issue Price
$40.00, '08
Set of 3

Purchased ________, Price $ ________

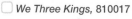

☐ *We Three Kings,* 810017

$80.00
$80.00

Open, Issue Price $80.00, '08

Purchased ________, Price $ ____________

☐ *Peace,* 810018

$75.00
$75.00

Open, Issue Price $75.00, '08

Purchased ________, Price $ ____________

☐ *My Art Says "I Love You" – Girl,* 810019

$35.00
$35.00

Open, Issue Price $35.00, '08
Series: *Crayola® Collection*
Official Licensed Product

Purchased ________, Price $ ____________

☐ *My Art Says "I Love You" – Boy,* 810020

$35.00
$35.00

Open, Issue Price $35.00, '08
Series: *Crayola® Collection*
Official Licensed Product

Purchased ________, Price $ ____________

☐ *The Color Of Love,* 810021

$42.00
$42.00

Open, Issue Price $42.00, '08
Series: *Crayola® Collection*
Official Licensed Product

Purchased ________, Price $ ____________

☐ *Drawing Us Closer Together,* 810022

$55.00
$55.00

Open, Issue Price $55.00, '08
Series: *Crayola® Collection*
Official Licensed Product

Purchased ________, Price $ ____________

☐ *A Season Of Joy And Togetherness,* 810023

$75.00
$75.00

Open, Issue Price $75.00, '08
Series: *Crayola® Collection*
Official Licensed Product

Purchased ________, Price $ ____________

☐ *Filled With Wonder And Joy On This Special Night,* 810024

$65.00
$65.00

Open, Issue Price $65.00, '08

Purchased ________, Price $ ____________

☐ *Holidays Are A Time For Comfort And Warmth,* 810025

$60.00
$60.00

Open, Issue Price $60.00, '08

Purchased _____

Price $_________

☐ *Nurses Are There In Our Time Of Need,* 810026 (Ornament)

$20.00
$20.00

Open, Issue Price $20.00, '08

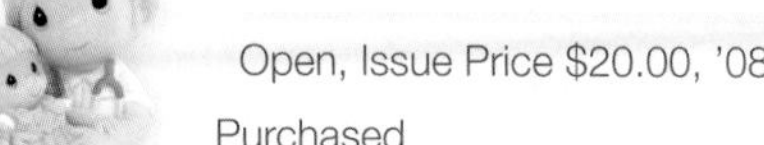

Purchased ____________

Price $ ______________

☐ *Sisters Are Precious Gifts,* 810027 (Ornament)

$20.00
$20.00

Open, Issue Price $20.00, '08

Purchased____________

Price $______________

☐ *Grandmother, Your Memories Fill My Heart,* 810028 (Ornament)

$20.00
$20.00

Open, Issue Price $20.00, '08

Purchased ____________

Price $ ______________

☐ *Behold The Spirit Of Christmas In Your Hands,* 810029

$50.00
$50.00

Open, Issue Price $50.00, '08

Purchased ____

Price $ ______

☐ *Wishing For Wonderful Things This Joyous Season,* 810030 (Ornament)

$20.00
$20.00

Open, Issue Price $20.00, '08

Purchased____________

Price $____________

☐ *Now You Can Fly,* 810037

$60.00
$60.00

Open, Issue Price $60.00, '08 Disney Showcase Collection

Purchased__________

Price $__________

☐ *Birthday Wishes From My World To Yours,* 810039

$65.00
$65.00

Open, Issue Price $65.00, '08 Disney Showcase Collection

Purchased ______

Price $ ______

☐ *A Warm Holidays Wish For You,* 810031 (Ornament)

$20.00
$20.00

Open, Issue Price $20.00, '08

Purchased ____________

Price $____________

☐ *Now You Can Fly,* 810037DW

First 250 pieces sold at Disney World Resort featured a special debut date and bottom stamp.

$85.00
$85.00

LImited 250, Issue Price $60.00, '08 Disney Showcase Collection

Purchased ________, Price $ ____________

☐ *Birthday Wishes From My World To Yours,* 810039DW

First 250 pieces sold at Disney World Resort featured a special debut date and bottom stamp.

$75.00
$75.00

LImited 250, Issue Price $65.00, '08 Disney Showcase Collection

Purchased ________, Price $ ____________

☐ *The Spirit Of Christmas Shines This Season,* 810032 (Ornament)

$20.00
$20.00

Open, Issue Price $20.00, '08

Purchased ______________

Price $ ______________

☐ *It Is In Giving That We Receive,* 810038

$70.00
$70.00

Open, Issue Price $70.00, '08 Disney Showcase Collection

Purchased _____

Price $________

☐ *Knowing You're In Love With Me Is The Greatest Gift Of All,* 810040

$200.00
$200.00

LImited Ed. 5,000, Issue Price $200.00, '08 Disney Showcase Collection

Purchased ________, Price $ ____________

☐ *It Is A Happy Heart That Holds A Friend,* 810035 (Ornament)

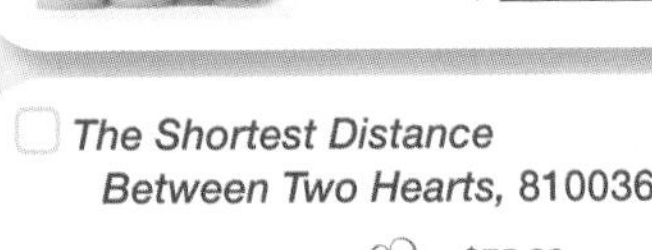

$25.00
$25.00

Open, Issue Price $20.00, '08

Purchased____________

Price $ ____________

☐ *It Is In Giving That We Receive,* 810038DW

First 250 pieces sold at Disney World Resort featured a special debut date and bottom stamp.

$70.00
$70.00

LImited 250, Issue Price $70.00, '08 Disney Showcase Collection

Purchased ________, Price $ ____________

☐ *The Season Is More Joyous Amongst Friends,* 810041

$70.00
$70.00

Open, Issue Price $70.00, '08 Disney Showcase Collection

Purchased________

Price $__________

☐ *The Shortest Distance Between Two Hearts,* 810036

$75.00
$75.00

Open, Issue Price $75.00, '08 Disney Showcase Collection

Purchased ______________

Price $______________

☐ *The Shortest Distance Between Two Hearts,* 810036DW

First 250 pieces sold at Disney World Resort featured a special debut date and bottom stamp

$85.00
$85.00

LImited 250, Issue Price $75.00, '08 Disney Showcase Collection

Purchased______________

Price $ ______________

☐ *The Season Is More Joyous Amongst Friends,* 810041DW

First 250 pieces sold at Disney World Resort featured a special debut date and bottom stamp.

$80.00
$80.00

LImited 250, Issue Price $70.00, '08 Disney Showcase Collection

Purchased ________, Price $ ____________

☐ *Hanging My Stocking With Care,* 810042 (Ornament)

$20.00
$20.00

Open, Issue Price $20.00, '08

Purchased ____________

Price $ ____________

☐ *Trim The Tree With Angelic Beauty,* 810043 (Ornament)

$20.00
$20.00

Open, Issue Price $20.00, '08

Purchased ____________

Price $____________

☐ *Dressing Up For The Holidays,* 810044 (Ornament)

$20.00
$20.00

Open, Issue Price $20.00, '08

Purchased ____________

Price $____________

☐ *May All Of Your Wishes Come True,* 810045

$55.00
$55.00

Open, Issue Price $55.00, '08

Purchased ________, Price $ ____________

☐ *A Heart Filled With Warmth And Wishes,* 810046

$45.00
$45.00

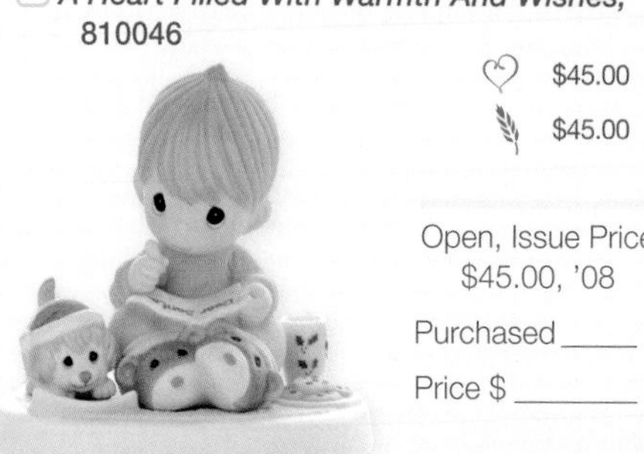

Open, Issue Price $45.00, '08

Purchased _____

Price $ _______

☐ *A Picture Perfect Memory Of A Special Day,* 810047

$60.00
$60.00

Open, Issue Price $60.00, '08

Purchased _____

Price $ ________

☐ *Wishing You Every Wonderful Thing That The Season Brings,* 810048

$55.00
$55.00

Open, Issue Price $55.00, '08

Purchased _____

Price $ ________

☐ *A Candid Christmas,* 810049 (Ornament)

$20.00
$20.00

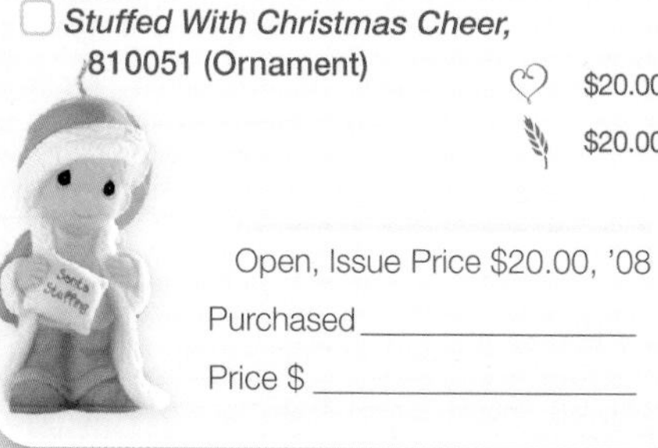

Open, Issue Price $20.00, '08

Purchased ____________

Price $ ____________

☐ *Stuffed With Christmas Cheer,* 810051 (Ornament)

$20.00
$20.00

Open, Issue Price $20.00, '08

Purchased ____________

Price $ ____________

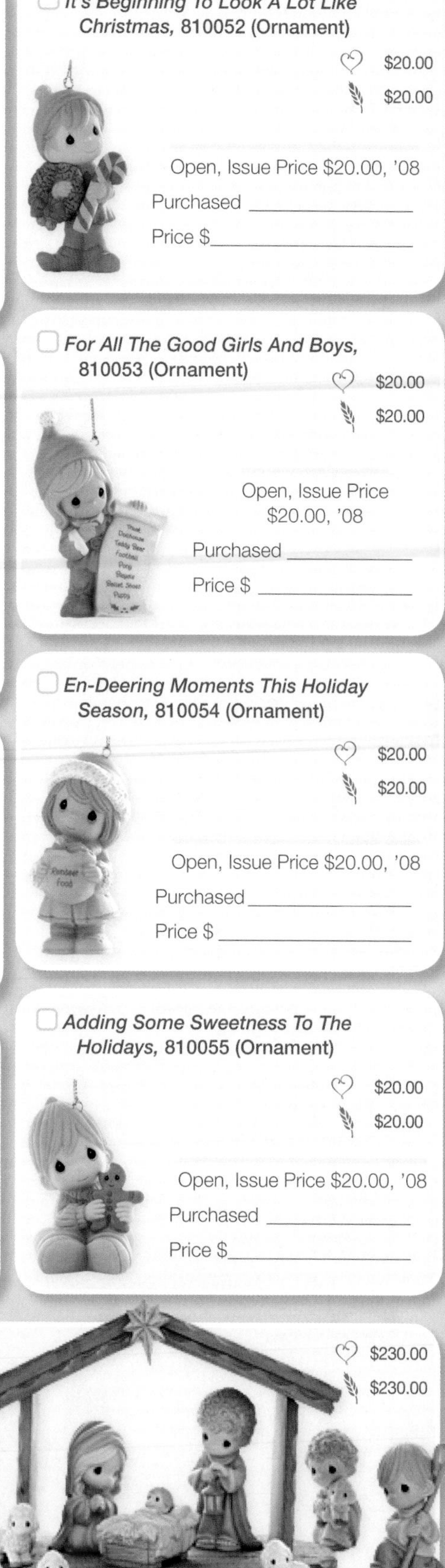

☐ *It's Beginning To Look A Lot Like Christmas,* 810052 (Ornament)

$20.00
$20.00

Open, Issue Price $20.00, '08

Purchased ____________

Price $____________

☐ *For All The Good Girls And Boys,* 810053 (Ornament)

$20.00
$20.00

Open, Issue Price $20.00, '08

Purchased ____________

Price $ ____________

☐ *En-Deering Moments This Holiday Season,* 810054 (Ornament)

$20.00
$20.00

Open, Issue Price $20.00, '08

Purchased ____________

Price $ ____________

☐ *Adding Some Sweetness To The Holidays,* 810055 (Ornament)

$20.00
$20.00

Open, Issue Price $20.00, '08

Purchased ____________

Price $____________

☐ *Collector's Edition 13 Piece Nativity Set,* 810056

$230.00
$230.00

Open, Issue Price $230.00, '08 Set of 13

Purchased ____________

Price $____________

Includes Nativity Set #810011, We Three Kings #810017 and Creche with embedded 30th Anniversary Medallion.

☐ *A Godchild Close To My Heart (Girl), 811807*

$35.00 · $35.00 · $35.00 · $35.00 · $35.00 · $35.00 · $35.00 · $35.00 · $35.00

Open, Issue Price $35.00, '01

Purchased ________, Price $ ___________

☐ *A Godchild Close To My Heart (Boy), 811815*

$35.00 · $35.00 · $35.00 · $35.00 · $35.00

Suspended, Issue Price $35.00, '01

Purchased___________

Price $___________

☐ *A Winning Spirit Comes From Within, 813044*

$50.00 · $43.00 · $48.00 · $40.00 · $45.00 · $40.00

Retired 2004, Issue Price $35.00, '01

Special Olympics Exclusive

Purchased _____________

Price $ _______________

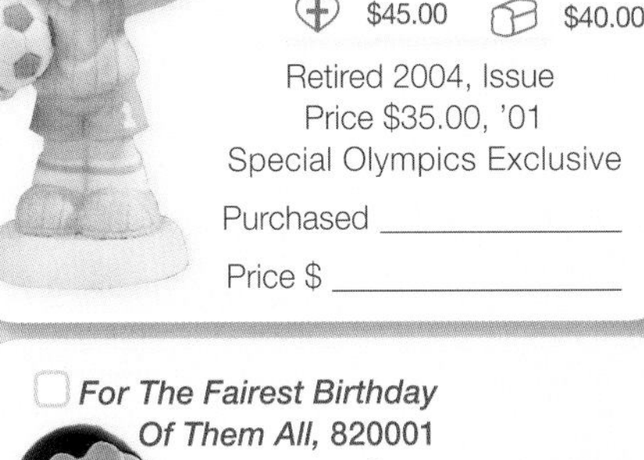

☐ *For The Fairest Birthday Of Them All, 820001*

$45.00 · $45.00

Open, Issue Price $45.00, '08

Disney Showcase Collection

Purchased _____________

Price $_______________

☐ *For The Fairest Birthday Of Them All, 820001DW*

Limited number of the first pieces sold at World Disney Resort featured a special debut date bottom stamp.

$55.00 · $55.00

LImited Ed., Issue Price $45.00, '08

Disney Theme Park Exclusive

Purchased ________, Price $ ___________

☐ *Wishing All Of Your Dreams Come True, 820002*

$45.00 · $45.00

Open, Issue Price $45.00, '08

Disney Showcase Collection

Purchased _____________

Price $ _______________

☐ *Wishing All Of Your Dreams Come True, 820002DW*

Limited number of the first pieces sold at World Disney Resort featured a special debut date bottom stamp.

$55.00 · $55.00

LImited Ed., Issue Price $45.00, '08

Disney Theme Park Exclusive

Purchased ________, Price $ ___________

☐ *Be Our Guest For Our Birthday Best, 820003*

$70.00 · $70.00

Open, Issue Price $70.00, '08

Disney Showcase Collection

Purchased ______

Price $ _________

☐ *Be Our Guest For Our Birthday Best, 820003DW*

Limited number of the first pieces sold at World Disney Resort featured a special debut date bottom stamp.

$75.00 · $75.00

LImited Ed., Issue Price $70.00, '08

Disney Theme Park Exclusive

Purchased ________, Price $ ___________

☐ *In My Book You Are The Best Friend There Is, 820005*

$65.00 · $65.00

Open, Issue Price $65.00, '08

Purchased ________, Price $ ___________

☐ *The World Is A Better Place With Friends, 820006*

$60.00 · $60.00

Open, Issue Price $60.00, '08

Purchased ________, Price $ ___________

☐ *The Path Of Friendship Is Not Measured In Miles, But In Moments Shared, 820007*

$40.00 · $40.00

Open, Issue Price $40.00, '08

Purchased ________, Price $ ___________

☐ *It Is A Happy Heart That Holds A Friend, 820008*

$50.00 · $50.00

Open, Issue Price $50.00, '08

Purchased ________, Price $ ___________

☐ *You Serve And Protect, 820009*

$40.00 · $40.00

Open, Issue Price $40.00, '08

Purchased ________, Price $ ___________

☐ *You Are A Cut Above The Rest,* 82010

$40.00
$40.00

Open, Issue Price $40.00, '08

Purchased ________

Price $ ___________

☐ *You Help Me Realize That Life Is Full Of Beauty,* 820015

$35.00
$35.00

Open, Issue Price $35.00, '08

Purchased ________, Price $ ___________

☐ *Love One Another,* 822426

$550.00
$500.00

Limited Ed. 1,500, Issue Price $500.00, '01
Easter Seals Commemorative

Purchased ________, Price $ ___________

☐ *You Make Life A Little Sweeter,* 820011

$40.00
$40.00

Open, Issue Price $40.00, '08

Purchased ______

Price $_________

☐ *You Are My Source Of Comfort And Inspiration,* 820016

$35.00
$35.00

Open, Issue Price $35.00, '08

Purchased ________, Price $ ___________

☐ *A Beary Loving Collector,* 823945 (Medallion)

$200.00

Given to those who attended the 11th Annual 2000 Local Club Chapter Convention)

Limited Ed., Gift, '00

Purchased ________, Price $ ___________

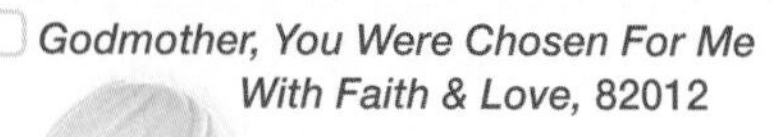

☐ *Godmother, You Were Chosen For Me With Faith & Love,* 82012

$40.00
$40.00

Open, Issue Price $40.00, '08

Purchased ________

Price $___________

☐ *I Will Make My Country Proud,* 820423

$50.00	$35.00
$48.00	$35.00
$40.00	$35.00
$35.00	$35.00
$35.00	$35.00

Open, Issue Price $37.50, '00
Canadian Exclusive

Purchased ________, Price $ ___________

☐ *A Beary Loving Collector,* 823953C

Given to those who attended the 11th Annual 2000 Local Club Chapter Convention)

$250.00

Limited Ed. 2,000, Gift, '00
2000 Convention Exclusive

Purchased ___________

Price $ ___________

☐ *A True Friend Is Someone Who Reaches For Your Hand And Touches Your Heart,* 820014

$35.00
$35.00

Open, Issue Price $35.00, '08

Purchased____

Price $______

☐ *Hisssterrically Sweet,* 821969

	$16.00
$16.00	$16.00
$16.00	$16.00
$16.00	$16.00
	$16.00
	$16.00
	$16.00

Open, Issue Price $15.00, '01
Japanese Exclusive

Purchased ________, Price $ ___________

☐ *Our Love Will Never Be Endangered,* 824119

Also issued in 2001 as a Reef Hallmark Fortieth Anniversary Limited Edition (824119S); Egg mark, $90.00.

$60.00

Limited Ed. of 5,000, Issue Price $50.00, '01
CCR Exclusive

Purchased ________, Price $ ___________

A Mother's Job Is Never Done, 829269

$30.00

Limited Ed., Issue Price $20.00, '01
Series: *Little Moments*
Avon Exclusive
Purchased ________
Price $__________

You Are Loved Today And Always, 830005

$35.00
$35.00

Open, Issue Price $35.00, '08
Purchased __________
Price $____________

Gathering Friends Together, 830010

$80.00
$80.00

Open, Issue Price $80.00, '08
Disney Showcase Collection
Purchased ________, Price $ __________

Be Mine, 830001

$30.00
$30.00

Open, Issue Price $30.00, '08
Purchased ______________
Price $ ______________

Laughter Gives Friends The Power To Share, 830006

$85.00
$85.00

Open, Issue Price $85.00, '08
Disney Showcase Collection
Purchased ________, Price $ __________

Discover Your Beautiful Strength Winthin, 830011

$40.00
$40.00

Open, Issue Price $40.00, '08
Purchased ________
Price $__________

My Heart Is Yours, 830002

$40.00
$40.00

Open, Issue Price $40.00, '08
Purchased ____________
Price $ ____________

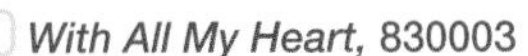

Friends Share Caring Hearts, 830008

$80.00
$80.00

Open, Issue Price $80.00, '08
Disney Showcase Collection
Purchased ________, Price $ __________

Make The Most Of Today With Hope For Tomorrow, 830012

$40.00
$40.00

Open, Issue Price $40.00, '08
Purchased __________
Price $ __________

With All My Heart, 830003

$45.00
$45.00

Open, Issue Price $45.00, '08
Series: *Crayola® Collection*
Official Licensed Product
Purchased_____
Price $_______

Anything Is Possible With Friends, 830009

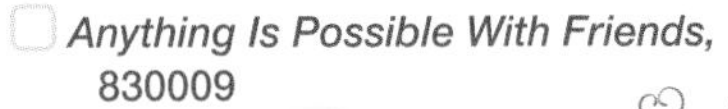

$75.00
$75.00

Open, Issue Price $75.00, '08
Disney Showcase Collection
Purchased ________, Price $ __________

You Fill My Heart With Joy, 830004

$45.00
$45.00

Open, Issue Price $45.00, '08
Purchased__________
Price $__________

Believe In The Wonder That Is You, 830013

$40.00
$40.00

Open, Issue Price $40.00, '08
Purchased __________
Price $ __________

☐ *Grow In The LIght Of His Love,* 830014

$55.00
$55.00

Open, Issue Price $55.00, '08

Purchased ________

Price $ ___________

☐ *Hands Build A House, Hearts Build A Home,* 830016

$125.00
$125.00

LImited Ed. 5,000, Issue Price $125.00, '08

Purchased ________, Price $ ___________

☐ *Love Is The Fountain Of Life,* 830017

$125.00
$125.00

LImited Ed. 5,000, Issue Price $125.00, '08

Purchased ________, Price $ ___________

☐ *A Best Friend Wherever You Go,* 830018

$40.00
$40.00

Open, Issue Price $40.00, '08
Series: *Raggedy Ann and Andy*

Purchased ________, Price $ ___________

☐ *Best Friends Forever,* 830019

$45.00
$45.00

Open, Issue Price $45.00, '08
Series: *Raggedy Ann and Andy*

Purchased ________, Price $ ___________

☐ *Your Heart Speaks Through Dance,* 830020

$40.00
$40.00

Open, Issue Price $40.00, '08

Purchased ________, Price $ ___________

☐ *You Shine In Every Arena,* 830021

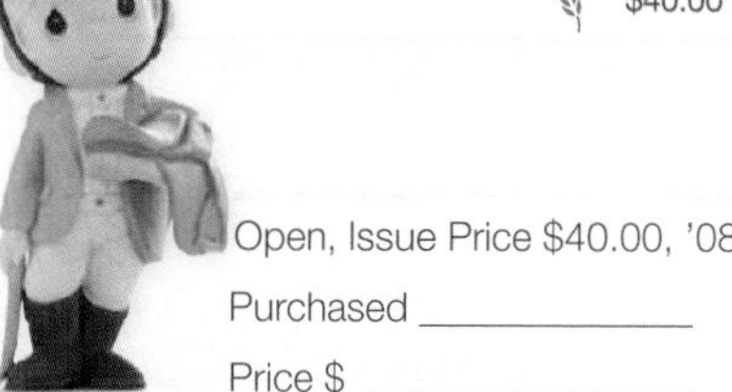

$40.00
$40.00

Open, Issue Price $40.00, '08

Purchased ___________

Price $ ___________

☐ *You Capture Beauty With All You Do,* 830022

$40.00
$40.00

Open, Issue Price $40.00, '08

Purchased ________, Price $ ___________

☐ *To Have And To Hold Forevermore,* 830023

$55.00
$55.00

Open, Issue Price $55.00, '08

Purchased ________, Price $ ___________

☐ *We Join Hands And Hearts,* 830024

$60.00
$60.00

Open, Issue Price $60.00, '08

Purchased ________

Price $ ___________

☐ *Always And Forever, Daddy's LIttle Girl,* 830025

$55.00
$55.00

Open, Issue Price $65.00, '08

Purchased ________, Price $ ___________

☐ *Bridesmaid, A Best Friend At My Side,* 830026

$30.00
$30.00

Open, Issue Price $30.00, '08

Purchased ________, Price $ ___________

☐ *Flower Girl,* 830027

$30.00
$30.00

Open, Issue Price $30.00, '08

Purchased ________, Price $ ____________

☐ *Baptized In His Name — Girl,* 830028

$40.00
$40.00

Open, Issue Price $40.00, '08

Purchased ________, Price $ ____________

☐ *Baptized In His Name — Boy,* 830029

$40.00
$40.00

Open, Issue Price $40.00, '08

Purchased ________, Price $ ____________

☐ *Put A Little Bounce In Your Step,* 830031

$55.00
$55.00

Open, Issue Price $55.00, '08
Series: *Crayola® Collection*
Official Licensed Product

Purchased ___________

Price $___________

☐ *You Brighten My Day,* 830032

$45.00
$45.00

Open, Issue Price $45.00, '08
Series: *Crayola® Collection*
Official Licensed Product

Purchased _______

Price $__________

☐ *A Box of Possibilities,* 830033

$42.50
$42.50

Open, Issue Price $42.50, '08
Series: *Crayola® Collection*
Official Licensed Product

Purchased ________, Price $ ____________

☐ *Embrace His Love,* 830036

$40.00
$40.00

Open, Issue Price $40.00, '08

Purchased ________, Price $ ____________

☐ *With Faith, All Things Are Possible,* 830037

$40.00
$40.00

Open, Issue Price $40.00, '08

Purchased ________, Price $ ____________

☐ *Holding On To Hope,* 830051

$45.00
$45.00

A 3 year partnership with St. Jude Children's Research Hospital. The proceeds will benefit St. Jude Hospital.

St. Jude Children's Research Hospital
ALSAC • Danny Thomas, Founder

Open, Issue Price $45.00, '08

Purchased ________, Price $ ____________

☐ *Mom, Your Love Makes Me Blossom — Girl,* 840001

$35.00
$35.00

Open, Issue Price $35.00, '08

Purchased ___________

Price $ _______________

☐ *Mom, Your Love Makes Me Blossom — Boy,* 840002

$35.00
$35.00

Open, Issue Price $35.00, '08

Purchased___________

Price $_______________

☐ *Tender Is Mother's Love,* 840003

$40.00
$40.00

Open, Issue Price $40.00, '08

Purchased _________

Price $ ___________

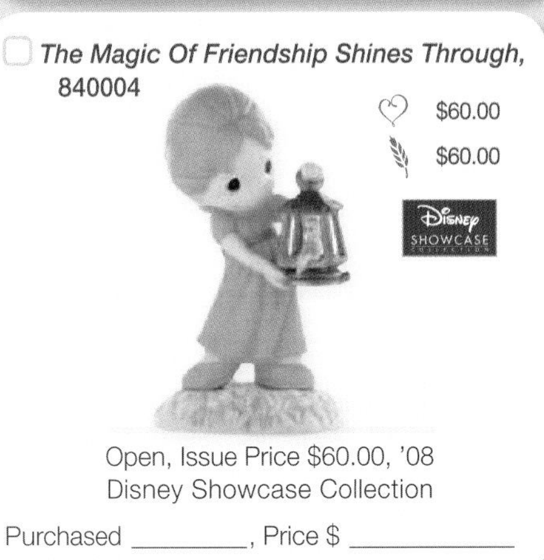

☐ *The Magic Of Friendship Shines Through,* 840004

$60.00
$60.00

Open, Issue Price $60.00, '08
Disney Showcase Collection

Purchased ________, Price $ ____________

☐ ***Fair In Beauty And In Spirit,* 840006**

$65.00

$65.00

Open, Issue Price $65.00, '08
Disney Showcase Collection

Purchased ________, Price $ ____________

☐ ***Mom, Your Love Is My Greatest Gift,* 840007**

$50.00

$50.00

Open, Issue Price $50.00, '08

Purchased ________, Price $ ____________

☐ ***Friendship Has A Way Of Finding You,* 840008**

$65.00

$65.00

Open, Issue Price $65.00, '08
Disney Showcase Collection

Purchased ________, Price $ ____________

☐ ***Blessed Be The Bread Of LIfe — Girl,* 840011**

$45.00

$45.00

Open, Issue Price
$45.00, '08

Purchased______

Price $________

☐ ***Blessed Be The Bread Of LIfe — Boy,* 840012**

$45.00

$45.00

Open, Issue Price
$45.00, '08

Purchased __________

Price $____________

☐ ***Love Accepts, Forgives and Never Ceases,* 840014**

$40.00

$40.00

Open, Issue Price $40.00, '08
Series: *Words Of Grace*

Purchased ____________

Price $ ____________

☐ ***Trust There Is A Reason For All Things,* 840015**

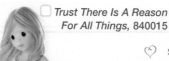

$40.00

$40.00

Open, Issue Price
$40.00, '08
Series: *Words Of Grace*

Purchased__________

Price $____________

☐ ***May Peace Dwell In Your Heart And Soul,* 840016**

$125.00

$125.00

Comes with wooden base.

Open, Issue Price $125.00, '08
Series: *Words Of Grace*

Purchased ________, Price $ ____________

☐ ***You Are Always In Our Hearts,* 840020**

Portion of the proceedes to benefit Boys and Girls Clubs of America.

$75.00

$75.00

Open, Issue Price $75.00, '08
Pays Tribute to Eugene Freedman

Purchased ________, Price $ ____________

☐ ***Our Love Is The Bridge To Happiness,* 840030**

$125.00

$125.00

LImited Ed. 5,000, Issue Price $125.00, '08

Purchased ________, Price $ ____________

☐ ***Today I Confirm My Faith,* 840034**

$35.00

$35.00

Open, Issue Price
$35.00, '08

Purchased __________

Price $ ____________

☐ ***To Your Rescue,* 840035**

$35.00

$35.00

Open, Issue Price
$35.00, '08
Series: *Moments Remembered*

Purchased ________, Price $ ____________

☐ *May Your Spirit Always Soar,* 840036

$35.00

$35.00

Open, Issue Price $35.00, '08 Series: *Moments Remembered*

Purchased ________, Price $ ____________

☐ *Thanks For Being There,* 840040

$70.00

$70.00

Open, Issue Price $70.00, '08 John Deere Collection

Purchased ________, Price $ ____________

☐ *The Key To Success Is In The Heart,* 840060

$40.00

$40.00

Open, Issue Price $40.00, '08

Purchased_______

Price $__________

☐ *I Feel The Need For Speed,* 840037

$35.00

$35.00

Open, Issue Price $35.00, '08 Series: *Moments Remembered*

Purchased ________, Price $ ____________

☐ *Give All Your Worries And Cares To God,* 840041

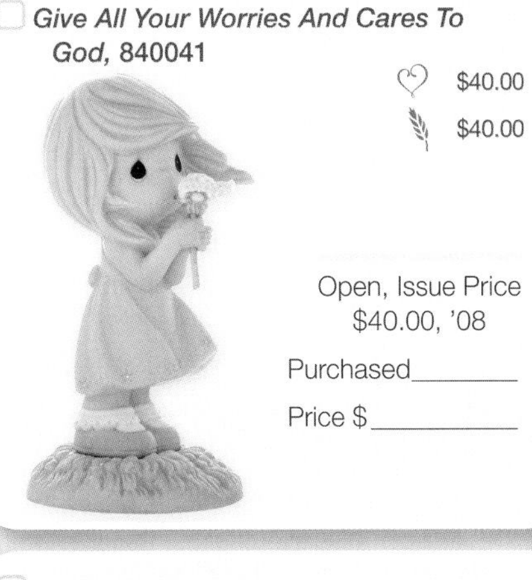

$40.00

$40.00

Open, Issue Price $40.00, '08

Purchased_______

Price $__________

☐ *My Love Is Always In Bloom For You,* 840061

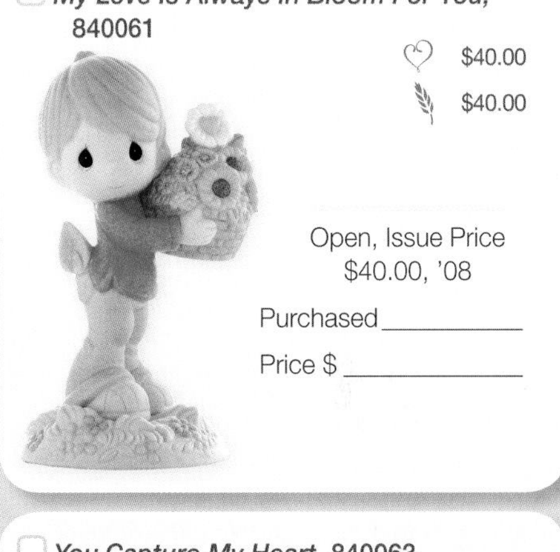

$40.00

$40.00

Open, Issue Price $40.00, '08

Purchased__________

Price $____________

☐ *A Cut Above The Rest,* 840038

$75.00

$75.00

Open, Issue Price $75.00, '08 John Deere Collection

Purchased ________, Price $ ____________

☐ *An Act Of Kindness Makes All The Difference,* 840042

$45.00

$45.00

Open, Issue Price $45.00, '08

Purchased_____

Price $ ________

☐ *You Capture My Heart,* 840063

$55.00

$55.00

Open, Issue Price $55.00, '08

Purchased_______

Price $__________

☐ *A Friend Is Someone Who Is Always There To Help,* 840039

$70.00

$70.00

Open, Issue Price $70.00, '08 John Deere Collection

Purchased ________, Price $ ____________

☐ *I'm With You Every Step Of The Way,* 840043

$55.00

$55.00

Open, Issue Price $55.00, '08

Purchased ____

Price $ _______

☐ *Love Is Always In Bloom,* 840064

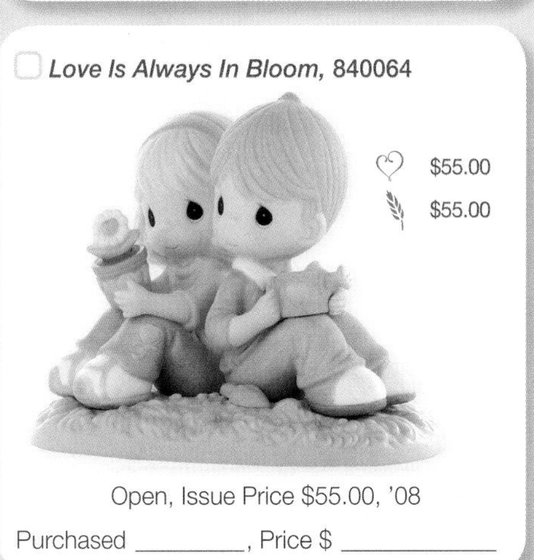

$55.00

$55.00

Open, Issue Price $55.00, '08

Purchased ________, Price $ ____________

☐ ***Mom (Blonde),*** **848735**

UM $20.00

Open, Issue Price $20.00, '01
Series: *Build A Family — Little Moments*

Purchased ________
Price $ ________

☐ ***Dad (Blond),*** **848743**

UM $20.00

Open, Issue Price $20.00, '01
Series: *Build A Family — Little Moments*

Purchased ________
Price $ ________

☐ ***Teenage Daughter (Blonde),*** **848751**

UM $17.50

Open, Issue Price $17.50, '01
Series: *Build A Family — Little Moments*

Purchased ________
Price $ ________

☐ ***Teenage Son (Blond),*** **848778**

UM $17.50

Open, Issue Price $17.50, '01
Series: *Build A Family — Little Moments*

Purchased ________
Price $ ________

☐ ***Toddler Daughter (Blonde),*** **848786**

UM $15.00

Open, Issue Price $15.00, '01
Series: *Build A Family — Little Moments*

Purchased ________
Price $ ________

☐ ***Toddler Son (Blond),*** **848794**

UM $15.00

Open, Issue Price $15.00, '01
Series: *Build A Family — Little Moments*

Purchased ________
Price $ ________

☐ ***Infant Daughter (Blonde),*** **848808**

UM $12.50

Open, Issue Price $12.50, '01
Series: *Build A Family — Little Moments*

Purchased ________
Price $ ________

☐ ***Infant Son (Blond),*** **848816**

UM $12.50

Open, Issue Price $12.50, '01
Series: *Build A Family — Little Moments*

Purchased ________
Price $ ________

☐ ***Dog,*** **848824**

UM $10.00

Open, Issue Price $10.00, '01
Series: *Build A Family — Little Moments*

Purchased ________
Price $ ________

☐ ***Cat,*** **848832** UM $10.00

Open, Issue Price $10.00, '01
Series: *Build A Family — Little Moments*

Purchased ________
Price $ ________

☐ ***Bride And Groom,*** **848840 (Frame)**

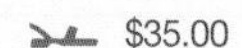

$35.00 $35.00 $35.00
$35.00 $35.00

Open, Issue Price $35.00, '01

Purchased ________, Price $ ________

☐ ***Victorious In Jesus,*** **850942**

UM $150.00

Limited Ed. 2,400,
Issue Price $85.00, '00
Chapel Exclusive

Purchased ________
Price $ ________

☐ ***Victorious In Jesus,*** **850950**

UM $50.00 $50.00 $50.00
$50.00 $50.00 $50.00

Retired 2004, Issue Price $50.00, '01
Chapel Exclusive

Purchased ________, Price $ ________

☐ ***Mary Had A Little Lamb,*** **850969**

UM $40.00
$35.00
$35.00
$35.00
$35.00
$35.00
$35.00

Retired 2004, Issue Price $35.00, '00
Chapel Exclusive

Purchased ________, Price $ ________

☐ ***Bride (Brunette),*** **874485**

$50.00 $43.00
$48.00 $40.00
$45.00 $40.00

Suspended, Issue
Price $30.00, '01
Series: *The Lord Bless You And Keep You*

Purchased ________, Price $ ________

☐ *Groom (Brunette)*, 874493

$50.00
$48.00
$45.00
$43.00
$40.00
$40.00

Suspended, Issue Price $30.00, '01
Series: *The Lord Bless You And Keep You*

Purchased ________, Price $ ___________

☐ *I Give You My Love Forever True*, 876143 (Musical)

$135.00
$125.00
$125.00
$125.00
$125.00
$125.00
$125.00

Open, Issue Price $125.00, '01
Tune: *Pachelbel's Canon in D*

Purchased ________, Price $ ___________

☐ *Bridal Arch*, 876151 (Musical)

$55.00
$50.00
$50.00
$50.00
$50.00
$50.00

Out of Production, Issue Price $50.00, '01
Tune: *Pachelbel's Canon in D*

Purchased ________, Price $ ___________

☐ *The Lord Is The Hope Of Our Future*, 877123

$45.00 $40.00
$40.00 $40.00
$40.00 $40.00
$40.00 $40.00

Open, Issue Price $40.00, '01

Purchased ___________

Price $____________

☐ *The Lord Is The Hope Of Our Future*, 877131

$45.00 $40.00
$40.00 $40.00
$40.00 $40.00
$40.00 $40.00

Open, Issue Price $40.00, '01

Purchased _________

Price $__________

☐ *May Your Christmas Begin With A Bang!* 877433

$40.00

Annual 2001, Issue Price $30.00, '01

Purchased _____

Price $________

☐ *May Your Christmas Begin With A Bang!* 877441 (Ornament)

$28.00

Annual 2001, Issue Price $19.00, '01

Purchased__________

Price $ ____________

☐ *Baby's First Christmas*, 877506 (Ornament)

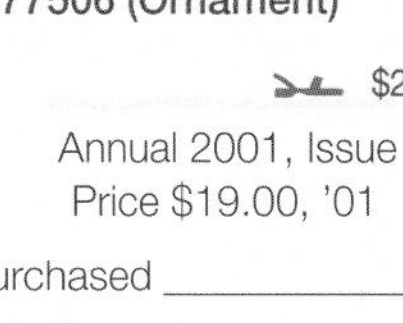

$28.00

Annual 2001, Issue Price $19.00, '01

Purchased ___________

Price $_______________

☐ *Baby's First Christmas*, 877514 (Ornament)

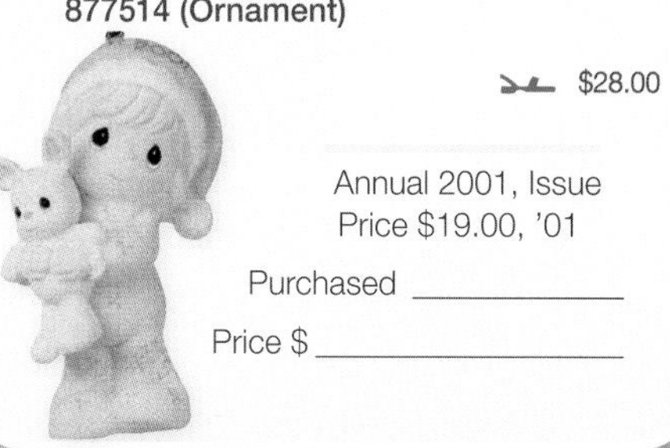

$28.00

Annual 2001, Issue Price $19.00, '01

Purchased ___________

Price $ _______________

☐ *Our First Christmas Together*, 878855 (Ornament)

$35.00

Annual 2001, Issue Price $25.00, '01

Purchased ________, Price $ ___________

☐ *May Your Days Be Merry And Bright*, 878901

$50.00
$45.00
$45.00
$45.00
$45.00
$45.00
$45.00
$45.00
$45.00

Open, Issue Price $45.00, '01
Series: *Christmas Remembered*

Purchased ________, Price $ ___________

☐ *On A Scale From 1 To 10 You Are The Deerest*, 878944

$45.00
$40.00

Retired 2002, Issue Price $30.00, '01

Purchased___________

Price $___________

☐ *Celebrating His Arrival,* 878952

$45.00
$40.00
$40.00
$40.00
$40.00
$40.00
$40.00

Open, Issue Price $40.00, '01

Purchased ________, Price $ ___________

☐ *The Royal Budge Is Good For The Soul,* 878987

$50.00 $45.00
$45.00
$45.00
$45.00
$45.00
$45.00

Open, Issue Price $45.00, '01
Nativity Addition

Purchased ________, Price $ ___________

☐ *Life Is So Uplifting,* 878995

$40.00 $35.00
$35.00 $35.00
$35.00 $35.00
$35.00 $35.00
$35.00

Open, Issue Price $35.00, '01

Purchased ________, Price $ ___________

☐ *Roll Away, Roll Away, Roll Away,* 879002

$40.00 $35.00
$35.00 $35.00
$35.00 $35.00
$35.00

Open, Issue Price $35.00, '01

Purchased ________

Price $__________

☐ *Building Special Friendships,* 879029

$105.00
$100.00
$100.00
$98.00
$98.00
$80.00
$80.00

Open, Issue Price $80.00, '01
Boys & Girls Club of America Commemorative

Purchased ________, Price $ ___________

☐ *Oh, What A Wonder-Fall Day,* 879096

$60.00
$58.00
$55.00
$53.00
$50.00

Suspended, Issue Price $40.00, '01
Series: *Country Lane Collection*

Purchased ________, Price $ ___________

☐ *Lord Let Our Friendship Bloom,* 879126

$65.00
$58.00
$55.00

Suspended 2003, Issue Price $40.00

Purchased ________, Price $ ___________

☐ *Our Friendship Was Made To Order,* 879134

$55.00 $50.00
$53.00 $48.00
$45.00

Suspended, Issue Price $35.00, '01

Purchased__________

Price $__________

☐ *Up To Our Ears In A White Christmas,* 879185

$85.00

Limited Ed., Issue Price $55.00, '01

Purchased ________, Price $ ___________

☐ *Count Your Many Blessings,* 879274

$70.00

Limited Ed., Issue Price $50.00, '01

Purchased ________, Price $ ___________

☐ *O Holy Night,* 879428 (Nativity Scene)

$450.00

Limited Ed. 3,000, Issue Price $375.00, '01
GoCollect.com and CCR Exclusives
Worldwide, Hand Numbered

Purchased ________, Price $ ___________

God's Love Is Crystal Clear, 879436

$65.00

Limited Ed., Issue Price $45.00, '01
CCR Event Exclusive

Purchased ____________

Price $ ____________

God's Love Is Crystal Clear, 879487 (Ornament)

$40.00

Annual 2001, Issue Price $25.00, '01
CCR Event Exclusive

Purchased ____________

Price $____________

House Of Bells Vignette, 879614

$125.00

$115.00

Retired 2003, Issue Price $85.00, '02
Series: *The Heavenly Daze* —
Fourth Issue, Set of 3

Purchased ________, Price $ ____________

Star Smith Vignette, 879568

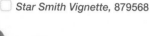

$150.00

$125.00

$115.00

Retired 2003, Issue Price $85.00, '01
Series: *The Heavenly Daze* —
First Issue, Set of 3

Purchased ________, Price $ ____________

The Good Book Library, 879622

$125.00

$115.00

Retired 2003, Issue Price $85.00, '02
Series: *The Heavenly Daze* —
Fifth Issue, Set of 3

Purchased ________, Price $ ____________

Halo Maker, 879576

$150.00

$125.00

$115.00

Retired 2003, Issue Price $85.00, '01
Series: *The Heavenly Daze* —
Second Issue, Set of 3

Purchased ________, Price $ ____________

The Golden Gown Seamstress, 879606

$125.00

$115.00

Retired 2003, Issue Price $85.00, '02
Series: *The Heavenly Daze* — Third Issue, Set of 3

Purchased ____________

Price $ ____________

Dream Makers, 879630

$115.00

Retired 2003, Issue Price $85.00, '03
Series: *The Heavenly Daze* —
Sixth Issue, Set of 3

Purchased ________, Price $ ____________

☐ ***We Would See Jesus*, 879681**

UM $500.00

Limited Ed. 1,500, Issue Price $300.00, '01
Chapel Exclusive

Purchased ________, Price $ ____________

☐ ***He Is The Rose Of Sharon*, 879703**

UM $35.00
$30.00
$30.00
$30.00
$30.00
$30.00
$30.00

Open, Issue Price $30.00, '01
Chapel Exclusive

Purchased ________, Price $ ____________

☐ ***The Most Precious Place On Earth*, 879711**

UM $50.00
$45.00
$40.00
$40.00
$40.00

Retired 2004, Issue Price $40.00, '01
Chapel Exclusive

Purchased ________, Price $ ____________

☐ ***The Lord Is Our Chief Inspiration*, 879738 (Ornament)**

UM $50.00
$45.00
$40.00
$37.50
$35.00
$32.50
$32.50

Open, Issue Price $20.00, '01
Chapel Exclusive

Purchased ________, Price $ ____________

☐ ***Sleep In Heavenly Peace*, 879746 (Ornament)**

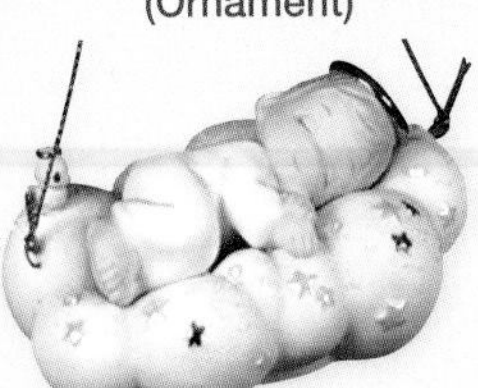

UM $30.00
$25.00
$25.00
$25.00
$25.00
$25.00

Open, Issue Price $25.00, '01
Chapel Exclusive

Purchased ________, Price $ ____________

☐ ***Sleep In Heavenly Peace*, 879754**

UM $45.00
$40.00
$35.00
$35.00
$35.00

Retired 2004, Issue Price $35.00, '01
Chapel Exclusive

Purchased ________, Price $ ____________

☐ ***Mom (Brunette)*, 880833**

UM $20.00

Open, Issue Price $20.00, '01
Series: *Build A Family — Little Moments*

Purchased______________

Price $ ______________

☐ ***Dad (Brunette)*, 880841**

UM $20.00

Open, Issue Price $20.00, '01
Series: *Build A Family — Little Moments*

Purchased______________

Price $ ______________

☐ ***Teenage Daughter (Brunette)*, 880868**

UM $17.50

Open, Issue Price $17.50, '01
Series: *Build A Family — Little Moments*

Purchased ______________

Price $ ______________

☐ ***Teenage Son (Brunette)*, 880876**

UM $17.50

Open, Issue Price $17.50, '01
Series: *Build A Family — Little Moments*

Purchased ______________

Price $______________

☐ ***Toddler Daughter (Brunette)*, 880884**

UM $15.00

Open, Issue Price $15.00, '01
Series: *Build A Family — Little Moments*

Purchased ______________

Price $ ______________

☐ ***Toddler Son (Brunette)*, 880892**

UM $15.00

Open, Issue Price $15.00, '01
Series: *Build A Family — Little Moments*

Purchased ______________

Price $ ______________

Infant Daughter (Brunette), 880906

UM $12.50

Open, Issue Price $15.00, '01
Series: *Build A Family — Little Moments*

Purchased ____________

Price $ ____________

Infant Son (Brunette), 880914

UM $12.50

Open, Issue Price $15.00, '01
Series: *Build A Family — Little Moments*

Purchased ____________

Price $ ____________

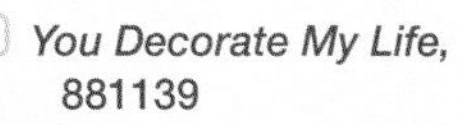

You Decorate My Life, 881139

$50.00

Limited Ed., Issue Price $35.00, '01
2001 Fall Catalog Exclusive

Purchased ____________

Price $ ____________

You Decorate My Life, 881147 (Ornament)

$35.00

Limited Ed., Issue Price $20.00, '01
2001 Fall Catalog Exclusive

Purchased ____________

Price $ ____________

You Decorate My Life, 881163 (Ornament)

$37.00

Dated 2001, Issue Price $30.00, '01

Purchased ____________

Price $ ____________

Hug Me Before I Melt, 883875

UM $25.00

$20.00

Limited Ed., Issue Price $20.00, '01
Series: *Little Moments*
Avon Exclusive

Purchased ____________

Price $ ____________

Grandma's Little Angel (Blonde), 887900

$25.00
$25.00
$25.00
$25.00

Suspended, Issue Price $25.00, '01

Purchased ________, Price $ ____________

Grandma's Little Angel (Brunette), 887927

$25.00
$25.00
$25.00
$25.00

Suspended, Issue Price $25.00, '02

Purchased ________, Price $ ____________

Daddy's Little Angel (Brunette), 887935

$25.00 $25.00
$25.00 $25.00

Suspended, Issue Price $25.00, '02

Purchased ________, Price $ ____________

Daddy's Little Angel (Blonde), 887951

$25.00 $25.00
$25.00 $25.00

Suspended, Issue Price $25.00, '02

Purchased ____________

Price $ ____________

Grandma's Little Angel (Blond), 887978

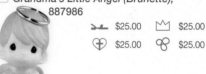

$25.00 $25.00
$25.00 $25.00

Suspended, Issue Price $25.00, '02

Purchased ____________

Price $ ____________

Grandma's Little Angel (Brunette), 887986

$25.00 $25.00
$25.00 $25.00

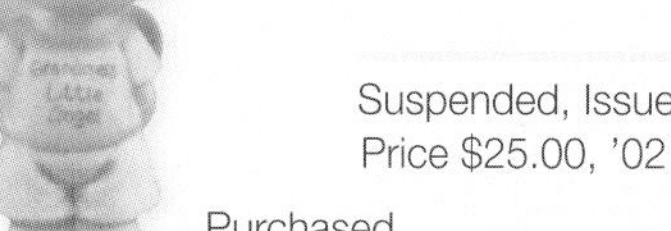

Suspended, Issue Price $25.00, '02

Purchased ____________

Price $ ____________

Mommy's Little Angel (Brunette), 887994

$25.00 $25.00
$25.00 $25.00

Suspended, Issue Price $25.00, '02

Purchased ____________

Price $ ____________

Mommy's Little Angel (Blond), 888001

$25.00 $25.00
$25.00 $25.00

Suspended, Issue Price $25.00, '02

Purchased ____________

Price $ ____________

The Lord Is The Hope Of Our Future (Hispanic), 889563

$48.00
$45.00
$45.00
$40.00
$40.00

Suspended, Issue Price $40.00, '02

Purchased ________

Price $ __________

Let's Have A Ball Together, 889849

$45.00

Annual 2001, Issue Price $35.00, '01 Boys & Girls Club of America Commemorative

Purchased __________

Price $__________

God's Love Is My Guiding LIght, 890008

UM $100.00
$100.00
$100.00

Open, Issue Price $100.00, '07 Chapel Exclusive

Purchased ________, Price $ __________

Love Is Always With Us, 890009

UM $50.00
$50.00
$50.00

Open, Issue Price $50.00, '07 Chapel Exclusive

Purchased ________, Price $ __________

Your Friendship Keeps Me Warm Even On The Coldest Of Days, 890013

$45.00
$45.00

Open, Issue Price $45.00, '08 Hallmark Exclusive

Purchased ________, Price $ __________

Would You Be Mine, 890015

$40.00

Limited Ed., Issue Price $40.00, '09 Hallmark Exclusive

Purchased ________

Price $ __________

I Hold Your Heart Forever, 890016

$35.00

Limited Ed., Issue Price $35.00, '09 Carlton Early Release

Purchased ________

Price $ __________

Cherish The Treasure Within, 890019

$130.00

Open, Issue Price $45.00, '08 30th Anniversary Exclusive

Purchased ________

Price $ __________

May The Blessings Of The Holy Family Be With You, 890020

$45.00
$45.00

Open, Issue Price $45.00, '08 Carlton Cards/American Greeting Exclusive

Purchased ________, Price $ __________

Making Music Together For 30 Years, 890021

$350.00

Given to those that attended the 2008 Branson Event.

LImited Ed. 640, Gift, '08 30th Anniversary Event

Purchased ________, Price $ __________

A Smile Means Friendship To Everyone, 890047

$150.00
$100.00

First 500 figurines sold at the Walt Disney World Resort featured the bottom stamp and event date of September 12 – 13, 2008.

Open, Issue Price $100.00, '08 Disney Theme Park Exclusive

Purchased ________, Price $ __________

***A Magical Moment To Rmemeber*, 890049**

First 500 figurines sold at the Walt Disney World Resort featured the bottom stamp and event date of September 12 – 13, 2008.

$150.00
$100.00

Open, Issue Price $100.00, '08
Disney Theme Park Exclusive

Purchased ________, Price $ ___________

***Let Love Reign*, 890596**

$75.00
$70.00

Limited Ed., Issue Price $60.00, '02

Purchased__________

Price $ ______________

***You Have A Heart Of Gold*, 890626**

$30.00 $30.00
$30.00 $30.00
$30.00 $30.00
$30.00 $30.00
$30.00

Open, Issue Price $25.00, '02

Purchased ___________

Price $______________

***Nearer To The Heart Of God*, 890731**

$65.00
$60.00

Retired 2002, Issue Price $40.00, '02

Purchased__________

Price $ ____________

***God's Love Has No Measure*, 890871**

$35.00 $30.00
$33.00 $28.00

Retired 2004, Issue Price $25.00, '02

Purchased ___________

Price $______________

***You Are The Cat's Meow*, 890952**

$35.00
$33.00
$30.00
$28.00
$28.00

Has been redesigned with the cat's head slightly raised.

Suspended, Issue Price $25.00, '02
Series: *Special Wishes*

Purchased ________, Price $ ___________

***Just A Happy Note*, 890960**

$30.00 $25.00
$25.00 $25.00
$25.00 $25.00
$25.00 $25.00
$25.00

Open, Issue Price $25.00, '02
Series: *Special Wishes*

Purchased____________

Price $_____________

***Best Friends Share The Same Heart*, 890987**

$55.00
$50.00
$50.00
$50.00
$50.00
$50.00
$50.00

Open, Issue Price $50.00, '02
Set of 2

Purchased ________, Price $ ___________

***Daddy's Little Girl*, 891045**

$48.00 $45.00
$45.00 $43.00
$40.00

Suspended, Issue Price $40.00, '02
Series: *Family*

Purchased__________

Price $ ___________

***You Are My Gift From Above*, 891738**

$60.00 $53.00
$58.00 $53.00
$55.00 $50.00
$50.00

Open, Issue Price $50.00, '02
Series: *Family*

Purchased ________, Price $ ___________

***Healing Begins With Forgiveness*, 892157**

$60.00 $58.00
$55.00

Suspended 2003, Issue Price $45.00, '02
Series: *Family*

Purchased ______

Price $ ________

***Ewe Are So Precious To Me*, 892726**

$60.00
$58.00
$55.00
$53.00
$50.00

Suspended, Issue Price $45.00, '02

Purchased ________, Price $ ___________

Overalls, I Think You're Special, 898147

$65.00
$63.00
$60.00
$58.00
$45.00

Retired 2005, Issue Price $45.00, '02
Series: *Country Lane Collection*

Purchased ________, Price $ ____________

Loving, Caring And Shearing, 898414

$70.00
$70.00

Limited Ed. 10,000, Issue Price $60.00, '01

Purchased ________, Price $ ____________

Jesus Loves Me (African-American), 899771

$25.00 $20.00
$23.00 $20.00
$20.00

Suspended 2004, Issue Price $20.00, '01

Purchased __________

Price $ ____________

How Can I Says Thanks, 898309

$35.00
UM $35.00 $35.00
$35.00 $35.00

Retired 2004, Issue Price $35.00, '02
Chapel Exclusive

Purchased ____________

Price $ ______________

You Are My Favorite Dish, 898457

$45.00
$45.00

898457S comes with a cookie cutter, has Cross in Heart mark, and is valued at $55.00.

Retired 2002, Issue Price $25.00, '02

Purchased __________

Price $ ____________

Jesus Loves Me (African-American), 899879

$25.00 $20.00
$23.00 $20.00
$20.00

Suspended 2004, Issue Price $20.00, '01

Purchased ________

Price $ __________

How Can I Says Thanks, 898317 (Ornament)

UM $20.00 $20.00
$20.00 $20.00
$20.00

Open, Issue Price $20.00, '02
Chapel Exclusive

Purchased ______________

Price $ ________________

Jesus Loves Me (Asian), 900575

$25.00 $20.00
$23.00 $20.00
$20.00

Suspended 2004, Issue Price $20.00, '01

Purchased ________

Price $ __________

Jesus Loves Me (Latino), 899526

$25.00 $20.00
$23.00 $20.00
$20.00

Suspended 2004, Issue Price $20.00, '01

Purchased ________

Price $ __________

Scent From Above To Share His Love, 898325

UM $35.00
$30.00
$30.00
$30.00
$30.00
$30.00

Open, Issue Price $30.00, '05
Chapel Exclusive

Purchased ________, Price $ ____________

Jesus Loves Me (Asian), 901555

$25.00 $20.00
$23.00 $20.00
$20.00

Suspended 2004, Issue Price $20.00, '01

Purchased__________

Price $ ____________

Jesus Loves Me (Latino), 899542

$25.00 $20.00
$23.00 $20.00
$20.00

Suspended 2004, Issue Price $20.00, '01

Purchased __________

Price $____________

Best Man (Hispanic), 901563

$30.00 $25.00
$28.00 $25.00
$25.00

Suspended, Issue Price $25.00, '02

Purchased ____________

Price $____________

☐ *Maid Of Honor (Hispanic),* 901571

$30.00 $25.00
$28.00 $25.00
$25.00

Suspended, Issue Price $25.00, '02

Purchased ____________

Price $ ____________

☐ *Best Man (African-American),* 902020

$30.00 $25.00
$28.00 $25.00
$25.00 $25.00
$25.00

Open, Issue Price $25.00, '02

Purchased ____________

Price $ ____________

☐ *Maid Of Honor (African-American),* 902039

$30.00 $25.00
$28.00 $25.00
$25.00 $25.00
$25.00

Open, Issue Price $25.00, '02

Purchased ____________

Price $ ____________

☐ *Best Man (Asian),* 902047

$30.00 $25.00
$28.00 $25.00
$25.00 $25.00
$25.00

Open, Issue Price $20.00, '01

Purchased ____________

Price $ ____________

☐ *Maid Of Honor (Asian),* 902055

$30.00 $25.00
$28.00 $25.00
$25.00 $25.00
$25.00

Open, Issue Price $20.00, '01

Purchased ____________

Price $ ____________

☐ *Un Dia Muy Especial (A Very Special Day),* 902098

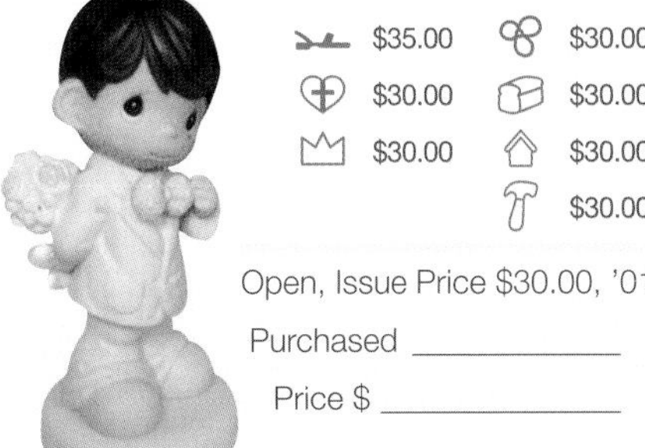

$35.00 $30.00
$30.00 $30.00
$30.00 $30.00
$30.00

Open, Issue Price $30.00, '01

Purchased ____________

Price $ ____________

☐ *Una Madres Es El Corazon De La Familia (A Mother Is The Heart Of The Family),* 902101

$35.00 $30.00
$30.00 $30.00
$30.00

Suspended, Issue Price $30.00, '01

Purchased ____________

Price $ ____________

☐ *May Your Faith Light The Way,* 910001

$35.00

Annual 2009, Issue Price $35.00, '09

Purchased ____

Price $________

☐ *May Your Faith Light The Way,* 910002 (Ornament)

$23.00

Annual 2009, Issue Price $23.00, '09

Purchased ____________

Price $ ____________

☐ *May Your Faith Light The Way,* 910003 (Ornament)

$30.00

Annual 2009, Issue Price $30.00, '09

Purchased ____________

Price $ ____________

☐ *Our First Christmas Together,* 910004 (Ornament)

$27.50

Annual 2009, Issue Price $27.50, '09

Purchased ____________

Price $ ____________

☐ *Baby's First Christmas — Girl,* 910005 (Ornament)

$22.50

Annual 2009, Issue Price $22.50, '09

Purchased ____________

Price $ ____________

☐ *Baby's First Christmas — Boy,* 910006 (Ornament)

$22.50

Annual 2009, Issue Price $22.50, '09

Purchased ____________

Price $ ____________

☐ *My Peace, Hope And Love Shine Throughout The Year,* 910007 (Ornament)

$22.50

Annual 2009, Issue Price $22.50, '09

Purchased ____________

Price $ ____________

☐ *It's What's Inside That Counts,* 910008

$45.00

Open, Issue Price $45.00, '09
Series: *Country Lane Collection*

Purchased ________, Price $ ________

☐ *Sharing The Seeds Of Love This Holiday Season,* 910009

$45.00

Open, Issue Price $45.00, '09
Series: *Heart Of Christmas*
Purchased ______
Price $__________

☐ *Delivering Smiles Is The Best Gift of All,* 910010

$50.00

Open, Issue Price $50.00, '09
Series: *Heart Of Christmas*
Purchased _____
Price $ ________

☐ *The Fruits Of Love Are A Gift To Cherish,* 910011 (Ornament)

$22.50

Open, Issue Price $22.50, '09
Series: *Heart Of Christmas*
Purchased ______________
Price $ ________________

☐ *Merry Kiss-mas To You,* 910012 (Ornament)

$22.50

Open, Issue Price $22.50, '09
Series: *Heart Of Christmas*
Purchased ______________
Price $ ________________

☐ *May Your Christmas Be Filled With Sweet Surprises,* 910013 (Ornament)

$22.50

Open, Issue Price $22.50, '09
Series: *Heart Of Christmas*
Purchased ______________
Price $ ________________

☐ *You Have The Sweetness Of The Season All Wrapped Up,* 910014 (Ornament)

$22.50

Open, Issue Price $22.50, '09
Series: *Heart Of Christmas*
Purchased ______________
Price $ ________________

☐ *All Is Merry and Bright,* 910015 (Ornament)

$22.50

Open, Issue Price $22.50, '09
Series: *Heart Of Christmas*
Purchased ______________
Price $ ________________

☐ *Blessed Is The Giving Hand,* 910016 (Ornament)

$22.50

Open, Issue Price $22.50, '09
Series: *Heart Of Christmas*
Purchased ______________
Price $ ________________

☐ *Do You See What I See?,* 910017

$60.00

Open, Issue Price $60.00, '09
Series: *Holiday Carols*
Purchased_______
Price $_________

☐ *On The First Day Of Christmas,* 910019

$45.00

Open, Issue Price $45.00, '09
Series: *Holiday Carols*
Purchased _______
Price $ _________

☐ *Glory To The Newborn King,* 910020

$55.00

Open, Issue Price $55.00, '09
Series: *Holiday Carols*
Purchased_______
Price $ _________

☐ *Glory To God In The Highest,* 910022 (Ornament)

$22.50

Open, Issue Price $22.50, '09
Series: *Holiday Carols*
Purchased ______________
Price $ ________________

☐ *Boughs Of Holly,* 910023 (Ornament)

$22.50

Open, Issue Price $22.50, '09
Series: *Holiday Carols*
Purchased ______________
Price $________________

☐ *My Gift For Him,* 910024 (Ornament)

$22.50

Open, Issue Price $22.50, '09
Series: *Holiday Carols*
Purchased ______________
Price $ ________________

☐ *Here Comes Santa Claus,* 910025 (Ornament)

$22.50

Open, Issue Price $22.50, '09
Series: *Holiday Carols*
Purchased ______________
Price $ ________________

☐ *Be Of Good Cheer,* 910026 (Ornament)

$22.50

Open, Issue Price $22.50, '09
Series: *Holiday Carols*
Purchased ______________
Price $ ________________

☐ *Daughter, Your Beauty Radiates From Within*, 910027 (Ornament)

$22.50

Open, Issue Price $22.50, '09

Purchased ______________

Price $ ______________

☐ *Firefighters LIght Up The Holidays*, 910028 (Ornament)

$22.50

Open, Issue Price $22.50, '09?

Purchased ______________

Price $ ______________

☐ *You LIght Up My Life Goddaughter*, 910029 (Ornament)

$22.50

Open, Issue Price $22.50, '09

Purchased ______________

Price $ ______________

☐ *Your Hospitality Is A Sweet Gift*, 910030 (Ornament)

$22.50

Open, Issue Price $22.50, '09

Purchased ______________

Price $ ______________

☐ *Mom, You Make The Season Merry*, 910031 (Ornament)

$22.50

Open, Issue Price $22.50, '09

Purchased ______________

Price $ ______________

☐ *You're The Best Grandmother Around*, 910032 (Ornament)

$22.50

Open, Issue Price $22.50, '09

Purchased ______________

Price $ ______________

☐ *He Will Bring Us Goodness And Light — Camel*, 910033

$30.00

Open, Issue Price $30.00, '09
Nativity

Purchased ________, Price $ ___________

☐ *His Burden Is Never Too Heavy — Donkey*, 910034

$30.00

Open, Issue Price $30.00, '09
Nativity

Purchased ____

Price $ ______

☐ *Before Him The Most Mighty Bow — Cow*, 910035

$30.00

Open, Issue Price $30.00, '09
Nativity

Purchased ________, Price $ ___________

☐ *My Gift For Him — Drummer Boy*, 910036

$35.00

Open, Issue Price $35.00, '09
Nativity

Purchased ________

Price $ ________

☐ *Born Is The King Of Israel*, 910037

$25.00

Open, Issue Price $25.00, '09
Mini Nativity

Purchased ___________

Price $ ___________

☐ *Friends Help You Find Your Way*, 910039

$60.00

Open, Issue Price $60.00, '09 Disney Showcase Collection

Purchased ________

Price $ ________

☐ *Your Beautiful Heart Warms The Coldest Day*, 910040

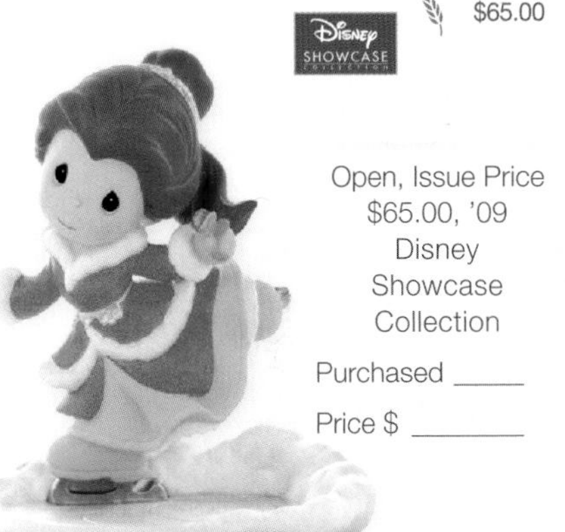

$65.00

Open, Issue Price $65.00, '09 Disney Showcase Collection

Purchased _____

Price $ ________

☐ *There's Magic Under The Mistletoe*, 910041

$50.00

Open, Issue Price $50.00, '09 Disney Showcase Collection

Purchased ________

Price $ ________

A Tractor To Call My Very Own, 910042

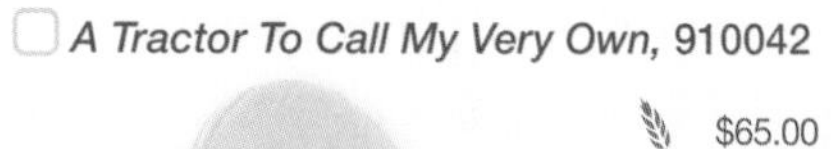

$65.00

Open, Issue Price $65.00, '09
John Deere Collection

Purchased ________, Price $ ___________

My First Set Of Wheels, 910043

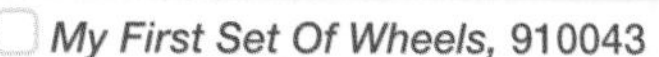

$45.00

Open, Issue Price $45.00, '09
John Deere Collection

Purchased ______

Price $ ________

You Light Up The Holidays, 910044

$75.00

Open, Issue Price $75.00, '09
John Deere Collection

Purchased ________, Price $ ___________

Noel, 910047

$120.00

Open, Issue Price $120.00, '09
Set of 5
Nativity

Purchased ________, Price $ ___________

Rejoice, 910048

$40.00

Open, Issue Price $40.00, '09
Series: *Word Of Grace*

Purchased ________, Price $ ___________

Holiday Surprises Are Filled With Love, 910052

$125.00

Limited Ed. 5,000, Issue Price $125.00, '09
Collector's Series

Purchased ________, Price $ ___________

I'm Forever By Your Side, 910053

$150.00

Limited Ed. 5,000, Issue Price $150.00, '09
Collector's Series

Purchased ________, Price $ ___________

May The Spirit Of Hope Embrace This Holiday Season, 910054 (Ornament)

The proceeds will benefit St. Jude Hospital.

$22.50

St. Jude Children's Research Hospital

Open, Issue Price $22.50, '09

Purchased ________________

Price $ __________________

Cruising Through The Holidays, 910055 (Ornament)

$30.00

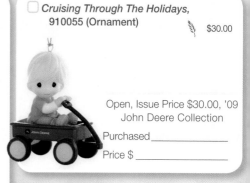

Open, Issue Price $30.00, '09
John Deere Collection

Purchased ____________

Price $ ______________

There's Nothing Better Than A LIttle Green For The Holidays, 910056 (Ornament)

$27.50

Open, Issue Price $27.50, '09
John Deere Collection

Purchased ____________

Price $______________

The Christmas Spirit Is A Part Of My World, 910057

Disney Showcase

$85.00

Open, Issue Price $85.00, '09
Disney Showcase Collection

Purchased ________, Price $ ___________

Love, 910058

$75.00

Open, Issue Price $75.00, '09

Purchased ________, Price $ ___________

☐ ***Believe In The Power Of True Love,*** **910059**

$75.00

Open, Issue Price $75.00, '09
Disney Showcase Collection

Purchased ________, Price $ ____________

☐ ***Shepherds Abiding In The Field,*** **910060**

$45.00

Open, Issue Price $45.00, '09
Set of 3
Nativity

Purchased ________________

Price $________________

☐ ***We Three Kings,*** **910061**

$60.00

Open, Issue Price $60.00, '09
Set of 3
Mini Nativity

Purchased ________, Price $ ____________

☐ ***Believe In The Magic Of Christmas,*** **910062**

$40.00

Open, Issue Price $40.00, '09
First in series: *Annual Santa Collection*

Purchased ________, Price $ ____________

☐ ***Believe In The Magic Of Christmas,*** **910063 (Ornament)**

$22.50

Open, Issue Price $22.50, '09
First in series:
Annual Santa Collection

Purchased ________________

Price $________________

☐ ***Shepherds Abiding In The Field,*** **910064**

$30.00

Open, Issue Price $30.00, '09
Set of 2
Mini Nativity

Purchased ________, Price $ ____________

☐ ***Our Love Makes A Lasting Impression,*** **910065**

$125.00

LImited Ed. 5,000, Issue
Price $125.00, '09
Collector's Series

Purchased __________

Price $__________

☐ ***Born Is The King Of Israel!,*** **910066 (Ornament)**

$25.00

Open, Issue Price
$25.00, '09
Series: *Holiday Carols*

Purchased __________

Price $ __________

☐ ***My Gift For HIm,*** **910067**

$22.50

Open, Issue Price $22.50, '09
Mini Nativity

Purchased________________

Price $ ________________

☐ ***Porcelain Backdrop,*** **914005**

Can be used for the Standard or the Mini Nativity — UM $40.00

Open, Issue Price $40.00, '09

Purchased ________, Price $ ____________

☐ ***Mini Wooden Creche,*** **914006**

For Mini Nativity — UM $20.00

Open, Issue Price $20.00, '09

Purchased ________, Price $ ____________

☐ ***Your Kiss Can Put A Smile On The Grumpiest Face,*** **920001**

$40.00

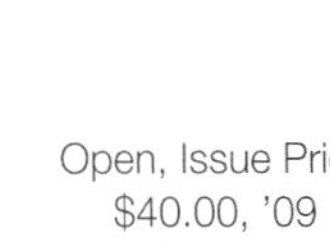

Open, Issue Price
$40.00, '09
Disney
Showcase Collection

Purchased __________

Price $__________

☐ *I'm Swept Away By You*, 920002

$40.00

Open, Issue Price
$40.00, '09
Disney
Showcase Collection

Purchased____________

Price $____________

☐ *Your An Ace On Any Court*, 920006

$40.00

Open, Issue Price
$40.00, '09
Series: *Special Wishes*

Purchased__________

Price $__________

☐ *I Get By With A Little Shopping With My Friends*, 920010

$65.00

Open, Issue Price
$65.00, '09
Series:
Friendship

Purchased_____

Price $ _______

☐ *Rounding Up A Gang Full Of Fun*, 920003

$65.00

Open, Issue Price
$65.00, '09
Disney
Showcase Collection

Purchased _______

Price $ __________

☐ *You Bring A Song To My Heart*, 920007

$40.00

Open, Issue Price
$40.00, '09
Series: *Special Wishes*

Purchased__________

Price $ ____________

☐ *Your Everday Kindness Is My Everyday Joy*, 920012

$35.00

Open, Issue Price
$35.00, '09
Series: *Heart Of An Angel*

Purchased _________

Price $__________

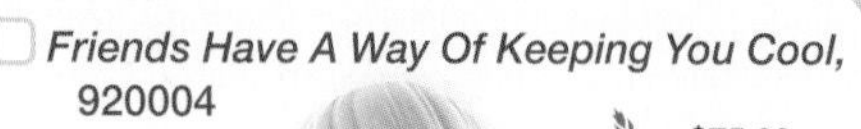

☐ *Friends Have A Way Of Keeping You Cool*, 920004

$75.00

Open, Issue Price $75.00, '09
Disney Showcase Collection

Purchased ________, Price $ __________

☐ *You're The Piece That Completes My Picture*, 920008

$45.00

Open, Issue Price
$45.00, '09
Series: *Special Wishes*

Purchased _________

Price $ __________

☐ *Your Comfort Speaks Directly To My Heart*, 920013

$35.00

Open, Issue Price
$35.00, '09
Series: *Heart Of An Angel*

Purchased _________

Price $ _________

☐ *Your Style Is So Striking*, 920005

$40.00

Open, Issue Price
$40.00, '09
Series: *Special Wishes*

Purchased___________

Price $____________

☐ *Friends Listen With Their Hearts*, 920009

$50.00

Open, Issue Price
$50.00, '09
Series: *Friendship*

Purchased ____

Price $ ______

☐ *Your Friendship Brings Light To My Life*, 920014

$35.00

Open, Issue Price
$35.00, '09
Series: *Heart Of An Angel*

Purchased _________

Price $____________

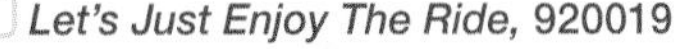

☐ *Your Strength Sustains Me,* 920015

$35.00

Open, Issue Price $35.00, '09
Series: *Heart Of An Angel*
Purchased ________
Price $ __________

☐ *Let's Just Enjoy The Ride,* 920019

$35.00

Open, Issue Price $35.00, '09
Series: *Moments Remembered*
Purchased ___
Price $ _____

☐ *We're Always On The Same Page,* 920031

$40.00

Open, Issue Price $40.00, '09
Disney Showcase Collection
Purchased_______
Price $__________

☐ *Always Ready To Serve And Protect,* 920016

$35.00

Open, Issue Price $35.00, '09
Series: *Moments Remembered*
Purchased __________
Price $ ___________

☐ *A Rebel With A Cause,* 920020

$35.00

Open, Issue Price $35.00, '09
Series: *Moments Remembered*
Purchased______
Price $ _________

☐ *Oceans Of Love For You,* 920032

$40.00

Open, Issue Price $40.00, '09
Disney Showcase Collection
Purchased _________
Price $ ___________

☐ *I've Got Things To Do And Places To Go,* 920017

$35.00

Open, Issue Price $35.00, '09
Series: *Moments Remembered*
Purchased _______________
Price $ _________________

☐ *All For The Love Of You On A Bicycle Build For Two,* 920025

$135.00

Open, Issue Price $135.00, '09
Collector's Series
Purchased_____
Price $ _______

☐ *God's Precious Pearl Of The Ozarks,* 927899

UM $38.00
$35.00
$33.00
$30.00
$30.00
$30.00
$30.00

Open, Issue Price $30.00, '01
Chapel Exclusive
Purchased__________
Price $ ____________

☐ *I'll Be There In A Flash,* 920018

$35.00

Open, Issue Price $35.00 '09
Series: *Moments Remembered*
Purchased ____
Price $ _______

☐ *Your Sweet Song Fills The Air,* 920030

$40.00

Open, Issue Price $40.00, '09
Disney Showcase Collection
Purchased ___________
Price $ ______________

☐ *Preparado Con Amor (Prepared With Love),* 928445

$40.00
$35.00
$35.00
$35.00

Suspended 2004, Issue Price $35.00, '01
Purchased__________
Price $ ____________

☐ *Seguro In Los Brazos De Padrinos (Safe In The Arms Of Godparents),* 928453

$55.00
$50.00
$50.00
$50.00
$50.00
$50.00
$50.00

Open, Issue Price $50.00, '01

Purchased ________, Price $ ____________

☐ *Mi Pequeno Amor (My Little Sweetheart),* 928461

$35.00 $30.00
$30.00 $30.00
$30.00

Suspended 2004, Issue Price $40.00, '01

Purchased____________

Price $______________

☐ *Una Bendesion Del Cielo (A Blessing From Heaven),* 928488

$45.00 $40.00
$40.00 $40.00
$40.00 $40.00
$40.00

Open, Issue Price $40.00, '01

Purchased____________

Price $______________

☐ *I Am A Bee-liever,* 928534

$45.00 $38.00
$40.00 $35.00
$33.00

Suspended 2005, Issue Price $30.00, '02
Series: *Trusting Is Bee-lieving*

Purchased ____________

Price $ ______________

☐ *Precious Friends,* 928542

$55.00
$53.00
$53.00
$50.00
$50.00

Suspended, Issue Price $40.00, '02

Purchased ________, Price $ ____________

☐ *The Lord Is Always Bee-side Us,* 928550

$50.00
$48.00
$45.00
$43.00
$40.00

Suspended, Issue Price $37.50, '02

Purchased ________, Price $ ____________

☐ *Worthy Is The Lamb,* 928569

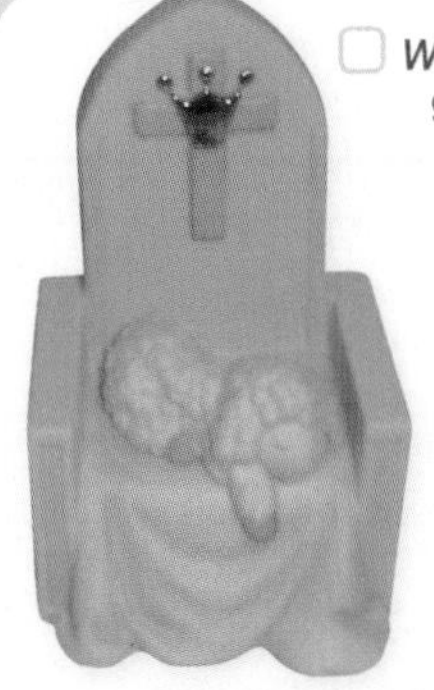

UM $35.00
$30.00
$30.00
$30.00
$30.00
$30.00

Open, Issue Price $30.00, '02
Chapel Exclusive

Purchased ________, Price $ ____________

☐ *Worthy Is The Lamb,* 928577 (Ornament)

UM $20.00 $18.50
$18.50 $18.50

Retired 2004, Issue Price $18.50, '02
Chapel Exclusive

Purchased____________

Price $______________

☐ *It Came Upon A Midnight Clear,* 928585 (Tree Topper)

UM $135.00
$130.00

Retired 2004, Limited Ed. 2,500, Issue Price $125.00, '02
Chapel Exclusive

Purchased__________

Price $____________

☐ *My Teacher, My Friend,* 928607

UM $75.00
$73.00
$73.00
$70.00
$70.00

Retired 2004, Issue Price $70.00, '02
Chapel Exclusive

Purchased ________, Price $ ____________

☐ *Loads Of Love For You,* 930001

$50.00

Open, Issue Price $50.00, '09

Purchased____________

Price $______________

☐ *I've Got Extra! Extra! Love For You,* 930002

$35.00

Open, Issue Price $35.00, '09

Purchased ____________

Price $ ______________

☐ *I'd Fall In Love With You All Over Again,* 930003 $40.00

Open, Issue Price $40.00, '09
Purchased ______
Price $__________

☐ *You Make My World A Wonderland,* 930007 $60.00

Open, Issue Price $60.00, '09
Disney Showcase Collection
Purchased____________
Price $______________

☐ *Forever Embraced In God's Warm Love — Girl,* 930011 $35.00

Open, Issue Price $35.00, '09
Purchased ________, Price $ ____________

☐ *Will You Share Your Heart With Me?,* 930004 $70.00

This figurine comes with a red heart ring box or a lavender ring box. The original came with the red box. It was later decided that the ring box would change to lavender as a running change.

Open, Issue Price $70.00, '09
Purchased ________, Price $ ____________

☐ *You Always Bounce Back Up,* 930008 $45.00

Open, Issue Price $45.00, '09
Purchased____________
Price $ ______________

☐ *In The Radiance Of Heaven's Light,* 930012 $40.00

Open, Issue Price $40.00, '09
Purchased________
Price $__________

☐ *Ahoy Mate! It's Smooth Sailing Ahead,* 930009 $50.00

Open, Issue Price $50.00, '09
Purchased__________
Price $ ____________

☐ *Heaven Just Became A Fetchingly Better Place,* 930013 $35.00

Open, Issue Price $35.00, '09
Purchased ________, Price $ ____________

☐ *Our Love Is Forever In Bloom,* 930005 $60.00

Open, Issue Price $60.00, '09
Disney Showcase Collection
Purchased ________
Price $ __________

☐ *The Joy You Bring Awakens My Heart,* 930006 $60.00

Open, Issue Price $60.00, '09
Disney Showcase Collection
Purchased ________
Price $ ___________

☐ *Whatever The Weather, We're Always Together,* 930010 $65.00

Open, Issue Price $65.00, '09
Purchased ________, Price $ ____________

☐ *Riding Toward Greener Pastures — Girl,* 930014 $80.00

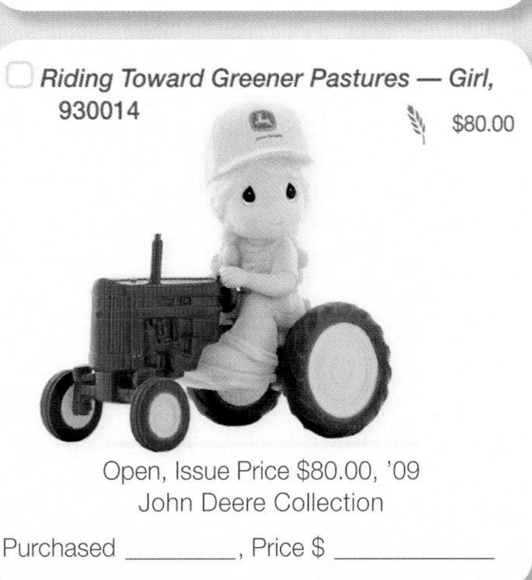

Open, Issue Price $80.00, '09
John Deere Collection
Purchased ________, Price $ ____________

☐ ***Riding Toward Greener Pastures — Boy,* 930015**

$80.00

Open, Issue Price $80.00, '09
John Deere Collection

Purchased ________, Price $ ____________

☐ ***Your Sweet Nature Sweeps Me Away,* 930016**

$35.00

Open, Issue Price $35.00, '09

Purchased _______

Price $ __________

☐ ***A Helpful Heart Is Always In The Mix,* 930017**

$35.00

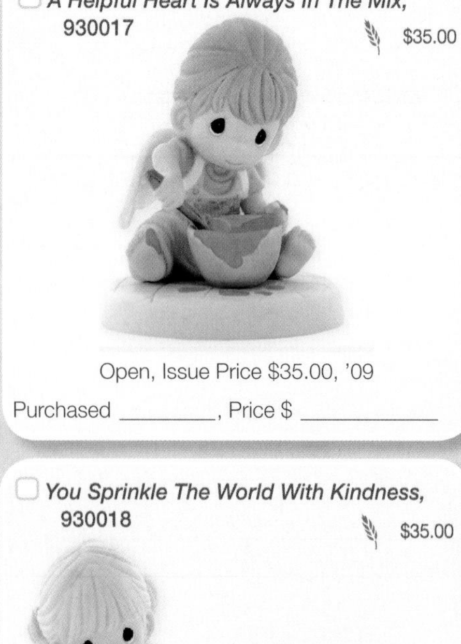

Open, Issue Price $35.00, '09

Purchased ________, Price $ ____________

☐ ***You Sprinkle The World With Kindness,* 930018**

$35.00

Open, Issue Price $35.00, '09

Purchased __________

Price $ ____________

☐ ***Hip Hop Hooray, You're One Year Old Today! — Girl,* 930020**

$45.00

Open, Issue Price $45.00, '09

Purchased ____________

Price $ ______________

☐ ***Hip Hop Hooray, You're One Year Old Today! — Boy,* 930021**

$45.00

Open, Issue Price $45.00, '09

Purchased ____________

Price $ ______________

☐ ***It's Your Birthday, Cake It Easy!,* 930022**

$50.00

Open, Issue Price $50.00, '09

Purchased _____

Price $________

☐ ***Double The Fun,* 930023**

$60.00

Open, Issue Price $60.00, '09

Purchased ________, Price $ ____________

☐ ***Bless The Day You Arrived,* 930024**

$55.00

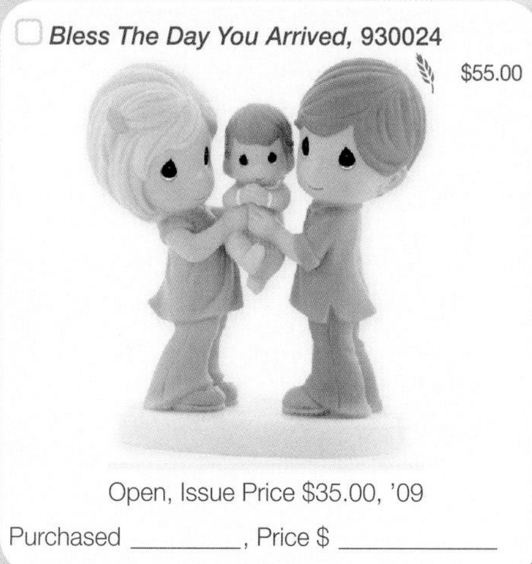

Open, Issue Price $35.00, '09

Purchased ________, Price $ ____________

☐ ***I Can't Spell Success Without "U,"* 930025**

$40.00

Open, Issue Price $40.00, '09

Purchased ________, Price $ ____________

☐ ***Your Caring Heart Is Easy To See,* 930026**

$40.00

Open, Issue Price $40.00, '09

Purchased __________

Price $ ____________

☐ ***You Go The Extra Smile,* 930027**

$40.00

Open, Issue Price $40.00, '09

Purchased____________

Price $______________

☐ ***Light On Your Feet And Oh So Sweet,* 930029** $125.00

Limited Ed. 3,000, Issue Price $125.00, '09

Purchased ________, Price $ ____________

☐ ***Miss You — Girl,* 930030**

$30.00

Open, Issue Price $30.00, '09

Purchased ____________

Price $ ______________

☐ ***Miss You — Boy,* 930031**

$30.00

Open, Issue Price $30.00, '09

Purchased______________

Price $______________

☐ ***Congrats,* 930032**

$30.00

Open, Issue Price $35.00, '09

Purchased_____________

Price $ ______________

☐ ***Love You — Girl,* 930033** $30.00

This figurine also comes as blank to be personalized. Girl Blank,109011.

Open, Issue Price $30.00, '09

Purchased______

Price $_________

☐ ***Love You — Boy,* 930034** $30.00

This figurine also comes as blank to be personalized. Boy Blank,109012.

Open, Issue Price $30.00, '09

Purchased _________

Price $__________

☐ ***Have A Hot Diggetty Dog Day!,* 930035**

$45.00

Open, Issue Price $45.00, '09

Purchased ________

Price $ ___________

☐ ***Thank You — Girl,* 930036**

$30.00

Open, Issue Price $30.00, '09

Purchased ________, Price $ ___________

☐ ***Forever Embraced In God's Warm Love,* 930037**

$35.00

Open, Issue Price $35.00, '09

Purchased _________

Price $ ___________

☐ ***Baby's First Christmas (Boy),* 934038 (Ornament)**

UM $10.00

Dated 2001, Issue Price $6.50, '01 Avon Exclusive

Purchased__________

Price $____________

☐ ***Baby's First Christmas (Girl),* 934046 (Ornament)**

UM $10.00

Dated 2001, Issue Price $6.50, '01 Avon Exclusive

Purchased _________

Price $____________

☐ ***Ice See In You A Champion,* 934852 (Ornament)**

$55.00

$50.00

Limited Ed., Issue Price $25.00, '02 Canadian Exclusive

Purchased__________

Price $ ____________

☐ ***We've Got The Right Plan,* 937282**

$95.00

$90.00

$88.00

$85.00

Suspended 2004, Issue Price $80.00, '02

Purchased ________, Price $ ___________

☐ ***Happy Birthday*, 934007 (Cake Topper)**

$20.00

Open, Issue Price $20.00, '09

Purchased ________, Price $ ___________

☐ ***Our Heroes In The Sky*, 958832**

$48.00
$45.00
$43.00
$40.00

Suspended, Issue Price $35.00, '02

Purchased ___________

Price $ ___________

☐ ***Our Heroes In The Sky*, 958840**

$48.00
$45.00
$43.00
$40.00

Suspended 2004, Issue Price $35.00, '02

Purchased ___________

Price $ ___________

☐ ***Galloping Towards Tomorrow*, 958859**

$57.00
$55.00
$53.00

Retired 2003, Issue Price $17.50, '02
Japan Early Release

Purchased ________, Price $ ___________

☐ ***I See Bright Hope In Your Future*, 973912**

$68.00

Limited Ed., Issue Price $50.00, '02
2002 Show Exclusive

Purchased ________, Price $ ___________

☐ ***Faith Is Heaven's Sweet Song*, 975893**

$130.00 $125.00 $125.00
$125.00 $125.00 $125.00

Open, Issue Price $125.00, '02
Easter Seals Exclusive
First in series: *Heaven's Grace*

Purchased ________

Price $________

☐ ***The Perfect Catch*, 990009**

$125.00

Open, Issue Price $125.00, '09
Chapel Exclusive

Purchased ________, Price $ ___________

☐ ***Merry Christmas To All*, 990010**

$75.00

Limited Ed., Issue Price $75.00, '09
Disney Theme Park Exclusive

Purchased ________, Price $ ___________

☐ ***20 Years Of Blessing You*, 990016**

Given at the June 2009 Reunion Event "To God Be The Glory."

$65.00
$65.00

Limited Ed. 1,000, Gift, '09
20th Anniversary Chapel Event Exclusive

Purchased ________, Price $ ___________

☐ ***Never Let Go Of Hope*, 990030**

$38.00

"St. Jude" logo printed on cape. Includes special dates certificate tent card marking the date of October 17, 2009. The proceeds will benefit St. Jude Hospital.

Limited Ed./Retired 10/17/2009, Issue Price $38.00, '09

St. Jude Children's Research Hopsital Exclusive

Purchased ________, Price $ ___________

☐ ***Never Let Go Of Hope*, 990070 (Medallion)**

UM $45.00

Presented to those who attended Memphis, Tennessee, for the Precious Moments 2009 Local Club and Collector Conference benefiting St. Jude, Novermber 7 – 8, 2009.

Precious Moments® Ambassadors of Hope
November 7 – 8, 2009 • Memphis, Tenn.

Limited Ed., Gift, '09

St. Jude Children's Research Hopsital Exclusive

Purchased ________, Price $ ___________

We're Behind You All The Way, 994863

$25.00
$20.00
$20.00
$20.00
$20.00
$20.00

Open, Issue Price $20.00, '02
Series: *Animal Affections*

Purchased ________, Price $ ____________

Miracles Can Happen, 994871

$25.00 $20.00
$20.00 $20.00
$20.00
$20.00

Open, Issue Price $20.00, '02
Series: *Animal Affections*

Purchased ________, Price $ ____________

Holy Mackerel It's Your Birthday! 994898

$25.00 $20.00
$20.00 $20.00
$20.00
$20.00

Out of Production, Issue Price $20.00, '02
Series: *Animal Affections*

Purchased ________, Price $ ____________

For His Precious Love, 0000364

$30.00 $30.00
$30.00 $30.00
$30.00 $30.00

Open, Issue Price $30.00, '04

Purchased ______________

Price $ ________________

For His Precious Love, 0000365

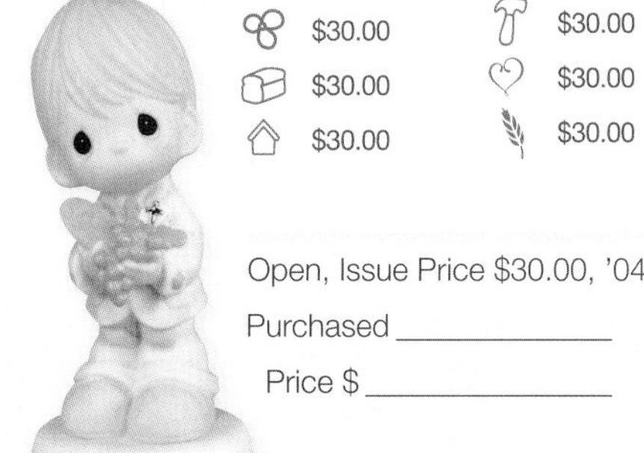

$30.00 $30.00
$30.00 $30.00
$30.00 $30.00

Open, Issue Price $30.00, '04

Purchased ____________

Price $ ______________

A Family Of Love, 0000366

$45.00
$45.00
$45.00
$45.00

Limited Ed., Issue Price $45.00, '04
GCC Exclusive

Purchased ________, Price $ ____________

You're Purr-fect, Pumpkin, 0000367

$37.50
$37.50
$37.50
$37.50

Open, Issue Price $37.50, '04

Purchased ________, Price $ ____________

Give With A Grateful Heart, 0000382

$30.00

Benefits Habitat for Humanity Event piece 11/13/04. A portion of the proceeds will be donated to Habitat For Humanity.

Retired 2004, Issue Price $30.00, '04
GCC Exclusive

Purchased _________

Price $ ______________

Arose On Her Toes, 0000383

$40.00 $40.00
$40.00 $40.00
$40.00 $40.00

Open, Issue Price $40.00, '05

Purchased _________

Price $ ____________

Twinkle, Twinkle, You're A Star, 0000384

$37.50
$37.50

Limited Ed. 10,000,
Issue Price $37.50, '04
Series: *Pretty As A Princess*

Purchased_________

Price $ ___________

Love Is Reflected In You, 0000385

$37.50
$37.50

Limited Ed. 10,000,
Issue Price $37.50, '04
Series: *Pretty As A Princess*

Purchased ________

Price $ ________

Sunshine Brings A Purr-fect Friend, 0000386

$37.50
$37.50

Limited Ed. 10,000, Issue Price $37.50, '04
Series: *Pretty As A Princess*

Purchased ________, Price $ ____________

☐ *Too Dog-Gone Sweet,* 0000387

$37.50
$37.50

Limited Ed. 10,000, Issue Price $37.50, '04
Series: *Pretty As A Princess*

Purchased _______

Price $ __________

☐ *I Love You Just Be-Claus,* 0000664

$50.00
$50.00
$50.00

Limited Ed., Issue Price $50.00, '04
Carlton Cards Exclusive

Purchased____

Price $______

☐ *Calling All My Party Girls,* 4001029

$45.00
$45.00
$45.00
$45.00
$45.00
$45.00

Open, Issue Price $45.00, '05

Purchased ________, Price $ ___________

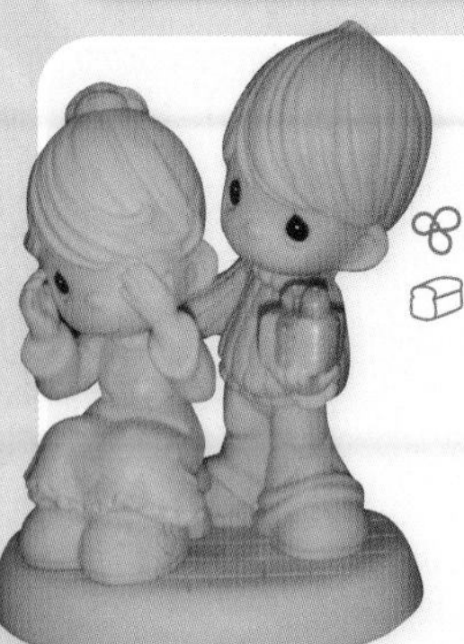

☐ *Guess Who Loves You,* 0000515

$45.00 $45.00
$45.00 $45.00

Limited Ed., Issue Price $45.00, '04
Hallmark Exclusive

Purchased _______

Price $ _________

☐ *May Your Christmas Be Filled With Holiday Cheer,* 0000860

$45.00
$45.00
$45.00

Limited Ed., Issue Price $45.00, '04
Hallmark Plus Exclusive

Purchased _____

Price $ ________

☐ *Blooming In God's Love,* 4001245

$50.00 $50.00
$50.00 $50.00
$50.00
$50.00

Open, Issue Price $50.00, '04

Purchased ________

Price $__________

☐ *Friends To The Very End,* 0000571

$50.00
$50.00
$50.00
$50.00

Limited Ed., Issue Price $50.00, '05
Hallmark Exclusive

Purchased ________, Price $ ___________

☐ *I Give You My Heart,* 0000974

$40.00
$40.00

Limited 2005, Issue Price $40.00, '05

Purchased______

Price $________

☐ *Love Will Carry You Through,* 4001246

$50.00 $50.00
$50.00 $50.00
$50.00 $50.00

Open, Issue Price $50.00, '04

Purchased ______

Price $ ________

☐ *You Color My World,* 0000615

$50.00
$50.00

Limited Ed., Issue Price $50.00, '04
Carlton Cards/ American Greetings Early Release

Purchased _____

Price $ ________

☐ *Find Your Wings And Fly,* 4001025

$35.00
$35.00
$35.00

Open, Issue Price $35.00, '05
GCC Early Introduction

Purchased__________

Price $ ___________

☐ *Some Bunny Loves You,* 4001247

$50.00 $50.00
$50.00 $50.00
$50.00 $50.00

Open, Issue Price $50.00, '04

Purchased _____

Price $ ________

☐ *Actions Speak Louder Than Words*, 4001570

$100.00

Limited Ed. 3,000, Issue Price $100.00, '05
Precious Moments Premier Collection
Charter Figurine

Purchased ________, Price $ ___________

☐ *An Angel In Disguise*, 4001573

$135.00

Limited Ed. 3,000, Issue Price $115.00, '05
Precious Moments Premier Collection
Charter Figurine

Purchased ________, Price $ ___________

☐ *Always Close To My Heart*, 4001645

$35.00
$35.00
$35.00
$35.00

Open, Issue Price $35.00, '05

Purchased ___________

Price $ ___________

☐ *Count Your Blessings*, 4001646

$50.00
$50.00
$50.00
$50.00
$50.00
$50.00

Open, Issue Price $50.00, '05

Purchased ________, Price $ ___________

☐ *Make Everything A Masterpiece*, 4001571

$155.00

Limited Ed. 3,000, Issue Price $135.00, '05
Precious Moments Premier Collection
Charter Figurine

Purchased ________, Price $ ___________

☐ *We Fix Souls*, 4001574

$155.00

Limited Ed. 3,000, Issue Price $135.00, '05
Precious Moments Premier Collection
Charter Figurine

Purchased ________, Price $ ___________

☐ *S'More Time Spent With You*, 4001647

$55.00 $55.00
$55.00 $55.00
$55.00 $55.00

Open, Issue Price $55.00, '05

Purchased ____

Price $ ______

☐ *Praise Him With Resounding Cymbals*, 4001572

$135.00

Limited Ed. 3,000, Issue Price $115.00, '05
Precious Moments Premier Collection
Charter Figurine

Purchased ________, Price $ ________

☐ *A Mother's Love Is A Warm Glow*, 4001650

$50.00
$50.00

Comes with a tulip candle.

Suspended 2005, Issue Price $45.00, '05

Purchased ________, Price $ ___________

☐ *'Til The End Of Time*, 4001653

$60.00 $60.00 $60.00 $60.00 $60.00 $60.00

Open, Issue Price $60.00, '05

Purchased_____

Price $ ________

☐ *Can I Have This Dance For The Rest Of My Life*, 4001655

$50.00 $50.00 $50.00 $50.00 $50.00 $50.00

Open, Issue Price $50.00, '05

Purchased ________, Price $ ____________

☐ *You Are A Precious Gift*, 4001656

$25.00 $25.00 $25.00 $25.00 $25.00 $25.00

Open, Issue Price $25.00, '05

Purchased________________

Price $__________________

☐ *I'm Always Bee-Side You*, 4001661

$45.00 $45.00

LImited Ed. 2005, Issue Price $45.00, '04
Easter Seals Exclusive

Purchased ________, Price $ ____________

☐ *Walk. Run. Empower.* 4001662

$37.50 $37.50 $37.50

Received a free lapel pin ($4 value) with this figurine. A portion of proceeds benefit the Y-Me National Breast Cancer Organiation."

Open, Issue Price $37.50, '06

Purchased_____________

Price $_______________

☐ *It's Time To Blow Your Own Horn*, 4001664

$50.00 $50.00 $50.00 $50.00 $50.00 $50.00

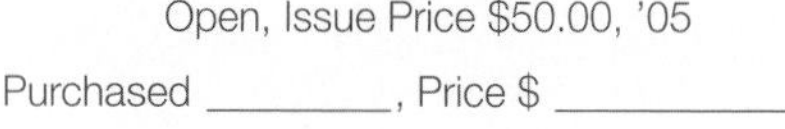

Open, Issue Price $50.00, '05

Purchased ________, Price $ ____________

☐ *You Make My Heart Shine*, 4001666

$35.00 $35.00 $35.00

LImited Ed., Issue Price $35.00, '05
American Greetings/ Carlton Cards Early Release

Purchased ____________

Price $_______________

☐ *Cent With Love*, 4001667

$25.00 $25.00 $25.00 $25.00 $25.00 $25.00

Open, Issue Price $25.00, '05

Purchased_____________

Price $ _______________

☐ *I Love You This Much*, 4001668

$30.00 $30.00 $30.00 $30.00 $30.00 $30.00

Open, Issue Price $30.00, '05

Purchased ____________

Price $ ______________

☐ *Tuning In To Happy Times*, 4001669

$50.00 $50.00

Limited Ed. 7,500, Issue Price $50.00, '05
Series: *Through The Years*

Purchased ________, Price $ ___________

☐ *Hopping For The Best*, 4001670

$50.00 $50.00

Limited Ed. 7,500, Issue Price $50.00, '05
Series: *Through The Years*

Purchased ________, Price $ ___________

☐ *From Small Beginnings Come Great Things*, 4001671

$35.00 $35.00

Limited Ed. 7,500, Issue Price $35.00, '05
Series: *Through The Years*

Purchased ________

Price $ ___________

I Love You This Much, 4001673

$30.00 $30.00
$30.00 $30.00
$30.00 $30.00

Open, Issue Price $30.00, '05

Purchased ____________

Price $ ____________

By Your Side Forever And Always, 4001778

UM $95.00
$90.00

Limited Ed. 1,500, Issue Price $90.00, '05
Chapel Exclusive

Purchased ________, Price $ ____________

I'm Yours Heart And Soul, 4001779

UM $400.00
$350.00

Limited Ed. 2005, Issue Price $100.00, '05
Chapel Exclusive

Purchased ________, Price $ ____________

Renew Faith, Restore Hope, Replenish Love, 4001784

$75.00

Limited Ed. 2,000, Issue Price $75.00, '05
Precious Moments Premier Collection
CCR Exclusive
Series: *Four Seasons Carousel Horse*

Purchased ________, Price $ ____________

Reflect And Give Thanks For All Of Life's Bounty, 4001786

$75.00

Limited Ed. 2,000, Issue Price $75.00, '05
Precious Moments Premier Collection
CCR Exclusive
Series: *Four Seasons Carousel Horse*

Purchased ________, Price $ ____________

Allow Sunshine And Laughter To Fill Your Days, 4001785

$75.00

Limited Ed. 2,000, Issue Price $75.00, '05
Precious Moments Premier Collection
CCR Exclusive
Series: *Four Seasons Carousel Horse*

Purchased ________, Price $ ____________

A Winter Wonderland Awaits, 4001787

$75.00

Limited Ed. 2,000, Issue Price $75.00, '05
Precious Moments Premier Collection
CCR Exclusive
Series: *Four Seasons Carousel Horse*

Purchased ________, Price $ ____________

You Take The Cake, 4001780

UM $60.00 $50.00 $50.00
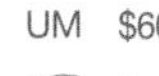 $55.00  $50.00  $50.00

Open, Issue Price $50.00, '05
Chapel Exclusive

Purchased ________, Price $ ____________

☐ *I Picked You To Love*, 4001810

$35.00
$35.00
$35.00
$35.00
$35.00
$35.00

Open, Issue Price $30.00, '05

Purchased ________

Price $ ________

☐ *I Picked You To Love*, 4001811

$35.00
$35.00
$35.00
$35.00
$35.00
$35.00

Open, Issue Price $30.00, '05

Purchased ________

Price $________

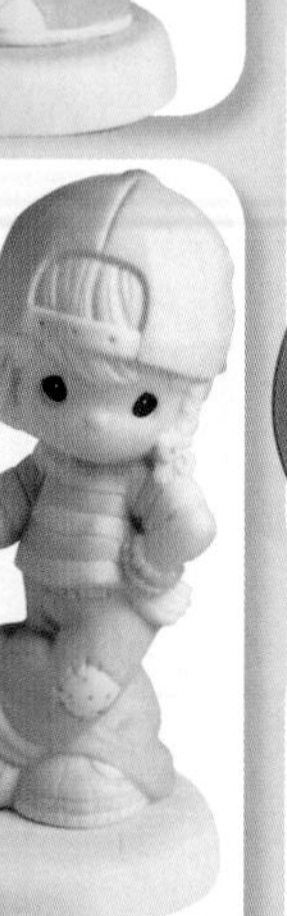

☐ *The Tassel Was No Hassle*, 4001812

$40.00
$40.00
$40.00
$40.00
$40.00
$40.00

Open, Issue Price $40.00, '05

Purchased ________, Price $ ________

☐ *A Bead-azzling Friendship*, 4001947

$40.00
$40.00

Open, Issue Price $40.00, '05
Carlton Cards Exclusive

Purchased ________, Price $ ________

☐ *You Shalt Not Stumble*, 4002981

$25.00
$25.00
$25.00
$25.00
$25.00

Open, Issue Price $25.00, '05
Japanese Collection

Purchased ________, Price $ ________

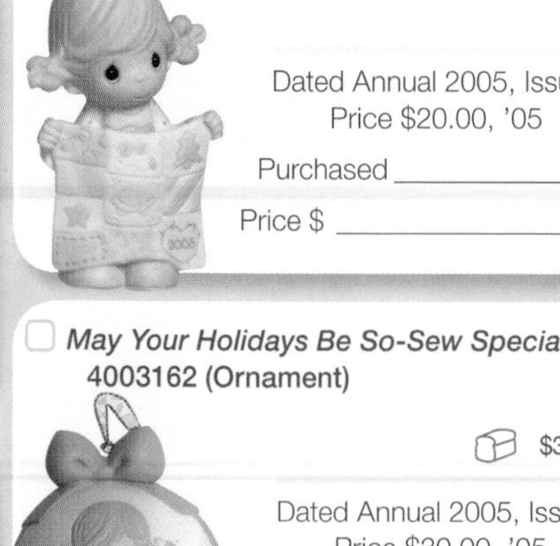

☐ *May Your Holidays Be So-Sew Special*, 4003161 (Ornament)

$20.00

Dated Annual 2005, Issue Price $20.00, '05

Purchased ________

Price $ ________

☐ *May Your Holidays Be So-Sew Special*, 4003162 (Ornament)

$30.00

Dated Annual 2005, Issue Price $30.00, '05

Purchased ________

Price $ ________

☐ *Our First Christmas Together*, 4003163 (Ornament)

$20.00

Dated Annual 2005, Issue Price $20.00, '05

Purchased________

Price $________

☐ *True Friends Have One Heart*, 4003164

$60.00
$60.00
$60.00
$60.00
$60.00

Open, Issue Price $60.00, '05

Purchased ________, Price $ ________

☐ *You Light Up My Holly-Days*, 4003165

$45.00
$45.00
$45.00
$45.00
$45.00

Open, Issue Price $45.00, '05

Purchased ________

Price $ ________

☐ *Thankful For My Family*, 4003166

$70.00
$70.00
$70.00
$70.00
$70.00

Open, Issue Price $70.00, '05

Purchased ________, Price $ ________

☐ *"A Hui Hou," Til We Meet Again*, 4003167

$2,500.00

2005 Precious Moments Collectors Club 25th Anniversary Hawaiian Celebration Exclusive Figurine. 100 were awarded to Collectors in drawings held during the event, May 18 – 23, 2005.

Limited Ed. 100, Gift, '05
2005 Hawaii Event Exclusive

Purchased ________

Price $________

☐ *Merry Christmas Two Ewe*, 4003168

$35.00
$35.00
$35.00
$35.00
$35.00

Open, Issue Price $35.00, '05

Purchased ________

Price $________

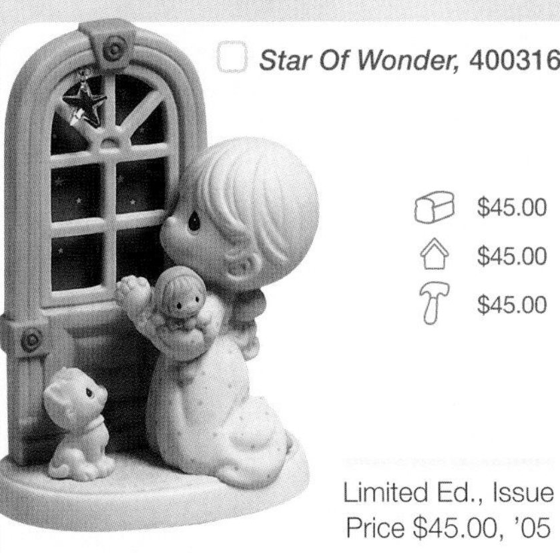

Star Of Wonder, 4003169

$45.00
$45.00
$45.00

Limited Ed., Issue Price $45.00, '05

Purchased ________, Price $ ___________

There's No Place Like Home For Christmas, 4003172

$35.00
$35.00
$35.00
$35.00
$35.00

Comes with photo frame stocking ornament.

Open, Issue Price $35.00, '05

Purchased ________, Price $ ___________

Rejoicing In God's Gift Of You, 4003174

$35.00
$35.00
$35.00
$35.00
$35.00

Open, Issue Price $35.00, '05

Purchased ___________

Price $ ___________

Together Is The Nicest Place To Be, 4003175

$75.00
$75.00
$75.00
$75.00
$75.00

Open, Issue Price $75.00, '05

Purchased ________, Price $ ___________

Sing Songs Of Praise To Him, 4003176 (Musical)

$145.00

Limited Ed. 5,000, Issue Price $145.00, '05
Tune: *Silent Night*

Purchased ________, Price $ ___________

You're The Cymbal Of Perfection, 4003177

$35.00 $35.00
$35.00 $35.00
$35.00

Open, Issue Price $35.00, '05
Nativity Addition

Purchased___________

Price $ ___________

His Truth Is Marching On, 4003178

UM $20.00 $20.00
$20.00 $20.00
$20.00 $20.00

Open, Issue Price $20.00, '05
Mini Nativity Addition

Purchased ___________

Price $___________

Angels Keep While Shepherds Sleep, 4003179

$125.00
$125.00

Limited Ed., Issue Price $65.00, '05
Limited to 2005 Production Only

Purchased ________, Price $ ___________

Sprinkled In Sweetness, 4003182

$60.00
$60.00
$60.00
$60.00
$60.00

Open, Issue Price $60.00, '05

Purchased ________, Price $ ___________

Until We Meet Again, 4003183

UM $55.00
$55.00
$55.00
$55.00
$55.00
$55.00

Open, Issue Price $55.00, '05
Chapel Exclusive

Purchased ________, Price $ ___________

"A Hui Hou," Til We Meet Again, 4003245

$150.00

Given to those who attended the Hawaiian Celebration held May 18 – 23, 2005.

Limited Ed.1,200, Gift, '05
2005 Hawaii Event Exclusive

Purchased ___________

Price $ ___________

"Pi'I Mai Ka Nalu," Surf's Up! 4003247

$150.00

Given to those who attended the Hawaiian Celebration held May 18 – 23, 2005.

Limited Ed. 1,200, Gift, '05
2005 Hawaii Event Exclusive

Purchased ___________

Price $___________

☐ **"Mahlo Hawi'I," Thank You Hawaii, 4003248**

$150.00

Given to those who attended the Hawaiian Celebration held May 18 – 23, 2005.

Limited Ed. 1,200, Gift, '05
2005 Hawaii Event Exclusive

Purchased ________, Price $ ____________

☐ **"Aloha Kakou A Pau," Aloha Everyone, 4003249**

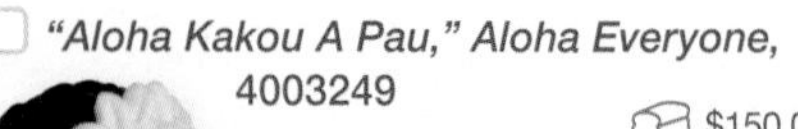

$150.00

Given to those who attended the Hawaiian Celebration held May 18 – 23, 2005.

Limited Ed.1,200, Gift, '05
2005 Hawaii Event Exclusive

Purchased____________

Price $______________

☐ **"Aloha Aina" Love Of The Land, 4003250**

$150.00

Given to those who attended the Hawaiian Celebration held May 18 – 23, 2005.

Limited Ed.1,200, Gift, '05
2005 Hawaii Event Exclusive

Purchased ________, Price $ ____________

☐ **"Wiki Wiki Transit" Quick Transportation, 4003251**

$150.00

Given to those who attended the Hawaiian Celebration held May 18 – 23, 2005.

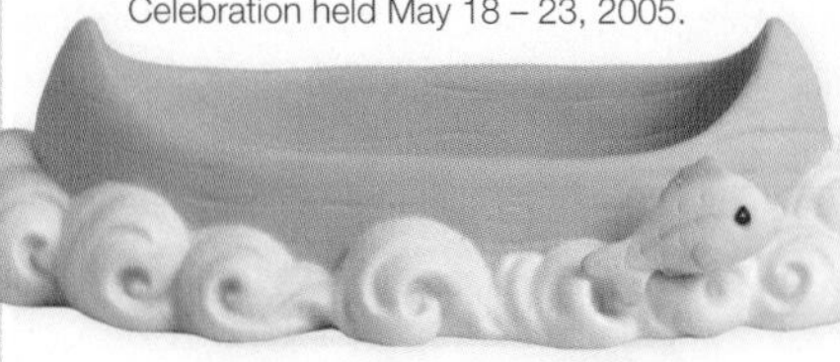

Limited Ed.1,200, Gift, '05
2005 Hawaii Event Exclusive

Purchased ________, Price $ ____________

☐ **Snowman in Top Hat — Streetlight, 4003322**

$20.00

Open, Issue Price $20.00, '05

Purchased ________, Price $ ____________

☐ **Snowman Christmas Tree, 4003323**

$20.00

Open, Issue Price $20.00, '05

Purchased ________, Price $ ____________

☐ **Snowman Holding Lantern, 4003324**

$15.00

Open, Issue Price $15.00, '05

Purchased ___________

Price $____________

☐ **Snowman Holding Wreath, 4003325**

$15.00

Open, Issue Price $15.00, '05

Purchased____________

Price $______________

☐ **Boy Placing Star On Tree, 4003327 (Nightlight)**

$40.00

Open, Issue Price $40.00, '05

Purchased ________, Price $ ____________

☐ **Nativity, 4003328**

$20.00

Open, Issue Price $20.00, '05

Purchased ________, Price $ ____________

☐ **Special Times With Mom Create Special Memories, 4003585**

$65.00
$65.00
$65.00

Open, Issue Price $50.00, '05
Carlton Card Exclusive

Purchased ___

Price $ _____

☐ **Love From Hawaii, 4003777**

$37.50 $37.50
$37.50

Limited Ed. 1,200, Issue Price $37.50, '05
Cathedral Gift Shop Exclusive

Purchased______________

Price $ ______________

☐ *Your Heart Is Forever,* 4003778

$40.00 $40.00
$40.00 $40.00
$40.00

Open, Issue Price $40.00, '05

Purchased ______

Price $ ________

☐ *Make Every Day Magical,* 4004159

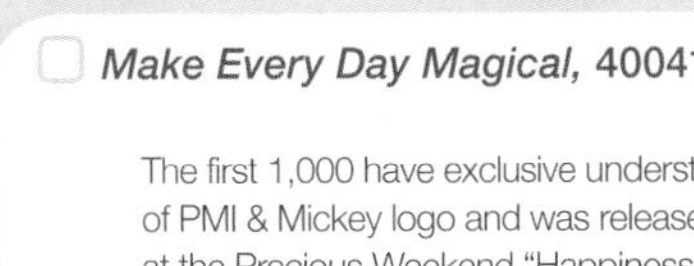

The first 1,000 have exclusive understamp of PMI & Mickey logo and was released at the Precious Weekend "Happiness Shared Together" September 3 – 4, 2005, Disney World in FL.

UM $125.00 $85.00
$100.00 $60.00

Open, Issue Price $45.00, '05
Disney Showcase Collection

Purchased ____________________

Price $____________________

☐ *Happiness Is Best Shared Together,* 4004156

$75.00
$75.00
$75.00

Open, Issue Price $75.00, '05
Disney Theme Park Exclusive,
Disney Showcase Collection

Purchased ________, Price $ ____________

☐ *This Bears My Love For You (Girl),* 4004371

$35.00 $35.00
$35.00 $35.00
$35.00

Open, Issue Price $35.00, '05

Purchased ________

Price $ __________

☐ *The Same Today, Yesterday And Forever,* 4004373

$35.00 $35.00
$35.00 $35.00
$35.00

Open, Issue Price $35.00, '05

Purchased ________, Price $ ___________

☐ *You're My Mouseketeer* 4004157

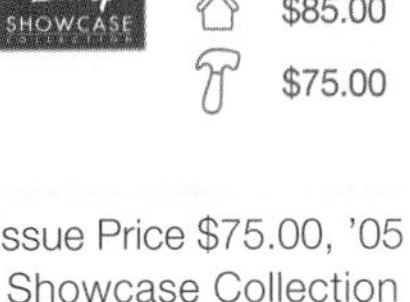

$100.00
$85.00
$75.00

Retired, Issue Price $75.00, '05
Disney Showcase Collection

Purchased ___________

Price $____________

☐ *I M The One You Love,* 4004372

$25.00
$25.00
$25.00
$25.00
$25.00

Open, Issue Price $25.00, '05

Purchased ________, Price $ ___________

☐ *Heaven Sent,* 4004374

$35.00 $35.00
$35.00 $35.00
$35.00

Open, Issue Price $37.50, '05

Purchased _______

Price $ _________

☐ *Everything's Better With A Friend,* 4004158

UM $125.00 $85.00
$100.00 $60.00

The first 1,000 have exclusive understamp of PMI & Mickey logo and was released at the Precious Weekend "Happiness Shared Together" September 3 – 4, 2005, Disney World in FL.

Open, Issue Price $60.00, '05
Disney Showcase Collection

Purchased ________, Price $ ___________

☐ *You Were Made For Me,* 4004375

$35.00

Available at Distinguished Service Retailers during a special one-day event on 11/19/05.

Event Piece, Issue Price $35.00, '05

Purchased ________, Price $ ___________

☐ ***You Were Made For Me,*** 4004376 (Ornament)

UM $20.00

$20.00

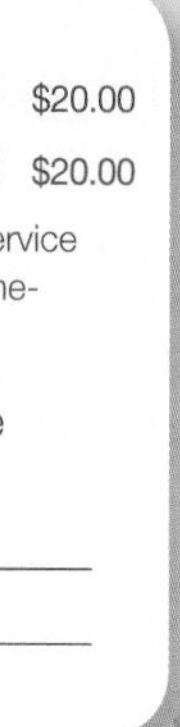

Available at Distinguished Service Retailers during a special one-day event on 11/19/05.

Event Piece, Issue Price $12.00, '05

Purchased__________

Price $ __________

☐ ***I'm So Glad I Picked You,*** 4004380

UM $35.00

$35.00

$35.00

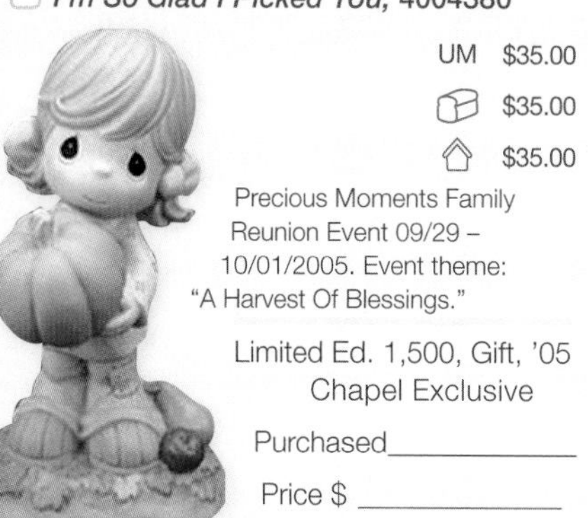

Precious Moments Family Reunion Event 09/29 – 10/01/2005. Event theme: "A Harvest Of Blessings."

Limited Ed. 1,500, Gift, '05 Chapel Exclusive

Purchased__________

Price $ __________

☐ ***Birthday Wishes With Hugs And Kisses,*** 4004682

$37.50

$37.50

$37.50

$37.50

$37.50

Open, Issue Price $35.00, '05

Purchased __________

Price $ __________

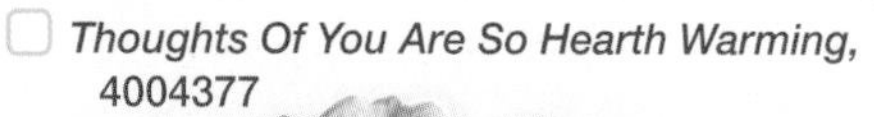

☐ ***Thoughts Of You Are So Hearth Warming,*** 4004377

$55.00

$55.00

$55.00

$55.00

Limited Ed., Issue Price $50.00, '05 2005 Syndicated Catalog Exclusive

Purchased ________, Price $ __________

☐ ***A Loving Heart Is Forever,*** 4004679

$35.00 $35.00

$35.00 $35.00

$35.00

Open, Issue Price $35.00, '05

Purchased__________

Price $ __________

☐ ***Our Friendship Is Like A Breath Of Fresh Air,*** 4004683

$37.50

$37.50

$37.50

$37.50

$37.50

Open, Issue Price $37.50, '05

Purchased __________

Price $ __________

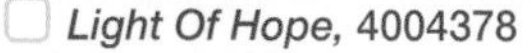

☐ ***Light Of Hope,*** 4004378

UM $40.00

$40.00

$40.00

$40.00

$40.00

$40.00

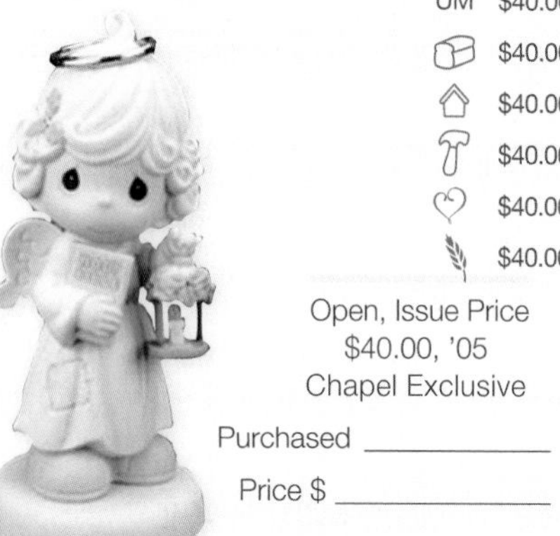

Open, Issue Price $40.00, '05 Chapel Exclusive

Purchased __________

Price $ __________

☐ ***Immersed In God's Love,*** 4004680

$40.00

$40.00

$40.00

$40.00

$40.00

Open, Issue Price $40.00, '05

Purchased ________, Price $ __________

☐ ***I'm A Fool For You,*** 4004737

$35.00

$35.00

$35.00

$35.00

$35.00

Gift Set Recieved a heart shaped pillow with the figurine.

Open, Issue Price $35.00, '05

Purchased ________, Price $ __________

☐ ***Light Of Hope,*** 4004379 (Ornament)

UM $25.00 $25.00

$25.00 $25.00

$25.00 $25.00

Open, Issue Price $25.00, '05 Chapel Exclusive

Purchased__________

Price $ __________

☐ ***You Are A Child Of God (Girl),*** 4004681

$35.00

$35.00

$35.00

$35.00

$35.00

Open, Issue Price $30.00, '05

Purchased __________

Price $ __________

☐ ***May Love Blossom Wherever You Go,*** 4004738

$50.00

LImited Ed. 2005, Issue Price $50.00, '05

Purchased __________

Price $ __________

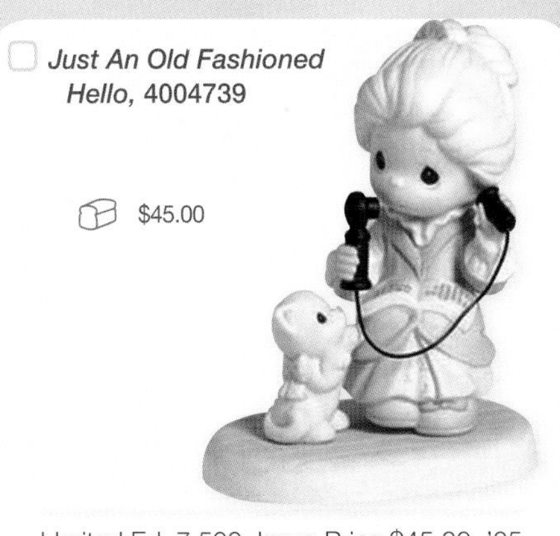

Just An Old Fashioned Hello, 4004739

$45.00

LImited Ed. 7,500, Issue Price $45.00, '05

Purchased ________, Price $ ___________

Mixing Up A Brighter Tomorrow, 4004740

$45.00

LImited Ed. 7,500, Issue Price $45.00, '05

Purchased ________, Price $ ___________

One Small Step, 4004741

$45.00

LImited Ed. 7,500, Issue Price $45.00, '05

Purchased ________, Price $ ___________

You Are A Child Of God (Boy), 4004880

$35.00
$35.00
$35.00
$35.00
$35.00

Open, Issue Price $30.00, '05

Purchased___________

Price $ ___________

Your Love Reigns Forever In My Heart, 4004985

$45.00
$45.00
$45.00
$45.00
$45.00

Open, Issue Price $45.00, '05

Purchased ________, Price $ ___________

You Take The Cake, 4004986

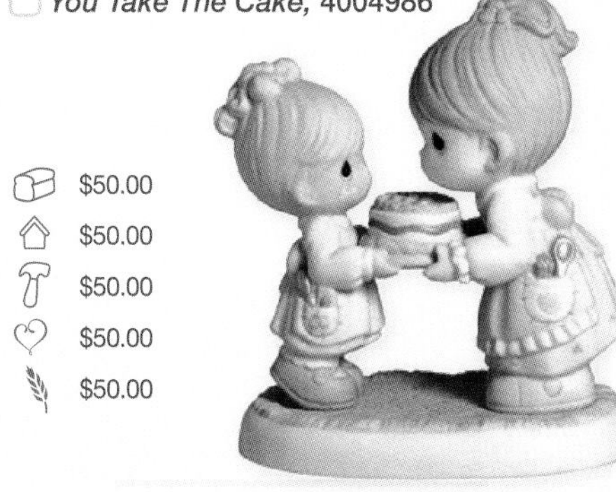

$50.00
$50.00
$50.00
$50.00
$50.00

Open, Issue Price $50.00, '05

Purchased ________, Price $ ___________

Baby's First Christmas, 4024080 (Ornament)

$20.00

Dated Annual, Issue Price $20.00, '05

Purchased ___________

Price $ ___________

Baby's First Christmas, 4024081 (Ornament)

$20.00

Dated Annual, Issue Price $20.00, '05

Purchased ___________

Price $ ___________

The Purr-fect Gift, 4024082 (Ornament)

$20.00

Dated Annual, Issue Price $20.00, '05

Purchased ___________

Price $ ___________

This Bears My Love For You (Boy), 4024083

$35.00
$35.00
$35.00
$35.00
$35.00

Open, Issue Price $35.00, '05

Purchased ___________

Price $ ___________

Love Is A Warm Heart On A Cold Day, 4024084

$30.00
$30.00
$30.00
$30.00

Retired 2007, Issue Price $30.00, '05

Purchased ________

Price $ ___________

His Hope Lights My Way, 4024085

$50.00
$50.00
$50.00
$50.00
$50.00

Open, Issue Price $50.00, '05

Purchased ________, Price $ ___________

Faithful Follower, 4024086

$40.00
$40.00
$40.00
$40.00
$40.00

Open, Issue Price $40.00, '05

Purchased ________, Price $ ___________

☐ *Scatter Joy*, 4024087

$50.00 $50.00 $50.00
$50.00 $50.00

Open, Issue Price $50.00, '05

Purchased ________, Price $ ____________

☐ *May Your Holidays Be So-Sew Special*, 4024088

$45.00

Dated Annual 2005, Issue Price $35.00, '05

Purchased ________, Price $ ____________

☐ *No Rest For The Weary*, 4024100 (Ornament)

$20.00
$20.00
$20.00
$20.00
$20.00

Open, Issue Price $20.00, '05

Purchased ________, Price $ ____________

☐ *Grandma, I'll Never Outgrow You!* 4024101 (Ornament)

$20.00
$20.00
$20.00
$20.00
$20.00

Open, Issue Price $20.00, '05

Purchased ________, Price $ ____________

☐ *Sister, You Have A Heart Of Gold*, 4024102 (Ornament)

$20.00 $20.00
$20.00 $20.00
$20.00

Open, Issue Price $20.00, '05

Purchased ____________

Price $ ____________

☐ *Daughter, You'll Always Be My Princess*, 4024103 (Ornament)

$20.00 $20.00
$20.00 $20.00
$20.00

Open, Issue Price $20.00, '05

Purchased____________

Price $ ____________

☐ *Blessed With A Loving Godmother*, 4024104 (Ornament)

$20.00 $20.00
$20.00 $20.00
$20.00

Open, Issue Price $20.00, '05

Purchased____________

Price $____________

☐ *Grandma's Little Angel*, 4024105 (Ornament)

$20.00
$20.00
$20.00
$20.00
$20.00

Open, Issue Price $20.00, '05

Purchased ________, Price $ ____________

☐ *I Can't Give You Anything But Love*, 4024106 (Ornament)

$20.00 $20.00
$20.00 $20.00
$20.00

Open, Issue Price $20.00, '05

Purchased ____________

Price $ ____________

☐ *You're A Gem Of A Friend*, 4024107 (Ornament)

$20.00 $20.00
$20.00 $20.00
$20.00

Open, Issue Price $20.00, '05

Purchased ____________

Price $ ____________

☐ *A Nurse's Care Is The Best Medicine*, 4024108 (Ornament)

$20.00 $20.00
$20.00 $20.00
$20.00

Open, Issue Price $20.00, '05

Purchased ____________

Price $____________

☐ *Teacher, You're A Precious Work Of Art,* 4024109 (Ornament)

$20.00
$20.00
$20.00
$20.00
$20.00

Open, Issue Price $20.00, '05

Purchased ________, Price $ ____________

☐ *You'll Always Be A Winner To Me,* 4024111 (Ornament)

$20.00
$20.00
$20.00
$20.00
$20.00

Open, Issue Price $20.00, '05

Purchased ________, Price $ ____________

☐ *Your Spirit Is An Inspiration,* 4024112 (Ornament)

$20.00
$20.00
$20.00
$20.00
$20.00

Open, Issue Price $20.00, '05

Purchased ________, Price $ ____________

☐ *Serving Up Fun,* 4024110 (Ornament)

$20.00 $20.00
$20.00 $20.00
$20.00

Open, Issue Price $20.00, '05

Purchased __________

Price $______________

Collector's Club

I Will Make You Fishers Of Men (Lithograph)

UM $35.00

Club members entitled to this exclusive lithograph free with purchase of $25.00 on January 25, 2002.

Members Only, Gift, '02

Purchased ____________________

Price $____________________

The Sweetest Treat Is Friendship, 110855

$60.00

$60.00

Members Only, Issue Price $55.00, '03

Purchased ________, Price $ ____________

God Bless Our Years Together, 12440

$350.00

There have been reports of this piece being completely unpainted.

Members Only,
Issue Price $175.00, '85
Fifth Anniversary Club
Commemorative

Purchased ________________

Price $________________

You Make My Heart Soar, 118316

$45.00

$40.00

Open, Issue Price $35.00, '05

Purchased ________, Price $ ____________

Bubble Your Troubles Away, 101730

$55.00

$50.00

Members Only, Issue Price $45.00, '02

Purchased ________, Price $ ____________

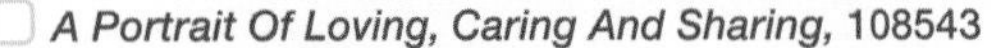

A Portrait Of Loving, Caring And Sharing, 108543

$450.00

$400.00

Available for preorder from January 25 through February 19, 2003.

Members Only, Issue Price $375.00, '03 Limited Ed.

Purchased ______________

Price $ ______________

A Perfect Display Of 15 Happy Years, 127817

Club's fifteenth anniversary commemorative figurine.

$150.00

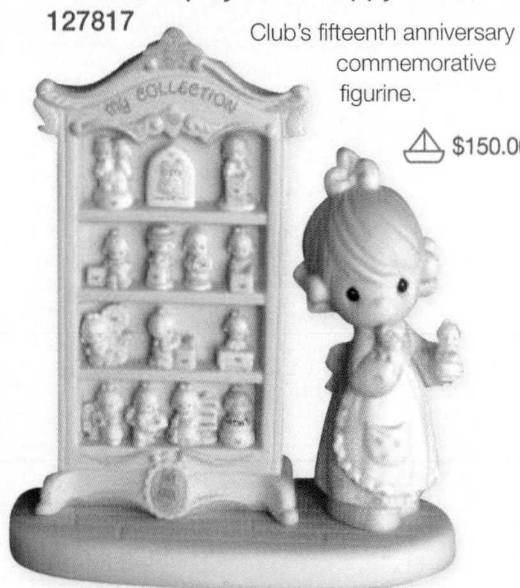

Members Only, Issue Price $100.00, '95

Purchased ________, Price $ ____________

☐ *Celebrating A Decade Of Loving, Caring And Sharing,* 227986 (Ornament)

UM $18.00

Members Only, Issue Price $7.00, '89

Purchased ______________

Price $______________

☐ *Our Club Is Soda-licious,* 266841 (Ornament)

$375.00

Members Only, Gift, '96 Convention Ornament

Purchased ________

Price $____________

☐ *Rejoice In The Victory,* 283541

$75.00

$70.00

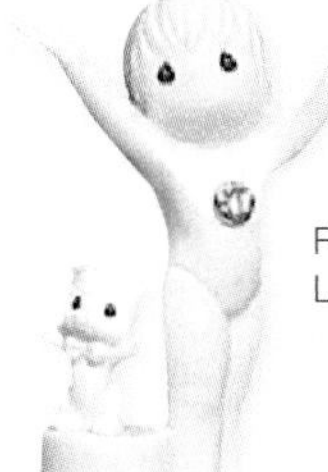

Precious Rewards Frequent Buyer Program, Level 1: 300 points.

Members Only, Issue Price $30.00, '97

Purchased__________

Price $ ____________

☐ *God Bless You With Bouquets Of Victory,* 283584

$85.00

$80.00

Precious Rewards Frequent Buyer Program, Level 2: 500 points.

Members Only, Issue Price $50.00, '97

Purchased ______________

Price $ ______________

☐ *Faith Is The Victory,* 283592

$145.00

$140.00

Precious Rewards Frequent Buyer Program, Level 3: 1,000 points.

Members Only, Issue Price $75.00, '97

Purchased _____

Price $ _______

☐ *Put On A Happy Face,* 440906 (Mask)

UM $450.00

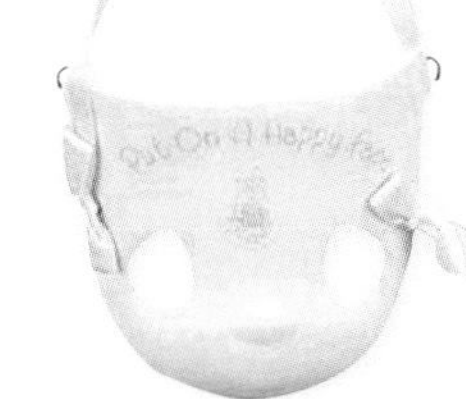

Given to attendess of the 1997 Local Club Chapter Convention.

Convention Gift, '97

Purchased ________, Price $ ____________

☐ *Delivering Good News To You,* 488135

$65.00

$60.00

Gift to club members who purchased $35.00 or more during June 21, 2003 event.

Members Only, Gift, '03 DSR & CCR Event

Purchased__________

Price $____________

☐ *God Loveth A Cheerful Giver,* 495891 (Box)

UM $38.00

Gift to club members joining by June 30, 1998.

Members Only, Gift, '98

Purchased__________

Price $____________

☐ *A Growing Love,* 520349 (Ornament)

$85.00

Members Only, Issue Price $15.00, '88

Purchased __________

Price $ ______________

☐ *Always Room For One More,* 522961 (Ornament)

$90.00

Members Only, Issue Price $15.00, '89

Purchased _________

Price $____________

☐ *This Land Is Our Land,* 527386

500th anniversary voyage of Columbus commemorative.

$425.00

$400.00

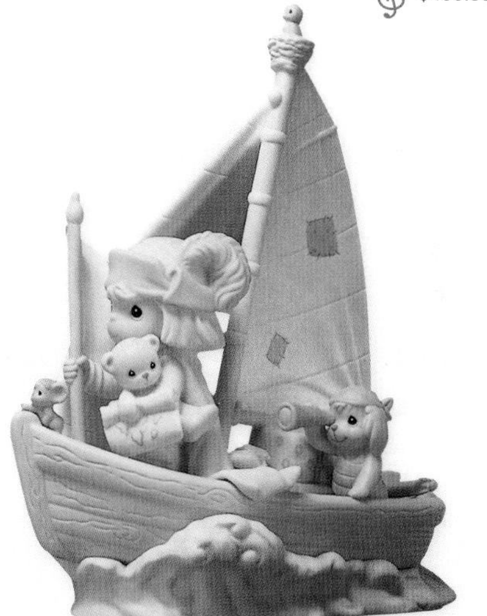

Members Only, Issue Price $350.00, '92

Purchased ________, Price $ ____________

☐ *You Fill The Pages Of My Life,* 530980

$75.00

Came with collector's edition of the book *Precious Moments Last Forever.*

Members Only, Issue Price $32.50, '94

Purchased ________, Price $ ____________

☐ **A Salute To Our Stars, 549614 (Medallion)**

$400.00

Convention Gift, '98

Purchased ________, Price $ ____________

☐ **Thank You For Your Membership, 635243**

$70.00 · $60.00 · $50.00 · $40.00 · $40.00 · $40.00 · $40.00 · $40.00 · $40.00 · $40.00 · $40.00

Five-year membership piece.

Members Only, Issue Price $30.00, '99

Purchased____________

Price $______________

☐ **A Club Where Friendships Are Made, 635251**

$90.00 · $80.00 · $70.00 · $60.00 · $50.00 · $40.00 · $40.00 · $40.00 · $40.00 · $40.00 · $40.00

Ten-year membership piece.

Members Only, Issue Price $40.00, '99

Purchased ________, Price $ ____________

☐ **A Club Where Fellowship Reigns, 635278**

$70.00 · $60.00 · $50.00 · $50.00 · $50.00 · $50.00 · $50.00 · $50.00 · $50.00 · $50.00 · $50.00

Fifteen-year membership piece.

Members Only, Issue Price $50.00, '99

Purchased ________, Price $ ____________

☐ **Companionship Happens In Our Club, 635286**

Twenty-year membership piece.

$70.00 · $60.00 · $60.00 · $60.00 · $60.00 · $60.00 · $60.00 · $60.00 · $60.00 · $60.00 · $60.00

Members Only, Issue Price $60.00, '99

Purchased ________, Price $ ____________

☐ **Club Friendships Are Unsinkable, 635290**

Twenty-five year membership piece.

$120.00 · $115.00 · $90.00 · $75.00 · $65.00 · $65.00

Members Only, Issue Price $65.00, '05

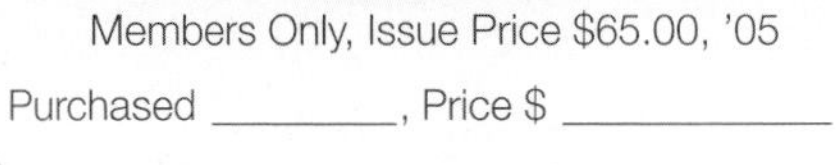

Purchased ________, Price $ ____________

☐ **You Are The Heart Of Precious Moments, 681016 (Medallion)**

UM $275.00

$250.00

1999 local club chapter convention.

Limited Ed. 600, Members Only, '99

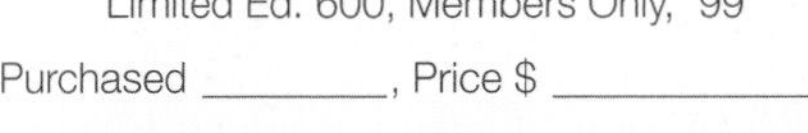

Purchased ________, Price $ ____________

☐ **A Beary Loving Collector, 823953**

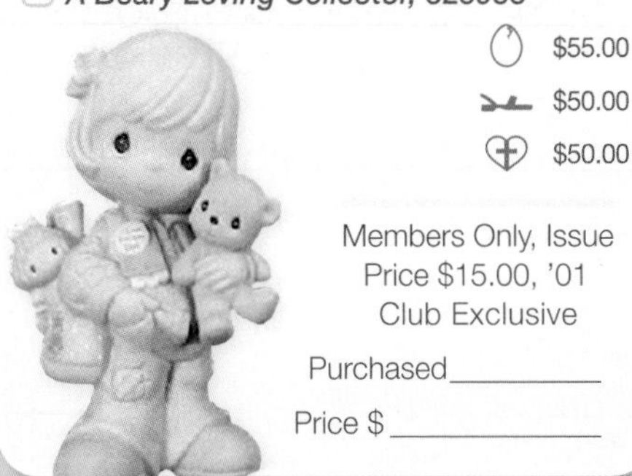

$55.00 · $50.00 · $50.00

Members Only, Issue Price $15.00, '01 Club Exclusive

Purchased__________

Price $____________

☐ **Loving Every Precious Moment With You, 4004612**

$85.00 · $85.00

Members Only, Issue Price $85.00, '05

Purchased ________, Price $ ____________

☐ **Always Room For One More, C-0009**

$55.00 · $50.00 · $48.00

Members Only, Issue Price $19.50, '89

Purchased ____

Price $________

☐ **Always Room For One More, C-0109**

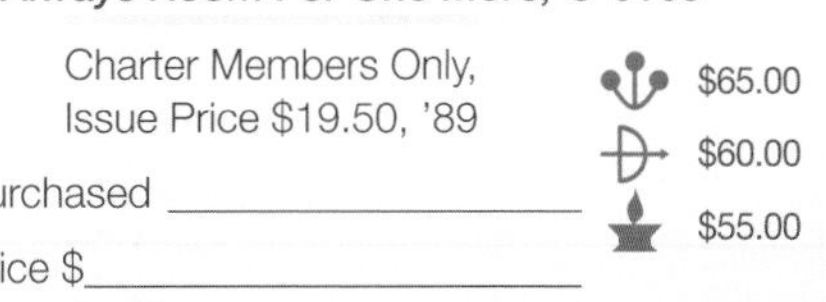

Charter Members Only, Issue Price $19.50, '89

$65.00 · $60.00 · $55.00

Purchased ________________

Price $__________________

☐ **My Happiness, C-0010**

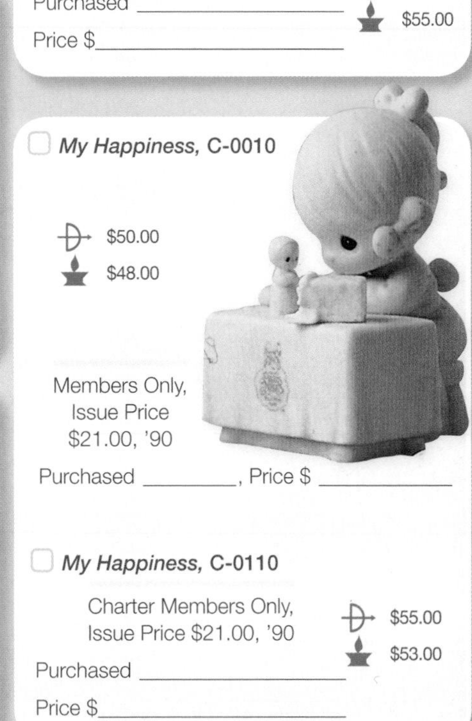

$50.00 · $48.00

Members Only, Issue Price $21.00, '90

Purchased ________, Price $ ____________

☐ **My Happiness, C-0110**

Charter Members Only, Issue Price $21.00, '90

$55.00 · $53.00

Purchased ________________

Price $__________________

☐ *Sharing The Good News Together, C-0011*

$55.00
$50.00

Members Only, Issue Price $22.50, '91

Purchased ________

Price $ ___________

☐ *Sharing The Good News Together, C-0111*

Charter Members Only, Issue Price $22.50, '91

$60.00
$55.00

Purchased ________________

Price $________________

☐ *You Are The End Of My Rainbow, C-0014*

$40.00
$35.00
$38.00

Members Only, Issue Price $26.00, '94

Purchased __________

Price $ ___________

☐ *You Are The End Of My Rainbow, C-0114*

Charter Members Only, Issue Price $26.00, '94

$55.00
$53.00
$50.00

Purchased ________________

Price $________________

☐ *A Special Toast To Precious Moments, C-0017*

$48.00
$45.00

Members Only, Issue Price $25.00, '97

Purchased ________

Price $ ___________

☐ *A Special Toast To Precious Moments, C-0117*

Charter Members Only, Issue Price $25.00, '97

$55.00
$53.00

Purchased ________________

Price $________________

☐ *The Club That's Out Of This World, C-0012*

$55.00
$50.00

Members Only, Issue Price $25.00, '92

Purchased ________

Price $________________

☐ *The Club That's Out Of This World, C-0112*

Charter Members Only, Issue Price $25.00, '92

$60.00
$55.00

Purchased ________________

Price $________________

☐ *You're The Sweetest Cookie In The Batch, C-0015*

$55.00
$53.00

Members Only, Issue Price $27.00, '95

Purchased ______________

Price $ ______________

☐ *You're The Sweetest Cookie In The Batch, C-0115*

Charter Members Only, Issue Price $27.00, '95

$60.00
$58.00

Purchased ________________

Price $________________

☐ *Focusing In On Those Precious Moments, C-0018*

$45.00
$40.00

Members Only, Issue Price $28.00, '98

Purchased ____________

Price $ ____________

☐ *Focusing In On Those Precious Moments, C-0118*

Charter Members Only, Issue Price $28.00, '98

$50.00
$48.00

Purchased ________________

Price $________________

☐ *Loving, Caring And Sharing Along The Way, C-0013*

$45.00
$40.00

Members Only, Issue Price $25.00, '93

Purchased__________

Price $____________

☐ *Loving, Caring And Sharing Along The Way, C-0113*

Charter Members Only, Issue Price $25.00, '93

$55.00
$53.00

Purchased ________________

Price $________________

☐ *You're As Pretty As A Picture, C-0016*

$43.00
$40.00

Members Only, Issue Price $25.00, '96

Purchased ______

Price $ _________

☐ *You're As Pretty As A Picture, C-0116*

Charter Members Only, Issue Price $25.00, '96

$50.00
$48.00

Purchased ________________

Price $________________

☐ *Wishing You A World Of Peace, C-0019*

$50.00
$48.00

Members Only, Issue Price $25.00, '99

Purchased ____

Price $_________

☐ *Wishing You A World Of Peace, C-0119*

Charter Members Only, Issue Price $25.00, '99

$60.00
$58.00

Purchased ________________

Price $________________

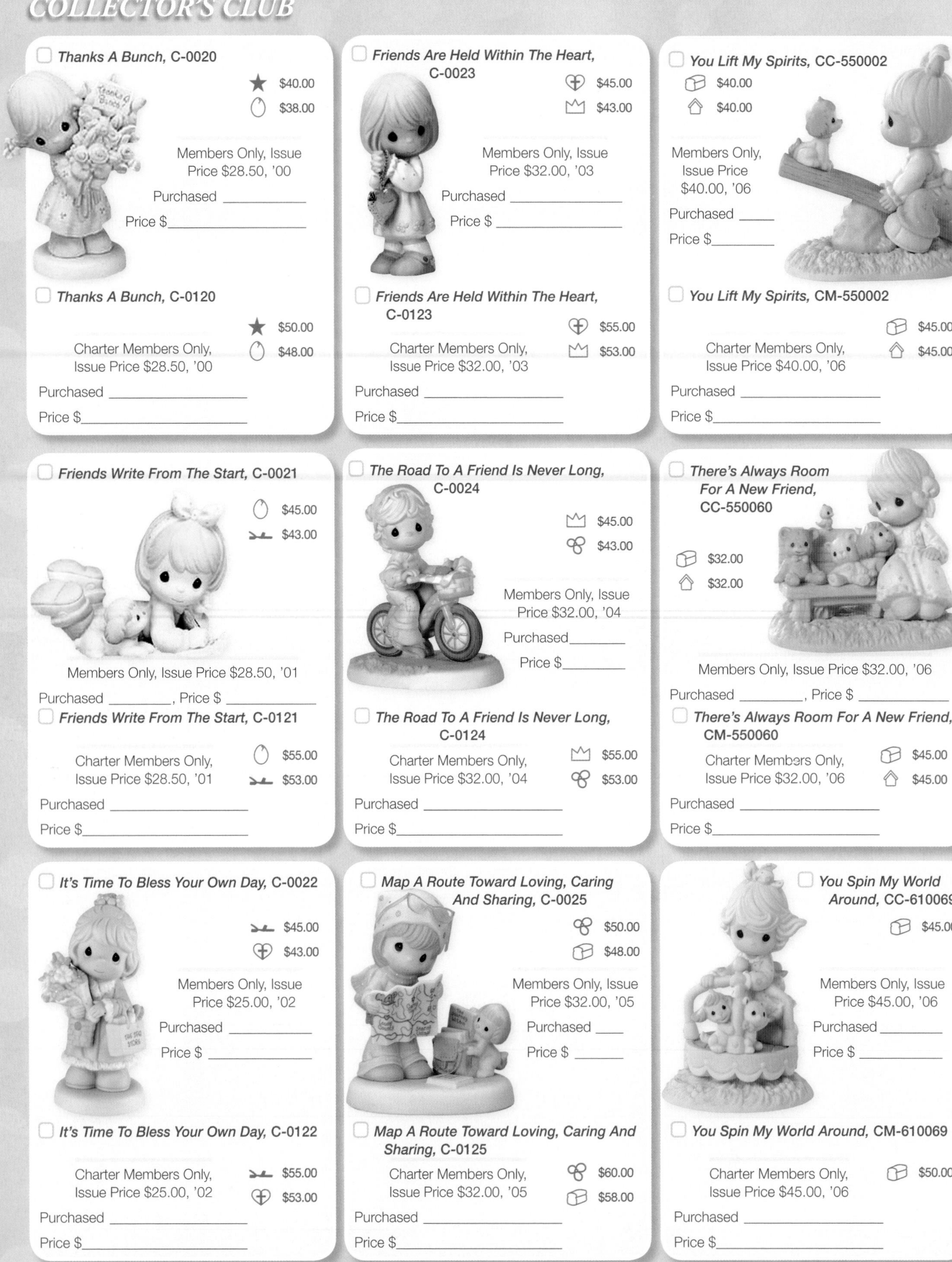

☐ *Thanks A Bunch, C-0020*

$40.00
$38.00

Members Only, Issue Price $28.50, '00

Purchased ___________

Price $___________

☐ *Thanks A Bunch, C-0120*

$50.00
$48.00

Charter Members Only, Issue Price $28.50, '00

Purchased ___________

Price $___________

☐ *Friends Are Held Within The Heart, C-0023*

$45.00
$43.00

Members Only, Issue Price $32.00, '03

Purchased ___________

Price $ ___________

☐ *Friends Are Held Within The Heart, C-0123*

$55.00
$53.00

Charter Members Only, Issue Price $32.00, '03

Purchased ___________

Price $___________

☐ *You Lift My Spirits, CC-550002*

$40.00
$40.00

Members Only, Issue Price $40.00, '06

Purchased _____

Price $_________

☐ *You Lift My Spirits, CM-550002*

$45.00
$45.00

Charter Members Only, Issue Price $40.00, '06

Purchased ___________

Price $___________

☐ *Friends Write From The Start, C-0021*

$45.00
$43.00

Members Only, Issue Price $28.50, '01

Purchased ________, Price $ ___________

☐ *Friends Write From The Start, C-0121*

$55.00
$53.00

Charter Members Only, Issue Price $28.50, '01

Purchased ___________

Price $___________

☐ *The Road To A Friend Is Never Long, C-0024*

$45.00
$43.00

Members Only, Issue Price $32.00, '04

Purchased________

Price $_________

☐ *The Road To A Friend Is Never Long, C-0124*

$55.00
$53.00

Charter Members Only, Issue Price $32.00, '04

Purchased ___________

Price $___________

☐ *There's Always Room For A New Friend, CC-550060*

$32.00
$32.00

Members Only, Issue Price $32.00, '06

Purchased ________, Price $ ___________

☐ *There's Always Room For A New Friend, CM-550060*

$45.00
$45.00

Charter Members Only, Issue Price $32.00, '06

Purchased ___________

Price $___________

☐ *It's Time To Bless Your Own Day, C-0022*

$45.00
$43.00

Members Only, Issue Price $25.00, '02

Purchased ___________

Price $ ___________

☐ *It's Time To Bless Your Own Day, C-0122*

$55.00
$53.00

Charter Members Only, Issue Price $25.00, '02

Purchased ___________

Price $___________

☐ *Map A Route Toward Loving, Caring And Sharing, C-0025*

$50.00
$48.00

Members Only, Issue Price $32.00, '05

Purchased ____

Price $ _______

☐ *Map A Route Toward Loving, Caring And Sharing, C-0125*

$60.00
$58.00

Charter Members Only, Issue Price $32.00, '05

Purchased ___________

Price $___________

☐ *You Spin My World Around, CC-610069*

$45.00

Members Only, Issue Price $45.00, '06

Purchased ________

Price $ ___________

☐ *You Spin My World Around, CM-610069*

$50.00

Charter Members Only, Issue Price $45.00, '06

Purchased ___________

Price $___________

☐ *It Only Takes A Moment To Show You Care,* CC-790001

⌂ $32.00
⚲ $32.00

Members Only, Issue Price $32.00, '07

Purchased ________, Price $ ____________

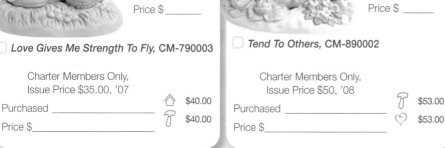

☐ *It Only Takes A Moment To Show You Care,* CM-790001

Charter Members Only, Issue Price $32.00, '07

⌂ $38.00
⚲ $38.00

Purchased ________________

Price $________________

☐ *Your Song Fills The Air With Love,* CC-790004

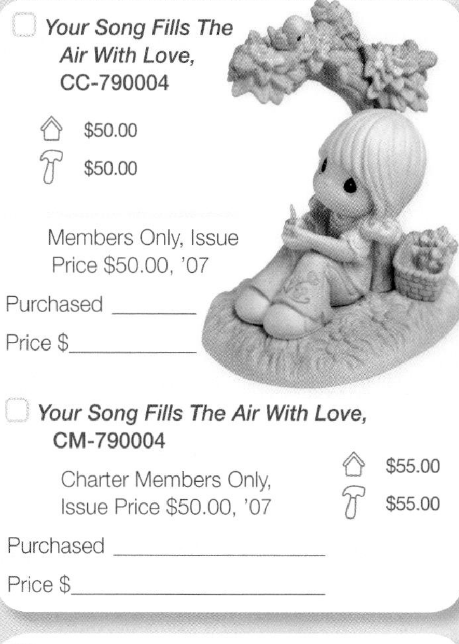

⌂ $50.00
⚲ $50.00

Members Only, Issue Price $50.00, '07

Purchased ________

Price $__________

☐ *Your Song Fills The Air With Love,* CM-790004

Charter Members Only, Issue Price $50.00, '07

⌂ $55.00
⚲ $55.00

Purchased ________________

Price $________________

☐ *Gather For The Good,* CC-890003

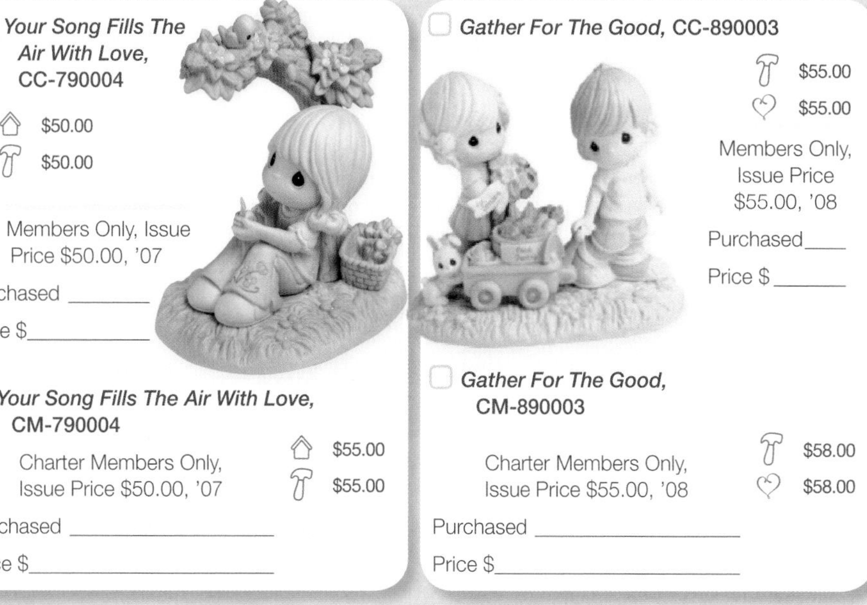

⚲ $55.00
♡ $55.00

Members Only, Issue Price $55.00, '08

Purchased____

Price $ ______

☐ *Gather For The Good,* CM-890003

Charter Members Only, Issue Price $55.00, '08

⚲ $58.00
♡ $58.00

Purchased ________________

Price $________________

☐ *You Make A World Of Difference,* CC-790002

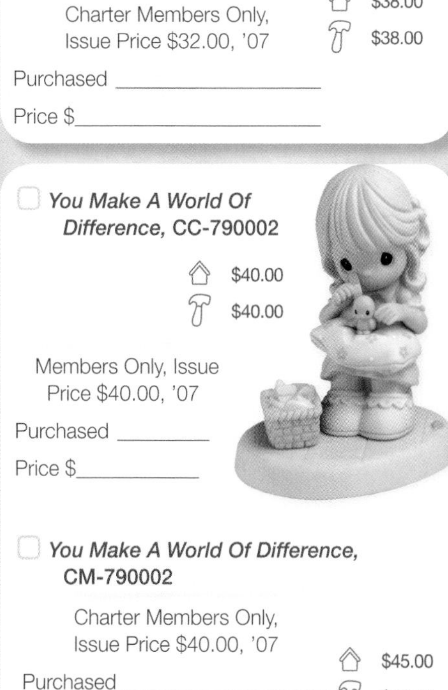

⌂ $40.00
⚲ $40.00

Members Only, Issue Price $40.00, '07

Purchased ________

Price $__________

☐ *You Make A World Of Difference,* CM-790002

Charter Members Only, Issue Price $40.00, '07

⌂ $45.00
⚲ $45.00

Purchased ________________

Price $________________

☐ *Sow Much To Do,* CC-890001

⚲ $32.00
♡ $32.00

Members Only, Issue Price $32.00, '08

Purchased ________

Price $__________

☐ *Sow Much To Do,* CM-890001

Charter Members Only, Issue Price $32.00, '08

⚲ $35.00
♡ $35.00

Purchased ________________

Price $________________

☐ *Sing For Joy With Each New Day,* CC-990001

♡ $36.00
⚘ $36.00

Members Only, Issue Price $36.00, '09

Purchased ____

Price $ ______

☐ *Sing For Joy With Each New Day,* CM-990001

Charter Members Only, Issue Price $36.00, '09

♡ $36.00
⚘ $36.00

Purchased ________________

Price $________________

☐ *Love Gives Me Strength To Fly,* CC-790003

⌂ $35.00
⚲ $35.00

Members Only, Issue Price $35.00, '07

Purchased______

Price $ ______

☐ *Love Gives Me Strength To Fly,* CM-790003

Charter Members Only, Issue Price $35.00, '07

⌂ $40.00
⚲ $40.00

Purchased ________________

Price $________________

☐ *Tend To Others,* CC-890002

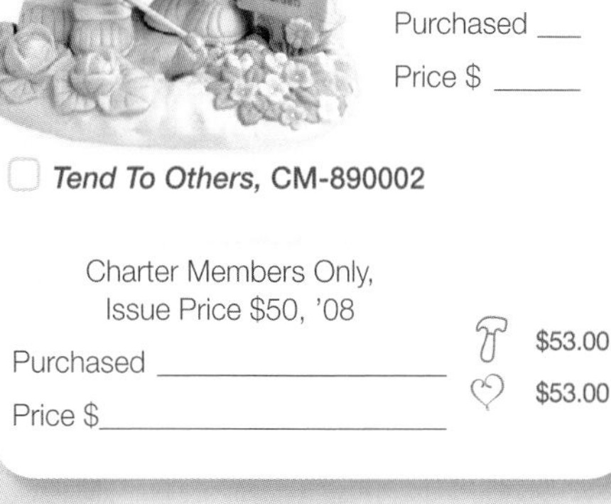

⚲ $50.00
♡ $50.00

Members Only, Issue Price $50.00, '08

Purchased ___

Price $ ______

☐ *Tend To Others,* CM-890002

Charter Members Only, Issue Price $50, '08

⚲ $53.00
♡ $53.00

Purchased ________________

Price $________________

☐ *I Come To You With Joy,* CC-990002

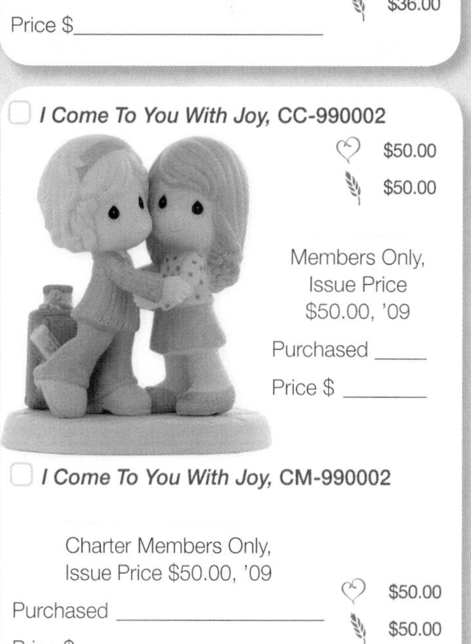

♡ $50.00
⚘ $50.00

Members Only, Issue Price $50.00, '09

Purchased ____

Price $ ______

☐ *I Come To You With Joy,* CM-990002

Charter Members Only, Issue Price $50.00, '09

♡ $50.00
⚘ $50.00

Purchased ________________

Price $________________

☐ ***Your Warm Greeting Is Pure Joy,* CC-990003**

$55.00
$55.00

Members Only, Issue Price $55.00, '09

Purchased ____

Price $ ______

☐ ***Your Warm Greeting Is Pure Joy,* CM-990003**

Charter Members Only, Issue Price $55.00, '09

$55.00
$55.00

Purchased ________________

Price $________________

☐ ***LIfe Is Souper' With You In The Mix,* CC-109001**

$39.00
$39.00

Members Only, Issue Price $39.00, '10

Purchased____

Price $ _____

☐ ***LIfe Is Souper' With You In The Mix,* CM-109001**

Charter Members Only, Issue Price $39.00, '10

$39.00
$39.00

Purchased ________________

Price $________________

☐ ***The Sweetest Times Are Shared With You,* CC-109002**

$50.00
$50.00

Members Only, Issue Price $50.00, '10

Purchased _______

Price $ _________

☐ ***The Sweetest Times Are Shared With You,* CM-109002**

Charter Members Only, Issue Price $50.00, '10

$50.00
$50.00

Purchased ________________

Price $________________

☐ ***Your Love And Guidance Nourish Our Lives,* CC-109003**

$65.00
$65.00

Members Only, Issue Price $65.00, '10

Purchased____

Price $ ______

☐ ***Your Love And Guidance Nourish Our Lives,* CM-109003**

Charter Members Only, Issue Price $65.00, '10

$65.00
$65.00

Purchased ________________

Price $________________

☐ ***But Love Goes On Forever,* E-0001**

UM $255.00
$225.00
$220.00

Charter Members Only, Issue Price $15.00, '81

Purchased __________

Price $ __________

☐ ***Seek And Ye Shall Find,* E-0005**

Also E-0105, Charter Members only. Values are $70.00 and $60.00.

$55.00
$53.00

Members Only, Issue Price $17.50, '85

Purchased ______________

Price $______________

☐ ***Birds Of A Feather Collect Together,* E-0006**

$50.00
$48.00

Also E-0106, Charter Members only. Values are $60.00 and $55.00

Members Only, Issue Price $17.50, '86

Purchased___________

Price $___________

☐ ***Sharing Is Universal,* E-0007**

Also E-0107, Charter Members only. Values are $60.00 and $58.00.

$50.00
$48.00

Members Only, Issue Price $17.50, '87

Purchased ________

Price $__________

☐ ***A Growing Love,* E-0008**

$45.00
$40.00

Also E-0108, Charter Members Only. Values are $60.00 and $57.00.

Members Only, Issue Price $18.50, '88

Purchased __________

Price $ ____________

☐ ***But Love Goes On Forever,* E-0102 (Plaque)**

UM $175.00
$105.00
$100.00

PRECIOUS MOMENTS LAST FOREVER

Also E-0202, Members Only. Values are $150.00, $85.00, and $75.00. *Precious Moments Last Forever* inscription on front confused many because the title of this piece is *But Love Goes On Forever.* Termed the "Canadian Plaque Error," approximately 750 pieces of this 1982 symbol of membership were produced in 1985 and shipped to Canada. These pieces are stamped TAIWAN and have a Dove annual production symbol. Value for the "Canadian Plaque Error" is $125.00.

Charter Members Only, Issue Price $15.00, '82

Purchased ________, Price $ ___________

☐ ***Let Us Call The Club To Order,* E-0103**

$78.00
$75.00
$73.00

Also E-0303, Members Only.

Charter Members Only, Issue Price $15.00 '83

Purchased ___________

Price $ ___________

☐ ***Join In On The Blessings,*** **E-0104**

Also E-0404, Members Only. Values are $125.00, $70.00, and $60.00.

$75.00

$70.00

Charter Members Only, Issue Price $17.50, '84

Purchased ________, Price $ ____________

☐ ***Loving, Caring And Sharing,*** **PCC-112 (Medallions)**

UM $35.00

Members Only, Issue Price $22.50, '93
Set of 3, with case

Purchased ________, Price $ ____________

☐ ***1993 Local Club Chapter Convention,*** **PCC-172 (Plate)**

UM $50.00

Given to those who atteneded the Local Club Chapter Convention in Chicago November 5 – 6, 1993.

Members Only, '93

Purchased ________, Price $ ____________

☐ ***Lord It's Hard To Be Humble,*** **PCC-489 (Lithograph)**

UM $70.00

Signed lithograph, Precious Rewards Frequent Buyer Program, Level 4.

Members Only, Gift, '98

Purchased ________, Price $ ____________

☐ ***My Collection,*** **PM-001**

$45.00

$40.00

Members Only, Issue Price $20.00, '00

Purchased ________

Price $____________

☐ ***Collecting Friends Along The Way,*** **PM-002**

$130.00

$125.00

Club's twentieth anniversary commemorative figurine.

Members Only, Issue Price $100.00, '00

Purchased ________, Price $ ____________

☐ ***Calling To Say You're Special,*** **PM-0011**

$65.00

$63.00

Members Only, Issue Price $50.00, '01
Set of 2

Purchased ________, Price $ ____________

☐ ***You're A Computie Cutie,*** **PM-0012**

$45.00

$40.00

Members Only, Issue Price $35.00, '01

Purchased ________, Price $ ____________

☐ ***You Are My In-Spa-ration,*** **PM-0021**

$55.00

$53.00

Members Only, Issue Price $45.00, '02

Purchased ________, Price $ ____________

☐ ***You Are My Favorite Pastime,*** **PM-0022**

$55.00

$50.00

$48.00

Members Only, Issue Price $40.00, '02

Purchased ________, Price $ ____________

☐ ***Goose Girl,*** **PM-030 (Medallion)**

UM $600.00

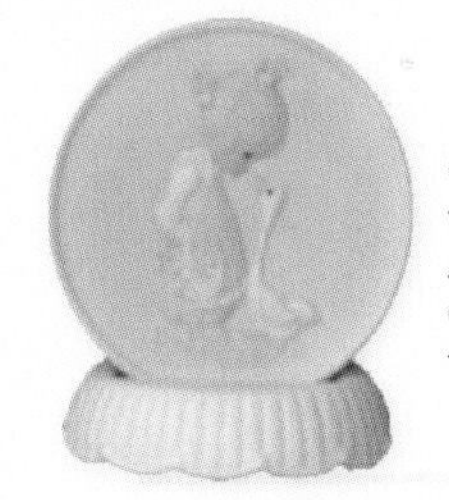

Given to those who atteneded the Annual Tour of the Orient and visited the factory in 1988.

Limited Edition 25, Gift, '88

Purchased ________, Price $ ____________

☐ ***Blessed With Small Miracles,*** **PM-0031**

$50.00

$45.00

$45.00

Members Only, Issue Price $40.00, '03

Purchased ________, Price $ ____________

☐ ***Safe In The Hands Of Love,*** **PM-0032**

$70.00
$65.00
$45.00

Members Only, Issue Price $55.00, '03
Purchased ________, Price $ ____________

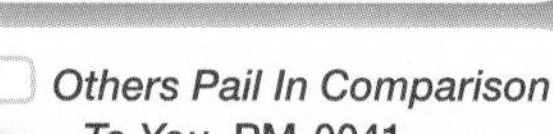

☐ ***Others Pail In Comparison To You,*** **PM-0041**

$35.00
$33.00

Members Only, Issue Price $30.00, '04
Purchased ____________
Price $ ____________

☐ ***Friendship Is Waiting To Be Discovered,*** **PM-0042**

$45.00
$43.00

Members Only, Issue Price $40.00, '04
Purchased ________, Price $ ____________

☐ ***Friends Help Us Keep Moving Up,*** **PM-0051**

$65.00
$65.00
$65.00

Members Only, Issue Price $65.00, '05
Purchased ________, Price $ ____________

☐ ***Getting There Is Half The Fun,*** **PM-0052**

$50.00
$50.00
$50.00

Members Only, Issue Price $50.00, '05
Purchased ________, Price $ ____________

☐ ***Mug,*** **PM-032** UM $7.00

Members Only, Issue Price $7.00, '90
Purchased ____________
Price $ ____________

☐ ***Desk Flag,*** **PM-034**

UM $10.00

Members Only, Issue Price $4.00, '90
Purchased ____________
Price $ ____________

☐ ***Sharing The Good News Together,*** **PM-037 (Ornament)**

$85.00

Members Only, Issue Price $17.50, '91
Purchased ____________
Price $ ____________

☐ ***The Club That's Out Of This World,*** **PM-038 (Ornament)**

$85.00

Members Only, Issue Price $17.50, '92
Purchased ____________
Price $____________

☐ ***Loving, Caring And Sharing,*** **PM-040 (Ornament)**

$48.00
$45.00

Members Only, Issue Price $15.00, '93
Purchased ____________
Price $____________

☐ ***You Are The End Of My Rainbow,*** **PM-041 (Ornament)**

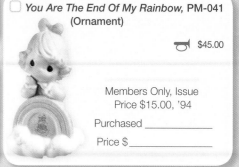

$45.00

Members Only, Issue Price $15.00, '94
Purchased ____________
Price $____________

☐ ***Blessed Are The Poor In Spirit, For Theirs Is The Kingdom Of Heaven,*** **PM-190 (Ornament)**

UM $35.00

Members Only, Issue Price $15.00, '90
Purchased____________
Price $____________

☐ ***Blessed Are They That Mourn, For They Shall Be Comforted,*** **PM-290 (Ornament)**

UM $35.00

Members Only, Issue Price $15.00, '90
Purchased____________
Price $____________

☐ ***Blessed Are The Meek, For They Shall Inherit The Earth,*** **PM-390 (Ornament)**

UM $35.00

Members Only, Issue Price $15.00, '90
Purchased ____________
Price $ ____________

Blessed Are They That Hunger And Thirst After Righteousness, For They Shall Be Filled, PM-490 (Ornament)

UM $35.00

Members Only, Issue Price $15.00, '90

Purchased ______________

Price $ ______________

Blessed Are The Merciful, For They Shall Obtain Mercy, PM-590 (Ornament)

UM $35.00

Members Only, Issue Price $15.00, '90

Purchased ______________

Price $ ______________

Blessed Are The Pure In Heart, For They Shall See God, PM-690 (Ornament)

UM $35.00

Members Only, Issue Price $15.00, '90

Purchased ______________

Price $ ______________

Blessed Are The Peacemakers, For They Shall Be Called Sons Of God, PM-790 (Ornament)

UM $35.00

Members Only, Issue Price $15.00, '90

Purchased ______________

Price $______________

Hello Lord, It's Me Again, PM-811

$450.00

$425.00

Members Only, Issue Price $25.00, '81

Purchased ________

Price $________

Smile, God Loves You, PM-821

$225.00

$205.00

Members Only, Issue Price $25.00, '82

Purchased ________, Price $ ____________

Put On A Happy Face, PM-822

$255.00

$225.00

$205.00

Members Only, Issue Price $25.00, '83

Purchased ___________

Price $ ___________

Dawn's Early Light, PM-831

$85.00

$80.00

$78.00

Members Only, Issue Price $25.00, '83

Purchased ________, Price $ ____________

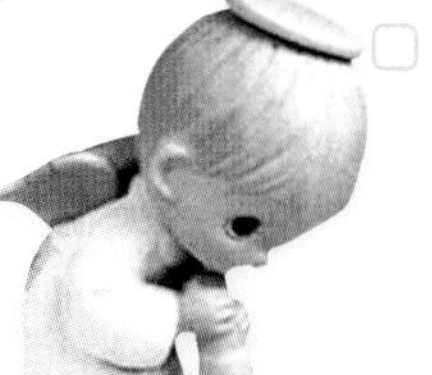

God's Ray Of Mercy, PM-841

$95.00

$85.00

$80.00

Members Only, Issue Price $25.00, '84

Purchased ________, Price $ ____________

Trust In The Lord To The Finish, PM-842

$80.00

$73.00

Members Only, Issue Price $25.00, '84

Purchased ____________

Price $____________

Trust In The Lord To The Finish, PM-843 (Cross-stitch)

UM $20.00

Members Only, Issue Price $11.00, '84

Purchased ________, Price $ ____________

The Lord Is My Shepherd, PM-851

UM $100.00

$95.00

$90.00

$88.00

Members Only, Issue Price $25.00, '85

Purchased ________, Price $ ____________

I Love To Tell The Story, PM-852

$75.00

$70.00

Members Only, Issue Price $27.50, '85

Purchased ________, Price $ ____________

The Lord Is My Shepherd, PM-853 (Cross-stitch)

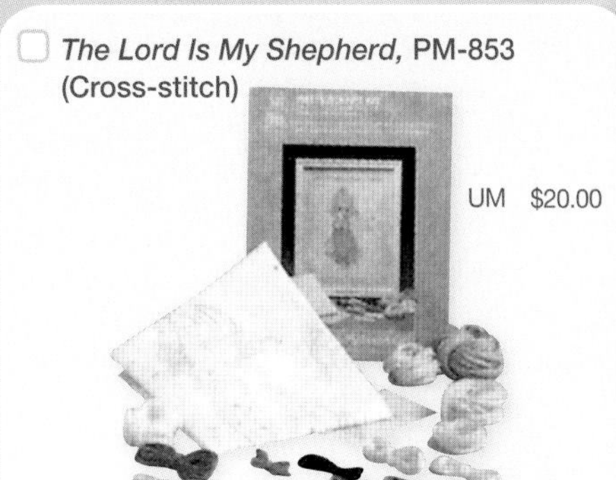

UM $20.00

Members Only, Issue Price $13.00, '85

Purchased ________, Price $ ____________

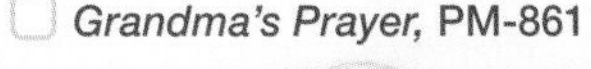

Grandma's Prayer, PM-861

$105.00
$100.00
$98.00

Members Only, Issue Price $25.00, '86

Purchased ________, Price $ ____________

I'm Following Jesus, PM-862

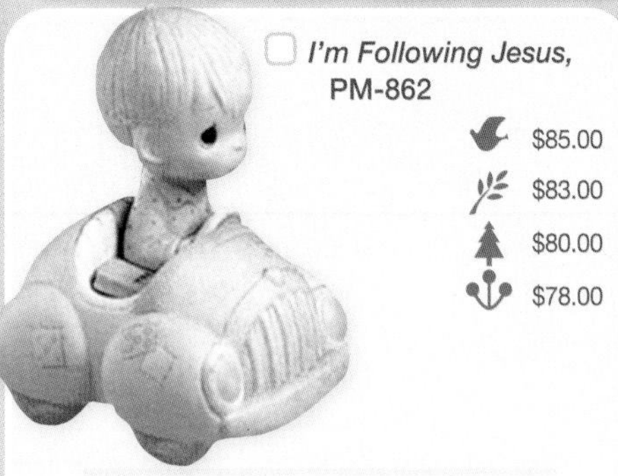

$85.00
$83.00
$80.00
$78.00

Members Only, Issue Price $25.00, '86

Purchased ________, Price $ ____________

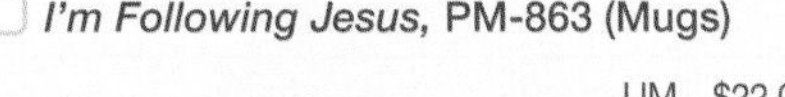

I'm Following Jesus, PM-863 (Mugs)

UM $22.00

Members Only, Issue Price $17.50, '86
Set of 2

Purchased ________, Price $ ____________

Birds Of A Feather Collect Together, PM-864 (Ornament)

$165.00

Members Only,
Issue Price $12.50, '86

Purchased____________

Price $____________

Feed My Sheep, PM-871

$105.00
$100.00
$90.00

Members Only, Issue Price $25.00, '87

Purchased ________, Price $ ____________

In His Time, PM-872

$75.00
$73.00
$70.00

Members Only, Issue Price $25.00, '87

Purchased ________, Price $ ____________

Loving You Dear Valentine (Boy), PM-873

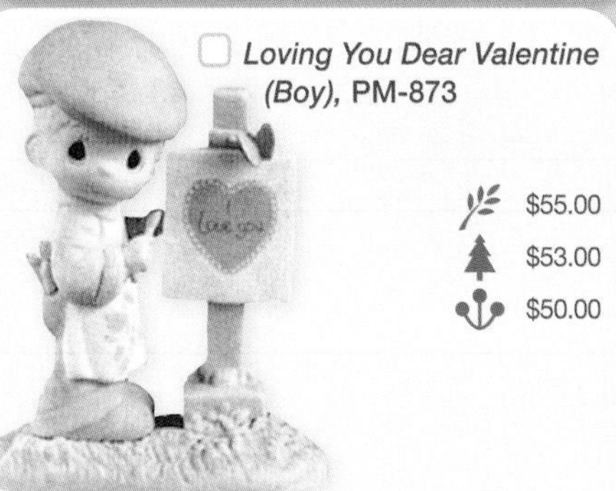

$55.00
$53.00
$50.00

Members Only, Issue Price $25.00, '87

Purchased ________, Price $ ____________

Loving You Dear Valentine (Girl), PM-874

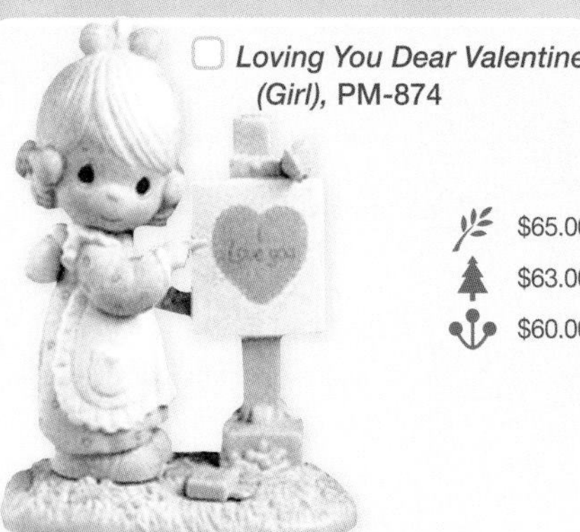

$65.00
$63.00
$60.00

Members Only, Issue Price $25.00, '87

Purchased ________, Price $ ____________

Goose Girl, PM-877 (Medallion)

UM $700.00

Given to those who attended the Annual Tour of the Orient and visited the factory in 1987.

LImited Ed. 25, Gift, '87

Purchased ________, Price $ ____________

God Bless You For Touching My Life, PM-881

$80.00
$78.00
$75.00

Members Only, Issue Price $27.50, '88

Purchased ________, Price $ ____________

You Just Cannot Chuck A Good Friendship, PM-882

$70.00
$65.00

Members Only, Issue Price $27.50, '88

Purchased ________, Price $ ____________

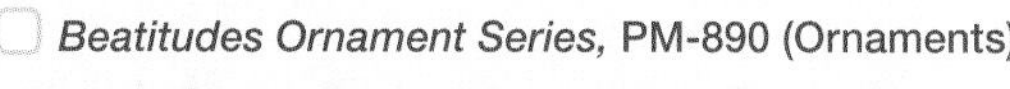

Beatitudes Ornament Series, PM-890 (Ornaments)

UM $300.00

Members Only, Issue Price $105.00, '90
Set of 7, Individually Numbered
PM-190 through PM-790

Purchased ______________________

Price $______________________

Lord, Keep Me In Teepee Top Shape, PM-912

$75.00
$73.00
$70.00

Members Only, Issue Price $27.50, '91

Purchased ________, Price $ ____________

You Will Always Be My Choice, PM-891

$60.00
$55.00

Members Only, Issue Price $27.50, '89

Purchased ________, Price $ ____________

You Are A Blessing To Me, PM-902

$75.00
$70.00

Members Only, Issue Price $27.50, '90

Purchased ________

Price $ ____________

Only Love Can Make A Home, PM-921

$75.00
$70.00

Members Only, Issue Price $30.00, '92

Purchased ________, Price $ ____________

You Are A Blessing To Me, PM-903 (Needlepoint Pillow)

UM $10.00

Members Only, Issue Price $7.00, '90

Purchased ____________

Price $ ____________

Mow Power To Ya, PM-892

$75.00
$70.00

Members Only, Issue Price $27.50, '89

Purchased ________, Price $ ____________

My Happiness, PM-904 (Ornament)

$100.00

Members Only, Issue Price $15.00, '90

Purchased____________

Price $ ____________

Sowing The Seeds Of Love, PM-922

$55.00
$50.00

Members Only, Issue Price $30.00, '92

Purchased ________, Price $ ____________

Ten Years And Still Going Strong, PM-901

$60.00
$60.00

Members Only, Issue Price $30.00, '90

Purchased ________, Price $ ____________

One Step At A Time, PM-911

$65.00
$63.00
$60.00

Members Only, Issue Price $33.00, '91

Purchased ________, Price $ ____________

His Little Treasure, PM-931

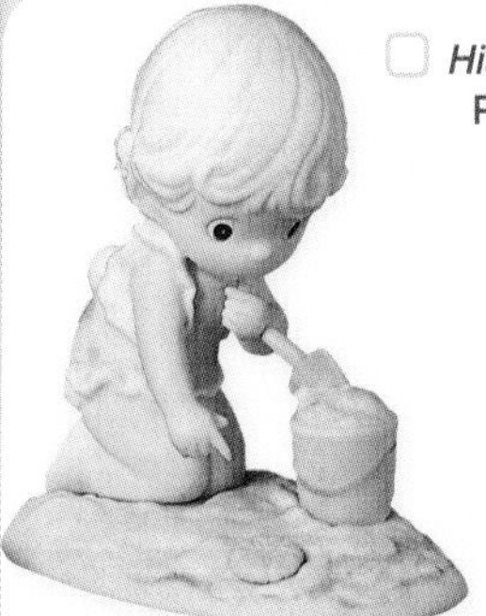

$60.00
$55.00

Members Only, Issue Price $30.00, '93

Purchased ________, Price $ ____________

☐ ***Loving*, PM-932**

$85.00

$80.00

Members Only, Issue Price $30.00, '93

Purchased ___________

Price $ ___________

☐ ***Caring*, PM-941**

$70.00

$65.00

Members Only, Issue Price $35.00, '94

Purchased ________, Price $ ___________

☐ ***Sharing*, PM-942**

$75.00

$70.00

Members Only, Issue Price $35.00, '94

Purchased ________, Price $ ___________

☐ ***You're One In A Million To Me*, PM-951**

$55.00

Members Only, Issue Price $35.00, '95

Purchased ________, Price $ ___________

☐ ***Always Take Time To Pray*, PM-952**

$60.00

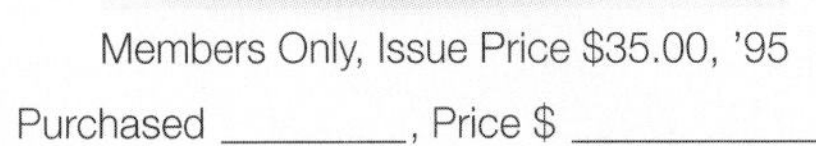

Members Only, Issue Price $35.00, '95

Purchased ________, Price $ ___________

☐ ***Teach Us To Love One Another*, PM-961**

$65.00

$60.00

Sam Butcher honors Aunt Cleo.

Members Only, Issue Price $40.00, '96

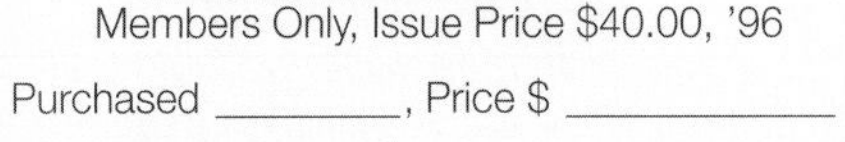

Purchased ________, Price $ ___________

☐ ***Our Club Is Soda-licious*, PM-962**

$65.00

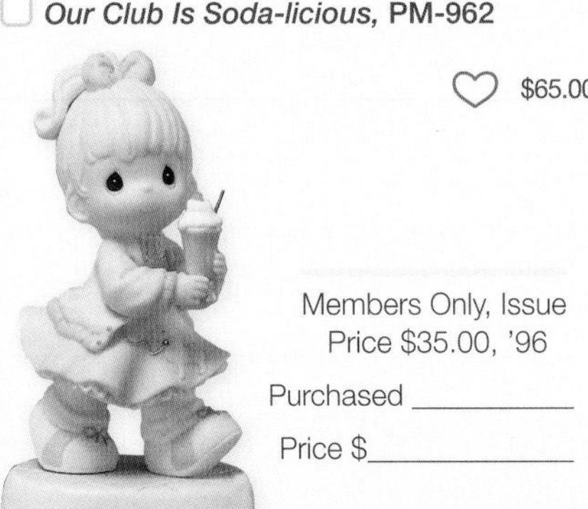

Members Only, Issue Price $35.00, '96

Purchased ___________

Price $___________

☐ ***You Will Always Be A Treasure To Me*, PM-971**

$65.00

$60.00

Members Only, Issue Price $50.00, '97

Purchased ________, Price $ ___________

☐ ***Blessed Are The Merciful*, PM-972**

$60.00

$55.00

Members Only, Issue Price $40.00, '97

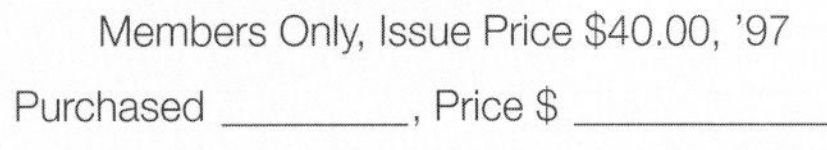

Purchased ________, Price $ ___________

☐ ***Happy Trails*, PM-981**

$65.00

$60.00

Members Only, Issue Price $50.00, '98

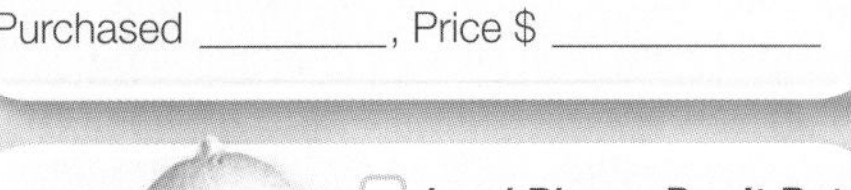

Purchased ________, Price $ ___________

☐ ***Lord Please Don't Put Me On Hold*, PM-982**

$55.00

$50.00

Members Only, Issue Price $40.00, '98

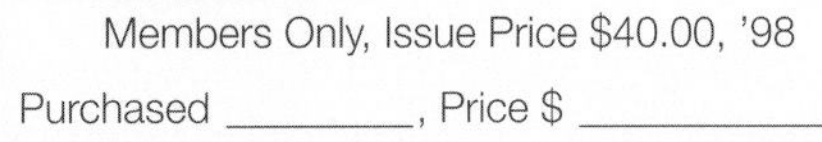

Purchased ________, Price $ ___________

☐ ***How Can Two Work Together Except They Agree*, PM-983**

$155.00

$150.00

Members Only, Issue Price $125.00, '98

Purchased ________, Price $ ___________

Jumping For Joy, PM-991

$45.00

$40.00

Members Only, Issue Price $30.00, '99

Purchased ____________

Price $ ________________

God's Speed, PM-992

$55.00

$50.00

Members Only, Issue Price $30.00, '99

Purchased ____________

Price $____________

He Watches Over Us All, PM-993

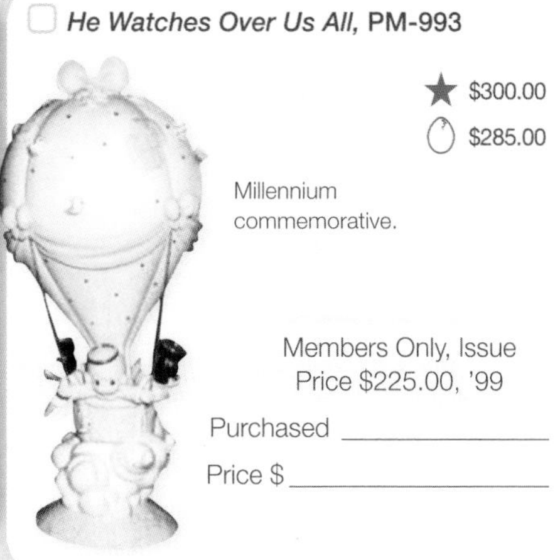

$300.00

$285.00

Millennium commemorative.

Members Only, Issue Price $225.00, '99

Purchased ______________

Price $ __________________

You Fill The Pages Of My Life, PMB-034 (Book & Figurine)

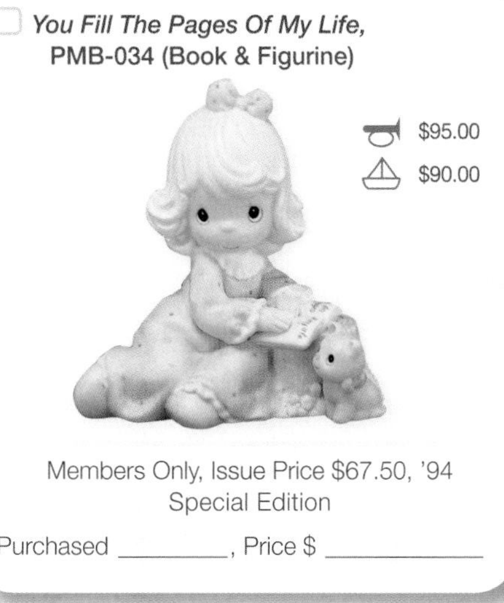

$95.00

$90.00

Members Only, Issue Price $67.50, '94 Special Edition

Purchased _________, Price $ ____________

Home For The Holidays, PMB-225 (Ornament)

UM $35.00

$30.00

Ornament item number is 150231, but this item was sold as a set with a Christmas CD.

Members Only, "Gift To Go" Program, Limited Ed., Issue Price $25.00, '01

Purchased _________, Price $ ____________

Birthday Club/Fun Club

☐ ***Cecilia*, 100018**

UM $12.00

Members Only, Gift, '02
Tender Tails, Club Exclusive

Purchased ________, Price $ ____________

☐ ***I'm So Glad You Sled Into My Life*, 101731**

$33.00

Members Only, Issue Price $20.00, '02

Purchased ________, Price $ ____________

☐ ***Friendship Begins With Caring*, 110858**

UM $70.00
$65.00
$60.00
$58.00
$55.00

Members Only, Issue Price $35.00, '02

Purchased ________, Price $ ____________

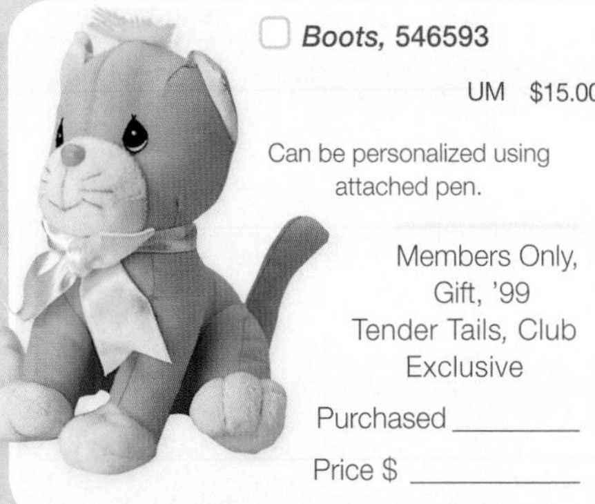

☐ ***Boots*, 546593**

UM $15.00

Can be personalized using attached pen.

Members Only, Gift, '99
Tender Tails, Club Exclusive

Purchased ________
Price $ ____________

☐ ***Gorilla*, 602361**

UM $10.00

Pink Heart version, $25.00; Yellow Star version, $20.00.

Members Only, Gift, '99
Tender Tails

Purchased ________, Price $ ____________

☐ ***Twinkle The Star*, 646237**

UM $20.00

Members Only, Gift, '99
Tender Tails

Purchased ________, Price $ ____________

☐ ***Iris The Caterpillar*, 720976 (Attachable)**

UM $20.00

Members Only, Gift, '00
Tender Tails, Club Exclusive

Purchased ________, Price $ ____________

☐ ***Iris The Caterpillar*, 721050**

UM $18.00

Add wings to make her a butterfly.

Members Only, Gift, '00
Tender Tails, Club Exclusive

Purchased ________, Price $ ____________

☐ ***Zelda The Zebra*, 819417**

UM $15.00

Members Only, Gift, '01
Tender Tails, Club Exclusive

Purchased ________, Price $ ____________

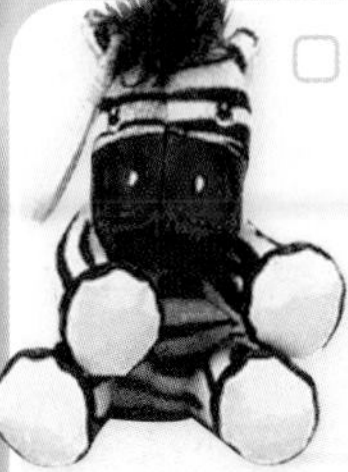

☐ ***Zelda The Zebra*, 826758 (Attachable)**

UM $12.00

Members Only, Gift, '01
Tender Tails, Club Exclusive

Purchased ________, Price $ ____________

☐ ***Our Club Can't Be Beat*, B-0001**

$90.00
$85.00
$85.00

Members Only, Issue Price $10.00, '86

Purchased ________, Price $ ____________

☐ ***A Smile's The Cymbal Of Joy*, B-0002**

$90.00
$85.00

Also issued as B-0102 for Charter Members only.

Members Only, Issue Price $10.00, '87

Purchased ________, Price $ ____________

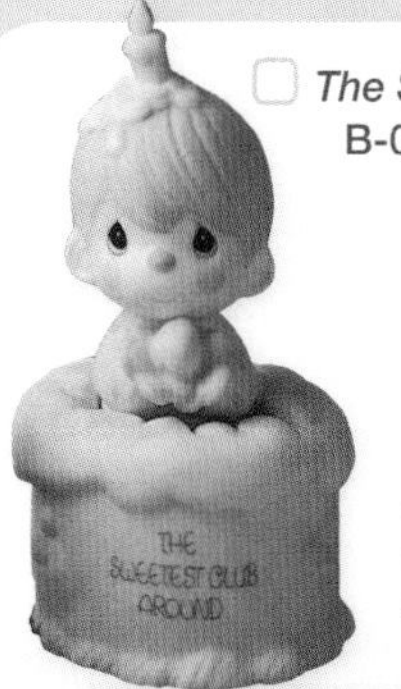

The Sweetest Club Around, B-0003

$55.00
$50.00

Also issued as B-0103 for Charter Members only. Add $10.00 to values.

Members Only, Issue Price $11.00, '88

Purchased ________, Price $ ____________

Have A Beary Special Birthday, B-0004

$50.00
$45.00

Also issued as B-0104 for Charter Members Only. Add $5.00 to values.

Members Only, Issue Price $11.50, '89

Purchased ________, Price $ ____________

Our Club Is A Tough Act To Follow, B-0005

$48.00
$45.00

Also issued as B-0105 for Charter Members only. Values are $45.00 and $40.00.

Members Only, Issue Price $13.50, '90

Purchased ________, Price $ ____________

Jest To Let You Know You're Tops, B-0006

$45.00
$40.00

Also issued as B-0106 for Charter Members only. Values are $45.00 and $30.00.

Members Only, Issue Price $15.00, '91

Purchased ________, Price $ ____________

All Aboard For Birthday Club Fun, B-0007

$43.00
$40.00

Also issued as B-0107 for Charter Members only. Values are $50.00 and $45.00.

Members Only, Issue Price $16.00, '92

Purchased ________, Price $ ____________

Happiness Is Belonging, B-0008

$40.00
$35.00

Also issued as B-0108 for Charter Members only.

Members Only, Issue Price $17.50, '93

Purchased ________, Price $ ____________

Can't Get Enough Of Our Club, B-0009

$40.00
$35.00

Also issued as B-0109 for Charter Members only. Add $10.00 to value.

Members Only, Issue Price $17.50, '94

Purchased ________, Price $ ____________

Hoppy Birthday, B-0010

$45.00
$40.00
$35.00

Also issued as B-0110 for Charter Members only.

Members Only, Issue Price $20.00, '95

Purchased ________, Price $ ____________

Scootin' By Just To Say Hi! B-0011

$40.00
$35.00

Also issued as B-0111 for Charter Members only. Add $5.00 to value.

Members Only, Issue Price $21.00, '96

Purchased ________, Price $ ____________

The Fun Starts Here, B-0012

$35.00
$33.00

Also issued as B-0112 for Charter Members only. Values are $45.00 and $40.00.

Members Only, Issue Price $22.50, '97

Purchased ________, Price $ ____________

You Are My Mane Inspiration, B-0014

Also issued as B-0114 for Charter Members only.

$60.00
$55.00
$53.00

Members Only, Gift, '97

Purchased ________, Price $ ____________

Fishing For Friends, BC-861

$145.00
$135.00

Members Only, Issue Price $10.00, '86

Purchased ________, Price $ ____________

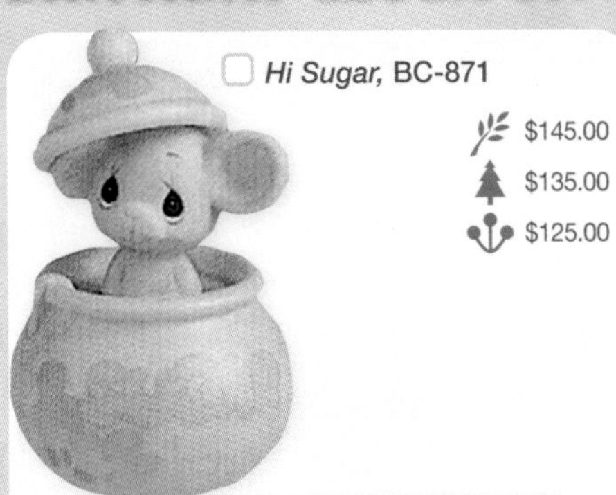

☐ *Hi Sugar,* BC-871

$145.00
$135.00
$125.00

Members Only, Issue Price $11.00, '87

Purchased ________, Price $ ____________

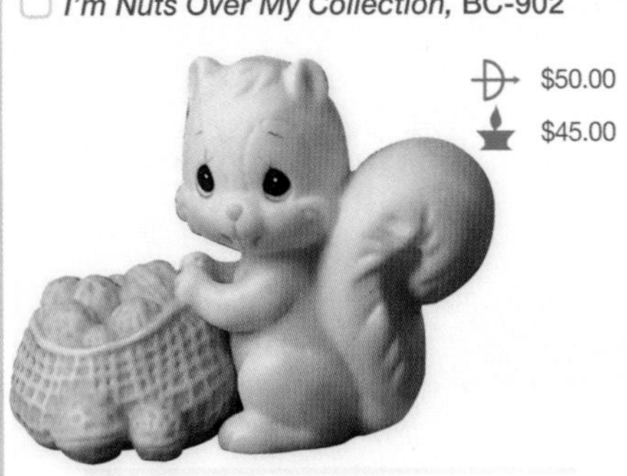

☐ *I'm Nuts Over My Collection,* BC-902

$50.00
$45.00

Members Only, Issue Price $15.00, '90

Purchased ________, Price $ ____________

☐ *I Got You Under My Skin,* BC-922

$45.00
$40.00

Members Only, Issue Price $16.00, '92

Purchased ________, Price $ ____________

☐ *Somebunny Cares,* BC-881

$65.00
$60.00
$60.00

Members Only, Issue Price $13.50, '88

Purchased ________, Price $ ____________

☐ *Love Pacifies,* BC-911

$60.00
$55.00
$50.00

Members Only, Issue Price $16.00, '91

Purchased ________, Price $ ____________

☐ *Put A Little Punch In Your Birthday,* BC-931

$45.00
$40.00

Members Only, Issue Price $15.00, '93

Purchased ________, Price $ ____________

☐ *Can't Bee Hive Myself Without You,* BC-891

$65.00
$60.00

Members Only, Issue Price $13.50, '89

Purchased ________, Price $ ____________

☐ *True Blue Friends,* BC-912

$60.00
$55.00
$50.00

Members Only, Issue Price $15.00, '91

Purchased ________, Price $ ____________

☐ *Owl Always Be Your Friend,* BC-932

$43.00
$38.00

Members Only, Issue Price $16.00, '93

Purchased ________, Price $ ____________

☐ *Collecting Makes Good Scents,* BC-901

$55.00
$50.00

Members Only, Issue Price $15.00, '90

Purchased ________, Price $ ____________

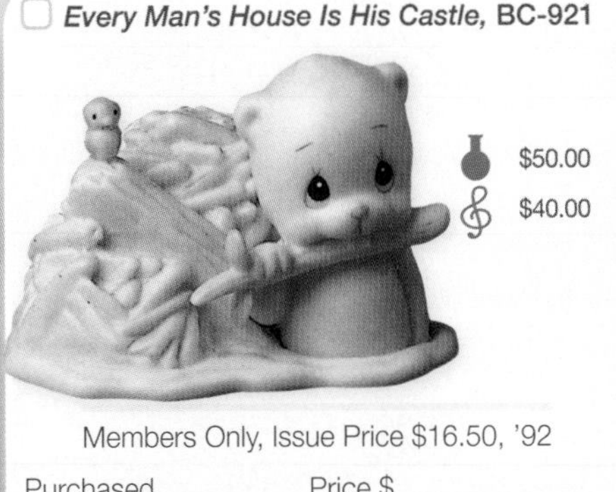

☐ *Every Man's House Is His Castle,* BC-921

$50.00
$40.00

Members Only, Issue Price $16.50, '92

Purchased ________, Price $ ____________

☐ *God Bless Our Home,* BC-941

$50.00
$45.00

Members Only, Issue Price $16.00, '94

Purchased ________, Price $ ____________

☐ ***Yer A Pel-I-Can Count On,* BC-942**

$40.00
$38.00

Members Only, Issue Price $16.00, '94

Purchased ________, Price $ ____________

☐ ***Making A Point To Say You're Special,* BC-951**

$40.00
$35.00

Members Only, Issue Price $15.00, '95

Purchased ________, Price $ ____________

☐ ***10 Wonderful Years Of Wishes,* BC-952**

$95.00
$90.00

Members Only, Issue Price $50.00, '95

Purchased ________, Price $ ____________

☐ ***There's A Spot In My Heart For You,* BC-961**

$45.00
$40.00

Members Only, Issue Price $15.00, '96

Purchased ________, Price $ ____________

☐ ***You're First In My Heart,* BC-962**

$45.00
$40.00

Members Only, Issue Price $15.00, '96

Purchased ________, Price $ ____________

☐ ***Hare's To The Birthday Club,* BC-971**

$35.00
$30.00

Members Only, Issue Price $16.00, '97

Purchased ________, Price $ ____________

☐ ***Holy Tweet,* BC-972**

$40.00
$35.00

Members Only, Issue Price $18.50, '97

Purchased ________, Price $ ____________

☐ ***Slide Into The Celebration,* BC-981**

Commemorates the twentieth anniversary of Precious Moments.

$35.00
$30.00

Members Only, Issue Price $15.00, '98

Purchased ________, Price $ ____________

☐ ***Ewe Are So Special To Me,* BC-991**

$40.00
$35.00

Members Only, Issue Price $25.00, '99

Purchased ________, Price $ ____________

☐ ***Chester,* BC-992**

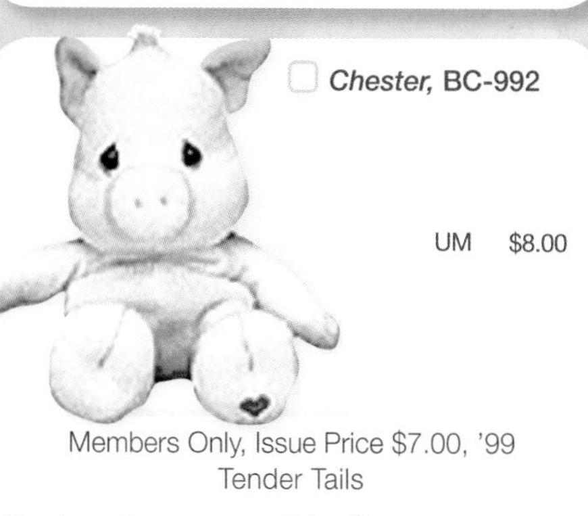

UM $8.00

Members Only, Issue Price $7.00, '99
Tender Tails

Purchased ________, Price $ ____________

☐ ***Chippie,* BC-993**

UM $7.00

Members Only, Issue Price $10.50, '99
Tender Tails

Purchased ________, Price $ ____________

☐ ***Don't Fret, We'll Get There Yet!* F-0002**

$33.00
$28.00

Also issued as F-0102 for Charter Members only. Values are $35.00 and $33.00.

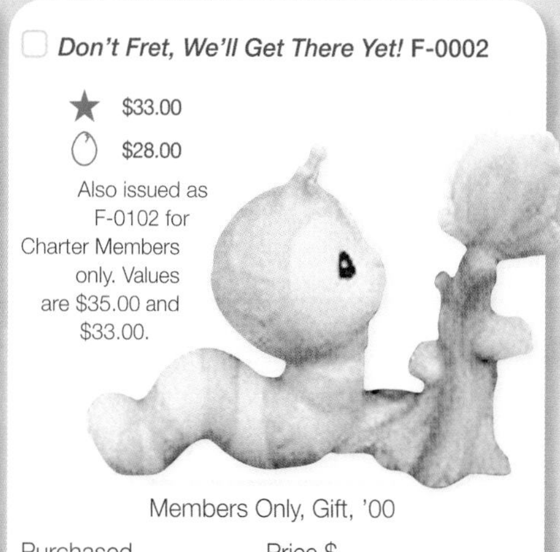

Members Only, Gift, '00

Purchased ________, Price $ ____________

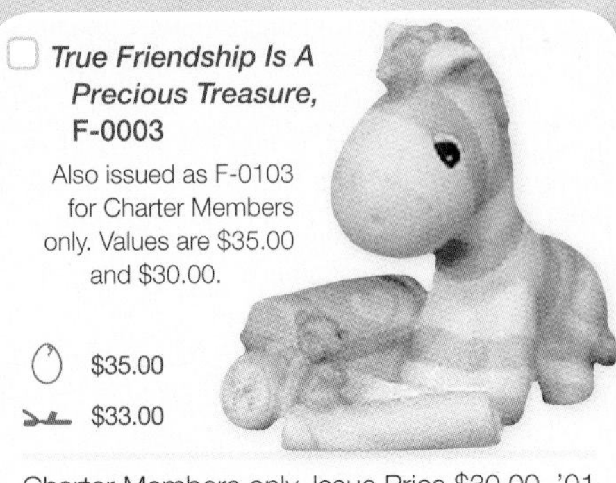

☐ ***True Friendship Is A Precious Treasure,* F-0003**

Also issued as F-0103 for Charter Members only. Values are $35.00 and $30.00.

$35.00

$33.00

Charter Members only, Issue Price $30.00, '01

Purchased ________, Price $ ___________

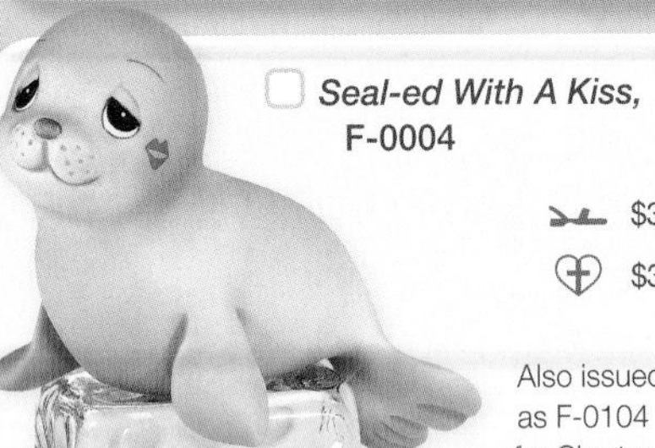

☐ ***Seal-ed With A Kiss,* F-0004**

$35.00

$33.00

Also issued as F-0104 for Charter Members only. Values are $35.00 and $30.00.

Members Only, Gift, '02

Purchased ________, Price $ ___________

☐ ***I'm All Ears For You,* F-0005**

$33.00

$28.00

Also issued as F-0105 for Charter Members only. Values are $30.00 and $25.00.

Members Only, Gift, '03

Purchased ________, Price $ ___________

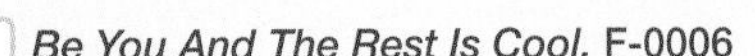

☐ ***Be You And The Rest Is Cool,* F-0006**

$30.00

$30.00

Also issued as F-0106 for Charter Members only, with Crown and Three-Petal Flower marks. $25.00 each.

Members Only, Issue Price $25.00, '04

Purchased ________

Price $ ___________

☐ ***When You Play With Heart, Music Is Art,* F-0007**

$35.00

$35.00

Also issued as F-0107 for Charter Members only, with Crown and Three-Petal Flower marks. $25.00 each.

Members Only, Issue Price $25.00, '04

Purchased ________

Price $ ___________

☐ ***Daring To Have True Fun,* F-0008**

$35.00

$35.00

$35.00

Also issued as F-0108 for Charter Members only, with Three-Petal Flower and Bread marks. $25.00 each.

Members Only, Issue Price $25.00, '05

Purchased ________, Price $ ___________

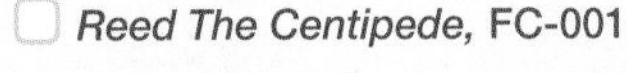

☐ ***Reed The Centipede,* FC-001**

UM $12.00

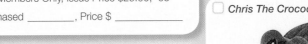

Members Only, Issue Price $6.99, '00
Tender Tails

Purchased ________, Price $ ___________

☐ ***Ronnie The Rhino Beetle,* FC-002**

UM $12.00

Members Only, Issue Price $6.99, '00
Tender Tails

Purchased ________, Price $ ___________

☐ ***Hold On To The Moment,* FC-003**

★ $35.00

$33.00

Members Only, Issue Price $25.00, '00

Purchased ________, Price $ ___________

☐ ***I'm Always Happy When You're A-long,* FC-011**

$35.00

$33.00

Members Only, Issue Price $18.50, '01

Purchased ________, Price $ ___________

☐ ***Chris The Crocodile,* FC-012**

UM $12.00

Members Only, Issue Price $6.99, '01
Tender Tails

Purchased ________, Price $ ___________

☐ ***Monty The Mandrill,* FC-013**

UM $12.00

Members Only, Issue Price $6.99, '01
Tender Tails

Purchased ________, Price $ ___________

Wade The Water Buffalo, FC-014

UM $12.00

Members Only, Gift, '01
Tender Tails, Club Exclusive

Purchased ________, Price $ ____________

You Are The Coolest Friend, FC-021

$55.00
$50.00

Members Only, Issue Price $35.00, '02

Purchased ________, Price $ ____________

Gwen The Penguin, FC-022

UM $12.00

Members Only, Issue Price $9.99, '02
Tender Tails

Purchased ________, Price $ ____________

You're So Bear-y Cool, FC-023

$30.00
$28.00

Members Only, Issue Price $20.00, '02

Purchased ________, Price $ ____________

So Happy To Be Together, FC-031

$29.00
$26.00

Members Only, Issue Price $20.00, '03

Purchased ________, Price $ ____________

Lost Without You, FC-032

$50.00
$48.00

Members Only, Issue Price $40.00, '03

Purchased ________, Price $ ____________

Sam, FC-033

UM $12.00

Members Only, Issue Price $9.99, '03
Tender Tails

Purchased ________, Price $ ____________

Shelly The Turtle, FC-034

UM $12.00

Shell opens. Comes with frog figurine.

Members Only, Issue Price $9.99, '03
Tender Tails

Purchased ________, Price $ ____________

Brought Together Through The Beat, FC-041

$40.00
$40.00

Members Only, Issue Price $35.00, '04

Purchased ________, Price $ ____________

Never Too Young For Sleepover Fun, FC-051

$38.00
$38.00

Members Only, Issue Price $35.00, '05

Purchased ________, Price $ ____________

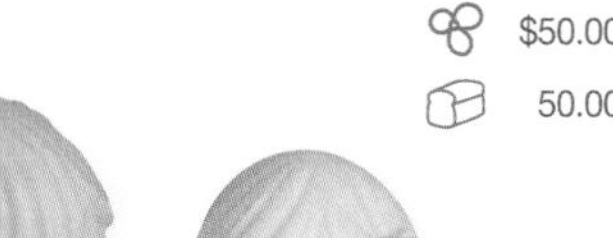

The Best Is Yet To Comb, FC-052

$50.00
50.00

Members Only, Issue Price $45.00, '05

Purchased ________, Price $ ____________

☐ *Simply Charming,* FC-550046

$35.00
$35.00

Members Only, Issue Price $35.00, '06

Purchased ________, Price $ ____________

☐ *You Fill The Air With Giggles And Laughter,* FC-790006

$40.00
$40.00

Members Only, Issue Price $40.00, '07

Purchased ________, Price $

☐ *You're On A Roll With Heart And Soul,* FC-890005

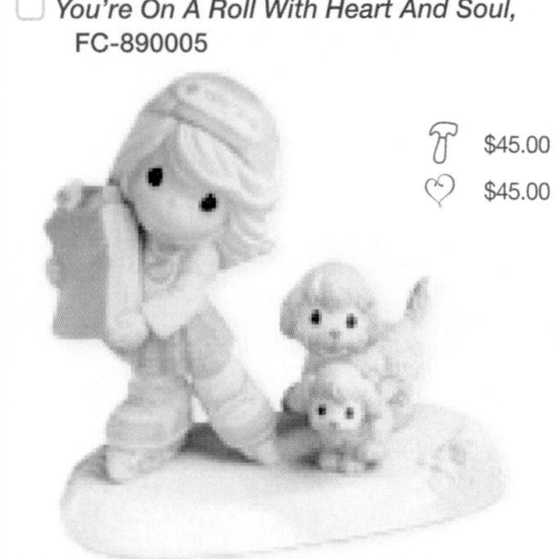

$45.00
$45.00

Members Only, Issue Price $45.00, '08

Purchased ________, Price $ ____________

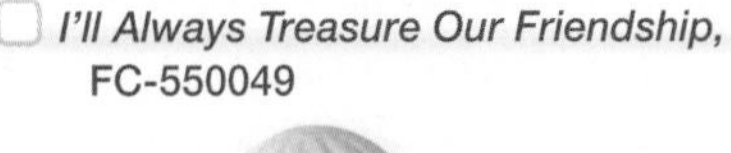

☐ *I'll Always Treasure Our Friendship,* FC-550049

$25.00
$25.00

Members Only, Issue Price $25.00, '06

Purchased ________, Price $ ____________

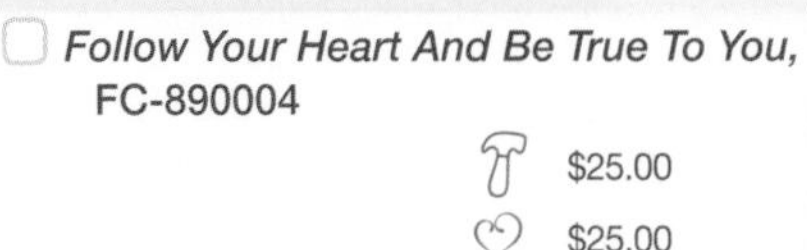

☐ *Follow Your Heart And Be True To You,* FC-890004

$25.00
$25.00

Members Only, Issue Price $25.00, '08

Purchased ______________

Price $______________

☐ *Bubbling Over With Fun,* FC-790005

$25.00
$25.00

Members Only, Issue Price $25.00, '07

Purchased ________, Price $ ____________

Special Pieces

The following pieces in this section are some fo the hardest to find. These pieces were presented from Sam or Gene for very special occasions.

☐ *God Bless The USA, 527572* $3,000.00

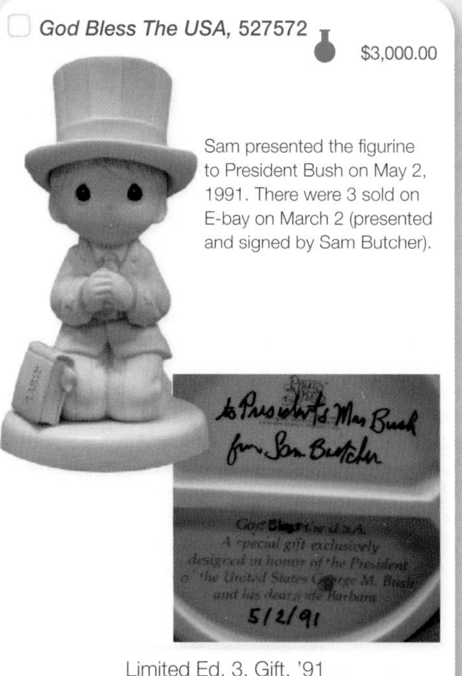

Sam presented the figurine to President Bush on May 2, 1991. There were 3 sold on E-bay on March 2 (presented and signed by Sam Butcher).

Limited Ed. 3, Gift, '91

Purchased ________, Price $ ____________

☐ *You Tug On my Heart Strings, 795526S*

UM Priceless

Presented by Gene Freedman, 2000.

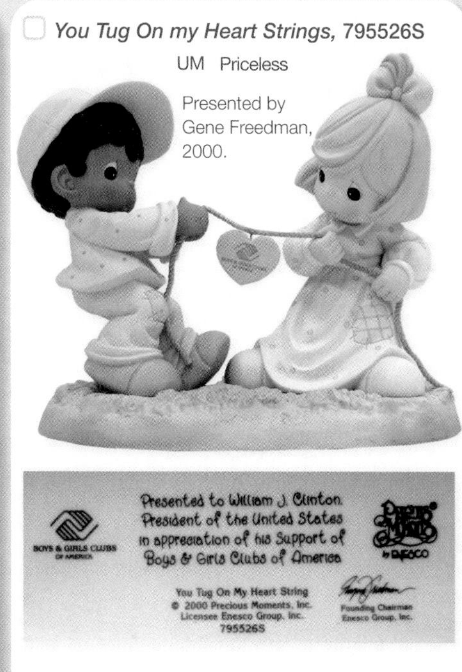

Purchased ________, Price $ ____________

☐ *I Couldn't Make It Without You, 635030S*

UM Priceless

Presented by Gene Freedman in 1999.

Purchased ________, Price $ ____________

☐ *America, You're Beautiful,*

UM Priceless

Purchased ________, Price $ ____________

☐ *Love Is Color Blind, 524204S*

UM Priceless

Presented by Gene Freedman in 1998.

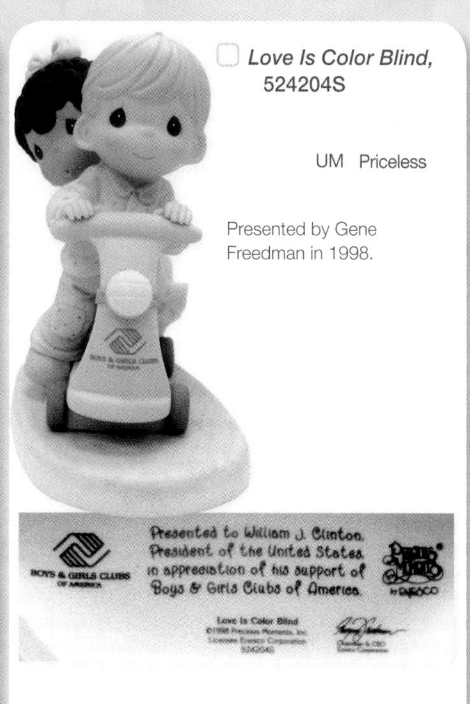

Purchased ________, Price $ ____________

☐ *Blessed Are They That Overcome, 115479S*

UM Priceless

Presented by Gene Freedman in 1997.

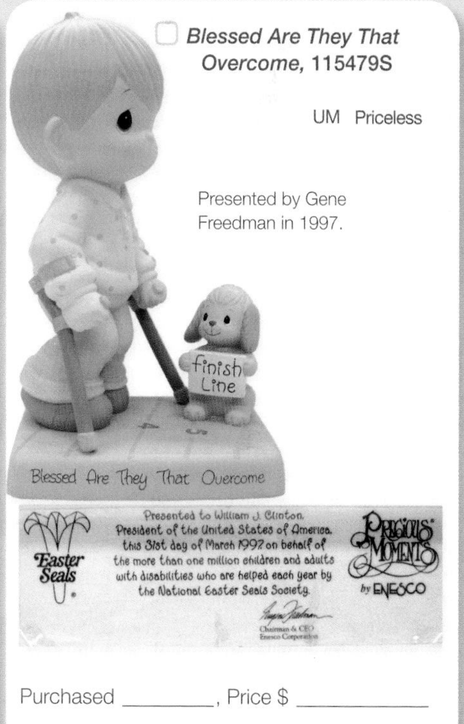

Purchased ________, Price $ ____________

☐ *He Is Our Shelter From The Storm, 523550S* UM Priceless

Presented by Gene Freedman in 1997.

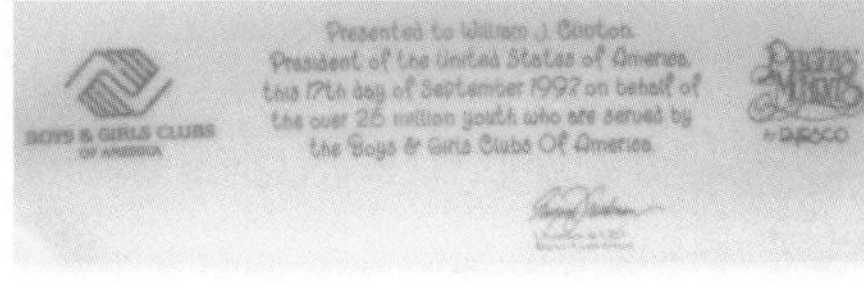

Purchased ________, Price $ ___________

☐ *How Can Three Work Together Except When They Agree, 527572* 👓 $3,000.00

All were signed by Artist Sam Butcher, Master Sculptor Yasuhei Fujioka, and Enesco Founding Chairman Eugene Freedman. Each received a figurine and the rest were available to collectors.

Limited Ed. 20, '98

Purchased ________, Price $ ___________

☐ *Happy Trails To You* UM Priceless

Presented to Roy Rogers at Roy's Museum in Victorville, California by Sam.

HAPPY TRAILS TO YOU
PRESENTED TO
ROY ROGERS AND DALE EVANS
BY PRECIOUS MOMENTS ARTIST
Samuel J Butcher

One of two made

Purchased ________, Price $ ___________

☐ *Turn Your Eyes Upon Jesus* UM Priceless

This is a prototype to be released as Sam Butcher's legacy after his death.

Purchased ________

Price $ ___________

☐ *Loretta Lynn* UM Priceless

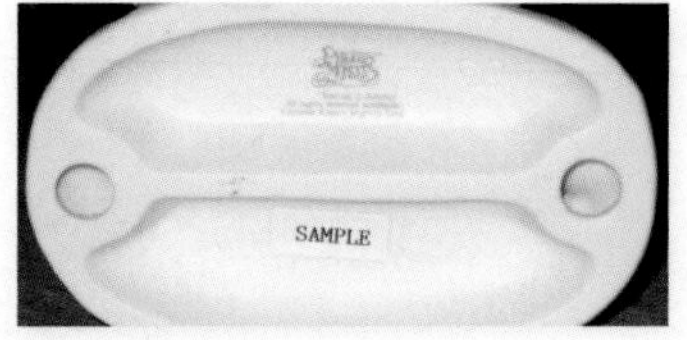

This is a duplicate of the fi...ine that the artis... sented to one of his favorite country singers Loretta Lynn.

Only 2 made

Purchased ___________

Price $___________

☐ *You Are The Wind Beneath My Wings* UM Priceless

Sam's response to September 11, 2001. The wounded baby eagle represents America. (Can only be seen at the Precious Moments Museum in Carthage, Missouri.)

One of a Kind

Purchased ________

Price $___________

☐ *To The Queen Of Hearts* UM Priceless

In honor of Princess Diana.

One of a Kind

Purchased ________, Price $ ___________

☐ ***Congratulations Frank & Willie***

Made for Sam's in-laws (Frank and Willie Cushman) on their 50th Anniversary

UM Priceless

Only 2 made

Purchased ________, Price $ ___

☐ ***Noah's Ark*** UM Priceless

This Noah's Ark is all one piece not like the original in separate pieces.

One of a Kind

Purchased ______________________

Price $__________________________

Convention Items

☐ ***1992 Convention,*** **PME-001 (Mini Plate)**

UM $25.00

The Enesco Precious Moments Collector's Club Chapter Convention, October 30 – 31, 1992.

Gift, '92

Purchased ________, Price $ ____________

☐ ***1993 Convention,*** **PCC-172 (Mini Plate)**

UM $25.00

The Enesco Precious Moments Collector's Club Chapter Convention, November 5 – 6, 1993.

Gift, '93

Purchased ________, Price $ ____________

☐ ***1994 Convention*** **(Mini Tablet)**

UM $20.00

The Enesco Precious Moments Collector's Club Local Club Chapter Convention, October 21 – 22,1994.

Gift, '94

Purchased ________, Price $ ____________

Websites

Precious Moments Chapel and Shop	www.preciousmoments.com
Precious Moments Company Dolls	www.pmcdolls.com
Precious Moments Community	www.preciousmom.net
Cherrylane Keepsakes	www.cherrylanecollection.com
Stone Fence Collectibles	www.stonefence.net
Collectibles Database	www.collectiblesdatabase.com
eBay online auction site	www.ebay.com
The Limited of Michigan, ltd.	www.limitedweb.com
Collector Books	www.collectorbooks.com

Reference Guide

4th Quarter Exclusive

0000974 Here's My Heart

25th Anniversary

108531 Collecting Life's Most Precious Moments
108532 Collecting Life's Most Precious Moments
108543 A Portrait Of Loving, Caring, And Sharing Members
108544 Marching Ahead To Another 25 Years Of Precious Moments
110238 Precious Moments From The Beginning
110239 God Loveth A Cheerful Giver
110254 Celebrating 25 Years Of Sunshine & Smiles
114982 May Your Christmas Be Delightful
115272 Celebrating 25 Years Of Sunshine & Smiles
115476 Collecting Life's Most Precious Moments
118259 The World Is A Stage Featuring Precious Moments
488135 Delivering Good News To You
522139 I Will Make You Fishers Of Men
804444 Happy Anniversary
4004612 Loving Every Precious Moment With You

30th Anniversary

730031 Celebrating The Gift Of Life Now And Forever
810056 Come Let Us Adore Him
890021 Making Music Together For 30 Years

Adoption

100145 God Bless The Day We Found You
100153 God Bless The Day We Found You
100145R God Bless The Day We Found You
100153R God Bless The Day We Found You

American Greeting/Carlton Cards Exclusive

110269 Friendship Is Always A Sweet Surprise
115873 I Pick You As My Friend
115873 I Pick You As My Friend
119301 Wishing You A Heavenly Holiday
523607 A Friend Like You Is Heaven-Scent
619002 Your Friendship Brightens Each Day
690005 Safe In Mother's Arms
690006 The Purr-Fet Christmas Morning
690011 There's Magic In Those Ears
690012 The Warmth Of Christmas Comes From The Heart
690013 Christmas Morning Is Just The Sweetest
690015 Merry Christmas Express-Ly For You
690019 Sending All My Love To You
690022 Wrapped In Mom's Love
710054 Love And Joy Come To You
790018 I Give This Rose As A Token Of My Love
790021 The Greatest Joy Is Motherhood
790023 Your Love Is Perfect
890020 May The Blessings Of The Holy Family Be With You
4001666 You Make My Heart Shine
4001947 A Bead-Azzling Friendship
4003585 Special Times With Mom Create Memories Of A Lifetime
0000615 You Color My World
0000664 I Love You Just Be-Claus
104311C A Mother's Love Is From Above
113369C A Mother's Story Is One Of Love
115926C Happiness Is Being A Mom
634980C Take Time To Smell The Roses
781770C May All Your Days Be Rosy
12149 Part Of Me Wants To Be Good
12351 Halo, And Merry Christmas
12408 We Saw A Star
12424 Aaron
12432 Bethany
16020 God Bless You With Rainbows
104825 Sitting Pretty
108540 May Your Faith Grow With Daily Care
108541 Forever In Our Hearts
111869 Mommy's Little Angel
113980 Rejoice O Earth
120114 Safely Home
150320 Joy To The World
153338 Joy To The World
163856 Sewing Seeds Of Kindness
183350 Peace On Earth... Anyway
183377 Peace On Earth... Anyway
183776 Angels On Earth
183830 Sing In Excelsis Deo
272558 I Think You're Just Divine
272566 Joy To The World
521868 The Greatest Of These Is Love
524107 Missing You
524921 Angels We Have Heard On High
525979 Going Home
526835 The Lord Is With You
531693 You Deserve A Halo-Thank You
587818 May Your Wishes For Peace Take Wing
887900 Grandma's Little Angel
887927 Grandma's Little Angel
887935 Daddy's Little Angel
887951 Daddy's Little Angel
887978 Grandma's Little Angel
887986 Grandma's Little Angel
887994 Mommy's Little Angel
888001 Mommy's Little Angel
890871 God's Love Has No Measure
E-0509 Bringing God's Blessing To You
E-0526 He Upholdeth Those Who Fall
E-2343 Joy To The World
E-2351 Holy Smokes
E-2801 Jesus Is Born
E-2804 Peace On Earth
E-5629 Let The Heavens Rejoice
E-5642 Silent Knight
E-6901 Collection Plaque
E-7168 My Guardian Angel
E-7169 My Guardian Angel

Angels On A Cloud

12335 You Can Fly
100056 Sending My Love
101826 No Tears Past The Gate
109967 Sending You My Love
520640 I'm So Glad You Fluttered Into My Life
522252 He Is The Star Of The Morning
E-3115 But Love Goes On Forever
E-5205 My Guardian Angel
E-5206 My Guardian Angel
E-5207 My Guardian Angel
E-5627 But Love Goes On Forever
E-5628 But Love Goes On Forever
E-9260 God's Promises Are Sure
E-9274 Taste And See That The Lord Is Good
E-9288 Sending You A Rainbow
E-9289 Trust In The Lord

Animals

15857 Honk If You Love Jesus
102474 Rocking Horse
104209 There's Sno One Like You
183903 When The Skating's Ruff, Try Prayer
261122 Lettuce Pray
272590 I'm Dreaming Of A White Christmas
325368 There Are Two Sides To Every Story
521671 Hope You're Over The Hump
524492 Can't Be Without You
531014 My World's Upside Down Without You
733008 You Should Be As Proud As A Peacock
890952 You Are The Cat's Meow
E-2371 Unicorn
E-2386 Camel, Donkey And Cow
E-9266 Our Love Is Heaven Scent
E-9266 I'm Falling For Some Bunny And It Happens To You
E-9267A Teddy Bear
E-9267B Dog With Slipper
E-9267C Bunny With Carrot
E-9267D Cat With Bow Tie
E-9267E Lamb
E-9267F Pig
E-9282 To Some Bunny Special
E-9282 You're Worth Your Weight In Gold
E-9282 Especially For Ewe
E-9282A To Some Bunny Special
E-9282B You're Worth Your Weight In Gold
E-9282C Especially For Ewe

Anniversary

106798 Puppy Love Is From Above
114021 Happy Birthday To Our Love
115909 Our Love Was Meant To Be
115910 A Whole Year Filled With Special Moments
115911 Our Love Still Sparkles In Your Eyes
115912 We Share A Love Forever Young
163783 A Year Of Blessings
163805 Ten Years Heart To Heart
163813 A Silver Celebration To Share
163821 Sharing The Gift Of 40 Precious Years
163848 Precious Moments To Remember
730006 I Fall In Love With You More Each Day
730007 A Decade Of Dreams Come True
730009 Our Picture Book Of Love
E-2853 God Blessed Our Years Together With So Much Love & Happiness
E-2854 God Blessed Our Years Together With So Much Love & Happiness
E-2855 God Blessed Our Years Together With So Much Love & Happiness
E-2856 God Blessed Our Years Together With So Much Love & Happiness
E-2857 God Blessed Our Years Together With So Much Love & Happiness
E-2859 God Blessed Our Years Together With So Much Love & Happiness
E-2860 God Blessed Our Years Together With So Much Love & Happiness

Art From The Heart

930030 Miss You — Girl
930031 Miss You — Boy
930032 Congrats
930033 Love You — Girl
930034 Love You — Boy
930036 Thank You

Avon Exclusives

102913 Mom, You're A Sweetheart
104850 Mom, You're A Sweetheart
384386 Thank You For The Times We Share
482242 Love Is The Key
588083 Mom, You're A Royal Gem
730238 I'm A Reflection Of Your Love
829269 A Mother's Job Is Never Done
883875 Hug Me Before I Melt

Baby

12475 P.D.
12033 God's Precious Gift
12041 God's Precious Gift
12483 Trish
100021 To My Favorite Paw
100285 Heaven Bless You
101500 The Sweetest Baby Boy
101501 The Sweetest Baby Girl
102970 I Would Be Sunk Without You
104817 A Tub Full Of Love
109231 The Greatest Gift Is A Friend
112313 A Tub Full Of Love

113962 A Child Is A Gift Of God
115923 A Special Moment Just For You
119916 Baby (Boy Standing)
119917 Baby (Boy Kneeling)
119918 Baby (Girl Standing)
119919 Baby (Girl Sitting)
119920 Baby (Boy Crawling)
119921 Baby (Girl Crawling)
429570 The Eyes Of The Lord Are Upon You
429589 The Eyes Of The Lord Are Upon You
487929 You're My Honey Bee
520934 Heaven Bless You
521493 A Special Delivery
523178 Joy On Arrival
524360 Something Precious From Above
527165 The Good Lord Always Delivers
740016 It's A Girl – Blonde
740017 It's A Girl – Brunette
804096 A Godchild Close To My Heart — Baby
163651B Baby Figurine
163651G Baby Figurine
930023 Double The Fun
930024 Bless The Day You Arrived
E-0521 Blessed Are The Pure In Heart
E-2852 Baby Figurines
E-2852A Baby Boy Sitting
E-2852B Baby Girl Standing With Bow
E-2852C Boy Sitting
E-2852D Girl Clapping Hands
E-2852E Boy Crawling
E-2852F Girl Lying Down
E-3104 Blessed Are The Pure In Heart
E-3108 The Hand That Rocks The Future
E-5204 The Hand That Rocks The Future

Baby's First

12211 Baby's First Haircut
15539 Baby's First Christmas
15547 Baby's First Christmas
16012 Baby's First Trip
520705 Baby's First Pet
524069 Baby's First Birthday
524077 Baby's First Meal
527238 Baby's First Word
E-2840 Baby's First Step
E-2841 Baby's First Picture

Baby's First Christmas

15539 Baby's First Christmas
15547 Baby's First Christmas
15903 Baby's 1st Christmas
15911 Baby's 1st Christmas
102504 Baby's 1st Christmas
102512 Baby's 1st Christmas
104204 Baby's 1st Christmas
104206 Baby's 1st Christmas
109401 Baby's 1st Christmas
109428 Baby's 1st Christmas
112842 Baby's 1st Christmas
112843 Baby's 1st Christmas
115282 Baby's 1st Christmas
117787 Baby's 1st Christmas
117788 Baby's 1st Christmas
142719 Baby's 1st Christmas
142727 Baby's 1st Christmas
183938 Baby's 1st Christmas
183946 Baby's 1st Christmas
272744 Baby's 1st Christmas
272752 Baby's 1st Christmas
455644 Baby's 1st Christmas
455652 Baby's 1st Christmas
520241 Baby's 1st Christmas
523194 Baby's 1st Christmas
523208 Baby's 1st Christmas
523771 Baby's 1st Christmas
523798 Baby's 1st Christmas
527084 Baby's 1st Christmas
527092 Baby's 1st Christmas
527475 Baby's 1st Christmas
527483 Baby's 1st Christmas
530255 Baby's 1st Christmas
530263 Baby's 1st Christmas
530859 Baby's 1st Christmas
530867 Baby's 1st Christmas
587826 Baby's 1st Christmas
587834 Baby's 1st Christmas
610005 Baby's 1st Christmas
610006 Baby's 1st Christmas
710005 Baby's 1st Christmas
710006 Baby's 1st Christmas
730092 Baby's 1st Christmas
730106 Baby's 1st Christmas
810005 Baby's 1st Christmas
810006 Baby's 1st Christmas
877506 Baby's 1st Christmas
877514 Baby's 1st Christmas
910005 Baby's First Christmas
910006 Baby's First Christmas
4024080 Baby's 1st Christmas
4024081 Baby's 1st Christmas
E-0518 Blessed Are The Pure In Heart
E-2362 Baby's 1st Christmas
E-2372 Baby's 1st Christmas
E-5392 Blessed Are The Pure In Heart
E-5631 Baby's 1st Christmas
E-5632 Baby's 1st Christmas

Back To School Event

E-1379BR God Understands

Back To The 80's Event

E-5213R God Is Love

Baptism

488232 Dedicated To God
620016 In Thy Light Shall We See Light (Girl)
620017 In Thy Light Shall We See Light (Boy)
830014 Grow In The Light Of His Love
830028 Baptized In His Name
830029 Baptized In His Name

Benefits Ronald McDonald House

119460 Take My Hand

Benefits Habitat For Humanity

0000382 Give With A Grateful Heart

Bereavement

930011 Forever Embraced In God's Warm Love — Girl
930012 In The Radiance Of Heaven's Light
930013 Heaven Just Became A Fetchingly Bettter Place
930037 Forever Embraced In God's Warm Love — Boy

Birthday

12157 This Is The Day (Which) The Lord Has Made
102466 Reindeer
104209 There's Sno One Like You
104418 Friends To The End
104515 Bear The Good News Of Christmas
105945 Showers Of Blessing
105953 Brighten Someone's Day
106836 Happy Birthday Poppy
108534 Wishing You A Birthday Fit For A Princess
112876 May The Holidays Keep You Bright And Bushy Tailed
115920 Sixteen …Sweet
116948 Sixteen And Feline Fine
128686 Another Year And More Grey Hares
128708 Owl Be Home For Christmas
136204 It's A Girl
163686 Birthday Personalized
183792 Snowbunny Loves You Like I Do
260940 From The First Time I Spotted You I Knew We'd Be Friends
272523 Happy Birthday Jesus
272760 Slow Down For The Holidays
455660 I'll Be Dog-Ged It's That Season Again
520292 Hang On For The Holly Days
520403 Hippo Holidays
520411 I'm Nuts About You
520438 Sno-Bunny Falls For You Like I Do
520446 Sno-Ball Without You
520462 Christmas Is Ruff Without You
520489 Slow Down And Enjoy The Holidays
520497 Wishing You A Purr-Fect Holiday
520659 Wishing You A Happy Dear Hug
521043 To My Favorite Fan
521078 Merry Christmas, Little Lamb
521086 Heaven Bless Your Special Christmas
521094 God Bless You This Christmas
521108 May Your Christmas Be Gigantic
521116 Christmas Is Something To Roar About
521124 Christmas Keeps Looking Up
521175 Hello World
522260 To Be With You Is Uplifting
524298 May Your Every Wish Come True
524301 May Your Birthday Be A Blessing
524506 Oinky Birthday
526924 How Can I Ever Forget You
527270 Let's Be Friends
527343 Happy Birdie
527769 I Only Have Arms For You
530972 You Are Always In My Heart
531057 I Haven't Seen Much Of You Lately
531561 Happy Birthday To Ewe
630016 Wishing You A Year Filled With Birthday Cheer
680184 Wishing You A Blow Out Birthday
720021 Let Your Heart Give You Joy In The Day Of Your Youth
720022 Felicidades Quinceanera
930020 Hip, Hip, Hooray, You're One Year Old Today! — Girl
930021 Hip, Hip, Hooray, You're One Year Old Today! — Boy
930022 It's Your Birthday, Cake It Easy!
930035 Have A Hot Diggetty Dog Day!
934007 Happy Birthday
136204B It's A Girl
524301B May Your Birthday Be A Blessing
E-2826 May Your Birthday Be A Blessing
E-2826Q May Your Birthday Be A Blessing

Birthday/Fun Club

101731 I'm So Glad You Sled Into My Life
110858 Friendship Begins With Caring
116611 Express Who You Are And You'll Be A Star
116612 Friends Let You Be You
B-0001 Our Club Can't Be Beat
B-0002 A Smile's The Cymbol Of Joy
B-0003 The Sweetest Club Around
B-0004 Have A Beary Special Birthday
B-0005 Our Club Is A Tough Act To Follow
B-0006 Jest To Let You Know You're Tops
B-0007 All Aboard For Birthday Club Fun
B-0008 Happiness Is Belonging
B-0009 Can't Get Enough Of Our Club
B-0010 Hoppy Birthday
B-0011 Scootin' By Just To Say Hi
B-0012 The Fun Starts Here
B-0014 You Are My Mane Inspiration
B-0102 A Smile's The Cymbal Of Joy
B-0103 The Sweetest Club Around
B-0104 Have A Beary Special Birthday
B-0105 Our Club Is A Tough Act To Follow
B-0106 Jest To Let You Know You're Tops
B-0107 All Aboard For Birthday Club Fun
B-0108 Happiness Is Belonging
B-0109 Can't Get Enough Of Our Club
B-0110 Hoppy Birthday
B-0111 Scootin' By Just To Say Hi
B-0112 The Fun Starts Here
B-0114 You Are My Mane Inspiration
BC-861 Fishing For Friends
BC-871 Hi, Sugar
BC-881 Somebunny Cares
BC-891 Can't Bee Hive Myself Without You
BC-901 Collecting Makes Good Scents
BC-902 I'm Nuts Over My Collection
BC-911 Love Pacifies

BC-912 True Blue Friends
BC-921 Every Man's Home Is His Castle
BC-922 I've Got You Under My Skin
BC-931 Put A Little Punch In Your Birthday
BC-932 Owl Always Be Your Friend
BC-941 God Bless Our Home
BC-942 Yer A Pel-I-Can Count On
BC-951 Making A Point To Say You're Special
BC-952 10 Wonderful Years Of Wishes
BC-961 There's A Spot In My Heart For You
BC-962 You're First In My Heart
BC-971 Hare's To The Birthday Club
BC-972 Holy Tweet
BC-981 Slide Into The Celebration
BC-991 Ewe Are So Special To Me
F-0002 Don't Fret, We'll Get There Yet
F-0003 True Friendship Is A Precious Treasure
F-0004 Seal-Ed With A Kiss
F-0005 I'm All Ears For You
F-0006 Be You And The Rest Is Cool
F-0007 When You Play With Heart, Music Is Art
F-0008 Daring To Have True Fun
F-0102 Don't Fret, We'll Get There Yet
F-0103 True Friendship Is A Precious Treasure
F-0104 Seal-Ed With A Kiss
F-0105 I'm All Ears For You
FC-003 Hold On To The Moment
FC-011 I'm Always Happy When You're A-Long
FC-021 You Are The Coolest Friend
FC-023 You're So Bear-Y Cool
FC-031 So Hoppy To Be Together
FC-032 Lost Without You
FC-041 Brought Together Through That Beat
FC-051 Never Too Young For Sleepover Fun
FC-052 The Best Is Yet To Comb
FC-550046 You're Simply Charming
FC-550049 I'll Always Cherish Our Friendship
FC-790005 Bubbling Over With Fun
FC-790006 You Fill The Air With Giggles And Laughter
FC-890004 We're Pullin' For You
FC-890005 You're On A Roll With Heart And Soul

Birthday Train

15938 May Your Birthday Be Warm
15946 Happy Birthday Little Lamb
15954 Heaven Bless Your Special Day
15962 God Bless You On Your Birthday
15970 May Your Birthday Be Gigantic
15989 This Day Is Something To Roar About
15997 Keep Looking Up
16004 Bless The Days Of Our Youth
109460 Isn't Eight Just Great
109479 Wishing You Grrrr-eatness
116945 It's Your Birthday Live It Up Large
116946 It's Your Birthday Go Bananas
116948 Sixteen And Feline Fine
119424 Birthday Train Frame
470279 May Your Christmas Be Warm
488003 Take Your Time, It's Your Birthday
488011 Give A Grin And Let The Fun Begin
488038 You Mean The Moose To Me
521825 May Your Birthday Be Mammoth
521833 Being Nine Is Just Divine

Birthday Train Ornaments

470279 May Your Christmas Be Warm (Caboose)
521078 Merry Christmas, Little Lamb (Lamb)
521094 God Bless You This Christmas (Seal)
521086 Heaven Bless Your Special Christmas (Pig)
521108 May Your Christmas Be Gigantic (Elephant)
521116 Christmas Is Something To Roar About (Lion)
521124 Christmas Keeps Looking Up (Giraffe)

Boy

100269 Help, Lord I'm In A Spot
104027 Love Is The Glue That Mends
106151 We're Pulling For You
108604 I Love You Knight And Day
113947 Hold On To Your Faith
114011 I'm Sorry
114014 This Too Shall Pass
163899 It May Be Greener, But It's Just As Hard To Cut
183849 You're Just To Sweet To Be Scary
325279 Wait Patiently On The Lord
325309 Only One Life To Offer
488321 You Can't Take It With You
520683 Sending You Showers Of Blessings
520756 Jesus Is The Only Way
521272 Take Heed When You Stand
521515 Water-Meloncholy Day Without You
521884 Pizza On Earth
521957 High Hopes
521981 Marching To The Beat Of Freedom's Drum
522872 On My Way To A Perfect Day
523763 I Can't Spell Success Without You
525952 All About Heaven
531022 Potty Time
531073 Money's Not The Only Green Thing Worth Saving
532002 Hallelujah For The Cross
532061 Who's Gonna Fill Your Shoes
681008 Precious Moments Will Last Forever
730041 Gradtitudes With Attitude
795186 You Will Always Be Mine
795275 You're As Sweet As Apple Pie
811815 A Godchild Close To My Heart
878987 The Royal Budge Is Good For The Soul
E-0525 You Can't Run Away From God
E-2823 To God Be The Glory
E-3107 Blessed Are The Peacemakers
E-3110B Loving Is Sharing
E-4723 Peace Amid The Storm
E-5203 Let Not The Sun Go Down On Your Watch
E-5397 Timmy
E-6214B Mikey
E-7156 I Believe In Miracles
E-7156R I Believe In Miracles
E-7159 Lord Give Me Patience
E-7161 His Sheep Am I
E-7163 God Is Watching Over You
E-7164 Bless This House
E-7170 Jesus Loves Me
E-9253 The End Is In Sight
E-9268 Nobody's Perfect
E-9275 Jesus Loves Me
E-9278 Jesus Loves Me
E-9280 Jesus Loves Me (Boy)
E-9281 Jesus Loves Me (Girl)
E-9285 If God Be For Us, Who Can Be Against Us

Boys And Girls Clubs Of America

104276 Twogether We Can Move Mountians
114918 Friends Make Life More Fun
120123 Sharing Fun And Games Together
521701 Shoot For The Stars And You'll Never Strike Out
523550 He Is Our Shelter From The Storm
524204 Love Is Color Blind
635030 I Couldn't Make It Without You
795526 You Tug On My Heart String
840020 You Are Always In Our Hearts
879029 Building Special Friendships
889849 Let's Have A Ball Together

Breast Cancer Awareness

104277 A Journey Of Hope
680982 Life Is Worth Fighting For
4001662 Walk. Run. Empower
680982B Life Is Worth Fighting For

Bridal Party

102369 Arch
488224 You'll Always Be Daddy's Little Girl
E-2831 Bridesmaid
E-2833 Ringbearer
E-2835 Flower Girl
E-2836 Groomsman
E-2837 Groom
E-2838 This Is The Day That The Lord Hath Made
E-2845 Junior Bridesmaid
E-2846 Bride

Calendar Girl

101515 January — Snowdrop "Pure And Gentle"
101517 February — Carnation "Bold And Brave"
101518 March — Violet "Modest"
101519 April — Lily "Virtuous"
101520 May — Hawthorne "Bright And Hopeful"
101521 June — Rose "Beautiful"
101522 July — Daisy "Wide-Eyed And Innocent"
101523 August — Poppy "Peaceful" - 2nd Edition
101525 September — Morning Glory "Easily Contended"
101526 October — Cosmos "Ambitious"
101527 November — Chrysanthemum "Sassy And Cheerful"
101528 December — Holly "Full Of Foresight"
109983 January
109991 February
110019 March
110027 April
110035 May
110043 June
110051 July
110078 August
110086 September
110094 October
110108 November
110116 December

Canadian Event Exclusive

101234C A Penny A Kiss, A Penny A Hug

Care-A-Van Exclusive

456268 How Can Two Work Together Except They Agree
634999 Scootin' Your Way To A Perfect Day
745413 You Add Sparkle To My Life
109487R Believe The Impossible
12416R Have A Heavenly Journey

Carlton Cards Greeting Early Release

890016 I Hold Your Heart Forever
115926C Happiness Is Being A Mom
801313C I Give You My Heart

Catalog Exclusive

000366 A Family Of Love, A Gift From Above
115625 You Are Such A Heavenly Host
212520 The Most Precious Gift Of Them All
521469 I'll Weight For You
529931 Happiness Is At Our Fingertips
531588 You Make Such A Lovely Pair
788031 Your Love Keeps Me Toasty Warm
798290 I'll Give You The World
881139 You Decorate My Life
4001025 Find Your Wings
4004377 Thoughts Of You Are So Heartwarming

Catalog Early Exclusive

456276 You Have Mastered The Art Of Caring
183814S The Most Precious Gift Of All
272957S My Love Will Keep You Warm
526037S A Prince Of A Guy

Catalog Syndicate Exclusive

101555 Dew Remember Me

Century Circle Exclusive

101548 Planting The Seeds Of Love
101549 Precious Moments In Paradise
101550 A Beary Warm Aloha
103175 Living Each Day With Love
103176 You Are The Rose In My Bouquet
103177 A Smile Is Cherished In The Heart
108544 Marching Ahead Another 25 Years Of Precious Moments
108602 Thanks For A Quarter Century Of Loving, Caring And Sharing
110238 Precious Moments From The Beginning
115922 May Love Blossom All Around You
115923 A Special Moment Just For You
118873 Caring

118874 Sharing
139475 Love Makes The World Go 'Round
163724 Blessed Are They With A Caring Heart
177091 Peace On Earth
184209 Loves Makes The World Go 'Round
184217 May The Sun Always Shine On You
261580 We Have The Sweetest Times Together
261599 In God's Beautiful Garden Of Love
261629 In God's Beautiful Garden Of Love
325503 Marvelous Grace
456349 Sharing Our Time Is So Precious
475084 Even The Heaven Shall Praise Him
523186 Yes Dear, You're Always Right
523569 I Will Always Love You
730262 The Fun Is Being Together
731048 Squeaky Clean
801313 I Give You My Heart
824119 Our Love Will Never Be Endangered
879428 O Holy Night
879436 God's Love Is Crystal Clear
879487 God's Love Is Crystal Clear

Century Circle Early Release

524115 Sharing Our Christmas Together

Century Circle Event Exclusive

104282 Hugs Can Tame The Wildest Heart
526061 The Pearl Of Great Price

Chapel Exclusive

110271 The Power Of Youth
111749 You're Worth Waiting On
111752 Everybody's Grandmother
111753 If Only You Could See Heaven
111754 Fairytales Can Come True!
111757 Every Precious Moment Needs A Smile
111760 Holding Him Close To My Heart
111762 Holding Him Close To My Heart
115248 Your Love Reigns Forever In My Heart
115925 May Love Blossom All Around You
116712 Praise Him With The Sound Of The Trumpet
119642 You Are Always Welcome Here
119643 Uphold His Name
119839 Uphold His Name
129259 Grandpa's Island
129275 Lighting The Way To A Happy Holiday
129967 Lighting The Way To A Happy Holiday
135976 Gone But Never Forgotten
135992 Heaven Must Have Sent You
136018 Going To The Chapel
163872 His Presence Is Felt In The Chapel
163880 His Presence Is Felt In The Chapel
204862 The Lord Is Our Chief Inspiration
204870 The Lord Is Our Chief Inspiration
204889 Coleenia
212547 We're Just A Passin' Through
261602 Crown Him Lord Of All
261610 Crown Him Lord Of All
271586 Seeds Of Love From The Chapel
349852 I'm Gonna Let It Shine
354406 A Prayer Warrior's Faith Can Move Mountains
354414 A Prayer Warrior's Faith Can Move Mountains
384844 Fountain Of Angels
475092 Toy Maker
475106 Toy Maker
496596 There's A Christian Welcome Here
497126 Timmy The Angel
523011 There's A Christian Welcome Here
523038 He Is My Inspiration
523291 Blessed Are The Merciful, For They Shall Obtain Mercy
523305 He Leads Me Beside The Still Waters
523313 Blessed Are The Meek, For They Shall Inherit The Earth
523321 Blessed Are They That Hunger And Thirst For Righteousness
523348 Blessed Are The Peacemakers, For They Shall Be Called Sons Of God
523356 I Will Fear No Evil
523364 He Restores My Soul
523372 You Prepare A Table Before Me
523380 Blessed Are They That Mourn, For They Shall Be Comforted
523399 Blessed Are The Pure In Heart, For They Shall See God
523402 The Lord Is My Shepherd, I Shall Not Want
523410 And I Will Dwell In The House Of The Lord Forever
523429 You Anoint My Head With Oil
523437 Blessed Are The Poor In Spirit, For Theirs Is The Kingdom Of Heaven
527106 He Is Not Here For He Is Risen As He Said
528021 There Is A Christian Welcome Here
531677 Surrounded With Joy
531685 Surrounded With Joy
531928 Death Can't Keep Him In The Ground
532088 A King Is Born
540013 Happy 10th Anniversary
542636 Sleep Tight
543722 Feed My Lambs
550021 He Is My Guiding Light
588040 Happy 10th Anniversary
588067 He Is The Birght Morning Star
588075 He Is The Birght Morning Star
603503 On The Hill Overlooking The Quiet Blue Stream
604151 A King Is Born
680761 Share In The Celebration
690007 Mommy's Love Goes With You
731668 There Shall Be Fountains Of Blessings
731676 Our Loss Is Heaven's Gain
748382 Let Earth Receive Her King
748390 Let Earth Receive Her King
795518 On Our Way To The Chapel
810043 Trim The Tree With Angelic Beauty
850942 Victorious In Jesus
850950 Victorious In Jesus
850969 Mary Had A Little Lamb
879681 We Would See Jesus
879703 Rose Of Sharon
879711 The Most Precious Place On Earth
879738 The Lord Is Our Chief Inspiration
879746 Sleep In Heavenly Peace
879754 Sleep In Heavenly Peace
890008 God's Love Is My Guiding Light
890009 Love Is Always With Us
898309 How Can I Say Thanks
898317 How Can I Say Thanks
898325 Scent From Above To Share His Love
927899 God's Precious Pearl
927899 God's Precious Pearl
928569 Worthy Is The Lamb
928577 Worthy Is The Lamb
928585 It Came Upon A Midnight Clear
928607 My Teacher, My Friend
4001778 By Your Side Forever And Always
4001779 I'm Yours Heart And Soul
4001780 You Take The Cake
4003183 Until We Meet Again
4004378 Light Of Hope
4004379 Light Of Hope
4004380 I'm So Glad I Picked You
588059C Our Love Will Flow Eternal
644463C You Color Our World With Loving, Caring And Sharing
990009 The Prefect Catch

Chapel Anniversary Pieces

540013 Happy 10th Anniversary
588040 Happy 10th Anniversary
680761 Happy 10th Anniversary

Chapel Event

644463 You Color Our World With Loving, Caring And Sharing
790011 Get Your Kicks On Route 66

Child Evangelism Fellowship

521922 Safe In The Arms Of Jesus
527556 Bring The Little Ones To Jesus
531359 Bring The Little Ones To Jesus

Christening

104217 And To All A Good Night
633001 Baptism Or Christening Frame
633002 Baptism Or Christening Frame
E-4724 Rejoicing With You
E-7165 Let The Whole World Know
E-7172 Rejoicing With You
E-7186 Let The Whole World Know

Christmas

12416 Have A Heavenly Christmas
15482 May Your Christmas Be Delightful
15768 God Sent His Love
15822 May Your Christmas Be Happy
15849 May Your Christmas Be Delightful
15865 God Sent His Love
15881 God Sent His Love
102288 Shepherd Of Love
102326 Wishing You A Cozy Christmas
102334 Wishing You A Cozy Christmas
102342 Wishing You A Cozy Christmas
102490 Sharing Our Christmas Together
104215 You Are My Christmas Special
104218 Merry Christ-Miss
109749 Peace On Earth
109754 Wishing You A Yummy Christmas
109770 Love Is The Best Gift Of All
109800 Meowie Christmas
109819 Oh What Fun It Is To Ride
109843 Love Is The Best Gift Of All
110930 Love Is The Best Gift Of All
111163 Tis The Season
111465 Retailer's Wreath
112372 I'm Sending You A White Christmas
112402 I'm Sending You A White Christmas
112839 Icy Good Times Ahead
112840 Icy Good Times Ahead
112876 May The Holidays Keep You Bright And Bushy Tailed
112880 May Your Heart Be Filled With Christmas Joy
112881 Warmest Wishes For The Holidays
115312 Time To Wish You A Merry Christmas
115320 Time To Wish You A Merry Christmas
115339 Time To Wish You A Merry Christmas
117784 S'mitten With The Christmas Spirit
117785 S'mitten With The Christmas Spirit
117786 Our First Christmas
117790 Bea-Ver-Y Good This Year
117792 Tidings Of Comfort & Joy
118267 Happy Hula Days
128694 Happy Hula Days
142654 He Covers The Earth With His Beauty
142662 He Covers The Earth With His Beauty
142670 He CoVers The Earth With His Beauty
150096 Soot Yourself To A Merry Christmas
150118 Making Spirits Bright
150126 Joy From Head To Mistletoe
150142 You're "A" Number One In My Book, Teacher
272671 Cane You Join Us For A Merry Christmas
272698 Cane You Join Us For A Merry Christmas
272701 Cane You Join Us For A Merry Christmas
272760 Slow Down For The Hoidays
272892 Puppies On Sled
272957 My Love Will Keep You Warm
451312 20 Years And The Vision's Still The Same
455601 I'm Sendingyou A Merry Christmas
455628 I'm Sending You A Merry Christmas
455660 I'll Be Dog-ged It's That Season Again
455768 Peas On Earth
455776 I'm Just Nutty About The Hoidays
455784 Alaska Once More, How's Yer Christmas
455792 You Can Always Fudge A Little During The Season
455806 Things Are Poppin' At Our House This Christmas
455814 Wishing You A Yummy Christmas
455822 I Saw Mommy Kissing Santa

455849	Time For A Holy Holiday
455873	Have A Cozy Country Christmas
469327	I'm Sending You A Merry Christmas
488348	Holiday Surprises Come In All Sizes
520349	A Growing Love
520446	Sno-Ball Without You
520454	Happy Holidaze
521213	The Fruit Of The Spirit Is Love
521302	May All Your Christmases Be White
521507	The Light Of The World Is Jesus
521566	Glide Through The Holidays
521574	Dashing Through The Snow
521590	Don't Let The Holidays Get You Down
521914	Perfect Harmony
521949	Wishing You A Cozy Season
522058	Now I Lay Me Down To Sleep
522082	May Your World Be Trimmed With Joy
522112	Don't Let The Holldays Get You Down
522120	Wishing You A Very Successful Season
522244	Do Not Open Until Christmas
522317	Merry Christmas Deer
522546	Oh Holy Night
522554	Oh Holy Night
522848	Oh Holy Night
523747	Blessings Fom Above
523755	Just Poppin' In To Say Halo!
523836	Once Upon A Holy Night
523844	Once Upon A Holy Night
523852	Once Upon A Holy Night
524166	May Your Christmas Be Merry
524174	May Your Christmas Be Merry
524190	May Your Christmas Be Merry
524468	A Special Chime For Jesus
524484	Not A Creature Was Stirring
525057	Bundles Of Joy
525898	Ring Those Christmas Bells
527211	Share The Warmth Of Christmas
527327	Onward Christian Soldiers
527378	You Are My Favorite Star
527580	Tied Up For The Holidays
527599	Bringing You A Merry Christmas
527629	Wishing You A Ho Ho Ho
527637	Waiting For A Merry Christmas
527688	But The Greatest Of These Is Love
527696	But The Greatest Of These Is Love
527718	But The Greatest Of These Is Love
527742	But The Greatest Of These Is Love
528218	Sending You A White Christmas
528226	Bringing You A Merry Christmas
528676	Alive With The Spirit Of The Season
528846	It's So Uplifting To Have A Friend Like You
529451	The Best Gifts Are Loving, Caring And Sharing
529532	Welcome Are Those With Happy Hearts
530166	Wishing You The Sweetest Christmas
530182	Wishing You The Sweetest Christmas
530204	Wishing You The Sweetest Christmas
530212	Wishing You The Sweetest Christmas
530395	You're As Pretty As A Christmas Tree
530409	You're As Pretty As A Chrlstmas Tree
530425	You're As Pretty As A Christmas Tree
530840	15 Happy Years Together — What A Tweet!
530956	I Only Have Ice For You
531820	Boughs Of Holly To Make You Jolly
531863	May Joy Bloom Within You
532193	Remember The Sweetness Of The Season
532916	Luke 2:10-11
532932	It's Almost Time For Santa
587885	May Your Seasons Be Jelly And Bright
587931	May Your Christmas Be Delightful
587958	Pretty As A Princess
603171	Ornament Holder
604135	May Your Christmas Be Delightful
610008	Christmas Together
610025	Guide Us To Thy Perfect Light
610026	Christmas Bells Are Ringing
610030	Daughter, You Bring Me Joy
610035	Grandma, Your Love Keeps Me Warm
634778	Wishing You An Old Fashioned Christmas
710001	Dancing For Joy On Christmas Morning
710002	Dancing For Joy On Christmas Morning
710003	Dancing For Joy On Christmas Morning
710007	Jump For Joy On Christmas Morning
710012	His Eyes How They Twinkled
710021	Clearing A Path To You
710022	Deck The Halls
720008	Godmother, You're An Inspiration To Me
730076	The Future Is In Our Hands
730122	There's Sno-Boredom With You
730130	Raisin' Cane On The Holidays
737550	Sure Could Use Less Hustle And Bustle
737569	One Good Turn Deserves Another
810001	Blessings Of Peace To You
810002	Blessings Of Peace To You
810007	Peace Be Within You
810023	A Season Of Joy And Togetherness
810024	Filled With Wonder And Joy On This Special Night
810025	Holidays Are A Time For Comfort And Warmth
810026	Nurses Are There In Our Time Of Need
810027	Sisters Are Precious Gifts
810028	Grandmother, Your Memories Fill My Heart
810029	Behold The Spirit Of Christmas In Your Hands
810030	Wishing For Wonderful Things This Joyous Season
810031	A Warm Holiday Wish For You
810032	The Spirit Of Christmas Shines This Season
810035	It Is A Happy Heart That Holds A Friend
810042	Hanging My Stocking With Care
810044	Dressing Up For The Holidays
810045	May All Of Your Wishes Come True
810046	A Heart Filled With Warmth And Wishes
810047	A Picture Perfect Memory Of A Special Day
810048	Wishing You Every Wonderful Thing That The Season Brings
810049	A Candid Christmas
810051	Stuffed With Christmas Cheer
810052	It's Beginning To Look A Lot Like Christmas
810053	For All The Good Girls And Boys
810054	En-Deering Moments This Holidays Season
810055	Adding Some Sweetness To The Holidays
877433	May Your Christmas Begin With A Bang
877441	May Your Christmas Begin With A Bang
878952	Celebrating His Arrival
4003165	You Light Up My Holly-Days
4024101	Grandma, I'll Never Out Grow You
4024103	Daughter, You'll Always Be My Princess
4024104	Blessed With A Loving Godmother
4024105	Grandma's Little Angel
4024106	I Can't Give You Anything But Love
4117785	May You Have An Old Fashioned Christmas
521302R	May All Your Christmases Be White
E-0501	Sharing Our Season Together
E-0502	Jesus Is The Light That Shines
E-0503	Blessings From My House To Yours
E-0504	Christmastime Is For Sharing
E-0505	Christmastime Is For Sharing
E-0506	Surrounded With Joy
E-0513	Surround Us With Joy
E-0519	Sharing Our Season Together
E-0520	Wee Three Kings
E-0531	O Come All Ye Faithful
E-0532	Let Heaven And Nature Sing
E-0533	Tell Me The Story Of Jesus
E-0534	To Thee With Love
E-0535	Love Is Patient
E-0536	Love Is Patient
E-2305	Dropping In For Christmas
E-2345	May Your Christmas Be Cozy
E-2346	Let Heaven And Nature Sing
E-2348	Mat Your Christmas Be Warm
E-2349	Tell Me The Story Of Jesus
E-2352	O Come All Ye Faithful
E-2353	O Come All Ye Faithful
E-2359	I'll Play My Drum For Him
E-2361	Christmas Joy From Head To Toe
E-2367	The First Noel
E-2368	The First Noel
E-2369	Dropping In For Christmas
E-2374	Bundles Of Joy
E-2375	Dropping In For Christmas
E-2376	Dropping In For Christmas
E-2381	Mouse With Cheese
E-2537	Jesus Is The Light That Shines
E-2802	Christmas Is A Time To Share
E-2805	Wishing You A Season Filled With Joy
E-2806	Christmas Is A Time To Share
E-2810	Come Let Us Adore Him
E-2829	I'm Sending You A White Christmas
E-4725	Peace On Earth
E-4726	Peace On Earth
E-5376	May Your Christmas Be Blessed
E-5377	Love Is Kind
E-5387	Wishing You A Merry Christmas
E-5388	Joy To The World
E-5389	Peace On Earth
E-5390	May God Bless You With A Perfect Holiday Season
E-5394	Wishing You A Merry Christmas
E-5395	Unto Us A Child Is Born
E-5634	Wee Three Kings
E-5645	Rejoice O Earth
E-5833	Wishing You A Merry Christmas
E-6120	We Have Seen His Star

Christmas Blessing

523860	Blessings From Me To Thee
527742	But The Greatest Of These Is Love
523801	Wishing You A Yummy Christmas
530204	Wishing You The Sweetest Christmas

Christmas Love

101834	I'm Sending You A White Christmas
102954	My Peace I Give Unto Thee
520284	Merry Christmas Deer
523003	May Your Christmas Be A Happy Home

Clown

12238	Clown Figurines
12262	I Get A Bang Out Of You
12270	Lord Keep Me On The Ball
12459	Waddle I Do Without You
12467	The Lord Will Carry You Through
15504	God Sent You Just In Time
15830	Happiness Is The Lord
100455	Bong Bong
100463	Candy
100668	Clowns
101842	Smile Along The Way
101850	Lord, Help Us Keep Our Act Together
102520	Let's Keep In Touch
104396	Happy Days Are Here Again
106216	Lord, Help Me Make The Grade
109584	Happiness Divine
112364	Waddle I Do Without You
113964	Smile Along The Way
113972	God Sent You Just In Time
520632	A Friend Is Someone Who Cares
795267	You Are The Wind Beneath My Wings
12238A	Clown Figurine
12238B	Clown Figurine
12238C	Clown Figurine
12238D	Clown Figurine

Collector's Christmas Event

111413	Ma-Holo Day Wishes For You
116710	Christmas Around The World
191353	Warm Hands, Warm Heart, Warm Wishes
681032	His Name Is Jesus
804088	Ready In The Nick Of Time

Collector's Licensee Event

106109	The Heart Of The Home Is Love
106672	Land Of The Free, Home Of The Brave
119840	We're All Cut From The Same Cloth
119841	Throwing A Holiday Wish Your Way
795496	Friendship Grows From The Heart

Collector's Series

640002 The Heart Of A Mother Is Reflected In Her Child
640004 A Mother's Love Grows By Giving
640031 Having A Sister Is Always Having A Friend
640041 Dreams Really Do Come True
640042 Follow Your Heart
640046 You Are My Work Of Art
710026 I Will Be Glad And Rejoice In You
710027 Rock Around The Clock
740001 You Color My World With Love
740002 You Color My World With Love
740006 The Simple Bare Necessities
740007 With A Smile And A Song
740048 My Solidier, My Hero
840030 Our Love Is The Bridge To Happiness
920025 All For The Love Of You On A Bicycle Built For Two
7400004 Gentle Is A Mother's Love

Columbus

527777 The Land Is Our Land

Communion

640022 Do This In Memory Of Me
640023 Do This In Memory Of Me
679852 This Day Has Been Made In Heaven
740050 Do This In Memory Of Me
840011 Blessed Be The Bread Of Life
840012 Blessed Be The Bread Of Life
0000364 For His Precious Love
0000365 For His Precious Love

Compassionate Friends

680990 God Gives Us Memories So That We Might Have Roses

Confirmation

488178 Confirmed In The Lord
840034 Today I Confirm My Faith

Country Lane Collection

104270 I Get A Cluck Out Of You
261106 Hogs And Kisses
261106S Hogs And Kisses
307017 You're Just As Sweet As Pie
307025 Oh, Taste And See That The Lord Is Good
307033 Fork Over Those Blessing To Others
307041 Nobody Likes To Be Dumped
307068 I'll Never Tire Of You
307076 Peas Pass The Carrots
307084 Bringing In The Sheaves
455865 Wishing You A Moo-Ie Christmas
539910 Shear Happiness And Hare Cuts
587842 Eat Ham
587850 You Brighten My Fields Of Dreams
588091 Dear Jon, I Will Never Leave You
649732 Hay Good Lookin
763225 Eat Turkey
795356 Life Would Be The Pits Without Friends
879096 Oh, What A Wonder-Fall Day
898147 Overalls, I Think You're Special!

Cowboy

105821 Hallelujah Country
455733 Praise The Lord And Dosie-Do
455830 Warmest Wishes For The Holidays

Cross Stitch

531707 The Lord Is Counting On You

Crown

526053 Pretty As A Princess

Cruise

110254 Celebrating 25 Years Of Sunshine & Smiles
150061 Sailabration
325511 Our Future Is Looking Much Brighter
529079 Friends Never Drift Apart
748412 Whale Have Oceans Of Fun

790013 Thankful For The Memories Of Good Times With Friends
790014 Sharing Of Ourselves Brings A Wealth Of Joy

Dated Annual

104202 May Your Holidays Sparkle With Joy
104203 May Your Holidays Sparkle With Joy

Dated Cross Series

127019 Love Blooms Eternal
163732 Standing In The Presence Of The Lord
306835 Under His Wings I Am Safely Abiding

Daughter

104269 I'm So Lucky To Have You As Daughter

Disney Collection

620031D A Dream Is A Wish Your Heart Makes
640041 Dreams Really Do Come True
640042 Follow Your Heart
690011 There's Magic In The Ears
710036 Aren't You Sweet
710037 The Stockings Were Hung By The Chimney With Care
710038 There's Nothin' To It When It Comes To You
710039 Nothing's Sweeter Than Time Together
710050 The Magic Of The Season
710051 Old Friends Make The Season Bright
710052 Smiles For The Season
710055 Close Friends Make The Season Special
710056 Making A List And Checking It Twice
710058 I'll Be Home For Christmas
730004 Your Love Is A Perfect Fit
740006 The Simple Bare Necessities
740007 With A Smile And A Song
740009 Come Along And Sing The Song
740010 You Are The Bright Spot Of My Day
810036 The Shortest Distance Between Two Hearts
810037 Now You Can Fly
810038 It Is In Giving That We Receive
810039 Birthday Wishes From My World To Yours
810040 Knowing You're In Love With Me Is The Greatest Gift Of All
810041 The Season Is Most Joyous Amounst Friends
820001 For The Fairest Birthday Of Them All
820002 Wishing All Of Your Dreams Come True
820003 Be Our Guest For Birthday Best
830006 Laughter Gives Friends The Power To Share
830009 Anything Is Possible With Friends
830010 Gatherng Friends Together
840004 The Magic Of Friendship Shines Through
840006 Fair In Beauty And In Spirit
840008 Friendship Has A Way Of Finding You
910039 Friends Help You Find Your Way
910040 Your Beautiful Heart Warms The Coldest Days
910041 There's Magic Under The Mistletoe
910057 The Christmas Spirit Is A Part Of My World
910059 Believe In The Power Of True Love
920001 Your Kiss Can Put A Smile On The Grumpiest Face
920002 I'm Swept Away By You
920004 Friends Have A Way Of Keeping You Cool
920030 Your Sweet Song Fills The Air
920031 We're Always On The Same Page
920032 Oceans Of Love For You
4004157 You're My Mouseketeer
620030D Magically Ever After
630037D The Wonderful Things About Tiggers
810036DW The Shortest Distance Between Two Hearts
810037DW Now You Can Fly
810041DW The Season Is Most Joyous Amount Friends
920003 Rounding Up A Gang Full Of Fun
930005 Our Love Is Forever In Bloom
930006 The Joy You Bring Awakens My Heart
930007 You Make My World A Wonderland

Disney Showcase Collection

620030 Magically Ever After
620031 A Dream Is A Wish Your Heart Makes
630037 The Wonderful Things About Tiggers
630038 Heigh Ho, It's Off To Play We Go
630039 Part Of Your World
690016 A Dream Is A Wish Your Heart Makes
690017 Everything's Better With A Friend
720017 A Friend In Need
720018 You Make The Best Of A Rainy Day
720019 It's So Much More Friendly With Two
720020 Always Reach For The Stars
730011 It's Never Too Late For Fun With Friends
730012 You Make All My Wishes Come True
730013 Discover The Beauty All Around You
4004158 Everything's Better With A Friend
4004159 Make Every Day Magical

Disney Theme Park Exclusive

690010 When You Wish Upon A Star
710053 Oh Boy! It Must Be Christmas
710057 Adorn Every Branch With Love
790010 Where Dreams Come True
890047 A Smile Means Friendship To Everyone
890049 A Magical Moment To Remember
4004156 Happiness Is Best Shared Together
690003D A World Of My Own
690004D A World Of My Own
690011D There's Magic In The Ears
790015D Spread Your Wings And Fly
790016D You Are My Cup Of Tea
790022DL Minnie And Me
790022DW Minnie And Me
810039DW Birthday Wishes From My World To Yours
820001DW For The Fairest Birthday Of Them All
820002DW Wishing All Of Your Dreams Come True
820003DW Be Our Guest For Our Birthday Best
990010 Merry Christmas To All

DSR Exclusive

104281 Carry A Song In Your Heart
115921 A Bright And Shining Moment
635049 Scoopin' Up Some Love
730173 The Peace That Passes Understanding
804444 Happy Anniversary

DSR Catalog Promotion

521329 Have I Toad You Lately I Love You
524379 So Glad I Picked You As A Friend
528609 Sending My Love Your Way
532223 Merry Giftness

DSR Event

104784 The True Spirit Of Christmas Guides The Way
272949 Pack Your Trunk For The Holidays
325457 Life Can Be A Jungle
4004375 You Were Made For Me
4004376 You Were Made For Me

Early Release

532061S Who's Gonna Fill Your Shoes

Easter

109886 Wishing You A Happy Easter
109924 Wishing You A Basket Full Of Blessings
521892 Easter's On Its Way
521906 Hoppy Easter, Friend Easter Seals
104531 Jesus Loves Me
107999 He Walks With Me
110367 Love Is A Heavenly Song
112966 Joy Is The Music Of Angels
112967 Hope Is A Gentle Melody
112969 Happiness Is A Song From Heaven
115479 Blessed Are They That Overcome
128899 Take Time To Smell The Roses
152277 He Loves Me
152579 You Can Always Count On Me
192368 Give Ability A Chance
192376 Love Is Universal
192384 Give Ability A Chance

225290 Always In His Care
233196 Sharing A Gift Of Love
238899 A Universal Love
244570 It Is No Secret What God Can Do
250112 You're My Number One Friend
272922 Somebody Cares
272981 Love Grows Here
456314 Heaven Bless You Easter Seal
475068 We Are All Precious In His Sight
475076 Heaven Bless You Easter Seal
490245 Give Your Whole Heart
520322 Make A Joyful Noise
522325 Somebody Cares
522376 His Love Will Shine On You
523283 You Have Touched So Many Hearts
523879 We Are God's Workmanship
524387 Take Time To Smell The Flowers
524522 Always In His Care
526010 You Are Such A Purr-Fect Friend
526827 You Can Always Count On Me
526886 He's Got The Whole World In His Hands
527114 Sharing A Gift Of Love
527173 A Universal Love
529680 Gather Your Dreams
530026 You're My Number One Friend
531111 It Is No Secret What God Can Do
531243 You Are The Rose Of His Creation
634735 Jesus Loves Me
634751 Give Your Whole Heart
730254 You Have The Beary Best Heart
822426 Love One Another
975893 Faith Is Heaven's Sweet Song
4001661 I'm Always Bee-Side You

e-Bay Exclusive

119836 Saving Sweet Memories

Event Exclusive

101551 Home, Home On The Range
E-2823R To God Be The Glory

Fall

730149 Everything Is Beautiful In It's Own Way
732494 Harvest Festival
0000367 You're Purr-Fect, Pumpkin

Fall Celebration

112874 Squashed With Love

Fall Syndiated Catalog Exclusive

E-2804R Peace On Earth

Family

101502 I'm A Big Sister
101503 I'm A Big Brother
101504 Precious Grandma
101505 Precious Grandpa
108526 Family's Fur-Ever
108527 Adopting A Life Of Love
108528 My Most Precious Moments Are With You
111898 Simple Pleasure Make Holiday Treasures
112870 To A Niece With A Bubbly Personality
163597 You Are Always There For Me
163600 You Are Always There For Me
163619 You Are Always There For Me
163627 You Are Always There For Me
163635 You Are Always There For Me
488089 He'll Carry Me Through
520918 Blessed Be The Tie That Binds
524409 Be Fruitful And Multiply
679844 We Knead You Grandma
730165 I'll Never Let You Down
730211 Home Made Of Love
790021 The Greatest Joy Is Motherhood
797693 You're Just Too Tweet
840001 Mom, Your Love Makes Me Blossom
840002 Mom, Your Love Makes Me Blossom
840007 Mom, Your Love Is My Greatest Gift
891045 Daddy's Little Girl
891738 You Are My Gift From Above
892157 Healing Begins With Forgiveness
892726 Ewe Are So Precioius To Me
937282 We've Got The Right Plan

Family Ornament Collection

104785 No One's Sweeter Than Mom
104786 Papas Make The Season Bright
104788 Making The Holidays Special
104789 Delivering Lots Of Love
104790 Bringing Bouquets Of Love
104791 Packed With Love
104792 Overflowing With Holiday Joy
104793 Holiday Surprises Come In All Sizes
104794 Hooked On The Holidays
104796 Hanging Out For The Holidays

Father

115906 Like Father Like Son
E-0515 To A Special Dad
E-5212 To A Special Dad

Friendship

100048 To My Deer Friend
100072 To My Favorite Friend
104219 Friends Share A Special Bond
108535 I-Rish You Lots Of Luck
108536 Grounds For A Great Friendship
108538 Friends Always Deserve Special Treatment
108539 I'm So Glad I Spotted You As A Friend
112356 You Have Touched So Many Hearts
112577 You Have Touched So Many Hearts
112882 You're A Gem Of A Friend
113956 To My Forever Friend
113991 Glad We See Eye To Eye
114018 Dear Friend, My Love For You Will Never Fade Away
114019 Friends Of A Feather Shop Together
114020 Let's Always Preserve Our Friendship
117800 Remember, We're In It Together
119094 Our Friendship's In The Bag
261068 Friends From The Very Beginning
427527 You Have Touched So Many Hearts
455903 Friends Are Forever, Sew Bee It
487953 You Can Always Count On Me
487988 What Better To Give Than Yourself
488054 You Just Can't Replace A Good Friendship
488240 A Very Special Bond
488372 You Count
520675 Your Love Is So Uplifting
520721 Just A Line To Wish You A Happy Day
520748 Friendship Hits The Spot
520764 Puppy Love
521000 There Is No Greater Treasure Than To Have A Friend Like You
521183 That's What Friends Are For
521299 Hug One Another
521817 Good Friends Are Forever
521973 Caught Up In Sweet Thoughts Of You
522287 Thinking Of You Is What I Really Like To Do
522937 Friends Never Drift Apart
523623 I'm So Glad That God Blessed Me With A Friend Like You
523631 I Will Always Be Thinking Of You
524018 You're The Best Friend On The Block
524084 My Warmest Thoughts Are You
524123 Good Friends Are For Always
524131 Good Friends Are For Always
524271 Friendship Grows When You Plant A Seed
524336 Our Friendship Is Soda-Licious
524395 You Are Such A Purr-Fect Friend
525049 Good Friends Are Forever
525901 We All Need A Friend Through The Ruff Times
526150 Friends To The Very End
526185 You Are My Happiness
526487 Sharing Sweet Moments Together
527661 You Have Touched So Many Hearts
531626 Our Friendship Goes A Long Way
531944 Sharing Our Christmas Together
634964 Friendship's A Slice Oif Life
720011 Your Friendship Grows Sweeter With Each Day
720012 Friendship Is A Sweet Journey
720013 Your Friendship Sweetens My Life
890987 Best Friends Share The Same Heart
920008 You're The Piece That Completes My Picture
920009 Friends Listen With Their Hearts
920010 I Get By With A Little Shopping With My Friends
E-4722 Love Cannot Break A True Friendship
E-5200 Bear Ye One Another's Burdens
E-5201 Love Lifted Me
E-5202 Thank You For Coming To My Ade
E-5391 Love Is Kind
E-6613 God Sends The Gift Of His Love
E-9252 Forgiving Is Forgetting
E-9259 We're In It Together
E-9283A Forever Friends
E-9283B Forever Friends

Garden Angels

114027 Hope Blooms In A Garden Of Glory
114028 Kindness Of Spirit Knows No Bounds
114029 Humble Prayers Make Hearts Bloom
114031 Dreams Bloom With A Seed Of Faith
176958 Some Plant, Some Water, But Giveth The Increase

Gift Sets

104275 Life's Ups 'N Downs Are Smoother With You
104781 There's Sno-One Quite Like You
110267 A Mother's Love Is Beyond Measure
114023 Nothing Is Stronger Than Our Love
119374 May Your Holidays Be Warm And Fuzzy
312444 Holiday Wishes, Sweety Pie!
553867 I Pray The Lord My Soul To Keep
553875 I Pray The Lord My Soul To Keep
553875 I Pray The Lord My Soul To Keep
630001 How Sweet It Is To Be Loved By You
640003 Mom, You Are A Bouquet Of Love & Understanding
690024 Birthday Train Gift Set
708518 I Will Love You All Ways
723011 Squeaky Clean
724007 Mi Quinceañera
724008 My Sweet Sixteen
730002 You Crafted A Place In My Heart
740003 A Mother's Loving Touch Is A Gift From God
740012 Your Future Is So Rosy
740015 Growing In Grace Starter Set - Blonde
740040 Growing In Grace Starter Set - Brunette
740050 Do This In Memory Of Me
745510 A Collection Of Precious Moments
798223 Grandma, I'll Never Outgrow You
798231 Grandma, I'll Never Outgrow You
4001650 A Mother's Love Is A Warm Glow
4003172 There's No Place Like Home For Christmas
4004737 I'm A Fool For You
526096S I'm Completely Suspended With Love
795232V You're A Dandy Mom And I'm Not Lion
E-4721B The Lord Bless You And Keep You
E-4721DB The Lord Bless You And Keep You — Girl
12343 Jesus Is Coming Soon
100102 Make Me A Blessing
100196 The Spirit Is Willing, But The Flesh Is Weak
100226 The Lord Giveth And The Lord Taketh Away
100277 He Cleansed My Soul
100528 Scent From Above
101497 It's What Inside That Counts
102903 We Are All Precious In His Sight
103632 I Believe In The Old Rugged Cross
104267 You're O.K., Buy Me
105643 Something's Missing When You're Not Around
108533 Just For Your Knowledge, I'll Miss You At College
112380 He Cleansed My Soul
113946 Hold On To Your Faith
113949 This Little Light Of Mine, I'm Gonna Let It Shine
113966 His Blessings Are Without Measure
115871 La Quinceañera
128309 Dreams Really Do Come True

135984 He Is My Salvation
163775 The Sun Is Always Shining Somewhere
183814 The Most Precious Gift Of All
204854 You're A Life Saver To Me
242673 Life's Beary Precious With You
260916 Lead Me To Calvary
261157 We All Have Our Bad Hair Days
272531 Sharing The Light Of Love
307009 Charity Begins In The Heart
455687 Mornin' Pumpkin
520667 Eggspecially For You
520802 My Days Are Blue Without You
520829 You Are My Number One
521205 Hope You're Up And On The Trail Again
521310 Yield Not To Temptation
521434 To A Very Special Mom And Dad
521450 Lord, Help Me Stick To My Job
521477 Tell It To Jesus
521485 There's A Light At The End Of The Tunnel
522104 It's No Yoke When I Say I Love You
522279 A Reflection Of His Love
522910 Make A Joyful Noise
522953 I Believe In The Old Rugged Cross
523224 Happy Trails Is Trusting Jesus
523496 This Day Has Been Made In Heaven
523542 You Are The Type I Love
523593 The Lord Will Provide
523615 Good News Is So Uplifting
523682 This Day Has Been Made In Heaven
524212 Walk In The Sonshine
524425 May Only Good Things Come Your Way
524913 We're Going To Miss You
526142 I Would Be Lost Without You
526916 Wishing You Were Here
531030 You Are My Once In A Lifetime
531138 What A Difference You're Made In My Life
531146 Vaya Con Dios (To Go With God)
531162 Bless Your Sole
531634 Who's Gonna Fill Your Shoes
532037 I Can't Bear To Let You Go
587869 Witch Way Do You Spell Love
587923 Thank You Sew Much
604208 A Poppy For You
634972 Reach For The Stars
642673 Life's Beary Precious With You
650013 Giving My Heart Freely
692409 Alleluia, He Is Risen
731064 Take Thyme For Yourself
731129 A Collection Of Precious Moments
737623 Auntie, You Make Beauty Blossom
742880 To The Sweetest Girl In The Cast
781770 May All Your Days Be Rosy
786152 Sharing Sweet Moments Together
790068 The Future Is In Our Hands
795151 You Are The Queen Of My Heart
795208 The Lord Can Dew Anything
795259 It's A Banner Day, Congratulations
795283 You're A Honey
795313 Wishing You A Birthday Full Of Surprises
811807 A Godchild Close To My Heart
878901 May Your Days Be Merry And Bright
878944 On A Scale From 1 To 10 You Are The Deerest
878995 Life Is So Uplifting
879002 Roll Away, Roll Away, Roll Away
879126 Lord Let Our Friendship Bloom
879134 Our Friendship Was Made To Order
890731 Nearer To The Heart Of God
890960 Just A Happy Note!
E-0530 His Eye Is On The Sparrow
E-0539 Katie Lynne
E-2851 Kristy
E-3110G Loving Is Sharing
E-5213 God Is Love
E-6214G Debbie
E-7164 Bless This House
E-7171 Jesus Loves Me
E-9258 We Are God's Workmanship
E-9273 Let Love Reign
E-9276 Jesus Loves Me
E-9279 Jesus Loves Me
E-9287R And A Child Shall Lead Them
E-9287R Peace On Earth

GCC Exclusive

104273 You Cane Count On Me
104274 You Cane Count On Me
115927 Sprinkled With Kindness
679259 Peace On Earth
795577 Your Love Keeps Me Toasty Warm
881147 You Decorate My Life

Globe

524352 What The World Needs Now

God's Creature

795194 You Can't Hide From God

Godmother

115904 Godmother & Me
115905 Godmother & Me
795348 Blessed With A Loving Godmother

Graduation

101498 You're An All Star Graduate
101499 You're An All Star Graduate
106194 God Bless You Graduate
106208 Congratulations, Princess
261564 The Lord Is The Hope Of Our Furture
532126 The Lord Bless You And Keep You
532134 The Lord Bless You And Keep You
550032 Your Future Is So Rosy
740011 I Know Who Holds The Future
740013 A World Of Possibilities Lies Ahead
840060 The Key To Success Is In Your Heart
877123 The Lord Is The Hope Of Our Furture
877131 The Lord Is The Hope Of Our Furture
889563 The Lord Is The Hope Of Our Furture
261564B The Lord Is The Hope Of Our Furture
261564G The Lord Is The Hope Of Our Furture
261564L The Lord Is The Hope Of Our Furture
E-4720 The Lord Bless You And Keep You
E-4721 The Lord Bless You And Keep You
E-4721D The Lord Bless You And Keep You
E-7177 The Lord Bless You And Keep You
E-7178 The Lord Bless You And Keep You
E-9261 Seek Ye The Lord
E-9262 Seek Ye The Lord

Grandfather

522864 Just A Line To Say You're Special
120107 There's More To Life Than Nine To Five
520810 We Need A Good Friend Through The Ruff Times
E-0517 The Perfect Grandpa
E-7160 The Perfect Grandpa

Grandmother

13307 The Purr-Fect Grandma
115902 Grandma & Me
115903 Grandma & Me
117801 A Grandma's Love Is One Size Fits All
731587 Grandma, I'll Never Out Grow You
731595 Grandma, I'll Never Out Grow You
E-0516 The Purr-Fect Grandma
E-3109 The Purr-Fect Grandma
E-7184 The Purr-Fect Grandma
E-7242 The Purr-Fect Grandma

Hallmark

104782 Bakin' The Holidays Even Sweeter
119436 Mom, No One Measures Up To You!
283452 May Your Prayers Be Answered
524034 Life's Filled With Little Surprises
590009 A Mother's Love Is Forever
590037 A Teaspoon Of Friendship Sweetens The Pot
619005 Sharing The Joys Of Christmas
690010 When You Wish Upon A Star
690021 Mom, You're Never Too Close For Comfort
690025 A Friend Like You Leads Me To The Sunny Side Of Life
702862 Sharing The Season With You
710052 Smiles For The Season
790007 Love Wrapped Up With A Bow
790019 I Give My Heart To You
810021 The Color Of Love
890013 Your Friendship Keeps Me Warm Even On The Coldest Of Days
890015 Would You Be Mine?
0000515 Guess Who Loves You
0000571 Friends To The Very End
0000860 May Your Holidays Be Filled With Christmas Cheer

Hawaiian Celebration Exclusive

108608 Gotta Hula-T Love For You
4003167 A Hui Hou (Till We Meet Again) (9")
4003245 A Hui Hou (Till We Meet Again)
4003247 Pi'I Mai Nalu (Surf's Up)
4003248 Mahalo Hawaii (Thank You Hawaii)
4003249 Aloha Kahou A Pau (Aloha Everyone)
4003250 Aloha Aina (Love Of The Land)
4003251 Wiki Wiki Transit (Quick Transportation)
4003777 Love From Hawaii

Heart Of An Angel

920015 Your Strength Sustains Me
920013 Your Comfort Speaks Directly To My Heart
920014 Your Friendship Brings Light To My Life
920012 Your Everyday Kindness Is My Everyday Joy

Heart Of Christmas

910008 It's What's Inside That Counts
910009 Sharing The Seeds Of Love
910010 Delivering Smiles Is The Best Gift Of All
910011 The Fruits Of Love Are A Gift To Cherish
910012 Merry Kiss-Mas To You
910013 May Your Christmas Be Filled With Sweet Surprises
910014 You Have The Sweetness Of The Season All Wrapped Up
910015 All Is Merry And Bright

Heroes

113963 Blessed Are They Who Serve
958832 Our Heroes In The Sky
958840 Our Heroes In The Sky

Holiday Preview Event

520470 Take A Bow Cuz You're My Christmas Star

Holiday Carols

910017 Do You See What I See?
910019 On The First Day Of Christmas
910020 Glory To The Newborn King
910022 Glory To God In The Highest
910023 Boughs Of Holly
910024 My Gift For Him
910025 Here Comes Santa Claus
910026 Be Of Good Cheer
910066 Born Is The King Of Israel
12319 God Bless Our Home

Housework

106844 Sew In Love
111155 Faith Takes The Plunge
521779 Sweep All Your Worries Away
587907 My Life Is A Vacuum
E-3111 Be Not Weary In Well Doing
E-3118 Eggs Over Easy
E-9265 Press On

Humor

104271 Owl Always Be There For You
114010 If The Shoe Fits, Buy It
358959 Catch Ya Later
521345 Life's Journey Has Its Ups And Downs
525944 Lord, I'm In It Again
587877 Snow Man Like My Man
587893 God Loves A Happy Camper
587915 Rv Havin' Fun Or What
679860 Lovingcaringsharing.Com

679879 Bless You
E-2827 I Get A Kick Out Of You

Indian

306991 Missum You
520772 Many Moons In Same Canoe

Blessum You

527335 Bless-Um You

Inspirations

113965 You Shall Receive A Crown Of Glory
261130 Have You Any Room For Jesus
490318 God Knows Our Ups And Downs
679828 Good Advice Has No Price
840041 Give All Your Worries And Cares To God
840042 An Act Of Kindness Makes All The Difference
840043 I'm With You Every Step Of The Way

Japanese Collection

103178 Hang Onto Your Happiness
103180 We Are The Sheep Of His Pasture
103181 The Dawn Of A New Beginning
103182 Good Forture Is Right Around The Corner
103183 Life Is No Boar With You
103184 Life's Blessings Are Bountiful
103185 Ringing In A Good Year Of Health
103186 Strength Comes From Within
103188 I'm Bouncing With You
111904 The Lord Bless You And Keep You
481602 On Our Way To A Special Day
481610 On Our Way To A Special Day
481629 Shiny New And Ready For School
481637 Shiny New And Ready For School
481645 Growing In Wisdom — Boy
481653 Growing In Wisdom — Girl
481661 All Girls Are Beautiful
481688 Make Me Strong
731625 Everybody Has A Part
731633 Good Fortune
791091 Rhythm And Flute
791113 Courteous Service
791121 Bringing In Another Grrreat Year
791148 Different Beats Can Still Come Together
821969 Hissterically Sweet
4002981 Thou Shalt Not Stumble

John Deere Collection

840038 A Cut Above The Rest
840039 A Friend Is Someone Who Is Always There To Help
840040 Thanks For Being There
910042 A Tractor To Call My Very Own
910043 My First Set Of Wheels
910044 You Light Up The Holidays
910055 Cruising Through The Holidays
930014 Riding Toward Greener Pastures — Girl
930015 Riding Toward Greener Pastures — Boy

Kirlin's Exclusive

104778 Lots Of Good Things Are Coming Your Way
104780 Lots Of Good Things Are Coming Your Way
119436 Mom, No One Measures Up To You!
690016 A Dream Is A Wish Your Heart Makes

Limited Edition

101543 Friends Are Never Far Behind
101545 Lord, Help Me Clean Up My Act
101546 Our Love Is Heaven Scent
101547 Life Never Smelled So Sweet
101552 Where The Deer And The Antelope Play
108522 Your Love Fills My Heart
110268 My Heart Belongs To You
110855 The Sweetest Treat Is Friendship
111896 Your Love Means The World To Me
114023 Nothing Is Stronger Than Our Love
115915 You Are The Apple Of My Eye
115917 You're Pear-Fectly Sweet
116710 Christmas Around The World
117793 Bring You The Gift Of Peace
117794 Simple Joys Put A Song In Your Heart
117795 All Wrapped Up With Love
117798 Twas The Night Before Christmas
118129 There's Snow Place Like Home
118259 The World Is A Stage Featuring Precious Moments
118302 Nature Provides Us With Such Sweet Pleasures
118316 You Make My Heart Soar
118728 Bringing You My Heart
118875 Friendship Has No Limit
119559 Heavenly Angels
120007 You Have The Sweetest Smile
120106 Love Is The Color Of Rainbows
127930 He Shall Lead The Children Into The 21st Century
184241 Winter Wishes Warm The Heart
261351 We're So Hoppy You're Here
325473 Mom, You're My Special-Tea
455970 Flight Into Egypt
495891 God Loveth A Cheerful Giver
522139 I Will Make You Fishers Of Men
550012 My Mona Lisa
550025 Her Children Will Rise Up And Call Her Blessed
610070 Your Love Gives Me Wings
610071 My Dream Boat
620027 Gloria In Excelsis Deo
630040 Life's A Picnic With My Honey
630041 Embraced In Your Love
730032 Washed Away In Your Love
804088 Ready In The Nick Of Time
4003169 Star Of Wonder
4004738 May Love Blossom Wherever You Go
4004739 Just An Old Fashioned Hello (1910s)
4004740 Mixing Up A Brighter Tomorrow (1930s)
4004741 One Small Step (1960s)
15849R May Your Christmas Be Delightful
183814S The Most Precious Gift Of All
523186E Yes Dear, You're Always Right
E-2347 Let Heaven And Nature Sing
E-9267 Animal Collection

Little Moments

101554 Nurses Are Blessed With Patients
102726 There's Sno-One Quite Like You
102913 Mom, You're A Sweetheart
104781 There's Sno-One Quite Like You
115914 You're A-Peeling To Me
115918 You're Just Peachy
118875 Friendship Has No Limit
139491 Where Would I Be Without You
139505 All Things Grow With Love
139513 You're The Berry Best
139521 You Make The World A Sweeter Place
139548 You're Forever In My Heart
139556 Birthday Wishes With Hugs & Kisses
139564 You Make My Spirit Soar
184241 Winter Wishes Warm The Heart
261173 Bless Your Little Tutu
261203 January
261211 May
261238 September
261246 February
261254 June
261262 October
261270 March
261289 July
261297 November
261300 April
261319 August
261327 December
272612 You Will Always Be A Winner To Me
272639 It's Ruff To Always Be Cheery
283460 You Will Always Be A Winner To Me
312444 Holiday Wishes, Sweety Pie!
320560 You're Just Perfect In My Book
320579 Loving Is Caring
320595 Loving Is Caring
320625 You Set My Heart Ablaze
320668 Just The Fact… You're Perfect
320706 You Have Such A Special Way Of Caring Each And Every Day
320714 What Would I Do Without You
384386 Thank You For The Times We Share
456373 You Are A Dutch-Ess To Me (Holland)
456381 Life Is A Fiesta (Spain)
456403 Don't Rome Too Far From Home (Italy)
456411 You Can't Beat The Red, White And Blue (United States)
456446 Love's Russian Into My Heart (Russia)
456454 Hola, Amigo! (Mexico)
456462 Afri-Can Be There For You, I Will Be (Kenya)
456470 I'd Travel The Highlands To Be With You (Scotland)
456896 Sure Would Love To Squeeze You (Germany)
456918 You Are My Armour (France)
456926 Our Friendship Is Always In Bloom (Japan)
456934 My Love Will Stand Guard Over You (England)
488283 Jonah And The Whale
488291 Daniel And The Lion's Den
488305 Joseph's Special Coat
490342 Soap Bubbles, Soap Bubbles, All Is Soap Bubbles
491586 World's Greatest Student
491594 World's Sweetest Girl
491608 World's Best Helper
491616 World's Greatest Student
491624 You're No. 1
491640 You're No. 1
524034 Life's Filled With Little Surprises
553867 I Pray The Lord My Soul To Keep
553875 I Pray The Lord My Soul To Keep
553875 I Pray The Lord My Soul To Keep
632341 I Pray The Lord My Soul To Keep
632430 I Pray The Lord My Soul To Keep
649457 Highway To Happiness
649465 I'll Never Stop Loving You
649473 There's No Wrong Way With You
649481 God's Children At Play
649511 Cross Walk
649538 Go For It
649546 Yield To Him
649554 Let Him Enter Your Heart
649562 Give 'Em A Brake For Jesus
649953 Baby Moses
649961 Ruth And Naomi
649988 The Good Samaritan
649996 The Great Pearl
650005 The Sower And The Seed
650064 David And Goliath
692077 The Child That's Born On The Sabbath Day
692085 Monday's Child Is Fair Of Face
692093 Tuesday's Child Is Full Of Grace
692107 Wednesday's Child Is Full Of Woe
692115 Thursday's Child Has Far To Go
692123 Friday's Child Is Loving & Caring
692131 Saturday's Child Works Hard For A Living
730238 I'm A Reflection Of Your Love
731579 Sharing Sweet Moments Together
848735 Blonde Mother
848743 Blonde Dad
848751 Blonde Teen Daughter
848778 Blonde Teen Son
848786 Blonde Toddler Girl
848794 Blonde Toddler Son
848808 Blonde Infant Daughter
848816 Blonde Infant Son
848824 Dog
848832 Cat
880833 Brunette Mother
880841 Brunette Dad
880868 Brunette Teen Daughter
880876 Brunette Teen Son
880884 Brunette Toddler Daughter
880892 Brunette Toddler Son
880906 Brunette Infant Daughter
880914 Brunette Infant Son
883875 Hug Me Before I Melt

4003177 You're The Cymbal Of Perfection
E-0502 It's A Perfect Boy
E-0507 God Sent His Son
E0508 Prepare Ye The Way Of The Lord
E-0511 Tubby's First Christmas
E-2355 I'll Play My Drum For Him
E-2356 I'll Play My Drum For Him
E-2357 I'll Play My Drum For Him
E-2360 I'll Play My Drum For Him
E-2363 Camel
E-2364 Goat
E-2365 The First Noel
E-2366 The First Noel
E-2800 Come Let Us Adore Him
E-2803 Crown Him Lord Of All
E-5178 Joy To The World
E-5379 Isn't He Precious
E-5382 For God So Loved The World
E-5619 Come Let Us Adore Him
E-5621 Donkey
E-5624 They Followed The Star
E-5633 Come Let Us Adore Him
E-5635 Wee Three Kings
E-5636 Rejoice O Earth
E-5637 The Heavenly Light
E-5638 Cow With Bell
E-5639 Isn't He Wonderful
E-5640 Isn't He Wonderful
E-5641 They Followed The Star
E-5644 Nativity Wall

Open House Event

529648 The Magic Starts With You
529974 An Event For All Seasons

Original 21

E-1372B Jesus Loves Me
E-1372G Jesus Loves Me
E-1373B Smile, God Loves You
E-1373G Jesus Is The Light
E-1374B Praise The Lord Anyhow
E-1374G Make A Joyful Noise
E-1375A Love Lifted Me
E-1375B Prayer Changes Things
E-1376 Love One Another
E-1377A He Leadeth Me
E-1377B He Careth For You
E-1378 God Loveth A Cheerful Giver
E-1379A Love Is Kind
E-1379B God Understands
E-1380G His Burden Is Light
E-1381 Jesus Is The Answer
E-2010 We Have Seen His Star
E-2011 Come Let Us Adore Him
E-2012 Jesus Is Born
E-2013 Unto Us A Child Is Born

Our First Christmas Together

E-2385 Our First Christmas Together
E-2378 Our First Christmas Together
102350 Our First Christmas Together
101702 Our First Christmas Together
112399 Our First Christmas Together
520233 Our First Christmas Together
115290 Our First Christmas Together
521558 Our First Christmas Together
525324 Our First Christmas Together
522945 Our First Christmas Together
528870 Our First Christmas Together
530506 Our First Christmas Together
529206 Our First Christmas Together
142700 Our First Christmas Together
183911 Our First Christmas Together
272736 Our First Christmas Together
455636 Our First Christmas Together
587796 Our First Christmas Together
730084 Our First Christmas Together
878855 Our First Christmas Together
104207 Our First Christmas Together
112841 Our First Christmas Together
117786 Our First Christmas Together
4003163 Our First Christmas Together
610004 Our First Christmas Together
710004 Our First Christmas Together
810004 Our First Christmas Together
E-2377 Our First Christmas Together

Orphan

520853 I Belong To The Lord

Pacific Rim Exclusive

690002 Life Is Full Of Golden Opportunities

Parade Of Gifts Catalog

163686E Birthday Personalized
488364 Purr-fect Friends
531634S Who's Gonna Fill Your Shoes

Patriotic

102938 God Bless America
681059 Let Freedom Ring

Prayer

100064 O Worship The Lord
102229 O Worship The Lord
163767 Take To The Lord In Prayer
525316 May Your Future Be Blessed
530697 Serenity Prayer Girl
530700 Serenity Prayer Boy
E-5214 Prayer Changes Things
E-7155 Thanking Him For You

Precious Moments Day

108606 Mom Hits A Home Run Every Day
112995 Mom, I Always Have A Ball With You
120008 Mom, Thanks For Always Supporting Our Team
619001 Moms Always Support Their Cubs

Precious Rewards

283541 Rejoice In The Victory
283584 God Bless You With Bouquets Of Victory
283592 Faith Is The Victory

Precious Scapes

750123 Christmas Street Precious Scape

Precious Thots Exclusive

690020 Thots Of You Bring Out The Best In Me

Premier Collection

4001787 A Winter Wonderland Awaits
4001570 Actions Speak Louder Than Words
4001571 Make Everything A Masterpiece
4001572 Praise Him With Resounding Cymbals
4001573 An Angel In Disguise
4001574 We Fix Souls
4001784 Renew Faith, Restore Hope, Replenish Love
4001785 Allow Sunshine And Laugther To Fill Your Days
4001786 Reflect And Give Thanks For All Of Life's Bounty
4001570A Actions Speak Louder Than Words

Preview Event

531200 Wishing You A Bear-ie Merry Christmas

Professions

112845 A Nurse's Care Is The Best Medicine
112857 Everyday Hero
112858 Take A Note, You're Great
112861 Teacher, You're A Precious Work Of Art
112962 It's Only Gauze I Care
114017 Our Love Is Built On A Strong Foundation

Raggedy Ann And Andy

830018 A Best Friend Wherever You Go
830019 Best Friends Forever

Reef Hallmark 40th Anniversary Exclusive

824119S Our Love Will Never Be Endangered

Regional Event

128295 An Event Showered With Love
(A) Wisconsin
(C) Texas
(D) California
160334 An Event Filled With Sunshine and Smiles
Illinois
(A) Ohio
(B) California
(C) New Jersey
(D) Missouri
(E) Maryland
(F) Florida
(G) Ohio
(H) Canada
270741 A Festival Of Precious Moments
San Jose, California
(A) Cleveland, Ohio
(B) Houston, Texas
(C) Philadelphia, Pennsylvania
796581 Konnichiwa Friends
212563 Your Precious Spirit Comes Shining Through
Knoxville
(A) Indianapolis
(B) Minneapolis

Sammy's Circus

163708 Jennifer
528099 Markie
528196 Circus Tent
529168 Jordon
529176 Dusty
529184 Katie
529192 Tippy
529214 Collin
529222 Sammy
604070 Sammy's Circus Set

School

522015 To The Apple Of God's Eye
E-3119 It's What's Inside That Counts
E-7162 Love Is Sharing
E-7185 Love Is Sharing

Shepherd

103004 We Belong To The Lord
E-5630 Unto Us A Child Is Born

Shepherd Of The Hills Exclusive

453722 Feed My Lambs

Show Exclusive

261556 Blessed Art Thou Amoungst Women
487945 Jesus Is My Lighthouse
539988 Sharing Our Winter Wonderland
649929 Peace In The Valley
730114 We're A Family That Sticks Together
737534 You Have A Special Place In My Heart
879185 Up To Our Ears In A White Christmas
879274 Count Your Many Blessings
898414 Loving, Caring And Shearing
973912 I See Bright Hope In Your Future
325333C By Grace We Have Communion With God
681059E Let Freedom Ring

Signing Event (Gene Freedman, Scuptor and Shuhei Tour Event)

111897 With A Little Help From Above

Sister

E-2825 To A Very Special Sister
528633 To A Very Special Sister

Soldier

E-0523 Onward Christian Soldiers

Special Event Piece

101234 A Penny A Kiss, A Penny A Hug
114026 You Arrr A Treasure To Me

118872 Loving
490327 You Ought To Be In Pictures
529982 Memories Are Made Of This
768952 You Are Always In My Heart
768987 You Are Always In My Heart
781851 Mr. Fujioka

Special Issue

104279 His Love Is Reflected in You
106632 God Shed His Grace On Thee
108542 Simple Pleasures Are Life's True Treasures
118316 You Make My Heart Soar Special Olympics Commemorative
813044A Winning Spirit Comes From Within

Special Wishes

742872 You're A Real Barbe-cutie!
795321 No Bones About It — You're Grr-eat
920005 Your Style Is So Striking
920006 You're An Ace On Any Court
920007 You Bring A Song To My Heart
930008 You Always Bounce Back Up
930009 Ahoy Mate! It's Smooth Sailing Ahead
930010 Whatever The Weather, We're Always Together

Spring Catalog Exclusive

261378 Happiness To The Core
325481 Home Is Where The Heart is
625465 Mom, You Always Make Our House A Home

Spring Celebration Event

163864 Hallelujah Hoedown

Sports

100110 Lord, I'm Coming Home
100129 Lord Keep Me On My Toes
100161 Serving The Lord
100188 I'm A Possibility
100293 Serving The Lord
102423 Lord Keep Me On My Toes
102431 Serve With A Smile
102458 Serve With A Smile
103497 My Love Will Never Let You Go
104035 Cheers To The Leader
104798 I Trust In The Lord For My Strength
104799 I'd Jump Through Hoops For You
104800 You're A Perfect 10
104801 We're A Perfect Match
104802 Your Spirit Is An Inspriation
104803 Serving Up Fun
109487 Believe The Impossible
111120 I'm A Possibility
112859 Coach, You're A Real Sport
113999 Cheers To The Leader
114006 My Love Will Never Let You Go
520535 The Lord Turned My Life Around
520543 In The Spotlight Of His Grace
520551 Lord, Turn My Life Around
520578 You Deserve An Ovation
520691 Lord, Keep My Life In Balance
521191 Lord, Spare Me
521221 Enter His Courts With Thanksgiving
521280 Happy Trip
521396 Faith Is A Victory
522023 May Your Life Be Blessed With Touchdowns
524905 It's So Uplifting To Have A Friend Like You
525332 Lord Keep Me On My Toes
526193 You Suit Me To A Tee
532096 Lord Help Me To Stay On Course
E-3112 God's Speed

St. Jude Children's Research

830051 Holding on To Hope
910054 May The Spirit Of Hope Embrace This Holiday Season
990030 Never Let Go Of Hope

Sugartown

150150 Train Station
150169 Sam
150177 Railroad Crossing Sign
150185 Luggage Cart
150193 Train Station Set
150207 Bus Stop Sign
150215 Fire Hydrant
150223 Bird Bath
150231 God Bless Our Home
150304 Sugar Town Chapel
152269 Sugar Town Enhancement Set
152595 Sugar Town Express
184020 Skating Sign
184039 Lighted Tree
184047 Skating Pond
184055 Mazie
184063 Cocoa
184071 Leroy
184098 Hank And Sharon
184101 Train Station
184128 Sugar Town Skating Pond Set
184136 Flag Pole
184144 Hot Cocoa Stand
184152 Bonfire
184160 Sugar Town Enhancement Set
184187 Doctor's Office Set
184195 Sam's House Set
192341 Warming Hut
192406 Passenger Car
212725 Sugar Town Accessories
272795 Canadian School House
272795 Schoolhouse
272809 Chuck
272817 Aunt Cleo
272825 Aunt Bulah And Uncle Sam
272833 Heather
272841 Merry Go Round
272876 Schoolhouse Collector's Set
272914 Garbage Can
272930 Sugar Town Skating Pond Collector's Set
273007 Cargo Car
273015 3 Piece Enhancement Set
282906 Bike Rack
456217 Sugar Town Post Office Collector's Set
528064 Free Christmas Puppies
528072 Nativity Cart
528668 Sammy
528684 Evergreen Tree
529281 Doctor's Office Set
529435 Dusty
529443 Sam's Car
529486 Aunt Ruth & Aunt Dorothy
529494 Philip
529508 Nativity
529516 Grandfather
529524 Katy Lynne
529540 Park Bench
529559 Lamp Post
529567 Sam Butcher
529605 Sam's House
529621 Chapel
529788 Stork wit Baby Sam
529796 Fence
529818 Leon And Evelyn Mae
529826 Jan
529842 Sam Butcher
529850 Dr. Sam Sugar
529869 Doctor's Office
530441 Dr. Sugar's Office
530468 Sam's House
530484 Chapel
531774 Sam's House Set
531804 Bunnies
531812 Tammy And Debbie
531847 Mailbox
531871 Donny
532185 Street Sign
532908 Town Square Clock
533149 Curved Sidewalk
533157 Straight Sidewalk
533165 Sugar And Her Doghouse
533173 Single Tree
533181 Double Tree
533203 Cobblestone Bridge
770272 Sugar Town Enhancement Set

Syndicated Catalog Exclusive

108603 Love Is The True Reward

Thanksgiving

100544 Brotherly Love
109762 We Gather Together To Ask The Lord's Blessing
183857 Color Your World With Thanksgiving
455695 Praise God From Whom All Blessings Flow
522031 Thank You Lord For Everything

Third Quarter Exclusive

635006 Hail Mary, Full Of Grace

Turn Back The Clock Event

E-1379R Love Is Kind

Valentine's Day

12009 Love Covers All
12017 Loving You
12025 Loving You
12254 Love Covers All
100250 Friends Never Drift Apart
100625 God Is Love, Dear Valentine
523518 God Is Love, Dear Valentine
730001 I Give My Heart To You
730003 Our Hearts Are Intertwined With Love
730005 Sending All My Love To You
830001 Be Mine
830002 My Heart Is Yours
830004 You Fill My Heart With joy
830005 You Are Loved Today And Always
890015 Would You Be Mine?
890016 I Hold Your Heart Forever
890596 Let Love Reign
890626 You Have A Heart Of Gold
898457 You Are My Favorite Dish
930001 Loads Of Love For You
930002 I've Got Extra! Extra! Love For You
930003 I'd Fall In Love With You All Over Again
930004 Will You Share Your Heart With Me?
898457S You Are My Favorite Dish
E-7153 God Is Love, Dear Valentine
E-7154 God Is Love, Dear Valentine

Wedding

E-7167 The Lord Bless You And Keep You
100498 God Bless Our Family
100501 God Bless Our Family
100633 The Lord Bless You And Keep You
104019 With This Ring I...
106755 Heaven Bless Your Togetherness
117802 Beautiful & Blushing, My Baby's Now A Bride
129097 Love Vows To Always Bloom
129100 I Give You My Love Forever True
455938 I Now Pronounce You Man And Wife
520780 Wishing You Roads Of Happiness
520799 Someday My Love
520837 The Lord Is Your Light To Happiness
520845 Wishing You A Perfect Choice
530999 I Still Do
531006 I Still Do
532118 The Lord Bless You And Keep You
550027 From This Day Forward
550028 Have You Cake And Eat It Too
550029 Happily Ever After
795364 Bride (African-American)
795372 Groom (African-American)
795380 Bride (Hispanic)
795399 Groom (Hispanic)
795402 Bride (Asain)
795410 Groom (Asian)
830023 To Have And To Hold Forevermore

830024	We Join Hands And Hearts
830025	Always And Forever, Daddy's Little Girl
830026	Bridesmaid, A Best Friend At My Side
830027	Flower Girl
874485	Bride (Brunette)
874493	Groom (Brunette)
876143	I Give You My Love Forever True
876151	Bridal Arch
901563	Best Man
901571	Maid Of Honor
902020	Best Man
902039	Maid Of Honor
902047	Best Man
902055	Maid Of Honor
E-2832	God Bless The Bride
E-2834	Sharing Our Joy Together
E-3114	The Lord Bless You And Keep You
E-5216	The Lord Bless You And Keep You
E-7166	The Lord Bless You And Keep You
E-7180	The Lord Bless You And Keep You
E-9255	Bless You Two

Type Guide

9" Figurines

104531 Jesus Loves Me
152277 He Loves Me
192376 Love Is Universal
204870 The Lord Is Our Chief Inspiration
272981 Love Grows Here
354414 A Prayer Warrior's Faith Can Move Mountains
456225 God Loveth A Cheerful Giver
475068 We Are All Precious In His Sight
520322 Make A Joyful Noise
523283 You have Touched So Many Hearts
523879 We Are God's Workmanship
526010 You Are Such A Purr-fect Friend
526886 He's Got The Whole World In His Hands
527572 God Bless The USA
529680 Gather Your Dreams
531243 You Are The Rose Of His Creation
634735 Jesus Loves Me
822426 Love One Another
4003167 A Hui Hou ("Till We Meet Again")
E-7350 But Love Goes On Forever

Bells

15873 God Sent His Love
109835 Love Is The Best Gift Of All
102318 Wishing You A Cozy Christmas
112348 Retailer's Wreath Bell
115304 Time To Wish You A Merry Christmas
522821 Oh Holy Night
523828 Once Upon A Holy Night
524182 May Your Christmas Be Merry
527726 But The Greatest Of These Is Love
530174 Wishing You The Sweetest Christmas
604216 You're As Pretty As A Christmas Tree
E-0522 Surrounded With Joy
E-2358 I'll Play My Drum For Him
E-5208 Jesus Loves Me
E-5209 Jesus Loves Me
E-5210 Prayer Changes Things
E-5211 God Understands
E-5393 Wishing You A Merry Christmas
E-5620 We Have Seen His Star
E-5622 Let The Heavens Rejoice
E-5623 Jesus Is Born
E-7175 The Lord Bless You And Keep You
E-7176 The Lord Bless You And Keep You
E-7179 The Lord Bless You And Keep You
E-7181 Mother Sew Dear
E-7183 The Purr-fect Grandma

Candle Climbers

E-2343 Joy To The World
E-6118 But Love Goes On Forever

Covered Boxes

E-9266 I'm Falling For Some Bunny And It Happens To You
E-9280 Jesus Loves Me (Boy)
E-9281 Jesus Loves Me (Girl)
E-9283A Forever Friends
E-9283B Forever Friends

Date Annual Ball Ornaments

104208 Home Sweet Home
112875 I-cy Potential In You
114982 May Your Christmas Be Delightful
117789 Thoughts Of You Are So Heart Warming
142689 He Covers The Earth With His Beauty
183350 Peace On Earth... Anyway
272728 Cane You Join Us For A Merry Christmas
523704 May Your Christmas Be A Happy
526940 May Your Christmas Be Merry
527734 But The Greatest Of These Is Love
530190 Wishing You The Sweetest Christmas
530387 You're As Pretty As A Christmas Tree
610003 Ringing In The Season
710003 Dancing For joy On Christmas
800813 Your Love Keeps Me Toasty Warm
810003 Blessings of Peace to You
881163 You Decorate My Life
4003162 May Your Holidays Be So-Sew Special

Dolls

12424 Aaron
12432 Bethany
12475 P.D.
12483 Trish
12491 Angie, The Angel Of Mercy
100455 Bong Bong
100463 Candy
102253 Connie
408786 The Voice Of Spring
408794 Summer's Joy
408808 Autumn's Praise
408816 Winter's Song
417785 May You Have An Old Fashioned Christmas
427527 You Have Touched So Many Hearts
E-0539 Katie Lynne
E-2850 Mother Sew Dear
E-2851 Kristy
E-5397 Timmy
E-6214B Mikey
E-6214G Debbie
E-7267B Cubby
E-7267G Tammy

Eggs

523534 I Will Cherish The Old Rugged Cross
525960 We Are God's Workmanship
528617 Make A Joyful Noise
529095 A Reflection Of His Love

Hinged Boxes

335576 April — Diamond — Color of Purity
335533 January — Garnet — Color Of Boldness
335541 February — Amethyst — Color of Faith
335568 March — Aquamarine — Color Of Kindness
335584 May — Emerald — Color Of Patience
335592 June — Pearl — Color Of Love
335606 July — Ruby — Color Of Joy
335614 August — Peridot — Color of Pride
335622 September — Sapphire — Color Of Confidence
335657 October — Opal — Color Of Happiness
335665 November — Topaz — Color Of Truth
335673 December — Turquoise — Color Of Loyalty
488380 Jesus Loves Me
488399 Jesus Loves Me
488402 Make A Joyful Noise
488410 Love One Another
488429 His Burden Is Light
488437 Jesus Is The Light
495891 God Loveth A Cheerful Giver
798290 I'll Give You The World

Jack-In-The-Box

408735 The Voice Of Spring
408743 Summer's Joy
408751 Autumn's Praise
408778 Winter's Song
417777 May You Have An Old Fashioned Christmas
422282 You Have Touched So Many Hearts

Medallion

12246 Precious Moments Last Forever
110270 Reisen In Deutschland
115272 Celebrating 25 Years Of Sunshine And Smiles
115476 Collecting Life's Most Precious Moments
177083 A Perfect Display Of 15 Happy Years
493627 Goose Girl
495298 Goose Girl
495301 Goose Girl
529079 Friends Never Drift Apart
529087 15 Years, Tweet Music Together
529672 Goose Girl
549614 A Salute To Our Stars
680761 Share In The Celebration
681016 You Are The Heart Of Precious Moments
802484 Sweetheart Safari
823945 A Beary Loving Collector
PCC112 Loving, Caring and Sharing
PM030 Goose Girl
PM877 Goose Girl

Musical

12165 Lord, Keep My Life In Tune
12408 We Saw A Star
12580 Lord, Keep My Life In Tune
15504 God Sent You Just In Time
15814 Silent Night
100285 Heaven Bless You
101702 Our First Christmas Together
102520 Let's Keep In Touch
109746 Peace On Earth
112402 I'm Sending You A White Christmas
112577 You Have Touched So Many Hearts
118259 The World Is A Stage Featuring Precious Moments
152595 Sugar Town Train Set
307084 Bringing in the Sheaves
408735 The Voice Of Spring
408743 Summer's Joy
408751 Autumn's Praise
408778 Winter's Song
417777 May You Have An Old Fashioned Christmas
422282 You Have Touched So Many Hearts
429570 The Eyes Of The Lord Are Upon You
429589 The Eyes Of The Lord Are Upon You
520691 Lord, Keep My Life In Balance
521507 The Light Of The World Is Jesus
522244 Do Not Open Until Christmas
523682 This Day Has Been Made In Heaven

526916	Wishing You Were Here	E-2355	I'll Play My Drum For Him	E-5206	My Guardian Angel
617334	Rejoice, Oh Earth	E-2806	Christmas Is A Time To Share	E-5394	Wishing You A Merry Christmas
876143	I Give You My Love Forever True	E-2807	Crown Him Lord Of All	E-5642	Silent Knight
876151	Bridal Arch	E-2808	Unto Us A Child Is Born	E-5645	Rejoice O Earth
4003176	Sing Songs Of Praise To Him	E-2809	Jesus Is Born	E-7180	The Lord Bless You And Keep You
E-0519	Sharing Our Season Together	E-2810	Come Let Us Adore Him	E-7182	Mother Sew Dear
E-0520	Wee Three Kings	E-4726	Peace On Earth	E-7184	The Purr-fect Grandma
E-2346	Let Heaven And Nature Sing	E-5204	The Hand That Rocks The Future	E-7185	Love Is Sharing
E-2352	O Come All Ye Faithful	E-5205	My Guardian Angel	E-7186	Let The Whole World Know

Series Guide

12 Days Of Christmas
My True Love Gave To Me
We're Two Of A Kind
Saying "Oui" To Our Love
Ringing In The Season
The Golden Rings Of Friendship
Hatching The Perfect Holiday
Swimming Into Your Heart
Eight Mice A Milking
Nine Ladies Dancing
Leaping Into The Holidays
Piping In Perfect Harmony
Twelve Drummers Drumming

4H Commemorative
The Power Of Youth
Collecting Life's Most Precious Moments

23rd Psalm Plaques
He Leads Me Beside The Still waters
I Will Fear No Evil
He Restores My Soul
You Prepare A Table Before Me
The Lord Is My Shepherd, I Shall Not Want
And I Will Dwell In The House Of The Lord Forever
You Anoint My Head With Oil

Always Victorian
Charity Begins In The Heart
Hope Is Revealed Through God's Word
Have Faith In God

America Forever
Stand Beside Her and Guide Her
God Bless America
America, You're Beautiful

Angel
Bringing You The Gift Of Peace
All Wrapped Up With Love
Simple Joys Put A Song In Your Heart

Animal Affections
So You Finally Met Your Match, Congratulations
You Are A Real Cool Mommy
Rats, I Missed Your Birthday
I Just Go Bats Over You
It's Down Hill All The Way — Congratulations
Are You Lonesome Tonight
Remember To Reach For The Stars
I Love You A Bushel And A Peck
A Chip Off The Old Block
We're Behind You All The Way
Miracles Can Happen
Holy Mackeral It's Your Birthday

Artist Series
My Mona Lisa
You Are My Work Of Art

Attitude With Gratitude
Girls Rule

Baby Classics Series
Good Friends Are Forever
We Are God's Workmanship
Make A Joyful Noise
I Believe In Miracles
God Loveth A Cheerful Giver
You Have Touched So Many Hearts
Love Is Sharing
Love One Another
Friendship Hits the Spot
Loving You Dear Valentine
He Cleansed My Soul
Well, Blow Me Down It's Yer Birthday

Beatitude Windows
Blessed Are The Merciful, For They Shall Obtain Mercy
Blessed Are The Meek, For They Shall Inherit The Earth
Blessed Are They That Hunger And Thirst For Righteousness
Blessed Are The Peacemakers, For They Shall Be Called Sons Of God
Blessed Are They That Mourn, For They Shall Be Comforted
Blessed Are The Pure In Heart, For They Shall See God
Blessed Are The Poor In Spirit, For Theirs Is The Kingdom Of Heaven

Beauty Of Christmas
He Covers The Earth With His Beauty

Bible Stories
Jonah And The Whale
Daniel And The Lion's Den
Joseph's Special Coat
Baby Moses
Ruth and Naomi
The Good Samaritan
The Great Pearl
The Sower And The Seed
David And Goliath

Bible Story Heroes
I Have Set My Rainbow In The Clouds
The Lord Was With Joseph
How Mighty Are Wonders
Be Strong And Courageous
I Have Spoken To You From Heaven
The Lord Is My Rock

Birthstone
January
May
September
February
June
October
March
July
November
April
August
December
January — Garnet — Color Of Boldness
February — Amethyst — Color Of Faith
March — Aquamarine — Color Of Kindness
April — Diamond — Color of Purity
May — Emerald — Color Of Patience
June — Pearl — Color Of Love
July — Ruby — Color Of Joy
August — Peridot — Color of Pride
September — Sapphire — Color Of Confidence
October — Opal — Color Of Happiness
November — Topaz — Color Of Truth
December — Turquoise — Color Of Loyalty

Build A Family
Blonde Mother
Blonde Dad
Blonde Teen Daughter
Blonde Teen Son
Blonde Toddler Girl
Blonde Toddler Son
Blonde Infant Daughter
Blonde Infant Son
Dog
Cat
Brunette Mother
Brunette Dad
Brunette Teen Daughter
Brunette Teen Son
Brunette Toddler Daughter
Brunette Toddler Son
Brunette Infant Daughter
Brunette Infant Son

Canada Exclusive
Nature Provides Us With Such Sweet Pleasures
Canadian School House
Let's Keep Our Eyes On The Goal
Ice See In You A Champion
Let's Keep Our Eyes On The Goal
I Will Make My Country Proud
Ice See In You A Champion

Christmas Remembered
And To All A Good Night
God Rest Ye Merry Gentlemen
Tidings Of Comfort & Joy
Sure Could Use Less Hustle And Bustle

Christmas Collection
Wee Three Kings
Let Heaven And Nature Sing
Come Let Us Adore Him

Clown
Clown Figurines
I Get A Bang Out Of You
Lord Keep Me On The Ball
Waddle I Do Without You
The Lord Will Carry You Through
God Sent You Just In Time
Happiness Is The Lord

Bong Bong
Candy
Clowns
Smile Along The Way
Lord, Help Us Keep Our Act Together
Let's Keep In Touch
Happy Days Are Here Again
Lord, Help Me Make The Grade
Happiness Divine
Waddle I Do Without You
Smile Along The Way
God Sent You Just In Time
A Friend Is Someone who Cares
You Are The Wind Beneath My Wings
Clown Figurine
Clown Figurine
Clown Figurine
Clown Figurine

Collector's Series

The Heart Of A Mother Is Reflected In Her Child
A Mother's Love Grows By Giving
Having A Sister Is Always Having A Friend
Dreams Really Do Come True
Follow Your Heart
You Are My Work Of Art
I Will Be Glad And Rejoice In You
Rock Around The Clock
You Color My World With Love
You Color My World With Love
The Simple Bare Necessities
With A Smile And A Song
My Solidier, My Hero
Our Love Is The Bridge To Happiness
Holiday Surprises Are Filled With Love
I'm Forever By Your Side
Our Love Makes A Lasting Impression
All For The Love Of You On A Bicycle Built For Two
Gentle Is A Mother's Love

Crayola Collection

My Art Says "I Love You"
My Art Says "I Love You"
The Color Of Love
Drawing Us Closer Together
With All My Heart
Put A Little Bounce In Your Step
You Brigthen My Day
A Box of Possibilities

Decorate The Season

The Best Gifts Are Loving, Caring And Sharing
Welcome Are Those With Happy Hearts
May Joy Bloom Within You
Remember The Sweetness Of The Season

Endangered Species

I'd Be Lost Without You
Have You Herd How Much I Love You
Stay With Me A-Whale
Everything's Better When Shared Together
Head And Shoulders Above The Rest
Together Fur-ever

Everyday Angels

A True Friend Is Someone Who Reaches For Your Hand
You Help Me Realize That Life Is Full Of Beauty
You Are My Source Of Comfort And Inspiration

Fall Collector Series

I Will Be Glad And Rejoice In You
Rock Around The Clock

Family Christmas Scene

Tell Me A Story
May You Have The Sweetest Christmas
The Story Of God's Love
God Gave His Best
Silent Night
Have A Beary Merry Christmas
Christmas Fireplace

First Christmas Scene

There's Snow Place Like Home
My Last One For You

Four Seasons

The Voice Of Spring
Summer's Joy
Autumn's Praise
Winter's Song
The Voice Of Spring
Summer's Joy
Autumn's Praise
Winter's Song
Four Seasons
He Graces The Earth With Abundance
Besides The Still Waters
He Covers The Earth With His Glory
The Beauty Of God Blooms Forever
The Voice Of Spring
Summer's Joy
Autumn's Praise
Winter's Song
The Voice Of Spring
Summer's Joy
Autumn's Praise
Winter's Song

Four Seasons Carousel Horse

Renew Faith, Restore Hope, Replenish Love
Allow Sunshine And Laughter To Fill Your Days
Reflect And Give Thanks For All Of Life's Bounty
A Winter Wonderland Awaits

Fruitful Delights

You're A-Peeling To Me
You Are The Apple Of My Eye
You're Pear-fectly Sweet
You're Just Peachy

Good Samaritan

Nothing Can Dampen The Spirit Of Caring

Growing In Grace

Age 1
It's A Girl
Age 2
Age 3
Age 4
Age 5
Age 6
Age 16
Age 7
Age 8
Age 9
Age 10
Age 11
Age 12
Age 13
Age14
Age 15
It's A Girl — Blonde
It's A Girl — Brunette
Age 1
It's A Girl
Age 2
Age 3
Age 4
Age 5
Age 6
Age 16
Age 7
Age 8
Age 9
Age 10
Age 11
Age 12
Age 13
Age 14
Age 15

Growing In God's Garden Of Love

Sewing Seeds Of Kindness
Some Plant, Some Water, But Giveth The Increase
A Bouquet From God's Garden Of Love

Hark! The Herald Angel Sings

Christmas Is Loving
Christmas Is Caring
Christmas Is Sharing

Heavenly Daze

You Add Sparkle To My Life
Star Smith Vignette
Halo Maker
Golden Gown Seanstress
House Of Bells
The Good Book Library
Dream Makers

Heavenly Halos

God's Promises Are Sure
Trust In The Lord
Sending You A Rainbow
Taste And See That The Lord Is Good
Sending You My Love
Sending My Love

Heaven's Grace

Love Is A Heavenly Song
Joy Is The Music Of Angels
Hope Is A Gentle Melody
Happiness Is A Song From Heaven
Faith Is Heaven's Sweet Song

Herald Angels

Gloria in Excelsis Deo
Angels Keep While Shepherd Sleep

Highway To Happiness

Highway To Happiness
I'll Never Stop Loving You
There's No Wrong Way With You
God's Children At Play
Crosswalk
Go For It
Yield To Him
Let Him Enter Your Heart
Give'em A Brake For Jesus

In The Beginning

In The Beginning
God Made Heaven And Earth — Age 2
God Made The Plants And The Trees — Age 3
Let There Be Light In The Sky — Age 4
God Made The Fish And The Birds — Age 5
God Made The Animals — Age 6
God Rested — Age 7
God Made Night And Day — Age 1

Inspired Thoughts

Love Is Kind
Love One Another
Make A Joyful Noise
I Believe In Miracles

International

You Are A Dutch-ess To Me (Holland)
Life Is A Fiesta (Spain)
Don't Rome Too Far From Home (Italy)
You Can't Beat The Red, White and Blue (United States)
Love's Russian Into My Heart (Russia)
Hola, Amigo! (Mexico)
Afri-can Be There For you, I Will Be (Kenya)
I'd Travel The Highlands To Be With You (Scotland)
Sure Would Love To Squeeze You (Germany)
You Are My Armour (France)

Our Friendship Is Always In Bloom (Japan)
My Love Will Stand Guard Over You (England)

Joy Of Christmas

Tell Me The Story Of Jesus
Christmastime Is For Sharing
I'll Play My Drum For Him
The World Of Christmas

Limited Editions

Friends Are Never Far Behind
Lord, Help Me Clean Up My Act
Our Love Is Heaven Scent
Life Never Smelled So Sweet
Where The Deer And The Antelope Play
Your Love Fills My Heart
My Heart Belongs To You
The Sweetest Treat Is Friendship
Your Love Means The World To Me
Nothing Is Stronger Than Our Love
You Are The Apple Of My Eye
You're Pear-fectly Sweet
Christmas Around The World
Bring You The Gift Of Peace
Simple Joys Put A Song In Your Heart
All Wrapped Up With Love
Twas The Night Before Christmas
There's Snow Place Like Home
The World Is A Stage Featuring Precious Moments
Nature Provides Us With Such Sweet Pleasures
You Make My Heart Soar
Bringing You My Heart
Friendship Has No Limit
Heavenly Angels
Your Have The Sweetest Smile
Love Is The Color Of Rainbows
He Shall Lead The Children Into The 21st Century
Winter Wishes Warm The Heart
We're So Hoppy You're Here
Mom, You're My Special-Tea
Flight Into Egypt
God Loveth A Cheerful Giver
I Will Make You Fishers Of Men
My Mona Lisa
Her Children Will Rise Up And Call Her Blessed
Your Love Gives Me Wings
My Dream Boat
Gloria In Excelsis Deo
Life's A Picnic With My Honey
Embraced Your Love
Washed Away In Your love
Ready In The Nick Of Time
Star Of Wonder
May Love Blossom Wherever You Go
Just An Old Fashioned Hello (1910s)
Mixing Up A Brighter Tomorrow (1930s)
One Small Step (1960s)
May Your Christmas Be Delightful
The Most Precious Gift Of All
Yes Dear, You're Always Right
Let Heaven And Nature Sing
Animal Collection

Masterpiece Ornaments

Peace On Earth
May Your Christmas Be A Happy Home
May Your Christmas Be Merry
But The Greatest Of these Is Love

Moments Remembered

To Your Rescue
May Your Spirit Always Soar
I Feel The Need For Speed
Always Ready To Serve and Protect
I've Got Things To Do And Places to Go
I'll Be There In A Flash
Let's Just Enjoy The Ride
A Rebel With A Cause

Mother's Love

Loving Thy Neighbor
Mother Sew Dear
The Purr-fect Grandma
The Hand That Rocks The Future

Motherhood Series

Cherishing Each Special Moment
A Mother's Arms Are Always Open
A Love Like No Other
Cherish Every Step

Noah's Ark — Two By Two

Congratulations, You Earned Your Stripes
I'd Goat Anywhere With You
Noah's Ark
Sheep
Pigs
Giraffes
Bunnies
Elephants
Noah's Ark
Llamas
A Tail Of Love

Occupational

Get Into The Habit Of Prayer
It Is Better To Give Than To Receive
Love Never Fails
Angie, The Angel Of Mercy
Trust And Obey
Love Rescued Me
Love Rescued Me
Angel Of Mercy
It's A Perfect Boy
Angel Of Mercy
To Tell The Tooth You're Special
My Heart Is Exposed With Love
Time Heals
Lord, Police Protect Us
Teacher, You Are My Shining Star
I Can't Spell Success Without "U"
Your Caring Heart Is Easy To See
You Go The Extra Smile
There Is Joy In Serving Jesus
Love Bearth All Things
Love Is Patient
Praise The Lord Anyhow

PM Rocks

Brought Together Throught the Beat
Express Who You Are And You'll Be A Star
Friends Let You Be You
Be You And The Rest Is Cool
When You Play With Heart, Music Is Art

Precious Collectibles

Hands Build A House, Hearts Build A Home
Love Is The Fountain Of Life
Light On Your Feet And Oh So Sweet

Pretty As A Princess

Twinkle, Twinkle, You're A Star
Love Is Reflected In You
Sunshine Brings You A Purr-fect Friend
Too Dog-Gone Sweet

Rejoice In The Lord Band

Lord, Keep My Life In Tune
There's A Song In My Heart
Happiness Is The Lord
Lord Give Me A Song
He Is My Song
Lord, Keep My Life In Tune

Reunion Exclusive

Home, Home On The Range

Rose Petal

Living Each Day With Love
You Are The Rose In My Bouquet
A Smile Is Cherished In The Heart

Rose Series

Blooming In God's Love
Love Will Carry You Through
Some-Bunny Loves you

Sea Of Friendship

You Bring Me Out Of My Shell
Water I Do Without You
I'm Filled With Love For You
Let's Sea Where This Friendship Takes Us

Seeds Of Love

A Tender Touch Helps Love Bloom
Sow Love To Grow Love
Your Love Makes My Heart Blossom

Smiles Forever

Friends Are Never Far Behind
Love Is On It's Way
Lord, Help Me Clean Up My Act
Our Love Is Heaven Scent
Life Never Smelled So Sweet

Through The Years

Tuning in To Happy Times (1920s)
Hopping For The Best (1950s)
From Small Beginnings Come Great Things (1970s)
Just An Old Fashioned Hello (1910s)
Mixing Up A Brighter Tomorrow (1930s)
One Small Step (1960s)

To Have And To Hold

Love Vows To Always Bloom
The Sun Is Always Shining Somewhere
A Year Of Blessings
Each Hour Is Precious With You
Ten Years Heart To Heart
A Silver Celebration To Share
Sharing The Gift Of 40 Precious Years
Precious Moments To Remember

Trophies

World's Greatest Student
World's Sweetest Girl
World's Best Helper
World's Greatest Student
You're No. 1
You're No. 1

Trust Is Bee-lieving

I Am A Bee-liever
Precious Friends
The Lord Is Always Bee-side Us

Word Of Grace

Discover Your Beautiful Strength Within
Make The Most Of Today With Hope Of Tomorrow
Believe In The Wonder That Is You
With Faith, All Things Are Possible
Tender Is A Mother's Love
Love Accepts, Forgives And Never Ceases
Trust There Is A Reason For All Things
May Peace Dwell In Your Heart And Soul

General Index

Numerical Index

more great TITLES from collector books

GLASSWARE & POTTERY

2 American **Pattern Glass Table Sets**, Florence/Cornelius/Jones $24.95
2 Collectible **Cups & Saucers**, Book IV, Harran $29.95
1 Collecting **Head Vases**, Barron $24.95
036 Collector's Encyclopedia of **Depression Glass**, 19th Ed., Florence $24.95
6629 Collector's Encyclopedia of **Fiesta**, 10th Ed., Huxford $24.95
5842 Collector's Encyclopedia of **Roseville Pottery**, Vol. 2, Huxford/Nickel $24.95
6646 Collector's Ency. of **Stangl Artware**, Lamps, and Birds, 2nd Ed., Runge $29.95
7530 **Decorative Plates**, Harran $29.95
7749 Early American Pattern Glass **Cake Stands**, James & O'Brien $29.95
7755 Elegant Glassware of the **Depression** Era, 13th Edition, Florence $24.95
7935 Encyclopedia of **Cobalt Glass**, Felt & Girard $39.95
7638 Encyclopedia of **Universal Potteries**, Chorey $29.95
7628 **English China** Patterns & Pieces, Gaston $29.95
7630 **Fostoria Stemware**, The Crystal for America, 2nd Edition, Long/Seate $29.95
6320 Gaston's **Blue Willow**, 3rd Edition $19.95
6127 The **Glass Candlestick Book**, Vol. 1, Akro Agate to Fenton, Felt/Stoer $24.95
7353 Glass **Hen on Nest**, Smith $29.95
7758 **Hazel-Atlas** Glass Identification, 2nd Edition, Florence $24.95
7534 **Lancaster Glass** Company, 1908 –1937, Zastowney $29.95
7359 **L.E. Smith Glass** Company, Felt $29.95
5913 **McCoy Pottery**, Volume III, Hanson/Nissen $24.95
6335 Pictorial Guide to **Pottery & Porcelain Marks**, Lage, No values $29.95
7637 **RumRill Pottery**, Fisher $29.95
7623 Standard Encyclopedia of **Carnival Glass**, 11th Ed., Carwile $29.95
6241 Treasures of Very Rare **Depression Glass**, Florence $39.95
6476 **Westmoreland Glass**, The Popular Years, 1940 – 1985, Kovar $29.95

DOLLS & FIGURES

6315 **American Character Dolls**, Izen $24.95
7748 **Barbie**®, The First 30 Years, 1959 – 1989, 3rd Ed., Deutsch & Dorfmann $29.95
7346 **Barbie Doll Around the World**, 1964 –2007, Augustyniak $29.95
6319 **Barbie Doll Fashion**, Volume III, 1975 – 1979, Eames $29.95
6825 **Celluloid Dolls**, Toys & Plaything, Robinson $29.95
7621 Collectible **African American Dolls**, Ellis $29.95
6451 Collector's Ency. of **American Composition Dolls**, Vol. II, Mertz $29.95
6546 Collector's Ency. of **Barbie Doll Exclusives**, 3rd Ed., Augustyniak $29.95
6636 Collector's Ency. of **Madame Alexander Dolls**, 1948 – 1965, Crowsey $24.95
6456 Collector's Guide to **Dolls of the 1960s and 1970s**, Vol. II, Sabulis $24.95
6944 Complete Gde. to **Shirley Temple Dolls** and Collectibles, Bervaldi-Camaratta $29.95
7763 Encyclopedia of **Nancy Ann Stroybook Dolls**, Vol. 2, Pardee $29.95
6473 Encyclopedia of **Vogue Dolls**, 2nd Ed., Izen & Stover $29.95
7354 **Horsman Dolls**, The Vinyl Era, Jensen $29.95
7939 **Madame Alexander** Collector's Dolls Price Guide #34, Crowsey $14.95
6642 20th Century **Paper Dolls**, Young $19.95

JEWELRY & ACCESSORIES

4704 **Antique & Collectible Buttons**, Volume I, Wisniewski $19.95
7751 **Classic American** Costume Jewelry, Rehmann $24.95
4850 Collectible **Costume Jewelry**, Simonds $24.95
7529 Collecting **Costume Jewelry 101**, 2nd Edition, Carroll $24.95
7025 Collecting **Costume Jewelry 202**, Carroll $24.95
6468 Collector's Ency. of **Pendant & Pocket Watches**, 1500 – 1950, Bell $24.95
6554 **Coro Jewelry**, A Collector's Guide, Brown $29.95
5812 Fifty Years of Collectible **Fashion Jewelry**, 1925 – 1975, Baker $24.95
6833 **Handkerchiefs**: A Collector's Guide, Volume 2 $24.95
7761 Inside the **Jewelry** Box, Volume 3, Pitman $24.95
7535 Mueller's Overview of **American Compacts** $29.95
1181 100 Years of **Collectible Jewelry**, 1850 – 1950, Baker $9.95
6645 100 Years of **Purses**, Aikins $24.95
6942 **Rhinestone Jewelry**: Figurals, Animals, and Whimsicals, Brown $24.95
6038 **Sewing Tools** & Trinkets, Volume 2, Thompson $24.95
6039 Signed Beauties of **Costume Jewelry**, Brown $24.95
6341 Signed Beauties of **Costume Jewelry**, Volume II, Brown $24.95
4850 Unsigned Beauties of **Costume Jewelry**, Brown $24.95

FURNITURE

6928 Early **American Furniture**: A Guide to Who, When, and Where, Obbard $19.95
7038 The Marketplace Guide to **Oak Furniture**, 2nd Edition, Blundell $29.95

TOYS

7523 **Breyer** Animal Collector's Guide, 5th Ed., Browell/Korber-Weimer/Kesicki $24.95
7540 Classic 80s **Home Video Games**, Wicker & Brassard $24.95
7527 Collecting **Disneyana**, Longest $29.95
7356 Collector's Guide to **Housekeeping Toys**, Wright $16.95
7528 Collector's **Toy** Yearbook, Longest $29.95
7355 **Hot Wheels**, The Ultimate Redline Guide Companion, Clark/Wicker $29.95
7635 **Matchbox Toys**, 1947 to 2007, 5th Edition, Johnson $24.95
8042 **Schroeder's** Collectible Toys, Antique to Modern Price Guide, 12th Ed $19.95

PAPER COLLECTIBLES & BOOKS

6623 Collecting **American Paintings**, James $29.95
1441 Collector's Guide to **Post Cards**, Wood $9.95
7622 Encyclopedia of Collectible **Children's Books**, Jones $29.95
7636 The Golden Age of **Postcards**, Early 1900s, Penniston $24.95
6936 **Leather Bound Books**, Boutiette $24.95
7036 **Old Magazine Advertisements**, Clear $24.95
6940 **Old Magazines**, 2nd Ed., Clear $19.95
3973 **Sheet Music** Reference & Price Guide, 2nd Ed., Guiheen/Pafik $19.95

OTHER COLLECTIBLES

7747 **Arrowheads**, Early Man Projectile Points, Owens $29.95
7936 Antique & Vintage **Fashions**, Johnson $29.95
7767 Antique **Santa Claus** Collectibles, Longest $29.95
7759 **Hot Cottage** Collectibles for Vintage Style Homes, Zweig $29.95
7633 **Indian Bannerstones** & Related Artifacts, Hothem & Bennett $29.95
7940 **McCoy Pottery**, The Ultimate Reference & Value Guide, Hanson/Nissen $29.95
7746 19th Century Patterned Art Glass **Chamber Lamps**, Gibson $39.95
7757 Vintage **Hats & Bonnets**, 1770 – 1970, 2nd Edition, Langley $29.95
7766 Wonderful World of Collecting **Perfume Bottles**, 2nd Edition, Flanagan $29.95

1.800.626.5420 Mon. – Fri. 8 am – 4 pm CT   Fax: **1.270.898.8890**